PERSONALITY

PERSONALITY

NINTH EDITION

Jerry M. Burger

Santa Clara University

CENGAGE
Learning

Australia • Brazil • Mexico • Singapore • United Kingdom • United States

CENGAGE
Learning·

Personality, **Ninth Edition**
Jerry M. Burger

Product Director: Jon-David Hague

Content Developer: Jean L. Smith

Product Assistant: Nicole Richards

Media Developer: Jasmin Tokatlian

Marketing Director: Jennifer Levanduski

Art and Cover Direction, Production
Management, and Composition:
PreMediaGlobal

Manufacturing Planner: Karen Hunt

Cover Image: Rick Rhay/Getty Images

For product information and technology assistance, contact us at
Cengage Learning Customer & Sales Support, 1-800-354-9706.

For permission to use material from this text or product,
submit all requests online at **www.cengage.com/permissions**.
Further permissions questions can be e-mailed to
permissionrequest@cengage.com.

Library of Congress Control Number: 2013955319

ISBN-13: 978-1-285-74022-5

ISBN-10: 1-285-74022-X

Cengage Learning
200 First Stamford Place, 4th Floor
Stamford, CT 06902
USA

Cengage Learning is a leading provider of customized learning solutions
with office locations around the globe, including Singapore, the United
Kingdom, Australia, Mexico, Brazil, and Japan. Locate your local office at
www.cengage.com/global.

Cengage Learning products are represented in Canada by
Nelson Education, Ltd.

To learn more about Cengage Learning Solutions, visit **www.cengage.com**.

Purchase any of our products at your local college store or at our
preferred online store **www.cengagebrain.com**.

Printed in the United States of America
1 2 3 4 5 6 7 18 17 16 15 14

To Marlene

Brief Contents

Contents

Preface

The day after I sent the ninth edition of this book to the publisher, I went to my bookshelf and pulled out a copy of the first edition. Few will remember (I hope) the sickly gray cover depicting the Greek statue. There were only 12 chapters, and the book was printed in only one color. And the writing was—well, as a teacher once told me, wincing at how you used to write indicates how much you have improved. Thumbing through the pages, I was struck by how much the book has changed over the course of nine editions—changes that reflect, among other things, the vibrancy of the field. Of course, many topics remain from that initial edition; Freud hasn't added much to his theory in the past few decades. But the differences between the first and ninth editions far outweigh the similarities. There are new topics, new learning aids, new examples, and hundreds and hundreds of new references. And yet, I would argue, the essence of the book—the structure, the philosophy—has remained intact. Let me explain.

What's New?

As in previous revisions, each chapter has been updated to reflect new research findings and new developments in the field. More than 300 references have been added to this edition. I've devoted more space to topics that have generated an increasing amount of research in recent years. The expanded topics include the behavioral activation and behavioral inhibition systems (Chapter 9), unmitigated agency (Chapter 14), and programs to reduce aggression in children (Chapter 16). In Chapter 7, you will find an expanded discussion of recent attempts to replace the Big Five model. That chapter also includes some new historical information about research published in 1949 that foreshadowed the emergence of the Big Five decades later. I've also reduced or eliminated coverage of topics that seem to have fallen out of favor with personality researchers. Most noteworthy of the discarded topics is research on defensive pessimism that previously had appeared in Chapter 8.

Previous users also will find a few new personality inventories. This edition includes tests to measure coping flexibility and preference for solitude. On the other hand, tests measuring loneliness and assertiveness have been dropped from the last edition. There also are a couple of new *In the News* topics. These new topics include changes in the kinds of toys marketed to girls and boys (Chapter 14) and thinking about loneliness as a public health issue (Chapter 12).

Perhaps the biggest change in this edition is the addition of an Appendix. The new appendix is the result of comments from several students who enjoyed taking the personality inventories but wanted an easy way to combine all the information they gained about themselves into one comprehensive picture.

What's the Same?

The philosophy that guided the organization and writing of the first eight editions remains. I wrote this book to organize within one textbook the two approaches typically taken by instructors of undergraduate personality courses. Many instructors focus on the great theories and theorists—a chapter each on Freud, Jung, Rogers, Skinner, and so on. Students in these classes gain insight into the structure of the mind and issues of human nature, as well as a background for understanding psychological disorders and psychotherapy. However, these students are likely to be puzzled when they pick up a current journal of personality research only to find they recognize few, if any, of the topics. Other instructors emphasize personality research. Students in these classes learn about current studies on individual differences and personality processes. But they probably see little relationship between the abstract theories they may touch upon in class and the research topics that are the focus of the course.

However, these two approaches to teaching the course do not represent separate disciplines that happen to share the word *personality* in their titles. Indeed, the structure of this book is designed to demonstrate that the classic theories stimulate research and that research findings often shape the development and acceptance of the theories. Limiting a student's attention to either theory or research provides an unnecessarily narrow view of the field.

Something else that remains from the earlier editions is my belief that students learn about research best by seeing *programs* of research rather than a few isolated examples. Twenty-six research programs are covered in the seven research chapters in this edition. In each case I have tried to illustrate how the questions being investigated are connected to a larger theory, how early researchers developed their initial hypotheses and investigations, and how experimental findings lead to new questions, refined hypotheses, and ultimately a greater understanding of the topic. Through this process, students are exposed to some of the problems researchers encounter, the fact that experimental results are often equivocal, and a realistic picture of researchers who don't always agree on how to interpret findings.

I also have preserved the structure used in previous editions for the theory chapters. Each of these chapters contains a section on application and a section on assessment. The application sections demonstrate how the sometimes abstract theories relate to everyday concerns and issues. Students discover in the assessment sections how each approach to understanding personality brings with it unique assumptions and problems when attempting to measure relevant personality constructs.

I've retained the personality tests students can take and score themselves. There are now 14 "Assessing Your Own Personality" boxes scattered throughout the book. I've discovered in my own teaching that discussions about, for example, social anxiety are more engaging after students discover how they score on a social anxiety test. This hands-on experience not only gives students a better idea of how personality assessment works, but often generates a little healthy skepticism about relying too heavily on such measures. I've also retained the biographies of prominent personality theorists in this edition. Feedback from students indicates that knowing something about the person behind the theory helps to make the theory come alive. My students often speculate about how a theorist's life affected the development of his or her theory. Students and instructors also tell me they like the *In the News* boxes I introduced five editions ago. Consequently, these have been retained as well.

Acknowledgments

Thanks are extended to all the people who helped with the production of this book. This includes the many colleagues who reviewed various parts of the manuscript: Diane Mello-Goldner, Pine Manor College; Tanya Renner, Kapiolani Community College; James Casebolt, Ohio University—Eastern, Heather LaCost, Waubonsee Community College; Catherine Pitman, Saint Mary's College; Lee Shrader, Lorain County Community College; Karen Savarese, Southern Connecticut State University; Linda Lindman, University of South Alabama; W. Amory Carr, University of New Haven; and Howard Markowitz, Hawaii Pacific University—Honolulu.

And, as always, I thank Marlene, whose understanding and support through all nine editions have made this book possible.

About the Author

JERRY M. BURGER is professor of psychology at Santa Clara University. He is the author of more than a hundred journal articles and book chapters and has published two books: *Desire for Control: Personality, Social and Clinical Perspectives* and *Returning Home: Reconnecting with Our Childhoods.* He has been on the editorial board of several academic journals, including the *Journal of Personality* and the *Personality and Social Psychology Bulletin,* and has served as an associate editor for the "Personality Processes and Individual Difference" section of the *Journal of Personality and Social Psychology.* In his spare time he likes to run, read, and write. You can send comments about the book to him at jburger@scu.edu.

What Is Personality?

At 2:45 in the afternoon on May 22, 2013, a devastating tornado touched down in the suburbs of Oklahoma City. The 1.3-mile-wide tornado plowed a 17-mile path through the community, leaving piles of rubble and debris where minutes earlier homes, schools, hospitals, and businesses had been standing. Wind speeds reached as high as 210 miles per hour. By the time the storm lifted 50 minutes later, a large part of Moore, Oklahoma, and other nearby cities had been destroyed. More than 12,000 homes were damaged, many of them completely obliterated by the storm. Twenty-four people were dead, including 10 children.

In the days that followed, residents discovered the extent of their losses, considered how their lives were changed, and helped those who had lost the most. While the community grieved, condolences and concern for the victims and their families poured in from public officials and citizens from across the country.

Powerful events have a way of bringing out similar reactions in people. Someone might point to this tragedy to illustrate how much alike each of us really is, how all people are basically the same. Yet if we look a little more closely, even in this situation we can see that not everyone reacted in the same way. Some people joined rescue teams to search through the piles of bricks and boards. Others pitched tents on their lawns vowing to protect what remained of their possessions. Some opened their homes to strangers who no longer had a home of their own. Others expressed anger at officials who had failed to build storm shelters in the basements of the elementary schools where children had died. Some dropped off food, clothing, diapers, and checks at quickly assembled donation centers. Others struggled to cope with the emotional aftermath of the storm and a growing sense of helplessness. Many turned to religion to find meaning and comfort, but some struggled to find the hand of God in so much suffering. Some residents who had lost everything vowed to rebuild. Others decided it was time to leave.

In many ways, the reactions to the Oklahoma tornado are typical of people who are suddenly thrown into a unique and tragic situation. At first, the demands of the situation overwhelm individual differences, but soon each person's characteristic way of dealing with the situation and the emotional aftermath begins to surface. The more we look, the more we see that people are not all alike. The closer we look, the more we begin to see differences among people. These characteristic differences are the focus of this book. They are part of what we call personality. Moreover, personality psychologists have already studied many of the topics and issues that surfaced in the Oklahoma tragedy. Coping with stress, emotions, religion, anxiety, feelings of helplessness, and many other relevant topics are covered in various places in this book.

The Person and the Situation

Is our behavior shaped by the situation we are in or by the type of person we are? In the Oklahoma tornado tragedy, did people act the way they did because of the events surrounding them, or were their reactions more the result of the kind of people they were before the incident? This is one of the enduring questions in psychology. The generally agreed-upon answer today is that both the situation and the person contribute to behavior. Certainly we don't act the same way in all situations. Depending on where we are and what is happening, each of us can be outgoing, shy, aggressive, friendly, depressed, frightened, or excited. But it is equally apparent that not everyone at the same party, the same ball game, or the same shopping center behaves identically. The debate among psychologists has now shifted to the question of how the situation influences our behavior as well as how our behavior reflects the individual.

We can divide the fields of study within psychology along the answer to this question. Many psychologists concern themselves with how people *typically* respond to environmental demands. These researchers recognize that not everyone in a situation reacts the same. Their goal is to identify patterns that generally describe what most people will do. Thus a social psychologist might create different situations in which participants encounter someone in need of help. The purpose of this research is to identify the kinds of situations that increase or decrease helping behavior, but personality psychologists turn this way of thinking completely around. We know there are typical response patterns to situations, but what we find more interesting is why Peter tends to help more than Paul, even when both are presented with the same request.

You may have heard the axiom, "There are few differences between people, but what differences there are, really matter." That tends to sum up the personality psychologists' viewpoint. They want to know what makes you different from the person sitting next to you. Why do some people make friends easily, whereas others are lonely? Why are some people prone to bouts of depression? Can we predict who will rise to the top of the business ladder and who will fall short? Why are some people introverted, whereas others are so outgoing? Each of these questions is explored in this book. Other topics covered include how your personality is related to hypnotic responsiveness, reactions to stress, how well you do in school, and even your chances of having a heart attack.

This is not to say that situations are unimportant or of no interest to personality psychologists. Indeed, as discussed in Chapter 7, many of the questions posed by personality researchers concern how a certain kind of person behaves in a particular situation. However, the emphasis of this book is on what makes you different from the next person—that is, your personality. Before addressing that question, let's start by defining "personality."

Defining Personality

Anyone who has been in college a while can probably anticipate the topic of the first lecture of the term. The philosophy professor asks, "What is philosophy?" The first class meeting in a communication course centers on the question, "What is communication?" Those who teach geography, history, and calculus have similar lectures. And so, for traditional and practical reasons, psychology professors too begin with the basic question, "What is personality?"

Although a definition follows, bear in mind that psychologists do not agree on a single answer to this question. In fact, personality psychologists are engaged in an ongoing and perhaps never-ending discussion of how to describe human personality and what topics belong within this subfield of psychology (Mayer, 2005; McAdams & Pals, 2006). As you will see, each personality theorist covered in this book also has a different idea about what personality psychologists ought to study. Whereas one theorist points to unconscious mechanisms, another might look at learning histories, and still another at the way people organize their thoughts. Although some students might find this lack of agreement frustrating, let me suggest from the outset that these different viewpoints provide a rich and exciting framework within which to explore the complexities of the individual.

Personality can be defined as *consistent behavior patterns and intrapersonal processes originating within the individual.* Several aspects of this simple definition need elaboration. Notice that there are two parts to it. The first part is concerned with consistent patterns of behavior. Personality researchers often refer to these as *individual differences.* The important point here is that personality is *consistent.* We can identify these consistent behavior patterns across time and across situations. We expect someone who is outgoing today to be outgoing tomorrow. Someone who is competitive at work is also quite likely competitive in sports. We acknowledge this consistency in character when we say, "It was just like her to do that" or "He was just being himself." Of course, this does not mean an extraverted person is boisterous and jolly all the time, on solemn occasions as well as at parties. Nor does it mean people cannot change. But if personality exists and behavior is not just a reflection of whatever situation we find ourselves in, then we must expect some consistency in the way people act.

The second part of the definition concerns intrapersonal processes. In contrast to *inter*personal processes, which take place between people, intrapersonal processes include all the emotional, motivational, and cognitive processes that go on inside of us that affect how we act and feel. Thus, you will find that many personality psychologists are interested in topics like depression, information processing, happiness, and denial.

It also is important to note that, according to the definition, these consistent behavior patterns and intrapersonal processes originate within the individual. This is not to say that external sources do not influence personality. Certainly the way parents raise their children affects the kind of adults the children become. And, of course, the emotions we experience are often a reaction to the events we encounter. The point is that behavior is not solely a function of the situation. The fear we experience while watching a frightening movie is the result of the film, but the different ways we each express or deal with that fear come from within.

Six Approaches to Personality

What are the sources of consistent behavior patterns and intrapersonal processes? This is the basic question asked by personality theorists and researchers. One reason for the length of this book is that personality psychologists have answered this question in many different ways. To help make sense of the wide range of personality theories proposed over the past century, we'll look at six general approaches to explaining personality. These are the psychoanalytic approach, the trait approach, the biological approach, the humanistic approach, the behavioral/social learning approach, and the cognitive approach. Although the fit is not always perfect, each of the major theories of personality can be placed into one of these six general approaches.

Why so many theories of personality? Let me answer this question by way of analogy. Nearly everyone has heard the story about the five blind men who encounter an elephant. Each feels a different part of the animal and then tries to explain to the others what an elephant is like. The blind man feeling the leg describes the elephant as tall and round. Another feels the ear and claims an elephant is thin and flat, whereas another, holding onto the trunk, describes the animal as long and slender. The man feeling the tail and the one touching the elephant's side have still different images. The point to this story, of course, is that each man knows only a part of the whole animal. Because there is more to the elephant than what he has experienced, each man's description is correct but incomplete.

In one sense, the six approaches to personality are analogous to the blind men. That is, each approach does seem to correctly identify and examine an important aspect of human personality. For example, psychologists who subscribe to the *psychoanalytic approach* argue that people's unconscious minds are largely responsible for important differences in their behavior styles. Other psychologists, those who favor the *trait approach,* identify where a person might lie along a continuum of various personality characteristics. Psychologists advocating the *biological approach* point to inherited predispositions and physiological processes to explain individual differences in personality. In contrast, those promoting the *humanistic approach* identify personal responsibility and feelings of self-acceptance as the key causes of differences in personality. *Behavioral/social learning* theorists explain consistent behavior patterns as the result of conditioning and expectations. Those promoting the *cognitive approach* look at differences in the way people process information to explain differences in behavior.

It's tempting to suggest that by combining all six approaches we can obtain the larger, accurate picture of why people act the way they do. Unfortunately, the blind men analogy can only be stretched so far. Although different approaches to a given question in personality often vary only in emphasis—with each providing a legitimate, compatible explanation—in many instances the explanations from two or more approaches may be entirely incompatible. Thus people who work in the field often align themselves with one or another of the six approaches as they decide which of the competing explanations makes the most sense to them.

Returning to the blind men and the elephant, suppose someone were to ask how an elephant moves. The man feeling the trunk might argue that the elephant slithers along the ground like a snake. The man holding the elephant's ear might disagree, saying that the elephant must fly like a bird with its big, floppy wings. The man touching the leg would certainly have a different explanation. Although in some instances more than one of these explanations might be accurate (for example, a bird can both walk and fly), it should be obvious that at times not every theory can be right. It also is possible that one theory may be correct in describing one part of human personality, whereas another theory may be correct in describing other aspects.

No doubt some theories will resonate with you more than others. But it is worth keeping in mind that each approach has been developed and promoted by a large number of respected psychologists. Although not all of these men and women are correct about every issue, each approach has something of value to offer in our quest to understand what makes each of us who we are.

Two Examples: Aggression and Depression

To get a better idea of how the six approaches to understanding personality provide six different, yet legitimate, explanations for consistent patterns of behavior, let's look at two common examples. Aggressive behavior and the suffering that comes from depression are widespread problems in our society, and psychologists from many different perspectives have looked into their causes.

Example 1: Aggression

Unfortunately, there is no shortage of people who consistently engage in aggressive behavior. People arrested for assault typically have a history of violence that goes back to playground fights in childhood. Why are some people consistently more aggressive than others? Each of the six approaches to personality provides at least one answer. As you read these answers, think about an aggressive person you have encountered or read about. Which of the six explanations seems to do the best job of explaining that person's behavior?

The classic psychoanalytic explanation of aggression points to an unconscious death instinct. That is, we are all said to possess an unconscious desire to self-destruct. However, because people with a healthy personality do not hurt themselves, these self-destructive impulses may be turned outward and expressed against others in the form of aggression. Other psychoanalysts argue that aggression results when we are blocked from reaching our goals. A person who experiences a great deal of frustration, perhaps someone who is constantly falling short of a desired goal, is a likely candidate for persistent aggressive behavior. In most cases, the person is unaware of the real reasons for the aggression.

Personality theorists who follow the trait approach focus on individual differences and the stability of aggressive behavior (Bettencourt, Talley, Benjamin, & Valentine, 2006). For example, one team of researchers measured aggressiveness in 8-year-old children (Huesmann, Eron, & Yarmel, 1987). The investigators interviewed the participants again when the participants were 30 years old. The researchers discovered that the children identified as aggressive in elementary school were the most likely to have become aggressive adults. The children who pushed and shoved their classmates often grew into adults who abused their spouses and engaged in violent criminal behavior.

Personality psychologists from the biological perspective also are interested in stable patterns of aggressive behavior. They point to a genetic predisposition to act aggressively as one reason for this stability. Evidence now suggests that some people inherit more of a proclivity toward aggression than others (Miles & Carey, 1997). That is, some people may be born with aggressive dispositions that, depending on their upbringing, result in their becoming aggressive adults. Other psychologists explain aggression in terms of evolutionary theory (Cairns, 1986). For example, the fact that men tend to be more aggressive than women might be explained by the male's inherited need to exercise control over rivals so that he can survive and pass along his genes. Other researchers look at the role hormones and neurotransmitters play in aggressive behavior (Berman, McCloskey, Fanning, Schumacher, & Coccaro, 2009; Klinesmith, Kasser, & McAndrew, 2006).

Psychologists with a humanistic approach to personality explain aggression in yet another way. These theorists deny that some individuals are born to be aggressive. In fact, many argue that people are basically good. They believe all people can become happy, nonviolent adults if allowed to grow and develop in an enriching and encouraging environment. Problems develop when something interferes with this natural growth process. Aggressive children often come from homes in which basic needs are not met adequately. If the child develops a poor self-image, he or she may strike out at others in frustration.

The behavioral/social learning approach contrasts in many ways with the humanistic view. According to these psychologists, people learn to be aggressive the same way they learn other behaviors. Playground bullies find that aggressive behavior is rewarded. They get to bat first and have first choice of playground equipment because other children fear them. The key to the behavioral interpretation is that rewarded behavior will be repeated. Thus the bully probably will continue this aggressive behavior and try it in other situations. If the aggression is continually met with rewards instead of punishment, the result will be an aggressive adult. People also learn from watching models. Children may learn from watching aggressive classmates that hurting others is sometimes useful. As discussed in Chapter 14, many people are concerned that the aggressive role models children routinely watch on television may be responsible for increasing the amount of violence in society.

Cognitive psychologists approach the question of aggressive behavior from yet another perspective. Their main focus is on the way aggressive people process information. Certain cues in the environment, such as images of guns and fighting, often trigger a network of aggressive thoughts and emotions. When aggressive thoughts are highly accessible, people are more likely to interpret situations as threatening and respond to those perceived threats with violence. Although most of us ignore unintended insults and accidental bumps in the hallway, individuals with highly accessible aggressive thoughts are likely to respond with threats of violence and angry shoves.

Now, let's return to the original question: Why do some people show a consistent pattern of aggressive behavior? Each of the six approaches to personality offers a different explanation. Which is correct? One possibility is that only one is correct and that future research will identify that theory. A second possibility is that each approach is partially correct. There may be six (or more) different causes of aggressive behavior. Still a third possibility is that the six explanations do not contradict one another but rather differ only in their focus. That is, it's possible that aggressiveness is relatively stable and reflects an aggressive trait (the trait approach). But it might also be the case that some people tend to interpret ambiguous events as threatening (the cognitive explanation) because of past experiences in which they were assaulted (the behavioral/social learning explanation). These people may have been born with a tendency to respond to threats in an aggressive manner (the biological approach). But perhaps if they had been raised in a nonfrustrating environment (the psychoanalytic approach) or in a supportive home in which their basic needs were met (the humanistic approach), they would have overcome their aggressive tendencies. The point is that each approach appears to contribute something to our understanding of aggression.

Example 2: Depression

Most of us know what it is like to be depressed. We have all had days when we feel a little blue or melancholy. Like many college students, you may also have suffered through longer periods of intense sadness and a general lack of motivation to do anything. Although most of us fluctuate through changing moods and levels of interest and energy, some people seem more prone to depression than others. Once again, each of the six approaches to personality has a different explanation for individual differences in depression.

According to Sigmund Freud, the founder of the psychoanalytic approach, depression is anger turned inward. That is, people suffering from depression hold unconscious feelings of anger and hostility. They may want to strike out at family members, but a healthy personality does not express such feelings overtly. Psychoanalysts also argue that each of us has internalized the standards and values of society, which typically discourage the expression of hostility. Therefore, these angry feelings are turned inward, and people take it out on themselves. As with most psychoanalytic explanations, this process takes place at an unconscious level.

Trait theorists are concerned with identifying depression-prone individuals. Researchers find that a person's general emotional level today is a good indicator of that person's emotions in the future. One team of investigators measured depression in a group of middle-aged men and again 30 years later (Leon, Gillum, Gillum, & Gouze, 1979). The researchers found an impressively high correlation between the men's depression levels at the two different times. Yet another study found that depression levels in 18-year-olds could be predicted from looking at participants' behavior from as early as 7 years of age (Block, Gjerde, & Block, 1991).

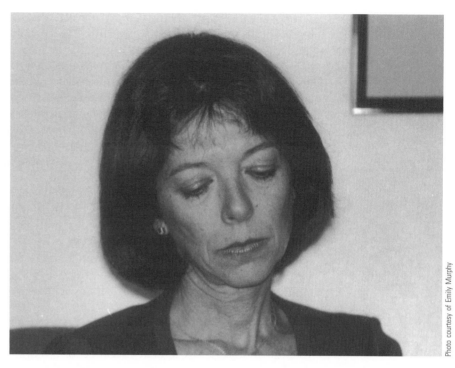

Photo courtesy of Emily Murphy

What causes depression? Depending on which approach to personality you adopt, you might explain depression in terms of anger turned inward, a stable trait, an inherited predisposition, low self-esteem, a lack of reinforcers, or negative thoughts.

Biological personality psychologists point to evidence that some people may inherit a genetic susceptibility to depression (McGue & Christensen, 1997). A person born with this vulnerability faces a much greater likelihood than the average individual of reacting to stressful life events with depression. Because of this inherited tendency, these people often experience repeated bouts of depression throughout their lives.

Humanistic personality theorists explain depression in terms of self-esteem. That is, people who frequently suffer from depression are those who have failed to develop a good sense of their self-worth. A person's level of self-esteem is established while growing up and, like other personality concepts, is fairly stable across time and situations. The ability to accept oneself, even one's faults and weaknesses, is an important goal for humanistic therapists when dealing with clients suffering from depression.

The behavioral/social learning approach examines the type of learning history that leads to depression. Behaviorists argue that depression results from a lack of positive reinforcers in a person's life. That is, you may feel down and unmotivated because you see few activities in your life worth doing. A more extensive behavioral model of depression, covered in Chapter 14, proposes that depression develops from experiences with aversive situations over which people have little control. This theory maintains that exposure to uncontrollable events creates a perception of helplessness that is generalized to other situations and may develop into classic symptoms of depression.

Some cognitive personality psychologists have taken this explanation one step further. These psychologists argue that whether people become depressed depends on how they interpret their inability to control events. For example, people who attribute their inability to get a promotion to a temporary economic recession will not become as depressed as people who believe it is the result of personal inadequacies. Other cognitive psychologists propose that some individuals use something like a depressive filter to interpret and process information. That is, depressed people are prepared to see the world in the most depressing terms possible. For this reason, depressed people can easily recall depressing experiences. People and places they encounter are likely to remind them of some sad or unpleasant time. In short, people become depressed because they are prepared to generate depressing thoughts.

Which of these accounts of depression strikes you as the most accurate? If you have been depressed, was it because of your low self-esteem, because you experienced an uncontrollable situation, or because you tend to look at the world through a depressing lens? As in the aggression example, more than one of these approaches may be correct. You may have found that one theory could explain an experience you had with depression last year, whereas another seems to better account for a more recent bout. In addition, the theories can at times complement each other. For example, people might interpret events in a depressing way because of their low self-esteem.

One more lesson can be taken from these two examples: You need not align yourself with the same approach to personality when explaining different phenomena. For example, you may have found that the cognitive explanation for aggression made the most sense to you, but that the humanistic approach provided the best account of depression. This observation demonstrates the main point of this section: Each of the six approaches has something to offer the student interested in understanding personality.

Personality and Culture

Psychologists have increasingly recognized the important role culture plays in understanding personality. To some students, this observation at first seems inconsistent with the notion of personality as distinct from situational influences on behavior. However, psychologists now recognize that many of the assumptions people in Western developed countries make when describing and studying personality may not apply when dealing with people from different cultures (Benet-Martinez & Oishi, 2008; Cheung, van de Vijver, & Leong, 2011). It is not just that different experiences in different cultures affect how personalities develop. Rather, psychologists have come to see that people and their personalities exist within a cultural context.

Perhaps the most important distinction cross-cultural researchers make is between individualistic cultures and collectivist cultures (Triandis, 1989, 2001). **Individualistic cultures,** which include most Northern European countries and the United States, place great emphasis on individual needs and accomplishments. People in these cultures like to think of themselves as independent and unique. In contrast, people in **collectivist cultures** are more concerned about belonging to a larger group, such as a family, tribe, or nation. These people are more interested in cooperation than competition. They obtain satisfaction when the group does well rather than from individual accomplishments. Many Asian, African, Central American, and South American countries fit the collectivist culture description. Consequently, concepts commonly studied by Western personality psychologists often take on very different meanings when people from collectivist cultures are studied. For example, research reviewed in Chapter 12 suggests that the Western notion of self-esteem is based on assumptions about personal goals and feelings of uniqueness that may not make sense to citizens of other countries (Markus & Kitayama, 1991, 2010).

Moreover, the kinds of behaviors examined in personality may have different meanings depending on the culture. For example, for many years personality psychologists have been concerned with achievement behavior. Traditionally, this means trying to predict who will get ahead in academic or business situations. However, this definition of achievement and success is not shared universally (Salili, 1994). In some collectivist cultures, success means cooperation and group accomplishments. Personal recognition may even be frowned upon by people living in these cultures. Similarly, we need to consider the culture a person comes from when identifying and treating psychological disorders (Benish, Quintana, & Wampold, 2011; Draguns, 2008; Pedersen, 2008). For example, behavior that suggests excessive dependency or an exaggerated sense of self in one culture might reflect good adjustment in another.

Thus it is worth remembering that most of the theories and much of the research covered in this book are based on observations in individualistic cultures. In fact, most of the research was conducted in the United States, the country that was found in one study to be the most individualistic of 41 nations examined (Suh, Diener, Oishi, & Triandis, 1998). This does not mean the research should be dismissed. Rather, we should keep in mind that whether a particular description applies to people in all cultures remains an open question. In some cases, such as the research on dream content presented in Chapter 4 and the studies on marriage patterns presented in Chapter 10, investigators find nearly identical results across very different cultural groups. In other cases, such as in the self-esteem and achievement examples, they find important differences among cultures. Identifying the cultural limitations or universality of various phenomena provides additional insight into the nature of the concepts we study.

The Study of Personality: Theory, Application, Assessment, and Research

If you spend a few minutes looking through the table of contents at the beginning of this book, you will notice that the book is divided into sections. Each section presents one of the different approaches to personality. Each of these sections is divided into four parts (in two chapters). These divisions represent the four components necessary for a complete understanding of personality. Each section begins with a presentation of *theory*. Each of the personality theorists covered in these pages presents a comprehensive model for how human personality is structured and how it operates. But psychologists have never been content to simply describe personality. Rather, we have a long history of applying the information gained from theories and research to questions and issues that directly affect people's lives. These *applications* include psychotherapy, education, and behavior in the workplace. An example of how psychologists apply their theories to these kinds of settings is presented for each approach. Psychologists working within each of the approaches also must develop ways to measure the personality constructs they study and use. Thus *assessment* is another important area of personality psychology covered within each approach. Examples of personality assessment are scattered throughout this book. If you take the time to try each of these inventories, not only will you obtain a better understanding of how psychologists from the different approaches measure personality, but you will also gain insight into your own personality. As you complete each inventory, you can record your scores in the Appendix of this book. In addition, within each section, an entire chapter is devoted to *research* relevant to that approach to personality. Personality psychology is, after all, a science. By examining a few research topics in depth for each of the approaches, you will see how theories generate research and how the findings from one study typically lead to new questions and more research.

> "There can scarcely be anything more familiar than human behavior. Nor can there be anything more important. Nonetheless, it is certainly not the thing we understand best."
>
> B. F. SKINNER

Theory

Each approach to understanding personality begins with a theory. This theory usually comes from the writings of several important psychologists who provide their own descriptions of consistent patterns of behavior and intrapersonal processes. They explain the mechanisms that underlie human personality and how these mechanisms are responsible for creating behaviors unique to a given individual. In most cases, the theorists also attempt to explain how differences in personality develop. And many describe methods for changing personality based on their theories.

If you were to develop your own theory of personality, like the theorists covered in this book, you would need to address several critical questions about the nature of human personality. Let's look briefly at a few of the most important questions you would need to consider. The way theorists from each of the six approaches generally deal with these issues is diagrammed in Figure 1.1.

Genetic Versus Environmental Influences

Are people born with the seeds for their adult personalities already intact? Or do we enter this world with no inherited personality orientation, with each healthy baby just as likely as any other to become a great humanitarian, a criminal, a leader, or a helpless psychotic? In one way or another, each major theory of personality addresses this question: To what extent are our

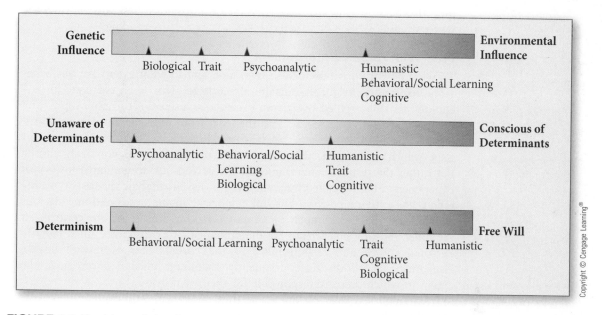

FIGURE 1.1 Position of the Six Approaches to Personality on Three Theory Issues

personalities the result of inherited predispositions, and to what extent are they shaped by the environment in which we grow up? Many biological and trait theorists argue that too often psychologists fail to recognize the importance of inherited predispositions. To a lesser degree, psychoanalytic theorists also emphasize innate needs and behavior patterns, albeit unconscious. However, humanistic, behavioral/social learning, and cognitive theorists are less likely to emphasize inherited influences on personality. Many of these theorists don't deny the role of genetics, but they place focus their attention on other determinants of personality. To some extent, the answer to these questions is an empirical one. And as we will see in Chapter 10, a growing amount of research implicates inherited factors in the development of personality.

Conscious Versus Unconscious Determinants of Behavior

To what extent are people aware of the causes of their behavior? Psychoanalyst Sigmund Freud argued that much of what we do is under the control of unconscious forces, which by definition are outside of our awareness. B. F. Skinner, an influential behavior theorist, argued that people assume they understand the reasons for their actions when in reality they do not. In contrast, trait and cognitive theorists rely heavily on self-report data in developing their theories and in their research. They assume people can identify and report, for example, their level of social anxiety or how they organize information in their memories. However, these psychologists hedge away from an extreme position on this issue. Increasingly, cognitive psychologists recognize that much information processing takes place at a level below awareness. Humanistic theorists often take a middle-ground position on this issue. Although these theorists argue that no one knows us better than ourselves, they also acknowledge that many people do not understand why they act the way they do.

Free Will Versus Determinism

To what extent do we decide our own fate, and to what extent are our behaviors determined by forces outside our control? This is an old issue in psychology that has spilled over from even older discussions in philosophy and theology. On one extreme we find theorists from the behavioral/social learning approach called radical behaviorists. Perhaps most outspoken on this issue was B. F. Skinner, who argued that our behavior is not freely chosen but rather the result of environmental forces and our accumulated history of experiences. Skinner called freedom a myth. Psychoanalytic theorists typically take a less extreme position but still emphasize innate needs and unconscious mechanisms that leave much of human behavior outside of our control. At the other end of the spectrum are the humanistic theorists, who often identify personal choice and responsibility as the cornerstones of mental health. Humanistic psychotherapists frequently encourage clients to recognize the extent to which they are responsible for their own lives.

Although less clear on this issue, trait, biological, and cognitive theorists probably fall somewhere between these others. Trait theorists and biological theorists often emphasize genetic predispositions that tend to limit development in certain areas. But none of these psychologists would argue that personality is completely dictated by these predispositions. Similarly, cognitive psychotherapists often encourage their clients to recognize how they cause many of their own problems and help clients to develop strategies to avoid future difficulties.

Application

The most obvious way personality psychologists use their theories to address problems is through psychotherapy. Many of the personality theorists covered in the book were also therapists who developed and refined their ideas about human personality as they worked with clients. Psychotherapy comes in many different styles, each reflecting assumptions the therapist makes about the nature of personality. For example, psychoanalytic therapists attend to unconscious causes of the problem behavior. Humanistic therapists are more likely to work in a nondirective manner to provide the proper atmosphere in which clients can explore their own feelings. Cognitive therapists try to change the way their clients process information, whereas behaviorists might structure the environment so that desired behaviors increase in frequency and undesired behaviors decrease. Personality theory and research are also used by psychologists working in educational, organizational, and counseling settings. In the following chapters, you will also see what personality psychologists tell us about religion, effective teaching, and choosing a career.

Assessment

How psychologists measure personality depends on which of the six approaches they adhere to. Many personality researchers use self-report inventories, in which test takers answer a series of questions about themselves. But psychoanalytic psychologists are more interested in what people are unable to describe directly. They learn about some of these unconscious thoughts by asking test takers to respond to ambiguous stimuli, which a trained psychologist then interprets. Traditional behavioral psychologists often take another tactic in assessing personality. They're not interested in structures and concepts that supposedly exist within people's minds. To determine consistent behavior patterns, these psychologists observe behavior. A behavioral psychologist who wants to measure cooperation might observe people working on a group task. A person who engages in a large number of cooperative behaviors (helping others in the group, complimenting others on their work) would be identified as a cooperative person. In short, how a psychologist measures personality depends on what he or she thinks personality is.

> "*Everyone else probably understand us better than we do ourselves.*"
> Carl Jung

Research

Although the focus thus far has been on the differences among the six approaches, one feature they all have in common is that each generates a great deal of relevant research. As you will see, sometimes this research tests

It's difficult to make it through college without taking a personality test somewhere along the way. One reason that self-report inventories are frequently used in personality research can be seen here—researchers can quickly collect information from a large number of people.

Jerry Burger

principles and assumptions central to the theory. Other times researchers are interested in further exploring some of the concepts introduced by a personality theory. You will also notice that several topics—health, relationships, depression, achievement, anxiety, aggression—surface in more than one place in the book. This is because a full understanding of these topics requires that we examine them from more than one approach. Several psychology journals are devoted to publishing research on personality, and many more publish articles relevant to the topics examined here. Psychology researchers employ a large number of methods in their efforts to uncover information about personality (Craik, 1986; Mallon, Kingsley, Affleck, & Tennen, 1998; Tracy, Robins, & Sherman, 2009). You won't need a complete understanding of these procedures to appreciate the research covered in this book. But it will help if you have a grasp of the hypothesis-testing approach and a few of the common procedures used by personality researchers. These topics are addressed in the next chapter.

Summary

1. Personality psychology is concerned with the differences among people. Although there is no agreed-upon definition, personality is defined here as consistent behavior patterns and intrapersonal processes originating within the individual.

2. For convenience, the many theories of personality are divided into six general categories: the psychoanalytic, trait, biological, humanistic, behavioral/social learning, and cognitive approaches. Each approach provides a different focus for explaining individual differences in behavior. The six approaches can be thought of as complementary models for understanding human personality, although occasionally they present competing accounts of behavior.

3. Personality psychologists need to consider the culture from which an individual comes. Most of the findings reported in this book are based on research in individualistic cultures, such as the United States. However, these results don't always generalize to people in collectivist cultures.

4. A thorough understanding of human personality requires more than the study of theory. Consequently, we'll also examine how each of the approaches is applied to practical concerns, how each deals with personality assessment, and some of the research relevant to the issues and topics addressed by the theories.

Key Terms

collectivist culture (p. 11)   individualistic culture (p. 10)   personality (p. 4)

Media Resources

Visit the book companion website at
www.cengagebrain.com to find a glossary,
flashcards, quizzing, and more.

Personality Research Methods

Not long ago, "Desperate in Dallas" wrote to a newspaper advice columnist about her husband's 16-year-old cousin, who was living with them. The boy didn't want to work, didn't want to go to school, and generally was a very messy houseguest. What was she to do? The columnist explained to "Desperate" that the boy's real problem was the rejection he had received from his parents earlier in his life. These early childhood experiences were responsible for the boy's lack of motivation. Within the next few weeks, the adviser also explained to "Wondering in Boston" that a 5-year-old boy became aggressive from watching too many violent programs on television. She told "Anonymous in Houston" that her 5-year-old daughter was going to be a leader, and "Intrigued in Norfolk" that, although some people are routinely incapacitated with minor aches and pains, others are capable of ignoring them.

In each of these examples, the columnist was explaining why a certain person engages in consistent behavior patterns—that is, the causes of that person's personality. Millions of people seem to think this columnist has something to say about human behavior. But how does she know? Experience? Intelligence? A keen insight into human nature? Perhaps. In a way, advice columnists represent one avenue for understanding personality—through expert opinion. In some ways, the columnist is similar to the great personality theorists who study the works of others, make their own observations, and then describe what they believe are the causes of human behavior. As you will see in Chapter 3, Sigmund Freud proposed many groundbreaking ideas about personality. Freud read widely about what his contemporaries were saying about behavior. He worked and consulted with some of the great thinkers of the day who also were concerned about psychological phenomena. And Freud carefully observed his patients, who came to him with a variety of psychological problems. From the information gathered from all of these sources, Freud developed a theory of personality that he spent the rest of his career promoting.

Although more scholarly than a columnist's one-paragraph diagnosis, Freud's writings often evoke a similar response: How does he know? Freud's ideas are intriguing, and his arguments at times persuasive, but most personality psychologists want more than an expert's viewpoint before they accept a personality theory. They want empirical research. They want studies examining key predictions from the theory. They want some hard numbers to support those predictions. This is not because an expert's views are of no value. Quite the contrary, the views and observations of personality theorists form the backbone of this book. But theories alone provide only part of the picture. Understanding the nature of human personality also requires an examination of what psychologists have learned from rigorous empirical investigations.

This chapter presents a brief introduction to personality research, beginning with a description of some basic concepts associated with the hypothesis-testing approach to research, with an emphasis on issues particularly relevant for personality researchers. Next we look at a research procedure that has played a significant role in the history of personality psychology—the case study method. We then briefly touch on what you will need to know about statistical analysis of data. Finally, because personality psychologists often rely on personality assessment, we quickly review some of the concepts associated with measuring individual differences in personality.

The Hypothesis-Testing Approach

Each of us on occasion speculates about the nature of personality. You may have wondered why you seem to be more self-conscious than others, why a family member is depressed so often, or why you have so much trouble making friends. In the latter case, you may have watched the way a popular student interacts with the people she meets and compared her behavior with the way you act around strangers. You may have even tried to change your behavior to be more like hers and then watched to see if this affected how people react to you.

In essence, the difference between this process and that used by personality psychologists lies only in the degree of sophistication. Like all of us, these researchers speculate about the nature of personality. From observations, knowledge about previous theory and research, and careful speculation, they generate hypotheses about why certain people behave the way they do. Then, using experimental methods, they collect data to see if their explanations about human behavior are correct. Like pieces in a large jigsaw puzzle, each study makes another contribution to our understanding of personality. However, by the time you get to the end of this book, it should be clear that this is one puzzle that will never be finished.

Theories and Hypotheses

Most personality research begins with a **theory**—a general statement about the relationship between constructs or events. Theories differ in the range of events or phenomena they explain. Some, such as the major personality theories discussed in this book, are very broad. Psychologists have used Freud's psychoanalytic theory to explain topics as diverse as what causes psychological disorders, why people turn to religion, and why certain jokes are funny. However, personality researchers typically work with theories considerably narrower in application. For example, they might speculate about the reasons some people are more motivated to achieve than others or about the relationship between a parent's behavior and a child's level of self-esteem. It might be useful to think of the larger theories, such as Freud's, as collections of more specific theories that share certain assumptions about the nature of human personality.

A good theory possesses at least two characteristics. First, a good theory is *parsimonious*. Scientists generally operate under the "law of parsimony"— that is, the simplest theory that can explain the phenomenon is the best. As you will see throughout this book, several theories can be generated to explain any one behavior. Some can be quite extensive, including many concepts and assumptions, whereas others explain the phenomenon in relatively simple terms. Which theory is better? Although it sometimes seems that scientists enjoy wrapping their work in fancy terms and esoteric concepts, the truth is that if two theories can account for an effect equally well, the simpler explanation is preferred.

Second, a good theory is *useful*. More specifically, unless a theory can generate testable hypotheses, it will be of little or no use to scientists. Ideas that cannot be tested are not necessarily incorrect. It's just that they do not lend themselves to scientific investigation. For example, throughout history some people have explained psychological disorders in terms of invisible demons taking over a person's body. This may or may not be a correct statement about the causes of disorders. But unless this explanation is somehow testable, the theory cannot be examined through scientific methods and therefore holds little value for scientists.

However, theories themselves are never tested. Instead, investigators derive from the theory hypotheses that can then be tested in research. A **hypothesis** is a formal prediction about the relationship between two or more variables that is logically derived from the theory. For example, many psychologists are interested in individual differences in loneliness (Chapter 12). That is, they want to know why some people frequently suffer from feelings of loneliness, whereas others rarely feel lonely. One theory proposes that lonely people lack the social skills necessary to develop and maintain satisfying relationships. Because this is a useful theory, many predictions can be logically derived from it, as shown in Figure 2.1. For example, if the theory correctly describes a cause of loneliness, we might expect consistently lonely people to make fewer attempts to initiate conversations than those who are not lonely. Another prediction might be that these lonely people have a poor idea of how they are being perceived by others. Yet another prediction might maintain that lonely people make more socially inappropriate statements than nonlonely people during conversations

Each of these predictions can be tested. For example, we might test the last prediction by recording conversations lonely and nonlonely people have with new acquaintances. Judges could evaluate the conversations in terms of number of appropriate responses, number of appropriate questions, and so on. If people who identify themselves as lonely make fewer appropriate responses during the conversation, the prediction is confirmed. We then say we have support for the theory. But notice that the theory itself is not tested directly. In fact, theories are never proved or disproved. Rather, a theory is more or less supported by the research and therefore is more or less useful to scientists trying to understand the phenomenon. The more often research confirms a prediction derived from a theory, the more faith psychologists have that the theory accurately describes the nature of things. However, if empirical investigations consistently fail to confirm predictions, we are much less likely to accept the theory. In these cases, scientists typically generate a new theory or modify the old one to better account for the research findings.

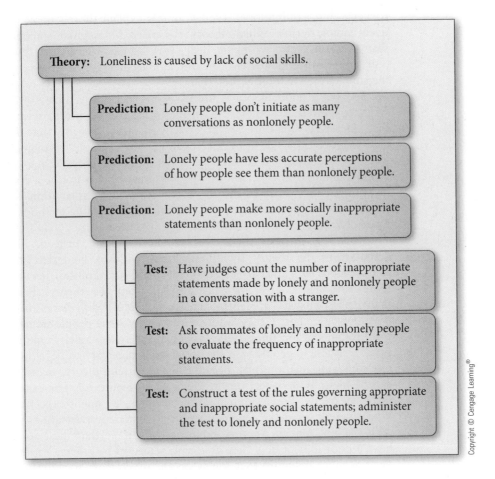

Copyright © Cengage Learning®

FIGURE 2.1 Example of the Hypothesis-Testing Approach

Experimental Variables

Good research progresses from theory to prediction to experiment. The basic elements of an experiment are the experimental variables, which are divided into two types: independent variables and dependent variables. An **independent variable** determines how the groups in the experiment are divided. Often this is manipulated by the experimenter, such as when participants are randomly assigned to different experimental conditions. An independent variable might be the amount of a drug each group receives, how much anxiety is created in each group, or the type of story each group reads. For example, if level of anxiety is the independent variable, a researcher might tell Group A that they will give a speech in front of a dozen critical people, Group B that they will give a speech in front of a few supportive people, and Group C nothing about a speech. Because each of the groups created by the independent variable receives a slightly different treatment, some researchers refer to the independent variable as the *treatment* variable.

Jerry Burger

Many personality researchers conduct laboratory studies to test their hypotheses. These investigations typically take place in university settings, often with undergraduate students as participants and graduate students as experimenters.

A **dependent variable** is measured by the investigator and used to compare the experimental groups. In a well-designed study, differences among groups on the dependent variable can be attributed to the different levels of the independent variable. Returning to the anxiety example, suppose the researcher's hypothesis was that people reduce anxiety about upcoming events by obtaining as much information about the situation as possible. The researcher might use level of anxiety as the independent variable, creating high-, moderate-, and low-anxiety conditions. The three groups might be compared on how many questions they ask the experimenter about the upcoming event. In this case, the number of questions is the dependent variable. The results of such an experiment might look like this:

	High Anxiety	*Moderate Anxiety*	*Low Anxiety*
Average number of questions	5.44	3.12	1.88

If the experiment has been designed correctly, the investigator will attribute the difference in the dependent variable (the number of questions) to the different levels of the independent variable (anxiety). Because experimenters want to say that differences in the dependent variable are the result of the

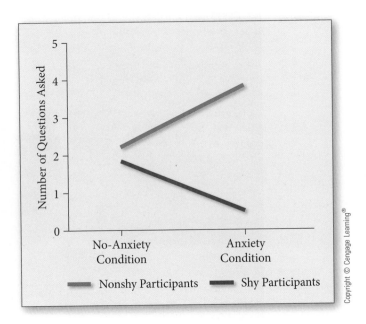

FIGURE 2.2 An Interaction Between Two Independent Variables

different treatment each of the groups received, some researchers refer to the dependent variable as the *outcome* variable.

However, most personality research is more elaborate than this example indicates. Researchers typically use more than one independent variable. In the information-seeking example, an experimenter might want to further divide participants into groups according to how shy they typically are. The researcher might predict that anxiety leads to a search for information, but only among people who are not shy. Researchers in this hypothetical study might use two independent variables to divide participants into groups. They might randomly assign participants to either an anxiety (anticipates speech) or a no-anxiety group, and within each of these groups identify those who are shy and those who are not. If the dependent variable remains the number of questions asked of the experimenter, the results might turn out like those shown in Figure 2.2. This figure illustrates what is called an *interaction*. That is, how one independent variable affects the dependent variable depends on the other independent variable. In this example, whether anxiety leads to an increase in questions depends on whether the participant is high or low in shyness.

Manipulated Versus Nonmanipulated Independent Variables

Sometimes personality researchers randomly assign participants to conditions, such as putting them into anxiety or no-anxiety groups. However, other times they simply identify which group the participant already belongs to, such as whether the person is shy or not shy. The significance of this difference is illustrated in the following example.

Suppose you are interested in the effect violent television programs have on the amount of aggression people display in real life. You recruit two kinds of participants—those who watch a lot of violent TV shows and those who watch relatively few. You then measure the participants' level of aggression in a number of situations. Consistent with the hypothesis, you find that people who watch a lot of violent television are more aggressive than those who watch relatively little violent TV. You might be tempted to conclude that watching violent television programs *causes* people to be more aggressive. However, based on this study alone, your conclusion must be tempered. For example, it's possible that some people watch violent TV shows precisely *because* they are aggressive. Perhaps they are more entertained by programs that include shootings, stabbings, and other violent acts. Thus, although the findings are consistent with the hypothesis, statements about cause and effect must be qualified.

This example illustrates the fundamental difference between research using manipulated independent variables and research using nonmanipulated independent variables. An investigator who uses a **manipulated independent variable** begins with a large number of participants and randomly assigns them to experimental groups. That is, each person has an equally likely chance of being assigned to Condition A as to Condition B (or C, or D, and so on). Investigators know all participants are not exactly alike at the beginning of the study. Some are naturally more aggressive than others, some more anxious, some more intelligent. Each has different life experiences that might affect what he or she does in the study. However, by using a large number of participants and randomly assigning them to conditions, researchers assume that all these differences will be evened out. Thus, although within any given condition there are people who are typically high or low in aggressiveness, each condition should have the same *average* level of aggressiveness at the beginning of the experiment.

The researcher then introduces the independent variable. For example, one group might be shown 30 minutes of violent television programming, another group might watch a baseball game, and still another group might sit quietly and watch no television. Because we assume participants in each condition are nearly identical on average at the start of the study, any differences among the groups *after* watching the program can be attributed to the independent variable. That is, if participants who watched the violent TV shows are more aggressive than those who watched the nonviolent shows or those who watched no TV, we can conclude with reasonable confidence that watching the violent TV shows *caused* the participants to act more aggressively.

This procedure contrasts with one that uses nonmanipulated variables. A **nonmanipulated independent variable** (sometimes referred to as a subject variable) exists without the researcher's intervention. For example, researchers might divide people into high self-esteem and low self-esteem groups, or into

> "*Personality is so complex a thing that every legitimate method must be employed in its study.*"
> GORDON ALLPORT

first-born, middle-born, or last-born categories. In these cases, the investigator does not randomly assign participants to a condition. Returning to the earlier example, the researcher who compared frequent and infrequent television viewers did not manipulate participants into those two categories. Instead, the participants had already determined which of the groups they belonged to without any action on the researcher's part.

The difficulty with this and other nonmanipulated independent variables is that the researcher cannot assume the people in the two groups are nearly identical on average at the beginning of the experiment. For example, people who watch fewer hours of television might be more intelligent or come from a higher socioeconomic level. We can be fairly certain that they have more time for activities other than television, such as reading or interacting with friends. The two kinds of participants also might differ in terms of self-esteem, diet, and, most notably, their level of aggression prior to participating in the experiment. Thus any differences we find between the two groups could be caused by any of these differences and not necessarily by the number of violent TV shows each group watches.

Because it is difficult to determine cause-and-effect relationships with nonmanipulated independent variables, researchers generally prefer to manipulate variables. However, doing so is not always possible. Sometimes manipulating the variable is too expensive, too difficult, or unethical. This is a particular problem in personality research because many of the variables researchers want to study simply cannot be manipulated. Returning to the violent television example, it would be next to impossible to tell some participants, "You watch a lot of violent television during the next few years," and tell others, "You watch no violent television until I tell you it's okay." Instead, if we want to know about the long-term effects of exposure to violent TV, we have to accept the participants as they are, understanding that many group differences exist at the outset of the study. Sometimes investigators try to control some of these known differences, such as by comparing the education levels of the two groups. However, researchers can never be sure that they have controlled all relevant variables.

This is not to say that research with nonmanipulated independent variables is useless. On the contrary, personality psychologists often find that relying on nonmanipulated variables is the only way to examine a topic of interest. How else can we study differences between introverts and extraverts or differences between men and women? A recent survey of academic journals found that the vast majority of personality research relies on nonmanipulated independent variables (Revelle & Oehlberg, 2008). Nonetheless, investigators who conduct this research must remain cautious when making statements about cause and effect.

Prediction Versus Hindsight

Which person is more impressive: the one who can explain *after* a basketball game why the winning team was victorious, or the one who accurately tells you *before* the game which team will win and why? Most of us are more impressed with the second person. After all, anyone can come up with an explanation after the facts are in. But people who really understand the game can make reasonable guesses about what will happen when two teams meet.

In a similar manner, if a scientist has a legitimate theory, we can expect him or her to make reasonably accurate predictions about what will happen in a study before the data are in. Remember, the purpose of research is to provide support for a hypothesis. Researchers generate a theory, make a hypothesis, and collect data that either support or do not support the hypothesis. Suppose a researcher examines the relationship between self-esteem and helping behavior, but the investigator has no clear prediction beforehand of what this relationship might be. If the study finds that high self-esteem people help more than low self-esteem people, the researcher might conclude that this is because people who feel good about themselves maintain that positive evaluation by doing good things. The explanation sounds reasonable, but do the data support the hypothesis? From a scientific standpoint, the answer is "No" because the hypothesis was generated *after* the results were seen. With that sequence, there is no way the hypothesis would not be supported. If the study found that low self-esteem people help more, the same researcher might conclude that this is because these people are trying to improve their self-image by doing good things. With no possibility that the hypothesis might not be supported, the hypothesis has not really been tested. This is not to say researchers should ignore findings they haven't predicted. On the contrary, such findings are often the basis for future hypotheses and further research. But explaining everything after the results are in explains nothing.

Replication

When investigators conduct a well-designed study and uncover statistically significant results, they usually report the findings in a journal or perhaps at a professional conference. Sometimes the findings are cited in popular media as something researchers *know* about the topic. However, most psychologists are cautious about relying on one research finding when drawing conclusions about human behavior.

There are many reasons a researcher might find a statistically significant effect in a given study. There could be something peculiar about the people in the sample. There might be something special about the time the research was conducted—perhaps an unusual mood in the country or on campus, caused by an important event. Or the finding could be the result of some unknown and inadvertent aspect of the particular experimental procedure. Whatever the reason, it is dangerous to assume that a significant finding from one study provides reliable evidence for an effect.

The way to deal with this problem is through *replication*. The more often an effect is found in research, the more confidence we have that it reflects a genuine relationship. Replications often examine participant populations different from those used in the original research. This helps to determine whether the effect applies to a larger number of people or is limited to the kind of individuals used in the original sample. Yet determining the strength of an effect by how often it is replicated is not always easy. One difficulty has been called the "File Drawer" problem (Rosenthal, 1979). That is, investigators tend to publish and report research only when they find significant effects. When an attempt at replication fails, the researcher may decide something has gone wrong—perhaps the wrong materials were used, perhaps something was not done the way the original researcher did it, and so on. And so the research is stored away in a file drawer and never reported. The result is that a well-known research finding may, in fact, be difficult to replicate. But because the failures at replication are stored away in file drawers, we might not realize the problem exists.

The Case Study Method

Like a carpenter or a physician, personality researchers must use many different tools to be effective in their job. Although most personality psychologists rely on empirical studies with large numbers of participants to test their ideas, there are other ways to examine individual differences and personality processes. One procedure occasionally used by personality researchers is the **case study method,** an in-depth evaluation of a single individual (or sometimes a few individuals). Typically, the participant in a case study is a psychotherapy client suffering from a problem of interest to the investigator. The researcher records in great detail the person's history, current behavior, and changes in behavior over the course of the investigation, which sometimes lasts for years. Case study data are usually descriptive. That is, rather than reporting a lot of numbers and statistical analyses, investigators describe their impressions of what the person did and what the behavior means. Researchers occasionally include quantitative assessments, such as recording how many times the person washes his or her hands in a 24-hour period. However, data comparing the individual with another group or another person are rarely reported.

As you will see throughout this book, case studies have played an important role in the history of personality psychology. Sigmund Freud relied almost exclusively on his own in-depth analysis of patients when formulating ideas about personality. In fact, many of Freud's initial insights into the functions of the human mind came from his observations of one early patient, Anna O., whose story is told in Chapter 3. Gordon Allport, the first psychologist to promote the concept of traits, argued that we cannot capture the essence of a whole personality without an in-depth analysis of a single individual. Humanistic theorists, most notably Carl Rogers, developed their unique concept of human nature through the extensive evaluation of psychotherapy clients. Behaviorists also sometimes rely on case studies to illustrate various aspects of their theories and the effectiveness of their therapies. For example, we will review John B. Watson's work with an infant named "Little Albert" in Chapter 13. This famous case study has been widely cited as evidence for the behaviorist explanation of abnormal behaviors.

Limitations of the Case Study Method

The widespread use of the case study method by prominent psychologists may surprise you at first given some of the obvious weaknesses of this method. First is the problem of generalizing from a single individual to other people. Just because one person reacts to events in a certain way does not mean all people do. In fact, many case study participants come to the attention of personality theorists when they seek out psychotherapy, often because they feel different from others. Most experimenters use a large number of participants in their studies as a way to eliminate the bias that comes from examining just a few people who may or may not represent a larger population.

Second is the problem of determining cause-and-effect relationships with the case study method. For example, a client with a fear of water may recall a traumatic experience of nearly drowning as a child. Although we can speculate that this earlier event is responsible for the fear, we cannot be certain that the fear wouldn't have developed without the experience. For this reason, researchers using case studies must be cautious when speculating about the causes of the behaviors they see.

Third, investigators' subjective judgments can often interfere with scientific objectivity in case study work. The expectancies researchers bring to a case study may cause them to see that which confirms their hypotheses and to overlook that which does not. It's possible that a different psychologist working with the same individual might come to different conclusions. As you will see in Chapter 3, Freud in particular has been criticized for approaching his cases with his own biases.

Strengths of the Case Study Method

With all these weaknesses, why do personality researchers ever rely on the case study method? One reason is that other research methods might not do the job. For example, Freud's concern with the deeper understanding of an individual's unconscious mind is not easily examined in other ways. The richness of a single person's life can be lost when he or she is reduced to a few numbers that are then added to other participants' numbers. This was one reason a team of researchers conducted a case study on Dodge Morgan, who at age 54 sailed around the globe by himself (Nasby & Read, 1997). The detailed analysis of Morgan's behavior and personality as he made his way through this adventure provides insights unavailable through other methods. The case study method is also valuable for generating hypotheses about the nature of human personality. Researchers sometimes follow up case studies with more traditional scientific investigations.

The case study method is a particularly useful research tool in at least four situations. It is the most appropriate method when examining a rare case. Suppose you wanted to investigate the personalities of political assassins. You probably would be limited to exploring the background and behavior of only a handful of people who fall into this category. Similarly, therapists working with patients described as having multiple personalities often report their observations in a case study manner when recording information about what is probably a once-in-a-lifetime encounter.

The case study method is also appropriate when researchers can argue that the individual being studied is essentially no different from all normal people on the dimension of interest. For example, case studies of "split-brain" patients have uncovered important information about the functioning of the human brain. Participants in these studies have had the corpus callosum (which connects the right and left halves of the cerebral hemisphere) severed as part of treatment for severe epilepsy. Because the physical functions of the brain are basically alike for all normally functioning people, studying the behavior of these few patients tells us much about the way our right and left brains would operate if not connected by the corpus callosum.

Still another appropriate use of the case study is to illustrate a treatment. Therapists often describe in detail the procedures they used to treat a particular client and the apparent success or failure of the therapy. A prudent therapist will not argue that all people suffering from the disorder should be treated in this way but rather will use the case study to suggest treatment programs other therapists might explore with their clients. A therapy procedure is most effectively demonstrated when the client's progress is compared at various stages of the treatment, such as comparing a no-treatment period with a treatment stage.

Finally, an investigator might choose the case study method simply to demonstrate possibilities. For example, a researcher using one or two easily hypnotizable people might demonstrate impressive changes in behavior. Some deeply hypnotizable people have been reported to change skin temperature on one part of the body but not on another or to form blisters on their hands when imagining their hands are on fire. These studies are not intended to argue that all people are able to do these things but rather to illustrate some of the possibilities obtainable with hypnosis.

Statistical Analysis of Data

Suppose a waitress wants to know, for obvious reasons, what kind of behavior elicits the largest tips from customers. Her hypothesis is that smiling and acting in a friendly manner will result in better tips than acting in a more professional and reserved manner. She tests her hypothesis by alternating between the friendly and professional styles each night for 14 nights. At the end of each evening, she counts her tips and records the data. Suppose these are her findings:

Friendly Approach	*Professional Approach*
$51.50	$56.90
62.75	51.75
59.60	58.00
52.00	52.25
61.10	53.60
49.45	59.30
50.20	50.60
$55.23 average	$54.63 average

The waitress concludes that the friendly approach indeed works best, and she changes to a friendly waitressing style from then on. But is her conclusion justified? We can see from the numbers that the friendly style came up with a higher average tip than the professional style. But by now you probably have already wondered if an average of $55.23 is reliably different from an average of $54.63. Because of naturally occurring variation in the amount of tips made in an evening, we would not expect the averages to come out exactly the same, even if the waitress never changed her style. One condition in this study would almost always come out at least a little higher than the other. So the question becomes: How much higher must one of the averages be before we conclude that the difference is not just a chance fluctuation but in fact represents a real difference between the two styles of waitressing? This is the question of statistical significance.

Statistical Significance

How can researchers tell if different group averages represent real effects or just chance fluctuations? Fortunately, statisticians have developed formulas that allow us to estimate the likelihood that the difference between the averages could have occurred by chance alone. There are many types of statistical tests, each appropriate for different types of data and different research designs. Some of the more common tests are an *analysis of variance,* a *chi-square test,* and a *correlation coefficient.*

Returning to the waitress example, if the two averages differed by an amount so small that it could have been caused by a chance fluctuation, we say the difference has not reached **statistical significance.** Conversely, if the difference is so large that in all likelihood it was not caused by chance but reflects a true difference between the two waitressing styles, we say the difference is statistically significant. In the latter case, the conclusion would be that one style of waitressing does seem to result in better tips than the other style.

However, statistical tests do not really provide a yes or no answer to our question. All they tell us is the statistical likelihood that the difference between the groups was caused by chance. But this observation raises another question. Suppose you apply a statistical test to the waitress' data and find that a difference this large would occur by chance only one out of every three times you conducted the study. What would you conclude? That the different averages represent a real effect? It would be difficult to have much confidence in such a statement. The difference might be real, but there is a high probability that the finding is just a fluke. So when *can* we say we have a real difference? Traditionally, psychologists use a significance level of .05 to answer this question. This means that if the difference between the scores is so large that it would occur less than 5% of the time by chance, the difference is probably genuine.

But keep in mind that statistically significant findings are not necessarily "significant" in all ways. When researchers use a large number of participants, even small differences can be *statistically* significant. Whether the difference is large enough to be important is another question. In response to this concern, investigators often examine and report the size of the difference through statistical values known as *effect size* indicators.

Correlation Coefficients

The **correlation coefficient** is a favorite statistic among personality researchers, and one that will pop up from time to time in this book. The correlation coefficient is the appropriate statistical test when we want to understand the relationship between two measures. For example, we might be interested in the relationship between loneliness and depression. We could ask a large number of people to complete a loneliness scale as well as a depression inventory. If loneliness and depression are related, we would expect people who score high on loneliness to also score high on depression. Similarly, those who score low on loneliness should score low on depression.

Figure 2.3 presents three possible outcomes for this study. Each point on the figure represents one participant's scores on both scales. The first outcome indicates that a person's score on one scale is a fairly good predictor of that person's score on the other scale. In this case, if we know someone is high on loneliness, we know that person is probably going to score high on depression as well. The second outcome indicates little or no relationship between the measures. Knowing a person's score on one scale tells us nothing about what the other score will be. The third outcome, like the first, indicates that knowing a person's loneliness score will help predict the depression score, but not in the way we might have anticipated. Here, a high score on one measure predicts a low score on the other.

After conducting the appropriate statistical test, we can reduce the data from our study to a single number, the correlation coefficient. This number can range from 1.00 to –1.00. Returning to the figure, the first outcome indicates a fairly strong relationship between loneliness and depression. The correlation coefficient for this figure might be .60. Because a high score on one measure indicates a high score on the other measure, this is a *positive correlation*. For the second outcome, the correlation coefficient is close to .00, indicating no relationship between the measures. The third outcome might yield a correlation of .60, also a fairly strong relationship between the variables.

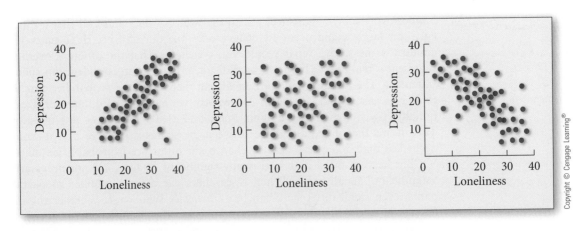

FIGURE 2.3 Three Possible Relations Between Loneliness and Depression

First They Tell You One Thing; Then They Tell You Another

Several years ago, four important health studies were reported in the news media within one 2-week period (Vo & Ostrov, 2006). A Women's Health Initiative study found no evidence that a low-fat diet for women over 50 reduced the risk of cancer or heart disease. We learned from another study that calcium and vitamin D supplements did not prevent broken bones for older women. We also read that estrogen supplements might not increase heart disease after all, followed by a report that exercise did not reduce the incidence of colon cancer. What makes these findings particularly interesting is that each contradicted current health care advice based on earlier studies. For those of us trying to keep up with the latest developments in nutrition and health, this is a familiar experience. Just like the advice on oat bran, salt, red wine, and caffeine, what researchers once told us suddenly seemed not to be the case. Even the value of getting an annual physical—for decades considered an essential step for maintaining good health—has been challenged by recent research (Rosenthal, 2012).

Personality researchers have little reason to feel smug. As discussed in Chapter 8, psychologists in the 1970s warned of the health consequences from a Type A lifestyle. But

research in the 1980s suggested that the warnings may have been premature. Similarly, the latest advice on how to lose weight, raise your children, and relate to your romantic partner often shifts with each new discovery. What's going on here? Perhaps, as a friend suggested recently, news media should stop reporting research findings until the investigators agree on what they know.

The problem is not that researchers can't make up their minds. Rather, consumers of scientific information may need a better understanding of how science works. A single study—even one reported with great fanfare in the news media—is but one step in a long-term, ongoing process. As revealed throughout this book, an important research finding does not merely provide data on an interesting question. It also raises new questions and stimulates new research. To understand what researchers know about a topic, we have to look at *programs* of research, not just isolated studies. Moreover, psychologists know that behavior is the result of many causes, and untangling the complex relationships between variables is a challenging task.

Sometimes findings can't be replicated. Sometimes additional information changes the interpretation

of earlier results. If we look at research findings over a long period of time, we often see an impressive amount of progress. But a closer inspection reveals that science moves in fits and starts. As a result, highly publicized "discoveries" often turn out to be incorrect. One journalist looked at 12 discoveries in the field of high-energy physics that were important enough to be reported in the *New York Times* (Taubes, 1998). He determined that 9 of the 12 discoveries were later found to be inaccurate. The Bayer pharmaceutical company recently announced that it failed to replicate nearly two-thirds of findings reported in academic journals that it tested (Naik, 2011).

What's the lesson here? First, scientific understanding of any interesting question comes from a series of investigations, not just one study. Second, the subject matter of this book—personality and behavior—is complex, and good psychological research is difficult. Third, recent findings represent our knowledge at the moment. It would be foolish to dismiss this information, but it would be equally ill advised to assume that the most recent study is the last word.

This last outcome is referred to as a *negative correlation,* but this does not mean it is less important than a positive correlation of the same magnitude. For example, if we had compared scores on a loneliness scale with scores on a sociability measure, we probably would have anticipated that a high score on one test would predict a low score on the other.

Personality Assessment

> *"The man with creative ideas in philosophy or art can give wings to them at once; but in science ... extensive painstaking experiment has to be done."*
>
> RAYMOND CATTELL

Sometimes our culture seems obsessed with measuring personality. Popular magazines often promote short tests, or "quizzes," to measure how good a roommate you are, what type of romantic partner you need, or the vacation spot that matches your personality. Although the magazines rarely claim their tests are based on scientific investigations, the popularity of these tests suggests that readers find them at least interesting, if not believable. There is something about calculating a score that gives credibility to an untested 10-item quiz.

Personality psychologists should also be concerned with the credibility of the numbers generated by their tests. Personality assessment is a central part of personality research. If we are going to study achievement motivation, self-esteem, social anxiety, and so on, we need to measure these concepts as accurately as possible. Similarly, psychologists working in education, human resources, and counseling often rely on personality tests to determine whether a child should be placed in a special class, whether an employee should be promoted to a new position, or whether a client needs to be admitted to a psychiatric hospital.

In each case, it is the responsibility of the people using the test to see that it accurately measures the concept they are interested in. Unfortunately, not all personality tests are as good as psychologists would prefer, and even the best tests can be used inappropriately. So how can we tell a good test from a bad one or determine whether the test measures what we want to measure? Before using any standardized test, we need to examine its reliability and validity.

Reliability

Suppose you took a personality test today and it indicated that, compared to others your age, you scored high on *independence*. That is, more than most people, you enjoy being on your own and making your own decisions. However, suppose next week you take the test again, and this time your score indicates you are relatively low on independence. Which of these scores reflects your true personality? Unfortunately, you have no way to know from this test whether you are an independent or a dependent person. The test suffers from poor reliability.

A test has good **reliability** when it measures consistently. One indication of a test's reliability is how consistently the test measures over time. Many factors can contribute to poor consistency from one time to the next. The test questions or the scoring procedures might be vague, or perhaps test responses fluctuate wildly depending on the test taker's mood. Nonetheless, because we assume personality is relatively consistent over time, tests designed to measure personality must provide consistent scores from one testing session to another.

A common way to determine a test's consistency is to calculate *a test–retest reliability coefficient*. Researchers first administer the test to a large number of people. Some time later, usually after a few weeks, the same people take the test again. The scores from the first administration are correlated with those from the second. Recall that correlation coefficients can range from 1.00 to –1.00. A high positive correlation coefficient indicates good consistency over time.

Unfortunately, whether a test is reliable is not a simple yes-or-no question. On one hand, a test–retest coefficient of .90 is probably reliable enough to meet most people's needs. On the other hand, a reliability coefficient of .20 is no doubt too low for most purposes. But what about something in between? Is a test with a reliability coefficient of .50 or .60 acceptable? The answer depends on the researcher's needs and the availability of alternative, more reliable tests. Sometimes the nature of the concept being measured contributes to low reliability. For example, tests given to young children, who often fluctuate in mood and attention, frequently have lower than desirable levels of reliability.

Another aspect of reliability is *internal consistency*. A test is internally consistent when all the items on the test measure the same thing. Let's say 10 items on a 20-item test of extraversion accurately measure the extent to which a test taker is an extraverted person. Because half the items measure extraversion, the overall score probably is somewhat indicative of the person's true level on this trait. But because half the items measure something besides extraversion, the usefulness of the score is limited. This test suffers from poor internal consistency.

Once again, statistical tests are available to help us determine how well responses on one test item correlate with responses on the other items. A statistic called an *internal consistency coefficient* can be calculated. A high coefficient indicates that most of the items are measuring the same concept; a low coefficient suggests items are measuring more than one concept. A careful test maker includes in the final version of a test only those items that "hang together" to measure the same concept.

Validity

Reliability data tell us whether a test is measuring something consistently. But they tell us nothing about *what* the test is measuring. That is why psychologists also examine data concerning the test's validity. **Validity** refers to the extent to which a test measures what it is designed to measure. As with reliability, the question is not whether a test does or does not have validity. Rather, the question is how well the validity of the test has been demonstrated.

Validity is relatively easy to determine for some kinds of tests. For example, if the purpose of a test is to predict how well students will do on an upcoming task, researchers can simply compare the test scores with the task scores to determine the *predictive validity* of the test. Unfortunately, demonstrating validity for most personality tests is not so easy. Personality psychologists often are interested in measuring hypothetical constructs, such as intelligence, masculinity, or social anxiety. *Hypothetical constructs* are useful inventions researchers employ to describe concepts that have no physical reality. That is, no one can be shown an *intelligence*. We can see behavior that suggests high intellectual functioning, but intelligence remains a theoretical entity.

The problem for personality researchers, then, is how to demonstrate that a test measures something that, in reality, is but a useful abstract invention. How do we know if a test measures self-esteem? Test takers who agree with the item, "I am not as competent in sports as most people," might have low self-esteem. Then again, they might just have poor athletic ability, or they might be depressed. Fortunately, there is much personality researchers can do to demonstrate the construct validity of their tests. Researchers can look at a test's face validity, congruent validity, discriminant validity, and behavioral validation.

Face Validity

Perhaps the most obvious way to decide whether a test measures what it says it measures is to look at the test items. Most of us would accept that a test asking people "Do you feel nervous interacting with others?" or "Are you uncomfortable meeting new people?" is probably measuring something like social anxiety.

The test would have good *face validity*. That is, on the face of it, the test appears to be measuring social anxiety. Although most tests have good face validity, not all do. Some hypothetical constructs don't lend themselves to obvious questions. For example, how would you design a test to measure creativity? Asking people "Are you creative?" probably won't help much. Instead, you might ask people to write an ending to a story or to name as many uses as they can think of for an ordinary object. These tests might be good measures of creativity, but the face validity would be less certain than with more straightforward measures.

Congruent Validity

Imagine that you developed a new intelligence test that takes less time to administer than most commonly used tests. You'd probably want to see how scores from your test compare with scores on an established intelligence test. But suppose you gave both tests to a group of people and found a correlation of only .20 between the two test scores. In this case, a person could attain a high score on one intelligence test and a low score on the other, leaving you to wonder which is the true measure of intelligence. This is not to say that the old scale is measuring intelligence and your scale is not, but the low correlation would mean that the two tests are not measuring the same construct.

The *congruent validity* of a test, sometimes called convergent validity, is the extent to which scores from the test correlate with other measures of the same construct. If two tests measure the same thing, scores from the two tests should be highly correlated. However, congruent validity data are not limited to personality tests. For example, to determine the construct validity of an anxiety scale, you might compare test scores with anxiety ratings provided by a team of professional psychologists.

Discriminant Validity

In contrast to congruent validity, *discriminant validity* refers to the extent to which a test score does *not* correlate with the scores of theoretically *unrelated* measures. Let's return to the problem of designing a creativity test. It is important to show that the test measures creativity instead of something that only resembles creativity, such as intelligence. To establish discriminant validity, you might give both the creativity test and an intelligence test to a group of people. If the two test scores are highly correlated, someone could argue that your creativity test does not measure creativity at all, but simply intelligence. However, if the correlation between the two tests is low, you have evidence that the two tests measure different constructs.

Behavioral Validation

Suppose you used scores on an assertiveness scale to predict how people respond when they receive poor service at a restaurant. Naturally, you would expect highly assertive individuals to complain about the service and people low in assertiveness to tolerate the inconvenience. But what if the test scores were completely unrelated to the behavior? What if people with low scores on the scale acted just as assertively as those with high scores? In this case, the validity of the test would be in doubt.

Another step in determining the construct validity of a test is *behavioral validation*. In other words, it is important that test scores predict relevant behavior. It is possible that test takers respond to assertiveness scales by indicating how they think they would act or how they wish they would act. It is possible for a test to have face validity, congruent validity, and discriminant validity, and still have questionable construct validity. If test scores cannot predict behavior, the usefulness of the test must be questioned. On the other hand, if the test does a good job of predicting how people will act in relevant situations, we have strong evidence for the test's validity.

Summary

1. Personality psychologists examine personality processes through scientific research. Most of this research is based on the hypothesis-testing approach in which hypotheses are derived logically from theories. These hypotheses are then tested in studies, and the theory either is or is not supported. A good theory is parsimonious and capable of generating many testable hypotheses.

2. The basic elements of a research design are the independent and dependent variables. One important distinction in personality research concerns whether independent variables are manipulated by the researcher. When researchers examine nonmanipulated variables, they have less confidence when making statements about cause and effect. Predicted results are better than those explained in hindsight because the latter approach does not allow for hypothesis testing. Researchers need to replicate their findings,

but obtaining reliable information about how often an effect is replicated is a problem.

3. Many personality researchers use the case study method. Although case studies have some limitations, such as questionable generalizability to other populations, they also possess some unique advantages over other methods.

4. Researchers use statistical tests to determine whether the differences they find between groups are the result of chance fluctuations or whether they represent genuine effects. Personality researchers often use correlation coefficients when analyzing their data. A correlation coefficient identifies the direction and size of a relationship between two measures.

5. Personality researchers often use personality tests in their work. To determine the usefulness of a test, researchers look at evidence for the test's reliability and validity. Reliability can be gauged through test–retest correlations and internal consistency coefficients. Validity is determined through face validity, congruent validity, discriminant validity, and behavioral validation. Researchers must make subjective judgments when deciding whether tests are reliable and valid enough for their needs.

Key Terms

case study method (p. 28)

correlation coefficient (p. 32)

dependent variable (p. 23)

hypothesis (p. 21)

independent variable (p. 22)

manipulated independent variable (p. 25)

nonmanipulated independent variable (p. 25)

reliability (p. 34)

statistical significance (p. 31)

theory (p. 20)

validity (p. 35)

Media Resources

Visit the book companion website at
www.cengagebrain.com to find a glossary,
flashcards, quizzing, and more.

CHAPTER 3

The Psychoanalytic Approach

Freudian Theory, Application, and Assessment

Although people have speculated about the nature of personality throughout history, the first acknowledged personality theorist did not emerge until the late 1800s. Then an Austrian neurologist began proposing such outrageous notions as the existence of sexual desires in young children, unconscious causes for baffling physical disorders, and treatment through a time-consuming, expensive procedure in which patients lie on a couch while the doctor listens to them talk about seemingly irrelevant topics. That neurologist, Sigmund Freud, continued to develop, promote, and defend his ideas despite intense criticism. By the time of his death in 1939, Freud had written numerous volumes, had established himself as the leader of an important intellectual movement, and had changed the thinking of psychologists, writers, parents, and laypeople for years to come.

Freud's influence on 21st-century thought is so widespread that most of us fail to appreciate the extent to which his theory has become part of our thinking. For example, if you are like most adults in this culture, you freely accept the idea that what you do is sometimes influenced by an unconscious part of your mind. Most of us have said something like "I must have done that unconsciously" or pondered what sort of hidden psychological conflict might be behind a friend or loved one's unusual behavior. Although Freud was not the first to talk about the unconscious, no one before or since has placed so much emphasis on unconscious processes in explaining human behavior. Similarly, when we wonder whether our dreams reveal inner fears and desires, we are espousing an idea Freud popularized. Although people have interpreted dreams for thousands of years, Freud was the first to incorporate dream interpretation into a larger psychological theory.

References to Freudian theory permeate our culture. As one writer put it, "Freud's theories of the subconscious mind … have had a dramatic impact on contemporary film, theater, novels, political campaigning, advertising, legal argument and even religion" (Fisher, 1995). English students learn Freudian psychology when studying the themes in great literature; theology students debate Freud's views on religion. Even our language has not escaped. It is not uncommon to hear people mention Freudian slips, denial, libido, repression, and other Freudian concepts in everyday conversations. But perhaps the most telling tribute to Freud's impact is that nearly every major theorist covered in this book has felt compelled to use Freud's works as a point of comparison for his or her own ideas about the nature of personality. Appropriately, this chapter begins with an examination of Freud's theory of personality.

Freud Discovers the Unconscious

How did a Viennese neurologist come to change the way we think of humankind? There is little in Freud's early history to indicate that greatness awaited him. Although Freud was a respected member of the medical community, his interests began to drift. In 1885 he went to Paris to study with another neurologist, Jean-Martin Charcot. Charcot was experimenting with early versions of hypnosis and its use in curing what were then believed to be unusual physiological problems. Shortly thereafter, Freud returned to Vienna and began work with a prominent physician, Joseph Breuer. Like Charcot, Breuer was using hypnosis to treat hysterical patients. Hysteria is a disorder that consists of a variety of physical symptoms. Patients often display blindness, deafness, an inability to walk or to use an arm, and so on. Most physicians of that day treated hysteria as if it were a physically based illness. However, Breuer and Freud developed another interpretation.

Discussions about one of Breuer's patients, a woman with the pseudonym Anna O., probably set the direction for the rest of Freud's career. According to Breuer, Anna O. experienced a number of hysterical symptoms, including paralysis of her left arm, hallucinations, and the ability to speak only in English even though her native tongue was German. Under hypnosis, Anna O. would talk about her daydreams and hallucinations and about past traumatic events. During her final hypnosis session, she discussed her dying father and some associated hallucinations about a black snake. After this session, the paralysis in her arm was gone, and she could once again speak German.

In 1895 Freud and Breuer published *Studies in Hysteria,* in which they presented the case of Anna O. and discussed their use of hypnosis in treating hysteria. Freud continued to use hypnosis to treat his hysterical patients, but he soon grew disillusioned with its limitations and began looking for alternative methods. Slowly he recognized the importance of allowing patients to say whatever came into their mind. He discovered that, even without hypnosis, under the right circumstances patients would describe previously hidden material that seemed related to the causes and cure of their hysterical symptoms. Refinement of this technique, called **free association**, was a significant step in the development of Freud's theory.

One startling discovery Freud reported in his early patients was that memories uncovered during free association often concerned traumatic sexual experiences, many of which supposedly had occurred in early childhood. He gradually concluded that these early sexual experiences were responsible for the hysterical symptoms expressed by his adult patients. At this point Freud was well along the way in his transition from neurologist to psychologist. He continued to work with hysterical patients and wrote about his observations and the development of his theories, convinced that he was on the threshold of important psychological discoveries.

But Freud's writings sold poorly at first. In fact, his work met with great opposition in the academic and medical communities. Freud's open discussion of infantile sexuality and omnipresent sexual motives did not sit well with the puritanical standards of Victorian Europe. His approach to treatment was so radical that many respected physicians considered it absurd. Nonetheless, Freud continued his work and his writing and soon developed a small following of scholars who traveled to Vienna to study with him. These scholars formed the Vienna Psychoanalytic Society, with Freud as its great figurehead and leader. Later, many members of the society would come to disagree with Freud and leave the ranks to develop their own personality theories and form their own professional organizations. However, as later chapters will reveal, the flavor of their theories remained unmistakably Freudian.

Sigmund Freud

1856–1939

Sigmund Freud was born in 1856 in Freiberg, Moravia (now part of the Czech Republic). In 1860 his family moved to Vienna, where Freud spent virtually the rest of his life. Freud's ambition to amount to something important surfaced early. He enrolled in medical school at the University of Vienna determined to make an important discovery and thereby a name for himself.

Freud began his quest while working in his instructor's medical laboratory. But immediate scientific breakthroughs were not forthcoming, and he soon became discouraged at his chances for advancement. In addition, he had fallen in love with Martha Bernays and wanted to earn enough money to marry her and give her a comfortable lifestyle. So, upon completing his degree, Freud left the lab and went into private practice.

During his subsequent 4-year engagement to Bernays (they were finally married in 1886), Freud won a research grant to travel to Paris to observe Jean-Martin Charcot's work with hypnosis. It

was during this time that he began to develop his ideas about the power of the unconscious mind. His work with Joseph Breuer, observations of his own patients, and a great deal of introspection led to his 1900 book, *The Interpretation of Dreams*. Although it took several years to sell the 600 original printings, the book's publication was the first step toward achieving the widespread recognition Freud had sought back in medical school.

Something about Sigmund Freud has attracted the attention of numerous biographers. The most complete of these is the three-volume biography by Ernest Jones (1953–1957). Although he sought fame, in many ways Freud was a private person. Consequently, most biographers have glued together the facts we have about Freud's life with a large amount of speculation. Perhaps the most interesting part of this speculation concerns the extent to which Freud's description of human personality reflects his own personality and life experiences. Not surprisingly, Freud's relationship with his parents is of particular interest. Although his father had several children from an earlier marriage, Sigmund was his mother's first child and apparently the apple of her eye. His mother was only 21 when he was born and almost as close in age to her son as she was to her husband. Biographers agree that an especially close relationship was formed. Freud's mother sometimes referred to him as her "Golden Sigi." In contrast, Freud's

relationship with his father appears to have been cold, if not occasionally hostile. Freud arrived late to his father's funeral, something he later identified as clearly unconsciously motivated. Freud struggled with guilt feelings over his relationship with his father many years after his father's death.

It is not difficult to see how Freud's description of the Oedipus complex—sexual attraction for the mother and competitive hostility toward the father—may have been a kind of projection of his own feelings toward his parents. Freud hints at this insight at many places in his writings. Indeed, he often relied on his own introspection to test the accuracy of his clinical intuition. He is reported to have reserved a half hour each night for this self-analysis.

Freud's marriage was a long and relatively happy one, producing six children. The youngest child, Anna, held a special place in her father's heart. She followed in his professional footsteps, eventually taking over a leadership role in the psychoanalytic movement and becoming a respected psychoanalytic theorist in her own right. Freud created a situation filled with interesting Oedipal possibilities when he conducted Anna's psychoanalysis himself.

Freud and his family fled from their home and Nazi persecution when Germany invaded Austria in 1938. They escaped to London, where Freud died of cancer the following year.

Gradually, Freud's ideas gained acceptance within the growing field of psychology. In 1909 Freud was invited to the United States to present a series of lectures on psychoanalysis at Clark University. For Freud the occasion marked the beginning of international recognition of his work. However, resistance to psychoanalysis by academic psychologists kept Freud's theory out of American textbooks for another quarter of a century (Fancher, 2000). Freud continued to develop his theory and write about psychoanalysis until his death in 1939. Many consider Freud the most influential psychologist in the history of the field. A *Time* magazine cover story at the end of the 20th century featured a picture of Albert Einstein and Sigmund Freud, identifying the two as "The Century's Greatest Minds."

We begin our examination of this influential perspective by looking at classic Freudian theory. Contemporary advocates of the psychoanalytic approach vary in the degree to which they agree with Freud's initial descriptions of personality (Westen, 1998). Most accept key psychoanalytic concepts, such as the importance of unconscious thoughts. But modern psychoanalytic psychologists typically back away from other aspects of Freudian theory, such as his description of infantile sexuality. Nonetheless, you need to understand what Freud said before deciding which parts make sense to you and which parts to jettison. More than a century after introducing psychoanalysis to the world, the Viennese neurologist still casts a shadow across the field of personality.

The Freudian Theory of Personality

The Topographic Model

The starting point for understanding the Freudian approach is the division of the human personality into three parts. Freud originally divided personality into the conscious, the preconscious, and the unconscious. This division is known as the **topographic model.** The **conscious** contains the thoughts you are currently aware of. This material changes constantly as new thoughts enter your mind and others pass out of awareness. When you say something is "on your mind," you probably mean the conscious part of your mind. However, the conscious can deal with only a tiny percentage of all the information stored in your mind. You could bring an uncountable number of thoughts into consciousness fairly easily if you wanted to. For example, what did you have for breakfast? Who was your third-grade teacher? What did you do last Saturday night? This large body of retrievable information makes up the **preconscious.**

Although many people consider the material in the conscious and preconscious to be fairly exhaustive of the thoughts in their minds, Freud described these as merely the tip of the iceberg. The vast majority of thoughts, and the most important from a psychoanalytic viewpoint, are found in the **unconscious.** This is material to which you have no immediate access. According to Freud, you cannot bring unconscious thoughts into consciousness except under certain extreme situations. Nonetheless, this unconscious material is responsible for much of your everyday behavior. Understanding the influence of the unconscious, particularly on what might be termed "abnormal behavior," is the key to appreciating the psychoanalytic perspective.

The Structural Model

"*In its relation to the id, [the ego] is like a man on horseback, who has to hold in check the superior strength of the horse, [but] is obliged to guide it where it wants to go.***"**

Sigmund Freud*

*Excerpts from *Collected Papers*, Vol. III by Sigmund Freud. Authorized translation under the supervision of Alix and James Strachey. Published by Basic Books, Inc. by arrangement with the Hogarth Press Ltd. and The Institute of Psycho-Analysis, London.

Freud soon discovered that the topographic model provided a limited description of human personality. He therefore added the **structural model,** which divides personality into the id, the ego, and the superego. Just as you often say, "One part of me wants to do one thing, and another part wants to do something else," so did Freud conceive of the personality as made up of parts often not at peace with one another.

Freud maintained that at birth there is but one personality structure, the **id.** This is the selfish part of you, concerned only with satisfying your personal desires. Actions taken by the id are based on the *pleasure principle.* In other words, the id is concerned only with what brings immediate personal satisfaction regardless of physical or social limitations. When babies see something they want, they reach for it. It doesn't matter whether the object belongs to someone else or that it may be harmful. And this reflexive action doesn't disappear when we become adults. Rather, Freud maintained, our id impulses are ever present, held in check by the other parts of a healthy adult personality.

Obviously, if the id were to rely only on reflexive action to get what it wants, our pleasure impulses would be frustrated most of the time. Therefore, Freud proposed that the id also uses *wish fulfillment* to satisfy its needs. That is, if the desired object is not available, the id will imagine what it wants. If a baby is hungry and doesn't see food nearby, the id imagines the food and thereby at least temporarily satisfies the need. As discussed later in this chapter, Freud argued that our dreams also are a type of wish fulfillment.

As shown in Figure 3.1, Freud described the id as buried entirely in the unconscious and therefore outside of our awareness. Indeed, because many id impulses center on themes of sexuality and aggression, it is probably good that we are not aware of this unconscious material.

As children interact with their environment during the first 2 years of life, the second part of the personality structure gradually develops. The actions of the **ego** are based on the *reality principle.* That is, the primary job of the ego is to satisfy id impulses, but in a manner that takes into consideration the realities of the world. Because id impulses tend to be socially unacceptable, they are threatening to us. The ego's job is to keep these impulses in the unconscious. Unlike the id, your ego moves freely among the conscious, preconscious, and unconscious parts of your mind.

However, the ego's function is not simply to frustrate the aims of the id. Freud maintained that human behavior is directed toward reducing tension, such as the tension we feel when impulsive needs—even unconscious ones—are unmet. Very young children might be allowed to grab food off their parents' plates and thereby reduce tension. But as infants mature, they learn the physical and social limits on what they can and cannot do. Your id impulse may be to grab whatever food is around. But your ego understands this

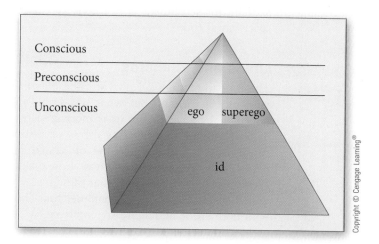

Conscious

Preconscious

Unconscious

ego   superego

id

Copyright © Cengage Learning®

FIGURE 3.1 Relationship of the Id, Ego, and Superego to the Three Levels of Awareness

action is unacceptable. The ego tries to satisfy the wants of the id, and thus lessen tension, but in a way that considers the consequences of the action.

By the time a child is about 5 years old, the third part of the personality structure is formed. The **superego** represents society's—and, in particular, the parents'—values and standards. The superego places more restrictions on what we can and cannot do. If you see a $5 bill sitting on a table at a friend's house, your id impulse might be to take the money. Your ego, aware of the problems this might cause, attempts to figure out how to get the $5 without being caught. But even if there is a way to get the money without being seen, your superego will not allow the action. Stealing money is a violation of society's moral code, even if you don't get caught. The primary weapon the superego brings to the situation is guilt. If you take the money anyway, you'll probably feel bad about it later and may lose a few nights' sleep before returning the $5 to your friend. Some people have roughly translated the concept of the superego into what is called conscience.

But the superego does not merely punish us for moral violations. It also provides the ideals the ego uses to determine if a behavior is virtuous and therefore worthy of praise. Because of poor child-rearing practices, some children fail to fully develop their superegos. As adults, these people have little inward restraint from stealing or lying. In other people, the superego can become too powerful, or supermoral, and burden the ego with impossible standards of perfection. Here the person could suffer from relentless *moral anxiety*—an ever-present feeling of shame and guilt—for failing to reach standards no human can meet.

Like forces pulling at three corners to form a triangle, the desires of the id, ego, and superego complement and contradict one another. In the healthy individual, a strong ego does not allow the id or the superego too much control over the personality. But the battle is never ending. In each of us, somewhere below our awareness, there exists an eternal state of tension between a desire for self-indulgence, a concern for reality, and the enforcement of a strict moral code.

Libido and Thanatos

The topographic model provides the playing field; the structural model provides the characters. But what sets Freud's system in motion? Freud maintained that human behavior is motivated by strong internal forces he called Triebe, roughly translated as drives or instincts. Freud identified two major categories of instincts: the life or sexual instinct, generally referred to as *libido,* and the death or aggressive instinct, known as *Thanatos*. Although Freud originally maintained that these forces were in opposition, he later suggested that the two often combine, thus intertwining much of what we do with both erotic and aggressive motives.

Freud attributed most human behavior to the life or sexual instinct. However, he used this description in a very broad sense. Sexually motivated behaviors not only include those with obvious erotic content but also nearly any action aimed at receiving pleasure. Late in his career Freud added the death instinct—the desire we all have to die and return to the earth. However, this unconscious motive is rarely expressed in the form of obvious self-destruction. Most often, the death instinct is turned outward and expressed as aggression against others. The wish to die remains unconscious.

Freud was greatly influenced by the scientific thought of his day. Among the ideas he adapted from other sciences was the notion of a limited amount of energy. Energy within a physical system does not disappear but exists in finite amounts. Similarly, Freud argued that we each have a finite amount of psychic energy that more or less powers the psychological functions. This means that energy spent on one part of psychological functioning is not available for other uses. Thus, if the ego has to expend large amounts of energy to control the id, it has little energy left to carry out the rest of its functions efficiently. One goal of Freudian psychotherapy is to help troubled clients release unconscious impulses being held in check, thereby freeing up energy for daily functioning.

Defense Mechanisms

"Freud recognized that most of what is real within ourselves is not conscious, and that most of what is conscious is not real."

ERICH FROMM

Freud's description of our unconscious minds can be a bit unsettling. Classic psychoanalytic cases involve such unconscious themes as hatred for one's parents, aggression toward one's spouse, incestuous thoughts, memories of traumatic childhood experiences, and similar notions too threatening for awareness. The ego attempts to reduce or avoid anxiety by keeping this material out of consciousness. Occasionally, people experience what Freud called *neurotic anxiety*. These are vague feelings of anxiety sparked by the sensation that unacceptable unconscious thoughts are about to burst through the awareness barrier and express themselves in consciousness.

Fortunately, the ego has many techniques at its disposal to deal with unwanted thoughts and desires. These are known collectively as **defense mechanisms.** Some of the principal defense mechanisms are reviewed in the following sections. Freud touched on each of these concepts at various places in his works. However, descriptions of many of the defense mechanisms were developed more completely by some of his followers. Among the later psychoanalysts who extended Freud's ideas about defense mechanisms was Anna Freud, Sigmund's daughter.

Repression

Freud called repression "the cornerstone on which the whole structure of psychoanalysis rests" (1914/1963, p. 116). It is clearly the most important of the defense mechanisms. *Repression* is an active effort by the ego to push threatening material out of consciousness or to keep that material from ever reaching consciousness. For example, one night a boy sees his father physically assault his mother. When later asked about the experience, the boy insists he has never seen anything at all like that. He may not be lying. Instead, he may have found the scene too horrifying to accept and therefore simply repressed it out of consciousness. According to Freud, each of us uses repression, for we all have material in our unconscious mind we would rather not bring into awareness. As efficient as this seems, it is not without cost. Because repression is a constant, active process, it requires that the ego constantly expend energy. Repressing a large number of powerful thoughts and impulses leaves our ego with little remaining energy with which to function. And without a strong ego, the battle for a stable personality can be lost.

Sublimation

Unlike repression, which drains our ability to function, the more we use *sublimation,* the more productive we become. Thus psychoanalysts often refer to sublimation as the only truly successful defense mechanism. When using sublimation, the ego channels threatening unconscious impulses into socially acceptable actions. Aggressive id impulses can be sublimated by playing hockey or football. In our society, aggressive athletes are often considered heroes and rewarded for their actions. The sublimation is productive because the id is allowed to express its aggression, the ego doesn't have to tie up energy holding back the impulses, and the athlete is admired for aggressive play.

Displacement

Like sublimation, *displacement* involves channeling our impulses to nonthreatening objects. Unlike sublimation, displaced impulses don't lead to social rewards. For example, as the result of mistreatment or abuse, a woman might carry around a great deal of unconscious anger. If expressing that anger toward her abuser is unacceptable or dangerous, she might instead direct her emotions toward her coworkers or children. Although doing so can create other problems, angry outbursts aimed at these less-threatening people may protect unacceptable thoughts from conscious expression. Freud maintained that many of our apparently irrational fears, or phobias, are merely symbolic displacements. He once speculated that a fear of horses expressed by a client's son was really a displaced fear of the father.

Marlene Somsak/Santa Clara University

According to Freud, participation in aggressive sports allows the expression of uncon-
scious aggressive impulses in a socially acceptable manner. Football players might be
engaging in sublimation with each tackle.

Denial

When we use *denial,* we refuse to accept that certain facts exist. This is more than saying we do not remember, as in repression. Rather, we insist that something is not true despite all evidence to the contrary. A widower who loved his wife deeply may act as if she were still alive long after her death. He may set a place for her at the table or tell friends that she is just away visiting a relative. To the widower, this charade is more acceptable than admitting consciously that his wife has died. Obviously, denial is an extreme form of defense. The more we use it, the less in touch with reality we are and the more difficulty we have functioning. Nonetheless, in some cases the ego will resort to denial rather than allow certain thoughts to reach consciousness.

Reaction Formation

When using *reaction formation,* we hide from a threatening unconscious idea or urge by acting in a manner opposite to our unconscious desires. Thus, a young woman who constantly tells people how much she loves her mother could be masking strong unconscious hatred for the mother. People who militantly get involved with antipornography crusades may hold a strong unconscious interest in pornography. It is as if the thought is so unacceptable that the ego must prove how incorrect the notion is. How could a woman who professes so much love for her mother really hate her deep inside?

Intellectualization

One way the ego handles threatening material is to remove the emotional content from the thought before allowing it into awareness. Using *intellectualization*—that is, by considering something in a strictly intellectual, unemotional manner—we can bring previously difficult thoughts into consciousness without anxiety. Under the guise of pondering the importance of wearing seat belts, a woman might imagine her husband in a gruesome automobile accident. A Freudian therapist might guess that the woman holds some unconscious hostility toward her spouse.

Projection

Sometimes we attribute an unconscious impulse to other people instead of to ourselves. This defense mechanism is called *projection*. By projecting the impulse onto another person, we free ourselves from the perception that we are the one who actually holds this thought. The woman who thinks everyone in her neighborhood is committing adultery may be harboring sexual desires for the married man living next door. The man who declares that the world is full of distrustful and cheating people may unconsciously know that he is distrustful and a cheater.

Psychosexual Stages of Development

Among the most controversial aspects of Freud's theory is his description of personality development. Freud argued that our adult personalities are heavily influenced by what happens to us during the first 5 or 6 years of life. Each child is said to progress through a series of developmental stages during these years. Because the chief characteristic of each stage is the primary erogenous zone, and because each stage has a specific influence on the adult personality, they are referred to as the **psychosexual stages of development**.

Freud maintained that children face specific challenges as they pass through each of the psychosexual stages and that small amounts of psychic energy are used up resolving these challenges. If all goes as it should, most of us still have an adequate amount of psychic energy left to operate a healthy personality by the time we become adults. But sometimes things go awry. Some children have a difficult time moving through a particular stage (or, for a few, find the stage excessively satisfying and wish to stay there). The result is *fixation,* the tying up of psychic energy. Not only does this leave less energy available for normal adult functioning, the adult is said to express behaviors characteristic of the stage at which the energy is fixated.

The first stage in Freud's model is the *oral stage.* During this period, which spans approximately the first 18 months of life, the mouth, lips, and tongue are the primary erogenous zones, that is, the source of pleasure. You need only watch a 6-month-old for a few minutes to realize that everything must go into the mouth. Traumatic weaning or feeding problems during this stage can result in fixation and the development of an *oral personality.*

Repressed Memories

One afternoon in 1969, 8-year-old Susan Nason disappeared on her way to visit a neighbor in Foster City, California. Two months later, her body was found in a nearby reservoir. The coroner concluded that Susan had died from a fractured skull. An investigation followed, but with little evidence to go on, police never found the killer. Twenty years later, Eileen Franklin-Lipsker, a childhood friend of the victim's, sat with her daughter in her Los Angeles home. Suddenly Franklin-Lipsker recalled images of Susan's death. She could see a man sexually assaulting the girl and then smashing her head with a rock. Franklin-Lipsker also knew the identity of the man in her memories—it was her own father, George Franklin.

Based on little more than his daughter's testimony, in 1990 George Franklin was tried and convicted for Susan Nason's murder. Jurors who listened to Franklin-Lipsker's testimony were convinced she could not have known the details she provided unless she had been at the scene of the crime. But why had the memories taken 20 years to surface? The prosecution argued that the nature of the memories was so traumatic Franklin-Lipsker had repressed them into an unconscious part of her mind. It was noticing the physical similarity between her daughter and Susan that triggered the long-repressed images and allowed them to enter consciousness. Superior Court Judge Thomas Smith called George Franklin "wicked and depraved" and sentenced him to life in prison. Franklin thus became the first person to be convicted on the basis of "repressed" memories.

The Franklin verdict provides an egregious example of how psychological principles can be misused. In this case, a handful of psychotherapists tore apart thousands of families by misapplying the psychoanalytic notion of repression (Brody, 2000). Over a period of several years in the 1990s, a huge number of adults going through psychotherapy suddenly "recalled" childhood memories of being victimized by parents, often sexually. In virtually every case, the client had not been aware of any such experience until the therapist suggested the event. In response to the near epidemic of repressed memory cases, many personality psychologists and memory researchers raised questions about the accuracy of the clients' claims. Researchers demonstrated that people often have great confidence in the accuracy of repressed memories that could not possibly have been true.

The fall of the repressed memory epidemic came quickly. Parents and family members falsely accused of abuse formed the False Memory Syndrome Foundation. Within the first year, the organization grew to include more than 3,000 families. Hundreds of clients came to see that their memories of abuse were in fact fictional creations and retracted their stories (de Rivera, 1997). But the issue has not gone away. New accusations of abuse based on suddenly remembered images still lead to occasional arrests and prosecutions ("Massachusetts: Court Upholds Ex-Priest's Conviction," 2010; Saulny, 2009; Zezima & Carey, 2009). Psychologists and the courts continue to grapple with questions surrounding repressed memories (Geraerts et al., 2009; McNally & Geraerts, 2009). Although psychologists have demonstrated that people often believe memories that are false, they cannot rule out the possibility that some cases of repressed memories might be based on fact.

In the meantime, prosecutors have revisited old cases that may have been unfairly decided on the basis of repressed memories. A man in Kentucky had his conviction thrown out after he had already served 5 years in prison (Dunbar, 2006). A man in Pennsylvania was granted a new trial after 12 years in prison (Conti, 2005). A federal judge in Nebraska voided a $1.75 million judgment against a clergyman accused of sexual abuse (Zezima & Carey, 2009). After more than 5 years in prison, George Franklin also was granted a new trial. His attorneys argued that the jury in the first case should have been allowed to see newspaper and television reports of Susan's death. Those reports contained details of the crime that could have been the basis of Franklin-Lipsker's memories. Prosecutors responded to the new information by dropping the charges. After serving several years for murder, George Franklin was released from prison.

Jerry Burger/Santa Clara University

According to Freud, adult oral personalities develop when traumatic childhood experiences cause the fixation of an excessive amount of psychic energy at the oral stage of development. Smoking, drinking, and excessive eating are characteristic of an oral personality.

Like a child, adults with an oral personality tend to be dependent on others, although fixation that occurs after the teething may instead result in excessive levels of aggression. People with an oral personality often express an infantile need for oral satisfaction. They may smoke or drink excessively and are constantly putting their hands to their mouth.

When children reach the age of about 18 months, they enter the *anal stage* of development. According to Freud, the anal region becomes the most important erogenous zone during this period. Not coincidentally, this is the time most children are toilet trained. Traumatic toilet training can result in fixation and an *anal personality*. An adult with an anal personality can be orderly, stubborn, or generous, depending on how the toilet training progressed.

Next comes the *phallic stage*, approximately ages 3 to 6, when the penis or clitoris becomes the most important erogenous zone. The key development during the phallic stage comes toward the end of this period when the child experiences the *Oedipus complex*, named for the Greek mythological character who unknowingly marries his mother. Freud argued that children this age develop a sexual attraction for their opposite-sex parent. Young boys have strong incestuous desires toward their mothers, whereas young girls have these feelings toward their fathers.

Needless to say, the children are not without their share of fear about this development. Boys develop *castration anxiety*, a fear that their father will discover their thoughts and cut off their penis. If the boy has seen his sister's genitals, he is said to conclude that this fate has already befallen her. Girls, upon seeing male genitals, are said to develop *penis envy*. This is a desire to have a penis, coupled with feelings of inferiority and jealousy because of its absence.

How do boys and girls resolve this conflict? Eventually the children repress their desire for their opposite-sex parent, whom they realize they can never have as long as the other parent is around. Then, as a type of reaction formation, children identify with the same-sex parent. Resolving the Oedipus complex serves several important functions. By identifying with the same-sex parent, boys begin to take on masculine characteristics and girls acquire feminine characteristics. Moreover, adopting the parents' values and standards paves the way for the emergence of the superego. However, Freud warned that Oedipal desires are never fully eliminated. Rather, they are merely repressed and have the potential to influence our behavior later in life in a number of ways. Businessmen who aggressively go after rivals are said to be expressing Oedipal urges left over from their earlier competition with their father.

After resolving the Oedipus complex, the child passes into the *latency stage*. Sexual desires abate during these years. Boys and girls seem fairly

After resolution of the Oedipus complex, children pass into the latency stage. For several years, boys will prefer to play with other boys, and girls with other girls. All of this ends with puberty.

uninterested in each other during the latency stage. A look at any playground will verify that boys play with other boys and girls play with other girls. But all of that changes with puberty. Erogenous urges return and are focused in the adult genital regions. If a child has progressed to this *genital stage* without leaving large amounts of libido fixated at earlier stages, normal sexual functioning is possible.

Getting at Unconscious Material

> " *Innocent dreams … are wolves in sheep's clothing. They turn out to be quite the reverse when we take the trouble to analyze them.* "
>
> Sigmund Freud

At first glance, it would appear that Sigmund Freud created a problem for himself. If the most important psychological material is buried in the unconscious and therefore outside of our awareness, how can psychologists study it? Moreover, how can a psychotherapist help his or her clients when the key to understanding the client's problems is unavailable for inspection? Not surprisingly, Freud had an answer to this dilemma. He maintained that strong id impulses do not simply disappear when they are pushed out of consciousness. Although the true nature of these impulses is repressed by a strong ego, the impulses are often expressed in a disguised or altered form. If psychologists know what to look for, they can catch a glimpse of unconscious thoughts by observing seemingly innocent behaviors. The following are seven techniques a Freudian psychologist might use to get at unconscious material.

Dreams

Freud called dreams the "royal road to the unconscious." In 1900 he published *The Interpretation of Dreams,* presenting for the first time a psychological theory to explain the meaning of these nighttime dramas. According to Freud, dreams provide id impulses with a stage for expression. They are, in fact, a type of wish fulfillment; our dreams represent the things we desire. This is not to say that we want the unpleasant and frightening things we sometimes dream about to literally come true. Freud drew a distinction between the *manifest content* of a dream (what the dreamer sees and remembers) and the *latent content* (what is really being said). Overt expression of many unconscious desires would be difficult to face upon waking. That's why they were repressed in the first place. However, these unacceptable images can surface in disguise in our dreams. Freud maintained that many of our unconscious thoughts and desires are represented symbolically. Dreams involving penises, sexual intercourse, and vaginas might be threatening to the dreamer. But we would have no problem with a dream about fountains, airplane rides, or caves. "The dreamer does know what his dream means," Freud wrote. "Only he does not know that he knows it, and for that reason thinks he does not know it" (1916/1961, p. 101).

Freud believed a trained psychoanalyst could identify many common dream symbols. A house is said to represent the human body, one's parents are disguised as a king and queen, children are represented as small animals, birth is associated with water, a train journey is a symbol for dying, and clothes and uniforms represent nakedness. Predictably, the vast majority of Freudian dream symbols are sexual. For example, male genitals are said to be represented by objects with a similar shape. Freud (1916/1961) listed several common phallic symbols, including sticks, umbrellas, trees, knives, rifles, pencils, and hammers. Female genitals are symbolically represented by bottles, boxes, rooms, doors, and ships. Sexual intercourse is hidden in such activities as dancing, riding, and climbing. In fact, reading Freud's long list of symbols, it's hard to think of many dreams that can't be interpreted sexually.

Projective Tests

We have all played the game of finding images in cloud formations. One person might describe a sailboat, another sees the Cowardly Lion, and a third can just make out a couple dancing the tango. Of course, there are no real pictures in the clouds. So where are these images coming from? The answer, from a Freudian perspective, is that these responses are projections of material in the perceiver's unconscious mind. The images we see in vague objects like clouds represent another way of getting at unconscious material. **Projective tests** present test takers with ambiguous stimuli and asks them to respond by identifying objects, telling a story, or perhaps drawing a picture. The responses are said to provide insights into what is going on in the unconscious. Some of the projective tests used by psychologists are reviewed later in this chapter.

Free Association

Try this exercise some time. Take a few minutes to clear your mind of thoughts. Then allow whatever comes into your mind to enter. Say whatever you feel like saying, even if it is not what you expect and even if you are a little surprised or embarrassed by what comes out. If you find strange, uncensored ideas flowing into your awareness, you may be experiencing free association. Clients undergoing psychoanalysis are often encouraged to use free association to temporarily bypass the censoring mechanism the ego employs. Ordinarily we block distasteful, seemingly trivial or silly thoughts to protect ourselves from this material or to keep from sounding foolish. But if we can slip by the ego's roadblocks and obstacles, even for a moment, glimpses into the unconsciousness may be possible.

However, free association is usually not so easy. The ego has invested considerable energy to repress threatening thoughts and is not likely to let them just ease into consciousness. Occasionally clients slip into long silences. Sometimes they report that nothing comes to mind or endlessly describe unimportant details in an effort to avoid any unconscious revelations. But when the client gives expression to whatever enters his or her awareness, both client and therapist are often surprised by what emerges.

Freudian Slips

We all occasionally make slips of the tongue. A husband might refer to his wife by her maiden name or say that her mind is really her "breast" feature. These slips can be embarrassing and funny, but to Freud they represented unconscious associations that momentarily slipped out. The husband who uses his wife's maiden name may unconsciously wish he'd never married this woman. We call these misstatements **Freudian slips**.

Hypnosis

Freud's early experiences with hypnosis told him there was more to the human mind than what we can bring into awareness. He came to believe that the ego was somehow put into a suspended state during a deep hypnotic trance, which allowed the hypnotist to bypass the ego and get directly to unconscious material. When people asked Freud for proof of the unconscious, he often pointed to hypnosis. "Anyone who has witnessed such an experiment," he wrote, "will receive an unforgettable impression and a conviction that can never be shaken" (1938/1964, p. 285).

If hypnosis is a pipeline to the unconscious, it is easy to see how the procedure would be a valuable tool for psychoanalysts. Yet Freud was quick to acknowledge some drawbacks. Chief among these is that not all clients are responsive to hypnotic suggestion. Moreover, as we will see in Chapter 4, not all psychologists agree with Freud's description of hypnosis as a pathway to the unconscious.

Accidents

Suppose you are having an argument with a friend and you "accidentally" knock off a shelf an irreplaceable statue belonging to that friend. The statue shatters beyond repair. You apologize, saying that you did not mean to do it. But is this really an accident? In Freud's view, many apparent accidents are in fact intentional actions stemming from unconscious impulses. Freud might argue that you were expressing an unconscious desire to hurt your friend when you broke his or her prized possession. Clients who claim to accidentally forget their regular therapy appointment might be displaying what Freud called *resistance*. Consciously, the clients believe they simply did not remember the appointment. Unconsciously, there has been a deliberate effort to thwart a therapist who may be close to uncovering threatening unconscious material. Similarly, reckless drivers might be setting themselves up for an accident to satisfy an unconscious desire for self-inflicted harm. To Freudian psychologists, many unfortunate events are accidents in the sense that people do not consciously intend them, but not in the sense that they are unintended.

Symbolic Behavior

Just like the events we dream, many of our daily behaviors can be interpreted by Freudian psychologists as symbolic representations of unconscious desires. Symbolic actions pose no threat to the ego because they are not perceived for what they are. But they may allow for the expression of unconscious impulses. An excellent example is found in the case of a client who held a great deal of hostility toward his mother, although he would not consciously acknowledge these feelings. To the therapist, the unconscious hostility was expressed through an interesting doormat the client purchased for his home. The doormat was decorated with images of daisies. Not coincidentally, the client's mother had a favorite flower, the daisy. She had daisies on her dishes and pictures of daisies all around the house. In short, the daisies symbolized the mother. The good son enjoyed rubbing his feet and stomping on the daisies—symbolically acting out his hostility toward his mother—every time he entered the house.

When we apply Freud's dream symbols to everyday acts, we can see psychologically significant behavior seemingly everywhere. What can we say about the woman who joins the rifle team? The man who explores caves? The person who constantly borrows pencils without returning them? It is interesting to note that Freud was a habitual cigar smoker who, despite painful operations for cancer of the jaw, continued to smoke until his death. Although the cigar is an obvious phallic symbol, Freud reportedly answered a query about his habit by saying, "Sometimes a cigar is just a cigar."

Application: Psychoanalysis

Not only was Freud the father of psychoanalytic theory, but he was also the first person to outline and advocate a system of psychotherapy. During his early years with Breuer, Freud recognized that many disorders were psychological rather than physical in origin. Through his experimentation with hypnosis, he came to see that the causes of these disorders were buried in a part of the mind not easily accessible to awareness. Slowly Freud developed various methods to get at this material, beginning with hypnosis and gradually changing to free association. As he gained insights into the causes of his clients' disorders and the structure and functioning of human personality, Freud developed a system of psychotherapy called **psychoanalysis.**

The primary goal of psychoanalysis is to bring crucial unconscious material into consciousness where it can be examined in a rational manner. However, once the unconscious material surfaces, it must be dealt with in such a way that it does not manifest itself in some new disorder. The therapist and the client work together to help the ego once again exercise appropriate control over the id impulses and the oppressive superego. In some ways, the therapist and the client are like explorers searching through the client's mind for crucial unconscious material. But the therapist also is like a detective, who must evaluate cryptic messages about the underlying cause of the disorder as the client unconsciously, and sometimes cunningly, works to mislead and frustrate the therapist.

Typically, psychoanalysis clients lie on a couch while the therapist sits behind them, out of sight. The client is encouraged to speak freely, without any distractions from the room or the therapist that might inhibit free association. Unfortunately, the process of digging through layers of conscious and unconscious material, as well as avoiding the obstacles and misdirection thrown in by the threatened ego, is a lengthy one. Clients usually require several hour-long therapy sessions a week for a period of perhaps several years. Consequently, traditional psychoanalysis is expensive and limited to those who can afford it.

The bulk of time spent in psychoanalysis is devoted to getting at the crucial unconscious material causing the disorder. Because the ego has devoted so much energy and is so strongly motivated to repress the material, this part of therapy can be difficult. Freud used several tactics to get into the unconscious, including free association, dream interpretation, and hypnosis. Unlike other systems of psychotherapy, in psychoanalysis the therapist actively interprets for clients the significance of their statements, behaviors, and dreams. But Freud cautioned that therapists should not reveal true meanings too soon. Beginning therapists are often tempted to interpret the unconscious meaning behind an act or a statement as soon as they perceive it. However, this early insight could be threatening for an unprepared ego, causing the client to construct new and stronger unconscious defenses.

Nonetheless, when the timing is right, the psychoanalyst interprets statements and dream symbols for clients until they understand their true meaning. An excellent example of this is found in one of Freud's famous case studies, the case of Dora. Dora was an 18-year-old patient from an affluent family. She complained of headaches and other physical problems. One area of trauma for Dora concerned a married couple, who Freud referred to as Mr. and Mrs. K. Mrs. K. was having an affair with Dora's father. To make matters worse, Mr. K. had made sexual advances toward Dora. One day during therapy, Dora related the following dream:

> A house was on fire. My father was standing beside my bed and woke me up. I dressed quickly. Mother wanted to stop and save her jewel-case; but Father said: "I refuse to let myself and my two children be burnt for the sake of your jewel-case." We hurried downstairs, and as soon as I was outside, I woke up. (1901/1953, p. 64)

To the untrained ear, the dream seems innocent and meaningless enough, similar to dreams we all have and give little thought to. But for Freud, the dream was filled with clues about the causes of Dora's problems. With a little questioning, Freud learned that shortly before the dream, Mr. K. had given Dora an expensive jewel case as a present. With this information, Freud had all the pieces to the puzzle he needed. As he explained to Dora,

> Perhaps you do not know that "jewel-case" is a favourite expression for the female genitals.... You said to yourself: "This man is persecuting me; he wants to force his way into my room. My 'jewel-case' is in danger, and if anything happens it will be Father's fault." For that reason in the dream you chose a situation which expresses the opposite—a danger from which your father is saving you. Mr. K. is to be put in the place of your father just as he was in the matter of standing beside your bed. He gave you a jewel-case; so you are to give him your jewel-case.... So you are ready to give Mr. K. what his wife withholds from him. That is the thought which has had to be repressed with so much energy, and which has made it necessary for every one of its elements to be turned into its opposite. The dream confirms once more what I had already told you before you dreamt it—that you are summoning up your old love for your father in order to protect yourself against your love for Mr. K. (p. 69)

Freud interpreted several important psychoanalytic concepts for Dora. He identified her use of symbols and her repression of her true desires. He explained how she used reaction formation—dreaming the opposite of what she really wanted—and how her repressed desires for her father affected her behavior. Not surprisingly, Dora had difficulty accepting this interpretation at first. As this example illustrates, clients must obtain a reasonable understanding of psychoanalytic theory before they can appreciate the therapist's interpretation of their dreams, thoughts, and behaviors.

Ironically, one of the first signs that therapy is progressing is the development of resistance. For example, clients might declare that the sessions aren't helping and that they want to discontinue therapy. Or they might lapse into long silences, return to material already discussed, miss appointments, or insist that certain topics aren't worth exploring. These attempts at resistance could indicate that the therapist and client are getting close to the crucial material. The threatened ego is desperately attempting to defend against the approaching demise of its defenses as crucial unconscious material is almost ready to burst into consciousness.

Another necessary step in traditional psychoanalysis is the development of *transference*. Here emotions associated with people from past situations are displaced onto the therapist. For example, a client might talk to and act toward the therapist as if the therapist were a deceased parent. Unconscious emotions and previously undelivered speeches buried deep and long ago are unleashed, feelings that often lie at the heart of the client's disorder. Freud warned that handling transference was a delicate and crucial part of the therapy process. He also cautioned therapists against *countertransference,* in which therapists displace their own feelings toward other individuals onto the client.

From the outset, psychoanalysis has been controversial, and the debate about its effectiveness has never ended (Gabbard, Gunderson, & Fonagy, 2002). Nonetheless, although many therapy options are available today, a large number of psychotherapists continue to identify their approach as "psychoanalytic" (Cook, Biyanova, Elhai, Schnurr, & Coyne, 2010; Thoma & Cecero, 2009). Recent reviews of carefully designed studies find evidence that psychoanalytic therapies are often effective when treating a wide variety of psychological disorders (Leichsenring, 2007; Leichsenring & Rabung, 2008; Shedler, 2010). Predictably, these claims of effectiveness have been met with skepticism (Beck & Bhar, 2009; McKay, 2011; Roepke & Renneberg, 2009). Critics also argue that psychoanalysis, if it works, can often take years and therefore is not as cost effective as many short-term therapies. As with most things associated with Freud, it is safe to say this controversy is likely to continue.

Assessment: Projective Tests

Psychoanalysts are faced with a unique problem when developing ways to measure the personality constructs of interest to them. By definition, the most important concepts are those the test taker is unable to report directly. If a client can readily describe a psychological conflict, that conflict obviously is not buried deeply in the unconscious and thus is unlikely to be the key to understanding the person's problem. So how do psychoanalytic therapists and researchers measure unconscious material? The solution is to bypass direct reports altogether.

Jerry Burger/Santa Clara University

This psychologist is administering one of the most widely used personality tests: the Rorschach ink blot test. The participant tells him what she sees on her card; whether these responses provide a valid assessment of her personality remains a controversy.

Projective tests present individuals with ambiguous stimuli, such as inkblots or vague pictures. Test takers respond by describing what they see, telling stories about the pictures, or somehow reacting to the material. The tests provide no clues about correct or incorrect answers, which makes each person's responses highly idiosyncratic. One person may see a circus and an elephant, whereas another identifies a cemetery and a woman in mourning. As the name implies, psychoanalysts consider these responses projections from the unconscious. The ambiguous material gives test takers an opportunity to express pent-up impulses. However, as with other expressions of unconscious impulses, the significance of the response is not apparent to the test taker.

Types of Projective Tests

In 1921, Hermann Rorschach published a paper in which he described a procedure for predicting behavior from responses to inkblots. Although Rorschach died the next year at age 38, his work stimulated other psychologists who continued to develop the test that still bears its creator's name. The Rorschach inkblot test consists of 10 cards, each containing nothing more than a blot of ink, sometimes in more than one color. Test takers are instructed to describe what they see in the inkblot. They are free to use any part of the inkblot and are usually allowed to give several responses to each card. Although some of the cards may be quite suggestive, they are in fact nothing more than inkblots.

Inkblot test responses can be analyzed with any of several scoring systems developed over the years. However, most psychologists probably rely on their personal insights and intuition when interpreting responses. Unusual answers and recurring themes are of particular interest, especially if they are consistent with information revealed during therapy sessions. For example, most therapists would probably take note if a client sees dead bodies, graves, and tombstones on each card. Similarly, clients who see suicidal acts, bizarre sexual behavior, or violent images probably provide therapists with topics to explore in future sessions.

Another widely used projective test is the Thematic Apperception Test (TAT). The test was designed by Henry Murray (Chapter 7) and consists of a series of ambiguous pictures. Test takers are asked to tell a story about each picture—who the people are, what is going on, what has led up to the scene, and what the outcome is going to be. Although most of the pictures contain images of people, facial expressions and the nature of the relationship between the people are intentionally vague. Thus test takers may see love, guilt, anger, or grief in the faces. The characters may be fighting, plotting, loving, or unaware of each other. They may be in for a happy, sad, horrifying, or disappointing end to their situation. What the test taker sees in the picture provides clues to the person's personality. Although therapists often rely on their intuition when interpreting TAT responses, many use relatively objective scoring procedures. Examples of how psychologists use the TAT in research are examined at length in Chapters 4 and 8.

Yet another projective test used by many therapists is the Human Figure Drawing test. Although initially developed in the 1920s as a measure of intelligence, psychologists soon recognized that the test also seemed to measure important personality constructs (Handler, 1996). The ambiguous stimulus here consists of a blank piece of paper and the instructions to draw a picture for the psychologist. In many cases, test takers are simply asked to draw a person, but sometimes psychologists instruct them to draw a family or a tree. The Human Figure Drawing test has many uses, including a measure of intelligence in children. However, most often it is used as an indicator of psychological problems, particularly in children (Bardos & Powell, 2001; Matto, 2002). Psychoanalysts typically view the person drawn by the test taker as a symbolic representation of the self.

The notion that children's drawings provide a peephole into their inner thoughts and feelings has strong intuitive appeal. Schoolteachers often take note of children who never seem to draw smiles on the faces of the characters they sketch. Similarly, children who frequently draw monsters or ghoulish creatures could be expressing some disturbing inward feelings. A glance at the drawings by emotionally disturbed children presented in Figure 3.2 makes a persuasive case that children sometimes express through drawing what they otherwise might not put into words.

Labels within drawing: robot hand made to kill · giant hand made to grab · He's half robot and half giant · robot leg · giant foot

FIGURE 3.2 Human Figure Drawings by Emotionally Disturbed Children

Source: From Koppitz, E. M. (1986). *Psychological Evaluation of Children's Human Figure Drawing.* Reprinted by permission of Grune & Stratton, Inc., and the author.

Evaluation of Projective Tests

Hundreds of studies have been conducted with projective tests, most often with the Rorschach inkblot test. Responses to the inkblots have been used to predict everything from intelligence to sexual orientation. Unfortunately, psychologists disagree on how to interpret this research (Garb, Wood, Lilienfeld, & Nezworski, 2005). Critics point to unacceptably low indices of reliability and frequent failures to find evidence for the validity of the test (Wood, et al., 2010; Wood, Nezworski, & Stejskal, 1996, 1997). One team of reviewers concluded that "there is currently no scientific basis for justifying the use of Rorschach scales in psychological assessment" (Hunsley & Bailey, 1999, p. 266). Another said bluntly that the Rorschach inkblot test was "not a valid test of anything" (Dawes, 1994, p. 146). Some psychologists challenge whether the inkblot procedure should be described as a test at all. They argue that the Rorschach is more accurately characterized as a highly structured interview.

But there are two sides to every controversy. Advocates for the Rorschach test raise several important points in its defense. First, one needs to separate good studies designed to test appropriate predictions from poor studies that attempt to tie test responses to any and all behaviors (Weiner, 1995, 1996). When reviewers look at results from sound studies making reasonable predictions, they find evidence for the usefulness of the test (Choca, 2013; Gronnerod, 2004; Mihura, Meyer, Dumitrascu, & Bombel, 2013; Parker, Hanson, & Hunsley, 1988; Viglione, 1999). Moreover, newer, more rigorous systems for coding Rorschach responses have proved far more reliable than earlier methods (Viglione & Hilsenroth, 2001; Weiner, 2001). Second, establishing good validity data for projective tests is more difficult than when using other kinds of personality measures. How can we demonstrate empirically that a Rorschach assessment is accurate? If a therapist concludes from an inkblot test that a client has a certain unconscious conflict, what objective criterion does the researcher use to establish the validity of this claim? Indeed, if objective indicators existed, therapists wouldn't need to use projective tests in the first place.

Despite the controversy, the Rorschach and many other projective tests continue to be widely used (Camara, Nathan, & Puente, 2000; Watkins, Campbell, Nieberding, & Hallmark, 1995). This use extends far beyond psychotherapy. For example, projective tests are often used by school psychologists to evaluate social and emotional adjustment in children (Hojnoski, Morrison, Brown, & Matthews, 2009) and by psychologists working with law enforcement and court officials (Gacono & Evans, 2008). One reason for this popularity is that the tests may uncover information not easily obtained through other procedures. For example, therapists working with children sometimes allow a child to play with a family of dolls. Imagine a child who acts out a drama in which the mother and father dolls are cruel to the child doll. The child might be expressing something about the situation at home that isn't easily revealed through other means.

Then again, many psychologists warn against overinterpreting responses to projective tests. The child in the previous example could merely be acting out a scene from a recent television program. Because the validity of projective tests remains open to challenge, psychologists usually are advised not to rely heavily on the tests when making diagnoses (Wood, Garb, Lilienfeld, & Nezworski, 2002). Instead, projective test results should be viewed as but one source of information about a client. They should be taken into consideration along with information collected through interviews, observations, case histories, and other psychological tests.

Strengths and Criticisms of Freud's Theory

None of the approaches to personality covered in this book can spark an argument as quickly as Freudian theory. Every clinical psychologist and personality researcher has an opinion on the value and accuracy of Freud's ideas. Although few accept all of Freud's observations and postulates unquestioningly, adherents of the Freudian view strongly defend the basic assumptions Freud made about the nature of human functioning. Critics tend to be equally passionate in their evaluations.

Strengths

Even if all of Freud's ideas were to be rejected by modern personality theorists, he would still deserve an important place in the history of psychology. Freud's was the first comprehensive theory of human behavior and personality. Most subsequent personality theorists have found it necessary to point out where their theories differ from or correct weaknesses in Freud's works. Many of these psychologists built their theories on the foundation laid by Freud, borrowing key psychoanalytic concepts and assumptions. As discussed in Chapter 5, many of those who studied with Freud or were trained in the Freudian tradition went on to develop and promote their own versions of psychoanalytic theory. In short, Freud's observations set the direction for subsequent personality theory and research. Even recent approaches to personality, although far removed from psychoanalytic theory, are probably influenced in many ways by Freud's ideas.

"Freud's greatest achievement probably consisted in taking neurotic patients seriously."
CARL JUNG

Freud also can be credited with developing the first system of psychotherapy. Today, treating psychological disorders through discussions with a therapist is an accepted and widely practiced procedure. Although psychotherapy might have evolved without Freud, it certainly would not have evolved the way it did. Techniques such as free association, hypnosis, and dream interpretation have become standard tools for many therapists. Indeed, some clients are disappointed to find their therapist has no couch and does not plan to hypnotize them or interpret their dreams. Nonetheless, surveys reveal that a large number of young as well as experienced psychotherapists identify their perspective as "psychoanalytic" (Cook et al., 2010; Thoma & Cecero, 2009).

In addition, Freud can be credited with popularizing and promoting important psychological concepts. For example, anxiety plays a key role in the work of many psychotherapists, personality theorists, and researchers from numerous areas of psychology. As discussed in Chapters 4, 6, and 16, many of the topics researched by psychologists today have their roots in one or more of Freud's concepts, even if they no longer carry much of the Freudian flavor. By placing these concepts on the menu of psychological topics many years ago, Freud influenced the subject matter of personality research today.

Criticisms

Although Freud's ideas were so revolutionary that they were rejected by many in the medical and academic communities at the time, some writers argue that

Freud's ideas may not have been so original or groundbreaking after all. For example, one investigator discovered that between 1870 and 1880 at least seven books were published in Europe that included the word *unconscious* in the title (Whyte, 1978). Because the educated elite in Europe was relatively small, one researcher concluded that "at the time Freud started his clinical practice every educated person must have [been] familiar with the idea of the unconscious" (Jahoda, 1977, p. 132). Other historians point out that Freud probably had access to the works of people already writing about different levels of consciousness, free association, and infantile sexuality (Jahoda, 1977; Jones, 1953–1957). In addition, many Freudian ideas appear in literature that predates Freud's work. For example, the Russian novelist Fyodor Dostoyevski, who died in 1881, described in his writing such things as unconsciously motivated behaviors, erotic symbolism in dreams, intrapsychic conflict, and even hints of an Oedipus complex.

Three points can be offered in Freud's defense. First, Freud often cited earlier works on topics similar to the ones he was introducing. This is especially true in his early writings. Second, Freud was the first person to organize many loosely related ideas into one theory of human behavior. Without a unified theory detailing the relationship among the unconscious, dream interpretation, and infantile sexuality, it is doubtful whether any of these notions would have been developed much further by the scientists who were familiar with them. Third, Freud initiated a lifelong program of investigating the various concepts in his theory. The work Freud and his followers did with their clients provided the data on which psychoanalytic theory was developed. Although many of Freud's contributions may have had precedents in earlier writings, there is a large difference between introducing an idea and organizing, integrating, and developing many ideas into a comprehensive model of human behavior.

A second criticism often made of Freudian theory is that many of the hypotheses generated from the theory are not testable. Recall that one criterion for a useful scientific theory is that it generates hypotheses that can be either supported or not supported with data. But critics question whether Freud's theory meets this standard. For example, if a Freudian therapist concludes that a client has a strong unconscious hatred for her sister, what sort of evidence would demonstrate that the conclusion is incorrect? What if the client says she cannot remember any negative feelings toward her sister? The client is obviously repressing them. What if the client describes how much she loves her sister? Obviously, this is a reaction formation. And if the client admits she harbors negative feelings toward her sister, then the therapist has been successful in bringing the material into consciousness. If the hypothesis cannot be unsupported, neither can it be truly supported. This makes the theory considerably less useful to scientists.

In Freud's defense, he can hardly be accused of being unconcerned with finding evidence to support his theory. Indeed, he referred to many parts of his theory as "discoveries," the products of detailed examinations of clients' statements during various stages of psychoanalysis. However,

Freud's heavy reliance on case study data is the basis of another criticism. These data were almost certainly biased. First, Freud's patients hardly represented typical adults. Not only did they come from relatively wealthy and well-educated European families, but they also were suffering from psychological disorders at the time. It is a large leap to say that the minds of these clients function in the same way as the mind of the average psychologically healthy adult. Second, all the information we have about these clients was filtered through Freud. It is possible that Freud recognized and recorded only the statements and behaviors that supported his theory and ignored or failed to notice those that did not. Third, it is possible that (consciously or unconsciously) Freud caused his patients to say the things he wanted to hear. Psychotherapy clients can be highly vulnerable to accepting whatever a person in a position of authority tells them and may be highly motivated to please that person. It is interesting to note that when interpreting Dora's dream, Freud wrote that the dream confirmed what he already knew.

A final group of criticisms concerns disagreements with the points of emphasis and tone of Freud's theory. Many of Freud's early followers eventually broke away from the group and developed their own theories because they felt Freud ignored or de-emphasized important influences on personality. Some were concerned about Freud's failure to recognize how experiences beyond the first few years of life could affect personality. Others disagreed with Freud's emphasis on an instinctual basis for personality at the expense of important social and cultural influences. Still others took issue with Freud's tendency to concentrate on psychological disorders rather than on daily functioning and positive aspects of personality. As discussed in Chapter 5, many subsequent psychoanalytic thinkers developed theories that corrected some of these limitations and omissions.

Summary

1. The first comprehensive theory of personality was developed by Sigmund Freud about 100 years ago. After working with hypnosis to help patients suffering from hysteria, Freud came to understand the power of unconscious influences on behavior. According to his theory, human personality can be divided into conscious, preconscious, and unconscious parts. In addition, personality can be divided into the id, ego, and superego. Psychological activity is powered by psychic energy, called libido. Intrapsychic conflict creates tension, and the goal of human behavior is to return to a tensionless state.

2. Within Freud's theory, a healthy personality is one in which the ego controls id impulses and superego demands. To this end, the ego often uses defense mechanisms. These include repression, in which traumatic information is pushed out of awareness. Other defense mechanisms include sublimation, displacement, reaction formation,

denial, intellectualization, and projection. With the exception of sublimation, the ego uses these defense mechanisms at a cost.

3. Among the most controversial aspects of Freud's theory is his description of the psychosexual stages of development. Freud maintained that young children pass through stages of development characterized by the primary erogenous zone for each stage. Children pass through oral, anal, and phallic stages on their way to healthy sexual expression in the genital stage. Excessive trauma during these early years may cause psychic energy to become fixated, and the adult personality will reflect the characteristics of the fixated stage of development. An important step in the development of adult personality takes place with the resolution of the Oedipus complex at the end of the phallic stage.

4. Psychoanalysts have developed several methods for getting at unconscious material. Freud called dreams the "royal road to the unconscious." He interpreted the symbols in his patients' dreams to understand unconscious impulses. In addition, Freudian psychologists use projective tests, free association, and hypnosis to get at this material. Clues about unconscious feelings also may be expressed in Freudian slips, accidents, and symbolic behavior.

5. Freud also developed the first system of psychotherapy, called psychoanalysis. Most of the time in this lengthy therapy procedure is spent bringing unconscious sources of the clients' problems into awareness. A Freudian therapist actively interprets the true (unconscious) meanings of the clients' words, dreams, and actions for them. One of the first signs that psychoanalysis is progressing is resistance, in which a client stops cooperating with the therapeutic process in order to halt the therapist's threatening efforts to bring out key hidden material.

6. Many Freudian psychologists rely on projective tests to measure the concepts of interest to them. Typically, test takers are asked to respond to ambiguous stimuli, such as inkblots. Because there are no real answers, responses are assumed to reflect unconscious associations. The use of projective tests is controversial. Critics point to unacceptably low indicators of reliability and validity. However, if used correctly, these tests may provide insights into clients' personalities and sources of psychological problems.

7. Among the strengths of the Freudian approach is the tremendous influence Freud had on personality theorists for many years to follow. In addition, Freud developed the first system of psychotherapy and introduced many concepts into the domain of scientific inquiry. Critics point out that many of Freud's ideas were not new and that many aspects of his theory are not testable. Others criticize his use of biased data in developing his theory. Many of those who studied with Freud also disliked his emphasis on instinctual over social causes of psychological disorders and the generally negative picture he painted of human nature.

Key Terms

conscious (p. 43)

defense mechanisms (p. 46)

ego (p. 44)

free association (p. 41)

freudian slips (p. 54)

id (p. 44)

preconscious (p. 43)

projective tests (p. 54)

psychoanalysis (p. 56)

psychosexual stages of
 development (p. 49)

structural model (p. 44)

superego (p. 45)

topographic model (p. 43)

unconscious (p. 43)

Media Resources

Visit the book companion website at
www.cengagebrain.com to find a glossary,
flashcards, quizzing, and more.

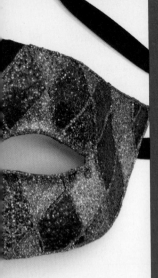

The Freudian Approach

Relevant Research

When I describe Freud's theory to undergraduates, I typically find two different reactions. On one hand, some students are impressed with Freud's insight into human behavior. Psychoanalytic theory helps them understand some of their own feelings and behaviors and the conflicts they wrestle with. "It really applies to me," a student told me, "Now I see why I do some of the things I do. Now I understand how symbolic some of my behaviors are."

On the other hand, some students eye Freudian theory with skepticism and even ridicule. Sexual feelings in children, unconscious meanings in dreams, Oedipal desires for one's opposite-sex parent and the like strike these students as little more than a Freudian fantasy taken too seriously. Although we probably embrace the personality theories that fit our own perceptions of human behavior, a scientific approach requires more than faith in one theory over another. What we need is evidence that Freud was correct in his characterization of human nature and psychological processes. In short, we need research.

Critics of the psychoanalytic approach sometimes charge that Freud was unconcerned with validating his theory. But that is not entirely correct. Freud's writings are filled with "a passionate desire to discover ways in which the validity of psychoanalytic findings could be established," wrote one historian. "The search for validation pervaded his entire work" (Jahoda, 1977, p. 113). Unfortunately, Freud's "validation" relied on methods other than empirical research, which left his work open to criticism. On the other hand, other psychologists have accepted the challenge of testing Freud's ideas through rigorous experimental procedures. Although some aspects of Freud's theory do not easily translate into experiments, investigators have succeeded in deriving several testable hypotheses from Freud's writings. In addition to direct tests of Freudian theory, a great deal of research has been conducted on topics either introduced or popularized by Freud. Hypnosis, slips of the tongue, anxiety, early developmental experiences, and other subjects of interest to Freud have been studied in depth by personality psychologists. Results from these investigations provide insight into many of the processes described by Freud.

In this chapter, we'll examine four areas of research relevant to Freud's theory. We begin with research on dream interpretation, with an eye to Freud's notions about the meaning and function of our dreams. Next, we look at how researchers study some of the defense mechanisms proposed by Freud and his followers and how these defense mechanisms change as we move from child to adult. This work is followed by research on Freud's ideas about humor. According to psychoanalytic theory, unconscious motives are often expressed through jokes, cartoons, and the things we find funny. Finally, we look at the phenomenon that first piqued Freud's curiosity about the unconscious—hypnosis. What is hypnosis, and why are some people more responsive to a hypnotist's suggestions than others?

Dream Interpretation

Next time you want to liven up a dull social gathering, ask the people around you to describe a recent dream. Although some of us remember dreams better than others, most people have little trouble recalling a funny, bizarre, or frightening dream they've experienced—sometimes more than once. In my dreams, I've walked on clouds, been visited by cartoon characters, and interacted with talking clocks. Friends have described dreams in which they fly like Superman, discover lost cities under the sea, live inside a potato, and fight with giant spiders. When unrestricted by the laws of time and physics, nearly anything is possible.

If you are like most people, you probably wonder from time to time just what your dreams really mean. Your curiosity reflects one of Freud's legacies to 21st-century Western culture. The notion that dreams contain hidden psychological meaning was promoted and popularized by Freud. Freud interpreted his patients' dreams in an effort to understand their unconscious conflicts and desires. Today, therapists from many different perspectives use dream interpretation as one of their therapeutic tools. But how accurate is dream interpretation? Although conducting research on dreams presents many challenges, a large number of investigators have studied this universal but mystical phenomenon. We'll look at two questions addressed in this research. First, what do people dream about? Can we use psychoanalytic theory to predict the content of our dreams? Second, why do people dream? Freud had some definite hypotheses about this, and researchers have produced findings relevant to some of these ideas. However, like other aspects of Freudian psychology, this research still leaves much room for interpretation by believers and skeptics.

> "*Dreams are never concerned with trivialities: we do not allow our sleep to be disturbed by trifles.*"
>
> SIGMUND FREUD

The Meaning of Dream Content

According to Freud, what we dream about provides clues about what's in our unconscious. Occasionally a dream contains images or evokes emotions that we feel must mean something. Yet for the most part, our dreams are absurd, vague, or just silly images that seemingly have no relation to anything. If you were to describe one of your dreams to a traditional Freudian therapist, you would likely be told that the objects and people in your dreams are symbols, which in the Freudian tradition usually means sexual symbols. Later psychoanalytic theorists argued that dreams represent unconscious preoccupations (Hall, 1953). That is, the unresolved conflicts we struggle with beneath our awareness surface during sleeping hours.

Dream researchers have developed various procedures to record and interpret the content of our dreams (Domhoff, 1996, 1999; Hill, 1996). Sometimes sleepers are awakened when physiological measures indicate they are probably dreaming. Other investigators rely on participants to record their dreams first thing in the morning in diaries they keep next to their beds. Still others simply ask participants to describe a recent dream or a recurrent dream.

Consistent with Freud's intuition, investigators find the content of our dreams is not random. Although there may be no apparent explanation for some of the bizarre material that makes its way into our nighttime productions, there is evidence that dream content is often influenced by the fears, problems, and issues that capture our thoughts before we go to bed

(Domhoff, 2001; Foulkes & Cavallero, 1993). One team of researchers compared the dreams of Palestinian children who lived under two very different circumstances (Valli, Revonsuo, Palkas, & Punamaki, 2006). Children living in the Gaza Strip during the time of the study had experienced years of violence and ever-present danger. In contrast, Palestinian children living in the Galilee area of Israel had a relatively peaceful existence. Dream reports revealed that the children living under constant stress had more dreams than the other children. Moreover, the stressed children's dreams included many more threatening events than the children who lived in a less stressful world. Clearly, the stressed children's dreams at night reflected the fears they faced during the day.

But what about unconscious conflicts? Can issues we are not consciously aware of also make their presence known in our dreams? Some research suggests they can. Consider a series of investigations comparing how often male and female characters appear in dreams. Think of a recent dream of your own. Were there more male or female characters? The answer will depend in part on your own gender. Several investigations find that women typically have an equal number of male and female characters in their dreams. However, despite stereotypes about men dreaming only of beautiful women, in truth men are much more likely to dream about male characters (Hall, 1984; Hall & Domhoff, 1963). As shown in Table 4.1, this difference is found at all ages and in nearly every culture. The combined findings of all these studies suggest that males make up about 50% of the characters in women's dreams, but about 65% of the characters in men's dreams.

But why are nearly two thirds of the characters in men's dreams other males? One explanation relates back to the Oedipus complex and its female counterpart, the Electra complex (Hall, 1984). According to Freudian theory, men never completely overcome their conflict with their fathers. Because some of these feelings are displaced onto other males, men typically experience more conflict with the men they encounter than do women. If men are preoccupied with this conflict at an unconscious level, as a psychoanalytic psychologist might guess, then this preoccupation should surface in the form of male characters in their dreams.

Can we say then that the universal prevalence of male characters in men's dreams proves this part of Freud's theory correct? Not entirely, because other interpretations are possible. For example, men may dream about men more than about women because they come into contact with more men during the day. And even if we accept that men have more conflicts with men than with women, it is still an open question as to whether this conflict is a manifestation of unresolved Oedipal feelings. Nonetheless, we can say that the findings from these studies are at least consistent with predictions from Freud's theory.

Another phenomenon of interest to dream researchers is the *recurrent dream*. Most of us have experienced a dream that we believe we have had before. For some people, the same dream occurs every night for several nights in a row. Sometimes a dream appears off and on for months or even years. From a psychoanalytic perspective, the dream reappears night after night

TABLE 4.1 Percentage of Male Dream Characters for Men and Women

Age of Participants	Country/Culture	Percent Male Characters	
		Men	Women
2–4	United States	59	49
7–12	United States	67	54
10–13	United States	69	52
	Guatemala	72	43
	Peru	68	50
14–17	United States	66	56
	Guatemala	68	46
	Peru	59	57
	Zulu	81	49
	Cuna	59	55
College	United States*	60	48
	Australia	55	48
	Mexico	59	61
	Peru*	34	39
	Zulu	82	54
	India	71	46
	Nigeria	81	50
Adult	United States	66	52
	Ifaluk	80	53
	Tinquian	61	66
	Alor	68	58
	Skolt	73	48
	Hopi	63	51

*Figures combined from more than one sample.

Source: From "A Ubiquitous Sex Difference in Dreams," by C. S. Hall, revisited, *Journal of Personality and Social Psychology,* 1984, 1109–1117.

because the conflict expressed in the dream is important yet remains unresolved. Consistent with this interpretation, researchers find most recurrent dreams include threatening images, usually situations in which the dreamer is in danger (Zadra, Desjardins, & Marcotte, 2006).

The psychoanalytic interpretation also helps to explain why recurrent dreamers are more likely to suffer from anxiety and generally poor adjustment during waking hours than people not experiencing recurrent dreams (Brown & Donderi, 1986; Zadra, O'Brien, & Donderi, 1998). The unconscious conflict surfaces in the dream at night but is expressed in the form of anxiety during the day. However, it is also possible that the cause-and-effect arrow runs in the opposite direction. The anxiety some people experience during the day might lead to recurring dreams at night. One study compared the number of recurrent dreams students experienced during exam weeks versus weeks without exams (Duke & Davidson, 2002). Students who experienced recurrent dreams had considerably more of these dreams during exam weeks than when they were under less stress.

But what of the most provocative aspect of Freud's dream interpretation theory—that seemingly innocent objects and actions are symbolic representations of sexuality and sexual activity? According to some psychoanalytic researchers, people who are anxious about sexual matters are unable to express their sexual desires directly. Instead, these individuals are left to express their sexual feelings through dream symbols. To test this hypothesis, one team of researchers asked participants to keep diaries of their dreams and their daily level of anxiety for 10 days (Robbins, Tanck, & Houshi, 1985). Consistent with the psychoanalytic position, the higher the participants' anxiety level, the more often classic Freudian sexual symbols (pencils, boxes, flying) appeared in their dreams.

So, was Freud correct about dream symbols? Although researchers sometimes find results that support psychoanalytic theory, direct and convincing tests of the notion that dream images are sexual symbols remain elusive. Most dream researchers agree that the content of our dreams is not random. But determining why some images appear in our dreams more often than others remains a challenge.

The Function of Dreams

A more difficult question than what people dream is *why* people dream at all. Freud maintained that unconscious impulses cannot be suppressed forever. Therefore, one of the major functions of dreams is to allow the symbolic expression of these impulses. Dreams provide a safe and healthy outlet for expressing unconscious conflicts. But researchers had to wait for technology to catch up with theory before they could investigate this aspect of Freud's theory.

In the 1950s researchers discovered that mammals experience two distinctly different kinds of sleep (Aserinsky & Kleitman, 1953). Each night we alternate between periods of *REM* and *non-REM sleep*. The acronym REM derives from the phrase "rapid eye movement"; this period is usually accompanied by rapidly moving eyes underneath closed lids. REM sleep is sometimes called paradoxical sleep because, although our muscles are especially relaxed during this time, our brain activity is similar to that of the waking state. Most adults spend 1½ to 2 hours a night in REM sleep, spread over several periods.

The significance of this discovery for personality researchers is that REM sleep is filled with dreams, whereas non-REM sleep has significantly fewer dreams. Thus the discovery of REM sleep created new opportunities for dream researchers. Researchers could look at the effects of depriving people of REM sleep, they could correlate psychological variables with the length and amount of REM sleep, and they could wake people during REM sleep to capture dreams that might be lost by morning (Arkin, Antrobus, & Ellman, 1978; Cohen, 1979).

What did REM sleep research reveal about the relationship between dreaming and mental health? Early researchers maintained that REM sleep, and therefore dreaming, was necessary for psychological health and that depriving someone of REM sleep might create serious psychological disturbances. Subsequent research has challenged this conclusion (Hoyt & Singer, 1978; Vogel, 1975), but dreaming does seem to have some psychological benefits. Emotional disorders are often associated with sleep difficulties and reduced REM sleep (Walker & van der Helm, 2009). In addition, individuals deprived of REM sleep have more difficulty with stressful tasks (McGrath & Cohen, 1978). Participants in one study were shown a film about autopsy procedures before and after a night's sleep (Greenberg, Pillard, & Pearlman, 1978). The film, depicting a physician performing an autopsy in gruesome detail, was selected for the study because it invariably created high levels of anxiety in viewers. Participants deprived of REM sleep had a difficult time coping with their anxiety. Participants allowed to dream between showings of the film were significantly less disturbed by the film the second time they saw it. Finally, researchers find that people deprived of REM sleep one night typically respond by increasing their amount of REM sleep the next night (Bulkeley, 1997). This *rebound effect* suggests that REM sleep serves some important function.

Other research finds at least partial support for Freud's notion that dreams provide an outlet for suppressed thoughts. Trauma victims who avoid thinking about their experience during the day often have dreams about the traumatic event at night (Mellman, David, Bustamante, Torres, & Fins, 2001). Participants in one study were asked before sleep to deliberately repress thoughts about someone they knew while engaging in a stream-of-consciousness writing exercise (Wegner, Wenslaff, & Kozak, 2004). That night, those participants had more dreams about the person they had tried not to think about than did participants allowed to write about the person they knew.

Interpreting the Evidence

What can we conclude about the experimental support for Freud's theory of dream interpretation? On one hand, researchers have produced a number of findings consistent with Freud's speculations. The content of our dreams is not random, and dreaming appears to serve some positive psychological functions. However, in almost all cases, psychologists can account for the findings without relying on Freudian concepts. Moreover, researchers have also uncovered results that are difficult to explain within Freudian theory (Domhoff, 2004). For example, why do newborn babies experience as much as 8 hours of REM sleep per day? What unconscious conflicts are they working out? For that matter, REM sleep has been found in nearly all mammals and possibly even in human fetuses (Crick & Mitchison, 1983). In short, the search for definitive answers to some of the questions Freud raised continues. Most of us have a difficult time abandoning the feeling that at least some of our dreams contain important psychological messages and that dreaming serves some important psychological function. Understanding the silly and frightening stories that play in our mind while we sleep no doubt will remain one of the irresistible mysteries for personality researchers for many years to come.

Defense Mechanisms

Among the discoveries Freud encountered when he first began to peek under the surface of human consciousness were the curious ways his patients dealt with emotional pain. As early as 1894, Freud wrote about his patients' unconscious efforts to conceal painful thoughts and described many of their neurotic symptoms as manifestations of defense mechanisms. Freud eventually identified the defense mechanism *repression* as the cornerstone of psychoanalysis. However, it was left to some of Freud's followers to fully develop the notion of defense mechanisms and to explore their psychological origins and function. In particular, Freud's daughter Anna identified 10 defense mechanisms depicted either directly or vaguely in her father's writings. She also described five additional mechanisms on her own, and subsequent psychoanalytic writers have added to the list. Thus, within the psychoanalytic approach, the ego has many tools at its disposal to fend off anxiety and guilt.

Defense mechanisms remain one of the most intriguing yet elusive aspects of Freud's theory. We are said to regularly employ a wide range of defenses, yet, by definition, we have no awareness that we are doing so. This is not to say that we are unaware of the behaviors that stem from these defenses. I may be quite in touch with my intense desire to compete, the anger I express at the grocery clerk, and the excuses I make to avoid my parents. But the defensive function that drives these behaviors could be buried at a level below consciousness. Of course, friends and family members often see the connection. Indeed, we frequently accuse people of being in denial, projecting their feelings onto others, or rationalizing away their bad habits. Most of us can think of times when friends displaced their anger onto us instead of onto whatever or whomever was really upsetting them. It also is the case that we often use anxiety-reducing techniques quite consciously. For example, you might deliberately distract yourself by going to a movie rather than thinking about an upcoming job interview. However, these conscious efforts to reduce anxiety are not the same as the unconscious defense mechanisms we are considering here (Cramer, 2000). The coping strategies we deliberately employ to reduce anxiety are covered in Chapter 6.

Identifying and Measuring Defense Mechanisms

Psychologists investigating defense mechanisms face the same set of problems that confront other researchers studying psychoanalytic concepts.

Because these processes operate at a level below consciousness, we cannot simply ask people to describe their defense mechanisms. Rather, investigators must rely on less direct methods to determine when and how often research participants use the various mechanisms identified by psychoanalysts (Davidson & MacGregor, 1998).

Not surprisingly, many of these researchers turn to projective tests. Some investigators measure defense mechanisms by interpreting responses to Rorschach inkblots (Lerner & Lerner, 1990) or to stories (Ihilevich & Gleser, 1993). Others use responses to Thematic Apperception Test (TAT) picture cards (Cramer, 1991; Porcerelli, Cogan, Kamoo, & Miller, 2010). Consider the response one psychiatric patient gave to a TAT card. The picture on the card features a boy and an unplayed violin. As with most projective stimuli, what the boy is feeling or thinking and his connection to the musical instrument is deliberately left unclear. The patient provided the following story:

> There's something wrong with this boy physically and mentally. He's unhappy. He wants to play the violin, and he can't. Maybe he's deaf. Somebody else was in the room earlier and put it in front of him, and left. He's not the kind of person who would pick it up and break it or anything. Is that enough? I don't know what the placemat's doing. It's obviously not something to eat. (Cramer, Blatt, & Ford, 1988, p. 611)

Researchers have developed detailed coding systems to turn this kind of response into scores indicating the extent to which test takers use various defense mechanisms (Cramer, 1991, 2006). In this example, the investigators found evidence of denial ("He's not the kind of person who would pick it up and break it") and projection ("Something's wrong with this boy physically and mentally"). The more frequently test takers make these kinds of statements, the more they are assumed to use defense mechanisms when dealing with the anxiety they face in their own lives.

College students in one study were given some threatening information about their masculinity and femininity (Cramer, 1998). The researcher reasoned that gender-related behavior is a particularly important aspect of identity for young men and women. In other words, it is important for most men entering adulthood to think of themselves as masculine, and for women to believe they are feminine. Information that threatens this part of the self-concept is potentially quite anxiety provoking. The investigator predicted that students would deal with this anxiety by using the defense mechanism *identification*. People who use identification associate themselves with powerful and successful individuals. For example, a young man might think about his association with a military leader or successful athlete. By unconsciously identifying with powerful others, we are said to fend off feelings of inadequacy and helplessness. Moreover, psychoanalysts argue that identification plays a particularly important role in the development of gender identity. Young men are said to identify with their fathers, whereas young women identify with their mothers as they develop gender-related characteristics. Thus, when one's masculinity or femininity is

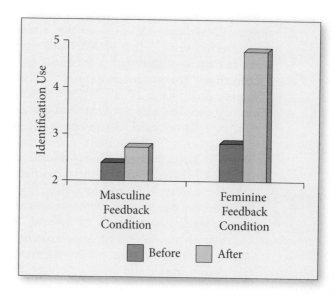

FIGURE 4.1 Men's Use of Identification as a Function of Feedback
Source: Adapted from Cramer (1998b).

threatened, the ego is likely to turn to identification to defend against the resulting anxiety.

To test this prediction, the investigator analyzed participants' stories for three TAT cards. The students then completed a short personality test that presumably measured their masculinity and femininity. Shortly thereafter the students were given bogus feedback on the test. Half the men were told they had scored high in masculinity. However, the other half were told they scored high in femininity. Similarly, half the women were told they were feminine and half that they were masculine. The students were then asked to provide three more stories from another set of TAT cards.

How did the participants respond to the threatening test feedback? As shown in Figure 4.1, men receiving the bogus feedback had a particularly strong emotional reaction. As predicted, they reacted to the threatening information by resorting to more identification. The use of identification was particularly strong for men who considered themselves highly masculine. In other words, to ward off this overt challenge to their sense of masculinity, the men unconsciously identified with powerful others, presumably masculine men. That the students became defensive in this study was illustrated well by the reaction of one male participant. When asked how he felt after being told he was feminine, he replied, "I didn't feel angry." Of course, no one had suggested that he was.

Developmental Differences

Adults have an arsenal of defenses they can use to ward off anxiety. But that is not the case for children (Cramer, 1991; Vaillant, 1992). Preschool children who experience a threat to their well-being may have no way to deal with their emotional reactions other than to simply deny the events ever took place. *Denial* consists of disavowing certain facts, from failure to see reality to distorting one's memory ("No, that's not what happened"), thereby reducing the anxiety associated with a traumatic event. Several studies find that young children rely heavily on denial (Brody, Rozek, & Muten, 1985; Cramer, 1997; Cramer & Brilliant, 2001). When one team of researchers asked kindergarteners if they had ever felt like a sad and crying boy in a drawing, few of the children acknowledged *ever* feeling sad (Glasberg & Aboud, 1982).

However, as children mature, they find that outright denial of facts and feelings is increasingly ineffective. By the time they enter the middle elementary school years, children understand that refusing to admit a fact does not make it go away. Unfortunately, the anxieties that brought about the use of denial do not disappear with this insight. Rather, the child comes to rely on more sophisticated methods of defense. In particular, older children often turn to *projection* to alleviate their anxieties and inward fears. Projection protects us from threatening anxiety by attributing unacceptable thoughts and feelings to someone else. In a sense, we move the anxiety-provoking material outside of ourselves. We recognize selfish behavior and sinister motives in others, but not in ourselves. Researchers in one study gathered TAT stories from children at several different times between the ages of 6½ and 9½ (Cramer, 1997). As shown in Figure 4.2, the children's use of denial and projection perfectly fit the expectations of the investigators. The children used

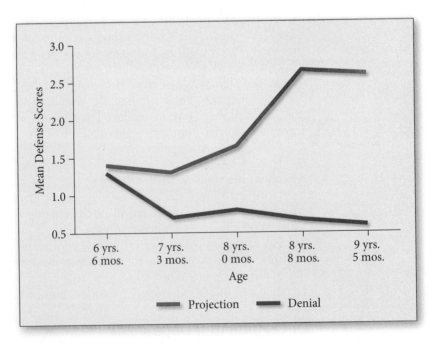

FIGURE 4.2 Use of Defenses as a Function of Age

Source: From "Evidence for Change in Children's Use of Defense Mechanisms," by Phebe Cramer, *Journal of Personality*, 1997, 65, 233–247.

increasingly less denial as they moved through these years but came to use projection more.

But projection also has its limitations. One study found that 9- to 11-year-old girls with few friends were quick to use both denial ("They're not really ignoring me") and projection ("Those girls are just mean") when faced with social rejection (Sandstrom & Cramer, 2003). By failing to acknowledge the reasons classmates rejected them, the girls most likely had a difficult time making the adjustments necessary to gain social approval. Thus, as they move into young adulthood, most men and women come to rely on more sophisticated defense mechanisms (Cramer, 2007). In fact, the use of defense mechanisms other than denial and projection is sometimes used as an indicator of emotional maturity (Cramer, 2012; Mahalik, Cournoyer, DeFranc, Cherry, & Napolitano, 1998). The tools used by the ego may change as we move through the childhood years and into adulthood, but the need to protect ourselves from unacceptable levels of anxiety remains.

Defensive Style

We all know people who are masters at rationalizing away their misdeeds and mistakes. You also may know someone who frequently displaces his anger onto employees, waiters, and telephone solicitors, or who constantly projects her own suspicions and fears onto others. Consistent with these observations, researchers have found that each of us tends to rely on some defense mechanisms more than others (Bond, 1992; Vaillant, 1992). Psychologists sometimes refer to these individual patterns as our *defensive style*.

Because some defense mechanisms are more effective than others, identifying a person's defensive style may tell us something about his or her general well-being. Freud often pointed to defense mechanisms to explain neurotic behavior. However, it is not clear whether he thought the use of defense mechanisms was necessarily pathological. Later psychoanalytic writers have argued that on occasion defense mechanisms can be normal and even adaptive (Fenichel, 1945; Vaillant, 1977, 1992). For example, *sublimation*—turning the unconscious impulse into a socially acceptable action—can serve the dual function of relieving anxiety and improving a person's life situation.

Whether a defense mechanism is adaptive or maladaptive may be a function of how often the person relies on it and how old that person is. Anna Freud (1965) suggested that defense mechanisms are maladaptive when used past an appropriate age. Five-year-olds may deny they did something unpleasant and still continue to function well. But adults who use the same defense strategy ("I never said that") will probably find it more and more difficult to interact with others or to make sense of their own behavior.

Why do some adults continue to rely on immature defense mechanisms like denial despite their ineffectiveness? According to Freud, adult defenses are related to early childhood experiences. One team of investigators tested this notion (Cramer & Block, 1998). The researchers began by measuring the amount of stress experienced by a group of 3-year-olds. They then waited 20 years before contacting the participants again and examining the kinds of defense mechanisms used by the now 23-year-old adults. As expected, the men who as adults frequently relied on denial were the participants who had experienced the highest levels of stress in their early childhood. The researchers reasoned that the men had relied heavily on the age-appropriate defense mechanism of denial when they were young. Because denial helped these boys deal with their psychological distress, they continued to rely on this defense mechanism as adults.

Unfortunately, in the real world we cannot simply insist that a problem does not exist. Not surprisingly, investigators find that using immature defenses is often associated with problems in psychological functioning (Cramer, 1999, 2002; Kwon, 2000; Segal, Coolidge & Mizuno, 2007; Vaillant, 1992; Zeigler-Hill, Chadha, & Osterman, 2008). One team of researchers found that adults who commonly rely on immature and ineffective defenses like denial have more problems with hostility, depression, and alcohol abuse than adults who use more effective defense mechanisms (Davidson, MacGregor, Johnson, Woody, & Chaplin, 2004).

Defensive style may also have implications for how people react to common sources of stress. Researchers in one study examined the use of defense mechanisms by parents during a particularly stress-filled time in their lives— the months immediately before the birth of their first child and the first year of the child's life (Ungerer, Waters, & Barnett, 1997). The demands of a newborn, coupled with the financial and personal burdens that come with parenthood, can be a major source of stress and anxiety. New parents who fail to deal with these stressors often experience a decline in general satisfaction with their relationship. Consistent with these observations, the investigators found that parents who typically relied on immature defense mechanisms such as denial and projection were less happy with their partners as they faced the anxieties of parenting. On the other hand, mothers and fathers who relied on more mature defense mechanisms, such as sublimation, remained satisfied with their relationship despite the challenges and anxieties the baby brought into their lives.

Humor

One type of humor has taken many forms over the years but never seems to disappear or go out of style. It is particularly popular among older elementary school children and early teenagers, but it is certainly not limited to these ages. You may have heard it in the form of "dead baby" jokes, "Helen Keller" jokes, or "Mommy Mommy" jokes. The point is to evoke shock and disgust by describing a particularly tasteless image or poking fun in an especially insensitive way. In Freud's day there were "marriage broker" jokes, which always began with a young man visiting a broker to arrange a marriage with a young woman. For example,

> The bridegroom was most disagreeably surprised when the bride was introduced to him, and drew the broker on the one side and whispered his remonstrances: "She's ugly and old, she squints and has bad teeth and bleary eyes...." "You needn't lower your voice," interrupted the broker, "she's deaf as well." (Freud, 1905/1960, p. 64)

Most of us agree that these jokes are in poor taste. Yet they remain popular and show up in each new generation in different forms. Why?

Freud's Theory of Humor

In his 1905 book *Jokes and Their Relation to the Unconscious,* Freud presented an extensive analysis of humor. Although he recognized "innocent" jokes, such as puns and clever insights, Freud was more concerned with *tendentious* jokes—the ones that provide insight into the unconscious of the joke teller as well as the person who laughs. Predictably, Freud saw two kinds of tendentious jokes, those dealing with hostility and those dealing with sex.

At first glance, it is difficult to understand how aggression can be funny. What is it about insults and biting satire that attracts and amuses us? Why do we laugh at another person's humiliation and embarrassment? According to Freud, aggressive jokes allow the expression of impulses ordinarily held in check. Although we may have unconscious urges to attack certain people or groups of people, our egos and superegos are generally effective in preventing outward acts of violence. But an insulting joke allows us to express these same aggressive desires in a socially appropriate manner. And, after all, who can take offense at an innocent joke? As Freud (1905/1960) wrote, "[b]y making our enemy small, inferior, despicable or comic, we achieve in a roundabout way the enjoyment of overcoming him" (p. 103).

Similarly, we can discuss taboo sexual topics through the socially appropriate outlet of sexual humor. Open discussions of sex are inappropriate in many social settings, yet jokes about sex are often not only tolerated but encouraged and rewarded. I have seen normally conservative and proper people who would never bring up the topic of sex in public deal with all kinds of taboo subject matter simply by repeating a joke "someone told me." One team of researchers found that sexual jokes provided adolescent girls with an easy way to introduce otherwise embarrassing topics into their lunchtime conversations (Sanford & Eder, 1984).

Freud also noticed that the laughter following a hostile or sexual joke is rarely justified by the humor content of the joke. If you stop to consider the next sexually oriented joke you hear, you'll probably notice that the joke often contains very little humor. So why do we laugh? Freud explained our reaction in terms of tension reduction, or **catharsis**. Descriptions of aggressive or sexual behavior create tension. The punch line allows a release of that tension. We get pleasure from many jokes not because they are clever or witty but because they reduce tension and anxiety. "Strictly speaking, we do not know what we are laughing at," Freud explained. "The technique of such jokes is often quite wretched, but they have immense success in provoking laughter" (1905/1960, p. 102).

Research on Freud's Theory of Humor

Look at the picture on page 82. Think of a caption that is as humorous or funny as possible. Now compare your answer to what one team of

> *"A person who laughs at [an obscene joke] ... is laughing as though he were the spectator of an act of sexual aggression."*
> SIGMUND FREUD

investigators found when they asked high school students to write funny captions to otherwise innocent pictures (Nevo & Nevo, 1983). According to the researchers, the students "used Freud's techniques as if they had read his writings." That is, the students' responses were filled with aggressive and sexual themes. One picture depicted only that a man was late for an appointment. Although the scene contained no obvious sexual or hostile content, students still came up with captions like, "I was late because I was with your wife." Interestingly, the students made almost no references to sex or aggression when asked what they might say if actually in the situation depicted in the picture.

Was Freud correct when he said that people find aggressive and sexual themes funny? Several investigations support this observation (Kuhlman, 1985; McCauley, Woods, Coolidge, & Kulick, 1983; Weinstein, Hodgins, & Ostvik-White, 2011). Participants in these studies typically rate cartoons containing aggression or sex as funnier than cartoons without these themes. Common observations point to the same conclusion. From one stooge poking another in the eye to cartoon characters being flattened by anvils, examples of pain and suffering permeate many sources of humor. And it's a rare situation comedy that goes more than a few minutes these days without a reference to sex.

Write a funny caption for this photo

Several other hypotheses derived from Freud's theory of humor also have been supported in empirical studies. For example, if hostile humor allows us to satisfy aggressive impulses, we should find a joke funnier when it pokes fun at a person or group we don't like. Several investigations find support for this prediction (Hodson, Rush, & MacInnis, 2010; Wicker, Barron, & Willis, 1980). Men and women in one study were presented with a series of hostile jokes and cartoons (Mundorf, Bhatia, Zillmann, Lester, & Robertson, 1988). Some of the material ridiculed men, whereas other jokes and cartoons made fun of women. Consistent with Freud's observations, men found humor that targeted women funnier than humor that aimed at men, whereas the women enjoyed humor that put down men more than humor that made fun of women.

Two predictions from Freud's theory are particularly intriguing because at first glance they appear to defy common sense. These have to do with the effect of hostile humor and how anxiety affects how funny we find a joke.

Reducing Aggression with Hostile Humor

We've often heard that humor can turn away anger. Suppose you were confronted with an angry person and wanted to defuse the situation with a joke. What kind would you tell—one with obvious hostile content or an innocent, nonhostile joke? Common sense tells you to try the nonhostile joke. But Freud made the opposite prediction. Remember, Freud said that hostile humor provides an outlet for aggressive feelings. If that is the case, hostile humor might do the trick better than nonhostile humor.

Although counterintuitive, several investigations find support for Freud's prediction. Participants in one study were insulted by the investigator and then read a series of either hostile or nonhostile jokes (Leak, 1974). When later asked what they thought about the insulting investigator, the participants who read the hostile jokes were less angry than those who read the nonhostile jokes. Angry participants in another study read cartoons that expressed hostility toward women (Baron, 1978b). Later these participants were given the opportunity to administer electric shocks to a woman under the guise of a learning experiment. These participants gave less intense and shorter shocks than angry participants who had not seen the cartoons.

However, other investigations find the relationship between humor and aggression is not that simple. Angry participants in one study were exposed to a hostile comedy routine and became more hostile toward a person who had insulted them (Berkowitz, 1970). In another investigation, angry participants allowed to shock an unseen victim gave more electric shocks after reading hostile cartoons than those who read nonhostile cartoons (Baron, 1978a). In short, hostile humor sometimes reduces aggressiveness, yet other times increases it.

So what's going on here? Quite possibly, as Freud speculated, hostile humor defuses aggressive tendencies in some situations. But hostile humor has the potential to do more than reduce tension. For example, as discussed in Chapter 14, people often imitate aggressive models. Thus the aggression described in hostile jokes or shown in cartoons might be imitated by an angry reader. In short, although Freud may be correct about the tension-reducing capabilities of hostile humor, we should be cautious about using that kind of humor when dealing with an angry audience.

Level of Tension and Funniness

Observe a group of listeners the next time a good storyteller delivers an obscene joke. Skilled joke tellers elaborate on the details. They allow the tension level to build gradually as they set up the punch line. Listeners smile or blush slightly as the joke progresses. According to Freud, this long buildup creates greater tension and thus a louder and longer laugh when the punch line finally arrives.

Freud said that the more tension people experience before a punch line, the funnier they'll find the joke. If that is the case, then a nervous and slightly frightened person is more likely to enjoy a joke than someone who is calm and therefore tensionless. Again, this prediction may not sound right at first. Shouldn't a relaxed person enjoy a funny story more than someone who is anxious?

The prediction was tested in a study in which people were asked to work with a laboratory rat (Shurcliff, 1968). Participants in the low-tension condition were asked to hold the rat for 5 seconds. They were told, "These rats are bred to be docile and easy to handle, and I don't think you will have any trouble." In the moderate-tension condition, people were asked to take a small sample of the rat's blood. They were told the task was easier than it looked. Participants in the high-tension group were given a bottle and syringe and asked to take two cubic centimeters of blood from the rat. The experimenter emphasized how difficult the task was and warned that the rat might bite.

The punch line occurred when participants reached into the cage and discovered a toy rat. Consistent with Freud's theory, participants in the high-tension group thought the situation was funnier than participants in the other conditions (Figure 4.3). The pleasure they derived from the release of tension apparently led to their enjoyment of the joke.

Interpreting the Findings

Drawing unequivocal conclusions from research is often difficult, but as you may have noticed by now, interpreting studies that test Freudian ideas is particularly challenging. On the plus side, researchers have uncovered considerable evidence in support of Freud's theory of humor. People often find jokes and cartoons funnier when they contain sexual and aggressive themes. We also appear to enjoy hostile humor more when it is aimed at someone we dislike. Hostile humor may reduce tension, although this does not necessarily reduce hostility, and jokes are funnier when the listener's tension level is built up before the punch line. Less direct tests of Freud's theory also suggest that laughter serves important psychological functions. For example, several studies find evidence to support the widely held belief that laughter is an effective means to combat daily tension and stressful events (Krokoff, 1990; Kuiper & Martin, 1998; Kuiper, McKenzie, & Belanger, 1995; Lefcourt,

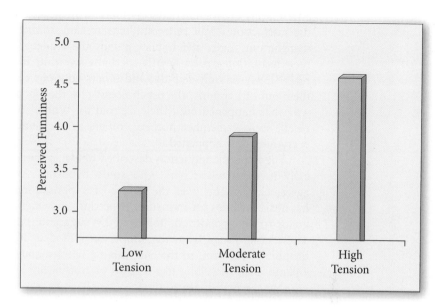

FIGURE 4.3 Perceived Funniness as a Function of Tension
Source: Based on Shurcliff (1968).

Davidson, Prkachin, & Mills, 1997). Some psychologists have even incorporated humor into their therapy procedures (McGuire, 1999).

On the other hand, alternative explanations are often possible for many of these findings (Kuhlman, 1985; Nevo & Nevo, 1983). For example, researchers find that humor often is the result of incongruity (McGhee, 1979). That is, we find a situation funny when what happens is inconsistent with what we expect. When applied to sexual and aggressive humor, it's possible that people find these kinds of jokes funny because sex and aggression are out of place in the joke setting. Imagine a movie scene in which two sophisticated women bump into each other at a department store. Imagine further that they either get into a physical fight or say something with sexual connotations. We may find this situation funny for the reasons outlined by Freud. But it might also bring a laugh because we do not expect sophisticated women to act this way in this setting.

Hypnosis

A psychologist is giving a classroom demonstration of hypnosis. Several student volunteers sit in the front of the room. They are told to relax and that they are becoming drowsy. The hypnotist tells them they are in a state of deep hypnosis and that they will do whatever he says. Soon the students close their eyes and sit peacefully yet attentively in their chairs. The hypnotist begins the demonstration by asking them to extend their left arm and to imagine a weight is pulling it down. Suddenly the arms of several students begin to move downward, just as if a weight were pulling on the arms.

A few arms drop immediately; others drop slowly over several repetitions of the instructions. Still other students remain unaffected, with arms extended straight out. Later the hypnotist tells the students a fly is buzzing around their head. Some react swiftly, perhaps swatting at the imaginary fly, others react slowly or only slightly, and others continue to sit calmly. Before taking them out of hypnosis, the psychologist tells the students they won't remember what has happened until they are told to. When later asked about what they recall, some remember nothing, others a few details, and others practically everything that happened.

The hypnotic induction described above is similar to the procedures typically used by researchers who study hypnosis. Although considerable disagreement remains over the nature of hypnosis, most researchers agree that hypnosis includes an induction procedure in which people are told they are going to be hypnotized, followed by suggestions to perform certain tasks. These tasks range from the simple ones used in hypnosis research, such as dropping your arm, to the entertaining performances of stage hypnosis participants, such as yelling like Tarzan or trotting up and down the aisles warning that the British are coming.

Although modern hypnosis has existed in some form for more than 200 years, it remains an intriguing and often misunderstood phenomenon. Hypnosis also has a number of potentially useful applications. Many people have dental work performed under hypnosis without the aid of painkillers. Police investigators sometimes use hypnosis to help witnesses remember crime details. And psychotherapists from many different perspectives find hypnosis a useful tool when dealing with a wide variety of client problems, especially chronic pain (Kirsch, 1996; Milling, Reardon, & Carosella, 2006; Patterson & Jensen, 2003). Despite these many uses, psychologists still quarrel about just what they are dealing with. We'll explore some of the different opinions on this matter in the next section, followed by an examination of individual differences in hypnotic responsiveness.

What Is Hypnosis?

There is no shortage of theories about the nature of hypnosis. Psychologists sometimes organize the various explanations for hypnosis along a continuum based on the extent to which the theory reflects psychoanalytic thinking (Kirsch & Lynn, 1995). At one end of this continuum we find psychologists who describe hypnosis in a manner similar to the way Freud did. They believe hypnosis taps an aspect of the human mind that is otherwise difficult to reach. These theorists sometimes say that hypnotic participants fall into a trance or that they experience an altered state of consciousness, like sleeping. At the other end of the continuum we find theorists who emphasize the role of cognitive and social processes. These psychologists reject the notion that hypnotized people operate under an altered state of awareness. They skeptically maintain there is nothing mysterious about hypnotic phenomena—that all the amazing things people do under hypnosis can be explained in terms of basic psychological processes applicable to hypnotized and nonhypnotized people. A great deal of research has been directed at determining which of these descriptions of hypnosis is correct. However, it may also be the case that both descriptions of hypnosis are partially correct and that each explains different aspects of the hypnotic experience (Kihlstrom, 1998, 2005; Spiegel, 2005).

Psychoanalytically Influenced Theories

> "*From being in love to hypnosis is evidently only a short step. There is the same humble subjection, the same compliance, the same absence of criticism toward the hypnotist as toward the love object.*"
>
> SIGMUND FREUD

Freud saw hypnosis as a passkey to a highly hypnotizable patient's unconscious mind. Somehow the barrier to the unconscious is weakened during hypnosis, allowing easier access to crucial unconscious material. Many psychoanalytic therapists still use hypnosis this way (Baker & Nash, 2008; Eisen, 2010; Lankton & Matthews, 2010). One account of hypnosis with a psychoanalytic flavor is called **neodissociation theory** (Hilgard, 1994; Sadler & Woody, 2010). According to this explanation, deeply hypnotized people experience a division of their conscious. One part of their conscious—the hypnotized part—enters a type of altered state. But another part remains aware of what is going on during the hypnotic session. This second part is said to act as a "hidden observer" monitoring the situation. The hypnotized part of the conscious is unaware of the observer part.

Highly responsive participants in one study were hypnotized and told they would not experience pain (Hilgard, 1977). Their arms were then lowered into ice water for up to 45 seconds. Like any of us, when not hypnotized, these people reported severe pain almost as soon as their arms touched the water. However, when hypnotized, they appeared to withstand the icy

Jerry Burger/Santa Clara University

Like the volunteers in this classroom demonstration, most people respond to simple suggestions during hypnosis. However, why these subjects go along with the hypnotist's suggestions remains a matter of controversy.

water with little evidence of suffering. But this ability to withstand pain under hypnosis has been demonstrated before. The new twist the investigator added was asking participants to report their experiences through automatic writing or automatic talking. The hand not immersed in the ice water was placed under a covered box where the participant used either a pencil or a keypad to write with. The researcher found that hypnotized participants could keep one arm in the cold water while writing with the other arm that the experience is quite painful. Advocates of neodissociation theory argue that the part of the participant's conscious that was in the altered state was able to deny the pain and keep the arm submerged in the water. However, the hidden observer part—presumably the part of consciousness that controls the automatic writing—was aware of the pain and could report it.

Sociocognitive Theories of Hypnosis

Although psychoanalytic accounts of hypnosis were once widely accepted among psychologists, some researchers began to challenge the notion that hypnosis involved a state of consciousness different than being awake (Barber, 1969). They pointed out there is nothing a person can do under hypnosis that cannot be done without hypnosis. For example, people who are relaxed but not hypnotized, and who are asked to imagine a weight pulling their arms down, will experience the same increased heaviness in their arms as hypnotized individuals.

But how do these psychologists explain some of the unusual things people do when hypnotized? Most use concepts such as expectancy, motivation, and concentration to account for hypnotic phenomena (Barber, 1999; Wagstaff, David, Kirsch, & Lynn, 2010). To illustrate the point, I sometimes ask a few students in my class to stand up and spin like a top. In every case the students comply. When I ask why they are doing this, they say it is because I asked them to. None have ever said it was because they were hypnotized. Yet most people who see hypnosis participants stand and spin like tops at the hypnotist's request say the people act that way because they are hypnotized. What is the difference between these two situations? Does the hypnotist use certain magical words that suddenly transform people into a trance? Sociocognitive theorists argue that hypnotized and nonhypnotized people stand up and spin for the same reason: They think they are supposed to.

These theorists are also critical of "hidden observer" demonstrations (Green, Page, Handley, & Rasekhy, 2005; Spanos & Katsanis, 1989). They argue that the highly responsive people in these experiments are told their hidden observer is supposed to feel pain, and they consequently report the pain they expect. When researchers told participants in one study that their hidden observer would experience less pain, the hidden observers indeed reported less, not more, pain (Spanos & Hewitt, 1980).

Sociocognitive theorists also argue that the psychoanalytic position sometimes can become circular. That is, if we ask why hypnosis participants run around making chicken noises, we are told it is because they are hypnotized. But if we ask how we can tell the participants are hypnotized, we are shown how they run around making chicken noises. The concept becomes inarguable and therefore useless in explaining the effect.

Which side is correct? Despite decades of research and discussion, the debate between psychoanalytic theorist and sociocognitive theorists continues (Kallio & Revonsuo, 2003; Kirsch, 2005; Lynn, Kirsch, Knox, Fassler, & Lilienfeld, 2007; Raz, Kirsch, Pollard, & Nitkin-Kaner, 2006). Nonetheless, in recent years there has been a growing consensus among researchers that the hypnotic trance notion alone does a poor job of explaining why hypnosis participants act the way they do (Kirsch, 2000; Kirsch & Lynn, 1998). Although psychoanalytic theorists point to unusual behavior under hypnosis, such as pain analgesia, deafness, and age regression, sociocognitive theorists counter with demonstrations of the same phenomena without hypnosis. In some cases, sociocognitive theorists challenge the accuracy of the participants' descriptions. For example, people who claim to go back to an earlier age typically do a poor job of re-creating what they were really like at that time (Nash, 1987).

Sociocognitive theorists also are skeptical of participants' reports concerning posthypnotic amnesia. Hypnosis participants are often told they will not remember what has happened during hypnosis until the hypnotist tells them to. Indeed, many of these people recall little or nothing of the experience until given permission. Posthypnotic amnesia has not escaped the attention of novelists and scriptwriters, whose characters sometimes engage in all manner of heinous acts while seemingly under the control of an evil hypnotist. Although there is no evidence that hypnosis can be used this way, some people do claim to forget what they did when hypnotized. Why?

Psychoanalytically oriented theorists explain that the experience either has been repressed out of consciousness or has been recorded in a part of the mind not accessible to consciousness. The information is said to remain inaccessible until the ego allows it to enter awareness. However, sociocognitive theorists argue that hypnosis participants expect not to recall what happens to them and therefore make no effort to remember (Coe, 1989; Sarbin & Coe, 1979; Spanos, Radtke, & Dubreuil, 1982). These researchers argue that under the right circumstances people can be persuaded to make that effort. For example, how long would posthypnotic amnesia continue if participants were offered $1,000 to describe what happened while they were hypnotized?

A team of researchers found a less expensive way to test this possibility (Howard & Coe, 1980; Schuyler & Coe, 1981). Some highly hypnotizable people were connected to a machine with a lot of lights and gauges and told the instrument could tell when they were lying. The experimenter explained that the machine "is very sensitive and functions in the same manner as a lie detector. It can tell if you are withholding information." In truth, the machine had no such capabilities, but the participants believed that it did. Although they were told under hypnosis they would remember nothing, when it came time to report what they could remember about the hypnotic experience, participants in the "lie detector" condition remembered significantly more than people in a control condition. Apparently, they believed they would be caught for saying they could not remember when they really could.

Although these studies challenge the psychoanalytically influenced theories of hypnosis, they do not dispute the usefulness of hypnosis or the honesty of the participants. Responsive participants are not intentionally deceiving the hypnotist. Rather, they are responding to normal social-psychological influences. Just as you act the way you believe a student is supposed to act when in school, hypnosis participants behave the way they believe people are supposed to when under hypnosis.

It also is safe to speculate that the debate between psychoanalytic and sociocognitive theorists will not go away any time soon. For example, recent advances in technology provide researchers with new opportunities to examine the neurological changes that accompany hypnosis. Not surprisingly, proponents of the psychoanalytic view have interpreted findings from these studies as evidence for a hypnotic trance, whereas psychologists who advocate a sociocognitive interpretation see the data in ways that support their position (Burgess, 2007; Lynn et al., 2007).

Hypnotic Responsiveness

Not everyone responds the same to a hypnotist's suggestions. Some people sing like an opera star, stick their arms in ice water, or report seeing objects that aren't really there. Others begrudgingly close their eyes but fail to react to any of the hypnotist's requests. Most people fall somewhere in between. One of the first things students ask me after a hypnosis demonstration is why some people are so responsive and others are not. What makes a good hypnotist? What kind of person makes the best participant?

Despite stage hypnotists' claims to be the best at their trade, research shows hypnotic responsiveness is largely a participant variable. The difference between hypnotists for the most part lies in showmanship (Meeker & Barber, 1971). Highly responsive people respond to anyone they perceive to be a legitimate hypnotist. In fact, to standardize procedures, many researchers put hypnotic induction procedures on tape. Research assistants play the tape for participants with no apparent loss in responsiveness. Beginning hypnotists are sometimes disappointed when people fail to respond to their suggestions, wondering what they did wrong. Had they given intelligence tests, they probably would not blame themselves for a test taker who did poorly. But so many performers have promoted the idea of good and bad hypnotists that it is a difficult concept to shake.

Nonetheless, there are a few techniques hypnotists can use to increase responsiveness, especially among people who are a bit skeptical at the beginning of the experience (Lynn et al., 1991). People are more responsive to hypnotic suggestions when the situation is defined as hypnosis and when their cooperation is secured and trust established before beginning. But most hypnotists use these techniques routinely and still find large differences in responsiveness.

Researchers find that hypnotic responsiveness is in fact a fairly stable individual difference. People who are highly responsive to one hypnotist's suggestions will probably be responsive to another hypnotist. Moreover, how responsive you are to hypnotic suggestions today is an excellent predictor of how responsive you will be years from now (Spanos, Liddy, Baxter, & Burgess, 1994). One team of researchers found an impressive correlation of .71 between hypnotic responsiveness scores taken 25 years apart (Piccione, Hilgard, & Zimbardo, 1989). The question thus becomes: What kind of person makes the most responsive participant?

For decades, investigators looked for personality trait measures that could predict hypnotic responsiveness. Researchers speculated that the most responsive participants might score high on measures of sensation seeking, imagination, or intelligence and low on measures of dogmatism, independence, extraversion, and so on. Unfortunately, few correlations between personality scores and hypnotic responsiveness were found, and replications were seldom reported (Green, 2004; Kirsch & Council, 1992; Laurence, Beaulieu-Prevost, & du Chene, 2008). Short of hypnotizing the person, no measure was discovered that reliably predicted responsiveness to hypnosis. Even Freud could not tell beforehand which patients would be highly responsive. He only observed that "neurotics can only be hypnotized with great difficulty, and the insane are completely resistant" (1905/1960, pp. 294–295).

However, later research identified a few personality variables other than neurosis and insanity that predict hypnotic responsiveness. These studies succeeded where earlier efforts had failed because investigators measured traits that more directly relate to the hypnotic experience. For example, a person's ability to become immersed in a role predicts hypnotic responsiveness (Sarbin & Coe, 1972). This may be why drama students are more responsive to hypnotic suggestions than other students (Coe & Sarbin, 1991). Recently, investigators have identified differences between highly responsive participants and poor responders when examining brain activity (Gruzelier, 2006; Oakley, 2008). Thus, some day it may be possible to predict how responsive you will be to hypnosis by examining electroencephalograph and fMRI data.

But the most successful efforts to date to predict hypnotic responsiveness from personality traits come from work on a trait called **absorption**. People who score high on measures of absorption have the ability to become highly involved in sensory and imaginative experiences. They are open to new experiences and are prone to fantasies and daydreams (Roche & McConkey, 1990; Tellegen & Atkinson, 1974). Numerous studies find that people who score high on measures of absorption are more responsive to hypnotic suggestions than those who score low (Glisky, Tataryn, Tobias, Kihlstrom, & McConkey, 1991; Nadon, Hoyt, Register, & Kihlstrom, 1991). Thus, if you are the kind of person who gets involved in a good book or a movie and blocks out all experiences around you, you probably can be responsive to hypnotic suggestions.

Beyond this, three important variables affect hypnotic responsiveness: attitude, motivation, and expectancy (Barber, 1999). People with a positive attitude toward hypnosis are more responsive than are those who view hypnosis with suspicion and mistrust. Participants taught to develop positive attitudes and to change their expectancies from passively receiving suggestions to actively taking part in the experience often become more responsive to suggestions (Gorassini, Sowerby, Creighton, & Fry, 1991; Gorassini & Spanos, 1986).

In addition, the more motivated people are to experience hypnosis, the more responsive they will be. Finally, what people expect to happen during the hypnotic experience affects their responsiveness (Benham, Woody, Wilson, & Nash, 2006; Fassler, Lynn, & Knox, 2008). Participants told in one study that responding to suggestions was difficult were not as responsive as those told it was easy (Barber & Calverley, 1964). Similarly, students who first watched a highly responsive participant were more responsive to hypnotic suggestions than those who watched a nonresponsive model (Klinger, 1970). In short, people tend to act under hypnosis the way they think they are supposed to act. This is why people who expect to see bizarre behavior at a hypnosis show often act bizarrely when they are brought up on stage and hypnotized.

Summary

1. A common thread runs through the four topics covered in this chapter. In each case, evidence supporting the Freudian position has been produced by researchers, yet questions about how to interpret these findings remain. Although it seems fair to conclude that some empirical support has been obtained for Freud's theory, in no case is this support clear and unequivocal.

2. Researchers examining the content of dreams find that men tend to dream about male characters twice as often as they dream about female characters. Some researchers interpret this finding as evidence of men's preoccupation with other men, a holdover from unresolved Oedipal impulses. The discovery of REM sleep allowed investigators to better examine the function of dreams. Although deprivation of REM sleep is not related to psychological disorders, some research indicates that dreaming may help the sleeper work through ongoing problems.

3. Researchers use projective tests and other procedures to determine which defense mechanisms people use. Studies find young children tend to rely on unsophisticated defense mechanisms, such as denial, whereas adults more often use defense mechanisms like identification. Researchers also find individual differences in preferred defense mechanisms. People who rely heavily on immature defense mechanisms may have more difficulties with personal adjustment and well-being than those who use more efficient and productive defense mechanisms.

4. Freud outlined a theory of humor, arguing that sexual and aggressive themes underlie much of what we find funny. In support of his theory, researchers find that people think hostile humor is funnier when it is aimed at someone they dislike. In addition, some research indicates that hostile humor reduces the likelihood of aggression, as Freud predicted. However, other studies find the opposite. The more tension people experience before receiving a punch line, the funnier they find a joke. Although many research findings are consistent with Freud's theory, many also are open to alternative interpretations.

5. Many researchers and therapists explain hypnosis in a manner similar to Freud's description. Although hypnotic participants often behave as if they are in an altered state of consciousness, skeptical researchers explain these phenomena in terms of expectancies, motivations, and relaxation. Hypnotic responsiveness is largely a participant variable. People who are generally able to become absorbed in a situation tend to be responsive to hypnotic suggestions.

Key Terms

absorption (p. 91)   catharsis (p. 81)   neodissociation theory (p. 87)

Media Resources

Visit the book companion website at
www.cengagebrain.com to find a glossary,
flashcards, quizzing, and more.

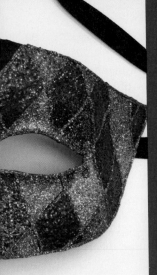

CHAPTER 5

The Psychoanalytic Approach

Neo-Freudian Theory, Application, and Assessment

Historians, scholars, teachers, and textbook writers use a number of images and metaphors to describe Sigmund Freud's work and influence. Some picture Freud defiantly marching against the stream of contemporary thought and values. Others describe him as a pioneer blazing new trails into the previously unknown territory of the unconscious mind. I've also seen Freud compared with a diligent detective piecing together clues about the true nature of the human mind or a shrewd lawyer cutting away the ego's defenses one by one. But the metaphor I like best compares Freud with a tree. Like a giant oak standing in the middle of a grove, Freud's theory is the oldest and most formidable of the many psychoanalytic approaches to understanding personality. Just as the oak drops acorns that sprout into their own trees, so did Freud's Psychoanalytic Society generate several scholars who went on to develop their own theories of personality. However, like the surrounding saplings that resemble the great oak, the ancestry of these later personality theories is clearly Freudian.

The collection of scholars who gathered in Vienna to study with Freud included some of the leading thinkers of the day. Not surprisingly, many of these psychologists eventually developed their own ideas about the nature of personality. Unfortunately, Freud and some of his followers often viewed these contributions as more than elaborations or professional disagreements. Sometimes the failure to adhere strictly to psychoanalytic theory as espoused by Freud was seen as blasphemy. Freud apparently viewed almost any deviation from or disagreement with his works as something akin to treason. Gradually, many followers left the Psychoanalytic Society, sometimes forming their own associations and new schools of psychology.

Although none of the theorists described in this chapter ever developed as much fame or influence as Freud, each made a substantial contribution to the psychoanalytic approach to personality theory. Although at the time their differences with Freud may have seemed great, with the perspective of time, we can see that their contributions were more accurately elaborations of Freud's theory rather than radically new approaches to personality. Hence, these theorists have come to be known as the neo-Freudians. For the most part, the neo-Freudian theorists retained the unconscious as a key determinant of behavior. Most also agreed with Freud about the impact of early childhood experiences on personality development, although many felt that later experiences also influenced adult personality. Most of these theorists also readily accepted such Freudian concepts as defense mechanisms and dream interpretation. In short, the neo-Freudian theories should be viewed as different perspectives within the general psychoanalytic approach to personality.

One feature that remains from the tradition of loyalty and divisions found in that early group of theorists is the tendency to treat the theory's developer more as a prophet than a theorist. People often identify themselves as a Jungian or an Adlerian psychologist. Although space doesn't allow more than a brief examination of a few of the major theorists' contributions, you may find that one or two of the neo-Freudians have a grasp on the nature of human personality that is particularly insightful and thought-provoking. In that spirit, I hope the following brief presentation provides a starting point for future reading and thought.

Limits and Liabilities of Freudian Theory

If you were to plow through the many volumes written by Sigmund Freud, you would most certainly find parts of his theory difficult to accept or in need of some elaboration. Although later students of psychoanalysis disagreed with many aspects of Freud's thinking, three of the theory's limits and liabilities often played key roles in the development of the neo-Freudians' approaches.

First, many of these theorists rejected the idea that the adult personality is formed almost in its entirety by experiences in the first 5 or 6 years of life. Most neo-Freudians acknowledged that early childhood experiences have a significant effect on personality development. But many argued that later experiences, particularly in adolescence and early adulthood, are also important in shaping personality. One neo-Freudian theorist in particular, Erik Erikson, maintained that important aspects of personality continue to develop into old age.

Second, many neo-Freudians challenged Freud's emphasis on instinctual sources of personality. In particular, Freud failed to recognize that many social and cultural forces also shape who we are. For example, Freud attributed many of the differences he saw between the personalities of men and women to inherent biological differences between the sexes. Later theorists, most notably Karen Horney, argued that the culture we grow up in plays a large role in creating these differences. Of course, Freud did not ignore social influences altogether. But he failed to give them enough attention to satisfy many of his detractors.

Third, many theorists disliked the generally negative tone of Freudian theory. Freud painted a pessimistic and in some ways degrading picture of human nature—people largely controlled by instincts and unconscious forces. Later theorists, both psychoanalytic and otherwise, presented a more positive view of humankind and human personality. Many described the constructive functions of the ego and emphasized the role of conscious rather than unconscious determinants of behavior. Other theorists spoke of growth experiences and the satisfaction people obtain from reaching their potential. These alternative views can be uplifting to those who find the Freudian perspective just a little depressing.

Alfred Adler

Alfred Adler was the first member of the psychoanalytic group to break with Freud. The year was 1911, and it was clear to both men that their differences were fundamental. Unfortunately, the professional dispute became personal as well. Freud saw Adler's disagreements more as defections than points of discussion. When Adler left the Vienna group, several members left with him. Friendships were severed, and accusations were tossed about. Adler went on to develop his own society, establish his own journal, and even select a name for his new psychology. He called his approach *individual psychology*. Among Adler's important contributions to our understanding of personality are the notion of striving for superiority, the role of parental influence on personality development, and the effects of birth order.

Alfred Adler

1870–1937

Bettmann/CORBIS

Alfred Adler's career provides an excellent example of one man's life-long striving to overcome feelings of inferiority. Adler was born in Vienna in 1870, the third of six children. Alfred spent much of his childhood in his older brother's shadow. A series of childhood illnesses, particularly rickets, left Adler physically unable to keep up with his brother and other playmates in athletic and outdoor games. He almost died of pneumonia at age 4 and twice was nearly killed when run over by carts in the streets. Because of his physical inferiority, Adler received special treatment from his mother. However, this ended with the birth of his brother. "During my first two years my mother pampered me," he recalled. "But when my younger brother was born she transferred her attention to him, and I felt dethroned" (cited in Orgler, 1963, p. 2).

Adler also experienced feelings of inferiority in the classroom. He achieved only mediocre grades and did so poorly at mathematics one year that he had to repeat the course. His teacher advised his father to take the boy out of school and find him an apprenticeship as a shoemaker. But this episode only seemed to motivate Adler. He studied furiously and soon became the best mathematics student in the class. He went on to receive his medical degree from the University of Vienna in 1895.

Adler never studied under Freud, nor did he ever undergo psychoanalysis, as required for becoming a practicing psychoanalyst (Orgler, 1963). The two theorists' association began in 1902 when Freud invited Adler to attend his discussion group after Adler had defended Freud's theory of dream interpretation against attacks in the local newspaper. Adler eventually was named the first president of the group in 1910.

However, growing disagreements with Freud led to Adler's resignation in 1911. Several members joined Adler in forming what was originally called the Society for Free Psychoanalytic Research—a name intended to express their objection to Freud's required adherence to his theory. Adler later changed the name of the association to Individual Psychology, established a journal, and received wide acceptance for his alternate interpretation of strict Freudian theory. As in his earlier battles to overcome feelings of inferiority, Adler devoted much of his professional life to catching and trying to surpass Sigmund Freud.

Striving for Superiority

One of the key differences between Freud and Adler was their description of human motivation. Whereas Freud depicted motivation in terms of sexual and aggressive themes, Adler identified a single motivating force he called **striving for superiority.** All other motives could be subsumed within this one construct. "I began to see clearly in every psychological phenomenon the striving for superiority," Adler wrote. "It lies at the root of all solutions of life's problems and is manifested in the way in which we meet these problems. All our functions follow its direction" (cited in Ansbacher & Ansbacher, 1956, p. 103).

Ironically, striving for superiority begins with feelings of inferiority. In fact, Adler maintained that each of us begins life with a profound sense of inferiority. This is to be expected from a weak and helpless child, dependent on larger and stronger adults for survival. The moment children become aware of their relative weakness marks the beginning of a lifelong struggle to overcome their sense of inferiority.

For Adler, virtually everything we do is designed to establish a sense of superiority over life's obstacles. Why do we work so hard to obtain good grades, to excel at athletics, or to reach a position of power? Because achieving these things moves us a step further away from our feelings of inferiority. Moreover, the more inferior we see ourselves, the stronger our striving for superiority. Franklin Roosevelt was disabled by polio. Nonetheless, Adler might have said that *because* of this disability, he aspired to become one of the most influential figures of the 20th century.

However, in some cases, excessive feelings of inferiority can have the opposite effect. Some people develop *an inferiority complex,* a belief that they are vastly inferior to everyone else. The result is feelings of helplessness rather than an upward drive to establish superiority. Children and adults who suffer from an excessive sense of inferiority avoid or run away from challenges rather than work to overcome them.

The contrast between Adler and Freud can be seen in their analysis of highly successful business people. Freud often described these individuals in terms of sublimation. Commercial and financial achievements are merely misplaced unconscious impulses. Freud also might say that, for businessmen, defeating business rivals satisfies an unconscious desire to compete with and defeat one's father, a motive left over from the Oedipus complex. In contrast, Adler saw business success as an expression of superiority striving. Each increase in salary and each step up the corporate ladder provides another reminder that one is not inferior.

But for Adler, achievement alone is not indicative of mental health. The key is to combine superiority striving with a concern for *Gemeinschaftsgefühl,* which roughly translates from German to *social interest.* Successful businesspeople achieve a sense of superiority *and* personal satisfaction through their accomplishments, but only if they reach these goals with consideration for the welfare of others. Success means providing consumers with a good product at a fair price that will make everyone's life a little happier. In contrast, poorly adjusted people express their striving for superiority through selfishness and a concern for personal glory at the expense of others. Politicians who seek public office for personal gain and a sense of power reflect a poor sense of social interest. Those who seek office to help right some of society's wrongs exhibit appropriate and constructive superiority striving.

Parental Influence on Personality Development

Like Freud, Adler believed the first few years of life are extremely important in the formation of the adult personality. However, Adler also placed great emphasis on the parents' role in this process. He identified two parental behaviors in particular that are almost certain to lead to problems for children later in life. First, parents who give their children too much attention run the risk of *pampering.* Pampering robs the child of independence and adds to feelings of inferiority. Parents who keep their children away from all fast

"*To be human
means to feel
inferior. At the
beginning of every
psychological life
there is a deep
inferiority
feeling.***"**
ALFRED ADLER

rides, aggressive playmates, and scary movies may leave their children unable to deal the inevitable setbacks and challenges life throws their way. You may know some of these formerly pampered children who have difficulty living on their own, making their own decisions, and dealing with the daily hassles and frustrations we all encounter. Allowing children to struggle with problems and make some of their own decisions, even if this means making mistakes, is good for them in the long run.

Parents can avoid pampering by allowing children the independence to make many of their own choices. However, it is also possible to do this too much. The second major mistake parents make is to *neglect* their children. Children who receive too little attention from their parents grow up cold and suspicious. As adults, they are incapable of warm personal relationships. They are uncomfortable with intimacy and may be ill at ease with closeness or touching.

Birth Order

Adler was the first psychologist to emphasize the role of *birth order* in shaping personality. That is, firstborn children in a family are said to be different in personality from middle-born children, who are different from last-borns. According to Adler, firstborn children are subjected to excessive attention from their parents and thus to pampering. First-time parents can never take enough photos and seldom miss an opportunity to tell friends and relatives about the new arrival. However, this pampering is short-lived. With the arrival of the second child, the firstborn is "dethroned." Now attention must be shared with, if not relinquished to, the newest member of the family. As a result, the firstborn's perception of inferiority is likely to be strong. Adler suggested that among firstborns we often find "problem children, neurotics, criminals, drunkards, and perverts."

On the other hand, Adler's assessment of middle children—Adler himself was a middle child—was more positive. These children are never afforded the luxury of being pampered, for even when they are the youngest there is always another sibling or two demanding much of the parents' time. Adler argued that middle children develop a strong superiority striving. The middle-borns are not quite as strong, not quite as fast, and not quite as smart as older brothers and sisters. It's as if they are always just a step behind. As a result, they are always looking at the person a little ahead of them in school or in the office, always putting in the extra effort to close the gap. Consequently, Adler said, middle-born children are the highest achievers.

According to Adler, second-born children will spend a lifetime trying to catch up with their older siblings.

Although Adler believed firstborns made up the greatest proportion of difficult children, he felt last-borns had their problems as well. Last-born children are pampered throughout their childhood by all members of the family. Older children often complain that their little brother or sister "gets away with murder," which would not have happened "when I was that age." However, Adler argued that this special treatment carries a price. A spoiled child is a very dependent child—a child without personal initiative. Last-born

According to Adler, second-born children will spend a lifetime trying to catch up with their older siblings.

children also are vulnerable to strong inferiority feelings because everyone in their immediate environment is older and stronger.

Before applying Adler's theory to the members of your own family, you should note that studies do not always support Adler's predictions. Birth order often does not predict how people will score on personality measures (Jefferson, Herbst, & McCrae, 1998; Parker, 1998), and effects found in one study frequently fail to replicate in another (Michalski & Shackelford, 2002; Pollet, Dijkstra, Barelds, & Buunk, 2010). Moreover, the structure and dynamics of the typical family have changed dramatically since Adler's time. Adler's descriptions may fit some families, but there are many exceptions. In short, although Adler's theorizing triggered a great deal of research, most likely the impact of birth order on personality and intellectual development is far more complex than he imagined (Rodgers, Cleveland, van den Oord, & Rowe, 2000; Wichman, Rodgers, & MacCallum, 2006; Zajonc, 2001; Zajonc & Sulloway, 2007).

Carl Jung

Perhaps the most bitter of the defections from the Freudian camp was Carl Jung's break with the psychoanalytic circle. In Freud's eyes, Jung was the heir apparent to the leadership of the movement. Jung served as the first president of the International Psychoanalytic Association. However, in 1914, after long and intense disagreement with some of the basic aspects of Freud's theory, Jung resigned from the association. In the years that followed, he continued his work as a psychotherapist, traveled extensively around the world to observe other cultures, and eventually established his own school of psychology, named *analytic psychology*.

At first blush, some students find Jung's ideas confusing. Part of the problem lies in Jung's frequent reliance on ancient mythology and Eastern religious views in his writings. The unfamiliar terms and abstract concepts can be perplexing to people reading Jung the first time. However, once the initial difficulty with unusual terms and concepts passes, many students find Jung's work among the most intriguing and thought provoking of the personality theories.

The Collective Unconscious

If you were like most newborn children, you had no difficulty recognizing and developing a strong attachment to your mother. When you were a little older, you most likely expressed at least some fear of the dark. When you became older yet, you probably had no difficulty accepting the idea that there was a God, or at least some superhuman existence that created and controlled nature. According to Jung, all people have these experiences. If we were to examine history, talk with people from other societies, and thumb through legends and myths of the past, we would find these same themes and experiences throughout cultures past and present. Why is this?

Jung's answer was that we all have a part of our mind that Freud neglected to talk about. He called this part the **collective unconscious,** as distinguished from the *personal unconscious*. Like the unconscious Freud described, the collective unconscious consists of thoughts and images that are difficult to bring into awareness. However, these thoughts were never repressed out of consciousness. Instead, each of us was born with this unconscious material, and it is basically the same for all people. According to Jung, just as we inherit physical characteristics from our ancestors, we also inherit unconscious psychic characteristics.

The collective unconscious is made up of *primordial images*. Jung described these images in terms of a potential to respond to the world in a certain way. Thus, newborns react quickly to their mothers because the collective unconscious holds an image of a mother for each of us. Similarly, we react to the dark or to God because of unconscious images inherited from our ancestors. Jung referred to these images collectively as *archetypes*. Among the many archetypes Jung described were the mother, the father, the wise old man, the sun, the moon, the hero, God, and death. The list is almost inexhaustible. Jung maintained there are "as many archetypes as there are typical situations in life."

Jung was aware of how mystical this theory sounds to many people encountering it for the first time. Some students scoff at the idea that each of us is born with a collection of unconscious material that directs our actions and that, like all unconscious material, we have no direct access to. However,

Jung argued that the collective unconscious was no more mysterious than the concept of instincts. People are comfortable saying a baby "instinctually" finds its mother or that humans "naturally" share a fear of darkness. He might add that many other theorists describe aspects of personality that we cannot perceive directly. Although the number of archetypes may be limitless, a few are particularly important in Jung's writings. Among the more interesting are the anima, the animus, and the shadow.

Some Important Archetypes

The *anima* is the feminine side of the male; the *animus* is the masculine side of the female. According to Jung, deep inside every masculine man is a feminine counterpart. Deep inside every feminine woman is a masculine self. A principal function of these archetypes is to guide the selection of a romantic partner and the course of the subsequent relationship. Jung explained that we look for a romantic partner by projecting our anima or animus onto potential mates. In his words, "a man, in his love choice, is strongly tempted to win the woman who best corresponds to his own unconscious femininity— a woman, in short, who can unhesitatingly receive the projection of his soul" (1928/1953, p. 70). Less poetically, Jung is saying that each of us holds an unconscious image of the man or woman we are looking for. The more someone matches our projected standards, the more we'll want to develop a relationship with that person. Whereas people in love might prefer to "count the ways," Jung believed the real reason for romance lies in the hidden part of our minds inherited from our ancestors through the centuries.

Although the name may be a bit melodramatic, the *shadow* contains the unconscious part of ourselves that is essentially negative, or to continue the metaphor, the dark side of our personalities. It is the evil side of humankind. The shadow is located partly in the personal unconscious in the form of repressed feelings and partly in the collective unconscious. Jung pointed out that evil is personified in the myths and stories of all cultures. In Judeo-Christian writings, this archetype is symbolized as the Devil. Good versus evil is perhaps the most common theme in literature from all cultures because the collective unconscious of all people readily grasps the concept. Similar to Freud's description of projection, Jung argued that we sometimes see our own objectionable characteristics in other people.

Evidence for the Collective Unconscious

One criticism sometimes directed at Jung's ideas is that his theory is difficult to examine with scientific research. But Jung did not create his ideas out of sheer fantasy. Rather, through a lifelong study of modern and ancient cultures, and through his career as a psychotherapist, Jung arrived at what was for him indisputable evidence for the collective unconscious and the other constructs in his theory.

However, Jung's evidence does not consist of hard data from rigorous laboratory experiments. Instead, he examined mythology, cultural symbols,

Jerry Burger/Santa Clara University

What attracts this woman and man to each other? According to Jung, these two have projected their anima and animus onto the partner and have apparently found a good fit.

dreams, and the statements of schizophrenics. Jung argued that if the collective unconscious is basically the same for each of us, then primordial images should be found in some form in all cultures and across time. He maintained that primordial images are often expressed in dreams. But they also serve as symbols in art, folklore, and mythology. People suffering from hallucinations are said to describe archetype-based images.

As evidence for the collective unconscious, Jung points to the recurrence of certain images and symbols in all of these sources. Why does a symbol like a vulture appear in the dreams of people today in the same basic way it appears in religious writings and ancient mythologies of cultures unknown to the dreamer? Jung described an early discovery of this type of evidence when he spoke with a mental patient suffering from a type of schizophrenia:

> One day I came across him there, blinking through the window up at the sun, and moving his head from side to side in a curious manner. He took me by the arm and said he wanted to show me something. He said I must look at the sun with eyes half shut, and then I could see the sun's phallus. If I moved my head from side to side the sun-phallus would move too, and that was the origin of the wind. (1936/1959, p. 51)

A few years later, while reading Greek mythology, Jung came across a description of a tube-like element hanging from the sun. According to the myth, the tube was responsible for the wind. How could such an image

Carl Gustav Jung

1875–1961

Bettmann/Corbis

Whereas biographers debate the extent to which Freud's personality theory reflected his unconscious thoughts, Carl Jung candidly described how his ideas about personality came from introspection and his own experiences. Jung was born in 1875 in Kesswil, a small town in Switzerland. He was a highly introspective child who kept to himself, largely because he felt no one would understand the inner experiences and thoughts with which he was preoccupied. Jung spent many childhood hours pondering the meaning of the dreams and supernatural visions he experienced. When he was 10, he carved a 2-inch human figure out of wood. He kept the figure hidden, spoke to it when alone, and sometimes wrote to it in secret codes. During his teenage years, he was preoccupied with the feeling that he was someone else. He began a lifelong search to identify what he called his "Number Two" personality.

Jung's desire to understand himself led him to the young field of psychiatry. He earned his medical degree from the University of Basel in 1900, and then went to Zurich to study with Eugen Bleuler, a leading authority on schizophrenia. Later he worked in Paris with Pierre Janet, who was conducting pioneering work on consciousness and hypnosis. Naturally, Jung's curiosity about the human mind soon brought him into contact with Freud's work. After reading *The Interpretation of Dreams,* Jung began a correspondence with Freud. When they finally met in 1907, the two men are said to have engaged in a conversation that lasted 13 hours. Jung soon became a close colleague of Freud's, even accompanying him on his 1909 trip to lecture at Clark University. It was during this trip that Jung came to appreciate how intolerant Freud was of their disagreements about the nature of personality. Jung formally parted with the Vienna group in 1914.

Jung spent the next 7 years in virtual isolation, exploring the depths of his own unconscious. He immersed himself in his fantasies, dreams, and visions in an effort to discover the true nature of personality. Scholars disagree on whether this was a period of voluntary introspection or a lengthy psychotic episode. Jung's autobiography, published just before his death, provides evidence

for both interpretations. "An incessant stream of fantasies had been released, and I did my best not to lose my head but to find some way to understand these strange things," he wrote. "From the beginning ... I had an unswerving conviction that I was obeying a higher will" (1961, pp. 176–177).

Jung reports visits by various figures and images during these years. He came to see these figures as the archetypal characters that make up the collective unconscious. Jung described in detail conversations with a figure he called Philemon. "I held conversations with him, and he said things which I had not consciously thought," Jung wrote. "For I observed clearly that it was he who spoke, not I.... I went walking up and down the garden with him, and to me he was what the Indians call a guru" (1961, p. 183).

Jung emerged from these years of introspection with a new theory of personality. He devoted the rest of his career to private practice, travel, reading, and studying. His observations during these experiences, combined with his continued introspection, resulted in numerous volumes and lectures. Many of Jung's writings have been controversial, including those that some say hint at anti-Semitism (Noll, 1997). Nonetheless, his ideas about human personality continue to mystify and excite readers from around the world.

appear in both the hallucinations of the patient and the stories of the ancient Greeks? Jung maintained that the image existed in the collective unconscious of the Greek storytellers as well as in those of psychotic patients and, therefore, in the collective unconscious of us all.

Jung was probably the most prolific writer among the neo-Freudians. Like Freud, he eventually managed to touch on most aspects of human behavior. His views on religion are reviewed later in this chapter. Although most of the neo-Freudians wrote of personality in less mysterious and more tangible terms than Freud, Jung's thinking took him in the opposite direction. Perhaps the unique flavor of his theory is what has kept his writings so popular for so many years.

Erik Erikson

In the summer of 1927, a young artist wandering about Europe took a job in a school established for the children of Sigmund Freud's patients and friends. That artist, Erik Homburger, who never received a university degree, became friendly with the psychoanalysts and was later trained by them. After changing his name from Homburger to Erikson, he began to practice psychotherapy and eventually to espouse his own views on the nature of human personality. Although Erikson retained several Freudian ideas in his theory, his own contributions to the psychoanalytic approach were numerous.

Whereas Freud saw the ego as the mediator between id impulses and superego demands, Erikson believed the ego performed many constructive functions. To Erikson, the ego is a relatively powerful, independent part of personality. For this reason, Erikson's approach to personality has been called *ego psychology*.

According to Erikson, the principal function of the ego is to establish and maintain a sense of identity. This sense of identity includes an awareness of our uniqueness as well as feelings of continuity with our past and our imagined future. The often overused and misused term *identity crisis* comes from Erikson's work. He used this phrase to refer to the confusion and despair we feel when we lack a strong sense of who we are. Perhaps you have experienced a time when you felt uncertain about your values or the direction your life was headed. Episodes of identity crises are typical in adolescence but are by no means limited to young people. Many middle-aged people experience similar trying periods.

Personality Development Throughout the Life Cycle

To Freud, personality development for the most part ends when the superego appears at about age 6. In contrast, Erikson (1950/1963) maintained that personality development continues throughout a person's lifetime. He outlined

Erik Homburger Erikson

1902–1994

Ted Streshinsky/Historical/Corbis

It is difficult to imagine a life filled with more identity issues than the one handed to Erik Erikson. Reflecting back on his formative years, Erikson observed that "it seems all too obvious … that such an early life would predispose a person to a severe identity crisis" (1975, p. 31). Indeed, Erikson's struggle with his identity led him to behavior he would later identify as somewhere between neurotic and psychotic. Yet these struggles also provided him with a keen insight into the problems associated with identity, particularly among adolescents and young adults.

Erik was born in Frankfurt, Germany, in 1902. His Danish father abandoned the family before Erik was born. Three years later his mother married a Jewish physician, Theodor Homburger, and for many years told her son that Dr. Homburger was his real father. It was not until he was an adolescent that Erikson learned the truth—that his birth was the result of an extramarital affair, a fact Erikson kept secret until he was 68 (Hopkins, 1995). Erikson's identity was further confused by his physical features. Although living in a Jewish family, he retained most of the physical features of his Scandinavian father—tall, blond hair, blue eyes. "Before long, I was referred to as 'goy' in my stepfather's temple," he wrote, "while to my schoolmates I was a 'Jew'" (1975, p. 27). World War I broke out during Erik's early adolescence, leaving the boy with torn feelings of loyalty between Germany and his growing identity as a Dane.

Erik's need to find his own identity erupted upon graduation from public school. His stepfather pushed

medical school, but Erik resisted. He decided instead that he was an artist and spent the next few years wandering about Europe. His travels eventually brought him to Vienna and into contact with Anna Freud, Sigmund's daughter and a noted psychoanalyst herself. Except for a Montessori teaching credential, his psychoanalytic training with Anna Freud was the only formal education he received after leaving home. Somewhere during these years, Erik changed his name to Erik Homburger Erikson, obviously reflecting his changing sense of identity.

Erikson fled the rise of the Nazis in 1933 and settled in Boston. He held positions with numerous universities, including Harvard, Yale, the University of California at Berkeley, and the University of Pennsylvania. His first book, *Childhood and Society,* was not published until 1950, when Erikson was nearly 50 years old. Like the mature adults he wrote about, Erikson continued his personal and professional development well into the later years of his life.

eight stages we all progress through, each crucial in the development of personality (Figure 5.1).

Erikson's stages of personality development bring to mind the image of a path. We continue down this path from infancy to old age, but at eight different points along the way we encounter a fork—two directions in which to proceed. In Erikson's model, these forks represent turning points in personality development. He called these points *crises.* How we resolve each crisis determines the direction our personality development will take and influences how we resolve later crises. Of the two alternatives for resolving each crisis, one is said to be adaptive, the other not. As you read about these stages, you may want to recall how you resolved the crises for the stages you have

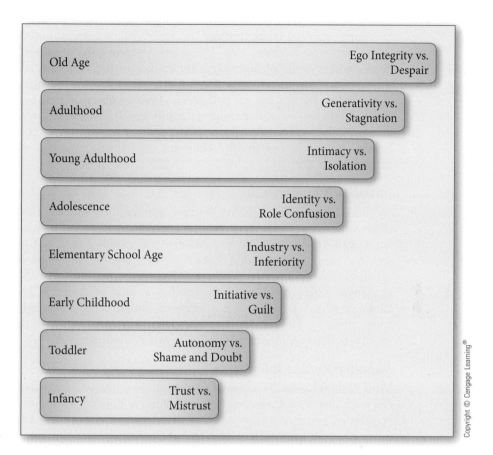

FIGURE 5.1 Erikson's Eight Stages of Development

already passed through, and perhaps reflect on the stage you now find your-self in.

Basic Trust Versus Mistrust

During the first year or so of life, newborns are almost totally at the mercy of those around them. Whether infants are given loving care and have their needs met or whether their cries go unnoticed is the first turning point in the development of personality. The child whose needs are met develops a sense of *basic trust*. For this child, the world is a good place and people are loving and approachable. Unfortunately, some infants never receive the loving care they need. As a result, they develop a sense of *basic mistrust*. These children begin a lifelong pattern of suspicion about and withdrawal from other people.

Autonomy Versus Shame and Doubt

By the second year of life, children want to know who they are relative to the rest of the world. Is the world something they control or something that controls them? When allowed to manipulate and control much of what they encounter, children come through this stage with a sense of *autonomy*. They feel powerful and independent. They have a strong sense of personal mastery. People with a sense of autonomy are confident that they can navigate their way through the sea of obstacles and challenges life has in store. However, just as Adler warned against pampering, Erikson observed that overly protective parents can hinder development at this age. If not allowed to explore and exercise influence over the objects and events in their world, children develop feelings of *shame and doubt*. They are unsure of themselves and become dependent on others.

Initiative Versus Guilt

As children begin to interact with other children, they face the challenges that come with living in a social world. Children must learn how to play and work with others and how to resolve the inevitable conflicts. Children who seek out playmates and who learn how to organize games and other social activities develop a sense of *initiative*. They learn how to set goals and tackle challenges with conviction. They develop a sense of ambition and purpose. Children who fail to develop a sense of initiative come through this stage with feelings of *guilt* and resignation. They may lack a sense of purpose and show few signs of initiative in social or other situations.

Industry Versus Inferiority

Most children enter elementary school thinking there is little they can't do. But soon they find themselves in competition with other children—for grades, popularity, teachers' attention, victories in sports and games, and so on. Inevitably, they compare their talents and abilities with other children their age. If children experience success, feelings of competence grow that set them well on their way to becoming active and achieving members of society. But experiences with failure lead to feelings of inadequacy and to a poor prognosis for productivity and happiness. It is during this time, before the turmoil of puberty and the teenage years, that we develop either a sense of *industry* and a belief in our strengths and abilities or a sense of *inferiority* and a lack of appreciation for our talents and skills.

Identity Versus Role Confusion

At last—or perhaps too soon—we reach the teenage years, a time of rapid changes and relatively short preparation for adulthood. Adolescence may be the most difficult time of life. The turmoil of transcending from playground concerns and simple solutions to a sudden bout with life's important questions can be disturbing, and maybe a little cruel. Erikson was well aware of the significance of these years. Young men and women begin to ask the all-important question, "Who am I?" If the question is answered successfully, they develop a sense of *identity*. They make decisions about personal values and religious questions. They understand who they are and accept and appreciate themselves. Unfortunately, many teens fail to develop this strong sense of identity and instead fall into *role confusion*.

In their search for identity, adolescents may join cliques, commit to causes, or drop out of school and drift from one situation to another. A friend of mine from high school bounced from devout Christianity to alcohol and drugs, to Eastern religions, to social causes, and to conservative politics—all during his high school years—in an effort to "find" himself. Ten years later, at our class reunion, I learned that he had spent the decade drifting to different parts of the country, different jobs, several colleges, and was currently thinking of becoming a rock star. His failure to develop a strong sense of identity clearly impeded subsequent personality development.

Intimacy Versus Isolation

The teen years dissolve swiftly into young adulthood and the next challenge in Erikson's model: developing intimate relationships. Young men and women search for that special relationship within which to develop *intimacy* and grow emotionally. Although these relationships typically result in marriage or a romantic commitment to one person, this is not always the case. One can share intimacy without marriage and, unfortunately, marriage without intimacy. People who fail to develop intimacy during this stage face *emotional isolation*. They may pass through many superficial relationships without finding the satisfaction of closeness promised by genuine relationships. Indeed, they may avoid emotional commitment. The single-person's lifestyle has its advantages and may be pleasant for a while, but failure to move beyond this lifestyle can seriously inhibit emotional growth and happiness.

Generativity Versus Stagnation

As men and women approach the middle years of life, they develop a concern for guiding the next generation. Parents find their lives enriched by the influence they have on their children. Adults without their own children find this enrichment by working with youth groups or playing an active role in raising nieces and nephews. Adults who fail to develop this sense of *generativity* may suffer from a sense of stagnation—a feeling of emptiness and questioning one's purpose in life. We've all seen parents whose lives are filled with continued meaning and interests through raising their children. Unfortunately, we've also seen parents who obtain little pleasure from this process. As a result, they become bored and generally dissatisfied with their lives. Failure to see the potential for personal growth in the development of their children is tragic for parent and child alike.

Ego Integrity Versus Despair

Inevitably, most of us keep our appointment with old age. But, according to Erikson, we still have one more crisis to resolve. Reflections on past experiences and the inevitability of life's end cause us to develop either a sense of *integrity or feelings of despair*. Men and women who look back on their lives with satisfaction will pass through this final developmental stage with a sense of integrity. "It is the acceptance of one's one and only life cycle ... as something that had to be and that, by necessity, permitted of no

Erikson described old age as a time for either feelings of integrity and satisfaction with life or feelings of despair and contempt for others.

substitution," Erikson wrote (1968, p. 139). People who fail to develop this sense of integrity fall into despair. They realize that time is now all too short, that the options and opportunities available to younger people are no longer there. A life has passed, and those who wish they could do it all differently will express their despair through disgust and contempt for others. Although few things in life are sadder than an older person filled with despair, few things are more satisfying than an elderly person filled with a sense of integrity.

Karen Horney

Unlike many neo-Freudians, Karen Horney (pronounced Horn-Eye) was not a student of Freud's. Instead, Horney studied Freud's work indirectly and later taught psychoanalysis at the Berlin Psychoanalytic Institute and the New York Psychoanalytic Institute. And, like many psychoanalysts, she began to question some of the basic tenets of Freudian theory. In particular, Horney found she could not accept some of Freud's views concerning women. Freud maintained that men and women were born with different personalities. Horney argued that cultural and social forces are far more responsible than biology for some of the apparent differences between the genders.

Eventually Horney became so disenchanted with the Freudian position that she and the members of the New York Psychoanalytic Institute agreed she should leave the institute. She resigned in 1941 and founded her own

A Sense of Personal Identity

Indicate how often each statement applies to you, using the following point scale: 1 = Never applies to me, 2 = Only occasionally or seldom applies to me, 3 = Fairly often applies to me, 4 = Very often applies to me.

_____ 1. I wonder what sort of person I really am.

_____ 2. People seem to change their opinion of me.

_____ 3. I feel certain about what I should do with my life.

_____ 4. I feel uncertain as to whether something is morally right or wrong.

_____ 5. Most people seem to agree about what sort of person I am.

_____ 6. I feel my way of life suits me.

_____ 7. My worth is recognized by others.

_____ 8. I feel freer to be my real self when I am away from those who know me very well.

_____ 9. I feel that what I am doing in life is not really worthwhile.

_____ 10. I feel I fit in well in the community in which I live.

_____ 11. I feel proud to be the sort of person I am.

_____ 12. People seem to see me very differently from the way I see myself.

_____ 13. I feel left out.

_____ 14. People seem to disapprove of me.

_____ 15. I change my ideas about what I want from life.

_____ 16. I am unsure as to how people feel about me.

_____ 17. My feelings about myself change.

_____ 18. I feel I am putting on an act or doing something for effect.

_____ 19. I feel proud to be a member of the society in which I live.

To obtain your score, first reverse the values you assigned to items 1, 2, 4, 8, 9, 12, 13, 14, 15, 16, 17, and 18. That is, for these items only, 1 = 4, 2 = 3, 3 = 2, 4 = 1. The values for the remaining items stay the same. Then add the values for all 19 items. Ochse and Plug (1986) found average scores for this scale of around 57 when they administered it to South African citizens between the ages of 15 and 60. The standard deviation for this score was around 7, indicating that the majority of people obtain scores that fall within 7 points of the average score. Scores considerably higher than this average range indicate a particularly well-developed sense of identity, whereas significantly lower scores suggest the test taker is still progressing.

Scale: Identity versus Identity Diffusion Scale
Source: Ochse and Plug (1986).

American Institute for Psychoanalysis. Horney explored cultural and social influences on personality development throughout her career. The prominent role she gave to these social influences can be seen in two of her contributions to the psychoanalytic approach: her views on neurosis and what she called "feminine psychology."

Neurosis

We all know people who fit Horney's description of neurotic. Let me give three examples of people I have met. One is a woman who at first appears friendly and warm. She's always involved in social activities and is quick to pass along a compliment. But people soon find that her attention turns into demands. She can't stand to be alone, can't accept the idea that her friends or romantic partners would be interested in doing anything without her. Although her relationships never work out for long, she inevitably "falls in love" almost as soon as she meets the next man. The second example is a man who was disliked by almost everyone he went to college with. Few people escaped his sarcastic, sometimes biting, comments. He seemed to hold everyone he encountered with contempt. I never heard him say a nice thing about anyone. Today he is a ruthless—albeit successful—businessman. The third example is a woman who works in a small office tabulating figures. She rarely socializes with the other employees, so now most of them have stopped asking her to join them. She has few friends and spends most of her evenings by herself.

According to Horney, what these three people have in common is that each is desperately fighting off feelings of inadequacy and insecurity. Although they eventually drive people away with their behavior, on the inside they are scared individuals. Horney would have identified all three of these people as *neurotic*. The key characteristic of neurotics in her theory is that they are trapped in a self-defeating interpersonal style. That is, the way these people interact with others prevents them from developing the social contact they unconsciously crave. Their destructive interpersonal style is a type of defense mechanism intended to ward off their feelings of anxiety.

What is it in the backgrounds of these people that brought them to the sad situations they find themselves in today? Freud explained neurosis in terms of fixated energy and unconscious battles between various aspects of the personality. But Horney pointed to disturbed interpersonal relationships during childhood. In particular, she believed children too often grow up in homes that foster feelings of anxiety. The ways parents can generate these feelings are almost endless:

> direct or indirect domination, indifference, erratic behavior, lack of respect for the child's individual needs, lack of real guidance, disparaging attitudes, too much admiration or the absence of it, lack of reliable warmth, having to take sides in parental disagreements, too much or too little responsibility, overprotection, isolation from other children, injustice, discrimination, unkept promises, hostile atmosphere, and ... [a] sense of lurking hypocrisy in the environment. (1945/1966, p. 41)

Karen Horney

1885–1952

Bettmann/Corbis

Karen Danielsen was born in Hamburg, Germany, the daughter of a sea captain and his young, second wife. From her earliest years on, she faced the injustices and rejection that came from being a rebellious woman in a man's world. Her father was a strict authoritarian who used Bible verse to promote his views on the superiority of men. Karen's older brother, Berndt, was awarded opportunities, including college and an eventual law degree,

that her father believed unnecessary for a female. Karen responded to these inequities by vowing in elementary school to always be first in her class, and at age 12 decided she would one day go to medical school.

Karen's mother persuaded her father to allow Karen to go to college, where she met and married Oskar Horney in 1909. In 1915 she received her medical degree from the University of Berlin, one of the few female students in one of the few schools to accept women. She underwent psychoanalysis as part of her psychoanalytic training but found it insufficient for dealing with her lifelong bouts with depression. At one point her husband was reported to have rescued her from a suicide attempt (Rubins, 1978). Despite her depression, her doubts about psychoanalysis, and a number of personal problems—including the premature death of her brother, a strained marriage

and eventual divorce—her career prospered. She worked at the Berlin Psychoanalytic Institute and later immigrated to America, where she joined the New York Psychoanalytic Institute in 1934.

However, it was not in Horney's character to check her growing dissatisfaction with several aspects of Freud's theory. This open questioning created great strain with the other members of the institute, who in 1941 voted to disqualify her as an instructor. According to most reports, Horney received the vote in a dramatically silent room. She responded by leaving the meeting in a dignified and proud manner, without uttering a word. Horney went on to establish her own highly successful American Institute for Psychoanalysis. By the time of her death, in 1952, it was clear she had made great progress in her battle against the male-dominated and paternalistic psychoanalytic school of thought.

In short, parenting is not easy. Although raising children is one of the most important tasks we face, there is practically no training for the job and few restrictions on who can raise children and how they should be raised. And so we end up with children who lack a sense of personal worth, who are afraid and unsure of how to deal with their parents, who fear unjust punishment from their parents for reasons they can't understand, who feel insecure and inadequate, and who desperately want but fail to receive the warmth and support they need. These children are confused, afraid, and anxious.

How do children deal with this anxiety? According to Horney, children growing up in anxiety-generating situations develop strategies for dealing with threatening people. On the positive side, these strategies usually succeed in alleviating anxiety in the short run. On the downside, these individuals may come to rely on these strategies even when dealing with people outside the family. As adults, their childhood fear of interacting with other people continues. In essence, they have learned that social relationships are a source of anxiety.

Horney identified three interaction styles neurotics adopt in their efforts to avoid anxiety-provoking experiences. She called these styles *moving toward people, moving against people, and moving away from people.* As you read about these styles, you'll no doubt see a little of yourself in each. That is healthy. Horney explained that most people use each of the three strategies on occasion to combat anxiety. In contrast, neurotic individuals inflexibly rely on just one of these styles for virtually all their social interactions.

Moving Toward People

Some children deal with anxiety by emphasizing their helplessness. They become dependent on others, compulsively seeking affection and acceptance from their parents and caregivers. The sympathy they receive provides temporary relief from their anxiety, but the children run the risk of relying on this strategy in later relationships. As adults, they have an intense need to be loved and accepted. They often believe that if only they can find love, everything else will be all right. They may indiscriminately attach themselves to whomever is available, believing that any relationship is better than loneliness and feeling unwanted. If you've ever been involved with someone who meets this description, you probably can appreciate the futility of pursuing a long-term relationship. These people don't love, they cling. They don't share affection, they can only demand it. Because of this neurotic style, each new relationship is almost certainly doomed.

Moving Against People

One way to handle anxiety is to cling to others, another is to fight. Some children find aggressiveness and hostility are the best way to deal with a poor home environment. They compensate for feelings of inadequacy and insecurity by pushing around other children. They are rewarded with a fleeting sense of power and respect from classmates, but no real friendships. This neurotic style takes on more sophisticated forms when these children become adults. They may take advantage of business partners or lash out at others with hurtful comments. In both child and adult, we find an ever-present need to exploit other people. Horney argued that this neurotic style is characterized by *externalization,* similar to Freud's concept of projection. That is, these individuals learned during childhood that people are basically hostile and out to get what they can. They respond to this perception by doing unto others before others can do unto them. They enter into relationships only when there is something to be gained. Consequently, relationships with these people are necessarily shallow, unfulfilling, and ultimately painful.

Moving Away from People

Some children adopt a third strategy to deal with their anxiety. Instead of interacting with others in a dependent or hostile manner, the child may simply tune out the world. Who needs them? The child's desire for privacy and self-sufficiency can be intense. As adults, these neurotics seek out jobs requiring little interaction with other people. As a rule, they avoid affection, love, and friendship. Because emotional attachment might lead to the kind of pain they remember from childhood, they develop a numbness to emotional experiences. The safest way to avoid anxiety is simply to avoid involvement. This is certainly the wrong person to fall in love with. Affection cannot be returned because it is not even experienced. Thus, for both participants, the relationship will be shallow and unrewarding.

Feminine Psychology

As a psychoanalyst in the 1930s, Horney found herself a woman in a man's world. Many of her initial doubts about Freudian theory began with some of Freud's disparaging views of women. Freud described *penis envy*—the desire every young girl has to be a boy. Horney (1967) countered this male-flattering position with the concept of *womb envy*—men's envy of women's ability to bear and nurse children. Horney did not mean that men are dissatisfied with themselves but rather that each gender has attributes that the other admires. However, she did suggest that men compensate for their inability to have children through achievement in other domains.

Horney also pointed out that Freud's observations and writings took place at a time when society often placed women in inferior positions. If a woman living in that era wished she were a man, it was probably because of the restrictions and burdens placed on her by the culture, not because of inherent inferiorities. In a society where both men and women are free to become whatever they desire, there is little reason to think that girls would want to be boys, or vice versa. In many ways, we can see that Horney's thinking was well ahead of its time. Horney's death in 1952 did not allow her to see how feminists would later use many of her ideas to promote the cause of gender equality.

Application: Psychoanalytic Theory and Religion

> *"The religions of mankind must be classed among the mass delusions. No one, needless to say, who shares a delusion ever recognizes it as such."*
>
> SIGMUND FREUD

The psychoanalytic theorists did more than describe personality and develop treatments for psychological disorders. These writers also offered important new perspectives on humankind and answers to some enduring philosophical questions about the human condition. Inevitably, their concerns overlapped with some of those traditionally addressed by theologians: Are people inherently good or bad? Should we sacrifice personal pleasure for the common good? Is the source of happiness within each of us or found in powers greater than our own?

In a style that typified his career, Freud directly challenged conventional thinking about many religious issues. Two books in particular, *The Future of an Illusion* and *Civilization and Its Discontents,* assaulted widely held religious beliefs. Although Freud understood that organized religion provided solace for the uneducated, he lamented its widespread acceptance by intelligent people. "The whole thing is so patently infantile, so foreign to reality,"

Freud wrote, "that to anyone with a friendly attitude to humanity it is painful to think that the great majority of mortals will never be able to rise above this view of life" (1930/1961, p. 21).

Why, then, do so many people believe? According to Freud, religious behavior represents a form of neurosis. It begins with the baby's feelings of helplessness and longing for a powerful protector, presumably the father. Freud called religion a type of collective wish fulfillment. To protect ourselves from a threatening and unpredictable world, we project our imagined savior from this predicament outward in the form of a God. Thus, to Freud, God is but an unconscious father figure generated in an infantile way to provide us with feelings of security.

Several neo-Freudian theorists also addressed religious questions in their writings, most notably, Carl Jung. Jung, whose father was a minister in the Swiss Reformed Church, struggled with religious issues throughout much of his life, often wavering between favorable and unfavorable impressions of modern religion. He once referred to "the religious myth," yet at another point he described religious experience as "a great treasure" providing "a source of life, meaning, and beauty" (Bechtle, 1984). Toward the end of his career, Jung seemed to take a more favorable approach to organized religion. He acknowledged that religion often provides followers with a sense of purpose and feelings of security.

Jung often insisted that the question of God's existence was outside the realm of science and hence nothing he could provide answers about. His interest was with humankind's eternal need to find religion. Why does religion surface in all cultures? Why is some entity similar to the Judeo-Christian God found in each of these cultures? Jung's answer was that each of us inherits a God archetype in our collective unconscious. This primordial image causes Godlike images to surface in the dreams, folklore, artwork, and experiences of people everywhere. We can easily conceive of a God, find evidence for His existence, and experience deep religious feelings because we were born with a kind of unconscious predisposition for Him. Scholars continue to debate whether Jung meant by this that God exists only in our collective unconscious and therefore that the traditional description of God as an external entity is a myth (Bianchi, 1988). Although at times Jung does appear to argue that God exists only in the human mind, other references suggest he was not ready to make such a bold statement.

Jung maintained that organized religions often took advantage of powerful archetypal symbols in promoting themselves to followers. Indeed, he described Christ as a symbol, with the four points on the cross representing the good-versus-bad and the spiritual-versus-material aspects of our being. In addition to religious art and scripture, Jung said, religious symbols are often found in our dreams and in the hallucinations of psychotic patients.

According to Jung, many people seek out psychotherapy when their religion fails to provide reassurance. Thus modern psychotherapy has taken on the role once reserved for the clergy. Of particular importance for many of Jung's patients was the need to resolve the good and evil sides of their personalities. Psychologists help these patients through a variety of therapy

Why do people feel deeply about their religious beliefs? This is one of the questions addressed by Freud and many of the neo-Freudian theorists. Freud declared religion a delusion, whereas Jung pondered the nature of religious experiences throughout his career.

techniques. However, Jung argued, modern religions have developed their own practices to achieve the same end. Churches use confession, absolution, and forgiveness to symbolically help followers reconcile the evil side of their selves with the good.

Erich Fromm was another neo-Freudian psychologist fascinated by the seemingly universal human need for religion (Fromm, 1950, 1966). He argued that people turn to the powerful authority of the church to escape a sense of powerlessness and loneliness. "People return to religion ... not as an act of faith but in order to escape an intolerable doubt," Fromm wrote. "They make this decision not out of devotion but in search of security" (1950, p. 4). Awareness that we are individuals, responsible for ourselves and for finding our own meaning in life, is frightening to many people. Religion provides an escape from these fears.

However, Fromm also drew a distinction between *authoritarian religions* and *humanistic religions*. The former emphasize that we are under the control of a powerful God, whereas in the latter God is seen as a symbol of our own power. Fromm argued that authoritarian religions deny people their personal identity, but humanistic religions provide an opportunity for personal growth. Thus, while condemning some religions, Fromm recognized the potential for individuation and finding happiness within others.

Today, the writings of Freud, Jung, Fromm, and other psychoanalytic theorists are studied and debated by theology students around the world. Some scholars have even looked into these theorists' backgrounds to understand what in their childhoods might have generated such hostility toward modern religion (Meissner, 1984). Although most theologians reject psychoanalytic interpretations of religious behavior, few are able to ignore them.

Assessment: Personal Narratives

Imagine that your life story were being made into a movie. Forget for the moment which actor will play you, but instead ask yourself what scenes would be needed for the audience to fully appreciate your character. What themes would run throughout the movie? What are the turning points, the lessons learned, the hardships overcome? In other words, what experiences have shaped or illustrate the kind of person you are?

Researchers sometimes use a variation of this procedure to study personality (McAdams, 2008; McAdams & McLean, 2013; Singer, 2004). They ask people to tell their life stories or some of the critical scenes in that story. When people tell stories about themselves, particularly those that supposedly shaped them into the kind of person they are today, they reveal their personality in a very telling way. They're saying, "This is the kind of person I am, and this is how I got to be that person." These descriptions provide personality researchers with a rich source of information not easily captured with other assessment procedures (Torges, Stewart, & Duncan, 2009).

Measuring Personality with Personal Narratives

Researchers who examine **personal narratives** typically interview participants, although sometimes participants respond to questions in writing (McAdams, 1993, 2004). In most cases, participants are asked to describe scenes from their life. These scenes might include a high point in their life, a turning point in their life, an important childhood memory, and so on. These accounts obviously tell us something about the character of the participant. But how do researchers turn these descriptions into data they can use to compare people and test hypotheses? First, interviews are recorded and probably transcribed. Next, judges review the interview transcripts or the written responses and code the stories according to preset criteria. For example, judges may count the number of times certain themes are mentioned, such as overcoming hardships. Or they may place the stories into one of several predefined categories. In most cases, two or more judges independently code the stories. If the judges agree on the vast majority of their assessments, then the ratings are considered reliable and useful (Chapter 2). However, if one judge rates a story high in achievement themes, while another rates the same story as low, then it's impossible to know which of these assessments is correct. The solution is to either clarify the coding criteria or retrain the judges on how to apply the criteria.

Like other measures of personality, scores from personal narratives tend to be consistent over time (McAdams et al., 2006). However, the procedure also raises some questions. Chief among these is how much credence researchers should give these autobiographical accounts (Pasupathi, McLean, & Weeks, 2009; Woike, 2008). That is, how accurately do people report their life stories? Even the best memory is likely to be a bit hazy when looking back several decades. Participants may selectively remember flattering portrayals of themselves and overlook failures and embarrassments. And most of us have stories we might not want to reveal to a researcher. Investigators acknowledge that personal narratives are selective presentations and most likely fall short of perfect accuracy (McAdams, Diamond, de St. Aubin, & Mansfield, 1997). However, they argue that what people choose to remember and the way they construct their past is revealing. It's more important that an individual believes a tragic event shaped his or her character than whether or not the event actually did so.

Generativity and Life Stories

Psychologists have found personal narratives especially useful for studying Erik Erikson's stages of personality development. In particular, much of this research has focused on the seventh stage in that model, *generativity versus stagnation* (Frensch, Pratt, & Norris, 2007; Mackinnon, Nosko, Pratt, & Norris, 2011; McAdams, Reynolds, Lewis, Patten, & Bowman, 2001; Pratt, Norris, Hebblethwaite, & Arnold, 2008). According to Erikson, middle-aged adults often are motivated to develop a sense of generativity. People this age obtain personal satisfaction and enrichment through the influence they have on the next generation. Erikson and his followers thought of generativity in much broader terms than parents influencing their children (McAdams, Hart, & Maruna, 1998). People can obtain a sense of generativity by working directly with youth as an uncle, scout leader, or Sunday school teacher. Adults also can satisfy their need for generativity by doing their part to create a better world for the next generation to live in.

One team of researchers asked elderly adults to write down memories from each decade of their lives (Conway & Holmes, 2004). Presumably the participants wrote about events that characterized the way they thought of their life during those decades. Judges then coded the stories according to which Eriksonian theme they portrayed. For example, a memory about falling in love was placed in the *intimacy versus isolation* category. A story about helping a grandchild overcome a personal problem fell into the *generativity versus stagnation* category. As shown in Figure 5.2, the number of stories reflecting a generativity theme peaked during the midlife decades, just as we would predict from Erikson's theory.

What is it about some people that enables them to develop a sense of generativity while others do not? One way to answer this question is to look at the life stories people tell. Compared to adults who fail to develop a sense of generativity, highly generative adults are likely to tell stories in which bad situations lead to good outcomes (McAdams et al., 1997; McAdams et al., 2001). In these stories a personal tragedy, such as the death of a loved one, eventually leads the storyteller to an increased sensitivity to the suffering of others and a commitment to help those going through similar experiences.

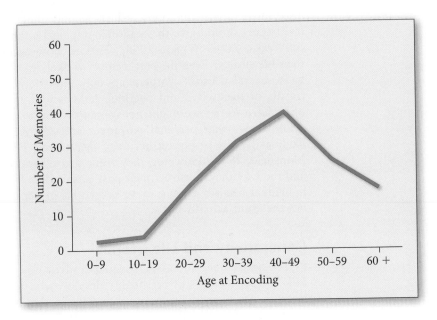

FIGURE 5.2 Number of Memories with a Generativity Theme

Source: Adapted from Conway and Holmes (2004).

Not surprising then, stories from highly generative adults tend to contain more themes about friendship, sharing, affiliation, and nurturance (Mansfield & McAdams, 1996). It's not difficult to see how middle-aged adults who have lived such lives—or who at least recall their lives in this way—would be concerned about helping and nurturing the next generation.

Strengths and Criticisms of Neo-Freudian Theories

Strengths

The primary strength of the neo-Freudian theories is their elaboration of important concepts that Freud had ignored or de-emphasized. Most of these theorists identified the role social factors play in the formation and change of personality. Many described the ways personality develops beyond the first few years of life. And most neo-Freudian theorists presented a much more optimistic and flattering picture of humankind than Freud had. They described the positive functions served by the ego rather than restricting its role to arbitrator between the demanding id and superego.

The neo-Freudians also introduced many new concepts into the psychological literature. As with Freudian theory, many of these ideas have made their way into everyday language. People speak of identity crises, introverts, and inferiority complexes without recognizing the references to Erikson, Jung, and Adler.

Another gauge of a personality theory's value is the extent to which it influences later theorists and psychotherapists. In this respect, the neo-Freudians can claim some success. The optimistic tone about humans that characterized many neo-Freudians' views helped pave the way for the humanistic personality theories. Similarly, the emphasis on social aspects of personality development was undoubtedly a considerable step in the evolution of social learning approaches to personality. And the techniques and approaches developed by each of the neo-Freudians have been adopted or adapted by many contemporary psychotherapists.

In sum, the neo-Freudian theorists did much to make parts of the psychoanalytic approach palatable to psychologists and nonpsychologists alike. In fact, these theories provide a bridge between Freud's concepts and many later personality theories. However, no individual neo-Freudian theorist, or even the theories taken as a whole, has ever reached the level of acclaim that Freud did.

Criticisms

Many of the limitations critics point to in Freud's theory also are present in some of the neo-Freudian works. Like Freudian theory, some of the neo-Freudian theories are supported with questionable evidence. In particular, many of Jung's conclusions about the nature of the collective unconscious are based on myths, legends, dreams, occult phenomena, and artwork. Neo-Freudians often based their conclusions about human personality largely on data from patients undergoing psychotherapy. As such, questions about biased interpretations and their applicability to normally functioning adults remain.

A second problem with the neo-Freudians as a group is that they often oversimplified or ignored important concepts. None dealt with so many topics in so much depth as Freud. Consequently, the neo-Freudians sometimes failed to effectively address questions central to psychoanalytic theory. This observation has led some people to criticize neo-Freudian works as incomplete or limited accounts of personality and human behavior. For example, Erikson has been criticized for what some consider a superficial treatment of anxiety's role in the development of psychological disorders. Similarly, Adler has been accused of oversimplifying in his attempt to explain many complex behaviors in terms of a single concept, the striving for superiority.

Summary

1. Many psychologists who studied with Freud eventually broke away from the Vienna group to develop their own theories of personality and establish their own schools of psychology. Collectively, these theorists are known as the neo-Freudians because they retained many basic Freudian concepts and assumptions. Among the limits they saw in Freud's theory were his failure to recognize personality change after the first few years of life, his emphasis on instinctual over social influences, and the generally negative picture he painted of human nature.

2. Alfred Adler introduced the concept of striving for superiority to account for most human motivation. He argued that we are motivated to overcome feelings of helplessness that begin in infancy. Adler also identified parental pampering and neglect as two sources of later personality problems. He argued that middle-born children were the most achieving and were less likely to experience psychological disorders than were firstborns or last-borns.

3. Carl Jung proposed the existence of a collective unconscious that houses primordial images he called archetypes. The collective unconscious contains material each of us inherited from past generations and is basically the same for all people. Among the most important of the archetypes are the anima, the animus, and the shadow. Jung pointed to the recurrent surfacing of archetypal symbols in folklore, art, dreams, and psychotic patients as evidence for their existence.

4. Erik Erikson emphasized the positive functions of the ego in his theory. One of the ego's most important functions is to develop and maintain a sense of identity. Erikson outlined eight stages of personality development that we pass through during our lifetimes. At each stage we are faced with a crisis and two means to resolve the crisis.

5. Karen Horney rejected Freud's emphasis on instinctual causes of personality development. She argued that the differences Freud saw between the personalities of men and women were more likely the result of social factors than inherited predispositions. Horney maintained that neurotic behavior is the result of interpersonal styles developed in childhood to overcome anxiety. She identified three neurotic styles, which she called moving toward people, moving against people, and moving away from people.

6. Freud was highly critical of organized religion, calling it wish fulfillment and a type of neurosis. Jung explained humankind's persistent need for religion in terms of a God archetype. He saw modern psychotherapists taking the place of religious leaders when patients become disenchanted with the answers provided by their religion. Erich Fromm argued that the universal need for religion stems from the need to escape from feelings of insecurity.

7. Personal narratives provide personality psychologists with a rich source of information about an individual's sense of identity. Participants are asked to describe parts of their lives, and these descriptions are coded by judges. Psychologists find personal narratives especially useful when examining Erikson's notion of generativity. Adults who develop a strong sense of generativity typically tell life stories that include themes of communion and learning from tragedy.

8. Among the strengths of the neo-Freudian theories are the contributions they made to psychoanalytic theory. In addition to correcting some of the limitations they found in Freud's work, many of the theorists introduced important concepts to the field of psychology. Many later approaches to personality were no doubt influenced by one or more of

these theorists. Criticisms of the neo-Freudians include their use of biased and questionable data to support the theories. In addition, critics have charged that some of the theories are oversimplified and incomplete.

Key Terms

collective unconscious (p. 101)   personal narratives (p. 118)   striving for superiority (p. 97)

Media Resources

Visit the book companion website at **www.cengagebrain.com** to find a glossary, flashcards, quizzing, and more.

The Neo-Freudian Theories

Relevant Research

Decades have passed since many of the neo-Freudian theorists broke away from the Freudian pack, allowing us to see how much more these theorists had in common with Freud than they probably realized at the time. Just as their theories are better thought of as elaborations of Freud's basic psychoanalytic approach, so is the research covered in this chapter relevant for both Freudian and neo-Freudian approaches to personality. In each case, researchers began with concepts introduced by psychoanalytic theory but, much like the theorists who followed Freud, soon took their thinking in new directions.

We begin by examining research on anxiety and coping strategies. Although traditional psychoanalytic theorists emphasize unconscious sources of anxiety and defense mechanisms, research on coping strategies is concerned with anxiety-provoking events that people are aware of. We'll look at some of the conscious efforts people make to cope with this anxiety.

Several decades ago, researchers borrowed some of Freud's concepts to explain the causes of aggression. Although subsequent research took these investigators far from their psychoanalytic starting point, the legacy is clear. A number of Freudian terms—sublimation, displacement, catharsis—can be found throughout this research, which tells us a lot about why people become violent and how their aggressive behavior affects them.

Finally, we'll examine the connection between infant–parent relationships and attachment styles in adults. Borrowing from a neo-Freudian approach known as object relations theory, researchers have identified patterns in the way people relate to their romantic partners. These adult attachment styles are said to have their origin in the attachment experiences children had with their parents. Studies suggest that these childhood experiences may affect adult romantic relationships.

Anxiety and Coping Strategies

Are we, as some popular writers suggest, in an "age of anxiety"? Have the good old days of afternoon strolls in the park and summer evenings on the porch been replaced with ever-present pressure to work harder and faster and be better than everyone else? The ubiquitous ads for massages, meditation, anti-anxiety drugs, get-away vacations, and the like seem to say that many of us have been pushed near some sort of anxiety breaking point. But are we really more anxious today, or do we just complain more? To answer this question, one investigator examined average anxiety scores reported in published studies throughout the second half of the 20th century (Twenge, 2000). Not only did anxiety scores rise throughout the five decades, but by the 1980s the average American child reported higher levels of anxiety than child psychiatric patients in the 1950s. The data suggest that we may indeed have entered an age of anxiety.

Anxiety and strategies for alleviating anxiety can be found throughout the works of psychoanalytic theorists. Although anxiety has been defined in many ways, most researchers would probably agree that it is above all else an unpleasant emotional experience. When you experience anxiety, you have feelings of worry, panic, fear, and dread. It is probably the emotional experience you would have if you were suddenly arrested or if you discovered that

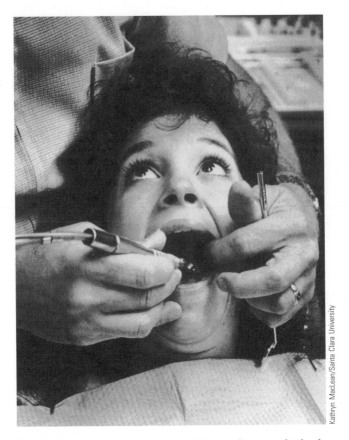

Kathryn MacLean/Santa Clara University

How do you handle the anxiety in this situation? You might try to think of something other than what the dentist is doing, or think about the value of good dental hygiene. What you probably won't do is concentrate on the potential pain.

a diary containing some of your deepest secrets had been passed around among friends.

Although Freud changed his thinking about anxiety several times during his career, his last major writing in this area identified three types of anxiety. First, there is *reality anxiety*, or objective anxiety, which is a response to a perceived threat in the real world. You probably experienced this type of anxiety if you were ever followed by a stranger or if you narrowly escaped a serious automobile accident. In cases of reality anxiety, you are aware of the source of your emotional reaction.

Predictably, these conscious thoughts were not particularly interesting to Freud. He focused on two other types of anxiety, neither of which has an obvious external source. *Neurotic anxiety* is experienced when unacceptable id impulses are dangerously close to breaking into consciousness. It's the type of anxiety that leads the ego to use defense mechanisms. *Moral anxiety* is brought about by the superego in response to id impulses that violate the superego's strict moral code. Generally, moral anxiety is experienced as guilt.

Many neo-Freudian theorists adopted and adapted Freud's ideas about anxiety in their writings. For example, the neurotic coping styles described by Horney are said to develop in an effort to reduce and avoid anxiety. Eventually, Adler, Anna Freud, and other neo-Freudians expanded the notion of defenses to include the conscious and deliberate methods people use to deal with their anxiety (Snyder, 1988). As if to acknowledge the Freudian legacy, these theorists often retained the names of the unconscious defense mechanisms when describing conscious efforts to cope with anxiety. Thus today, we sometimes speak of a person being "in denial" even when that individual is fully aware of the problem and intentionally trying to ignore it. To avoid confusion, we will draw a distinction here between *defense mechanisms*, which are unconscious processes, and *coping strategies*, which are conscious efforts.

Coping with Anxiety

What do you do when faced with a potentially stressful situation, such as waiting for your dentist to start drilling or getting ready for a job interview? If you are like most people, you don't just accept the distress and fear as an unavoidable part of life. Rather, most often we respond to stress-provoking situations with calculated efforts to reduce our anxiety (Lazarus, 1968, 1974). Participants in one early study were shown a rather grisly film on industrial safety (Koriat, Melkman, Averill, & Lazarus, 1972). The film depicted several serious accidents, including a scene in which a saw drives a board through the abdomen of a workman who dies writhing and bleeding on the floor. How did participants react to the film? As you might expect, each of them tried a number of tactics to reduce their discomfort. The most common strategy was to remind themselves that what they were seeing was only a film, not a real accident. Another common tactic was to watch the film in an emotionally detached manner, focusing on the technical aspects of the production rather than the gruesome content. Interestingly, these two approaches sound similar to two Freudian defense mechanisms: denial and intellectualization.

Psychologists refer to these efforts to cope with anxiety in the face of a perceived threat as **coping strategies**. The number of strategies people use when faced with a threatening situation is almost endless. People take long walks, talk to friends with similar problems, meet with professional counselors, drink alcohol, attack the source of the problem, ignore the source of the problem, exercise, avoid people, find a silver lining, and pray. Women report using more coping strategies than men (Tamres, Janicki, & Helgeson, 2002), but researchers don't know if this difference is real or perhaps reflects a difference in recall or the degree to which men and women find various problems stressful.

Investigators also find that not everyone uses the same coping strategies to reduce anxiety. After a lifetime of facing various threatening situations, each of us develops an arsenal of strategies that we believe work for us. Consequently, researchers can identify relatively stable patterns in the way people cope with anxiety (Ptacek, Pierce, & Thompson, 2006). Like other personality variables, our reliance on our favorite coping strategies tends to be consistent over time and across different anxiety-provoking situations. We sometimes refer to a person's general approach to dealing with stress as his or her *coping style*.

Types of Coping Strategies

I was once involved in a discussion at a local Red Cross office about whether to show a potentially anxiety-provoking film to expectant parents. The topic of the film was Sudden Infant Death Syndrome (SIDS), an illness that mysteriously kills thousands of infants annually. One group of parents did not want to expose themselves to anything that suggested their child could die in infancy. The other group argued that they wanted to know as much as possible about any such situation to prepare themselves in case the unfortunate event should happen to them.

TABLE 6.1 Examples of Coping Strategies

Problem-Focused Strategies
I obtained as much information as I could about the situation.
I made a plan of action.
I considered alternatives and weighed the pros and cons.
I talked with people who have had similar experiences.
I tried harder to make things work.
I sought out help from someone who knew more than I did.
I set aside time to work on the problem.

Emotion-Focused Strategies
I discussed my feelings with friends.
I thought about how I could learn from the experience.
I accepted what had happened and moved on.
I tried to put things in perspective.
I looked for the silver lining.
I found comfort in my religion.
I talked about my feelings with a professional counselor.

Avoidance Strategies
I tried not to think about the problem.
I pretended the problem didn't exist.
I used alcohol or drugs to feel better.
I tried to distract myself with other activities.
I avoided people and situations that reminded me of the problem.
I slept more than usual.
I refused to acknowledge the scope of the problem.

The differences in opinion clearly reflected different strategies for dealing with anxiety. Early researchers in this area probably would have divided the two groups of parents along a personality dimension called *repression-sensitization* (Byrne, 1964). At one end of this dimension are people who typically respond to threatening situations by avoiding them. These *repressors* try not to think about the situation and thereby succeed in avoiding the anxiety as much or as long as possible. We see this strategy at work when people advise us that "worrying about it will do no good" and to "try to think of something else to take your mind off it." If you have ever put off seeing a doctor or talking to a professor because you expected the encounter to be stressful, you have used the *repression* strategy. At the other end of the dimension are the *sensitizers*. These people typically deal with a stressful situation by finding out as much as possible, as soon as possible, and thereby put themselves in a position to take the most effective action. You may have employed this strategy if you read up on a scheduled medical procedure or spent a great deal of time preparing for an upcoming job interview.

Subsequent investigators have developed more sophisticated and complex systems to categorize the many different coping strategies people employ (Fok et al., 2012; Gol & Cook, 2004; Lazarus, 2006; Skinner, Edge, Altman, & Sherwood, 2003; Stanton, Kirk, Cameron, & Danoff-Burg, 2000; Zuckerman & Gagne, 2003). However, we can identify a few basic distinctions that most researchers find useful. First, we can divide coping strategies into those in which people take an active role to deal with the problem and those in which people try to avoid the problem. This is similar to the sensitization-repression distinction drawn by early investigators. Second, we can separate the active-role strategies into those aimed at the source of the stress and those that focus on the emotional reaction to the experience. This organization leaves us with three basic ways to deal with anxiety: problem-focused strategies, emotion-focused strategies, and avoidance strategies.

Problem-focused strategies are intended to take care of the problem and thereby overcoming the anxiety. If the problem is financial, we look for ways to earn more money or reduce expenses. If struggling in a class, we seek out a tutor or make extra time to work on assignments. People employing problem-focused strategies often find that simply making plans to deal with the problem makes them feel better than sitting back and doing nothing at all.

Emotion-focused strategies are designed to reduce the emotional distress that accompanies the problem. A student not accepted to law school might consider how this apparent setback could be for the best. Couples can deal with an emotionally painful divorce by talking about their feelings with friends or with a professional counselor.

People who use **avoidance strategies** deal with their emotions by pushing the anxiety-provoking situation out of awareness. When learning that a friend has a serious health problem, a woman might respond by not thinking about the friend or by convincing herself that the problem is not as serious as people are making it out to be. A man who fears he will lose his job might distract himself from his worries by going out with friends or by drinking excessively.

In one investigation, men and women were asked how they had coped with a series of real-life events they had experienced during the past 7 months (Folkman & Lazarus, 1980). Participants indicated their coping strategies on a checklist of possible responses. More than 1,300 examples of stressful experiences were examined. The researchers found that participants used an emotion-focused strategy, a problem-focused strategy, or both in more than 98% of the cases. Of course, most people used more than one tactic to deal with their stresses, and many used strategies from all three of the major categories when wrestling with a single event. Other research finds that women tend to use emotion-focused strategies more than men, whereas men are more likely than women to take steps to solve problems directly (Ptacek, Smith, & Dodge, 1994). This pattern is consistent with the research findings on gender roles presented in Chapter 14.

How Effective Are Coping Strategies?

Researchers consistently find that using some kind of coping strategy is almost always better than using no strategy (McCrae & Costa, 1986; Mitchell, Cronkite, & Moos, 1983). But are all coping strategies equally effective? We can answer this question by dividing it into two more specific questions. First, do active or avoidance strategies work better in alleviating anxiety? Second, when using an active strategy, is it better to focus on the problem or focus on the emotion?

Should you face a problem head on by using an active coping strategy or should you do what you can to avoid the source of anxiety? A great deal of research has been conducted on this question, and the answer is clear: In almost all cases, active strategies are more effective in helping people cope with stressors than avoidance strategies. In one study, military veterans exposed to moderate levels of combat were better able to deal with the long-term consequences of trauma when they took direct steps to deal with their situation than when they tried to ignore the problem (Suvak, Vogt, Savarese, King, & King, 2002). In another study, HIV patients who had lost a loved one to HIV/AIDS were hopeful and optimistic about their future when they used active coping strategies, but expressed helplessness when relying on avoidance strategies (Rogers, Hansen, Levy, Tate, & Sikkema, 2005). One team of researchers found that the more medical students relied on active coping, the better their physical health during the rigorous first year of medical school (Park & Adler, 2003).

On the other hand, avoidance strategies rarely are successful in reducing anxiety or helping people overcome tragedy. Researchers find this unfortunate outcome when looking at how people cope with a loved one's illness (Compas, Worsham, Ey, & Howell, 1996), a physical assault (Valentiner, Foa, Riggs, & Gershuny, 1996), or being diagnosed with breast cancer (Carver et al., 1993). Victims of Hurricane Katrina who used avoidance strategies to deal with the trauma of the storm and its aftermath were more likely to suffer from post-traumatic stress disorder than those who used more effective coping strategies (Glass, Flory, Hankin, Kloos, & Turecki, 2009).

Investigators also find long-term consequences from extensive reliance on avoidance strategies. In one study, adults who had learned to cope with adolescent bullying by relying on avoidance strategies often turned to these same ineffective strategies when faced with different problems as adults (Newman, Holden, & Delville, 2011). In addition to the psychological consequences that often flow from the failure to cope with stress, people who rely on avoidance strategies may be more vulnerable to stress-related health problems, such as hypertension and cardiovascular disease (Mund & Mitte, 2012).

Are avoidance strategies ever effective? Perhaps. Some research suggests that on occasion avoidance strategies may help in the short run (Suls & Fletcher, 1985). For example, you might decide to ignore relationship problems for a few days while you study for finals. However, at best this strategy only delays dealing with the problem. Moreover, research indicates that whatever short-term advantages there are to avoidance strategies may be limited to stressors that are relatively mild and at least partially under the individual's control (Terry & Hynes, 1998). And as if this weren't bad enough, extensive use of avoidance strategies can create additional problems. Because escape from anxiety sometimes includes drinking, people who typically rely on avoidance strategies may be at risk for alcohol problems (Simpson & Arroyo, 1998; Windle & Windle, 1996). One study found that adolescents who relied on avoidance coping were more likely than other students to engage in a number of delinquent behaviors, including substance abuse (Cooper, Wood, Orcutt, & Albino, 2003).

Clearly active coping strategies are superior to avoidance strategies, but the question of whether one should use a problem-focused or emotion-focused strategy is more difficult. Depending on the situation, either of these approaches might prove more effective for dealing with stress (Austenfeld & Stanton, 2004). The key is whether there is any way to correct the problem, or if the situation is one that eventually has to be accepted (Aldwin & Revenson, 1987; Zeidner, 2007). If a means to resolve the situation is available, taking quick action to eliminate a problem probably is the most effective course of action (Vitaliano, DeWolfe, Maiuro, Russo, & Katon, 1990). Students who fret over difficult material in their math classes probably could do themselves a favor by seeking help right away instead of hoping for sudden insight. However, we often encounter situations that we can't do anything about. In these cases, trying to make the problem go away is fruitless. One study found that parents who reacted to their infant's death with problem-focused strategies had a more difficult time coping with the loss than parents who used other coping tactics (Murray & Terry, 1999). When a situation can't be changed, working on your emotional reaction to the experience is probably the more effective approach.

One team of psychologists demonstrated this point in a dramatic way (Strentz & Auerbach, 1988). In conjunction with the FBI and some domestic airline companies, the researchers staged a 4-day hostage abduction. Pilots, copilots, and flight attendants who had volunteered to participate in the exercise experienced what it would be like to be taken hostage by terrorists. Great effort was taken to make the situation as realistic as possible. FBI agents dressed as terrorists fired automatic weapons (blanks), handcuffed the hostages, and made death threats. Measures taken throughout the study showed that, as expected, the participants experienced high levels of anxiety. How did they cope with this anxiety? Before the kidnapping, some participants were instructed in the use of emotion-focused coping strategies, whereas others were trained to use problem-focused strategies. Remember, there was little or nothing the hostages could do to change the situation. But they could deal with their emotional reactions. As a result, participants instructed in how to use the emotion-focused strategies experienced lower levels of anxiety than those who relied on problem-focused strategies.

Coping Flexibility

Fortunately, most of us have a number of coping strategies in our repertoires. If one approach for dealing with an anxiety-provoking situation does not work, perhaps another one will. But just having these strategies at hand may not be enough to cope effectively with the wide variety of stressors life throws our way. We also have to be able and willing to recognize when a coping strategy is not working and to try something new. Because different strategies work in different situations, the key to effective coping might be to know when to employ which type of strategy.

Researchers refer to this ability to effectively utilize different coping strategies as *coping flexibility* (Cheng, 2001, 2009; Cheng & Cheung, 2005). People who readily adjust their coping strategies to fit the realities of a given situation are likely to deal with life's problems more effectively than those who do not. As with other personality variables, some individuals have better coping flexibility than others (Bonanno, Pat-Horenczyk, & Noll, 2011; Kato, 2012). One team of researchers examined college students' reactions to traumatic events, such as accidents, serious health issues, or the death of a loved one (Galatzer-Levy, Burton, & Bonanno, 2012). Students high in coping flexibility experienced significantly less stress as a result of these traumas than did students who tended to rely on but a few familiar coping strategies. Because stressors large and small are a part of everyone's life, people who score high on measures of coping flexibility tend to have a higher sense of well-being and experience fewer emotional problems (Bonanno, Papa, Lalande, Westphal, & Coifman, 2004; Bonanno, et al., 2011; Kato, 2012).

Psychoanalytic Concepts and Aggression

Suppose you are in the library late one night trying to read an article from a professional journal for one of your classes. You wade through the big words and jargon on the first few pages, hoping to make more sense of the writing as it progresses. You come to what appears to be the main point of the article, so you read each word slowly and carefully. Still, you don't get it. So you read the last few paragraphs again. But again it doesn't make any sense. You try once more, but still no luck. You're running out of time and patience. What do you feel like doing? Most people react to this kind of

Assessing Your Own Personality

Coping Flexibility

When we feel stress, we try to cope using various actions and thoughts. The following items describe stress-coping situations. Please indicate how these situations apply to you by choosing one of the following for each situation: 0 = Not applicable; 1 = Somewhat applicable; 2 = Applicable; 3 = Very Applicable.

_____ 1. When a stressful situation has not improved, I try to think of other ways to cope with it.

_____ 2. I only use certain ways to cope with stress.

_____ 3. When stressed, I use several ways to cope and make the situation better.

_____ 4. When I haven't coped with a stressful situation well, I use other ways to cope with that situation.

_____ 5. If a stressful situation has not improved, I use other ways to cope with that situation.

_____ 6. I am aware of how successful or unsuccessful my attempts to cope with stress have been.

_____ 7. I fail to notice when I have been unable to cope with stress.

_____ 8. If I feel that I have failed to cope with stress, I change the way in which I deal with stress.

_____ 9. After coping with stress, I think about how well my ways of coping with stress worked or did not work.

_____ 10. If I have failed to cope with stress, I think of other ways to cope.

To obtain your scores, first reverse the answer values for items 2 and 7. That is, for these two items, 0 = 3, 1 = 2, 2 = 1, and 3 = 0. Next sum the answer values for items 2, 6, 7, 8 and 9 to obtain your Evaluation Coping score. Then sum the answer values for items 1, 3, 4, 5, and 10 to obtain your Adaptive Coping score. Evaluation coping refers to your tendency to abandon ineffective strategies. Adaptive coping refers to your tendency to consider and create alternative coping strategies. Kato (2012) found a mean of 10.10 (sd = 3.12) for Evaluation Coping and a mean of 7.29 (sd = 3.20) for Adaptive Coping in a sample of Japanese college students.

Scale: The Coping Flexibility Scale

Source: Kato, T. (2012). Development of the Coping Flexibility Scale: Evidence for the coping flexibility hypothesis. *Journal of Counseling Psychology, 59,* 262–273.

experience with a good amount of frustration. As a result, they might pound their fists on the table or swear under their breath at the author. If they could, they might throw the journal across the room. What these reactions illustrate is the commonly observed connection between frustration and aggression, an association that—as we will see—links psychoanalytic concepts to current research on violence in several important ways.

Few events in our lives command as much attention as those with an element of aggression. From playground fights to muggings to war, attempts by one human to inflict pain on another have been among the most widely researched human behaviors. Naturally, the psychoanalytic approach to personality has much to say about this topic. In fact, one of the first efforts to explain the association between frustration and aggression can be found in Freud's early writings. Freud initially proposed that aggression is the result of frustrated libido. When our pleasure-seeking impulse is blocked, we experience a "primordial reaction" to attack the obstacle. Naturally, our egos keep us from assaulting anyone and everyone who spoils our fun. Therefore, Freud argued, we often displace our aggression. Because we can't attack the police officer who won't let us drive as fast as we want, we express the aggressive impulse by yelling at employees, friends, or family members.

Freud later changed his views on the causes of aggression. After witnessing the mass destruction of human life in World War I, he introduced the concept of a death instinct, *Thanatos*. Freud claimed that we all have an instinctual desire to destroy ourselves. But because a fully functioning ego does not allow self-destruction, the instinct is turned outward toward others. However, it was Freud's original position that later inspired researchers interested in the connection between frustration and aggression. In 1939, a team of psychologists modified Freud's earlier thoughts to create the *frustration-aggression hypothesis* (Dollard, Doob, Miller, Mowrer, & Sears, 1939). Although many of these psychologists identified more closely with behaviorism (Chapter 13), the psychoanalytic flavor of their theorizing is unmistakable.

The frustration-aggression hypothesis states that "aggression is *always* a consequence of frustration … that the occurrence of aggressive behavior *always* presupposes the existence of frustration and, contrariwise, that the existence of frustration *always* leads to some form of aggression" (p. 1, italics added). One attractive feature of this hypothesis is its simplicity. Notice that the psychologists argued there is but one cause of aggression (frustration) and one response to frustration (aggression). A student frustrated in efforts to get on the honor roll, an unemployed worker frustrated by an economic recession, and a rat frustrated in its effort to find a piece of cheese all should respond with aggression. And anyone who acts aggressively should have experienced some earlier frustration.

The researchers adopted another psychoanalytic notion to explain when aggression will stop. They proposed that aggression ceases when we experience catharsis, loosely conceived of as a release of tension. Freud discussed catharsis in terms of a release of psychic energy. However, these early aggression researchers described tension in terms of arousal, energy levels, and muscle tension. The frustrated student who kicks her books across the room and the slumping batter who pounds his bat against the dugout wall should feel a cathartic release in tension. Until the frustration builds tension levels up again, we should expect no further outbreaks.

> "Men are not gentle creatures who want to be loved. They are, on the contrary, creatures among whose instinctual endowments [is] a powerful share of aggressiveness."
>
> SIGMUND FREUD

At first glance, the frustration-aggression hypothesis makes some intuitive sense. You may have felt the urge to kick a malfunctioning copy machine. We've all seen how a little shoving in a long line can lead to angry words. But a problem with the theory soon becomes apparent. Given all of the frustrating experiences in our lives, why don't we spend more of our time acting aggressively? To account for this complication, some of the original theorists modified the frustration-aggression hypothesis, again by borrowing from psychoanalytic theory (Doob & Sears, 1939; Miller, 1941; Sears, 1941). They proposed that frustration sometimes leads to *indirect* expressions of aggression. Indirect aggression can be expressed in many ways. One is by *displacing* the aggression to a new target, such as taking frustration at the office out on your spouse. Another is to attack the source of our frustration in an indirect manner. For example, people might not physically attack their supervisors, but they can make their supervisors' jobs a little harder or spread malicious gossip about them. We can also use *sublimation* (another concept adapted from psychoanalytic theory). For example, a frustrated person might run a few miles or play a hard game of basketball to work out tension. Thus, within the modified version of the frustration-aggression hypothesis, frustration always leads to aggression, but not always in the most obvious forms.

The frustration-aggression hypothesis and its subsequent variations have spawned a large amount of research. The following sections examine three topics addressed by that research, each of which has psychoanalytic roots: frustration, displacement, and catharsis.

Frustration and Aggression

The connection between frustration and aggression can be seen in many places. Elementary school children in one study were asked which of their classmates engaged in aggressive behavior, such as pushing or shoving (Guerra, Huesmann, Tolan, Van Acker, & Eron, 1995). The children identified as the most aggressive children were those who experienced the highest levels of stress and frustration at home. Another study looked at adults who had been laid off from their jobs (Catalano, Dooley, Novaco, Wilson, & Hough, 1993). These individuals were six times more likely to engage in an act of violence, such as striking a spouse, than those who were still employed. Consistent with this last observation, researchers find that when frustrating social conditions like unemployment rise, we usually see a corresponding increase in violent crime (Landau, 1988; Landau & Raveh, 1987).

Several direct tests of the frustration-aggression hypothesis demonstrate that frustrated people act more aggressively than nonfrustrated people (Berkowitz, 1989). Researchers in one study intentionally provoked unsuspecting people standing in lines in stores, banks, and at ticket windows (Harris, 1974). Because frustration is more intense the closer people are to their goal, the investigators cut in front of either the 3rd person in line (close to the goal) or the 12th person in line. The intruder then glanced back to notice the person's response and, after 20 seconds, apologized and left. Responses were coded for verbal aggression, such as making threatening

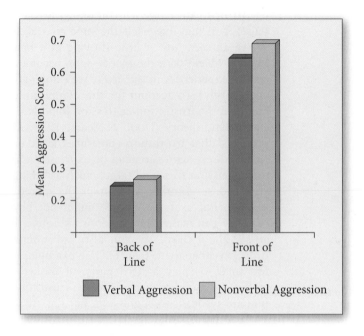

FIGURE 6.1 Verbal and Nonverbal Aggression as a Function of Place in Line

Source: Adapted from Harris (1974).

comments, and nonverbal aggression, such as pushing and shoving. The results are shown in Figure 6.1. As expected, highly frustrated people toward the front of the line expressed more aggression than the less frustrated people toward the end.

Although an abundance of evidence validates the link between frustration and aggression, most researchers believe the original frustration-aggression hypothesis was too limited. They argue that frustration is but one of many negative emotions that increase aggression (Berkowitz, 1989, 1994, 1998; Lindsay & Anderson, 2000). Things that frustrate us are unpleasant, and it is the unpleasantness that we respond to when frustrated. Consistent with this analysis, researchers find that uncomfortably high temperatures, at least up to a point, increase aggression (Anderson & Anderson, 1998). Similarly, irritating cigarette smoke and loud noise increase the amount of punishment people give to innocent bystanders (Berkowitz, 1989). Thus, the question is not whether a particular event is frustrating but rather how unpleasant the accompanying emotion is.

This newer way of looking at frustration and aggression has several advantages over the original hypothesis. First, the new model explains why frustration does not always lead to aggression. Frustration facilitates aggression only to the extent that it is perceived as unpleasant. Second, the model clarifies why certain thoughts increase or decrease the likelihood of acting aggressively. For example, you may be very frustrated if you do poorly on a test because your roommate drove home for the weekend with your textbooks in the back of his or her car. However, you will have a very different reaction to this frustration if you believe your roommate was unaware of the books than if you determine he or she deliberately took off with them. Thoughts that create negative feelings make the whole experience more unpleasant and increase the chances for aggression. Thoughts that decrease negative feelings reduce the likelihood of aggression.

Displacing Aggression

Like most people, you have probably had the regrettable experience of lashing out at a friend far more than the situation called for. The outburst was most likely met with a "What's the matter with you?" or "Someone had a bad day." After calming down, you may have recognized that the source of your anger wasn't really your friend at all but a poor grade on an assignment or a boss who would not let you off work this coming weekend. Incidents like these illustrate one prediction from early versions of the frustration-aggression hypothesis. That is, we don't always attack the source of our frustration directly; we sometimes direct our frustration-induced anger toward someone who does not deserve it (Denson, Pedersen, & Miller, 2006; Vasquez, Osman, & Wood, 2012). Expressing aggression toward these indirect targets is usually safer than going after a frustrating instructor or employer.

Dozens of studies find support for the notion that we sometimes displace aggression from a frustrating source to an innocent target (Marcus-Newhall, Pedersen, Carlson, & Miller, 2000). Participants in one of these investigations were asked to work on some anagrams (Konecni & Doob, 1972). Some people found the task frustrating, especially because another participant (a confederate of the experimenter) persistently annoyed them while they worked on the problems. Other participants were allowed to work on the task without interruptions. Participants were then given the opportunity to grade another individual on a creativity task. The means of grading was electric shock. Participants were told to give this other person painful (but not harmful) shocks whenever they heard uncreative responses. Although no actual shocks were delivered, the number of shocks participants thought they were giving was used to measure aggression.

The researchers added one more interesting twist to the study. Some participants were fortunate enough to find that the person who had earlier annoyed them was the one hooked up to the shock apparatus. For other participants, the person receiving the shock was a stranger. The results from the relevant conditions are shown in Figure 6.2. Not surprisingly, participants given the chance to get even with the person who had frustrated them gave more shocks than the nonfrustrated participants. However, frustrated participants given the opportunity to shock a stranger also delivered more shocks than the nonfrustrated participants. In other words, these people *displaced* their aggressive tendencies onto the innocent bystander. This tendency to displace aggression has been found in studies with adolescents as young as 13 (Reijntjes, Kamphuis, Thomaes, Bushman, & Telch, 2012).

One team of researchers looked for evidence of displaced aggression in the business world (Hoobler & Brass, 2006). They first measured the amount

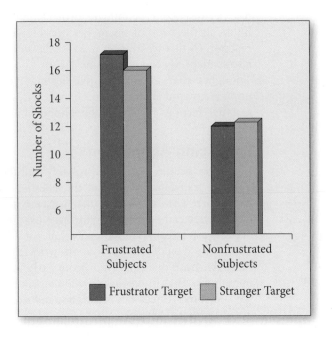

FIGURE 6.2 Mean Number of Shocks Delivered

Source: From "Catharsis through displacement of aggression," by V. J. Konecni and A. N. Doob, *Journal of Personality and Social Psychology*, 1972, 23, 379–387.

of frustration supervisors experienced at work, such as not being promoted or feeling as if they were treated unfairly by the company. Of course, these supervisors were reluctant to express their anger directly toward their bosses. However, the more frustration these supervisors experienced, the more the employees working directly below them felt abused by the supervisor. These employees complained about being put down in front of other people or being told their ideas were stupid. In other words, the frustrated supervisors appeared to displace their anger onto their subordinates in the organization. But the story does not stop there. The family members of those abused subordinates were also part of the study. The more the employees felt abused by their boss at work, the more unpleasant they were to their families. In short, displaced aggression may not simply disappear, but may get passed down to the next person in the hierarchy.

On the other hand, not all victims of displaced aggression are completely innocent. Sometimes the targets of displaced aggression have done something to annoy the person attacking them. The problem is that the reaction is often way out of proportion to the relatively small offense. Psychologists refer to this kind of overreaction as *triggered displaced aggression* (Miller, Pedersen, Earleywine, & Pollock, 2003). Researchers find that displaced aggression is most likely to occur when we encounter a minor annoyance that we otherwise would easily tolerate or ignore (Bushman, Bonacci, Pedersen, Vasquez, & Miller, 2005; Denson, et al., 2008; Pedersen, Bushman, Vasquez, & Miller,

2008; Vasquez, 2009; Vasquez, et al., 2013). We see examples of this effect when a frustrated mother overreacts to her child's messy room or a basketball player having a bad game lashes out at an opponent who happens to brush up against him too hard.

Catharsis and Aggression

Each of us has been told at one time or another that we needed to "let off a little steam" rather than do something in anger we'll later regret. We are told to punch a pillow or spend 10 minutes vigorously shooting baskets. Some therapists advise clients to strike plastic dolls or use foam-rubber bats to work off their tensions. The idea is to get the aggressive tendencies out of the client's system so therapy can continue in a violence-free atmosphere. These examples illustrate one more prediction from the frustration-aggression hypothesis: Our need to aggress is reduced after a cathartic release of tension. Conventional wisdom often agrees. The best way to deal with frustration, many people believe, is to express our feelings against some harmless target. Indeed, one team of researchers found that people are more likely to play violent video games when they believe the games provide them a safe means for releasing their anger (Bushman & Whitaker, 2010). The problem is, this widely dispensed advice appears to be wrong.

Consider the experience of participants in one investigation, who wrote essays that supposedly were graded by another participant (Bushman, 2002). The feedback from this other person was particularly harsh, ending with a handwritten comment that "This is one of the worst essays I have ever read!" Needless to say, this irritated the real participants. Some of these angry participants were then given the chance to hit a punching bag as hard and for as many times as they wished while looking at a picture of and thinking about the person who had just insulted them. Other participants also hit the punching bag, but were told to do so while thinking about how much exercise they were getting. Finally, some participants had no opportunity to hit anything and simply sat quietly for a few minutes. As shown in Figure 6.3, the conventional wisdom about letting off steam didn't work. Not only were the participants who hit the bag while thinking of their insulter the angriest, they also were the most aggressive when later given a chance to do something that would hurt the person they were mad at. Contrary to the advice we have all received, the least angry and least aggressive participants were those who calmly sat alone without punching anything.

These findings also contradict the original frustration-aggression hypothesis, which maintained that aggression leads to a tension-reducing catharsis that reduces the need for aggression. Consistent with the hypothesis, researchers often find a sudden drop in physiological arousal after participants are allowed to attack another person (Geen, Stonner, & Shope, 1975; Verona & Sullivan, 2008). But not only does this cathartic reaction not reduce aggression, several studies find that acting aggressively often *increases* the tendency to aggress (Bresin & Gordon, 2013; Bushman, Baumeister, & Stack, 1999; Geen et al., 1975; Verona & Sullivan, 2008).

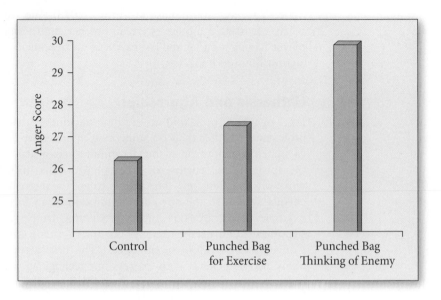

FIGURE 6.3 Anger After Cathartic Activity

Source: Adapted from Bushman (2002).

Why should this be the case? Researchers have identified several reasons (Geen & Quanty, 1977). Acting aggressively may lead to a kind of disinhibition. That is, most of us have strong reservations about physically hurting other people. However, once we violate that rule, we may find it easier to attack in the future. Another reason for the aggression-breeds-aggression effect may be the presence of aggressive cues. As described in Chapter 14, seeing something we associate with violence (for example, a gun) often increases aggression. By observing our own aggressive actions, we may be spurred on to more aggression. Moreover, as discussed in Chapter 16, these violent cues may tap into other memories and emotions related to aggression. Finally, because a cathartic release of tension feels good, aggressive acts may be reinforced. Researchers find that people sometimes feel better after punching a bag or blasting another participant with loud noise (Bushman, Baumeister, & Phillips, 2001; Bushman et al., 1999). As discussed in Chapter 13, behaviors that lead to pleasant consequences are likely to be repeated. Thus, rather than reducing aggression, catharsis may do the opposite.

Attachment Style and Adult Relationships

When people are asked what brings them happiness, they usually talk about their personal relationships (Myers, 1992). Career, personal accomplishments, and material possessions almost always come in a distant second to our loved ones when people stop to think about what they treasure most in their lives. Ironically, our relationships are also one of our biggest sources of distress.

Jerry Burger/Santa Clara University

According to attachment theory, infants who experience loving, secure relationships with their parents develop unconscious working models for secure, trusting relationships as adults.

Most adults have been in relationships that for one reason or another simply didn't work. You may have gone through the frustration of being involved with someone who remained emotionally distant. Or you may have suffered through a relationship in which your partner was so dependent and clinging that you felt smothered. If you are lucky, you also have found a romantic partner who is confident and emotionally engaging. But what is it that allows some people to enter relationships easily, whereas for others it is such a chore? There are, of course, many reasons relationships succeed and fail. But one approach to studying relationships maintains that understanding adult romantic behavior begins by looking at very early childhood experiences. The neo-Freudians who first presented these ideas maintained that how we relate to significant others as adults is a reflection of the relationship we had with our parents. Recent research finds considerable merit in this notion.

Object Relations Theory and Attachment Theory

Among the many theorists who expanded on Freud's personality theory in the middle part of the 20th century were a group of psychologists who became known as *object relations* theorists. Some of the most influential of these psychologists are Melanie Klein, Donald Winnicott, Margaret Mahler, and Heinz Kohut. Although these theorists often present different interpretations of object relations theory, some general principles unite most of the viewpoints. First, like other neo-Freudians, object relations theorists place great emphasis on early childhood experiences. Instead of focusing on the internal conflicts and drives that Freud described, these psychologists are interested in the infant's relationship with important people in his or her life. In most cases, this means the child's relationship with the parents, most often with the mother. Second, as the name suggests, object relations theorists postulate that the child develops an unconscious representation of significant objects in his or her environment. The child's unconscious representation of the parents does more than provide the infant with an object to relate to in the physical absence of the mother or father. The way the child internalizes the parent's image serves as a basis for how the child thinks of others when he or she enters into future relationships. In other words, the kind of attachment children feel with their parents influences their ability to develop meaningful attachments with significant others as adults.

Object relations theory became the springboard for what has been called *attachment theory*. Perhaps the two biggest contributors to this theory were John Bowlby (1969, 1973, 1980) and Mary Ainsworth (1989; Ainsworth, Blehar, Waters, & Wall, 1978). These psychologists examined the emotional bonds between infants and their caregivers, again usually the mother. Bowlby referred to these as *attachment relationships* because they meet our human need to form attachments with a supportive and protective other. Bowlby was particularly interested in the reactions of infants who are physically separated from their primary caregiver. Some children deal with the separation quite well. These infants seem to understand that mother is gone for the moment but that she will return and that the love and nurturance they need will not be lost. However, Bowlby observed that other children seem to protest the separation by crying. Still other infants react to their mother's absence by falling into a type of despair, and some respond with a kind of detachment to the mother even when she returns.

Ainsworth and her colleagues made similar observations in their studies with infants and mothers. They identified three types of parent–child relationships (Ainsworth et al., 1978). First, there are *secure* infant–mother pairs. Mothers in these dyads are attentive and responsive to their child. Infants who experience this type of attachment understand that mother is responsive and accessible even if she is not physically present. Secure children tend to be happy and self-confident. In contrast, we sometimes find *anxious-ambivalent* relationships. Mothers in these dyads are not particularly attentive or responsive to the child's needs. The children are anxious whenever mother leaves, sometimes breaking into tears as soon as they are separated. These children are not easily calmed by other adults and may be afraid in unfamiliar situations. Finally, there are *avoidant* relationships. Mothers in these relationships also are not very responsive to the child. However, the child reacts to this treatment by developing a type of aloofness or emotional detachment from the mother. These children do not become anxious when mother leaves and are not particularly interested in her attention when she returns.

Attachment theorists then took their observations about different attachment styles one step further. Like the object relations theorists, they argue that these different infant–parent relationships have long-term implications for the child's ability to enter into relationships later in life. Bowlby argues that the infant forms unconscious "working models" for interpersonal involvement. If the child experiences love and trust in this early relationship, the child will come to see him- or herself as lovable and trustworthy. However, if the infant's attachment needs are not met, the child will develop a less healthy self-image. "An unwanted child is likely not only to feel unwanted by his parents but to believe that he is essentially ... unwanted by anyone," Bowlby (1973) explained. "Conversely, a much-loved child may grow up to be not only confident of his parent's affection but confident that everyone else will find him lovable too" (pp. 204–205).

Thus our earliest experiences with caretakers become the foundation upon which we approach later relationships. If our parents were caring, attentive, and responsive, we come to see relations with others as sources of love and support. If our needs for attachment and attention were not met, we become suspicious and mistrusting. Consistent with the psychoanalytic flavor of the object relations theorists, these mental models of attachment relationships are said to be largely unconscious.

Adult Attachment Styles

If the attachment theorists are correct, we should be able to identify adults who fit the descriptions of the different attachment styles found among infants. In other words, the secure, avoidant, and anxious-ambivalent styles Ainsworth and her colleagues saw in children should surface when these same children become adults and enter into adult romantic relationships. We should find secure adults, who have little difficulty getting close to others. These are people who easily trust and depend on those they become romantically involved with. On the other hand, we should also find avoidant adults, who are suspicious of those who say they love them, who fear that getting too close means making themselves vulnerable. These people may be wary of making emotional commitments for fear of being hurt by the inevitable separation. We might also find anxious-ambivalent adults, who are so insecure about the partner's love that they become demanding and sometimes overwhelming in their relationships. These people may require so much attention that they scare away potential romantic partners.

Interestingly, one of the first attempts to identify and measure these three adult attachment styles came in the form of a survey printed in the *Rocky Mountain News* (Hazan & Shaver, 1987). More than a thousand readers mailed in their responses to the "love quiz" they found in the Lifestyle section of the Colorado newspaper. One of the questions in this quiz asked respondents to indicate which of the following three descriptions most closely captured them:

_____ I find it relatively easy to get close to others and am comfortable depending on them and having them depend on me. I don't often worry about being abandoned or about someone getting too close to me.

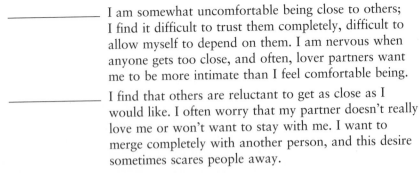

——————————— I am somewhat uncomfortable being close to others; I find it difficult to trust them completely, difficult to allow myself to depend on them. I am nervous when anyone gets too close, and often, lover partners want me to be more intimate than I feel comfortable being.

——————————— I find that others are reluctant to get as close as I would like. I often worry that my partner doesn't really love me or won't want to stay with me. I want to merge completely with another person, and this desire sometimes scares people away.

The first description depicts an adult with a *secure attachment style*. The second portrays an *avoidant style*, the third an *anxious-ambivalent style*. Although the sample was far from scientific, the results were enlightening. Fifty-six percent of the respondents placed themselves in the secure category, 25% said the avoidant description fit them best, and the remaining 19% identified themselves as part of the anxious-ambivalent group. A subsequent national survey with a large stratified sample found a similar breakdown among Americans: 59% secure, 25% avoidant, 11% anxious, and 5% unclassifiable (Mickelson, Kessler, & Shaver, 1997). The significance of these numbers was not lost on the investigators. They were quick to point out that the percentages of adults who fall into the three categories match quite closely those found by developmental psychologists who calculate the number of secure, avoidant, and anxious-avoidant infants (Campos, Barrett, Lamb, Goldsmith, & Stenberg, 1983). Although only suggestive, the similarity in numbers is consistent with the notion that the adult attachment styles were formed in childhood.

Results of additional studies indicate that the connection between early parent–child relationships and adult attachment style is more than speculative. When asked about family members, secure adults are more likely than others to describe positive relationships with parents and a warm and trusting family environment (Brennan & Shaver, 1993; Diehl, Elnick, Bourbeau, & Labouvie-Vief, 1998; Feeney & Noller, 1990; Hazan & Shaver, 1987; Levy, Blatt, & Shaver, 1998). In contrast, anxious-ambivalent people in these studies recall little parental support, and avoidant people describe their relationships with family members as distrustful and emotionally distant. People who describe their parents' marriage as unhappy are more likely to fall into the avoidant category and less likely to develop a secure attachment style.

Psychologists have also used longitudinal studies to demonstrate the link between early caregiver relationships and adult attachment styles (Fraley, Roisman, Booth-LaForce, Owen, & Holland, 2013; Simpson, Collins, Tran, & Haydon, 2007). One team of researchers videotaped mothers interacting with their children when the child was 18 months old (Zayas, Mischel, Shoda, & Aber, 2011). Coders rated the extent to which the mother acted in a sensitive, controlling, or unresponsive manner toward the child. Twenty years later, the investigators measured the attachment styles of the children (now adults). As expected, the mother's interaction style two decades earlier predicted quite well the romantic attachment styles of the adults.

Alternate Models and Measurement

The introduction of adult attachment styles resulted in an explosion of writings and research. This work includes new ideas about the number of adult attachment styles and new scales for determining how to classify individuals (Bartholomew, 1990; Bartholomew & Shaver, 1998; Carver, 1997; Sipley, Fischer, & Liu, 2005). In recent years, attachment researchers have found it useful to divide attachment style along two dimensions (Bartholomew & Horowitz, 1991; Brennan, Clark, & Shaver, 1998). Researchers first divide people into those who are and are not fearful that their romantic partner will abandon them. Drawing from attachment theory, we can say this fear of abandonment reflects the person's internalized feelings of self-worth. Those who rarely worry about abandonment see themselves as worthwhile and capable of being treasured. On the other hand, some people are burdened with self-doubts about their value and reservations about whether anyone would find them lovable. The second dimension concerns how comfortable people are with closeness and dependency. On one side of this dimension, we find people who believe that others can be trusted and will be there to provide for their emotional needs. At the other end are those who see people as unreliable and rejecting.

When we combine these two dimensions, we get the four-category model shown in Figure 6.4. Adults who are comfortable with closeness and who don't overly concern themselves about being abandoned are classified as *secure*. Like the secure adults in the three-category model, these people tend to seek out and are comfortable with intimate relationships. However, some people who don't fear abandonment still have a deep-seated mistrust of others. These *avoidant* individuals (sometimes called *dismissing*) shy away from close relationships. They are reluctant to trust others or to become too emotionally dependent for fear of being hurt.

People classified in the other two quadrants of the model suffer from feelings that they are unlovable, which burdens them with a constant fear that

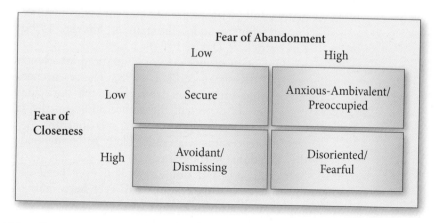

FIGURE 6.4 Four Types of Attachment
Source: Adapted from Brennan et al. (1998).

their loved ones will abandon them. Those who are comfortable with close-ness fall into the *anxious-ambivalent* category (sometimes called *preoccupied*). Because these individuals lack internal feelings of self-worth, they seek self-acceptance by becoming close and intimate with others. In a sense, they are trying to prove that they must be worthy of love if this other person finds them lovable. Unfortunately, their lack of self-worth leaves these people vul-nerable to heartbreak when their partner fails to meet their strong intimacy needs. Additionally, we have *disoriented* (sometimes called *fearful*) people. These adults see themselves as unworthy of love and doubt that romantic involvement will provide the much-needed intimacy. They avoid getting close to others because they fear the pain of rejection.

Students correctly ask whether the three- or four-category model best describes the different kinds of adult attachment styles. The answer is that both models are useful, although there is a clear trend in recent research toward using the four-category model. Because researchers sometimes divide participants into three categories and sometimes into four, occasion-ally it is difficult to compare results across studies. Nonetheless, because of the similarity between the two models, research using either scheme is valu-able, and the research reviewed in the next section relies on studies using both models.

Attachment Style and Romantic Relationships

Do attachment styles really affect our romantic relationships? A good start-ing point for answering this question might be to ask how happy people are with their romantic relationships. As you might expect, several studies find that adults with a secure attachment style tend to be more satisfied with their relationships than people in the other categories (Brennan & Shaver, 1995; Keelan, Dion, & Dion, 1994; Pistole, 1989; Simpson, 1990; Tucker & Anders, 1999). This phenomenon also works in the other direction. That is, people are more likely to be happy with their relationship if they have a partner with a secure attachment style. And perhaps not surpris-ingly, adults with secure attachment styles tend to have partners with a sim-ilar attachment style (Brennan & Shaver, 1995; Collins & Read, 1990; Kirkpatrick & Davis, 1994).

One team of investigators measured attachment style in a sample of 52-year-olds (Klohnen & Bera, 1998). The researchers already had measures of relationship satisfaction from when the participants were 21, 27, and 43 years old. As expected, the secure adults in the sample had a long history of stable and satisfying romantic relationships. As shown in Figure 6.5, the secure participants were more likely to be married and to stay married than the avoidant participants. By age 52, 95% of the secure adults had been married, and only 24% had ever been divorced. In contrast, only 72% of the avoidant adults had ever been married, and 50% of them had experienced a divorce.

But why are relationships with secure adults better? Researchers find that people with a secure attachment style are more likely than others to

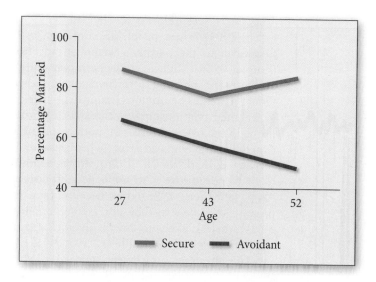

FIGURE 6.5 Marriage Rates as a Function of Attachment Style

Source: Adapted from "Behavioral and experimental patterns of avoidantly and securely attached women across adulthood," by Eva C. Klohnen, *Journal of Personality and Social Psychology*, 1998, 74, 211–223. Copyright 1998 American Psychological Association.

characterize their current romantic relationship as one with a great deal of love, a strong commitment, and a large amount of trust (Keelan et al., 1994; Simpson, 1990). Moreover, these secure individuals are able to accept and support their partner despite the partner's personal faults (Hazan & Shaver, 1987). Conversations between secure partners tend to be warmer and more intimate than conversations with avoidant or anxious-ambivalent partners (Simpson, 1990). And compared to people with other attachment styles, secure adults are more likely to share personal information when appropriate (Garrison, Kahn, Sauer, & Florczak, 2012; Tidwell, Reis, & Shaver, 1996).

This kind of relationship is very different from one with an avoidant adult. People with an avoidant attachment style are hampered by a fear of intimacy and problems with jealousy (Levy & Kelly, 2010; Spielmann, Maxwell, MacDonald, & Baratta, 2013). They tend to believe that real romance rarely lasts forever and that the kind of head-over-heels love depicted in movies and romance novels doesn't really exist. As a result, they are less likely than most people to show affection or share intimacy with their partners (Collins, Cooper, Albino, & Allard, 2002). And, because they are hesitant to become deeply committed to a relationship, they may be more vulnerable to cheating on their partners (DeWall, et al., 2011). Not surprisingly, 43% of the undergraduate students classified with an avoidant attachment style in one study said they had never been in love (Feeney, Noller, & Patty, 1993).

In contrast, people with an anxious-ambivalent attachment style fall in love many times but have difficulty finding the long-term happiness they desperately seek (Hazan & Shaver, 1987; Rholes, Simpson, Campbell, & Grich, 2001). These people are afraid of losing their partner and are quick to give in to the partner's wishes in an effort to keep him or her happy (Pistole, 1989). College students in one study watched their dating partners evaluate the physical attractiveness of other people (Simpson, Ickes, & Grich, 1999). The anxious-ambivalent participants were particularly likely to feel their relationship was threatened by the experience. Yet, like the newborns in the original research, both avoidant and anxious-ambivalent adults experienced heightened stress when separated from their romantic partners (Feeney & Kirkpatrick, 1996). Anxious-ambivalent people are also more likely to fall in love with someone who does not love them in return (Aron, Aron, & Allen, 1998). But because they fear abandonment or perhaps because they believe they don't deserve a better relationship, these individuals are less likely to break up with a partner who fails to meet their needs (Slotter & Finkel, 2009).

The effects of attachment style are likely to surface when couples face stress in their relationships. Romantic partners in one study were asked to discuss for 15 minutes an unresolved issue in their relationship (Powers, Pietromonaco, Gunlicks, & Sayer, 2006). Secure participants experienced fewer physiological indicators of stress as the conversation progressed than did insecure participants. For insecure individuals, even small relationship issues can be threatening. Insecure partners tend to see more conflict in their relationships than do secure partners (Campbell, Simpson, Boldry, & Kashy, 2005) and become more upset when they perceive small slights from their partners, such as not being comforted when they are feeling down (Collins, Ford, Guichard, & Allard, 2006).

One team of researchers asked couples in airport lounges to complete an attachment style inventory (Fraley & Shaver, 1998). The investigators then watched surreptitiously and coded various behaviors (e.g., hugs, eye contact, sitting close) while the couples waited for the departure. As expected, secure partners showed signs of closeness when one of them was leaving. In contrast, avoidant participants showed signs of pulling away from their partners as the departure approached. Presumably, these avoidant adults were experiencing anxiety and fear related to the impending separation from their partners.

Avoidant individuals also have difficulty giving and seeking emotional support from their partners just when they need support the most. This pattern has been found in a series of laboratory studies that look at couples' reactions to stress (Collins & Feeney, 2000; Feeney & Collins, 2001; Simpson, Rholes, Orina, & Grich, 2002). Women in one study were told they would soon be going through an anxiety-provoking experience involving an isolation chamber and some threatening electronic equipment (Simpson, Rholes, & Nelligan, 1992). Whereas secure women sought more comfort from their partners as their anxiety increased, avoidant women wanted less support when they became anxious. Secure male partners in this study offered more emotional support when their partners expressed anxiety, but avoidant men did not.

Before closing the door on this research, we should offer a bit of optimism to those who fear they might not have a secure attachment style. Although, like other personality variables, attachment style is relatively stable over time (Fraley, Vicary, Brumbaugh, & Roisman, 2011), it may be possible for people to change their attachment style when they enter a secure, long-lasting adult relationship (Carnelley, Pietromonaco, & Jaffe, 1994; Davila, Karney, & Bradbury, 1999). Specifically, a loving and trusting adult relationship may provide the secure working model some people were denied as children. Thirty percent of the young women in one study changed their attachment style classification over a 2-year span (Davila, Burge, & Hammen, 1997). This observation suggests that attachment style may not be as set early in life as Bowlby and others suggested. It also makes it difficult to know whether relationships last because people have secure attachment styles or whether people develop secure attachment styles because their relationships last.

Summary

1. People do not passively accept their discomfort when faced with an anxiety-provoking situation. Instead, each of us has learned to take steps to reduce that anxiety. Researchers divide these coping strategies into active and avoidant categories and into those that focus on the problem and those that deal with the emotional reaction. Which of these strategies will be more effective in reducing anxiety depends on the availability of means to solve the problem.

2. Researchers have applied many psychoanalytic concepts to understanding the causes and consequences of aggression. Studies find that frustration is a source of aggression, but not all frustrating events lead to aggression. Recent models suggest that frustration causes aggression because it is unpleasant. Other studies find that frustration-induced aggression can be displaced onto innocent targets. In addition, the widely held belief that aggression leads to catharsis and less aggression has not been supported in empirical investigations. Allowing people to act out their aggressive impulses appears to increase, not decrease, the likelihood of further aggression.

3. Researchers use concepts from object relations theory and attachment theory to explain adult romantic relationships. Based on the works of John Bowlby and Mary Ainsworth, investigators can identify adult attachment styles that presumably stem from early parent–child relationships. Researchers find adults with secure, avoidant, and anxious-ambivalent attachment styles approach and participate in romantic relationships differently.

Key Terms

avoidance strategies (p. 129)

coping strategies (p. 127)

emotion-focused strategies (p. 129)

problem-focused strategies (p. 129)

Media Resources

Visit the book companion website at **www.cengagebrain.com** to find a glossary, flashcards, quizzing, and more.

CHAPTER 7

The Trait Approach

Theory, Application, and Assessment

Suppose for the moment that, like many college freshmen living in on-campus housing, you have been assigned a roommate you don't know. A few weeks before classes, your new roommate sends you an e-mail message. After saying hello and introducing himself or herself, your roommate asks: "What kind of person are you?" Describing your physical features is relatively easy and giving facts about your hometown or number of siblings takes almost no time at all. But how do you describe your personality to someone you have never met?

If you are like most people, you probably tackle this problem in one of two ways. You might start by describing the type of person you are—a quiet type, an independent type, an outgoing type. The other strategy is to describe your characteristics—studious, shy, friendly. In either case, you would be using a rough variation of the trait approach to personality. That is, you would be identifying relatively stable features of your personality that distinguish you from other individuals.

People have tried to describe personality for probably about as long as humans have used language. Gordon Allport (1961), one of the original trait theorists, counted more than 4,000 adjectives in the English language that can be used for this purpose. Thus an early challenge for personality psychologists was combining all these characteristics into a usable structure. Some of the first attempts to identify and describe personality were *typology* systems. The goal was to discover how many types of people there are and identify each person's type. The ancient Greeks divided people into four types: sanguine (happy), melancholic (unhappy), choleric (temperamental), and phlegmatic (apathetic). Another early effort identified three basic personality types based on general physique: endomorphic (obese), mesomorphic (muscular), and ectomorphic (fragile). The three types were said to differ in personality as well as physical appearance (Sheldon, 1942).

Today personality researchers have largely abandoned typologies. The problem is that several assumptions underlying the approach cannot be justified. A typology assumes that each of us fits into one personality category and that all people within a category are basically alike. Further, the approach assumes that the behavior of people in one category is distinctly different from the behavior of people in other categories. You can't be a little of category A and a little of B. You must be either A or B. These assumptions simply don't stand up to empirical scrutiny. Although typologies are still popular outside of academia (zodiac signs, for instance), psychologists have replaced the type approach with the trait approach.

The Trait Approach

Almost any personality characteristic you can think of—optimism, self-esteem, achievement motivation—can be illustrated with the trait continuum shown in Figure 7.1. Several important characteristics about the trait approach are depicted in this simple diagram. First, trait psychologists identify characteristics that can be represented along a continuum. For example, achievement motivation can range from little interest in achieving at one

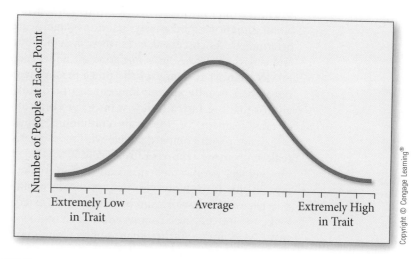

Number of People at Each Point

Extremely Low
in Trait

Average

Extremely High
in Trait

FIGURE 7.1 Trait Continuum

extreme to highly driven persistence at the other. Second, trait psychologists maintain that we can take any person and place him or her somewhere along the continuum. We are all more or less aggressive, more or less friendly, and so on. Finally, if we were to measure a large number of people and place their scores at appropriate points along the continuum, we probably would find that the scores are normally distributed; that is, they would form the well-known bell curve. Relatively few people score extremely high or extremely low. Instead, most of us fall somewhere toward the middle of the distribution.

A **trait** is a dimension of personality used to categorize people according to the degree to which they manifest a particular characteristic. The trait approach to personality is built on two important assumptions. First, trait psychologists assume that personality characteristics are relatively stable over time. It would make little sense to describe someone as high in sociability if that person loved being around people one day but shied away from social settings the next. Of course, we all have times we prefer to be alone and other times we seek out friends. But if we were to examine a given individual's behavior over a long period of time, we should see a relatively stable level of sociability. Someone who tends to be highly sociable today will probably tend to be sociable next month, next year, and many years down the road. This is not to say that personality does not change. Researchers find that our personalities continue to develop as we move through adulthood and into old age (Bleidorn, Kandler, Reimann, Angleitner, & Spinath, 2009; Roberts & Mroczek, 2008; Roberts, Walton, & Viechtbauer, 2006). However, these changes are gradual and typically evolve over a period of many years.

The second assumption underlying the trait approach is that personality characteristics are stable across situations. Aggressive people should exhibit higher-than-average amounts of aggression during family disagreements as well as when playing football. Again, we all act more aggressively in some situations than in others. But the trait approach assumes that over many different situations a relatively stable average degree of aggressiveness can be determined. As discussed later, these assumptions of trait stability over time and across situations have not gone unchallenged.

In contrast to many of the other perspectives covered in this book, trait researchers usually are *not* interested in predicting one person's behavior in a given situation. Instead, they want to predict how people who score within a certain segment of the trait continuum typically behave. Thus a trait researcher might compare people who score relatively high on a social anxiety scale with those who score relatively low. The investigators might find that, on average, people high in social anxiety make less eye contact than those low on this trait. However, they probably would not attempt to predict any one person's behavior. Surely a few high-anxiety people in the study would make a lot of eye contact and a few low-anxiety participants would make very little. Rather than singling out one individual, the researchers' goal would be to identify how the average person in either of these two groups acts.

It is also important to note that the significance of a person's score on a trait measure lies in how that individual compares with other people. When we say someone is feminine, we are saying only that the person is more feminine than most people. It is important to keep this notion in mind when interpreting the personality test scores. Test takers who, for example, think of themselves as outgoing are sometimes surprised to learn that they score in the middle of the distribution on a measure of extraversion. The score does not mean that these people are not sociable or that they don't enjoy parties. But it does suggest that they probably are not as extraverted as many other people who have taken the same personality test.

Finally, unlike most other approaches to personality, no major schools of psychotherapy have evolved from the trait approach to personality. Information collected by trait researchers can be useful to therapists making diagnoses and charting progress during therapy. In addition, many of the characteristics examined by trait researchers, such as self-esteem and social anxiety, are relevant to a client's well-being. But research findings on personality traits typically provide only a direction for how to change people who may be too high or too low on a personality dimension. Trait psychologists are more likely to be academic researchers than practicing therapists.

Important Trait Theorists

You will notice references to traits and trait measures scattered throughout most of the chapters in this book. This is testimony to how widely accepted the trait concept has become in personality psychology. Personality psychologists from nearly every approach, as well as researchers from many other fields of psychology, use traits and trait measures in their work. The expansion of the trait approach from virtually nothing less than a century ago to its prominent influence today can be attributed in part to the pioneering work of some early trait theorists.

Gordon Allport

The first recognized work on traits by a psychologist did not appear until 1921. That was the year Gordon Allport, along with his brother Floyd, published *Personality Traits: Their Classification and Measurement*. Gordon Allport also taught what is believed to be the first college course on personality in the United States, in 1925 (Nicholson, 1997). Only one year after receiving his bachelor's degree, the unconventional Allport somehow managed to arrange a meeting with Sigmund Freud. Allport wanted to talk psychology, but Freud spent much of the time inquiring about Allport's unconscious motives. As far as Allport was concerned, there were obvious, conscious reasons for his behavior. But Freud's limited orientation wouldn't allow him to see the obvious. "Psychologists would do well," Allport concluded from the visit, "to give full recognition to manifest motives before probing the unconscious" (1968, p. 384).

> *"Dispositions are never wholly consistent. What a bore it would be if they were—and what chaos if they were not at all consistent."*
>
> GORDON ALLPORT

Unlike Freud, whom he accused of blindly adhering to psychoanalytic theory, Allport acknowledged the limitations of the trait concept from the beginning. He accepted that behavior is influenced by a variety of environmental factors and recognized that traits are not useful for predicting what a single individual will do. Allport also believed that our traits have physical components in our nervous systems and predicted that scientists would one day develop technology advanced enough to identify personality traits by examining neurological structures.

Allport identified two general strategies researchers might use when investigating personality. So far, we have described traits and trait research along the lines of what Allport called the *nomothetic approach*. Researchers using this approach assume that all people can be described along a single dimension according to their level of, for example, assertiveness or anxiety. Each person in a study using the nomothetic approach is tested to see how his or her score for the given trait compares with the scores of other participants. Allport referred to these traits that presumably apply to everyone as *common traits*.

Allport called nomothetic research "indispensable" for understanding human personality. But he also championed another way to research personality that is often ignored. Rather than forcing all people into categories selected beforehand, researchers using the *idiographic approach* identify the unique combination of traits that best accounts for the personality of a single individual. To illustrate Allport's point, take a few minutes to list 5 to 10 traits you believe are the most important in describing your behavior. Have a friend do the same for himself or herself, and then compare your answers. You will most likely discover that the two of you have compiled very different lists. You may have used *independent* or *genuine* to describe yourself, but it may not have occurred to your friend to think in terms of independence or genuineness. Similarly, the traits your friend came up with might never have crossed your mind when you wrote your self-description.

Allport referred to these 5 to 10 traits that best describe an individual's personality as *central traits*. If you want to understand one particular person, Allport recommended that you first determine the central traits for this

Gordon Allport

1897–1967

Bettmann/CORBIS

Gordon Allport was born in Montezuma, Indiana, to a family with three older brothers, including 7-year-old Floyd. Even as a child, Gordon did not fit in. "I was quick with words, poor at games," he wrote. "When I was ten a schoolmate said of me, 'Aw, that guy swallowed a dictionary' " (1967, p. 4). Allport was persuaded by his brother Floyd to attend Harvard. This was the beginning of an academic and professional shadow in which the younger Allport was to spend many of his early adult years. Not only did Gordon follow his brother to both undergraduate and graduate degrees at Harvard, but he also chose Floyd's field of study, psychology. Floyd was the teaching assistant for Gordon's first psychology class. Later, Gordon took a course in experimental psychology from his brother, served as a participant in some of his research, and helped him with the editing of the *Journal of Abnormal and Social Psychology.*

But Gordon soon developed a very different view of psychology. Floyd was a social psychologist who went on to achieve substantial recognition in that field. However, Gordon had different ideas about the best way to understand human behavior. In graduate school Allport once again felt different from the other psychology students. "Unlike most of my student colleagues," he wrote, "I had no giftedness in natural science, mathematics, mechanics (laboratory manipulations), nor in biological or medical specialties" (1967, p. 8). After confessing these feelings to one of his professors, he was told, "But you know, there are many branches of psychology."

"I think this casual remark saved me," Allport later reflected. "In effect he was encouraging me to find my own way in the ... pastures of psychology" (1967, p. 8). This he did, despite much early resistance to his notion of personality traits. Perhaps the earliest of these confrontations came in graduate school when Allport was given 3 minutes to present his research ideas at a seminar at Clark University in front of the famous psychologist Edward Titchener. His presentation about personality traits was followed by total silence. Later, Titchener asked Allport's adviser: "Why did you let him work on that problem?"

But Allport was not discouraged. He went on to a distinguished career, most of it at Harvard. His 1937 book, *Personality: A Psychological Interpretation,* outlined his theory of personality traits and was well received by many psychologists. Two years later, Allport was elected president of the American Psychological Association. In 1964 he received the prestigious Distinguished Scientific Contribution Award from that same organization.

Allport's decision to wander off into different pastures of psychology was appropriate for the man who promoted the idea of individual differences. This decision also took him out of his brother's shadow, perhaps best symbolized when Gordon later became editor of the *Journal of Abnormal and Social Psychology* himself. He identified his confrontation with Titchener as a turning point in his career. "Never since that time have I been troubled by rebukes or professional slights directed at my maverick interests," he said. "Later, of course, the field of personality became not only acceptable, but highly fashionable" (1967, p. 9).

individual and then decide where he or she falls on each of these dimensions. Although the number of central traits varies from person to person, Allport proposed that occasionally a single trait will dominate a personality. These rare individuals can be described with a *cardinal trait*. Allport pointed to historical figures whose behavior was so dominated by a single trait that the behavior became synonymous with the individual. Thus we speak of people who are *Machiavellian, Homeric,* or *Don Juans.*

The advantage of using the idiographic approach is that the person, not the researcher, determines what traits to examine. With the nomothetic approach, the traits selected by the investigator might be central for some people, but only what Allport called *secondary traits* for others. A test score indicating a person's level of sociability is of great value when sociability is a central trait for that person, but of limited value when it is not. Allport employed the idiographic approach in his study of an elderly woman who used the pseudonym Jenny Masterson. In his book *Letters from Jenny,* Allport (1965) examined more than 300 letters written by Jenny over a 12-year period. Allport identified eight of the woman's central traits with this method. Although time-consuming, this procedure allowed for a much more enlightening portrait of Jenny than could have been obtained from a few test scores on some preselected dimensions.

Allport also was interested in the concept of "self," particularly the process by which children develop a sense of themselves. Like his work on personality traits, at the time Allport's writings about the self represented new territory for the discipline. Today the self occupies a central role in many personality theories and is the focus of a large amount of research by personality and developmental psychologists. We will touch on some of that work when we examine the humanistic (Chapters 11 and 12) and cognitive (Chapters 15 and 16) approaches to personality.

> "*Personality, like every other living thing, changes as it grows.*"
> GORDON ALLPORT

Henry Murray

Unlike Gordon Allport, who rejected much of psychoanalytic theory, Henry Murray's approach to personality was a blend of psychoanalytic and trait concepts. Early in his career, Murray had the opportunity to interact extensively with Carl Jung. As a result, Murray's writings are filled with references to the unconscious. The psychoanalytic influence on Murray's work also can be seen in one of his principal contributions to the field of personality, the *Thematic Apperception Test* (TAT). As described in Chapter 3, the TAT is a projective measure designed to get at material not readily accessible to conscious thought.

Murray called his approach *personology* and identified needs as the basic elements of personality. He was not very concerned with *viscerogenic needs,* such as the need for food and water. Rather, his work focused on *psychogenic needs,* which he described as a "readiness to respond in a certain way under certain given conditions" (1938, p. 124). In keeping with his psychoanalytic background, Murray postulated that these needs are largely unconscious. Murray eventually arrived at a list of 27 psychogenic needs, including the need for Autonomy, the need for Achievement, the need for Dominance, and the need for Order.

According to Murray, each of us can be described in terms of a personal hierarchy of needs. For example, if you have a strong need for a lot of close friends, you would be said to have a high need for Affiliation. The importance of this need is not so much how it compares with the Affiliation needs of other people but how intense it is compared to your other needs. Suppose

Henry Murray

1893–1988

Bettmann/Corbis

There is little in Henry Murray's background to suggest that he would become a psychologist or that he would come to be recognized as an influential personality theorist. In his own words, "[my] record consisted of nothing but items which correlated negatively … with the records of the vast majority of professional psychologists" (1967, p. 286). Murray attended one psychology lecture as an undergraduate. He found it boring and walked out. He earned his bachelor's degree in history in 1915, followed by a medical degree from Columbia in 1919. After working a few years in embryology, Murray went to Cambridge University in England, where he earned a doctorate in biochemistry in 1927.

How does a biochemist become an important personality theorist? During the latter years of his academic training, Murray was exposed to and enthusiastically embraced the writings of Carl Jung. He was particularly impressed with Jung's description of psychological types. In 1925, while studying in England, he arranged to meet with Jung in Vienna. His conversations with Jung persuaded Murray that his real interests were in the budding field of psychology. After working at the Harvard Psychological Clinic and receiving formal psychoanalytic training, Murray accepted a position at Harvard, where he taught until his retirement in 1962.

Like most turns in his career, Murray was struck by the improbability of becoming a lecturer in psychology. Not only did he have a relatively weak background in psychology, he also was a stutterer. Nonetheless, Murray's academic career was long and successful. But Murray's commitment to psychology did not end his professional diversity. He took a brief break from academia in 1943 when he was recruited by the Office of Strategic Services, a forerunner of the Central Intelligence Agency. His job was to apply personality in the selection of undercover agents. Murray also became something of a literary scholar, although he confessed once that "in school, [I] had received [my] consistently worst marks in English" (p. 286). He had a particular passion for the writings of Herman Melville and became an authority on Melville's life. Murray died in 1988 at the age of 95.

you have a big test tomorrow, but your friends are having a party tonight. If your Achievement need is higher on your personal hierarchy than your need for Affiliation or your need for Play, you'll probably stay with your books. If your Achievement need, although high, is not quite as strong as these other needs, your grade will probably suffer.

Murray recognized that whether a need is activated depends on the situation, which he called the *press*. For example, your need for Order won't affect your behavior without an appropriate press, such as a messy room. If you have a strong need for Order, you probably make time to clean your room even when it is only slightly disheveled. If you have a relatively weak need for Order, you might wait until the room is too messy to move around in—and even then the cleaning might be motivated more by a need to please your roommates than to see things arranged neatly.

In addition to the TAT, Murray's principal legacy to the field of personality is the research stimulated by his theory. Several of Murray's psychogenic needs have been subjected to extensive research, often by his students who went on to become important personality researchers in their own right. Among the more widely studied are the need for Power, the need for Affiliation, and as presented in Chapter 8, the need for Achievement.

Factor Analysis and the Search for the Structure of Personality

Alongside Allport and Murray, we find another pioneer of the trait approach, Raymond Cattell. Unlike many theorists, Cattell did not begin with insightful notions about the elements that make up human personality. Rather, he borrowed an approach taken by other sciences. Notably, Cattell's first college degree was in chemistry. Cattell argued that just as chemists did not begin by guessing what chemical elements might exist, psychologists should not begin with a preconceived list of personality traits.

Much of Cattell's work was devoted to discovering just how many basic personality traits there are. Psychologists have identified, measured, and researched hundreds of traits. But certainly many of these traits are related. For example, being sociable is not entirely different from being extraverted, although we can point to some fine distinctions. In his quest to discover the structure of human personality, Cattell employed a statistical technique called **factor analysis**. Although a complete understanding of the procedure is beyond the scope of this book, an example can illustrate how researchers use factor analysis to determine the number of basic personality traits.

Suppose you had tests to measure the following 10 traits: aspiration, compassion, cooperativeness, determination, endurance, friendliness, kindliness, persistence, productivity, and tenderness. You could give these tests to a group of people and obtain 10 scores per person. You might then use correlation coefficients (Chapter 2) to examine how scores on one test compare with scores on the other nine tests. For example, you might find that friendliness and tenderness scores are highly correlated. If a person scores high on one test, you can predict with some confidence that the person also will score high on the other test. Looking at the pattern of correlation coefficients, you might discover that the tests tend to cluster into two groups. That is, five of the tests are highly correlated with one another, but not with the other five tests. These other five tests are similarly correlated among themselves, but not with the tests in the first group. The two groups might look something like this:

Group A	*Group B*
aspiration	compassion
determination	cooperativeness
endurance	friendliness
persistence	kindliness
productivity	tenderness

Although you originally measured 10 traits, a reasonable conclusion would be that you actually measured two larger personality dimensions, one having to do with achievement and the other with interpersonal warmth. This is a simple illustration of Cattell's basic approach. By analyzing data from various sources with factor analyses, he attempted to determine how many of these basic elements exist. He called the basic traits that make up the human personality *source traits*.

Unfortunately, the data obtained from factor analysis typically are not as neat and clear-cut as this example suggests. If they were, we would have determined the number of source traits a long time ago. One serious limitation of factor analysis is that the procedure is confined by the type of data chosen for analysis. For example, what would happen if you took a few tests out of the previous example and inserted a few new ones, such as *independence, absentmindedness,* and *honesty*? Most likely, this would change the number of categories (called factors) and the traits associated with them (or, in factor analytic terms, "loaded on" them).

In response to this problem, Cattell looked at information about personality from many different sources. He examined data from records, such as report cards and ratings by employers, data about how people act when placed in lifelike situations, and data from personality questionnaires. He called these three *L-data, T-data,* and *Q-data.* Cattell identified 16 basic traits in his research and in 1949 published the first version of the Sixteen Personality Factor Questionnaire (16 PF) to measure these traits. A revised version of the 16 PF remains a widely used personality inventory today (Cattell, 2004; Cattell & Mead, 2008).

The Big Five

Efforts to identify and describe the basic dimensions of personality did not end with Cattell's original model. Rather, this question has been an ongoing issue in personality research for decades. One particularly interesting study often lost in the long history of this research was conducted by Donald Fiske (1949). In the summer of 1947, Fiske and his colleagues conducted extensive personality assessment of 128 men who had been admitted into the Veteran Administration's clinical psychology training program. In addition to many standard trait measures, the assessment included projective tests, biographical data, interviews, and ratings from peers. When the researchers factor analyzed all these data, they identified five basic personality factors. They described these five factors as *Social Adaptability* (talkative, makes good company), *Emotional Control* (easily upset, has sustained anxieties), *Conformity* (ready to cooperate, conscientious), *The Inquiring Intellect* (intellectual curiosity, an exploring mind), and *Confident Self-Expression* (cheerful, not selfish). Although the data were not quite as clean as these labels suggest, as we will see, the findings foreshadowed the direction personality research would take decades later.

Cattell, Fiske, and the other pioneers in this area were limited by some practical concerns. They had to calculate the extensive mathematical computations required of factor analysis by hand and, of course, double check each decimal point and each carried number. Personality researchers today have the benefit of larger and more varied sets of data, sophisticated statistical

TABLE 7.1 The Big Five Personality Factors

Factor	Characteristics
Neuroticism	Worried versus calm Insecure versus secure Self-pitying versus self-satisfied
Extraversion	Sociable versus retiring Fun-loving versus sober Affectionate versus reserved
Openness	Imaginative versus down-to-earth Preference for variety versus preference for routine Independent versus conforming
Agreeableness	Softhearted versus ruthless Trusting versus suspicious Helpful versus uncooperative
Conscientiousness	Well organized versus disorganized Careful versus careless Self-disciplined versus weak willed

tests, and—most important—computers that conduct extensive calculations quickly and accurately. These developments led to a burgeoning amount of research and a surprisingly consistent pattern in the findings. Although there may never be complete agreement, different teams of investigators using many different kinds of data repeatedly found evidence for five basic dimensions of personality (Digman, 1990; Goldberg, 1992; John, Nauman, & Soto, 2008; McCrae & Costa, 1997, 2008). Some disagreements remain, but researchers looking at the structure of personality typically uncover five basic factors that look like the ones listed in Table 7.1.

The five factors described in the table have shown up in so many studies using a variety of methods that researchers now refer to them as the **Big Five**. Remember, these investigators did not begin with a theory about how many factors they would find or what these basic dimensions of personality would look like. Rather, they let the data do the talking. Once researchers saw which traits clustered with one another, they had to come up with descriptive terms for the five dimensions. Although different researchers sometimes use different names, the most commonly used terms are Neuroticism, Extraversion, Openness, Agreeableness, and Conscientiousness. Alert students have recognized that the beginning letters of the five labels cover the OCEAN of human personality.

The *Neuroticism* dimension places people along a continuum according to their emotional stability and personal adjustment. People who frequently experience emotional distress and wide swings in emotions will score high on measures of Neuroticism. People high in Neuroticism tend to become more upset over daily stressors than those low on this dimension and are more vulnerable to bouts of anxiety and depression (Gunthert, Cohen, & Armeli, 1999; Kotov, Gamez, Schmidt, & Watson, 2010; Lahey, 2009). Although

Raymond B. Cattell

1905–1998

Cattell Estate

Raymond Cattell spent most of his childhood by the sea in the resort town of Torquay in the south of England. There he developed a life-long love for the ocean and sailing. Unfortunately, this happy child-hood was interrupted when England entered World War I. Cattell suddenly found himself treating wounded and maimed soldiers in a makeshift wartime hospital. He did not realize until many years later how these experiences would one day affect his choice of careers. Cattell won a scholarship to the University of London, the only member of his family to attend college. A few months before he graduated with honors in chemistry, images of the wounded soldiers returned to him. Suddenly his plans for a career in the physical sciences were no longer appealing. At about the same time, Cattell was impressed with a lecture he attended by the famous psychologist Cyril Burt, who argued that the science of psychology offered the best hope for solving many of society's problems (Horn, 2001).

"My laboratory bench began to seem small and the world's problems vast," Cattell wrote. "Gradually I concluded that to get beyond human irrationalities one had to study the workings of the mind itself" (1974, p. 64).

His decision to study psychology, which "was then regarded, not without grounds, as a subject for cranks," led him to graduate work at London University. There Cattell—and psychology—stumbled into a fortunate association. Cattell was hired as a research assistant for the famous psychologist and mathematician Charles Spearman, who was studying the relationship between measures of intelligence. Spearman found evidence for a single general concept of intelligence, as compared to models arguing for many unrelated aptitudes. In the course of this research, Spearman developed the statistical procedure known as factor analysis. Cattell would later use factor analysis to understand the structure of personality.

After 5 years working at various clinics in England, Cattell was tempted to come to the United States by an offer to work with the learning theorist E. L. Thorndike at Columbia. He also worked at Clark University until Gordon Allport invited him to join the faculty at Harvard in 1941. It was at Harvard, while working alongside Allport and Henry Murray, that Cattell developed the idea that factor analysis could be a useful tool for personality researchers (Raymond B. Cattell, 1997). He put this insight into practice after joining the faculty at the University of Illinois in 1945, where he spent most of his career.

Cattell was always a hard worker, sometimes going into his office on Christmas day. The result of this diligence was 56 books and more than 500 research articles. His decision to study personality clearly was psychology's gain and physical science's loss.

there are many different kinds of negative emotions—sadness, anger, anxiety, guilt—that may have different causes and require different treatments, research consistently shows that people prone to one kind of negative emotional state often experience others (Costa & McCrae, 1992). Individuals low in Neuroticism tend to be calm, well adjusted, and not prone to extreme emotional reactions.

The second personality dimension, *Extraversion,* places extreme extraverts at one end and extreme introverts at the other. Extraverts are very sociable people who also tend to be energetic, optimistic, friendly, and assertive. Introverts do not typically express these characteristics, but it would be incorrect to say that they are asocial or without energy. As one team of researchers explained, "Introverts are reserved rather than unfriendly, independent rather than followers, even-paced rather than sluggish" (Costa & McCrae, 1992, p. 15). As you might imagine, studies find that extraverts have more friends and spend more time in social situations than introverts (Asendorpf & Wilpers, 1998; Selfhout, et al., 2010; van der Linden, Scholte, Cillessen, te Nijenhuis, & Segers, 2010).

The *Openness* dimension refers to openness to experience rather than openness in an interpersonal sense. The characteristics that make up this dimension include an active imagination, a willingness to consider new ideas, divergent thinking, and intellectual curiosity. People high in Openness are unconventional and independent thinkers. Those low in Openness tend to prefer the familiar rather than seeking out something new. Given this description, it is not surprising that innovative scientists and creative artists tend to be high in Openness (Feist, 1998; Rubinstein & Strul, 2007). Some researchers refer to this dimension as *Intellect*, although it is certainly not the same as intelligence.

People who are high on the *Agreeableness* dimension are helpful, trusting, and sympathetic. Those on the other end tend to be antagonistic and skeptical. Agreeable people prefer cooperation over competition. In contrast, people low in Agreeableness like to fight for their interests and beliefs. Researchers find that people high in Agreeableness have more pleasant social interactions and fewer quarrelsome exchanges than those low on this dimension (Donnellan, Conger, & Bryant, 2004; Jensen-Campbell & Graziano, 2001; Malouff, Thorsteinsson, Schutte, Bhullar, & Rooke, 2010). They also are more willing to help those in need (Graziano &Habashi, 2010).

The *Conscientiousness* dimension refers to how controlled and self-disciplined we are. People on the high end of this dimension are organized, plan oriented, and determined. Those on the low end are apt to be careless, easily distracted from tasks, and undependable. Little wonder that those low in Conscientiousness tend to have more automobile accidents (Arthur & Graziano, 1996). In fact, researchers find that people high in Conscientiousness typically live longer than those low on this dimension (Hill, Turiano, Hurd, Mroczek, & Roberts, 2011). Because the characteristics that define Conscientiousness often show up in achievement or work situations, some researchers have referred to this dimension as *Will to Achieve* or simply *Work*.

Many researchers have been impressed with the pervasiveness of the Big Five regardless of how personality is measured. Of course, the five factors show up when researchers look at responses to self-report trait inventories. But researchers also find evidence for five basic factors when looking at other indicators of personality, such as the terms people use to describe their friends and acquaintances (Watson, Hubbard, & Wiese, 2000) and the way teachers describe their students (Digman & Inouye, 1986; Goldberg, 2001). The five factors also emerge in studies with elementary school children (Markey, Markey, Tinsley, & Ericksen, 2002; Measelle, John, Ablow, Cowan, & Cowan, 2005) and appear to be fairly stable over time

Assessing Your Own Personality

Conscientiousness

Indicate the extent to which each of the following terms describes you. Use a 9-point scale to indicate your response, with 1 = Extremely Inaccurate and 9 = Extremely Accurate.

_____ Careful   _____ Negligent*

_____ Careless*   _____ Organized

_____ Conscientious   _____ Practical

_____ Disorganized*   _____ Prompt

_____ Efficient   _____ Sloppy*

_____ Haphazard*   _____ Steady

_____ Inconsistent*   _____ Systematic

_____ Inefficient*   _____ Thorough

_____ Impractical*   _____ Undependable*

_____ Neat   _____ Unsystematic*

This scale was developed by Goldberg (1992) to measure Conscientiousness, one of the Big Five personality dimensions. Although different scoring procedures are possible, the most straightforward procedure is as follows (Arthur & Graziano, 1996): Reverse the answer values for the 10 items with an asterisk (that is, for these items only, 1 = 9, 2 = 8, 3 = 7, 4 = 6, 5 = 5, 6 = 4, 7 = 3, 8 = 2, 9 = 1). Then add all 20 answer values. Arthur and Graziano (1996) report a mean score of 123.11 for a sample of college students, with a standard deviation of 23.99.

*Scale: Big Five Factor Markers for Conscientiousness

(Terracciano, Costa, & McCrae, 2006; Vaidya, Gray, Haig, & Watson, 2002). One team of researchers used college student interviews and questionnaire data from 1939 to 1944 to determine Big Five scores (Soldz & Vaillant, 1999). These scores correlated highly with scores on Big Five measures participants completed when they were 45 years older. In short, evidence from many different sources indicates that the many traits comprising our personalities can be organized along five basic personality dimensions.

Ongoing Questions Related to the Big Five Model

Although research on the five-factor model has produced impressively consistent findings and an unusually high level of agreement among personality researchers, several questions about the model remain. First, there is some debate about what the five factors mean. For example, these factors may simply represent five dimensions built into our language. That is, although personality may in reality have a very different structure, our ability to describe personality traits is limited to the adjectives available to us, which may fall into five primary categories. It also may be the case that our cognitive ability to organize information about ourselves and others is limited to these five dimensions. Thus, although people may describe personality as if all traits can be subsumed under five factors, this model may not accurately capture the complexities and subtleties of human personality.

In response to these concerns, many researchers have looked at the structure of personality among people who speak languages other than English (McCrae et al., 2004, 2005a, 2005b). Although a few exceptions to the rule are found, the results from numerous studies indicate that the five-factor model does not merely reflect the structure of the English language but appears to be a universal pattern for describing personality.

Second, there remains some disagreement about the structure of the five-factor model (Ashton, Lee, Goldberg, & de Vries, 2009). Some factor analytic studies find patterns that do not fit well within the five-factor structure. In recent years, researchers have on occasion found evidence for seven (Simms, 2007), six (Ashton & Lee, 2007), three (De Raad, et al., 2010), two (Simsek, Koydemir, & Schutz, 2012), and even one (Loehlin, 2012) basic factor(s).

Some of the confusion about the number of personality dimensions goes back to the question of what kind of data to include in the factor analysis (McCrae & Costa, 1995). For example, most studies finding five factors do not include traits that are evaluative, such as *special* or *immoral*. When these terms are included, researchers sometimes find additional personality factors (Almagor, Tellegen, & Waller, 1995; Benet-Martinez & Waller, 1997). Beyond this, a few personality descriptors simply do not fit well within the five-factor model. These maverick traits include *religiousness, youthfulness, frugality, humor, and cunning* (MacDonald, 2000; Paunonen & Jackson, 2000; Piedmont, 1999; Saucier & Goldberg, 1998).

Different research outcomes may also reflect differences in how broadly or narrowly investigators conceive of personality structure. That is, if we think of personality structure in very broad terms, it may be possible to combine some of the Big Five factors to create a smaller number of dimensions. Similarly, if we want finer distinctions, we can probably divide some of the factors into smaller parts and thereby create a larger number of dimensions. Thus, it is not the case that one investigator's findings contradict another investigator's results. On the contrary, the similarities between the factor patterns uncovered using different methods and different populations are really quite remarkable (McCrae, 2001). Indeed, one would be hard-pressed to find many examples of such consistent findings within the field of personality research.

Third, many researchers have looked into the stability of the five factors over time. That is, do our personalities change as we age? The answer appears to be "yes and no." Let's start with the *no*. Researchers who follow individuals over long periods of time generally find that our personalities become fairly stable during our 20s and show little sign of change after the age of 30 (Costa & McCrae, 2006; Ferguson, 2010; Terracciano, McCrae, & Costa, 2010). That is, how you score on measures of the Big Five personality dimensions during your early adulthood is likely to be quite similar to how you will score on those same measures 20, 30, or 40 years from now.

On the other hand, researchers sometimes find general trends in Big Five scores over the lifespan (Roberts, Walton, & Viechtbauer, 2006; Soto, John, Gosling, & Potter, 2011; Specht, Egloff, & Schmukle, 2011). That is, even though a strong extravert is unlikely to ever become an introvert, people may experience small shifts along some of the dimensions as they age. Although to date research findings are not as consistent as we would like, we can identify a few general patterns (Anusic, Lucas, & Donnellan, 2012; Soto, et al., 2011). Older adults tend to be higher than younger adults in Conscientiousness and Agreeableness. People also tend to become lower in Neuroticism as they move through adulthood. However, no consistent patterns for age-related changes have been found for Extraversion or Openness.

Fourth, there are questions about when to use scores from Big Five measures versus scores from specific trait scales. That is, would psychologists be better off relying on only five main traits instead of the hundreds of smaller traits they now use? In most cases, the answer is "No." Examining a specific trait is usually better for predicting relevant behaviors than measuring a global personality dimension (Mershon & Gorsuch, 1988; Paunonen, 1998; Paunonen & Ashton, 2001). For example, being sociable and being adventurous may be part of the larger personality concept of Extraversion. However, if researchers want to understand how people act in social situations, it is probably more useful to examine their sociability scores than to measure the more general dimension of Extraversion. This is exactly what researchers found when they looked at cooperative and competitive behavior (Wolfe & Kasmer, 1988). Although Extraversion scores predicted who would act cooperatively and who would act competitively, researchers obtained even better predictions when they looked at scores for sociability.

Another example makes the point even clearer. Scales designed to measure the Big Five personality dimensions usually combine subscales measuring anxiety with subscales measuring depression as part of the global dimension Neuroticism. Although it makes sense that both anxiety and depression contribute to this larger dimension, surely psychotherapists and researchers would want to know whether their clients and participants suffer more from one of these emotional difficulties than the other.

This is not to say that understanding where an individual falls on the basic five dimensions is not useful. On the contrary, research suggests that the Big Five model can be valuable for diagnosing clinical disorders and working with therapy patients (Lamers, Westerhof, Kovacs, & Bohlmeijer, 2012; Widiger & Costa, 2013) and for identifying problem health behaviors (Booth-Kewley & Vickers, 1994; Marshall, Wortman, Vickers, Kusulas, & Hervig, 1994). In addition, as you will see later in this chapter, how people score on measures of the Big Five dimensions is often related to how they perform on the job.

The Situation Versus Trait Controversy

The trait concept has come a long way since Allport's early battles to gain acceptance for his theory. Trait measures have been embraced by psychologists from nearly every perspective and used by professionals working in a wide variety of settings. Patients admitted to mental health facilities often spend hours taking tests that yield scores on a variety of traitlike measures. Educators commonly use achievement and aptitude measures to classify children and identify problem cases. Anyone who has gone through the American education system in recent years can recall many such tests, often beginning in the first grade. And for several decades now, academic personality researchers have been busy developing trait measures and correlating scores with a number of behaviors.

Criticism of the Trait Approach

"Can personality psychologists predict behavior? Yes, of course we can—sometimes."

WALTER MISCHEL

Unfortunately, along with the widespread use of personality measurement comes the possibility of abuse. More than 40 years ago, one psychologist in particular criticized the way many psychologists were using and interpreting test scores. Walter Mischel (1968) pointed out that too many psychologists relied on one or two scores to make important decisions, such as psychiatric diagnoses or whether an individual should be imprisoned. Although critics accused Mischel of denying the existence of personality traits, he argues that this was never his point (Mischel, 1973, 1990, 2009). Mischel maintains his complaint was with the overinterpretation of personality test scores.

As a result of the discussion and debate that ensued, most psychologists today are aware of the dangers of overreliance on test scores. Psychologists who might have once used a single test score now consider information from a number of relevant sources before making diagnoses or recommending a certain type of education program. Although the trait approach today is as strong as it has ever been (Swann & Seyle, 2005), Mischel and other critics raised important questions about some of its key assumptions. It is useful to look at two of these criticisms in particular, as well as the responses trait researchers gave in their defense. First, critics argued that trait measures, as well as other types of test scores, do not predict behavior as well as many psychologists claim. Second, critics maintained that there is little evidence for the consistency of behavior across situations.

Trait Measures Do Not Predict Behavior Well

At the heart of this argument is the issue of whether personality or the situation determines your behavior. Do you act the way you do because of the situation you are in or because of the kind of person you are? Advocates on one extreme side of this debate argue that our behavior is almost entirely determined by the situation. Although these psychologists don't assert that everyone acts the same in a given setting, they often refer to individual differences in behavior as merely "error variance." Advocates on the other extreme claim that stable individual differences are the primary determinants of how we act.

Early in this debate, some psychologists sought an answer to the person-versus-situation question by measuring how well personality scores and situations predict people's behavior. Typically, this research found that both the person and the situation were related to behavior and that knowing about personality *and* the situation was better than having information about only one (Endler & Hunt, 1966, 1968). Unfortunately, this approach has a major weakness. The results of any such investigation are limited by the type of situation and the kind of personality variable examined. For example, we can think of situations in which nearly all people react the same. It would be absurd to try to predict whether high- or low-self-esteem people will run outside when a building catches fire. Although the situation would account for nearly all of the variance in this case, it also would be incorrect to conclude that differences in self-esteem are therefore not related to behavior. If we look at other behaviors in other situations, such as how people react to criticism, we will probably find large differences between high- and low-self-esteem people.

Today, most psychologists agree that the person and the situation interact to determine behavior (Funder, 2009). Knowing that a person is high in aggressiveness or that a particular situation is frustrating helps researchers predict behavior less well than knowing both of these facts. Thus, although people high in aggressiveness may be more prone to act aggressively than those scoring low on this dimension, and frustrating situations are more likely to produce aggression than are nonfrustrating situations, researchers would expect the highest amount of aggression when an aggressive person is placed in a frustrating situation. This way of looking at the relationship among traits, situations, and behaviors is called the **person-by-situation approach**.

Nonetheless, arguments remain over the validity of using personality trait scores to predict behavior. Mischel pointed out that personality trait scores rarely correlate with measures of behavior above the .30 or .40 correlation coefficient level. This "personality coefficient," as it is derogatorily called, statistically accounts for only about 10% of the variance in behavior. Although these numbers confirm that personality is related to behavior, a considerable amount of behavior remains that single trait scores do not explain.

There Is Little Evidence for Cross-Situational Consistency

In one of the earliest studies on personality traits, a research team spent several years looking at honesty in more than 8,000 elementary school children (Hartshorne & May, 1928). They measured honesty 23 different ways (lying, cheating, stealing, and so on) and found an average intercorrelation among these measures of only .23. Because personality traits are assumed to show some consistency across situations, this finding was widely cited as a challenge to the trait approach. Knowing that a child is honest in one situation, such as telling the truth to a parent, may reveal little about whether the child will cheat on the playground or steal something from another child's desk.

Mischel also challenged the evidence for cross-situational consistency in traits. Although people appear to show fairly strong consistency in behavior across situations, Mischel referred to this as "more apparent than real."

For many reasons, we tend to see consistent behavior that, on close examination, is not really there. For example, people often see what they expect to see. If you expect Karen to be unfriendly, you tend to notice when she insults someone but ignore the times when she pays a compliment. In addition, we typically see people in only one type of situation or role and fail to fully realize the extent to which the situation, not the person, is responsible for the behavior. Students are sometimes surprised to find that their stuffy, conservative professor is a fun-loving, adventurous person outside the classroom. And sometimes the way we treat people causes them to act more consistently than they otherwise might. If you assume Ron is going to be hostile, you will probably approach him in such a confrontational way that he will react with hostility. For all of these reasons, we may see people acting more consistently across situations than they really are.

In Defense of Personality Traits

Naturally, attacks on something as central to personality theory as the use of traits have not gone unchallenged. Responses to Mischel's criticisms center around the question of how behaviors and traits are measured and the importance of the variance these traits explain.

Measuring Behavior

Proponents of the trait approach argue that, on the surface, denying the existence of personality traits is absurd (Epstein, 1980, 1983). If behavior were completely inconsistent over time and across situations, how would we know whom to marry or whom to hire? Without predictable behavior patterns, we might as well marry someone at random because our spouse's behavior will change from day to day depending on the situation.

Trait psychologists argue that researchers often fail to produce strong links between personality traits and behavior because they don't measure behavior correctly. The typical investigation held up by critics uses trait scores to predict only one measure of behavior. For example, investigators might measure the number of minutes spent on an activity or ask people to indicate on a 7-point scale the likelihood that they will volunteer for a charity drive. This approach violates a basic concept in psychological testing. A behavior score based on one item or one measure is so low in reliability that it is almost impossible to find a correlation with any test score higher than the .30 to .40 "personality coefficient."

To understand this principle, think about why a final examination would never consist of just one true-false question. A student who knows the material might miss one particular item for any number of reasons. But over the course of, say, 50 items, the student who knows the material is likely to get a higher score than the student who does not. In psychometric terms, the 50-item test has greater internal consistency and is thus a better indicator of the student's knowledge. Unfortunately, at the time Mischel launched his attack, many trait studies measured behavior with what were essentially one-item tests. A personality trait may be a good predictor of behavior, but psychologists will never know if they don't measure behavior reliably.

As an alternative to one-item measurement, researchers can *aggregate* data. For example, if you want to measure how much time students spend studying, you'll obtain a much better score by observing their behavior each night over the course of a few weeks than by observing just one night. Consider a study in which scores on an extraversion scale were used to predict social behavior (Epstein, 1979). Undergraduates in this study recorded the number of social contacts they initiated each day. Although we would expect extraverts to initiate more social contacts than introverts, the researchers found an insignificant correlation between any one day's total of social contacts and extraversion scores. However, when the researchers looked at the relation between the scale score and the student's 2-week total of initiated social contacts, they found an impressive correlation of .52. Another investigation looked at trait measures of aggression and the number of aggressive acts students performed (e.g., getting into an argument, yelling at someone) over the course of 2 weeks (Wu & Clark, 2003). The researchers found a correlation of .51 between the aggregated aggression measure and the trait score.

Identifying Relevant Traits

Another reason personality trait measures usually fail to break the .30 to .40 barrier is that researchers may be looking at the wrong traits. Recall Allport's distinction between central and secondary traits. A trait is more likely to predict a person's behavior if that trait is important, or central, for the person. Suppose you were interested in the trait *independence*. You might give an independence scale to a large number of people, and then correlate the scores with how independently people acted in some subsequent situation. But in doing this, you probably would group together those people for whom independence is an important (central) trait and those for whom it is a relatively unimportant (secondary) trait. You undoubtedly would do a better job of predicting independent behavior by limiting your sample to people who consider independence an important personality dimension. By including people for whom the trait is only secondary, you are likely to dilute the correlation between the trait score and the behavior (Britt & Shepperd, 1999).

To illustrate this problem, one team of researchers identified people who were either fairly consistent or relatively inconsistent in two kinds of behavior, friendliness and conscientiousness (Bem & Allen, 1974). Some personality researchers refer to these two groups as *traited* and *untraited* people because the personality trait is either an important one for them or insignificant. The goal of this study was to predict six measures of friendly behavior (e.g., how friendly the participant was while waiting for the experiment to begin) and six measures of conscientiousness (e.g., how well the student kept up with class readings). As Table 7.2 shows, correlation coefficients obtained for high-consistency people and low-consistency people showed a noticeably different pattern. Correlations between measures of friendliness averaged .57 for the consistent (traited) participants, but only .27 for the inconsistent (untraited) ones. Similarly, correlations for the conscientiousness data averaged .45 for the high-consistency participants and .09 for the low-consistency people. Similar findings are found when researchers separate traited and untraited participants

TABLE 7.2 Mean Correlations Between Trait Measures in High- and Low-Consistency Participants

	High-Consistency Participants	Low-Consistency Participants
Friendliness Measures		
Self-report	.57	.39
Mother's report	.59	.30
Father's report	.60	.16
Peer's report	.54	.37
Group discussion	.52	37
Spontaneous friendliness	.59	.01
All friendliness variables	.57	.27
Conscientiousness Measures		
Self-report	.41	.11
Mother's report	.56	.10
Father's report	.49	.22
Peer's report	.49	.16
Returning evaluations	.40	.06
Course readings	.32	−.12
All conscientiousness variables	.45	.09

Source: From Bem, D. J., and Allen, A. (1974). On predicting some of the people some of the time: The search for cross-situational consistencies in behavior. *Psychological Review*, 81, 506–520.

on other personality measures (Baumeister,1991; Baumeister & Tice, 1988; Britt, 1993; Reise & Waller, 1993; Siem, 1998).

The Importance of 10% of the Variance

Another argument on the side of personality traits concerns the significance of .30 to .40 correlation coefficients. Critics have attacked trait theory on the basis of the weak relationship between trait measures and behavior. But how high does a correlation have to be before it is considered important? One team of researchers answered this question by looking at several social-psychological (situation-focused) investigations often cited for their "important" findings (Funder & Ozer, 1983). The researchers converted the data from these studies into correlation coefficients and found they ranged from .36 to .42. In short, the "important" effects of situational variables are, statistically speaking, no more important than the effects deemed weak by critics of personality traits.

Yet another way to examine the importance of these correlations is to compare the amount of variance accounted for in personality research with results from other fields. One psychologist looked at some highly acclaimed research in the field of medicine (Rosenthal, 1990). One large medical study he examined made headlines when researchers found that aspirin significantly reduced the risk of heart attacks. In fact, the investigators ended the experiment earlier than planned because the results were so clear. To continue to give one group of patients placebo pills instead of aspirin would have been unethical. Obviously, the researchers considered this an important finding. Yet when we examine the data, we find that the medical researchers were dealing with a correlation of around .03, which accounted for less than 1% of the variance! Another team of investigators looked at the relation between personality measures and important life events like mortality, divorce, and success at work (Roberts, Kuncel, Shiner, Caspi, & Goldberg, 2007). Not only were personality traits significant predictors of these events, but they accounted for as much or more variance than either socioeconomic status or cognitive ability (e.g., IQ), two concepts typically considered to be important determinants of behavior.

The point is that importance is a subjective judgment. When dealing with medical treatments, reliably saving a relatively small number of lives is important. When trying to predict behavior from personality test scores, we must remember that most of the behaviors we are interested in are determined by a large number of causes. No one will ever discover a single cause for why people suffer from schizophrenia or why consumers buy one product over another. Rather, the goal of most studies is to account for *some* of the variance. When we think about all the complex influences on our behavior, we probably should be impressed that personality psychologists can explain even 10%.

Application: The Big Five in the Workplace

Imagine you own your own business and have to make a quick hiring decision. You have five applications on your desk, all nearly identical. You notice that each applicant's file includes some personality test scores. Specifically, you have scores for each job candidate on each of the Big Five personality dimensions. A quick glance through the applications tells you that each applicant has one score that distinguishes him or her from the rest of the pack. One applicant is high in Extraversion, another scored very low on Neuroticism, and one is notably high in Openness. Predictably, another applicant is especially high in Agreeableness, whereas the final applicant's distinguishing score is his or her high level of Conscientiousness. Time is running out, and you have to make your decision based on this information alone. Looking back at the descriptions of the Big Five factors on pages 161–163 which of these five people do you suppose you will hire? Of course, the answer to the question depends on the kind of job and many other important variables. But if you had to make a quick decision based on this limited amount of information, you might consider a growing body of research that in fact points to the best answer.

Employers have used scores from personality tests to make hiring and promotion decisions for many years (Roberts & Hogan, 2001). And for just about the same length of time, critics have complained that employers misuse and misinterpret personality test scores when making these decisions. Just as

Mischel criticized clinical psychologists for relying too heavily on test scores to make diagnoses about psychological disorders, these critics point to research indicating low correlations between test scores and job performance (Reilly & Chao, 1982; Schmidt, Gooding, Noe, & Kirsch, 1984).

But the debate about using personality tests to predict success in the workplace changed with the development of the Big Five model (Goldberg, 1993; Landy, Shankster, & Kohler, 1994). Rather than examine a large number of personality variables that may or may not be related to how well people perform their jobs, researchers addressed the question of personality and job performance by using the five larger personality dimensions. The findings from that research provided much stronger evidence for the relationship between personality and job performance than had been previously demonstrated (Tett, Jackson, & Rothstein, 1991).

So, which of the five applicants is likely to make the best employee? Although a case can be made for each of the five, a great deal of research indicates that, of the Big Five factors, Conscientiousness may be the best predictor of job performance (Barrick & Mount, 1991; Barrick, Mount, & Judge, 2001; Hurtz & Donovan, 2000; Salgado, 1997). To understand why, we need only look at some of the characteristics that make up this personality dimension. People who score high in Conscientiousness are said to be careful, thorough, and dependable. That is, they don't rush through a job but take time to do the job correctly and completely. Highly conscientious people tend to be organized and to lay out plans before starting a big project. These individuals also are hardworking, persistent, and achievement oriented.

It's not difficult to see why people who exhibit this combination of traits make great employees. Researchers in one study looked at the way sales representatives for a large appliance manufacturer did their jobs (Barrick, Mount, & Strauss, 1993). As in other studies, the investigators found Conscientiousness scores were fairly good predictors of how many appliances the employees sold. But a closer examination of the work styles of these salespeople helped to explain their success. Highly conscientious workers set higher goals for themselves than did the other employees. From the beginning they had their eyes on fairly ambitious end-of-the-year sales figures. In addition, these highly conscientious salespeople were more committed to reaching their goals than were other workers. That is, they were more likely to expend extra effort to hit their targets and were more persistent when faced with the inevitable obstacles and downturns that got in their way.

In short, there are many reasons a person high in Conscientiousness would make an excellent employee. As one team of investigators put it, "It is difficult to conceive of a job in which the traits associated with the Conscientiousness dimension would not contribute to job success" (Barrick & Mount, 1991, pp. 21–22). And these efforts do not go unnoticed. Highly conscientious employees typically receive higher evaluations from their supervisors (Barrick et al., 1993). Moreover, one study found that workers who scored high on Conscientiousness were among the least likely to lose their jobs when companies were forced to lay off employees (Barrick, Mount, & Strauss, 1994). Not surprisingly, highly conscientious people do better in college (Kappe & van der Flier, 2010; Poropat, 2009; Richardson, Abraham, & Bond, 2012) and in their careers (Judge, Higgins, Thoresen, & Barrick, 1999) than people low on this dimension.

This is not to say that Conscientiousness is the only Big Five dimension related to job performance. On the contrary, a strong case can be made for hiring people high in Agreeableness (Tett et al., 1991). These individuals are trusting, cooperative, and helpful. They are pleasant to have around the office and probably work especially well in jobs calling for teamwork. Other studies indicate that extraverts often have an edge in the business world over introverts and that openness to experience can be beneficial in some job settings (Barrick & Mount, 1991; Caldwell & Burger, 1998; Mount, Barrick, & Strauss, 1994; Tett et al., 1991). In sum, knowing where an applicant falls on the Big Five personality dimensions may be useful when making a hiring decision.

Nonetheless, one caveat is in order. Although research relating Big Five personality characteristics and job performance has been encouraging, it would be an egregious oversimplification to conclude that one should always hire the person highest in Conscientiousness. Personality may account for a significant proportion of job performance variance, but it is only one of many important variables that contribute to how well an individual performs his or her job. Just as it is inappropriate to base decisions about mental health or education solely on personality test scores, making hiring and promotion decisions on test score data alone is unwise and unfair.

Assessment: Self-Report Inventories

It is unlikely you have reached college age without taking a number of self-report inventories. You may have received interest and abilities tests from a counselor, achievement and aptitude tests from a teacher, or personality and diagnostic inventories from a therapist. You may have even tried a few of those magazine quizzes for your own entertainment and curiosity. Self-report inventories are the most widely used form of personality assessment. Typically, these tests ask people to respond to a series of questions about themselves. Relatively simple scoring procedures allow the tester to generate a score or a set of scores that can be compared with others along a trait continuum. Over the years, hundreds if not thousands of self-report inventories have been created, some carefully constructed with attention to reliability and validity, others not.

Self-report inventories are popular among professional psychologists for several reasons. They can be given in groups or even online and can be administered quickly and easily by someone with relatively little training. Contrast this experience with the Rorschach inkblot test, which must be administered and interpreted by a trained psychologist one test at a time. Scoring a self-report inventory is also relatively easy and objective. Researchers typically count matched items or total response values. Self-report measures also are popular because they usually have greater face validity than other instruments. That is, we can be reasonably confident from looking at the items on a self-esteem test that they actually measure self-esteem. Although face validity alone does not establish the value of a test (Chapter 2), psychologists are less likely to disagree about what the test is measuring when the intent of the items is so obvious.

Self-report inventories come in all forms and sizes. Some have fewer than 10 items, others more than 500. Some provide detailed computer analyses on a number of subscales and comparison groups, others a single score for a specific trait dimension. Self-report inventories are used by researchers investigating individual differences, personnel managers making hiring decisions, and clinical psychologists getting a quick profile of their client's personality to aid in making diagnoses.

The Minnesota Multiphasic Personality Inventory

The prototypic self-report inventory used by clinical psychologists is the Minnesota Multiphasic Personality Inventory (MMPI). The original MMPI was developed in the late 1930s. A revised version of the scale, the MMPI-2, was published in 1989. A large number of clinical psychologists, counseling psychologists, personnel psychologists, and school psychologists give the MMPI-2 regularly to their patients and clients.

The MMPI-2 contains 567 true-false items. These items generate several scale scores that are combined to form an overall profile of the test taker. The original scales were designed to measure psychological disorders. Thus psychologists obtain scores for such dimensions as *depression, hysteria, paranoia,* and *schizophrenia.* However, most psychologists look at the overall pattern of scores rather than one specific scale when making their assessments. Of particular interest are scores that are significantly higher or lower than those obtained by most test takers. A sample profile is shown in Figure 7.2.

Many additional scales have been developed since the original MMPI scales were presented. Researchers interested in a particular disorder or concept usually determine those items that separate a normal population from the group they are interested in. For example, to develop a creativity scale, you would identify test items that highly creative people tend to answer differently from people who are not very creative.

For many years the MMPI (and now the MMPI-2) has ranked among the most widely used clinical assessment tools (Camara, Nathan, & Puente, 2000; Piotrowski & Keller, 1989; Watkins, Campbell, Nieberding, & Hallmark, 1995). One survey found nearly universal agreement among directors of graduate programs in clinical psychology that the MMPI-2 should be part of a clinical student's training (Piotrowski & Zalewski, 1993). The scale has also been used in an enormous amount of research (Butcher, 2006). However, this does not mean the MMPI-2 is without its critics. Psychologists continue to debate the validity of some scales, the appropriateness of some of the norm data provided by the test makers, and the nature of some of the constructs the test is designed to measure, among other issues (Helmes & Reddon, 1993). As you will see in the following section, scores from self-report inventories are not as easy to interpret as the seemingly precise and objective numbers generated from these tests sometimes suggest.

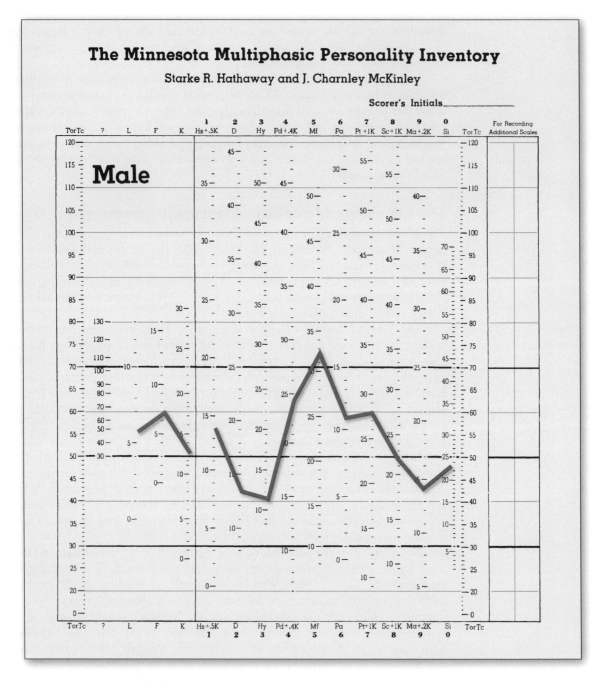

FIGURE 7.2 Sample MMPI Profile

The scales identified by numbers 1 through 0 are Hypochondriasis, Depression, Hysteria, Psychopathic Deviancy, Masculinity—Femininity, Paranoia, Psychasthenia (anxiety), Schizophrenia, Mania, and Social Introversion.

Source: Minnesota Multiphasic Personality Inventory Profile Form. Copyright 1943, 1948, (renewed 1970), 1976, 1982 by the Regents of the University of Minnesota. All rights reserved. Reprinted by permission of the University of Minnesota Press.

Problems with Self-Report Inventories

Despite their widespread use, self-report inventories have several limitations that need to be considered when constructing a scale or interpreting test scores. Researchers who use self-report inventories still must depend on participants' ability and willingness to provide accurate information about themselves. Sometimes these inaccuracies can be identified and test scores discarded, but more often the misinformation probably goes undetected. Clinical psychologists who rely too heavily on self-report measures run the risk of making inaccurate assessments of their clients' mental health (Shedler, Mayman, & Manis, 1993).

Faking

Sometimes test takers intentionally give misleading information on self-report inventories. Some people "fake good" when taking a test. This means they try to present themselves as better than they really are. This strategy is not uncommon when scales are used to make employment decisions (Rosse, Stecher, Miller, & Levin, 1998). Why would applicants admit something negative about themselves if an employer is using that information to decide whom to hire? On the other hand, sometimes people are motivated to "fake bad." These test takers want to make themselves look worse than they really are. A person who wants to escape to a "safe" hospital environment might try to come across as someone with psychological problems.

What can a tester do in these cases? To start, important decisions probably should not be made on test data alone. An employer would be foolish to promote a worker who scores high on a leadership measure if that person has never shown leadership qualities in 5 years of employment. Beyond this, test makers sometimes build safeguards into tests to reduce faking. If possible, the purpose of a test can be made less obvious, and filler items can be added to throw the test taker off track. However, these efforts are probably, at most, only partially successful. Another option is to test for faking directly (Bagby, Rogers, Nicholson, Buis, Seeman, & Rector, 1997; Nelson, Sweet, & Demakis, 2006; Nicholson, Mouton, Bagby, Buis, Peterson, & Buigas, 1997). Like many large personality inventories, the MMPI contains scales designed to detect faking. To create these scales, test makers compare responses of people instructed to fake good or fake bad with the responses of other populations. Test makers find certain items distinguish between fakers and, for example, genuine schizophrenics. People trying to look schizophrenic tend to check these items, thinking they indicate a psychological disorder, but real schizophrenics do not. When testers detect faking, they can either throw out the results or adjust the scores to account for the faking tendency. However, some psychologists challenge the usefulness of relying on these methods to obtain accurate scores (Piedmont, McCrae, Riemann, & Angleitner, 2000).

Carelessness and Sabotage

Although the person administering a test usually approaches the session very seriously, this cannot always be said for the test taker. Participants in experiments and newly admitted patients can get bored with long tests and not bother to read the test items carefully. Sometimes they don't want to admit to poor reading skills or their failure to fully understand the instructions. As a result, responses may be selected randomly or after only very briefly skimming the question. Moreover, this problem is not limited to poorly educated individuals. Researchers in one study allowed university students taking a standard personality test to indicate when they did not know the meaning of a word (Graziano, Jensen-Campbell, Steele, & Hair, 1998). The investigators found that some test questions were not understood by as many as 32% of the students.

Even worse, test takers sometimes report frivolous or intentionally incorrect information to sabotage a research project or diagnosis. I once found a test answer booklet that appeared normal at first, but at second glance discovered that the test taker had spent the hour-long research session filling in answer spaces to form obscene words. A similar lack of cooperation is not uncommon among those who resent medical personnel or law enforcement officials.

The best defense against this problem may be to explain instructions thoroughly, stress the importance of the test, and maintain some kind of surveillance throughout the testing session. Beyond this, tests can be constructed to detect carelessness. For example, some tests present items more than once. The tester examines the repeated items to determine if the test taker is answering consistently. A person who responds A one time and B the next when answering two identical items might not be reading the item or might be sabotaging the test.

Response Tendencies

Before reading this section, you may want to take the test presented on page 181. This test is designed to measure a response tendency called **social desirability**—the extent to which people present themselves in a favorable light. This is not the same as faking, in which people answer test items in a manner they know is inaccurate. People high in social desirability unintentionally present themselves in a way that is slightly more favorable than the truth. A look at the items on the scale illustrates the point. Few of us can say we have never covered up our mistakes. Yet someone who only rarely covers up mistakes might exaggerate the truth slightly and indicate that this statement is true for him or her. What can be done about this mild deception? By measuring social desirability tendencies directly, a tester can adjust the interpretation of other scores accordingly. When social desirability scores are especially high, researchers sometimes drop participants from the study. However, the extent to which social desirability undermines the validity of psychological tests and whether adjusting scores actually improves the validity of the test remain a matter of debate (McGrath, Mitchell, Kim, & Hough, 2010; Paunonen & LeBel, 2012).

Social desirability scores are also useful when testing the discriminant validity of a new personality scale (Chapter 2). Suppose you developed a self-report inventory to measure the trait *friendliness*. Most of your items would be fairly straightforward, such as "Do you make a good friend?" High scores on this

Gao Kao: The World's Largest Test

The use of entrance exams in admission decisions by American universities and colleges has been the subject of debate for decades. At the heart of this issue is the question of validity, that is, what do exams like the SAT and the ACT really measure? Are they valid indicators of a student's academic potential? Critics also raise questions about fairness. They point to test score differences based on gender, ethnicity, parent's income, and parent's education. These concerns have led several prominent universities to no longer consider entrance exam scores when evaluating prospective students (Wilner, 2013). And a commission created by the National Association for College Admission Counseling recommended that colleges and universities reduce their reliance on entrance exam scores when making admission and financial aid decisions (Rimer, 2008). Researchers continue to examine the validity of the tests for predicting academic performance (Sackett, Kuncel, Arneson, Cooper, & Waters, 2009). But there is general agreement among psychologists and educators that admission decisions should be based on more than test scores.

This trend stands in sharp contrast to the situation in China. Each summer more than nine million students take China's National College Entrance Examination, which is known as the *gao kao* (the "big" or "high" test). Scores on the 9-hour test are the single determinant of which students are admitted to Chinese universities. Higher scores earn admission to more prestigious institutions. Regardless of other achievements or skills, students whose scores fall in the bottom 25% have to take the test again if they want to go to college in China. Because a college degree is the only hope most Chinese have for obtaining a good paying, white-collar job, the pressure to do well is intense (LaFraniere, 2009).

The *gao kao* is offered only once a year, but students spend months and sometimes years preparing for the test. In large cities, police cordon off streets near test sites so that test takers are not disturbed by traffic noise, and airplanes that might fly overhead are rerouted (McDonald, 2012). In some areas, police are barred from using their sirens during testing hours and some cities halt construction

projects at night so that test takers can get a good night's sleep (Siegel, 2007). Parents often stand outside keeping vigil during the test. Although the competition for admission into the best Chinese universities is intense, the situation is better now than when the test was reinstated in 1977. That year nearly six million students competed for only 220,000 university spots (Siegel, 2007).

As in the United States, the Chinese entrance exam has its critics. Some Chinese educators complain that the test emphasizes memorization over problem solving and creativity (Siegel, 2007). Issues of fairness have also been raised. Students from rural areas tend to perform more poorly on the *gao kao* than urban students who typically receive a superior education (Wong, 2012). Despite these concerns, no one expects the system to change any time soon.

On the morning of the gao kao, after countless hours of preparation, many test takers eat a special breakfast—a bread stick next to two eggs. The meal is said to symbolize 100%, the hoped-for score on the test.

test might reflect an underlying trait of friendliness, but they might also reflect the test takers' desire to present themselves as nice people. For this reason, test makers often compare scores on their new inventory with scores on a social desirability measure. If the two are highly correlated, test makers have no way to know which of the two traits their test is measuring. However, if scores on your new friendliness inventory do not correlate highly with social desirability scores, you would have more confidence that high scorers are genuinely friendly people and not just those who want to be seen that way.

But presenting oneself in a favorable light is not the only response tendency testers have to worry about. Some people are more likely than others to agree with test questions. If you ask these people "Do you work a little harder when given a difficult task?" they probably will say "Yes." If you ask them a little later "Do you usually give up when you find a task difficult?" they will probably say "Yes" again. This *acquiescence* (or *agreement*) response can translate into a problem on some self-report scales. If the score for the trait is simply the number of "true" or "agree" answers on a scale, someone with a strong acquiescence tendency would score high on the scale regardless of the content of the items. Moreover, people susceptible to an acquiescence response tendency tend to differ from other test takers on several personality dimensions (Knowles & Nathan, 1997) and the response tendency may affect some personality scales more than others (Rammstedt & Kemper, 2011). Thus, if not accounted for, the tendency for some people to agree with test items could distort the meaning of scores on the personality test. Just how seriously acquiescence response tendencies affect test scores is still a matter of debate (Paulhus, 1991). However, to be safe, many test makers word half the items in the opposite manner. That is, sometimes "agree" is indicative of the trait, and sometimes "disagree" is. In this case, any tendency to agree or disagree with statements should not affect the final score.

Strengths and Criticisms of the Trait Approach

In many ways, the trait approach to personality is different from the other approaches examined in this book. Trait theorists tend to be academic researchers instead of therapists. Their focus is on describing and predicting behavior rather than on behavior change or development. In addition, trait researchers rarely try to understand the behavior of just one person. These differences give the trait approach some unique advantages, but they are also the source of criticism.

Strengths

The empirical nature of the work by Allport, Murray, and other early trait psychologists sets them apart from the founders of most personality theories. Rather than relying on intuition and subjective judgment as did Freud and many of the neo-Freudians, these trait theorists used objective measures to examine their constructs. Cattell specifically allowed the data to determine the theory, which was then subject to further empirical validation. This approach reduces some of the biases and subjectivity that plague other approaches.

Another strength of the trait approach is its many practical applications. Mental health workers routinely use trait measures when evaluating clients. Similarly, many educational psychologists have embraced trait measures in their work. Psychologists working in industrial and organizational settings often use personality trait measures in hiring and promotion decisions. Job counselors frequently rely on trait scores to match clients with careers.

●●● Assessing Your Own Personality

Response Tendencies

Indicate the extent to which you agree with each of the following statements. Use a 7-point scale to indicate your response, with 1 = Not True and 7 = Very True.

_____ 1. I sometimes tell lies if I have to.*

_____ 2. I never cover up my mistakes.

_____ 3. There have been occasions when I have taken advantage of someone.*

_____ 4. I never swear.

_____ 5. I sometimes try to get even rather than forgive and forget.*

_____ 6. I always obey laws, even if I'm unlikely to get caught.

_____ 7. I have said something bad about a friend behind his or her back.*

_____ 8. When I hear people talking privately, I avoid listening.

_____ 9. I have received too much change from a salesperson without telling him or her.*

_____ 10. I always declare everything at customs.

_____ 11. When I was young, I sometimes stole things.*

_____ 12. I have never dropped litter on the street.

_____ 13. I sometimes drive faster than the speed limit.*

_____ 14. I never read sexy books or magazines.

_____ 15. I have done things that I don't tell other people about.*

_____ 16. I never take things that don't belong to me.

_____ 17. I have taken sick-leave from work or school even though I wasn't really sick.*

_____ 18. I have never damaged a library book or store merchandise without reporting it.

_____ 19. I have some pretty awful habits.*

_____ 20. I don't gossip about other people's business.

This scale was designed to detect a social desirability response tendency. To obtain your score, give yourself one point for each 1 or 2 response to odd-numbered items (the ones with asterisks) and one point for each 6 or 7 response to even-numbered items. The test developer found a mean score of 4.9 and a standard deviation of 3.2 for female college students, and a mean score of 4.3 and a standard deviation of 3.1 for male college students. People who score high on this measure tend to present themselves in an overly favorable light.

*Scale: The Impression Management Scale from the Balanced Inventory of Desirable Responding

Source: From Lockard, J. S. and D. L. Paulhus (Ed.). *Self-Deception: An Adaptive Mechanism.* Prentice-Hall, 1988.

Although this widespread use of trait measures invites abuse if scores are used incorrectly, the popularity of these measures attests to the value many psychologists place on them.

Like any important theoretical perspective, the trait approach has generated a large amount of research. Personality journals are filled with investigations about a variety of personality traits. Predicting behavior from personality trait measures has become a standard feature in research by clinical, social, industrial-organizational, educational, and developmental psychologists.

Criticisms

Criticisms of the trait approach are often based not so much on what the approach says but on what it leaves out. Trait psychologists describe people in terms of traits, but they often do not explain how these traits develop or what can be done to help people who suffer from extreme scores. Knowing about these scores can help teachers and employers match people with the tasks and jobs best suited to them, but no schools of psychotherapy have originated from the trait approach.

Another criticism concerns the lack of an agreed-upon framework. Although all trait theorists use empirical methods and are concerned with the identification of traits, no single theory or underlying structure ties all the theories together. We can see the confusion this creates by asking how many basic traits there are. Murray reduced personality to 27 psychogenic needs. Cattell found 16 basic elements of personality. More recent investigations suggest the number is really 5, and a few studies even challenge this figure. Although research continues to determine which of these models is correct, without an agreed-upon framework, it is difficult to gain a cohesive overview of the approach or to see how research on one aspect of personality traits fits with research in other areas.

Summary

1. The trait approach assumes we can identify individual differences in behaviors that are relatively stable across situations and over time. Trait theorists are usually not concerned with any one person's behavior but rather with describing behavior typical of people at certain points along a trait continuum.

2. Gordon Allport was the first acknowledged trait theorist. Among his contributions were the notions of central and secondary traits, nomothetic versus idiographic research, and descriptions of the self. Henry Murray identified psychogenic needs as the basic elements of personality. According to Murray, a need will affect behavior depending on where it lies on a person's need hierarchy and the kind of situation the person is in.

3. Raymond Cattell was interested in identifying the basic structure of personality. He used a statistical procedure called factor analysis to

determine how many basic traits make up human personality. More recent research provides fairly consistent evidence that personality is structured along five basic dimensions. Although questions remain, the evidence to date tends to support the five-factor model.

4. An enduring controversy in personality concerns the relative importance of traits compared to situational determinants of behavior. Critics have charged that traits do not predict behavior well and that there is little evidence for cross-situational consistency. Trait advocates have answered that if traits and behaviors are measured correctly, a significant relationship can be found. In addition, they maintain that the amount of behavior variance explained by traits is considerable and important.

5. The development of the five-factor model renewed interest in the relationship between personality and job performance. Although several of the Big Five dimensions are related to performance in the business world, many studies indicate that Conscientiousness may be the best predictor of performance.

6. Trait researchers typically rely on self-report assessment procedures in their work. One of the most commonly used self-report inventories is the Minnesota Multiphasic Personality Inventory. Test users need to be aware of problems inherent in self-report inventories. These include faking, carelessness and sabotage, and response tendencies.

7. Like other approaches to personality, the trait approach has strengths and is subject to criticisms. The strengths include a strong empirical base, a host of practical applications, and the large amount of research generated. Criticisms include the limited usefulness of the approach for dealing with problem behaviors and the lack of an agreed-upon framework.

Key Terms

Big Five (p. 161)

factor analysis (p. 159)

person-by-situation approach (p. 168)

social desirability (p. 178)

trait (p. 153)

Media Resources

Visit the book companion website at **www.cengagebrain.com** to find a glossary, flashcards, quizzing, and more.

The Trait Approach

Relevant Research

I recently took some time to conduct a brief, partially scientific survey. I examined the three most recent issues of the *Journal of Personality*, the *Journal of Research in Personality*, and the personality section of the *Journal of Personality and Social Psychology*. These journals are prominent outlets for current research on personality. Of the 45 articles with empirical studies I found in these journals, 40 included at least one trait measure. That is, in 88.9% of these studies, researchers measured individual differences and used these scores either to compare people who fell on different parts of a trait continuum or to predict scores on another measure. This finding supports an assertion I have made for a while: The trait approach has become so entrenched in personality research today that, for many psychologists, personality research is synonymous with measuring and examining traits. A more rigorous study than mine found that the use of trait measures in personality research not only is extensive but has steadily increased over the past few decades (Swann & Seyle, 2005). Using trait measures has become so widespread that it is part of the research arsenal for experimenters in all of the approaches to personality covered in this book. In addition, if you were to conduct a similar survey of research journals in developmental psychology, social psychology, clinical psychology, industrial-organizational psychology, and other fields, I suspect you would find a liberal use of trait measures.

Although personality researchers have studied dozens and dozens of traits in depth, we'll look at five areas of research that illustrate the breadth and depth of the trait approach. We first examine research on achievement and achievement motivation. Then we'll examine a personality concept that came to the attention of trait researchers via the medical community. The Type A behavior pattern and measures of hostility have been used by medical professionals to identify candidates for heart disease. We'll also look at how personality research helps psychologists understand a common interpersonal problem, namely social anxiety or shyness. Next, we examine research on individual differences in emotions. Although our emotions vary depending on the events we encounter, personality psychologists can identify relatively stable patterns in how we experience and express our feelings. Finally, we look at research on optimism and pessimism. That work suggests that how typically optimistic or pessimistic we are in our approach to life has many important implications.

Achievement Motivation

Look at the picture on page 187. What is happening? Who do you think this person might be? Think of a story that might be told about him. How is the story resolved? There are no right or wrong answers to these questions. One person might see a man deep in thought, weighing all the possible solutions to an important problem, on his way to accomplishing something of value. Another person might say the man is bored with his job, daydreaming about where he would rather be, and contemplating an excuse to leave the office early to spend the afternoon with his friends or family.

This brief exercise is similar to one of the initial procedures developed by psychologists to tackle the question of why some people work hard and achieve in the business world, whereas others do not (McClelland, 1961). Predicting success in achievement situations has been a focus of personality research for more than half a century. Much of the early work on this question was concerned with individual differences in one of the needs identified by Henry Murray—the **need for Achievement**. Murray described the need for Achievement as the desire "to accomplish something difficult; to master, manipulate or organize ... to overcome obstacles and attain a high standard; to excel one's self" (1938, p. 164). To assess this need, researchers sometimes use another of Murray's contributions to psychology, the Thematic Appperception Test (TAT). As described in Chapter 3, test takers create stories about the scenes they see in the TAT cards. Investigators then use objective coding systems to obtain a need for Achievement score from the stories. For example, if you saw in the photograph a man working hard to reach an important goal, your story would probably indicate a high need for Achievement. On the other hand, if your story was about how this man was thinking about his loved ones and personal goals when he should have been working, your response would probably yield a low need for Achievement score.

The TAT has been used in a large number of investigations into achievement motivation (McClelland, 1961, 1985; McClelland, Atkinson, Clark, & Lowell, 1953; Stewart, 1982). However, the test is also time consuming and has been subject to questions about interpretation of scores (Blankenship et al., 2006; McClelland, 1980; Tuerlinckx, De Boeck, & Lens, 2002). Consequently, today many investigators rely on easier-to-administer, self-report inventories to assess achievement motivation (Schmalt, 1999; Spence & Helmreich, 1983). However, scores on the TAT are sometimes different than scores obtained through self-report measures (Brunstein & Schmitt, 2004; Thrash, Elliot, & Schultheiss, 2007). This observation has led some researchers to suggest there may be two kinds of achievement motivation: an *implicit* motive we are not aware of (as measured by the TAT) and a *self-attributed* or *explicit* motive we can readily describe (Brunstein & Maier, 2005; McClelland, 1980; Thrash & Elliot, 2002). Implicit achievement motivation might account for spontaneous actions, such as how we respond to a dart-throwing challenge at a party, whereas self-attributed motives come into play when we have time to ponder achievement options and decisions.

High Achievement Motivation Characteristics

What are people with high achievement motivation like? The original need for Achievement researchers were not interested in all types of achievement but only with *entrepreneurial* behavior. That is, they wanted to understand and predict behavior in the business world rather than, for example, the arts or sciences. These early investigators soon discovered that people with a need for Achievement do not always fit the stereotypes for a highly successful businessperson. For example, we might guess that someone with a high need for Achievement is not afraid to take huge risks to get ahead. But as it turns out, that is not the case. One of the prominent features of high need achievers is

Jerry Burger/Santa Clara University

Who is this person? What is he doing? How will things turn out? Whether you see a man thinking about a difficult business problem or dreaming about going fishing may indicate your own level of need for Achievement.

that they are *moderate* risk takers. They want to succeed, but they also are highly motivated to avoid failure. They take some risks, such as fairly secure business ventures with a moderate chance of failure. But they avoid highly speculative investments despite potentially large payoffs. People with strong achievement motivation are optimistic that their decisions are correct and that they will succeed (Puca & Schmalt, 2001). However, their desire to achieve does not mean they ignore the possibility of failure.

Predictably, people with a high need for Achievement tackle their work with a lot of energy. But high need achievers don't work hard at everything. Rather, they limit their enthusiasm for tasks with a potential for personal achievement. Routine and boring jobs hold no more interest for high need achievers than they do for anyone else. However, a job that requires creativity and provides an opportunity to demonstrate what they can do is very appealing.

High need achievers also prefer jobs that give them personal responsibility for outcomes. They want credit for success but also are willing to accept blame for failure. In particular, high need achievers want concrete feedback about their performance (Fodor & Carver, 2000). They want to find out how good they are and how they compare to others. This observation helps to explain why high need for Achievement people typically choose careers in the business world. Some professionals rarely receive clear feedback on how they are doing. For example, a social worker may never see clear evidence that he or she is helping clients who pass through a community mental health clinic. In contrast, sales, productivity, and profit figures provide members of the business world with constant barometers of their performance. This need for immediate feedback is complemented by the high need for Achievement person's desire to anticipate future possibilities and make long-range plans.

These people succeed in business in part because they look ahead, anticipate many courses of action and possible pitfalls, and thereby increase their chances of reaching their goal of personal achievement.

Predicting Achievement Behavior

Why do some people become highly successful entrepreneurs, whereas others show little interest in making millions in the business community? Is there something parents can do to create high achievement motivation in their children? These were some of the questions asked by the original need for Achievement investigators. Although no simple answers were found, researchers did identify a few parenting practices associated with high need for Achievement in children (McClelland, 1961; McClelland & Pilon, 1983). In essence, parents can promote achievement motivation by providing support and encouragement long enough to enable the child to develop a sense of personal competence, but not so long that the child is robbed of independence and initiative. The prescription for raising a high need for Achievement child

When to let go and when to hold on? The mother might decide to let the boy fall a few times, but in the process allow him to develop a sense of mastery and independence. However, she might also want to protect him just a little longer so that he can retain his sense of security and confidence. Psychologists argue that such decisions have an impact on the child's need for Achievement.

thus seems to be finding that fine line between too much parental involvement and not enough. Parents should encourage achievement in young children, reward them, and show enthusiasm for their accomplishments.

Predictably, people with a high need for Achievement are more likely than others to find economic prosperity (Littig & Yeracaris, 1965). But researchers also warn that a high need for Achievement can sometimes be a two-edged sword. The same high level of achievement motivation that helps some people succeed can also interfere with effective performance (Winter, 2010). Success in upper management and executive positions often depends on the manager's ability to delegate authority and motivate others. Someone too concerned about his or her own accomplishments might have a difficult time relinquishing control over details and effectively relying on subordinates. This may explain why one study found need for Achievement predicted success for low-level managers but not for those higher up the corporate ladder (McClelland & Boyatzis, 1982). One intriguing study examined the need for Achievement and effectiveness among American presidents (Spangler & House, 1991). Presidents whose inaugural speeches indicated a high need for Achievement were usually rated by historians as relatively ineffective leaders.

Gender, Culture, and Achievement

Much of the early work on need for Achievement was conducted with only male participants. There are reasons for this. When the research was initiated in the 1950s, relatively few women entered the business world and even fewer had opportunities to advance into high managerial positions. However, things have obviously changed quite a bit since then. As career aspirations and opportunities for women changed, researchers found a comparable increase in need for Achievement among women college students (Veroff, Depner, Kulka, & Douvan, 1980). And, as with men, researchers found that a high need for Achievement also predicts success in the business world for women. In one study, need for Achievement scores taken from female college students predicted job choice and job characteristics 14 years later (Jenkins, 1987).

Although the need for Achievement predicts success in the business world for both genders, studies suggest that many other variables come into play when comparing the achievement behavior of men and women (Hyde & Kling, 2001; Mednick & Thomas, 2008). For example, some researchers find that men and women often think about achievement in different ways (Eccles, 1985, 2005). Because of differences in gender-role socialization (Chapter 14), men and women may differ on the kinds of achievement they value and where achievement in the business world falls among their personal goals. For example, a businesswoman might value achievement, but on occasion she may put other concerns—such as the welfare of her customers—ahead of her personal accomplishments. We see examples of this in women who sometimes make sacrifices for their family rather than pursue career goals. Other investigators find that men and women sometimes differ in the way they define success (Gaeddert, 1985). Men in our society are more likely to see success in terms of external standards, such as gaining prestige or recognition for accomplishments. In contrast, women are more likely to rely on internal definitions of success, such as whether they accomplish what they set out to do. Rather than ask why women don't always act like men in achievement settings, a better question might be why men and women sometimes make different choices in these settings.

Similar caution should be exercised when looking at achievement behavior in different cultures (Salili, 1994; Shechter, Durik, Miyamoto, & Harackiewicz, 2011). In individualistic countries like the United States (Chapter 1), achievement is typically defined in terms of personal accomplishments. Individual effort is rewarded and people are singled out for their successes. However, in collectivist cultures success is more likely to be defined in terms of cooperation and group accomplishments. Workers in a collectivist culture might have a strong sense of accomplishment when they do their part and the entire company reaches its goal (Niles, 1998). Individual recognition is not sought and is not needed.

Workers in individualistic cultures often see themselves in competition with their coworkers, and this competition motivates them to work harder. In contrast, one team of researchers found that corporate professionals in India were concerned about the emotional and financial well-being of their coworkers (Tripathi & Cervone, 2008). Instead of trying to outperform them, these Indian businesspeople were motivated to help their coworkers succeed. In short, concepts like achievement motivation that focus on the individual may not be useful when studying behavior in a collectivist culture. New definitions for achievement and success may be needed to fully understand achievement behavior in different societies.

Attributions

Imagine for a moment that you have just received an F on a midterm exam (remember, this is only hypothetical). How would you react? Because passing the class is important to you, you will no doubt spend part of the next few days trying to figure out why you did so poorly. You might conclude there was something peculiar about the test—the professor selected bizarre points to test on or wrote ambiguous questions. Another possibility is that personal problems kept you from studying as much as you would have liked. Then again, you might decide that you really don't have what it takes to be a college student, no matter how hard you study. How you respond to the poor midterm grade and how well you do on the next test depend in part on which of these explanations you adopt. If the problem is not studying enough, you can set aside extra time for the next exam. But if the problem is a lack of ability, there may be little reason to try next time.

This example illustrates another approach researchers take when trying to understand achievement. Many psychologists are interested in the explanations people generate for why they do well or poorly in achievement situations (Weiner, 1985, 1990, 2006). According to this approach, we often ask ourselves why we have failed or succeeded. The answer to this question—our *attribution*—determines how we feel about the performance and how we perform in similar situations in the future.

TABLE 8.1 Three Dimensions for Attributions

Stability	*Stable Attributions*	*Unstable Attributions*
	Good coordination	Good luck
	Poor math attitude	Illness (such as cold)
Locus	*Internal Attributions*	*External Attributions*
	Extra effort	Easy test
	Poor skills	Difficult competition
Control	*Controllable Attributions*	*Uncontrollable Attributions*
	High motivation	From wealthy family
	Not enough practice	Weak national economy

There are many ways to analyze the kinds of attributions people give for their successes and failures, but researchers typically focus on three dimensions (Table 8.1). One is the *stability* dimension. We can explain our performance by pointing to stable causes, such as intelligence, or to unstable causes, such as luck. In addition, an attribution may be either internal to us, such as the amount of effort put forth, or external, such as a difficult test. Researchers refer to this dimension as *locus*. Finally there is the dimension of *control*—whether we can control or not control the cause of the success or failure.

By examining attributions along these three dimensions, researchers can predict how people respond to successes and failures. For example, performing well on a test, being promoted in an organization, or winning a tennis match should enhance your sense of well-being, but only if you believe the reason for success is internal. If you win a tennis game because your opponent is a lousy tennis player or had the sun in her eyes (external attributions), you probably won't feel very good about the victory. How a person responds to future events often depends on the perceived stability of the cause of the performance. If you lose the tennis match because your opponent is a better player (stable), you probably will not expect to win next time you two play. However, if you attribute the loss to some unstable bad luck, you might be eager for a rematch. This analysis helps explain why most people continue to participate in sports, even though not everyone can be a winner. Researchers find that most of us attribute our losses to unstable sources, thus keeping alive our hope of winning the next time (Grove, Hanrahan, & McInman, 1991).

This analysis also suggests a relatively easy way to improve achievement motivation: Change people's attributions. One team of researchers did just that with a group of college freshmen (Perry, Stupnisky, Hall, Chipperfield, & Weiner, 2010). The students were enrolled in a two-semester psychology course. After receiving their grade on the first fall semester exam, half the students attended an attributional retraining session. These students were told that many freshmen have difficulty with their classes but that is was possible to change. In particular, the students were encouraged to make controllable attribution for their performances (e.g., *I need to develop better studying*

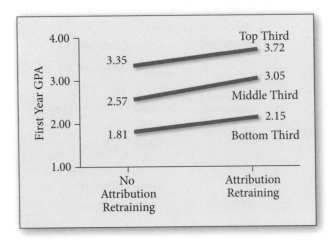

FIGURE 8.1 GPA as a Function of Attribution Retraining

Source: Perry, R. P., Stupnisky, R. H., Hall, N. C., Chipperfield, J. G., & Weiner, B. (2010). Bad starts and better finishes: Attributional retraining and initial performance in competitive achievement. *Journal of Social and Clinical Psychology, 29,* 668–700.

strategies). Not only did these students do better on their exams the next semester than students who did not attend the session, the attributional retraining helped them in other classes. As shown in Figure 8.1, regardless of how well they performed on the initial test, students who attended the attributional retraining sessions had higher overall GPAs than students who did not receive this training. The implications for education, sports, the business world, and other achievement domains are obvious.

Achievement Goals

Achievement is not only determined by how we account for performances after the fact, but also by the goals we set for ourselves at the outset (Elliot & McGregor, 2001; Kaplan & Maehr, 2007). **Achievement goals** provide targets that people aspire to in achievement situations. Although terminology and classification schemes vary, most investigators divide achievement goals into two broad categories: mastery goals and performance goals. *Mastery goals* are concerned with developing competence. Students motivated by a strong mastery goal will work hard to learn the subject matter in a course. Satisfaction comes from a sense of proficiency and a feeling that they understand the material. *Performance goals* are concerned with demonstrating accomplishments to others. Students motivated by strong performance goals want to obtain a high grade, possibly the highest grade in the class. Satisfaction comes from receiving the recognition that accompanies the achievement. In the typical classroom, we can usually find two students who work equally hard preparing for tests and completing assignments, and who achieve similar grades, yet who are motivated by very different goals. One of these achieving students wants to learn the material. This student is motivated to overcome challenges and to obtain a sense of competence. The other achieving student

⚫⚫⚫ Assessing Your Own Personality
⚫⚫⚫

Achievement Goals

Indicate with a number from 1 to 7 the extent to which each of the following statements is true about you in the class you are currently taking. A response of 7 indicates the statement is *very true* about you; 1 indicates the statement is *not at all true* about you.

_____ 1. It is important for me to do better than other students.

_____ 2. I worry that I may not learn all that I possibly could in this class.

_____ 3. I want to learn as much as possible from this class.

_____ 4. I just want to avoid doing poorly in this class.

_____ 5. It is important for me to do well compared to others in this class.

_____ 6. Sometimes I'm afraid that I may not understand the content of this class as thoroughly as I'd like.

_____ 7. It is important for me to understand the content of this course as thoroughly as possible.

_____ 8. My goal in this class is to avoid performing poorly.

_____ 9. My goal in this class is to get a better grade than most of the other students.

_____ 10. I am often concerned that I may not learn all that there is to learn in this class.

_____ 11. I desire to completely master the material presented in this class.

_____ 12. My fear of performing poorly in this class is often what motivates me.

The scale provides a score for each of the four kinds of achievement goals. Add the following answer values to obtain your scores: Mastery-Approach goals (items 3, 7, and 11); Mastery-Avoidance goals (items 2, 6, and 10); Performance-Approach goals (items 1, 5, and 9); Performance-Avoidance goals (items 4, 8, and 12). Use the following means and standard deviations obtained from college undergraduates (Elliot & McGregor, 2001) to interpret your scores:

	Mean	Standard Deviation
Master-Approach	5.52	1.18
Master-Avoidance	3.89	1.53
Performance-Approach	4.82	1.68
Performance-Avoidance	4.49	1.67

Scale: *The Achievement Goal Questionnaire*
Source: Elliot and McGregor (2001).

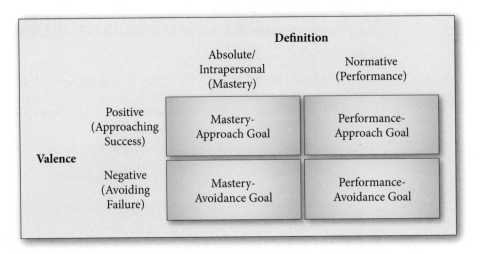

FIGURE 8.2 Achievement Goal Framework

Source: From Elliot and McGregor (2001).

is likely to ask what he or she needs to do to good grade and then arrange his or her study time to get the desired outcome.

But people aren't just motivated to succeed. Sometimes they are more concerned about not failing. Thus psychologists also find it useful to draw a distinction between *approach goals* and *avoidance goals* (Cury, Elliot, Da Fonseca, & Moller, 2006; Elliot & McGregor, 2001; Van Yperen, 2006). As shown in Figure 8.2, by dividing both mastery and performance into approach and avoidance categories, we create a 2 by 2 model of achievement goals. Within this framework, students trying to learn difficult material (mastery goal) can be motivated either by a desire to achieve a sense of mastery (approach) or by a wish to not feel incompetent (avoidance). Similarly, students who rely on performance goals might be motivated to gain recognition for their accomplishments or to avoid the embarrassment of a poor performance.

Because achievement motivation has important implications in education, business, and many other areas of our lives, psychologists have asked whether some achievement goals are more effective than others. Is it better for students to focus on learning the material or obtaining a good grade? Can teachers alter assignments and grading policies or should business managers change the way they evaluate and reward employees to improve learning and productivity? Although both mastery and performance goals motivate people to achieve, investigators often find differences between people who seek competence and those who focus on recognition.

Most of the research on this question has compared the effects of mastery and performance goals, and investigators consistently find that mastery goals lead to high achievement (Dompnier, Darnon, & Butera, 2009; Kaplan & Maehr, 2007; Payne, Youngcourt, & Beaubien, 2007). Students motivated by mastery goals often choose more challenging tasks and are more interested in their classes than students who rely on performance goals. When given the choice between two assignments, mastery-oriented students are likely to select the one they are more curious about, whereas students relying on performance goals want to know which will lead to a better grade. A student interested in learning the material is unlikely to ask, "Will this be on the test?"

People motivated by mastery goals also tend to retain the information and skills they learn longer than those driven by performance goals. A piano student whose goal is to master a difficult concerto is likely to remember the piece longer than the student who simply wants to sound good at the recital. Similarly, people motivated by mastery goals often continue their interest in the material after recognition for the achievement has passed (Rawsthorne & Elliot, 1999). The student who reads Charles Dickens with the goal of obtaining a deeper appreciation for fine literature is more likely to read good books during the summer than the student who reads Dickens only to do well on the exam. Performance goals also affect how well individuals work in groups (Darnon, Dompnier, Delmas, Pulfrey, & Butera, 2009; Poortvliet & Darnon, 2010). People who approach tasks with a mastery orientation are more likely to share information and work with others to achieve common goals, whereas those with a performance orientation tend to see others as competition.

This is not to say reliance on performance goals is all bad. Both mastery and performance goals can lead to achievement (Richardson, Abraham, & Bond, 2012), and it is possible to aspire to both a sense of mastery and recognition for accomplishments. In some cases, researchers find a combination of mastery and performance goals can be particularly effective (Barron & Harackiewicz, 2001; Harackiewicz, Barron, Pintrich, Elliot, & Thrash, 2002; Senko & Harackiewicz, 2005). However, the advantages of focusing on performance appear to be limited to performance *approach* goals (Darnon, Harackiewicz, Butera, Mugny, & Quiamzade, 2007; Elliot, Shell, Bouas, & Maier, 2005; Roney & O'Connor, 2008). Students motivated only by a desire to not receive a poor grade tend to do more poorly than those who come to class with other achievement goals.

Finally, research on achievement goals has implications for how educators structure the goals and assignments in their classes (Meece, Anderman, & Anderman, 2006; Murayama & Elliot, 2009). Researchers find higher levels of motivation and learning when teachers emphasize mastery and improving skills (Kaplan & Maehr, 2007; Meece et al., 2006). Unfortunately, many schools take the opposite approach by emphasizing grades, competition among students, and the threat of a poor performance. Although some students respond well to these incentives, many do not, and a focus on performance rather than learning can often lead to a decrease in academic motivation.

Type A, Hostility and Health

Several decades ago, some physicians and medical researchers were frustrated by their inability to identify which patients were likely to suffer from cardiovascular problems. Although they knew high blood pressure, smoking, obesity, and inactivity all contributed to the risk of heart disease, combinations of these factors were still unable to predict new cases with much accuracy (Jenkins, 1971, 1976). But these medical professionals also noticed that their heart attack patients seemed to act differently than other patients (Friedman & Rosenman, 1974). Heart attack victims were more active, more energetic, and more driving than those without cardiovascular problems. In short, they seemed to have different personalities.

Initially researchers identified this personality dimension the *coronary-prone behavior pattern* because it seemed to consist of a combination of behaviors associated with coronary disease. Later, this individual difference was called *Type A–Type B*, or sometimes just Type A. Strictly speaking, the name is inappropriate because it is not a true typology. Instead of identifying two types of people, A and B, we should think of a trait continuum with extreme Type A people at one end and extreme Type B people at the other. Typical Type A individuals are strongly motivated to overcome obstacles and are driven to achieve. They are attracted to competition, enjoy power and recognition, and are easily aroused to anger and action. They dislike wasting time and tend to do things in a vigorous and efficient manner. Type A people often find more easygoing people a source of frustration. On the other hand, typical Type B people are relaxed and unhurried. They may work hard on occasion, but rarely in the driven, compulsive manner of Type A people. These people are less likely than Type A's to seek competition or to be aroused to anger or action.

Type A people often have a sense of urgency and like to do more than one thing at a time.

Jerry Burger/Santa Clara University

Type A as a Personality Variable

What the medical researchers were examining, of course, is a personality trait. Naturally, a trait as intriguing as Type A soon caught the attention of personality researchers. Before long, psychologists identified three major components that appear to make up the Type A trait (Glass, 1977). First, Type A people have a higher competitive achievement striving than Type B's. Type A's work harder at achievement tasks regardless of outside pressure, such as deadlines. Second, Type A individuals show a sense of time urgency. They feel time is important and shouldn't be wasted. Whereas Type B people might procrastinate, Type A's jump right in. Studies find that Type A students volunteer for experiments earlier in the term than Type B's, and they show up earlier to participate (Gastorf, 1980; Strube, 1982). Third, Type A's are more likely to respond to frustrating situations with anger and hostility (Bettencourt, Talley, Benjamin, & Valentine, 2006). As you will see, it's this third component that soon became the most significant.

Personality researchers have compared Type A and Type B people on a wide variety of behaviors, including driving habits, study habits, reactions to failure, and reactions to persuasive messages. One particularly interesting hypothesis to come out of this work explains differences in Type A and Type B behavior in terms of a motivation for control. That is, achievement striving, time urgency, and hostility reflect the Type A individuals' desire to exercise effective control over the people and situations they encounter. Type A's are more likely than Type B's to dominate a group discussion (Yarnold, Mueser, & Grimm, 1985). Type A's are less likely to give up control over a task, even to someone who might do a better job (Strube, Berry, & Moergen, 1985). Type A's are also more likely than Type B's to want something after being told they can't have it (Rhodewalt & Comer, 1982; Rhodewalt & Davison, 1983).

Naturally, researchers have looked at whether Type A or Type B individuals achieve more. Numerous laboratory studies find Type A participants typically outperform Type B's on achievement tasks. One reason for this difference is that Type A's tend to set higher goals for themselves (Ward & Eisler, 1987). But what really fires them up is competition. What greater threat to a Type A's sense of control than to be told there can be but one winner? Sometimes their blood pressure and heart rate go up when simply told they are going to compete against another person (Lyness, 1993). In some cases, Type A's actually seem to be attracted to competition. Type A participants in one study were more confident in their ability to do well in a game when told they were competing against another participant (Gotay, 1981).

Researchers also find differences in academic performance between Type A and Type B college students. Type A students tend to take more classes than Type B students and expect to do better in those classes (Ovcharchyn, Johnson, & Petzel, 1981). One investigation found that Type A students receive more academic honors and participate in more extracurricular activities than Type B students (Glass, 1977). This study also found that Type A students participate in more sports, receive more athletic awards, and participate in more social activities in high school than their Type B classmates.

Hostility and Health

As the medical researchers who first identified the trait anticipated, early studies found Type A was a good predictor of heart disease (Cooper, Detre, & Weiss, 1981). Type A men in one 8½-year study had more than twice the incidence of heart disease than Type B men (Rosenman et al., 1975). In another investigation, Type A was a better predictor of heart attacks than cholesterol level or cigarette smoking (Jenkins, Zyzanski, & Rosenman, 1976). Naturally, findings like these caught the attention of the medical community as well as the media. Not only did the concept help physicians do a better job of predicting heart attacks, but the findings hinted at lifestyle changes that might reduce the risk of heart disease.

However, as is often the case, results from subsequent studies found that the connection between Type A and health is more complex than the original research suggested. In particular, several investigators reported low or nonexistent relationships between Type A behavior and coronary disease (Matthews & Haynes, 1986; Siegman, 1994), which left researchers with the difficult task of explaining inconsistent findings. It seemed unlikely that Type A behavior once caused heart disease but that suddenly it did not. It also did not seem probable that all the earlier studies somehow identified a relationship where one did not exist.

Researchers found the answer to this puzzle by breaking Type A into its components. As you may recall, Type A is actually a collection of several behavior tendencies that tend to go together. In essence, when we measure Type A, we are measuring more than one trait. It is possible that only one or two of these components are responsible for health problems. In that case, we would expect to find only weak and sometimes nonsignificant associations between Type A and cardiovascular disease.

This line of reasoning led some researchers to look for the "toxic component" of Type A behavior. What did they find? A large amount of evidence now points to the hostility component as the culprit (Bunde & Suls, 2006; Krantz & McCeney, 2002; Smith, 2006; Smith, Glazer, Ruiz, & Gallo, 2004; Williams, 2010). People high in hostility aren't necessarily violent or even bossy. Rather, they tend to have a strong reaction to the small frustrations and inconveniences we all experience. They respond to even minor annoyances with "expressions of antagonism, disagreeableness, rudeness, surliness, criticalness, and uncooperativeness" (Dembroski & Costa, 1987). People high in hostility might become upset when stuck in a slow-moving line at the post office or when they misplace something and can't find it right away. Most of us have learned to take these minor inconveniences in stride, but some people become highly irritated. We sometimes refer to these individuals as "quick-tempered" because it usually doesn't take much to send them into a fit of anger. It should be noted that researchers sometimes use the terms *anger* or *aggression* to refer to this trait (Smith et al., 2004). However, for clarity's sake, I will simply use the term *hostility* here.

Several investigations find that scores on hostility and anger measures do a good job of predicting coronary artery disease (Kawachi, Sparrow, Spiro, Vokonas, & Weiss, 1996; Niaura, Todaro, Stroud, Spiro, Ward, &

Weiss, 2002; Williams, Nieto, Sanford, Couper, & Tyroler, 2002; Williams, Nieto, Sanford, & Tyroler, 2001). One study followed 12,986 healthy middle-aged men and women over a 4½-year period (Williams et al., 2000). Compared to participants low in trait anger, participants who scored high on this trait were more than twice as likely to suffer some form of coronary heart disease during this time. More alarming, the high-anger participants were nearly three times as likely to be hospitalized or die from heart disease during the study.

Why is hostility related to cardiovascular problems? Researchers have identified several possible connections, including unhealthy lifestyles (Siegler, 1994), poor social support (Smith, Fernengel, Holcroft, Gerald, & Marien, 1994), immune system weaknesses (Uchino, Cacioppo, & Kiecolt-Glaser, 1996), and blood lipid levels (Richards, Hof, & Alvarenga, 2000). Other studies find that people high in hostility frequently exhibit the kind of physiological reactions associated with cardiovascular problems, such as high blood pressure (Jackson, Kubzansky, Cohen, Jacobs, & Wright, 2007; Jorgensen, Johnson, Kolodziej, & Schreer, 1996; Martin & Watson, 1997; Powch & Houston, 1996; Raikkonen, Matthews, Flory, & Owens, 1999).

Male participants in one investigation wore a blood pressure monitor for an entire day (Guyll & Contrada, 1998). The men also kept a record of their activities and their moods. As shown in Figure 8.3, participants high in hostility showed elevated levels of blood pressure when they interacted with other people, whereas the low-hostility participants showed no such reaction. Apparently the high-hostility participants found many of their conversations

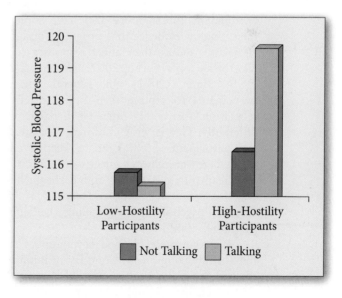

FIGURE 8.3 Blood Pressure Response to Social Interactions

Source: From "Trait hostility and ambulatory cardiovascular activity: Responses to social interaction," by M. Guyll and R. J. Contrada in *Health Psychology*, 17, 1998, p. 30–39. Copyright © 1998 by the American Psychological Association.

TABLE 8.2 Some Health Consequences of High Anger and Hostility

Physical Illness	High hostility scores predict increased incidence of many illnesses, including asthma, liver disease, and arthritis.
Immune System	High anger is related to weakness in the immune system, especially after conflict.
Pain	High anger scores are associated with lower pain tolerance in lab studies and with complaints of greater pain among patients experiencing pain.
Cholesterol	High trait anger is correlated with higher cholesterol levels.
Cardiovascular Disease	High hostility is related to higher incidence of many cardiovascular diseases, including atherosclerosis and coronary artery blockage.
Death	High scores on measures of anger and hostility are associated with death from cardiovascular disease as well as death from other causes.

Source: From "The terrible twos–anger and anxiety: Hazardous to your health," by R. M. Suinn in *American Psychologist*, 56, 2001, p. 27–36. Copyright 2001 by the American Psychological Association.

frustrating or annoying, and this reaction resulted in higher blood pressure. Interestingly, the high-hostility women in the study did not have this reaction. Perhaps this is because women generally find social interactions more pleasant and less a source of frustration than do men.

As shown in Table 8.2, the results from numerous studies paint a consistently dangerous picture for those high in hostility (Suinn, 2001). Fortunately, investigators also have some encouraging findings to report. First, there is evidence that programs designed to help potential cardiovascular victims reduce their anger responses can be effective (Davidson, Gidron, Mostofsky, & Trudeau, 2007; Fernandez, 2010; Gidron, Davidson, & Bata, 1999; Suinn, 2001). In general, these programs train anger-prone participants to replace their initial reaction to frustrating situations with relaxation. Instructors often teach participants to think about the situation differently. That is, instead of making a small inconvenience out to be a disaster, participants are taught to keep events in perspective and recognize that there are more effective solutions to the problem than anger. One team of investigators found these training procedures to be especially effective for drivers whose "road rage" had gotten so out of hand they required psychological counseling (Deffenbacher, Huff, Lynch, Oetting, & Salvatore, 2000).

A second piece of good news applies to those who are Type A but lack the hostility component. Contrary to initial warnings, Type A is not necessarily bad for your health. Workaholics who push themselves to meet ever greater challenges and who prefer to work through lunch might not be headed for an early heart attack after all. If these people don't let minor setbacks and little frustrations upset them, it may be possible to be productive *and* healthy.

Social Anxiety

I took a few moments at a recent psychology conference to note the different ways my colleagues went about meeting and greeting other professionals. I positioned myself in the corner of a large room and watched as people entered what was designated as a "social hour." The event was scheduled so that people in the field could meet one another and perhaps exchange a few ideas about each other's work. Some people seemed quite at home in this setting. One woman in particular amazed me with her ability to introduce herself to someone she obviously had never met and immediately begin what appeared to be a lively and pleasant conversation. But other people approached the social hour in a very different manner. One man stopped about 2 feet inside the door and examined the proceedings. Then he slowly worked his way around the exterior of the room, looking for someone to talk to. When people did speak to him, he appeared to smile nervously. The man looked at the floor more than at the person he was speaking to, and his conversations never seemed to last more than 30 seconds. After about 10 minutes, he left.

It would be easy to speculate that these two visitors to the social hour probably fall on opposite ends of the personality trait we call social anxiety. The man was very anxious in this situation and behaved in a manner most people would identify as shy. I would guess that the woman has never suffered from shyness. Although most people would probably consider the woman's behavior normal and appropriate for a social gathering, researchers find that the shy man's experience may be more common than most of us

Speaking in front of a group creates high levels of nervousness for someone high in social anxiety. High social-anxiety people are often concerned about negative evaluation.

realize. In fact, shyness appears to be a widespread social problem. Researchers consistently find about 40% of the people they survey identify themselves as shy (Zimbardo, 1986). Another 40% to 50% say they have been shy before or are shy in certain situations. This leaves only a small percentage of people who do not know the pain of social anxiety or shyness.

Social anxiety is anxiety related specifically to social interactions or anticipated social interactions. People suffering from social anxiety experience many of the usual anxiety symptoms: increased physiological arousal, inability to concentrate, feelings of nervousness. But socially anxious people recognize that the source of their discomfort is the social encounter they are now or will soon be engaged in. Although everyone has on occasion been at least a little nervous about an upcoming interview or date, we can identify a relatively stable tendency for people to experience social anxiety. That is, each of us can be placed along a continuum for how much social anxiety we typically experience.

Social anxiety is the same as or related to many other constructs investigated by psychologists. The names for these concepts include shyness, dating anxiety, communication anxiety, reticence, and stage fright. Although some psychologists draw a distinction between social anxiety and some of these related concepts (Buss, 1980; Leary, 1983b), most researchers today appear to use the terms *social anxiety* and *shyness* synonymously. Concepts like dating anxiety and stage fright are often regarded as specific examples of the larger concept of social anxiety. Moreover, scales designed to measure social anxiety, shyness, and related constructs are highly correlated with one another (Anderson & Harvey, 1988). Consequently, I will use the terms *social anxiety* and *shyness* interchangeably here.

It also is important to recognize that social anxiety is not the same as introversion. Whereas introverts often choose to be by themselves, the vast majority of socially anxious people do not like their shyness. Nearly two-thirds of the socially anxious people in one study identified their shyness as "a real problem," and one-quarter of the shy participants said they would be willing to seek professional help to overcome their social anxiety (Pilkonis, 1977a).

Characteristics of Socially Anxious People

People who suffer from social anxiety have a difficult time in many social situations. Socially anxious people report feeling awkward and nervous when they have to talk to others, particularly when interacting with people they don't know (Kashdan & Roberts, 2006; Shimizu, Seery, Weisbuch, & Lupien, 2011). They are very concerned about what others will think of them and become self-conscious when they meet new people or have to talk in front of an audience. Quite often, socially anxious people think about what they are doing wrong, how stupid they must sound, and how foolish they must look (Bruch, Hamer, & Heimberg, 1995; Ickes, Robertson, Tooke, & Teng, 1986; Ritts & Patterson, 1996). Shy people often stumble over their words, say the wrong thing, and show outward signs of nervousness, such as perspiration and shakiness. Shy people are more likely than most to feel ashamed or embarrassed about what they say or do in social situations, which is probably why shy people also are more likely than nonshys to blush (Leary & Meadows, 1991). Shy people sometimes report they are so self-conscious and nervous during a social encounter that they cannot think of anything to say. They may allow the conversation to fall into silence, which can be extremely uncomfortable for someone already suffering from social anxiety (Pilkonis, 1977b).

These feelings of awkwardness are not merely in the minds of socially anxious people. The people they interact with also identify shy people as more tense, inhibited, and unfriendly than nonshy people (Cheek & Buss, 1981; Papsdorf & Alden, 1998). College students in one study did a reasonable job of identifying shy and nonshy people just by looking at their Facebook pages (Fernandez, Levinson, & Rodebaugh, 2012). In general, conversations with socially anxious individuals are less pleasant than when speaking with nonanxious people (Heery & Kring, 2007).

As noted earlier, shy people are not introverts. Rather, most would like to have a larger network of friends than they do. In particular, shy people often say that they would like more people they could turn to when they need help. Unfortunately, their shyness often keeps them from developing more friends or asking the friends they have for help when they are in need. One study found that shy students were less likely than nonshy students to talk to a counselor about career advice (Phillips & Bruch, 1988). Researchers in another study gave participants a task that could be completed only by asking someone else for assistance (DePaulo, Dull, Greenberg, & Swaim, 1989). Nonetheless, the socially anxious people were more reluctant than the other participants to ask a nearby person for help.

Not only do socially anxious people fear that others will think poorly of them, they often assume incorrectly that other people simply are not interested in getting to know them (Wenzel & Emerson, 2009). Perhaps this is why shy individuals also tend to interpret the feedback they get from other people in a negative light (Amir, Beard, & Bower, 2005; Ledley & Heimberg, 2006). This self-defeating tendency was demonstrated in a study in which college students were asked to work on a series of tasks with other participants (DePaulo, Kenny, Hoover, Webb, & Oliver, 1987). When later asked what they believed the other students thought of them, the socially anxious students felt they were less liked and had come across as less competent than did the nonanxious participants. Participants in another experiment carried on what they believed to be a two-way discussion via a television hook-up (Pozo, Carver, Wellens, & Scheier, 1991). In reality, all participants watched a prerecorded videotape of a confederate posing as a participant. Although the feedback was identical, socially anxious people were more likely than nonanxious participants to interpret the other person's facial expressions as indicating disapproval.

In short, people high in social anxiety expect their social interactions to go poorly and look for evidence that the other person is rejecting them. Unfortunately, this pessimism may cause the social rejection that the socially anxious person fears in the first place. People sometimes mistake shyness for

●●● **Assessing Your Own Personality**

Social Anxiety

Indicate the extent to which each of the following statements describes you. Use a 0-to-4 scale to indicate your answers, with 0 = Extremely uncharacteristic and 4 = Extremely characteristic.

_____   1. I feel tense when I'm with people I don't know well.

_____   2. I am socially somewhat awkward.

_____   3. I am often uncomfortable at parties and other socialfunctions.

_____   4. When conversing, I worry about saying something dumb.

_____   5. I feel nervous when speaking to someone in authority.

_____   6. I have trouble looking someone right in the eye.

_____   7. I feel inhibited in social situations.

_____   8. I don't find it hard to talk to strangers.

_____   9. I am more shy with members of the opposite sex.

To obtain your score, first reverse the value of your answer to item #8 (that is, for this item only, 0 = 4, 1 = 3, 2 = 2, 3 = 1, 4 = 0). Then add all nine answer values. Researchers find a mean score on the scale of 14.8 (standard deviation = 5.6) for men and 14.4 (standard deviation = 5.9) for women (Cheek & Buss, 1981). Higher scores indicate higher levels of social anxiety.

Scale: *The Shyness Scale*

a lack of interest or a lack of intelligence (Paulhus & Morgan, 1997). Moreover, because they feel the other person dislikes them, socially anxious people may cut conversations short or avoid them altogether. As a result, they may nip pleasant interactions and potential friendships in the bud before they have a chance to bloom. Indeed, researchers find that shy teenagers have fewer friends than nonshy classmates (Van Zalk, Van Zalk, Kerr, & Stattin, 2011) and that shyness reduces satisfaction even in long-term romantic relationships (Baker & McNulty, 2010).

Explaining Social Anxiety

Why are some people so anxious in social situations? What are they afraid of? Many researchers believe **evaluation apprehension** is an underlying cause of social anxiety. That is, socially anxious people are afraid of what other people think of them (Catalino, Furr, & Bellis, 2012; Leary & Kowalski, 1995; Weeks, Jakatdar, & Heimberg, 2010). In particular, they fear negative evaluation. Socially anxious people worry that the person they are talking with is going to find them foolish, boring, or immature. Situations that lend themselves to evaluation by others are particularly anxiety provoking. Just thinking about going on a blind date, giving a speech in front of a large audience, or meeting people for the first time can be a nightmarish experience for someone high in social anxiety.

How do socially anxious people deal with this fear of negative evaluation? Often, they simply avoid social encounters altogether. They skip parties where they might not know anyone, avoid blind dates, and opt for a term paper instead of a class presentation. When getting out of the situation is not realistic, shy people will do what they can to reduce the amount of social interaction. One way they do this is by avoiding eye contact (Farabee, Holcom, Ramsey, & Cole, 1993; Garcia, Stinson, Ickes, Bissonnette, & Briggs, 1991). Making eye contact with someone signals a readiness or willingness to talk. By refusing to give this signal, shy people tell those around them that they would prefer to avoid social interaction. In this way, socially anxious people limit the opportunities for others to evaluate them.

When their efforts to avoid potentially awkward social situations fail, shy people do what they can to keep the conversation short and nonthreatening. Shy people typically limit the amount of personal information they reveal to a person they've just met (Meleshko & Alden, 1993). Participants in one experiment were asked to tell four stories about themselves to an interviewer (DePaulo, Epstein, & LeMay, 1990). Some of the participants believed the interviewer would use these stories to evaluate them afterward. The socially anxious people who thought they were going to be evaluated told shorter and less revealing stories than the other participants. Apparently these shy people were worried about creating a poor impression in the mind of the interviewer.

Participants in another experiment were asked to engage in a 5-minute "get-acquainted" conversation with someone they had just met (Leary, Knight, & Johnson, 1987). When researchers examined tapes of these conversations, they found several differences in the way shy and nonshy participants acted. Socially anxious participants were more likely to agree with what the other person said and to merely restate or clarify their partner's remarks when it was their turn to talk. This interactive style allows socially anxious people to create an image of politeness and interest without becoming too involved in the conversation. In this way, shy people hope to minimize opportunities for this other person to find something objectionable about them.

Not surprisingly, we find higher rates of shyness in cultures that emphasize concern for what others think of you and the importance of avoiding criticism (Okazaki, 1997). Recall from Chapter 1 that people from collectivist cultures are more concerned about fitting in with their community and culture, whereas people from individualistic cultures are more interested in drawing attention to themselves. Consistent with these differences, researchers typically find more shyness in collectivist cultures than in individualistic cultures (Heinrichs et al., 2005; Paulhus, Duncan, & Yik, 2002).

In short, the shy person's interaction style is a type of self-protective strategy. Because they are so concerned with negative evaluations, socially anxious people do what they can to control the impressions others have of them (Schlenker & Leary, 1982; Shepperd & Arkin, 1990). Shy people deliberately keep conversations short and pleasant and avoid potentially controversial or embarrassing topics. In this way, they reduce the likelihood that the other person will form a negative impression of them.

Although this picture of the shy person may sound rather hopeless, one research finding suggests that socially anxious people may not be as incapable of conversation as they seem. Researchers sometimes find that shy people have little difficulty interacting with others once they get started. That is, for at least some shy people, it's *initiating* a conversation that seems to be the real stumbling block (Curran, Wallander, & Fischetti, 1980; Paulhus & Martin, 1987). In one study, shy and nonshy participants were left alone to carry on a conversation with a member of the opposite sex (Pilkonis, 1977b). Although the nonshy people spoke more often and were more likely to break periods of silence than the shy participants, there was no difference in how long these two kinds of people spoke when they did say something.

Shy individuals also find their anxiety is less of a problem when they are with friends than when they interact with strangers. When one team of researchers asked college students who they had eaten lunch with the previous day, shy students were more likely than nonshy students to say they had eaten with a friend (Arkin & Grove, 1990). Just having a friend nearby is often enough to alleviate some of the negative thoughts that surface when shy people are forced to interact with strangers (Pontari, 2009). When a friend was present, socially anxious participants in one study were just as likely as other participants to describe themselves in a positive manner and to disclose personal information to a stranger (Pontari & Glenn, 2012).

Observations like these lead some researchers to speculate that what socially anxious people really lack is confidence in their ability to make a good impression (Hill, 1989; Leary & Atherton, 1986; Maddux, Norton, & Leary, 1988). Fear that they might say the wrong thing often keeps shy people from saying anything. Consequently, therapy programs designed to help people overcome problems with shyness often focus on getting clients to believe that they can say the right thing and can make a good impression (Glass & Shea, 1986; Haemmerlie & Montgomery, 1986; Leary & Kowalski, 1995).

Emotions

At first glance, you might wonder why a topic like emotions is included in a chapter on personality traits. After all, traits are consistent characteristics, and common observation tells us that our moods fluctuate constantly. Each of us goes through good days and bad—times when we are extremely happy, tremendously sad, proud, ashamed, enthusiastic, or guilty. Common sense also suggests that how we feel depends on the situation. We're happy when good things happen to us, proud when we accomplish something, sad when unfortunate events occur. However, if I ask you to think of someone you know who always seems to be in a good mood, my guess is you will have little difficulty coming up with an example. Similarly, I find people can easily think of individuals they would describe as "gloomy," "confident," or "grouchy." In other words, after a little reflection it also is apparent that, although each of us experiences a wide range of positive and negative emotions, we can also identify relatively stable patterns in emotions that distinguish each person from the people around him or her.

What are some of these consistent patterns? Researchers identify at least three ways our emotions can be examined as relatively stable personal characteristics. First, each of us differs in the extent to which we typically experience positive and negative emotions. Second, we differ in the typical strength of the emotions we experience. Third, we differ in the way we express our emotions. Personality psychologists refer to these three aspects of emotion as *affectivity, intensity,* and *expressiveness.*

Emotional Affectivity

Thumb through a dictionary, and you will find dozens and dozens of words that describe human emotions. People can be happy, irritated, content, nervous, embarrassed, and disgusted. We experience shame, joy, regret, rage, anxiety, and pride. But it is reasonable to ask if these are all different emotions or, as researchers have found when examining personality traits, connected to one another along a few major dimensions. Like psychologists studying the Big Five personality dimensions, researchers use factor analysis to examine the relation among various emotions (Watson & Clark, 1991; Watson & Tellegen, 1985). These researchers look at emotions as indicated by self-report inventories, use of words, facial expressions, and evaluations from others. And like Big Five researchers, they find that certain emotions indeed tend to go together. People who are happy also tend to be enthusiastic, those who are irritable are also often sad.

Eventually, these investigators discovered that affect could be organized around two general dimensions. As shown in Table 8.3, researchers identified one of these dimensions simply as *positive affect*. At one extreme we find such emotions as *active, content,* and *satisfied*. At the other extreme we find *sad* and *lethargic*. The other dimension that emerged in this research was identified, perhaps predictably, as *negative affect*. At one extreme of this dimension we find *nervousness, anger,* and *distress*. At the other end we find *calm* and *serene*.

The same two dimensions can be used to identify our typical emotional experiences. As with other traits, our general tendencies to experience positive affect and negative affect are relatively stable over time. That is, if I know where to place you on the two affect dimensions today, I can predict with reasonable accuracy your general tendency to experience positive and negative affect years from now (Charles, Reynolds, & Gatz, 2001). Psychologists refer to these individual differences as **emotional affectivity**.

Among the first issues addressed by researchers was the relationship between positive and negative affect. Initial investigations indicated that these two affect dimensions are relatively independent from one another (Diener & Emmons, 1984; Mayer & Gaschke, 1988; Meyer & Shack, 1989; Watson, Clark, & Tellegen, 1988). If that is the case, knowing your score on a test

TABLE 8.3 Positive and Negative Affect Examples

High Positive Affect	High Negative Affect
Active	Distressed
Elated	Fearful
Enthusiastic	Hostile
Excited	Jittery
Peppy	Nervous
Strong	Scornful
Low Positive Affect	**Low Negative Affect**
Drowsy	At rest
Dull	Calm
Sleepy	Placid
Sluggish	Relaxed

measuring positive affect would tell me nothing about how you score on a test measuring negative affect. However, later studies found support for the more intuitive notion that being high on one of these dimensions means being low on the other, and vice versa (Russell & Carroll, 1999). In other words, the more I experience positive emotions like happiness and contentment, the less likely I am to experience anger and anxiety. Currently, the relation between positive and negative affect remains an issue of discussion and continuing investigation (Leue & Beauducel, 2011; Schmukle, Egloff, & Burns, 2002; Segura & Gonzalez-Roma, 2003; Terracciano, McCrae, Hagemann, & Costa, 2003). Most likely, the relation is more complex than researchers initially recognized. Although common observations tell us that doing something fun helps to take away the blues, most of us can identify a time when we felt both a little bit happy and a little bit sad at the same time. Indeed, researchers find that people often report mixed emotions when recalling past experiences or when watching a motion picture with a bittersweet message (Ersner-Hershfield, Mikels, Sullivan, & Carstensen, 2008; Larsen & McGraw, 2011).

Regardless of the outcome of this debate, psychologists find that individual differences in positive and negative affect predict a number of important behaviors. For example, people who are high in trait positive affect tend to be in better health than those who are low on this dimension (Cohen & Pressman, 2006; Robles, Brooks, & Pressman, 2009; Steptoe, Dockray, & Wardle, 2009). But the behavior most consistently associated with high positive affect is social activity (Watson & Naragon, 2009). People high in trait positive affect tend to engage in more social events and tend to enjoy those activities more than people who score low on this trait (Berry & Hansen, 1996; Clark & Watson, 1988; Robins, Caspi, & Moffitt, 2002; Watson, 1988). This finding also extends to romance. People high in trait positive affect are more likely to be involved in a romantic relationship and are more satisfied with their partners than are people low in positive affect (Berry & Willingham, 1997).

Why is positive affect related to social activity? One reason may be that social activity *causes* positive affect. That is, because some people are more social, they experience more positive emotions. Students in one study completed a scale measuring positive and negative mood each week for 13 consecutive weeks (Watson, Clark, McIntyre, & Hamaker, 1992). Participants also completed a questionnaire each week indicating how often they had engaged in each of 15 different social activities (e.g., attending a party, having a serious discussion, or going to a movie or concert). The researchers found the more social activities the students engaged in, the higher their positive affect that week. A similar finding was uncovered when researchers looked at the mood and activity levels of Japanese students (Clark & Watson, 1988). However, it is important to note that this research is correlational (Chapter 2). In other words, it is possible that the causal arrow runs the other way as well. People may engage in social activity *because* they experience positive affect. Consistent with this interpretation, studies find that when we feel good, we are more likely to seek out friends and to act friendly toward the people we meet (Cunningham, 1988).

People high in trait positive affect also act in ways that most people find attractive, which leads to more friends and more social activity. Participants in one study were asked to engage in a 6-minute conversation with a stranger (Berry & Hansen, 1996). When judges examined videotapes of these conversations, they found high positive affect participants generally were more pleasant and engaging than low positive affect participants. Consistent with this research, high positive affect people report fewer conflicts with their friends (Berry, Willingham, & Thayer, 2000) and are more likely to be accommodating when they have a disagreement with their romantic partners (Berry & Willingham, 1997). That is, they are better at resolving conflicts and thus maintaining solid, happy relationships. In short, people high in trait positive affect tend to be happy, enthusiastic, and attentive. Little wonder they develop and keep friendships and romantic partners.

What kinds of behaviors are associated with negative affect? Not surprisingly, high scores on negative affect are generally related to psychological stress (Brissette & Cohen, 2002; Merz & Roesch, 2011). People on the high end of this dimension suffer from a diverse list of emotional problems. Studies also find that negative affect is related to complaints about health (Finch, Baranik, Liu, & West, 2012; Howren & Suls, 2011; Williams, et al., 2002). That is, people who score high on measures of negative affect report more health problems than people with low negative affect. And we are more likely to find high negative affect people in a doctor's office than people who are low on this dimension.

But these findings raise another question: Do people high in negative affect really suffer from more health problems, or do they simply complain more? Maybe people high in negative affect simply think about their symptoms more than most of us. To test this possibility, one group of healthy volunteers was deliberately exposed to cold and flu viruses (Cohen et al., 1995). The participants were then quarantined in a hotel for several days where they were monitored for real symptoms and provided daily self-reports of their perceived symptoms. Consistent with earlier research, participants characteristically high in negative affect reported more cold and flu symptoms than those who scored low on this dimension. However, when the investigators looked at actual symptoms (such as mucus excretions), they found no difference between those high and low in negative affect.

But before we dismiss the higher rate of health problems among negative affect people as exaggerated complaining, consider that both of these possibilities may be true—perhaps people high in negative affect complain more, but they also may experience more genuine symptoms. This was the conclusion of a 7-year study looking at patients suffering from rheumatoid arthritis (Smith, Wallston, & Dwyer, 1995). Patients high in negative affect did report more symptoms and more severe symptoms than those on the other end of this dimension. However, it also was the case that these patients had higher levels of physical ailments that could not be explained away simply by their tendency to focus on the negative. In short, patients high in negative affect complained more than the symptoms warranted, but they also had more legitimate reasons to complain.

This last observation leads to a final question: Why should different levels of negative affect be related to one's physical health? As of yet, no clear answers to this question are available. One possibility is that people high in negative affect have difficulty dealing with stress, which subsequently affects their health. It might also be the case that mood affects health-related behaviors. High and low negative affect people might have different exercise, eating, or health habits. Finally, it's possible that people who suffer from a lot of health problems become more negative about their lives in general.

Affect Intensity

Students participating in one psychology experiment were asked to keep daily records of their emotions for 84 consecutive days (Larsen, 1987). Each day the students completed a short scale indicating the extent to which they had experienced positive emotions, such as happiness and fun, and negative emotions, such as sadness and anger. The researchers plotted each person's emotional pattern for the length of the study.

What were these investigators looking for? Consider the data from two of the participants in that study, shown in Figure 8.4. The average amount of positive and negative emotion was about the same for each of these students over the nearly 3-month period. But this is a case in which averages tell only part of the story. Clearly, the two students lead very different emotional lives. Student A has highs and lows, but these typically aren't extreme. We all know people like this; we call them steady and even-tempered. They enjoy themselves but rarely become ecstatic. They get irritated but rarely irate. Each of us also knows people like Student B. When they get happy, they get very happy. When they get down, they get very down. We say these people are unpredictable, that they fly off the handle, or

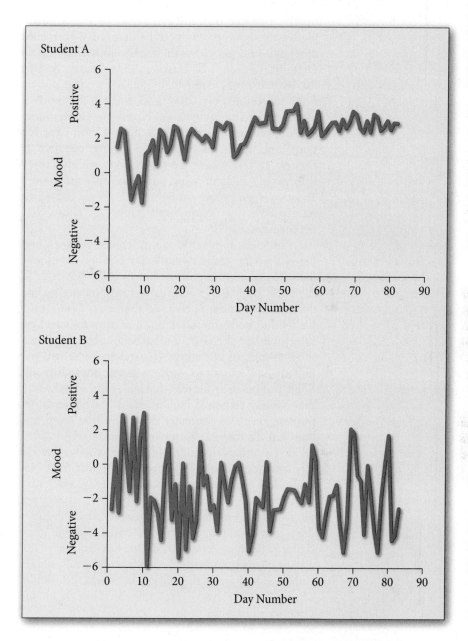

FIGURE 8.4 Examples of Daily Mood Fluctuations in Two People

Source: Adapted from "The stability of mood variability: A spectral analytic approach to daily mood assessments," by R. J. Larsen, *Journal of Personality and Social Psychology*, 1987, 52, 1195–1204. Copyright 1987 by the American Psychological Association.

that they're moody. Today they might be pumped up and enthusiastic, tomorrow frustrated and hostile.

Personality researchers would say the two students differ in terms of their affect intensity (Larson, 2009). **Affect intensity** refers to the strength or degree to which people typically experience their emotions. At one end we find people who respond to emotional situations with relatively mild reactions; at the other we find people with strong emotional reactions (Jones, Leen-Feldner, Olatunji, Reardon, & Hawks, 2009; Larsen & Diener, 1987). As shown in the two students' data, high-intensity people not only experience their emotions more intensely, they also tend to be more variable. They experience higher highs and lower lows. Notice that affect intensity applies to both positive and negative emotions. A person who experiences strong positive emotions also tends to experience strong negative emotions (Schimmack & Diener, 1997). Where we find peaks, we also find valleys. Researchers find that people high in affect intensity also are more aware of their emotions and may spend more time thinking about and reliving emotional experiences than people low on this trait (Gohm & Clore, 2002; Thompson, Dizen, & Berenbaum, 2009).

We might think that the difference between high- and low-intensity people is that the former simply have more emotionally loaded events in their lives. However, this does not seem to be the case. When researchers compare the kinds of activities high- and low-intensity people experience, they find no differences (Larsen, Diener, & Emmons, 1986). High- and low-intensity people tend to go to the same number of parties and concerts, and they have the same number of hassles and setbacks. The difference lies in how they react to those events. In one study, researchers presented participants with a series of hypothetical situations, such as being praised by an instructor or discovering a flat tire on their bicycle (Larsen et al., 1986). When asked to imagine how they would respond, high-intensity participants said they would enjoy the positive events to a greater degree and be more upset by the negative events than did the low-intensity participants.

Even relatively mild situations can evoke strong reactions in high-intensity individuals. High-intensity participants in one study had stronger emotional reactions than lows to magazine ads for alcoholic beverages (Geuens & De Pelsmacker, 1999). Other studies find that high-intensity people tend to overestimate the extent to which events will affect them and often draw unwarranted conclusions based on one good or one bad experience (Larsen, Billings, & Cutler, 1996; Larsen, Diener, & Cropanzano, 1987). To a high-intensity individual, one friendly smile suggests a blossoming relationship, one bad grade the end of the world. No doubt high-intensity people are often told they are overreacting by those from the other end of the affect intensity dimension.

These observations lead to another question: Is it better to be high on affect intensity and really experience life or low on this dimension and maintain a steady and calm approach to achievements and calamities? In other words, how does affect intensity relate to well-being? The answer is that high- and low-intensity people tend to score about the same on measures of happiness and well-being (Larsen, Diener, & Emmons, 1985). High-intensity people experience more positive affect, of course. But this seems to be offset by the fact that they also experience more negative affect (Kring, Smith, & Neale, 1994).

However, there does seem to be a difference in *how* these two kinds of people experience happiness. For high-intensity people, happiness means a lot of exhilarating and enlivening experiences. For low-intensity people, happiness takes the form of a calm and enduring sense of contentment (Larsen & Diener, 1987). In short, these people simply lead different—but not necessarily better or worse—emotional lives. Moreover, both kinds of individuals can be productive, but again in different ways. One researcher found that scientists tend to be low in affect intensity, whereas artists tend to be high (Sheldon, 1994). These findings fit the stereotypes of the pondering scientist satisfied with incremental steps toward his or her goal and the temperamental artist operating on bursts of inspiration-driven energy. Both get where they want to be, but each takes a different emotional route.

Emotional Expressiveness

If I tell you Maria is an emotional person, you probably have little difficulty imagining what she is like. The "emotional" people I know cry at sad movies, tell friends they are loved, and move about excitedly when given good news. If Maria is an emotional person, you could probably tell me what kind of mood she is in just by seeing the expression on her face. No doubt her friends share her joys as well as her disappointments. Most of us know someone like Maria, but what is it that makes these people stand out from the crowd?

By now it should be clear that the kinds of emotions we experience (affectivity) and the strength of our emotions (intensity) represent important aspects of our emotional lives. Yet when we identify someone as an "emotional" person, we probably aren't referring exactly to either of these individual differences. Rather, I suspect what distinguishes these people from most of us is that they are high in what researchers call emotional expressiveness.

Emotional expressiveness refers to a person's outward display of emotions. Some people tend to be particularly expressive of their feelings. We say these individuals "wear their emotions on their sleeves" or that we can "read them like a book." If they're feeling a little sad today, it shows. They move slowly; their shoulders sag; they wear sad faces. And if these same people have just received good news or simply feel good about what they're doing, we can tell in a minute. They bounce when they walk; they grin. We hear the enthusiasm in their voices. When highly expressive women in one study were told they had answered some difficult problems correctly, they could not keep themselves from smiling (Friedman & Miller-Herringer, 1991).

As with affectivity and intensity, researchers find relatively stable differences in the extent to which we express our emotions (Friedman, Prince, Riggio, & DiMatteo, 1980; Gohm & Clore, 2000; Kring, Smith, & Neale, 1994). Like other personality traits, we can place people along a continuum ranging from those who are highly expressive to those who show few outward signs of how they are feeling. Consistent with common observations, researchers find that women tend to be more expressive of their emotions than men (Gross & John, 1998; Kring & Gordon, 1998; Lavee & Ben-Ari, 2004; Timmers, Fischer, & Manstead, 1998). Interestingly, women also tend

Assessing Your Own Personality

Emotional Expressiveness

Indicate the extent to which each of the following statements describes you. Indicate your response using a 6-point scale with 1 = Never true and 6 = Always true.

_____   1. I think of myself as emotionally expressive.

_____   2. People think of me as an unemotional person.*

_____   3. I keep my feelings to myself.*

_____   4. I am often considered indifferent by others.*

_____   5. People can read my emotions.

_____   6. I display my emotions to other people.

_____   7. I don't like to let other people see how I'm feeling.*

_____   8. I am able to cry in front of other people.

_____   9. Even if I am feeling very emotional, I don't let others see my feelings.*

_____   10. Other people aren't easily able to observe what I'm feeling.*

_____   11. I am not very emotionally expressive.*

_____   12. Even when I'm experiencing strong feelings, I don't express them outwardly.*

_____   13. I can't hide the way I'm feeling.

_____   14. Other people believe me to be very emotional.

_____   15. I don't express my emotions to other people.*

_____   16. The way I feel is different from how others think I feel.*

_____   17. I hold my feelings in.*

To calculate your score, first reverse the answer values for the items with asterisks. That is, for these items only, 6 = 1, 5 = 2, 4 = 3, 3 = 4, 2 = 5, 1 = 6. Then add all 17 answer values. The higher your score, the more expressive you tend to be. When the test developers gave this scale to a group of undergraduates, they came up with the following norms:

	Mean	Standard Deviation
Females	66.60	2.71
Males	61.15	12.69
Total Sample	64.67	12.97

Scale: *The Emotional Expressivity Scale*

Source: Copyright © 1998 by the American Psychological Association. Reproduced with permission. Kring, A. M., Smith, D. A., & Neale, J. M. (1994). Individual differences in dispositional expressiveness: Development and validation of the Emotional Expressivity Scale. *Journal of Personality and Social Psychology, 66,* 934–949. doi: 10.1037/0022-3514.66.5.934. No further reproduction or distribution is permitted without written permission from the American Psychological Association.

to be better than men at reading the emotions in other people's faces (McClure, 2000). How well we express our feelings has important implications for how we get along with others. In particular, the more people express their emotions, the fewer problems they have in romantic relationships (Cordova, Gee, & Warren, 2005; Lavee & Ben-Ari, 2004; Noller, 1984). Communication is aided when partners understand what the other person is feeling, and communication almost always contributes to harmony and satisfaction in relationships. Moreover, people who express their emotions freely tend to experience less confusion when trying to read another person's emotions (King, 1998).

Expressing emotions also seems to be good for our psychological health. Participants in one study completed a series of well-being measures and kept daily records of their moods for 21 consecutive days (King & Emmons, 1990). The participants identified as highly expressive were happier and experienced less anxiety and guilt than those who were low in expressiveness. Other researchers using similar procedures found that expressive people were less prone to depression (Katz & Campbell, 1994). Highly expressive people also tend to be higher in self-esteem than those on the other end of this trait dimension (Friedman et al., 1980). In short, emotional expressiveness is good for us. In Chapter 12 we'll return to some of the reasons for this relation between well-being and expressing one's emotions.

Optimism and Pessimism

Winston Churchill once noted, "A pessimist sees the difficulty in every opportunity; an optimist sees the opportunity in every difficulty." Consistent with this observation, psychologists find that a positive outlook is often associated with high achievement and a positive mood (Taylor, 1989). People who approach an upcoming event believing they will do well tend to perform better and feel better about themselves than those who enter the situation thinking things will likely turn out poorly. Similarly, when people face a specific problem, those who believe they will beat the odds tend to do better and feel better than those who think the odds will beat them. Heart transplant patients in one study were asked about their expectations prior to the surgery (Leedham, Meyerowitz, Muirhead, & Frist, 1995). Those with positive expectations did a much better job of adjusting to life after the surgery than those with a more pessimistic outlook.

But optimism and pessimism aren't simply tied to specific events or problems. Rather, like the other traits reviewed in this chapter, psychologists can identify individual differences in the manner in which we typically approach life's challenges (Scheier & Carver, 1985). We can place people on a continuum ranging from those who look at life in the most optimistic light to those who view the world through the most pessimistic lenses. Because people are relatively consistent in the extent to which they adopt these viewpoints, psychologists sometimes refer to this personality variable as **dispositional optimism.**

When researchers compare people high in dispositional optimism with those who are not, they usually find clear advantages for the optimists. People who take an optimistic approach to life tend to achieve more than those who don't (Crane & Crane, 2007; Brown & Marshall, 2001; Segerstrom, 2007). Optimists set their goals higher, effectively prioritize their goals, and believe they can reach those goals (Geers, Wellman, & Lassiter, 2009). Optimistic college students tend to achieve higher grades and are less likely to drop out of college than pessimistic students (Richardson, Abraham, & Bond, 2012; Solberg Nes, Evans, Segerstrom, 2009).

Just like the moral of so many stories, researchers find that having confidence in one's abilities is often the key to success. In particular, optimists are less likely to allow setbacks and temporary failures to get them down (Gibbons, Blanton, Gerrard, Buunk, & Eggleston, 2000). One team of researchers looked at how new life insurance agents reacted to the inevitable rejections they face when selling policies (Seligman & Schulman, 1986). They found the pessimists were more than twice as likely as the optimists to quit within the first year. When the going got tough, many of the pessimists decided it was never going to get any better. Meanwhile, the undiscouraged and persistent optimists sold more insurance policies than their pessimistic colleagues.

As with many other personality variables, researchers find optimism and pessimism are related to culture (Chang, 2001; Fischer & Chalmers, 2008). Much of this research has compared people in individualistic cultures with those from collectivist cultures (Chapter 1). One study asked Canadian and Japanese students to estimate the likelihood that certain events (e.g., live a long life, develop skin cancer) would happen to them (Heine & Lehman, 1995). The Japanese students consistently expressed a more pessimistic outlook than the Canadians. Other investigators have compared scores on measures of optimism and pessimism between cultures (Chang, 1996; Lee & Seligman, 1997; You, Fung & Isaacowitz, 2009). These researchers also find Asian participants are more pessimistic than participants from individualistic cultures. Because, as we will see, optimism and pessimism are related to coping, well-being, and health, these cultural differences have important implications for counselors working with people from diverse cultural backgrounds (Chang, 2001).

Dealing with Adversity

Differences between optimists and pessimists are likely to be seen when people are faced with stressful events (Carver, Scheier, & Segerstrom, 2010; Nes & Segerstrom, 2006; Rasmussen, Wrosch, Scheier, & Carver, 2006). Consider the stress experienced by Israeli citizens in a study conducted during the Persian Gulf War (Zeidner & Hammer, 1992). The researchers looked at coping and adjustment among residents of Haifa, an area repeatedly threatened with SCUD missile attacks during the time the study was conducted. The investigators found that the dispositional optimists living in this region experienced less anxiety and less depression than those identified as pessimists. Similar reactions are found in people dealing with less acute sources of stress. One team of researchers looked at adjustment levels in men and women who had spent at least one year caring for a spouse diagnosed with Alzheimer's disease (Hooker, Monahan, Shifren, & Hutchinson, 1992). The spouses who generally approached life with an optimistic outlook experienced less stress and less depression than the pessimistic caregivers. Another study examined the health of individuals who experienced the death or severe illness of a loved one (Kivimaki et al., 2005). Optimistic participants had fewer health problems in the 18 months following the event than those low in optimism.

Other investigators look at how optimists and pessimists react to health problems and medical procedures. In one study, optimistic women who had surgery for breast cancer reported less distress during the year following the surgery and showed higher levels of adjustment several years later than pessimistic women going through the same experience (Carver et al., 1993, 2005). In another investigation, rheumatoid arthritis patients high in dispositional optimism scored higher on measures of psychological adjustment than did pessimistic patients (Long & Sangster, 1993). In yet another study, men recovering from coronary artery bypass surgery were compared for general mood and quality of life 6 months after the surgery (Scheier et al., 1989). As in the other investigations, the dispositionally optimistic men looked much better after their surgery than did the pessimists.

The results of these studies clearly demonstrate that optimists deal with adverse situations better than pessimists. But the benefits of optimism are not limited to extreme situations like war and surgery. Investigators also find that optimism affects how well students adjust to the challenges that come with the transition to college life. Freshman students with an optimistic outlook have a significantly easier time adjusting to the demands of their first quarter of college life than do pessimistic students (Aspinwall & Taylor, 1992; Condren & Greenglass, 2011).

Clearly, dispositional optimists do a better job of handling stressful situations than pessimists. But why is this the case? What is it about an optimistic disposition that helps some people come through life's crises and challenges so well? One answer is that optimists and pessimists use different strategies to cope with their problems (Carver, et al, 2010; Scheier, Carver, & Bridges, 2001). Optimists are more likely to deal with their problems head-on—that is, to use active coping strategies (Chapter 6). On the other hand, pessimists are more likely to distract themselves or resort to denial when faced with a difficult problem. Consider an investigation that compared the coping strategies optimistic and pessimistic college students used when facing a big exam (Chang, 1998). As shown in Figure 8.5, the optimists dealt with the stress of the upcoming exam by using direct problem solving, such as preparing for the test and talking with other students about their experience. In contrast, the pessimists dealt with their anxiety by relying on wishful thinking and withdrawing from others.

Researchers find a similar pattern when examining optimists and pessimists facing other types of stressors. Optimistic cancer patients in one study were more likely than pessimists to use active coping strategies (Friedman et al., 1992). The optimistic patients did what they could to deal with their cancer and talked to other people about their feelings. The pessimistic patients avoided thinking about their situation and kept their feelings to themselves. The optimistic women in the breast cancer study mentioned earlier were more likely than the pessimists to make plans early in the course of the disease and

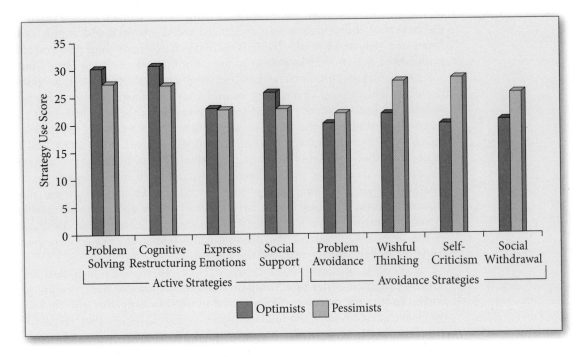

FIGURE 8.5 Use of Coping Strategies

Source: From "Dispositional optimism and primary and secondary appraisal of a stressor," by E. C. Chang, *Journal of Personality and Social Psychology*, 1998, 74, 1109–1120. Copyright © 1998 by the American Psychological Association.

to rely on such positive coping strategies as humor (Carver et al., 1993). The pessimistic patients were more likely to use denial. A similar pattern was found for the men recovering from bypass surgery (Scheier et al., 1989). Even the freshman students dealing with the stresses of entering college showed this different use of coping strategies. The optimistic students dealt with the stress of new classes, new friends, and new social pressures by trying to do something about these problems directly. The pessimistic students were more likely to pretend the problems did not exist or simply avoided dealing with them for as long as possible.

Optimism and Health

Researchers also find that optimism may be good for your health. Optimists are typically in better physical health than pessimists (Baker, 2007; Conway, Magai, Springer, & Jones, 2008; Rasmussen, Scheier, & Greenhouse, 2009; Segerstrom, 2007). In one study, researchers used essays written years earlier to determine how optimistic or pessimistic a group of men had been when they were 25 (Peterson, Seligman, & Vaillant, 1988). The investigators found that the optimists were in better health at ages 45 through 60 than the pessimists in their sample.

Why are optimists healthier than pessimists? The relationship between optimism and health appears to be complex, but investigators have identified several possible links (Peterson & Bossio, 2001). For example, we know that optimists are more likely to develop wide social networks and turn to friends in times of crisis (Brissette, Scheier, & Carver, 2002; Schollgen, Huxhold, Schuz, & Tesch-Romer, 2011), and numerous studies find social support often contributes to better health. In contrast, one study found pessimistic women diagnosed with breast cancer tended to reduce contact with friends (Carver, Lehman, & Antoni, 2003).

Other investigators have looked at physiological changes that affect the health of optimists and pessimists. One team of researchers examined optimism among law students during their first year of law school (Segerstrom & Sephton, 2010). Changes in optimism were related to changes in the strength of the students' immune systems. When the law students felt more optimistic, they had stronger immune systems than when they were feeling more pessimistic. Because they more often experience negative emotions, pessimists also tend to have higher blood pressure, and this can have an impact on their health (Raikkonen & Matthews, 2008).

Perhaps the most likely reason that optimists are healthier than pessimists is that an optimistic outlook leads to the kinds of attitudes and behaviors that contribute to good health. One team of researchers looked at patients in a cardiac rehabilitation program (Shepperd, Maroto, & Pbert, 1996). Each participant entered the program after suffering a heart attack or having been diagnosed with some other cardiovascular problem. Compared to the pessimists in the program, the optimistic patients were more successful in reducing saturated fat from their diet, decreasing body fat, and increasing their aerobic capacity. These optimistic patients apparently decided they could reach their rehabilitation goals and did what it took to succeed. Other studies find that optimists pay more attention to relevant health information than do pessimists (Aspinwall & Brunhart, 1996), are more physically active, eat healthier foods (Geers, Wellman, Seligman, Wuyek, & Neff, 2010; Giltay, Geleijnse, Zitman, Buijsse, & Kromhout, 2007), and are less prone to health-destructive habits, such as substance abuse (Carvajal, Clair, Nash, & Evans, 1998). In addition, the fatalistic view taken by pessimists may prevent them from practicing reasonable safety and health precautions, such as wearing a seat belt or using a designated driver. One team of investigators found pessimists—particularly those who expect bad events to occur in a wide range of situations—were more likely than optimists to be involved in fatal accidents (Peterson, Seligman, Yurko, Martin, & Friedman, 1998). In sum, when people expect good or bad health outcomes, they act in ways that make those outcomes more likely to occur.

Summary

1. Achievement motivation has been an important research topic for several decades. Much of the early work in this area was based on Henry Murray's description of people high in need for Achievement. More recent investigations look at the effects of attributions and achievement goals on

achievement behavior. Researchers find mastery goals often lead to more achievement than performance goals.

2. Research on the Type A behavior pattern developed out of observations by medical professionals about people who suffer heart attacks. Although early researchers found a strong link between Type A behavior and cardiovascular problems, later studies did not always replicate these findings. Researchers now know that one Type A component—hostility—is responsible for the increase in cardiovascular problems found in the earlier studies.

3. Research on socially anxious people finds a number of characteristic behaviors that interfere with the shy person's ability to interact effectively with others. Shy people tend to be self-conscious during social encounters, are reluctant to ask others for help, and often interpret feedback from their conversation partners as rejection. Research suggests that socially anxious people suffer from evaluation apprehension. Shy people avoid negative evaluation from others by limiting their social interactions or by keeping these interactions short and pleasant. The socially anxious persons' lack of confidence makes initiating conversations especially difficult for them.

4. Although emotions fluctuate considerably over time and across situations, researchers have identified three ways our emotions can be examined in terms of relatively stable individual differences. Researchers place our emotions along two major dimensions, which they identify as positive affect and negative affect.

5. Personality researchers also look at emotional intensity and at individual differences in the extent to which people express their emotions.

6. People can be identified along a continuum from dispositionally optimistic to dispositionally pessimistic. Researchers find optimists typically deal more effectively with adversity, probably because they use more active and direct coping strategies than pessimists. Optimists also tend to be in better health than pessimists. Among the reasons for this difference is that optimists are more likely to act in ways that lead to better health outcomes.

Key Terms

achievement goals (p. 192)

affect intensity (p. 211)

dispositional optimism (p. 215)

emotional affectivity (p. 207)

emotional expressiveness (p. 213)

evaluation apprehension (p. 204)

need for Achievement (p. 186)

social anxiety (p. 202)

Media Resources

Visit the book companion website at **www.cengagebrain.com** to find a glossary, flashcards, quizzing, and more.

CHAPTER 9

The Biological Approach

Theory, Application, and Assessment

Have you ever been told that you act like one of your parents? Perhaps a relative has said, "You're your mother's son (daughter), all right." My brother's quick temper has often been described as "inherited from his father." I know one couple who were more interested in learning about the family of their daughter's fiancé than about the fiancé. They told me that meeting the new in-laws would help them see what their future grandchildren would be like. As these examples suggest, the notion that children inherit characteristics from their parents is widely held in this society. Not only do people accept that parents pass physical characteristics, such as eye color or height, through their genes, but we often expect children's personalities to resemble their parents'.

Although conventional wisdom has for years acknowledged the role of biology in the development of personality, the same cannot be said of many psychologists. Several decades ago, many academic psychologists looked at all healthy newborns as blank slates, perhaps limited by differences in intelligence or physical skills but otherwise equally likely to develop into any kind of adult personality. Different adult personalities were attributed to differences in experiences, particularly in the way parents raised their children during the child's early years. However, this view has changed. No reputable psychologist would argue that people are born with their adult personalities intact, but today few psychologists would deny that personality is at least partly the result of inherited biological differences.

This acceptance of a genetic influence on personality has coincided with a growing recognition that personality cannot be separated from other biological factors. Research tells us that not all people have identical physiological functioning. We can identify differences between people in terms of brainwave activity, hormone levels, heart-rate responsiveness, and other physiological features. More important for personality psychologists, researchers find these biological differences often translate into differences in behavior. We'll review an example of this later in this chapter when we look at individual differences in brainwave patterns.

We also have seen in recent years a growing recognition that human personality, like other human features, is the product of many generations of evolutionary development. Just as biologists find it useful to ask about the evolutionary function of the physical characteristics of a species, some psychologists have found this same question useful in understanding certain features of personality.

This growing acceptance of a biological influence on personality is partly a reflection of behaviorism's declining influence on the thinking of academic psychologists. As described in Chapter 13, early behaviorists tended to ignore individual differences among newborns, and a few even claimed that with enough control over the child's experiences they could shape a child into whatever personality they wanted. Probably no behaviorist would argue such an extreme position today. The movement away from the "blank slate" position has also been stimulated by research demonstrating rather clearly that at least some of our personality is inherited from our parents. This research is reviewed in Chapter 10.

In this chapter, we'll look at three ways psychologists have used biological concepts to explain personality. First, we examine Hans Eysenck's description of personality, which has been an influential model in personality research for several decades. From the beginning, Eysenck maintained that the individual differences in personality he described are based on physiological differences. Second, we look at individual differences in general dispositions, called temperaments. A strong case can be made that temperaments are based on biological differences. Psychologists have identified some of these temperamental differences among very young children. Third, we examine an area of personality research called evolutionary personality psychology. Psychologists using this approach borrow the concept of natural selection from biology to explain a large number of human behaviors.

What each of these three theoretical perspectives makes clear is that a complete understanding of human personality requires us to go beyond some of the early boundaries of the discipline. It is no longer useful to think of our personality as somehow separate from our physiological makeup.

Hans Eysenck's Theory of Personality

Many years ago, when the conventional wisdom in psychology traced an individual's personality to his or her experiences, a respected psychologist argued that personality was, in fact, determined more by biological makeup than by any actions or mistakes made by one's parents. Although Hans Eysenck's (pronounced Eye-Zinc) theory of personality has always been accorded respect within the field, his initial claims about a large biological determinant of personality were met by many with a mix of skepticism and tolerance. But today Eysenck's emphasis on biological aspects of individual differences is increasingly compatible with the recognition of biology's role in personality.

The Structure of Personality

Like Raymond Cattell and other psychologists described in Chapter 7, Eysenck was concerned with discovering the underlying structure of personality. Also like these trait researchers, Eysenck employed factor analysis to identify the basic number of what he called types, or supertraits. However, unlike most of the trait researchers, Eysenck's conclusion after years of research was that all traits can be subsumed within *three* basic personality dimensions. He called these three dimensions extraversion–introversion, neuroticism, and psychoticism.

Eysenck's research strategy began by dividing the elements of personality into various units that can be arranged hierarchically (Figure 9.1). The basic structure in this scheme is the *specific response level,* which consists of specific behaviors. For example, if we watch a man spend the afternoon talking and laughing with friends, we would be observing a specific response. If this man spends many afternoons each week having a good time with friends, we have evidence for the second level in Eysenck's model, a *habitual*

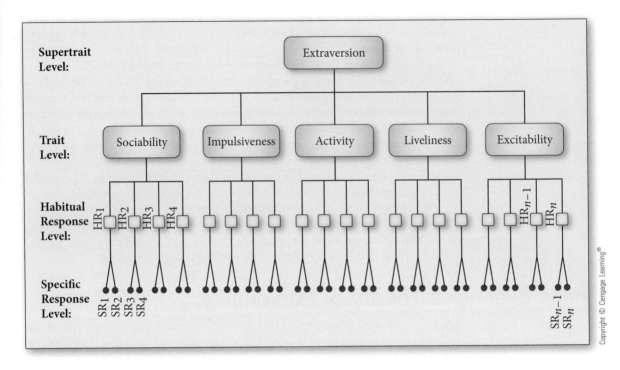

FIGURE 9.1 Eysenck's Hierarchical Model of Personality

response. But it is unlikely that this man limits himself to socializing just in the afternoon and just with these friends. Suppose this man also devotes a large part of his weekends and quite a few evenings to his social life. If you watch long enough, you might find that he lives for social gatherings, group discussions, parties, and so on. You might conclude, in Eysenck's terms, that this person exhibits the *trait* of sociability. Finally, Eysenck argued that traits such as sociability are part of a still larger dimension of personality. That is, people who are sociable also tend to be impulsive, active, lively, and excitable. All of these traits combine to form the *supertrait* Eysenck called extraversion.

How many of these supertraits are there? Originally, Eysenck's factor analytic research yielded evidence for two basic dimensions that could subsume all other traits: *extraversion–introversion* and *neuroticism*. Because the dimensions are independent of one another, people who score on the extraversion end of the first dimension can score either high or low on the second dimension. Further, as shown in Figure 9.2, someone who scores high on extraversion and low on neuroticism possesses traits different from a person who scores high on both extraversion and neuroticism.

If you are the prototypic extravert, you are "outgoing, impulsive, and uninhibited, having many social contacts and frequently taking part in group activities. The typical extravert is sociable, likes parties, has many friends, needs to have people to talk to, and does not like reading or studying by

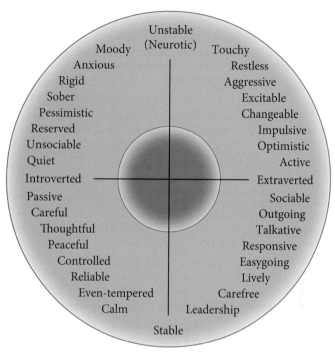

FIGURE 9.2 Traits Associated with Eysenck's Two Major Personality Dimensions

Source: From Eysenck, H. J., and Eysenck, B. G. (1968), *Manual for the Eysenck Personality Inventory*, San Diego: EDITS. Reprinted by permission of Educational and Industrial Testing Service.

himself" (Eysenck & Eysenck, 1968, p. 6). An introvert is "a quiet, retiring sort of person, introspective, fond of books rather than people; he is reserved and distant except to intimate friends" (p. 6). Of course, most people fall somewhere between these two extremes, but each of us is perhaps a little more one than the other.

The second major dimension in Eysenck's model is *neuroticism*. High scores on this dimension indicate a tendency to respond emotionally. We sometimes refer to people high in neuroticism as unstable or highly emotional. They often have strong emotional reactions to minor frustrations and take longer to recover from these. They are more easily upset, angered, and depressed than most of us. Those falling on the other end of the neuroticism dimension are less likely to fly off the handle and less prone to large swings in emotion.

Research findings later led Eysenck to add a third supertrait: *psychoticism*. People who score high on this dimension are described as "egocentric, aggressive, impersonal, cold, lacking in empathy, impulsive, lacking in concern for others, and generally unconcerned about the rights and welfare of other people" (Eysenck, 1982, p. 11). Needless to say, people scoring particularly high on this dimension are good candidates for some type of judicial correction or psychotherapy.

A Biological Basis for Personality

Eysenck (1990) provided three arguments when making the case that individual differences in personality are based in biology. First, he noted the consistency of extraversion–introversion over time. One study found that participants' scores on measures of extraversion–introversion remained fairly consistent over a span of 45 years (Conley, 1984, 1985). Of course, this finding alone does not establish that extraversion–introversion is determined through biology. It is possible that people remain in similar environments throughout their lives. Or the finding may simply mean that after this part of personality is established it is difficult to change.

Second, Eysenck pointed to the results of cross-cultural research. Investigators often find the same three dimensions of personality—extraversion–introversion, neuroticism, and psychoticism—in studies conducted in many different countries with people from very different cultures (Barrett & Eysenck, 1984; Lynn & Martin, 1995). Moreover, the same three superfactors appear in studies using different data-gathering methods (Eysenck & Long, 1986). Eysenck maintained that this level of cross-cultural consistency would be unlikely unless biological factors were largely responsible for personality.

Third, Eysenck noted the results of several studies indicating that genetics plays an important role in determining a person's placement on each of the three personality dimensions. As presented in detail in Chapter 10, that research strongly suggests that how introverted or extraverted you are is a result of your genetic makeup.

After examining the evidence from all of these sources, and no doubt adding a bit of his own intuition, Eysenck (1982) asserted that about two-thirds of the variance in personality development can be traced to biological factors. Although the exact figure may not be this high, data from a continuing stream of studies suggests that extraverts and introverts differ on a number of biological measures (Cox-Fuenzalida, Gilliland, & Swickert, 2001; Doucet & Stelmack, 2000; Stelmack & Pivik, 1996). This is not to say that environmental factors do not play a role. But, as the evidence reviewed in the next chapter makes clear, biology probably sets limits on how much we can change an introverted friend into a highly sociable individual or the likelihood of shaping an impulsive, outgoing child into a calm, easygoing adult.

Physiological Differences: Stimulation Sensitivity and Behavioral Activation/Inhibition Systems

Eysenck argued that extraverts and introverts differ not only in terms of behavior but also in their physiological makeup. He originally maintained that extraverts and introverts have different levels of cerebral cortex arousal when in a nonstimulating, resting state (Eysenck, 1967). Although it may sound backward at first, he proposed that extraverts generally have a lower level of cortical arousal than do introverts. Extraverts seek out highly arousing social behavior because their cortical arousal is well below their desired level when doing nothing. In a sense, highly extraverted people are simply trying to avoid unpleasant boredom. Their problem is feeding their need for stimulation. Introverts have the opposite problem. They typically operate at cortical arousal level that is near or perhaps even above the optimal amount. These people select solitude and nonstimulating environments in an effort to keep their already high arousal level from becoming too aversive. For these reasons, extraverts enjoy a noisy party that introverts can't wait to leave.

Sensitivity to Stimulation

Unfortunately, a great deal of research has failed to uncover the different levels of base-rate cortical arousal proposed by Eysenck. Introverts and extraverts do differ in how certain parts of their brains respond to emotional stimuli (Canli, 2004). However, they show no differences in brain-wave activity when at rest or when asleep (Stelmack, 1990). But this does not mean that Eysenck's original theorizing was entirely off base. Rather, there is ample evidence that introverts are more sensitive to stimulation than extraverts (Bullock & Gilliland, 1993; Stelmack, 1990; Swickert & Gilliland, 1998). That is, introverts are more quickly and strongly aroused when exposed to external stimulation. Introverts are more likely to become aroused when they encounter loud music or the stimulation found in an active social encounter. Introverts are even more responsive than extraverts when exposed to chemical stimulants, such as caffeine or nicotine.

As a result of these research findings, many researchers now describe extraverts and introverts in terms of their different sensitivity to stimulation rather than differences in cortical activity. However, the effect is essentially the same. Because of physiological differences, introverts are more quickly overwhelmed by the stimulation of a crowded social gathering, whereas extraverts are likely to find the same gathering rather pleasant. Extraverts are quickly bored by slow-moving movie plots and soft music, but introverts often find these subtle sources of stimulation engaging.

Sensitivity to Reinforcement: The Behavioral Approach System and the Behavioral Inhibition System

Other researchers tie differences in extraversion and neuroticism to biologically based differences in sensitivity to reinforcement (Smillie, 2013). According to *reinforcement sensitivity theory* (Gray, 1982, 1987; Gray & McNaughton, 2000), each human brain has a **behavioral approach system (BAS)** and a **behavioral inhibition system (BIS)**. The exact regions of the brain and the specific processes involved in each of these hypothetical systems remain to be determined. Nonetheless, like other personality concepts, individuals are said to differ in the strength of these two systems, and these individual differences are relatively stable over time. People with a highly active BAS are intensely motivated to seek out and achieve pleasurable goals. Compared to people low on this dimension, they get more pleasure out of rewards and more enjoyment out of simply anticipating that rewards are coming. Individuals with an active BAS also experience more anger and frustration when they fall short of reaching anticipated sources of pleasure. People with a highly active BIS tend to be more apprehensive than others. They approach new situations warily, are on

Hans J. Eysenck

1916–1997

If heredity plays a large role in determining personality, we might say that Hans Eysenck was born to be the center of attention in whatever field he entered. Eysenck was born in Germany into a family of celebrities. His father, Eduard Eysenck, was an accomplished actor and singer, something of a matinee idol in Europe. His mother, whose stage name was Helga Molander, was a silent film star. They planned a glamorous career in the entertainment field for Hans, who at age 8 had a small role in a motion picture. However, like many Hollywood marriages today, Eysenck's parents divorced when he was young (only to marry other show business people later). Most of Eysenck's early years were spent with his grandmother in Berlin.

Upon graduating from public school in Berlin, the rebellious Eysenck decided not only to pursue a career in physics and astronomy, much to his family's displeasure, but to do so abroad. After a year in France, he moved to England, where he eventually completed his PhD at the University of London. Like so many others at the time, Eysenck left Germany in 1934 in part to escape the rise of the Nazis. "Faced with the choice of having to join the Nazi storm troops if I wanted to go to a university," he wrote, "I knew that there was no future for me in my unhappy homeland" (Eysenck, 1982, p. 289). Because he was a German citizen, Eysenck was prohibited from joining the British military and spent World War II working in an emergency hospital. Following the war, Eysenck returned to the University of London, where his long career produced 79 books and more than 1,000 journal articles (Farley, 2000).

Although he never pursued the career in show business his parents desired, he did not avoid the public's eye. Eysenck appeared to seek out and dive right into some of the biggest controversies in psychology. In 1952 he published a paper challenging the effectiveness of psychotherapy. He was especially critical of psychoanalysis, pointing out that empirical evidence at the time showed psychoanalysis to be no better than receiving no treatment at all. More controversy occurred when he stated that individual differences in intelligence are largely inherited. As a result, Eysenck was sometimes unfairly associated with those who proposed inherent racial differences in intelligence. In 1980 Eysenck published a book arguing that the case for cigarettes as a cause of health problems was not as strong as many people claimed. Critics were particularly harsh when they discovered that some of this work had been sponsored by American tobacco companies.

This lifelong combative style caused one biographer to call Eysenck the "controversialist in the intellectual world" (Gibson, 1981, p. 253). Eysenck would no doubt have enjoyed this title. "From the days of opposition to Nazism in my early youth, through my stand against Freudianism and projective techniques, to my advocacy of behavior therapy and genetic studies, to more recent issues, I have usually been against the establishment and in favor of the rebels," he wrote. "[But] I prefer to think that on these issues the majority were wrong, and I was right" (1982, p. 298).

the constant lookout for signs of danger, and are quick to retreat from a situation that they sense might lead to problems. Not surprisingly, they also are more likely to experience anxiety than people low on this dimension.

Just how these two hypothetical systems are related to extraversion and neuroticism remains a matter of debate (Smillie, Pickering, & Jackson,

2006). But most researchers see a connection between the BAS and extraversion and a connection between the BIS and neuroticism. That is, people with a highly active BAS are similar to those scoring high in extraversion, and those with a highly active BIS are similar to people scoring high in neuroticism. Consistent with this analysis, scales designed to measure BAS and BIS correlate with scales measuring extraversion and neuroticism, respectively. However, the correlation is far from perfect (Jackson, 2009). Thus, although the concepts are related, they probably are not exactly the same.

Nonetheless, when looked at within this framework, we can think of extraverts as people who are more aware of and more attracted to situations that promise rewards. When extraverts encounter an opportunity to have a good time, they are motivated to approach the object of their desire. As a result, extraverts are more impulsive than introverts and are more likely to find themselves in the middle of a party or riding on a roller coaster. One

Marlene Somsak/Santa Clara University

How do you spend your spare time? If you're an extravert, it probably never occurs to you to take a long walk by yourself. If you're an introvert, you may rely on a long walk to reduce your arousal level after an intense and active day.

implication of this description is that extraverts aren't necessarily attracted to all social situations, but only to those that are likely to be enjoyable (Lucas, Diener, Grob, Suh, & Shao, 2000). Consistent with this hypothesis, one team of researchers found that extraverts actually preferred nonsocial situations, such as going for a walk alone, more than introverts did *if* they thought the experience would be pleasant (Lucas & Diener, 2001).

Temperament

If you were to spend a few minutes watching toddlers in a nursery school, you most likely would notice that even before they are a year old, some children clearly act differently than others. If you were to spend a week working in the nursery, you could probably identify the active babies, the ones who cry frequently, and (hopefully) a few who are usually quiet and happy. Although it is possible these differences are the result of different treatment the children receive at home, a growing number of researchers are convinced these general behavioral styles are present at birth. Further, they argue that these general styles are relatively stable and influence the development of personality traits throughout a person's life.

But does this mean that some people are born to be sociable and others are born to be shy? Probably not. More likely we are born with broad dispositions toward certain types of behaviors. Psychologists refer to these general behavioral dispositions as **temperaments**. Temperaments are general patterns of behavior and mood that can be expressed in many different ways and that, depending on one's experiences, develop into different personality traits. How these general dispositions develop into stable personality traits depends on a complex interplay of one's genetic predispositions and the environment that a person grows up in.

Temperament and Personality

Although researchers agree that temperaments are general behavioral patterns that can often be seen in newborns, they do not always agree on how to classify the different kinds of temperaments they observe (Caspi, 1998; Clark, 2005; Dyson, Olino, Durbin, Goldsmith, & Klein, 2012; Evans & Rothbart, 2007; Shiner, 1998). Indeed, researchers often disagree on the number of basic temperaments. One popular model identifies three temperament dimensions—emotionality, activity, and sociability (Buss & Plomin, 1984, 1986). *Emotionality* refers to the intensity of emotional reactions. Children who cry frequently, are easily frightened, and who often express anger are high in this temperament. As adults, these individuals are easily upset and may have a "quick temper." *Activity* refers to a person's general level of energy. Children high in this temperament move around a lot, prefer games that require running and jumping, and tend to fidget and squirm when forced to sit still for an extended period of time. Adults high on this dimension are always on the go and prefer high-energy activities like playing sports and dancing. *Sociability* relates to a general tendency to affiliate and interact with others. Sociable children seek out other children to play with. Adults high in this temperament have a lot of friends and enjoy social gatherings.

Where do temperaments come from? Because we can identify temperamental differences in babies, it is not surprising that researchers find evidence that temperaments are largely inherited (Kandler, Riemann, & Angleitner, 2013; Mullineaus, Deater-Deckard, Petrill, Thompson, & DeThrone, 2009). In contrast to the approach taken by many physicians and psychologists a few decades ago, it is now widely agreed that not all babies are born alike. Parents with difficult-to-manage babies are often troubled by descriptions of the "typical" newborn who sleeps whenever put into a crib, eats meals on a regular schedule, and responds to parental attention with calm, loving sounds. Fortunately, most popular baby books today assure parents that some babies are going to be more active and more emotional than others.

Consistent with common observation, researchers also find gender differences in temperament (Else-Quest, Hyde, Goldsmith, & Van Hulle, 2006). Girls are more likely than boys to exhibit an *effortful control* temperament, which includes the ability to focus attention and exercise control over impulsive urges. On the other hand, boys are more likely than girls to be identified with a *surgency* temperament. This temperament pattern includes high levels of activity and sociability. These gender differences can be seen in children as young as 3 months of age.

Can we look at temperament levels in preschool children and determine what kind of adult personalities they will have? To a certain degree, the answer is "Yes." Consider the results of an ongoing longitudinal study conducted in Dunedin, New Zealand (Caspi, 2000; Caspi et al., 2003; Moffitt et al., 2007; Slutske, Moffitt, Poulton, & Caspi, 2012). Ninety-one percent of the children born in this town between April 1, 1972, and March 31, 1973, were tested for temperament at age 3. The researchers identified three temperament types in these toddlers. The *well-adjusted* children exhibited self-control and self-confidence and were capable of approaching new people and situations with little difficulty. The *undercontrolled* children were impulsive and restless and easily distracted. The *inhibited* children were fearful, reluctant to get involved in social activities, and uneasy in the presence of strangers. The investigators then examined personality development and behavior at several points as the children moved through childhood and adolescence and into their young adult years.

What did they find? As expected, the well-adjusted children became relatively healthy, well-adjusted adults. Also as expected, the undercontrolled and inhibited children's lives had their difficulties. During the elementary school and adolescent years, undercontrolled children were more likely to have problems with fighting, lying, and disobeying at both school and home. As young adults, they were more likely to experience legal, employment, and relationship problems. By the time they reached 32, these individuals were twice as likely to have a problem with excessive gambling as the people who had been classified as well-adjusted. Compared to the other two groups, inhibited children showed more signs of worrying and fussing when growing up, and as adults they were less socially engaged and more likely to suffer from depression. Although temperament by no means is the sole determinant of adult personality and behavior, this study and others make the case that temperament plays an important role in personality development.

The process through which general temperaments develop into personality traits is complex and influenced by a large number of factors (Caspi, 1998; Rothbart, 2007; Rothbart & Ahadi, 1994). Although the child's general level of emotionality or activity points the development of personality in a certain direction, that development is also influenced by the child's experiences as he or she grows up (Ganiban, Saudino, Ulbricht, Neiderhiser, & Reiss, 2008). For example, a highly emotional child has a better chance of becoming an aggressive adult than does a child low in this temperament. But parents who encourage problem-solving skills over the expression of anger may turn a highly emotional child into a cooperative, nonaggressive adult. A child low in sociability is unlikely to become an outgoing, highly gregarious adult, but that child might develop excellent social skills, be a wonderful friend, and learn to lead others with a quiet, respectful style.

Most temperament researchers accept that biologically based differences in temperament are directly related to differences in adult personality. But there is also a less direct connection. General behavioral dispositions also affect the development of personality traits because the child's temperament influences the type of environment he or she lives in (Caspi, 1998; Rothbart & Ahadi, 1994). That is, how other people react to us, and whether they will be a part of our environment at all, is partly determined by our temperament. For example, children high in sociability are likely to seek out situations with other people. Parents react differently to a baby who is constantly fussing and restless than to one who sleeps calmly. As a result, the restless baby experiences a different parent–child relationship than children with other temperaments. Temperament also generates expectations in other people that can affect the way they treat a child. Preschool teachers in one study expected different personalities in the children in their classes based on observations about the child's general activity level (Graziano, Jensen-Campbell, & Sullivan-Logan, 1998). It is not hard to imagine that these different teacher expectations lead to treating each student a little differently.

In short, adult personalities are determined by both inherited temperament and the environment. Moreover, temperament influences the environment, and the environment then influences the way temperament develops into stable personality traits. Within limits, two children born with identical temperaments can grow up to be two very different people. A child with a high activity level may become an aggressive, achieving, or athletic adult. But that child will probably not become lazy and indifferent. A child does not represent a blank slate on which parents may draw whatever personality they desire. But neither is a child's personality set at birth, leaving the parents and society to settle for whatever they get.

Inhibited and Uninhibited Children

Several decades ago, two developmental psychologists reported the results of an investigation on personality trait stability (Kagan & Moss, 1962). They had measured traits when the participants were 2 or 3 years old and again when these same people were 20. Although most traits showed at least a little change over time, one appeared remarkably stable. The researchers found that children who were passive and cautious when faced with a new situation usually grew up to be adults who showed a similar pattern of shyness around strangers. Because environmental explanations of behavior were prevalent at the time, the researchers assumed this stable trait was the result of some type of "acquired fearfulness" shaped by the parents during childhood.

Today those psychologists have a different interpretation. They argue that these different styles are the result of inherited dispositions (Kagan, 2003; Kagan & Snidman, 2004). Moreover, they find that approximately 10% of Caucasian American children fall into a category they refer to as "inhibited" (Kagan & Snidman, 1991a). **Inhibited children** are controlled and gentle. When they throw a ball or knock over a tower of blocks, they do so in a manner that is "monitored, restrained, almost soft." Inhibited children are the ones who cling to their mothers or fathers when entering a new playroom or when meeting new children. They are slow to explore new toys or equipment and may go for several minutes without saying a word.

Uninhibited children show the opposite pattern. Approximately 25% of the children in the researchers' samples fall into this category (Kagan & Snidman, 1991a). These children jump right in to play with a new toy or to climb on a new piece of playground equipment. They usually start talking soon after they enter a new play area, even if they don't already know the other children playing there.

On the surface, the difference between the two kinds of children appears to be their level of anxiety. But inhibited children are not simply more afraid of everything. Rather, they are vulnerable to a specific form of anxiety psychologists refer to as *anxiety to novelty*. These children are cautious about and at times fearful of new people and new situations. Inhibited toddlers often turn away from strangers and bury their face in mother's or father's leg. As adults, they may express their discomfort in a new situation by withdrawing socially and waiting for others to speak first.

Researchers find evidence from a number of sources that these inhibited and uninhibited styles represent inherited biological temperaments. Inhibited and uninhibited children show a number of physical differences almost from the moment of birth (Fox, Henderson, Rubin, Calkins, & Schmidt, 2001; Moehler, Kagan, Brunner, Wiebel, Kaufmann, & Resch, 2006; Rosenberg & Kagan, 1989). They differ in terms of body build, susceptibility to allergies, and even eye color (inhibited children are more likely to have blue eyes). Inhibited children are more likely than uninhibited children to show signs of irritability, sleep disturbances, and chronic constipation during the first few months of life. Newborns later identified as inhibited children respond to unfamiliar stimuli with increased heart rate and pupil dilation (LaGasse, Gruber, & Lipsitt, 1989).

Additional evidence for a biological foundation comes from research with older children and adults. In particular, neuroimaging studies find inhibited and uninhibited children's brains react differently to events and images (Bar-Haim et al., 2009). In one investigation, 10- to 12-year-old boys and girls classified as inhibited reacted to noises with different brain stem responses than did uninhibited children (Woodward et al., 2001). Other investigators find inhibited children have an abnormally high amygdala response (Perez-Edgar et al., 2007; Schwartz, Wright, Shin, Kagan, & Rauch, 2003) or increased striatum activity (Helfinstein, Fox, & Pine, 2012) when presented highly novel or uncertain stimuli.

Of course, how inhibited children express their anxiety changes as they mature. Nonetheless, researchers find evidence for a fear of the unfamiliar throughout childhood and into adulthood (Gest, 1997; Kagan & Snidman, 2004; Moehler et al., 2008). Trained judges in one study looked at motor activity—arm and leg movements, tongue protrusions, and crying—in 4-month-old infants to place the children into inhibited and uninhibited categories (Kagan, 1989; Kagan & Snidman, 1991a, 1991b). The psychologists observed the children again at ages 9, 14, and 21 months to see how the toddlers would react to unfamiliar events, such as seeing a puppet speaking in an angry tone or being shown a large metal robot they could play with. Forty percent of the infants classified as inhibited showed signs of fear, such as crying or hiding, at 14 and 21 months, but none of the uninhibited children did.

These temperamental differences can also be seen when the children reach school age (Rimm-Kaufman & Kagan, 2005). One team of investigators

Some children appear to inherit a tendency to respond to unfamiliar situations with increased arousal. When entering a new situation with new people, many of these children display what we typically call "shy" behavior.

TABLE 9.1 Correlations Between Inhibition Measures at 21 Months and Behaviors at Age 5 1/2 Years

Behavior at Age 5 1/2 Years	Correlation with Inhibition Score at 21 Months
Play with unfamiliar children	.43
Laboratory activity level	.38
Look at experimenter	.22
Play with new toys	.19
Spontaneous falling	.40
Ball-toss riskiness	.35
Social interaction in school	.34
Mother's rating of shyness.	.36

Note: The higher the score, the better the inhibition score predicts the behavior.

Source: From "Inhibited and uninhibited children: A follow-up study," by J. S. Reznick et al., *Child Development*, 1986, 57, 660–680. Reprinted by permission of the Society for Research in Child Development, Inc.

measured children's fear of unfamiliar situations at 21 months of age (Reznick et al., 1986). When the children reached age 5 1/2, they were brought back into the laboratory and examined in a number of situations. Experimenters coded how much the children played with unfamiliar children in the laboratory playroom, how spontaneously they allowed themselves to fall onto a mattress when playing a falling game, and how risky they were in a ball-tossing game. As shown in Table 9.1, the children who had shown an inhibited behavior pattern as infants exhibited similar behaviors at age 5 1/2. In other words, the toddler who clung to mother or father in a new situation showed a similar style of behavior when examined 4 years later.

It is easy to see how this fear of the unfamiliar can set inhibited children on a path toward shyness. Indeed, investigators find that inhibited children are significantly more likely than uninhibited children to become shy teenagers (Schwartz, Snidman, & Kagan, 1999). However, researchers also find that inhibited children are also at risk for developing social anxiety disorder (Chronis-Tuscano et al., 2009; Perez-Edgar et al., 2010). One team of reviewers estimated that inhibited children were seven times more likely to suffer from social anxiety disorder in adolescence than children not identified as inhibited (Clauss & Blackford, 2012).

But what about after that? Do inhibited children become inhibited adults? To answer this question, one study measured inhibition in a group of children between the ages of 8 and 12 (Gest, 1997). These same participants were tested again nearly 10 years later, just as they were entering early adulthood. The investigator found an impressively high correlation of .57 between the two measures, indicating that quiet, apprehensive children retain many of these characteristics when they become adults. Another study found that being an inhibited child was a risk factor for adult anxiety disorders, especially social phobia (Biederman et al., 2001).

Do these results mean inhibited children are sentenced to become shy adults? Fortunately, the answer is "No." Parents of inhibited children can do their offspring a favor by becoming sensitive to the child's discomfort in unfamiliar settings and by teaching the child how to deal with new situations and people. Research indicates that many business leaders, community workers, and entertainers have learned to overcome their shyness and lead very social lives. It also is an open question as to whether the connection between inhibited children and later social problems applies to all cultures. One study with Chinese children found that toddlers identified as inhibited at age 2 actually had better social relationships at age 7 than the average child (Chen, Chen, Li, & Wang, 2009).

Finally, although most of the research in this area has been focused on inhibited children, researchers also find that uninhibited children are susceptible to their own set of potential problems. In particular, uninhibited children are more likely than most to exhibit disruptive behavior disorders, including aggressiveness and attention problems (Biederman et al., 2001; Schwartz, Snidman, & Kagan, 1996). But once again, parents and others have a hand in determining how this inherited temperament expresses itself when these uninhibited children become adolescents and adults.

Evolutionary Personality Psychology

Think for a moment about a recent experience you have had with anxiety. That is, what was happening the last time you felt nervous, worrisome, or anxious? Although direct threats to our well-being—such as an earthquake or physical assault—are certainly sources of anxiety, these kinds of events are relatively rare and probably did not make your list. Instead, if you are like most people, you probably thought of something like talking in front of a group, making a fool of yourself at a party, or having a fight with a friend. In other words, it's likely you recalled a situation that involved some sort of negative evaluation and possibly even rejection by other people. Or you may have thought of a situation that only suggested that negative social evaluation might be coming, such as forgetting to turn in an assignment or discovering that you forgot to use deodorant one morning.

What this simple exercise illustrates is that negative evaluation by other people, either directly or potentially, is a common source of anxiety. But why might this be the case? Is this a learned behavior? Have we been conditioned to fear situations in which other people dislike us? That's certainly possible. Or could there be a psychoanalytic basis for this anxiety? At some deep level are we reminded of a traumatic separation from our childhood? Perhaps. But another explanation suggests that the roots of anxiety go back much further than this. According to this approach, we react to negative social evaluation in the same way our ancestors did. Moreover, this inherited tendency to become nervous and upset in certain situations allowed our species to survive.

This different approach is known as *evolutionary personality theory* (Buss, 2008, 2009). Proponents of this theory use the process of natural selection, borrowed from the theory of evolution, to explain universal human characteristics such as anxiety. These psychologists argue that many characteristics we call "human nature" make sense if we understand the evolutionary function they serve. We'll return to the example of anxiety later to illustrate this point. First, we need to examine some of the assumptions underlying evolutionary personality theory.

Natural Selection and Psychological Mechanisms

Evolutionary personality psychology is based on the theory of evolution, as developed in the field of biology for more than a century. According to evolution theory, physical features evolve because they help the species survive the challenges of the environment and reproduce new members of the species. The key to this process is *natural selection*. That is, some members of a species possess inherited characteristics that help them meet and survive the threats from the natural environment, such as severe climate, predators, and food shortages. These survivors are more likely than those less able to deal with the environment to reproduce and pass their inherited characteristics on to their offspring. The net result over many generations is the evolution of species-specific features. Through the process of natural selection, species developing features that help them survive prosper, and those failing to develop these features die out. In many cases, physical features evolve because they provide solutions to a serious threat to a species' survival. For example, in humans, the problem of disease was limited by the evolution of an immune system, and the potential problem of bleeding to death when cut or wounded was solved with the evolution of blood clotting (Buss, 1991). This is not to say that these features were created *because* they were needed. Rather, the theory of evolution maintains that because of these changes our species was better prepared to survive.

According to evolutionary personality theory, just as the natural selection process has led to the evolution of certain physical characteristics in humans, this process is also responsible for what are called *psychological mechanisms*. These psychological mechanisms are characteristically human functions that allow us to deal effectively with common human problems or needs. Through the process of natural selection, mechanisms that increased the chances of human survival and reproduction have been retained, and those that failed to meet the challenges to survival have not.

Psychologists have identified a large number of these mechanisms. For example, most humans have an innate fear of strangers. Evolutionary personality psychologists argue that this fear evolved to meet the problem of attack by those not belonging to the group or tribe (Buss, 1991). Similarly, anger might have assisted our ancestors in such survival behaviors as asserting authority and overcoming enemies (McGuire & Troisi, 1990). Thus it makes sense that anger is a common human characteristic. Some psychologists argue that humans have an innate need to belong to groups and form attachments (Baumeister & Leary, 1995). It is not difficult to imagine how a species that worked together would survive better than a species that did not. Similarly, some researchers maintain that the human characteristic of compassion helps the species survive because it leads to protection of individuals in need (Goetz, Keltner, & Simon-Thomas, 2010). But whereas the survival function of some human characteristics may be easy to explain, the advantages of other psychological mechanisms might not be so obvious. We return next to an example of one such mechanism.

Anxiety and Social Exclusion

Evolutionary personality theory maintains that human characteristics such as anxiety evolved because they proved beneficial to the survival of our ancestors. But how can this be? Anxiety is an unpleasant emotional state, something a normally functioning person would prefer to avoid. Moreover, anxiety is almost always problematic. It interferes with our ability to learn new tasks, remember information, perform sexually, and so on. How can something as disruptive as anxiety help the species?

We can answer this question by looking at what causes anxiety. Some psychologists have argued that one of the primary causes of anxiety is social exclusion (Baumeister & Tice, 1990). These investigators propose that all humans have a strong need to belong to groups and to be in relationships. Consequently, when we experience exclusion or rejection from social groups, we suffer great distress. This distress is not just limited to those relatively rare instances when we are literally rejected from a group or tossed out of a relationship. Rather, any information that suggests we might be excluded socially or that we are no longer attractive to other people is threatening to our need to belong.

As you thought about a situation that recently caused you to feel anxious, you may have recognized that your reaction was related to a fear of social rejection. You may also have noticed that you didn't have to experience actual exclusion from a group or relationship to feel anxious. Rather, information that even hints that someday you might be rejected by others is often enough to bring on anxiety. Thinking about anxiety as fear of social rejection helps us understand why people feel anxious when they have to give a speech in front of an audience or when they discover that first gray hair. The speaker is afraid the audience members will evaluate him or her negatively, a form of social rejection. The 30-ish adult discovering a gray hair worries about his or her attractiveness to others. Although outright social rejection is not common, fear of what others will think of us may be an everyday experience.

This social exclusion explanation of anxiety fits nicely with evolutionary personality theory. Primitive people who lived together in small groups were more likely to survive and reproduce than those living alone. An isolated person would be more susceptible to injury, illness, lack of shelter, and limited resources and would be less able to mate and raise offspring than individuals living in groups or tribes. Consequently, anything that motivates people to avoid behaviors that might lead to their exclusion from the group would help the species survive. Anxiety serves this purpose.

Proponents of this view point out that anxiety, although expressed in different ways, is found in nearly all cultures (Barlow, 1988). Moreover, the kinds of behavior that lead to social exclusion are typically those that impair the survival of the species (Buss, 1990; Sloman, 2008). These include adultery, aggression, and taking valuable resources away from others. In this sense, evolutionary theory crosses paths with Sigmund Freud. Freud also argued that primitive people came to live in groups and developed laws against many sexual and aggressive behaviors so that the species might survive. Although Freud was concerned with repressing unconscious impulses, his analysis is in many ways similar to that of more recent evolutionary theorists.

In short, what we call "human nature" can be thought of as a large number of psychological mechanisms that have allowed humankind to survive as long as we have. Advocates of this approach do not argue that all human characteristics are necessarily beneficial. It is even possible that some of our psychological mechanisms could someday contribute to the extinction of the species. Nonetheless, evolutionary personality psychology provides an interesting avenue for understanding some basic features of human personality.

Application: Children's Temperaments and School

Most of us have been exposed at one time or another to a parent's or grandparent's description of the strict and regimented way teachers used to run their classes "when I was a kid." According to these stories, all children were treated alike. Each was expected to sit quietly during reading period, to work at the pace set by the teacher, and above all, to pay full attention at all times. Any deviations from the routine were met with strict and sometimes severe punishment.

Although the accuracy of these descriptions might be challenged, teachers today do not approach their job the same way they did a few generations ago. One important difference between teaching then and teaching now is an awareness that not all children approach learning the same way. Because children are born with different temperaments, some jump right in and begin participating in lessons, but others are slow to warm up to new tasks. Some students have difficulty focusing their attention on any one activity for very long, whereas other students become frustrated when forced to move on to a new assignment before they are ready.

In fact, the transition from a familiar home environment to an unfamiliar classroom is just the kind of event that is likely to highlight differences in temperament. This was illustrated in a study in which researchers used measures of inhibition taken at age 21 months to predict how children would react upon entering kindergarten (Gersten, 1989). Observers watched the children during a relatively unstructured free-play period their first day of school. The children who had earlier been identified as inhibited responded to this unfamiliar situation by keeping to themselves and watching their new classmates. Compared to their classmates, the inhibited children were less likely to play with the other boys and girls, to touch other children, or even to laugh. Clearly inhibited and uninhibited children respond very differently to the first day of class, and researchers find these differences often continue throughout the school year (Gersten, 1989).

Although temperaments can be classified in a number of ways, many researchers find it convenient to examine three basic temperament patterns among elementary school children (Chess & Thomas, 1996; Thomas & Chess, 1977). First, there is the *easy child,* who eagerly approaches new situations, is adaptive, and generally experiences a positive mood. Most teachers would probably prefer an entire classroom full of these students. However, classes are likely to include some examples of the *difficult child.* These children have difficulty adapting to new environments and are often in a negative mood. A classroom is also likely to include some children who fall in the third general pattern, the *slow-to-warm-up child.* These children are similar to the inhibited children described earlier in the chapter. They tend to withdraw from unfamiliar situations and are slow to adapt to new academic tasks and new activities.

A 6-year study of children primarily from middle-class backgrounds found that about two-thirds of the elementary school children could be placed into one of these three categories (Thomas & Chess, 1977). Forty percent of the students fell into the easy child category, 10% into the difficult child group, and 15% into the slow-to-warm-up category. Thus, the typical elementary school classroom contains a mix of children with different temperament patterns. Obviously, this represents a significant challenge for the teacher.

Temperament and Academic Performance

Numerous studies find that a child's temperament affects how well that child does in school (Coplan, Barber, & Lagace-Seguin, 1999; Cowen, Wyman, & Work, 1992; Keogh, 2003; Rudasill & Konold, 2008; Stright, Gallagher, & Kelley, 2008). As you might expect, children with either the difficult or slow-to-warm-up pattern tend to perform more poorly than students with the easy child pattern. Children with an easy temperament get higher grades and better evaluations from their teachers. Differences related to temperament are also found in standardized achievement tests.

But studies indicate that temperament is not related to intelligence (Keogh, 1986). So how does temperament affect a child's academic performance? Researchers have identified several possibilities. First, some temperaments are probably more compatible with the requirements of the typical classroom than others. In most classes, children who are attentive, adaptable, and persistent are likely to do better than those who are low on these temperament dimensions. Children with short attention spans and children who are easily distracted may have difficulty completing assignments or paying enough attention to learn their lessons the first time. Students who take a long time to adapt to new situations often find themselves behind the rest of the class. Moreover, children who fall behind or do poorly on assignments may become discouraged or give up, thus adding to their academic problems.

Second, a student's behavior evokes responses from the teacher (Houts, Caspi, Pianta, Arseneault, & Moffitt, 2010). The student who is attentive and seemingly eager to learn is going to draw a different reaction from the typical elementary school teacher than the student who is easily distracted and withdrawn. Working with the former student probably will be pleasant and rewarding; working with the latter may be frustrating and demanding. Because they are less likely to initiate interactions with the teacher, inhibited children are less likely to get help when they need it and generally receive less attention from their teachers than do other students (Rudasill & Rimm-Kaufman, 2009). Thus, perhaps quite unintentionally, teachers may pay more attention to and work more closely with some students than with others. As a result, opportunities for learning and achievement may be shaped by the child's temperament.

Third, teachers sometimes misinterpret temperamental differences in their students (Keogh, 1989). Slow-to-warm-up children may be seen as unmotivated when they fail to eagerly attack an assignment or as unintelligent when they require several tries to master a new task. A highly active student might be identified as a troublemaker. An easily distracted student might be seen as uninterested in learning. These false impressions can color the way a teacher responds to the student. A large amount of research demonstrates that teachers' explanations for their students' behavior often affect how the teacher interacts with the student and subsequently how well the student does in school (Cooper & Good, 1983).

This indirect impact of temperament on learning is illustrated in the real-life case of an elementary school student who approached schoolwork with a high-intensity, high-persistence style (Chess & Thomas, 1986). This boy had a long attention span and preferred to spend an extensive amount of time absorbed in one lesson before moving on to the next. Unfortunately, the teacher's schedule rarely allowed for this. The boy became upset whenever the teacher interrupted his lessons. Initially, the teacher interpreted the boy's reaction as an indication of some underlying behavior disorder. Fortunately, the problem was resolved when the boy's parents transferred him to a school that encouraged the kind of persistent and intense involvement that had been limited in the earlier class.

Matching Temperament and Teaching

It is tempting to ask, "What temperament characteristics contribute to better school performance?" However, this is probably not the right question. Most researchers prefer to ask, "What kind of environment and procedures are most conducive to learning for *this* student, given his or her temperament?" The second question reflects the thinking behind what some researchers call the "goodness of fit" model. According to this approach, how well a child does in school is partly a function of how well the learning environment matches the child's "capabilities, characteristics, and style of behaving" (Thomas & Chess, 1977). In other words, not all children come to school with the same learning styles or abilities. We can't do much to change a child's temperament, but an optimal amount of learning can take place if lessons and assignments are presented in a way that matches the child's learning style. Several investigations find support for the goodness of fit approach (Keogh, 2003). Students get higher grades and better evaluations from teachers when the student's temperament matches the teacher's expectations and demands.

These research findings provide an obvious strategy for improved teaching. Classroom assignments that require extensive concentration create a problem for the easily distracted girl with a short attention span. However, this girl will probably have little difficulty mastering the assignment if the same material is presented in short, easily processed segments. A slow-to-warm-up boy will fall behind when his teacher works at a pace set for the average member of the class. If allowed to progress at his own rate, however, the boy eventually will do as well as his classmates.

The goodness of fit model can also be applied to preschool settings. Of particular importance is the child's ability to adjust to the regimen and rules of an organized social situation. Of course, as part of their preparation for elementary school, children must learn to follow rules and consider the needs of others. But impulsive children who have a difficult time sitting still are likely to be frustrated and get into trouble in a rigid one-size-fits-all preschool (Coplan, Bowker, & Cooper, 2003; De Schipper, Tavecchio, Van IJzendoorn, & Van Zeijl, 2004; Rudasill, Rimm-Kaufman, Justice, & Pence, 2006). Preschool teachers find fewer adjustment problems when they adapt their style in consideration of the child's temperament, and improved adjustment paves the way for academic development. One study found that a good match between Head Start teachers' styles and student temperament was associated with higher math and preliteracy scores (Churchill, 2003).

Teachers who match teaching style with temperament not only increase the child's chances of academic success, they also contribute to the child's feelings of self-worth (Chess & Thomas, 1991). Children who do poorly in school begin to blame themselves. These feelings are often reinforced by parents and teachers who accuse the child of not trying or who communicate to the child in various ways that he or she simply may not have the ability to keep up with classmates. The resulting decline in self-esteem may add to the child's academic difficulties, which can create a downward spiral effect. Fortunately, today most teachers are aware of differences in temperament and take steps to adapt their teaching to meet students' individual styles (Keogh, 2003). Although time and resources may limit teachers' abilities to meet the individual needs of all their students, recognizing temperament differences is an important step toward that goal.

Assessment: Brain Electrical Activity and Cerebral Asymmetry

The next time you're talking to some friends, you might try this quick experiment. Ask your friends some reflective questions, such as "How do you feel when you are anxious?" or "What's the most joyous scene you have recently been in?" When people engage in a little reflective thought, most tend to look off to one side. Some people consistently, although not always, glance to the right, whereas others tend to look to the left. As described later, the significance of this difference lies in what it may tell us about our friends' tendency to experience happiness or sadness. The direction in which people look when contemplating may be a general indicator of brain activity patterns psychologists associate with emotion.

The notion that we can examine personality with physiological measures has been around a long time. Freud speculated that scientists would one day discover the neurological underpinnings of personality. Similarly, Allport argued that future technological advances would identify differences in the central nervous system associated with different traits. Although we have yet to fulfill these prophecies, personality researchers have come to use a wide variety of physiological measures in their experiments. For many years now, researchers have used physiological indicators of arousal, such as heart rate, respiration, and galvanic skin response. Other investigators examine hormones, immune systems, neurotransmitters, respiration, automatic muscle reflexes, and enzymes in the blood. More recently, researchers have turned to neuroimaging techniques to pinpoint the location of neural activity in the brain (Mather, Cacioppo, & Kanwisher, 2013). These techniques include functional Magnetic Resonance Imaging (fMRI) and positron emission tomography (PET). In this section, we look at another example of how psychologists use physiological measures to examine differences in brain activity level.

Measuring Brain Activity

How can we measure brain activity without going into a person's skull? Fortunately, technology provides some relatively nonintrusive procedures for obtaining these measurements. One relatively simple and inexpensive procedure uses an instrument called an *electroencephalograph* (EEG) to measure electrical activity in different parts of the human brain. Personality researchers find EEG measurements particularly useful for several reasons. The procedure is relatively easy and does not harm the individual in any way. Typically, small electrodes are attached to the person's head with hair clips and elastic straps. Participants report that the procedure is not uncomfortable although electrode paste can sometimes leave messy spots in their hair. In addition, the EEG enables researchers to record brain activity in very quick intervals. Some instruments can measure this activity within milliseconds. This sensitivity is particularly important when looking at emotions, which often change very rapidly.

EEG data are usually described in terms of cycles per second, or waves. One kind of wave identified through this process, known as an *alpha wave,* has proven particularly useful for research on personality and emotion. The lower the alpha wave activity, the more activation in that region of the brain.

Cerebral Asymmetry

Although EEG data can be used to assess activity level in many different regions of the brain, research on alpha wave levels in the anterior (front) regions of the cerebral hemisphere has proven particularly useful in understanding individual differences in emotion. This region has considerable connections with the parts of the brain that regulate emotions. More important,

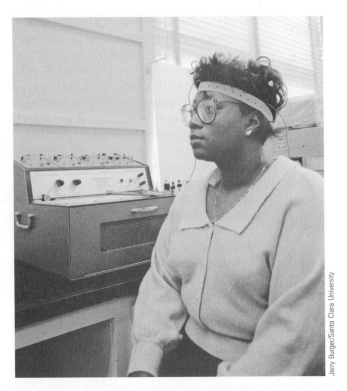

Jerry Burger/Santa Clara University

Researchers measure brain activity levels with an instrument known as an EEG. This information may tell us about the person's tendency to experience different emotions.

researchers find the anterior region of a person's right cerebral hemisphere often shows a different activity level than the anterior region of that same person's left cerebral hemisphere. Researchers refer to this difference in right and left hemisphere activity as **cerebral asymmetry**.

Investigators find that different patterns of cerebral asymmetry are associated with differences in emotional experience. Originally researchers noticed that higher activation in the left hemisphere was associated with positive moods, whereas higher activation in the right hemisphere was indicative of negative moods (Wheeler, Davidson, & Tomarken, 1993). In one study, researchers showed emotion-arousing films to participants while taking EEG measures of right and left hemisphere activity (Davidson, Ekman, Saron, Senulis, & Friesen, 1990). When participants experienced happiness, as determined by their facial expressions, the activity in their left cerebral hemisphere increased. When participants experienced disgust, there was more activity in the right hemisphere.

Similar patterns were found in children less than a year old. In one study with 10-month-old infants, smiling was associated with higher left hemisphere activity, whereas crying was associated with higher right hemisphere activity (Fox & Davidson, 1988). In other experiments, infants showed increases in left hemisphere activity when their mothers reached down to pick them up (Fox & Davidson, 1987), when they heard laughter (Davidson & Fox, 1982), and when they tasted something sweet (Fox & Davidson, 1986). In all cases, the children experiencing positive emotions had relatively more activity in their left hemisphere than in the right. Because the infants had not yet reached their first birthday, researchers argued that the association between cerebral asymmetry and emotion is something we are born with rather than the result of learning.

Individual Differences in Cerebral Asymmetry

Additional research has taken the association between cerebral asymmetry and emotion one step further. Most people typically have higher activation in one hemisphere than in the other, even when in a relatively nonemotional resting state. However, which hemisphere displays the higher activity level is not the same for everyone. Some people tend to have higher activity in the left hemisphere when resting, whereas others tend to more right hemisphere activity. Moreover, like other individual differences, differences in cerebral asymmetry tend to be fairly stable over time. If you show a higher level of activity in one hemisphere over the other today, you will show the same pattern when taking an EEG test next week or even next year.

This observation leads to another intriguing question. Because left and right hemispheric activity is associated with positive and negative moods, can we use EEG data to predict differences in emotion? The answer appears to be "Yes." Participants in one study were identified as having either higher left hemisphere or higher right hemisphere activity when resting (Davidson & Tomarken, 1989). These individuals then watched films designed to elicit certain emotions, such as happiness or fear. As expected, people with a higher level of left hemisphere activity were more responsive to the positive mood films, whereas participants with higher right hemisphere activity levels reacted more to the films that produced negative moods.

Again, similar patterns can be found in infants. Ten-month-old babies in one study were identified as having either higher left hemisphere or higher right hemisphere activity when resting (Davidson & Fox, 1989). The babies were then divided into those who cried and those who did not cry when separated from their mothers. As expected, the criers tended to have higher right hemisphere activity, whereas the noncriers were those with higher left hemisphere activity.

How can we account for these findings? Initially researchers explained the results in terms of thresholds for positive and negative mood (Davidson & Tomarken, 1989). They speculated that people with higher right hemisphere activity require a less intense negative event to experience fear or sadness. A minor disappointment or a rude remark might be enough to push them over the threshold into a negative emotional state. On the other hand, people who generally have a higher level of left hemisphere activity may require a less intense positive event before they experience happiness. An enjoyable conversation or a favorite song on the radio might be enough to trigger pleasant emotions.

However, subsequent research findings have caused psychologists to rethink the relationship between cerebral asymmetry and emotions. Instead of looking at positive and negative emotions, psychologists now describe the differences in terms of approach and withdrawal tendencies (Harmon-Jones & Allen, 1997; Harmon-Jones & Sigelman, 2001; Pizzagalli, Sherwood, Henriques, & Davidson, 2005). Studies find that left hemisphere activity is related to movement toward the source of the emotion, whereas right hemisphere activity is related to movement away. Thus higher right hemisphere activity is associated with sadness because depression is essentially an effort to withdraw from whatever is causing the emotion. Higher left hemisphere activity is associated with joy because happiness draws us toward the source of the emotion. Consistent with this analysis, researchers find that anger is related to higher left hemisphere activity (Harmon-Jones, Lueck, Fearn, & Harmon-Jones, 2006; Kelley, Hortensius, & Harmon-Jones, 2013; Chavanon, Leue, & Stemmler, 2008). Although anger is a negative emotion like depression, angry people tend to approach or even attack the source of their distress.

The demonstrated association between cerebral asymmetry and emotion leads researchers to yet another question: Do differences in hemispheric activity level play a role in the development of emotional disorders? Some research findings suggest that they may. Depressed participants in these studies show more right-side activation than nondepressed participants (Accortt & Allen, 2006; Nelson et al., 2012; Stewart, Bismark, Towers, Coan, & Allen, 2010; Thibodeau, Jorgensen, & Kim, 2006). In one investigation, researchers examined EEG patterns in people who were currently not depressed but who had suffered from previous bouts of depression (Henriques & Davidson, 1990). These individuals tended to have less left hemisphere activity in the anterior region of the brain when resting than a group of participants who had never suffered from depression. In other words, these previously depressed individuals may have a physiologically based vulnerability to experience bouts of depression. Other investigations find anxiety sufferers also have higher right-side activation than nonanxious individuals (Crost, Pauls, & Wacker, 2008; Mathersul, Williams, Hopkinson, & Kemp, 2008; Thibodeau et al., 2006).

Finally, if cerebral asymmetry is a marker for greater vulnerability to emotional disorders, can we use EEG patterns to predict who is likely to suffer from these disorders in the future? Once again, the answer appears to be "Yes." One team of researchers measured cerebral asymmetry in a group of college students who had no history of emotional problems (Nusslock et al., 2011). The students were then interviewed every four months for the next three years to determine whether the student had experienced a significant episode of depression. As expected, students with higher right-side activation were more likely to experience their first depressive episode during this time than those with higher left-side activation. Measures of cerebral asymmetry have also been used to predict whether people who suffer from mood swings will develop bipolar disorder (Nusslock et al., 2012). Clearly, whether we experience any emotional disorder depends on many factors, including the kinds of situations we encounter. But it may be that some people require fewer or less intense negative experiences than others before succumbing to feelings of depression or anxiety.

Let's return now to the eye-drift example at the beginning of this discussion. Although not nearly as reliable as EEG data, research suggests that right-handed people who typically glance to the left when engaged in reflective thought are likely to show a higher level of right hemisphere activation when resting. Those who tend to glance to the right are likely to be higher in left hemisphere activity (Davidson, 1991; Gur & Reivich, 1980). Of course, many other variables affect emotion, but studies suggest that which way you look during a reflective moment may be a telltale sign of your proclivity to experience certain emotions over others.

Strengths and Criticisms of the Biological Approach

Strengths

One of the strengths of the biological approach is that it provides a bridge between the study of personality and the discipline of biology. For too many years, personality psychologists often ignored the biological roots of human behavior. But it has become increasingly difficult to disregard the fact that we are the product of an evolutionary history and our individual genetic makeup. Human behavior is influenced by many factors, one of which is biology. By incorporating what biologists know about evolution and genetics, personality psychologists come closer to understanding what makes each of us the kind of person we are.

The biological approach also has succeeded in identifying some realistic parameters for psychologists interested in behavior change. The "blank slate" image of humankind can be very appealing. If the newborn personality is like clay, then with enough knowledge, resources, and effort we should be able to mold that personality any way we want. If all babies are essentially alike, then with enough research psychologists could advise parents and teachers on the "correct" way to raise all children and teach all students. Unfortunately, past acceptance of the blank slate notion created many problems. Parents with difficult-to-control babies were blamed for not knowing how to raise their children. Highly active children were punished for not sitting as still as their classmates. Advocates of the biological approach argue that our inherited biological differences probably place limits on the kind of children and adults we become. Some people are born with a tendency to be more introverted than others, and there is probably little a parent, teacher, or spouse can do to turn an introvert into an extravert.

Another strength of the biological approach is that most of its advocates are academic psychologists with a strong interest in testing their ideas through research. Consequently, investigators have generated empirical support for many of the hypotheses advanced from this perspective. In addition, psychologists from the biological approach have often modified their theories as a result of research findings. For example, after Eysenck outlined a comprehensive model of personality several decades ago, he and others conducted research on many of the predictions generated from the model. Much of this work supported Eysenck's ideas, but investigators altered other ideas to better reflect the research findings.

Criticisms

Despite their focus on research, advocates of the biological approach sometimes face limits on their ability to test their ideas. In particular, evolutionary personality psychologists often are left to argue from the relatively weak position of analogy and deduction (Eagly, 1997). A reasonable case can be made that anxiety helps the species survive because it prevents social isolation. But how can we test this hypothesis? Direct manipulation is often out of the question, making demonstrations of cause-and-effect relationships difficult, if not impossible. One problem with this limitation is that we can think of a potentially adaptive function for nearly every human attribute. For example, some psychologists have argued that depression is adaptive because it leads us to give up on unattainable goals and thereby save resources (Wrosch & Miller, 2009). There is some logic to this analysis, but it is quite a leap to say that we were better able to survive as a species because we have the capacity to become depressed.

To fully appreciate why this ability to explain everything is a problem, consider the example offered by one psychologist (Cornell, 1997). As discussed in Chapter 10, some researchers use evolutionary theory to explain gender differences, such as why men are more dominant, stronger, and more sexually promiscuous than women (Archer, 1996; Gangestad & Thornhill, 1997). But imagine if just the opposite were the case—that men were more timid and physically weaker than women, and less likely to seek out multiple sex partners. One could use evolutionary theory to explain these results as well. We could speculate that because men were free to roam and did not have to protect offspring, the tendency for them to timidly run away from potential fights evolved. Women evolved to be stronger because child-care responsibilities required them to carry children, lift them into trees for safety, and fight off predators. And sexual promiscuity allowed a woman to avoid the risk of pairing up with a man who might be unable to make her pregnant and thus not allow her to pass along her genes. As this example illustrates, if a theory can explain all possible outcomes, it cannot be tested.

Other critics of evolutionary personality theory challenge the assumption that every human characteristic must serve a survival function. It is entirely possible that a characteristic evolved that had no impact on survival or that even hurt our species' likelihood of survival. For example, a critic might ask what the survival value could possibly be for the tendency for men to grow hair in the ears as they age or for urine to smell funny after eating asparagus. Of course, with a little creativity, we can probably come up with an answer. But that exercise would only reinforce the problem of being able to explain everything.

Another criticism of the biological approach is directed at theory and research on temperament. Students and researchers may be bewildered by the lack of an agreed-upon model. One prominent model identifies three basic temperaments. Yet other models describe five, seven, and nine temperament dimensions (Bates, Wachs, & Emde, 1994). Students have a right to ask which of these is correct. More important, it is difficult to make comparisons across investigations when researchers rely on different names and descriptions for these temperaments. Is the "inhibited" child the same as the "slow-to-warm-up" child? We can hope that clearer answers about the number and description of basic temperaments will be forthcoming as researchers continue to work in this area.

Like the trait approach, the biological approach offers few suggestions for personality change. Although many ideas from this approach are probably useful for psychotherapists, there are no schools of psychotherapy based on this perspective. On the contrary, the message from the biological approach is that we need to be more aware of some of the limitations on how much we can change people. On the other hand, therapists might do well to recognize that, because of biological differences, not all clients respond the same to their treatments.

Summary

1. Hans Eysenck was an early proponent of the biological approach to personality. He argued that personality can be divided along three primary dimensions. He called these extraversion–introversion, neuroticism, and psychoticism. Eysenck argued that differences in personality are largely based in inherited biological differences. Research suggests that introverts are more sensitive to stimulation than extraverts and that extraverts may be more attracted to rewards.

2. Personality researchers have identified general inherited dispositions called temperaments. Psychologists argue that temperaments are largely inherited and that these inherited dispositions interact with experiences to form adult personality traits. Children identified as inhibited show a fear of unfamiliar situations that other children do not. There is evidence that this tendency is inherited and that it remains fairly stable throughout childhood.

3. Evolutionary personality psychology uses the concept of natural selection to explain the development and survival function of human personality characteristics. Theorists point out that anxiety often results from events related to social rejection. They argue that because social isolation decreases the chances of survival and reproducing, the evolution of anxiety has helped the species survive.

4. Research on temperament has important implications for education. Studies find that children identified with a difficult temperament pattern and those identified with a slow-to-warm-up pattern perform more poorly in school than children identified with an easy temperament pattern. Research suggests that children will learn best when the demands of the learning environment match the child's temperament.

5. Personality researchers often use physiological measures in their research. Some researchers use EEG data to look at individual differences in emotions. They find that differences in the activity levels of the right and left halves of the cerebral hemispheres are associated with differences in

mood. Some research indicates that people inherit different base-rate levels of brain activity in the two hemispheres and that this difference may make them more likely to have certain emotional experiences.

6. One strength of the biological approach is that it ties personality psychology to the discipline of biology. In addition, research in this area has identified realistic limitations for the blank slate model of personality development. Another strength of the biological approach is its strong emphasis on research. Criticisms of the approach include the difficulty researchers have when testing some of their ideas. Other criticisms are that researchers have not agreed upon a single model for temperament and that the biological approach provides little information about behavior change.

Key Terms

behavioral approach system
   (p. 227)
behavioral inhibition system
   (p. 227)

cerebral asymmetry (p. 244)
inhibited/uninhibited children
   (p. 233)

temperaments (p. 230)

Media Resources

Visit the book companion website at
www.cengagebrain.com to find a glossary,
flashcards, quizzing, and more.

The Biological Approach

Relevant Research

Today most psychologists readily embrace the notion that biology plays a role in human personality, but students are often surprised to hear that this was not always the case. In truth, many psychologists came to accept this conclusion rather reluctantly. Why the resistance? One reason is that the "blank slate" view of humankind has great appeal. If we accept that personality is formed largely or exclusively by experiences, in theory we can mold an individual into whatever kind of person we want. With enough knowledge and resources, we could eliminate low self-esteem, pessimism, neuroticism, and other personality traits that often create difficulties. But accepting that biology plays a role in personality development usually means limiting these possibilities for change. Another reason some psychologists were hesitant to accept the biological approach was a concern about inappropriate and even offensive interpretations that come from placing too much emphasis on biological determinants. In the past, some people have argued against social programs by maintaining that certain racial or gender differences are the result of biological rather than cultural factors.

Of course, accepting a biological component to personality does not mean that personality is fixed at birth. Those who resign themselves with "That's the way men/women are" or "It's just my nature" are foolishly ignoring the power of experience. But it would be equally foolish to ignore the wealth of evidence indicating that biology has a hand in shaping personality. The most persuasive case for the biological approach can be found in the growing amount of supportive research findings. We'll review some of those findings in this chapter. As with research from other approaches to personality, the studies reported here have limitations and are sometimes subject to alternate interpretations. However, taken together the data make it difficult to ignore the importance of biological determinants of personality.

We begin by looking at research on the heritability of personality characteristics. More specifically, we examine the methods researchers use to determine how much of our personality is inherited from our parents. As you will see, this research is not without its critics, and identifying the precise strength of the genetic component remains elusive.

Next we'll review research generated from Hans Eysenck's theory of personality. Specifically, we'll look at some of the differences between extraverts and introverts. This research suggests that your level of extraversion–introversion affects a wide range of behavior, including how happy you are and where you sit in the library. We'll also examine one application of evolutionary personality theory. According to this theory, men and women should differ in what they look for in a romantic partner.

Heritability of Personality Traits

How much of your personality is the result of your genetic makeup, and how much is the result of the environment you grew up in? This "nature–nurture" question is one of the oldest and most enduring issues in psychology.

Interestingly, people with little or no exposure to personality research seem to readily accept that both genetic background and experiences are important in shaping personality. Parents often point to personality traits their children "got from me," but few would deny that the way they raise their children also plays a large role in what kind of adults the children become. Thus the question is not which of these—genetics or environment—shapes our personalities but rather to what extent and how our personalities are shaped by each.

So we might rephrase the question this way: To what degree was the mold for your adult personality already cast by the time you were born? Researchers now agree that relatively stable abilities and aptitudes, such as intelligence, appear to have a genetic component (Plomin & DeFries, 1998). This is not to say that a highly intelligent child cannot be born to relatively unintelligent parents or that a child's environment plays no role in intellectual development. But it does appear we are born with a potential for intelligence that combines with environmental influences to determine adult intelligence levels. Similarly, many psychological disorders appear to be affected by the genes we inherited (Crabbe, 2002; DiLalla, Carey, Gottesman, & Bouchard, 1996; McGue & Christensen, 1997; Rhee & Waldman, 2002). Again, this does not mean people are born to be schizophrenic or depressed. Rather, some people are born with a higher susceptibility to these disorders than are others.

What about personality traits? Are people born to be aggressive or extraverted? There is now ample evidence that genetics also influences these and other personality traits. However, collecting good evidence on this issue is not easy, and questions remain about how to interpret the data that are available.

Separating Environmental from Genetic Influences

Psychologists working on the environment–genetics question have a somewhat different task facing them than those working in other areas of personality research. For technological and ethical reasons, it is not possible to manipulate people's genes and observe the kind of adults they become. Instead, researchers must rely on less direct means. Like detectives trying to piece together a picture of how we got to where we are, these researchers use innovative and sometimes clever experimental procedures to track down the roots of adult personalities. Each method has limitations and weaknesses, but data from a number of sources suggest a significant role for genetics in the development of our personalities.

The most obvious source of information on this question is the similarity of parents and children. Aggressive parents often have aggressive offspring; shy children often come from homes with shy parents. Similarly, we often see brothers who are both outgoing or sisters who are both sensitive and caring. Casual observers look at these relationships and often assume the

Identical twins not only share physical features but also have similar personalities. Researchers attribute this similarity in part to genetic influences although the extent of genetic influence on personality continues to be debated.

children inherited these traits from their parents. However, there is an obvious alternative explanation for these similarities. Members of a family not only share genes, they share living environments as well. Siblings' personalities may be similar because the parents raised them in the same basic manner. Children of introverted parents might become introverted because of the calm and quiet home they grow up in.

In most cases, therefore, shared genes and shared environments seem hopelessly confounded. Can we peel one of these influences away from the other? Fortunately, there are ways. The most popular procedure for separating the role of genetics from the role of environment is the **twin-study method**. This method takes advantage of a naturally occurring phenomenon: the two types of human twins. Some twins are *monozygotic* (MZ); that is, the two babies come from the same fertilized egg. These are the twins that look alike physically, the ones we commonly call identical twins. The important point for researchers is that MZ twins have identical genes. The other type, *dizygotic* (DZ) twins, come from different eggs. These two babies, commonly called fraternal twins, are no more alike genetically than any two siblings.

Genetics and Intelligence

A large amount of research indicates that, as with personality traits and psychological disorders, a significant portion of intelligence is determined by our genetic inheritance. Although at first glance this conclusion hardly seems surprising, it is in fact at the heart of a controversy that flares up periodically among psychologists and those who debate social policy. Several decades ago psychologist Arthur Jensen (1969) considered the research on intelligence and the finding that Black Americans typically score lower on standard intelligence tests than Whites. He suggested from these observations that Blacks might be genetically less intelligent than Whites. Richard Herrnstein and Charles Murray rekindled the debate in 1994 when they published *The Bell Curve: Intelligence and Class Structure in American Life.* These psychologists also began by pointing out that intelligence is largely inherited. They argued that any gains from educational intervention programs such as Head Start will be short-lived because a child's genetically determined aptitude will ultimately determine his or her success. Herrnstein and Murray then touched a social and political nerve when they tied their analysis to the question of race. They argued that if Black Americans on average score lower on IQ tests than White

Americans, perhaps efforts to provide educational opportunities for African Americans are a waste of time. A decade later, racist groups seized on the findings of genetics researchers who identified recent (within the past 40,000 years) evolutionary changes in brain-related genes (Regalado, 2006). Because differences were found between European and African samples, these individuals drew the scientifically inappropriate conclusion that the research verified claims of genetically based differences in intelligence among racial groups.

In each of these situations, reaction was strong and swift. News analysts, political commentators, and political leaders were quick to challenge the interpretations. Reaction from academic psychologists was equally intense. Not only do the vast majority of psychologists find the suggestion of inherent racial differences in intelligence offensive, they also maintain that such a conclusion is simply not supported by research findings (Flynn, 1999; Neisser et al., 1996; Nisbett, 2009; Sternberg, Grigorenko, & Kidd, 2005). Moreover, it is incorrect to say that intelligence level is fixed by nature and is not amenable to environmental influence (Nisbett et al., 2012). Psychologists are quick to point out that Black children often grow up in an environment that is less intellectually stimulating than

that of the average White family (Zernike, 2000). Indeed, researchers find that Black children adopted by White families of reasonable socioeconomic means develop IQ scores no different from those of adopted White children (Nisbett, 2007). Not surprisingly, as preschool and other educational opportunities have become more available to children of all backgrounds, the gap between White and Black students' IQ scores has narrowed considerably (Nisbett et al., 2012).

Beyond this, critics have raised the issue of culture-bound intelligence tests. They argue that the questions asked on most intelligence tests reflect what White, middle-class Americans consider important. One subtest on the widely used Wechsler intelligence tests asks about general knowledge. The assumption behind these questions is that although all children are exposed to this information, the more intelligent ones will attend to and retain it. But clearly a child growing up in an African American culture is exposed to different information from one growing up in a White, middle-class culture. Because of this problem, many psychologists have been working to develop "culture-free" intelligence tests, and recent versions of the adult and children's Wechsler tests have been revised to account for some of these concerns.

The logic behind the twin-study method is illustrated in Figure 10.1. We assume that two same-sex DZ twins and two MZ twins (who are always the same sex) share very similar environments. That is, in studies using this method, twin pairs, regardless of type, are the same age and the same sex and live in the same house under the same rules. Therefore, the extent to

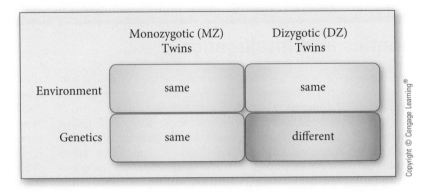

FIGURE 10.1 Twin-Study Research Diagram

which the environment is responsible for their personalities is going to be about the same for both types of twin pairs. However, if there is also a genetic influence on personality, we would expect the MZ twins to be more like each other than are the DZ twins because the MZ twins also have identical genes, but the DZ twins do not.

Researchers using the twin-study method give personality trait measures to both members of both kinds of twins. They then look at how similar the twin brothers and sisters are on the traits. If trait scores for the MZ twin pairs are more highly correlated than the scores for the DZ twin pairs, we have evidence for genetic influence on personality. Because the environmental influence is roughly the same for both kinds of twins, it is assumed that the MZ twins are more alike because they also have identical genes.

Twin-study research usually generates correlation tables similar to the one found in Table 10.1. In this example, adult MZ and DZ twin pairs were compared on the Big Five personality traits (Chapter 7). As seen in the table, the MZ twin pairs were more similar than the DZ twin pairs in each case (Riemann, Angleitner, & Strelau, 1997). The data in the table are similar to those obtained in other twin studies looking at different measures of the Big Five dimensions (Borkenau, Riemann, Angleitner, & Spinath, 2001; Jang, Livesley, &

TABLE 10.1 Correlations from a Twin Study

	MZ Twins	DZ Twins
Neuroticism	.53	.21
Extraversion	.56	.33
Openness	.54	.35
Agreeableness	.42	.24
Conscientiousness	.54	.23

Source: Riemann, Angleitner, and Strelau (1997).

Vernon, 1996; Jang, McCrae, Angleitner, Riemann, & Livesley, 1998; Loehlin, McCrae, & Costa, 1998; McCrae, Jang, Livesley, Riemann, & Angleitner, 2001).

Numerous investigations have been conducted across many cultures using the twin-study method to examine the role genetics plays in personality. One team of researchers estimated that perhaps 800,000 pairs of twins have participated in these studies (Johnson, Turkheimer, Gottesman, & Bouchard, 2009). The size of the effect varies depending on which traits we examine, but when researchers combine twin-study results from all of these investigations, they find that about 40% of the stability in our adult personalities can be attributed to what we inherit from our parents (Johnson et al., 2009; Krueger & Johnson, 2008; Loehlin, 1992).

Other methods for teasing apart genetic and environmental influences also find evidence for genetic influence, but usually not as strong as in the twin-study data (Plomin & Caspi, 1999). One example comes from research with adopted children. When children are raised from birth by someone other than their biological parents, genetic and environmental influences are not confounded. Think of a family in which parents raise one child they adopted and one they gave birth to. Which child should have a personality similar to the parents'? If genes are playing a role, we would expect the biological offspring to be more like the parents because that child shares not only the environment but also some genes with the parents. In fact, this is what researchers find (Bezdjian, Baker, & Tuvblad, 2011; Klump, Suisman, Burt, McGue, & Iacono, 2009; Scarr, Webber, Weinberg, & Wittig, 1981). However, calculations with the data from these studies indicate the genetic influence is less than that suggested by the twin-study data. In fact, data from adoption studies suggest that the heritability of personality is about half what the twin-study data suggest (Frisell, Pawitan, Langstrom, & Lichtenstein, 2012; Plomin, Corley, Caspi, Fulker, & DeFries, 1998).

But the adoption situation provides even more opportunities to test the genetic-environmental influence question. What would you expect if you compared the personalities of adopted children with those of their biological mothers? The children have shared no environment with the mothers but are still linked by genes. When the personality scores of adopted children are compared with those of their adoptive parents and their biological mothers, the children look more like the biological mothers, whom they have never known (Loehlin, Willerman, & Horn, 1982, 1987). Although the strength of the relationship is also weaker than that suggested by the twin-study data, these findings provide evidence from yet another source that genetics plays at least some role in the formation of adult personalities.

It is also possible to combine the twin-study and adoption situations. Although rare, some researchers have taken advantage of situations in which MZ twins are separated from their parents at birth and in addition are raised in two different households. The twins in these pairs share genes but not environments. These twins are then compared with MZ twins raised in the same household, who share both genes and environments. A summary of the findings from studies using this method is shown in Table 10.2. As you can

TABLE 10.2 Correlations for Twins Raised Apart and Twins Raised Together

	Identical Twins Raised Apart	Identical Twins Raised Together
Extraversion	.61	.51
Neuroticism	.53	.50
Intelligence	.72	.86

Source: From "Resolving the person-situation debate: Invitation to an interdisciplinary dialogue," by D. C. Rowe, *American Psychologist*, 1987, 42, 218–227. Reprinted by permission of the American Psychological Association

see, the MZ twins tend to be quite similar to each other regardless of whether they are raised with or separated from their twin brother or sister (Rowe, 1987). The obvious explanation for this similarity is that the twins' genes shaped their personalities in a similar manner regardless of the environments they grew up in.

In summary, investigators have used a variety of clever procedures to separate the influence of genetics on personality from the influence of the environment. The consistency of the findings from so many sources suggests that adult personalities clearly are affected by heredity. However, as we will see in the next section, researchers face a number of challenges when interpreting the results of this research, and determining the precise extent of the genetic influence on personality is still a matter of discussion and debate.

Interpreting the Heritability Findings

The strongest and most consistent evidence in favor of genetic influence on personality comes from twin-study research. However, researchers using this method make two key assumptions. The first is that twin pairs can be accurately identified as MZ or DZ twins. Many "identical" twins may in fact be DZ twins who look very much alike. Fortunately, biological advances have made this less of a problem than it once was. Today, zygosity can be determined in almost all cases through blood tests.

The second assumption presents a bigger problem. Researchers assume that MZ and DZ twins have equally similar environments. However, there is some evidence that MZ twins may share more of their environment than DZ twins (Hoffman, 1991; Lytton, 1977; Scarr & Carter-Saltzman, 1979). That is, identical twins may be treated more alike than are DZ twins. Identical twins are often thought of as one unit—they are dressed alike, given identical presents, and so on. DZ twins grow up in similar environments, but they are usually allowed to dress differently, join different clubs, and have different friends. DZ twins may even experience environments that are less similar than those typical for siblings (Hoffman, 1985) because parents may look for and emphasize their differences (for example, "Terry is the studious one"; "Larry is the troublemaker").

If this is the case, we would have to modify Figure 10.1. The environmental influence on personality traits may not be as similar for DZ twins as it is for MZ twins. This possibility creates a problem when interpreting the twin-study findings. We can't be certain if the higher correlations between MZ twins are caused by greater genetic similarities or greater environmental similarities. This interpretation problem may explain why data from twin-study research suggest a larger role for genetic influences than is found with other procedures.

However, some of these other procedures also rely on questionable assumptions (Evans, Gillespie, & Martin, 2002; Hoffman, 1991; Stoolmiller, 1999). Adoptions are not random events. Families who adopt children are typically older, more affluent, more stable, and without many of the problems found in families that do not adopt. Although separated twins may be placed in different homes, the homes typically selected for placement are very similar. As a result, the environmental influences on personality experienced by one twin may be similar to the environmental influences experienced by his or her sibling. We can also challenge the assumption that parents treat an adopted child the same way they do their biological offspring. It is likely parents have different expectations for adopted children. Because they don't know the biological parents, adopting parents may have few preconceived ideas about how the child's personality will unfold.

In short, some of the discrepancies between the results of twin studies and studies using other methods might be attributed to methodological issues. However, twin studies might produce higher estimates of heritability for another reason. Research suggests that personality traits aren't passed down from parents to child in a simple, direct manner. Rather, the inherited part of personality is often the result of a complex combination of more than one gene (Finkel & McGue, 1997; Plomin et al., 1998). That is, the genetic influence of some personality traits may not be seen unless a unique combination of more than one gene is inherited. Researchers refer to these complex influences as *nonadditive effects*. DZ twins share many genes, but they may not share the exact combination of genes that make up a specific personality trait. However, because MZ twins have identical genes, they also share any unique combinations of genes that come together to influence personality. Thus, nonadditive effects would show up in identical twins but not in fraternal twins. If this is the case, it could explain why twin studies find evidence for a larger genetic influence on personality than studies using other methods.

So where does this leave us? Exactly how or how much genes determine our adult personalities remains an open question. Some of the answers to this question may come from new methodological and technological developments (Krueger, South, Johnson, & Iacono, 2008). For example, researchers are beginning to identify connections between personality traits and DNA markers for specific genes (Canli, 2008; Gillespie et al., 2008; McCrae, Scally, Terracciano, Abecasis, & Costa, 2010). But regardless of what future discoveries tell us, at this point it seems foolish to ignore the relatively strong case that genetics has an influence on personality.

Extraversion–Introversion

Few personality variables have received as much attention from researchers as extraversion and introversion. However, space allows us to examine only three of the many topics investigators have tied to this personality dimension. First, we'll connect individual differences in extraversion–introversion to the research covered in the previous section by looking at the evidence for the heritability of this personality variable. Second, we'll look at research examining one of the basic differences between introverts and extraverts postulated by Eysenck: preference for arousal. Third, we'll address the question: Who is happier, introverts or extraverts?

The Heritability of Extraversion

If you are an introvert, it's likely you've been given some of the following pieces of advice: "You need to get out more often," "Why can't you be more sociable?" or "Loosen up and enjoy yourself a little." Extraverts have probably heard some of these: "There's more to life than having fun all the time," "Can't you think a little before you do something?" or "Slow down and enjoy life." In short, whether you are introverted or extraverted, someone has probably asked you to become more of the other. Even the most extreme extravert can sit still for a few minutes, and the most introverted person you know occasionally cuts loose and has a good time with friends. But is it possible for an extravert to become permanently more introverted? Can you raise your child to be less introverted or more extraverted?

The answer to these questions depends on what causes a person to become an extravert or an introvert. Hans Eysenck championed the role of genetics in determining personality. As seen in the previous chapter, the exact nature of the physiological differences between extraverts and introverts is still being investigated. Nonetheless, these inherited differences are said to remain fairly constant throughout one's life and eventually develop into the adult behavior styles of extraversion or introversion. Although little evidence for heritability was available when Eysenck first introduced his theory of personality, today an impressive body of work appears to support Eysenck on this point.

As described earlier, researchers often use the twin-study method to determine the role of genetics in the development of personality. Consequently, much of the evidence for the heritability of extraversion–introversion comes from research comparing correlations between pairs of MZ twins with correlations between pairs of DZ twins. Studies using this procedure find consistent evidence for a genetic component of extraversion–introversion (Baker & Daniels, 1990; Heath, Neale, Kessler, Eaves, & Kendler, 1992; Kandler, Bleidorn, Reimann, Angleitner, & Spinath, 2011; Kandler et al., 2010; Kandler, Riemann, Spinath, & Angleitner, 2010).

Two studies in particular deserve special attention. In one of these, a group of researchers measured extraversion–introversion in 12,898 adult twin pairs in Sweden (Floderus-Myrhed, Pedersen, & Rasmuson, 1980). This number represents virtually all of the contactable twins born in Sweden

TABLE 10.3 Within-Pair Extraversion Correlations for MZ and DZ Twins

	Males		Females	
	MZ Twins	DZ Twins	MZ Twins	DZ Twins
Swedish sample	.47	.20	.54	.21
Finnish	.46	.35	.48	.14

Source: From Floderus-Myrhed et al. (1980) and Rose et al. (1988).

between the years 1926 and 1958. Another team of researchers tested 7,144 adult twin pairs in Finland (Rose, Koskenvuo, Kaprio, Sarna, & Langinvainio, 1988). This is nearly every living twin in that country born before 1958. A couple of features of these studies make them particularly noteworthy. First, the samples are large. Second, the participants are composed of nearly every available twin in the designated population. This means researchers don't have to worry about only a certain kind of person volunteering to participate in the study.

When the within-pair correlations for DZ and MZ twins in these samples were compared, considerable evidence for a genetic component for extraversion–introversion was uncovered. As shown in Table 10.3, the MZ twins were more like each other than were the DZ twins, which argues for a genetic influence. Beyond this, the researchers in the Finnish study examined the amount of social contact between the members of the twin pairs as well as the amount of social contact the twins generally engaged in. Although the researchers did find that MZ twins were more likely to stay in communication with each other, this factor alone was not sufficient to explain the differences in MZ and DZ correlations on the extraversion–introversion measure.

Another study takes the twin-study method one step further (Pedersen, Plomin, McClearn, & Friberg, 1988). As in the earlier investigations, the researchers compared MZ and DZ twins who grew up together. However, these researchers also located 95 pairs of MZ twins and 220 pairs of DZ twins reared apart. Again, a positive correlation between the scores of identical twins separated at birth and reared in different environments would provide strong evidence for a genetic component. And indeed, as shown in Table 10.4, there was a relatively strong correlation between the scores of

TABLE 10.4 Within-Pair Correlations of Extraversion Scores for Twins Reared Apart and Together

Twins Reared Apart		Twins Reared Together	
MZ Twins	DZ Twins	MZ Twins	DZ Twins
.30	.04	.54	.06

Source: From "Neuroticism, extraversion, and related traits in adult twins reared apart and reared together," by N. L. Pedersen, R. Plomin, G. E. McClearn, and L. Friberg, *Journal of Personality and Social Psychology*, 1988, 55, 950–957. Reprinted by permission of the American Psychological Association.

Is this student an introvert or an extravert? According to research, his choice of study area provides a clue. Extraverts prefer this type of open study area where opportunities for interruptions and occasional social stimulation are possible.

MZ twins reared in separate environments, albeit not as strong as that for MZ twins reared together.

In short, extraversion appears to have one of the strongest genetic components of any personality variable studied. This observation makes extraversion–introversion an ideal subject for future studies on the heritability of personality. Recent scientific and technological advances have provided researchers with new ways to examine the connection between genes and personality (Canli, 2006). For example, one team of investigators conducted genome-wide scans on adolescents to see which chromosomes were related to various personality measures (Gillespie et al., 2008). They found links between extraversion and chromosomes 2, 3, 8, and 12.

None of this means that you can't be more outgoing at times if you are highly introverted or learn to stop and introspect for a few minutes if you're an extravert. It also does not mean that environmental influences aren't a factor. But we can say that most likely where you fall on the extraversion–introversion continuum was largely determined by the genetic hand you were dealt many years ago.

Extraversion and Preferred Arousal Level

Imagine it's a few days before a big test in one of your classes. You've put off preparing for the exam long enough, so tonight you'll go to the library and spend a few hours behind the books. There are two study areas in this library. One contains a series of one-person desks where you can isolate your-self behind the quiet of the book stacks. Few people walk by these desks, and the room is relatively free of whispers, photocopy machines, and other library noises. The other study area consists of long tables, sofas, and easy chairs. You can easily scan the room to see who else is there. Many people walk by on their way to other parts of the library, and short conversations with those passing through are common. Which of these study areas will you choose?

Your choice in this situation depends in part on whether you are an extravert or an introvert. One team of researchers demonstrated this phenom-enon when they asked students studying in the two kinds of library sections just described to complete an extraversion inventory (Campbell, 1983; Campbell & Hawley, 1982). Students in the noisy, open area were more likely to be extraverts, whereas the ones in the isolated, quiet places were more likely to be introverts. Those in the noisy section said they preferred the amount of noise and the opportunities for socializing. The others said they chose the quiet area to get away from these distractions.

These findings are entirely consistent with the descriptions of extraversion–introversion presented in the previous chapter. Introverted stu-dents are more sensitive to stimulation. Thus an introvert in a noisy room is probably so disturbed by all the activity that he or she will have a difficult time studying. On the other hand, the understimulated extravert probably finds the quiet room boring. Unless the study material is particularly exciting, the extravert will probably take a number of breaks, look around for distrac-tors, and generally have a difficult time keeping his or her mind on the task.

This difference in preferred stimulation level also is found in more con-trolled laboratory experiments (Geen, 1983). For example, extraverts more quickly press a button to change slides on a visual learning task, presumably because they become bored more quickly with the pictures and designs (Brebner & Cooper, 1978). One team of researchers found that extraverts, but not introverts, showed a sudden drop in their ability to perform a listen-ing exercise when the task was made less challenging by slowing down the pace (Cox-Fuenzalida, Angie, Holloway, & Sohl, 2006). In another study, extraverts and introverts worked on a word-memory task while listening to noise through earphones (Geen, 1984). When given the opportunity, intro-verted participants set their earphones at considerably lower levels than did extraverts. However, some introverts in this study were forced to listen to loud noise and some extraverts were restricted to soft noise. As expected, the introverts did worse when exposed to higher levels of stimulation, whereas the extraverts performed worse when listening to the softer noise. Even a pleasant distractor like music can soon become too much for introverts trying to concentrate on a difficult task (Dobbs, Furnham, & McClelland, 2011).

These findings help to explain why some students can study only with music or a TV blaring, whereas other students have to find a quiet library room and then stuff pieces of foam into their ears to block out any remaining noise. Too much stimulation makes it difficult to concentrate, and even extra-verts can reach a point when they have to turn their radios down. But for introverts this point comes much earlier. Of course, the other side of the coin is that too little stimulation also interferes with performance. Whereas it may take hours of solitude to bring an introvert to this point, a few minutes in quiet isolation might be tough on a high extravert.

Extraversion and Happiness

Clearly, extraverts and introverts lead different lives. We are more apt to find extraverts at parties, visiting friends, going places, and generally being active. Introverts are more likely to spend time alone, engaging in quiet, low-stimulation tasks. Who do you suppose is happier? Not surprisingly, I usually find introverts guess introverts are happier people, whereas extraverts can't imagine how anyone could lead a life as boring as the introverted style.

Although introverts may have difficulty understanding this at first, researchers find that on average extraverts report higher levels of happiness than introverts (DeNeve, 1999; DeNeve & Cooper, 1998; Lucas & Baird, 2004; Lucas, Le, & Dyrenforth, 2008). Extraverts and introverts in one investigation were asked to provide a daily mood report for 84 consecutive days (Larsen & Kasimatis, 1990). As shown in Figure 10.2, the researchers found an interesting pattern when they compared moods on days of the week. Perhaps not surprisingly, Monday was the students' least favorite day, with the week becoming progressively better as Saturday approached. But the figure also illustrates that no matter what the day of the week, extraverts reported higher levels of positive mood than introverts. One team of researchers found that extraversion scores could predict levels of positive affect measured 2 years later (Headey & Wearing, 1989). Another investigation used extraversion scores to predict the number of pleasant experiences

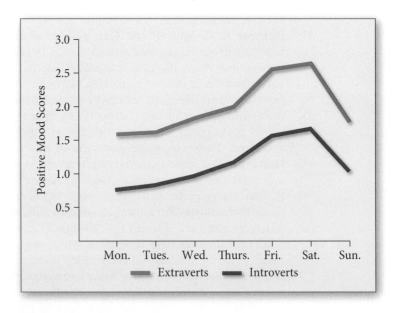

FIGURE 10.2 Happiness Ratings of Extraverts and Introverts

Source: Adapted from Larsen and Kasimatis (1990).

people would have over a 4-year period (Magnus, Diener, Fujita, & Pavot, 1993). Finally, one team of researchers found that the higher the average extraversion score in a country, the higher the average citizens' sense of well-being (Steel & Ones, 2002). However, as is often the case, the relationship between extraversion and happiness also varies from culture to culture. Although extraversion always predicts happiness, the correlation is slightly higher for cultures in which acting extraverted is consistent with the cultural norm (Fulmer et al., 2010).

In short, extraverts generally experience more happiness than introverts. But why might this be the case? Researchers have uncovered at least two reasons. First, extraverts tend to socialize more than introverts (Srivastava, Angelo, & Vallereux, 2008). Extraverts have more friends, and they interact with those friends more often. Researchers have repeatedly found that social contact is closely tied to feelings of well-being (Diener, 1984). Interacting with friends is usually pleasant, as are other extraverted behaviors, such as going to dances, parties, and football games. Many basic needs, such as feeling competent and worthwhile, are also satisfied in social settings. Introverts as well as extraverts find social contact pleasant. Introverts in one study found themselves in a better mood when instructed by the experimenter to act more extraverted in a group setting (Zelenski, Santoro, & Whelan, 2012). In addition, friends often serve as a buffer against stress (Cohen & Wills, 1985). That is, people usually cope with their problems better with friends' help than when they try to handle the situation alone. Consistent with this observation, one study found that extraverts were more likely than introverts to seek out friends when they had a problem (Amirkhan, Risinger, & Swickert, 1995).

The second explanation for extraverts' happiness is that, as explained in the previous chapter, they may be more sensitive to rewards or may simply enjoy the pursuit of rewards more than do introverts (Rusting & Larsen, 1998; Smillie, Cooper, Wilt, & Revelle, 2012). An extravert who receives a good grade on a test may be more pleased than an introvert receiving the same news. In a laboratory test of this hypothesis, extraverts and introverts were given a test of "Syncretic Skill," supposedly a new type of intelligence (Larsen & Ketelaar, 1989). Although the test was bogus, participants received information indicating either that they had done well on the test or that they had done poorly. Mood measures indicated that extraverts were much happier than introverts after receiving the positive feedback. Interestingly, extraverts were no more disappointed than introverts when told they had done poorly.

Other studies find extraverts are more likely than introverts to seek out tasks they think will make them happy (Tamir, 2009) and that extraverts find rewards in situations that introverts don't see (Noguchi, Gohm, & Dalsky, 2006). Participants in one investigation simply wrote down words as if taking a spelling test (Rusting, 1999). However, many of the words were homonyms (words that sound like other words). Thus in some cases it was possible to hear a happy word (*peace* instead of *piece*) and in other cases to hear a sad word (*mourning* instead of *morning*). Although either answer was correct, extraverted participants were more likely than introverts to hear the happy words.

Does this mean extraverts are always happier than introverts? Not necessarily. Extraverts are not only more sociable than introverts; they also are more impulsive. Extraverts are more likely to act on the spur of the moment, and this impulsivity can create problems (Emmons & Diener, 1986). Saying the first thing that comes to mind often is not a good idea. Doing what feels good at the moment without considering the eventual consequences is also fraught with danger. Anyone who has enjoyed a trip to the beach or an evening with friends instead of writing a term paper can appreciate the problem of acting impulsively. Thus extraversion appears to be a two-edged sword. Extraverts are more likely than introverts to have friends and have fun, but they also are more likely to act before thinking and get themselves into trouble. Introverts may not always reap the benefits of social interactions, but they avoid the price of lapses in judgment.

Evolutionary Personality Theory and Mate Selection

Imagine that, like many people these days, you decide to look for a romantic partner through an online dating service. As you move through the process of entering information about yourself, you find that you are faced with two challenging tasks. First, you must describe yourself in a way that will make you attractive to others. Second, you must identify the kind of person you are looking for. What do you say?

Once they get past favorite songs, dream evenings and references to piña coladas, researchers find that how people describe themselves and the kind of person they are looking for in these situations depends largely on whether they are male or female (Harrison & Saeed, 1977; Kelley & Malouf, 2013). Women tend to identify themselves as physically attractive and say they are looking for someone who is older and can provide financial security. Fortunately, these requests fit rather well with what the men say. Men typically are looking for someone who is younger and physically attractive. They also are likely to describe themselves as someone who can provide financial security.

In addition to their practical uses for someone seeking romance, do these results tell us something about the nature of personality? According to advocates of evolutionary personality theory, the answer is "Yes." These psychologists think of romantic relationships in terms of male and female members of a species getting together to (eventually) reproduce. Consequently, choosing a partner is based in part on concerns for parental investment (Geary, 2000; Trivers, 1972). That is, as members of a species, we are concerned about reproducing and passing our genes along to the next generation. Because of this concern, we select mates who are likely to be a part of successful reproduction and effective child rearing. This analysis does not suppose that we actively consider reproduction success when we select among potential dating partners but that certain mate-selection preferences have been passed down to us through the evolutionary process.

According to the evolutionary analysis, men and women have different ideas about parental investment. Because they bear and in most cases raise the offspring, females are more selective about whom they choose to mate and reproduce with. In contrast, in many species males are free to attempt to reproduce with as many females as they can. Frequent mating with many different females increases the probability that one will pass along the male's genes to the next generation. In evolutionary terms, the investment in selecting a mate is larger for women than for men. She has more to lose by making a poor choice than he does. Because they have different ideas about parental investment, evolutionary personality theory predicts that men and women look for very different characteristics in their partners.

What do men look for in a woman? What do women want in a man? Complete answers to these commonly asked questions have eluded the most insightful of us. Although they cannot explain everything, evolutionary personality psychologists argue that men and women select their mates based in part on what serves the needs of the species. As described in the next section, research supports many of these speculations.

What Men Look for in Women

From an evolutionary perspective, men can best serve the needs of the species by reproducing as frequently as possible (Buss, 1991). Consequently, men should be attracted to women with "high reproductive value." In other words, a man should select a woman who is likely to give him many children. But what outward signs do we have of a woman's likely fertility? One indicator is the woman's age. A young wife has the potential to produce more offspring than an older wife. Thus some evolutionary personality psychologists predict that men prefer younger women to older women. Moreover, physical features associated with young adult women, such as "smooth skin, good muscle tone, lustrous hair, and full lips," provide "cues to female reproductive capacity" (Buss, 1991, p. 2). Not coincidentally, these physical attributes are the ones our society associates with beauty.

Evolutionary personality psychologists thus predict that men prefer partners who are physically attractive and probably younger than they are. But can the same reasoning be applied to women? Probably not. If anything, a young man is probably less likely than an older man to provide a woman and her offspring with the kinds of material resources she seeks from a partner. As a result of these different preferences for men and women, we would expect most couples to consist of an older husband and a younger wife.

Research tends to support this speculation. A national survey of unmarried American adults found that men preferred younger women as potential marriage partners, whereas women expressed a preference for older men (Sprecher, Sullivan, & Hatfield, 1994). Married couples in one study were asked about the importance they placed on various characteristics when choosing their spouse (Buss & Barnes, 1986). As expected, husbands were more likely than their wives to rate *physically attractive* and *good looking* as features they sought in a marriage partner. Another study found the more attractive their partner, the more efforts men make to retain their relationship with that woman (Buss & Shackelford, 1997). Men also are more likely than women to be upset if their partner becomes less attractive (Cramer, Manning-Ryan, Johnson, & Barbo, 2000).

The importance of a woman's physical attractiveness can also be seen in the tactics women use to gain a man's attention (Buss, 1988). In evolutionary personality theory, this is known as *intrasexual selection*—the competition among members of one gender for mating access to the best members of the other gender. If men select partners who are youthful and beautiful, a woman can improve her chances of pairing up with the most desirable partner by emphasizing these attributes.

To test this possibility, newlyweds in one study were asked to describe what they did to attract their spouse when they first began dating (Buss, 1988). As predicted, the women tended to report that they altered their appearance with makeup and jewelry, wore stylish clothes, wore sexy clothes, and kept themselves clean and groomed. In another study, investigators scheduled undergraduate women to attend experimental sessions on two separate occasions (Durante, Li, & Haselton, 2008). Although the women did not know it, the sessions were scheduled for different times in their ovulatory cycle. Hormone tests verified that one of the visits was on a high-fertility day and the other on a low-fertility day. The women also did not know that the researchers were primarily interested in what they would wear to the session. Consistent with the intrasexual selection notion, the women wore clothes judges rated as more revealing and sexier on high-fertility days. These were the days in which the women presumably were more interested in capturing the attention of a potential partner. Finally, some evolutionary personality theorists point to the so-called "lipstick effect," that is, the tendency for women to spend more money on cosmetics during economic downturns (Hill, Rodeheffer, Griskevicius, Durante, & White, 2012). These researchers argue that economic insecurity heightens the need to find a mate with resources, which drives the women to try to make themselves more attractive.

In short, there is abundant evidence that men are more likely than women to look at physical attractiveness when selecting a dating or marriage partner (Feingold, 1990). However, it is important to keep in mind that it is fertility men are said to be seeking in younger women, not necessarily youthfulness. When one team of investigators interviewed teenage boys, they found a preference for slightly older women (Kenrick, Keefe, Gabrielidis, & Cornelius, 1996). In other words, the boys were attracted to the females most likely to reproduce regardless of their age.

Although the findings are consistent, there is one important limitation in the studies reviewed so far. That is, they tell us a lot about the preferences of American men and women, but little about romantic choices in other cultures. To make a strong case for the evolutionary personality position, we need to demonstrate that this effect is not limited to certain social or cultural groups. If men were found to rely on physical attractiveness only in Western cultures, a strong argument could be made that this behavior reflects social learning patterns rather than an inherited human characteristic.

To solve this problem, one team of researchers conducted an elaborate cross-cultural investigation (Buss, 1989). The researchers looked at gender differences in partner preferences in 37 cultural groups. These groups were located in 33 different countries, on six continents and five islands, and included people from cultural backgrounds very different from Americans, such as South African Zulus, Gujarati Indians, and Santa Catarina Brazilians. Participants in each of these samples were asked what they considered the ideal age for themselves and their partner when marrying. Participants were also asked how important each of 18 personality traits were for choosing a potential mate (for example, *intelligence, good financial prospect,* and *good looks*).

The findings provide strong support for evolutionary personality theory. As shown in Table 10.5, in each of the 37 samples men preferred partners who were younger than they were. Additional evidence was found when researchers looked at the actual age at which people first married. This information was available in 27 of the countries studied. Men in each of these cultures not only said they preferred younger partners but also tended to marry women younger than themselves. Although the investigators made no predictions about the women's preferences, the women in all 37 cultures said they preferred an older partner.

TABLE 10.5 Mean Age Difference in Years between Preferred Age of First Marriage for Spouse and for Self in 37 Cultures

Sample	Males	Females
Africa		
Nigeria	−6.45	4.90
South Africa(Whites)	−2.30	3.50
South Africa (Zulus)	−3.33	3.76
Zambia	−7.38	4.14
Asia		
China	−2.05	3.45
India	−3.06	3.29
Indonesia	−2.72	4.69
Iran	−4.02	5.10
Israel (Jewish)	−2.88	3.95
Israel (Palestinian)	−3.75	3.71
Japan	−2.37	3.05
Taiwan	−3.13	3.78
Eastern Europe		
Bulgaria	−3.13	4.18
Estonia	−2.19	2.85
Poland	−2.85	3.38
Yugoslavia	−2.47	3.61

(Continued)

TABLE 10.5 Mean Age Difference in Years between Preferred Age of First Marriage for Spouse and for Self in 37 Cultures (*continued*)

Sample	Males	Females
Western Europe		
Belgium	−2.53	2.46
Finland	−0.38	2.83
France	−1.94	4.00
Germany	−2.52	3.70
Great Britain	−1.92	2.26
Greece	−3.36	4.54
Ireland	−2.07	2.78
Italy	−2.76	3.24
Netherlands	−1.01	2.72
Norway	−1.91	3.12
Spain	−1.46	2.60
Sweden	−2.34	2.91
North America		
Canada (English)	−1.53	2.72
Canada (French)	−1.22	1.82
United States (Mainland)	−1.65	2.54
United States (Hawaiian)	−1.92	3.30
Oceania		
Australia	−1.77	2.86
New Zealand	−1.59	2.91
South America		
Brazil	−2.94	3.94
Colombia	−4.45	4.51
Venezuela	−2.99	3.62
Mean	−2.66	3.42

Note: Negative values indicate a preference for a younger mate; positive values indicate a preference for an older mate.

Source: From "Sex differences in human mate preferences: Evolutionary hypotheses tested in 37 cultures," by D. M. Buss, *Behavioral and Brain Sciences*, 1989, 12, 1–49. Reprinted by permission of the author and Cambridge University Press.

More evidence for the evolutionary personality position was found when the researchers looked at the importance men and women placed on physical attractiveness when selecting a mate. In each of the cultures, men were more likely than women to say that good looks are important. This difference was statistically significant in all but three of the samples. Thus the tendency for men to prefer youthful and physically attractive women appears to be fairly universal despite differences in cultures and social norms. Evolutionary personality psychologists interpret these findings as evidence for universal characteristics handed down from our ancestors.

What Women Look for in Men

According to evolutionary personality theory, men prefer a female partner who provides maximal opportunity for successful reproduction. But women have a different role to play in reproduction and child rearing. According to the parental investment analysis, women prefer to mate with men who can provide for their offspring. In nonhuman species this may simply mean a mate who can provide food and protection. In humans this means providing the financial resources required to raise the children. Some men are better able to do this than others. Men also differ in their ability to take care of and nurture their sons and daughters as well as in their ability to transfer status or power to their children. Evolutionary personality psychologists argue that women prefer partners who possess these abilities.

Again, some research supports this speculation. When investigators asked married couples to describe what they found attractive in their spouse, women were more likely to identify such characteristics as *dependable, good earning capacity, ambitious,* and *career-oriented* (Buss & Barnes, 1986). Other investigations find women are more interested in locating a partner high in socioeconomic status and ambitiousness (Ben Hamida, Mineka, & Bailey, 1998; Feingold, 1992). However, no gender difference is found for characteristics unrelated to parental investment, such as sense of humor (Feingold, 1992). In another study, more women than men said they would be upset if their partner was unable to hold a good job (Cramer et al., 2000). When forced to make choices about hypothetical romantic partners, women in one study were more willing to give up physical attractiveness in their partner than high status and resources (Fletcher, Tither, O'Loughlin, Friesen, & Overall, 2004)

Researchers find that men often are aware of these preferences and, like women, compete among themselves for the most desirable partner. Newlywed husbands in one study were more likely than their spouses to say they bragged about their financial resources as a way to catch their future wives' attention (Buss, 1988). In other words, the men let it be known that they made a lot of money or went out of their way to show off a new car or condominium. Men are more interested in purchasing flashy items like expensive cars and watches when looking for a romantic partner (Sundie et al., 2011). Similarly, men are more likely to display their material resources when trying to retain a partner's affection (Buss & Shackelford, 1997).

Other studies find that women prefer dominant men over relatively meek men (Sadalla, Kenrick, & Vershure, 1987). This preference for a dominant man is even stronger when women have first been made to think about objects related to being a parent (Miller & Ostlund, 2006). According to evolutionary personality theorists, a dominant man is better able to provide needed resources for his family than a man at the bottom of the pecking order. But do these findings mean that, given a choice, women prefer loud and brutish men? In other words, in the game of love, do nice guys finish last? Additional studies indicate that this is not necessarily the case

(Burger & Cosby, 1999; Graziano, Jensen-Campbell, Todd, & Finch, 1997). Mating with a dominant man may have its advantages, but not if he is unwilling to share resources or invest in the welfare of his children. In other words, dominance alone may not be a very attractive trait. In support of this reasoning, when undergraduate women observed and evaluated interactions between men, they reported that helpful and generous men were far more appealing for both short- and long-term relationships than men who were simply dominant (Jensen-Campbell, Graziano, & West, 1995).

In summary, research finds patterns of attraction that support evolutionary theory's predictions about what women find attractive in men. But once again, we need to ask if the findings are limited to American samples. Data from the 37-culture study described earlier indicate that women around the world report similar preferences (Buss, 1989). As shown in Table 10.6, women in each culture were more likely than men to prefer a spouse who had good financial prospects. Only in Spain did this difference fail to reach statistical significance. Similar patterns were found when the men and women rated the importance of characteristics like ambition and industriousness in a partner. In short, there is a nearly universal tendency for women to prefer men who can provide financial resources.

TABLE 10.6 Importance of "Good Financial Prospects" When Selecting a Mate

Sample	Males	Females
Africa		
Nigeria	1.37	2.30
South Africa (Whites)	0.94	1.73
South Africa (Zulus)	0.70	1.14
Zambia	1.46	2.33
Asia		
China	1.10	1.56
Indonesia	1.42	2.55
India	1.60	2.00
Iran	1.25	2.04
Israel (Jewish)	1.31	1.82
Israel (Palestinian)	1.28	1.67
Japan	0.92	2.29
Taiwan	1.25	2.21
Eastern Europe		
Bulgaria	1.16	1.64
Estonia	1.31	1.51
Poland	1.09	1.74
Yugoslavia	1.27	1.66

(Continued)

TABLE 10.6 Importance of "Good Financial Prospects" When Selecting a Mate (*continued*)

Sample	Males	Females
Western Europe		
Belgium	0.93	1.36
Finland	0.65	1.18
France	1.22	1.68
Great Britain	0.67	1.16
Germany	1.14	1.81
Greece	1.16	1.92
Ireland	0.82	1.67
Italy	0.87	1.33
Netherlands	0.69	0.94
Norway	1.10	1.42
Spain	1.25	1.39
Sweden	1.18	1.75
North America		
Canada (English)	1.02	1.91
Canada (French)	1.47	1.94
United States (Mainland)	1.08	1.96
United States (Hawaiian)	1.50	2.10
Oceania		
Australia	0.69	1.54
New Zealand	1.35	1.63
South America		
Brazil	1.24	1.91
Colombia	1.72	2.21
Venezuela	1.66	2.26

Note: Participants rated on a scale from 0 (Unimportant) to 3 (Indispensable).
Source: From Buss (1989).

Conclusions and Limitations

Research findings on what men and women look for in romantic partners tend to be consistent with the predictions from evolutionary personality psychology. Men around the world prefer younger and physically attractive women, whereas women look for a man who can provide the material resources they need to raise their children. However, as intuitive and consistent as these findings may be, there are reasons to take them with a grain of salt.

As described in the previous chapter, researchers testing these hypotheses are necessarily limited in their ability to make strong tests of causal relationships. Because they cannot manipulate variables like gender and physical attractiveness, investigators are unable to rule out many alternative explanations for their findings (Wood & Eagly, 2002). For example, differences in the ages men and women marry may simply have to do with differences in maturity level, with women becoming physically and perhaps emotionally mature more quickly than men.

Moreover, investigations do not always produce findings consistent with evolutionary personality theory's predictions (Costa, Terracciano, & McCrae, 2001; Eastwick & Finkel, 2008). For example, evolutionary personality psychologists argue that men should be more upset when discovering their spouse's sexual infidelity and that women will be more concerned about losing their partner's emotional fidelity. These predictions stem from the men's theoretical needs to be assured the offspring they raise are their own and from the women's desire that their partners continue to support them and the offspring after reproduction. However, studies often fail to support either of these predictions (Berman & Frazier, 2005; DeSteno, Bartlett, Braverman, & Salovey, 2002; Harris, 2003).

In addition, it's entirely possible that instincts inherited from our ancestors are largely overshadowed by learned preferences we develop for romantic partners. The basic needs of animals in the wild may be quite different from the needs of men and women in modern society. Many women probably prefer a partner who spends time with them rather than one devoted to an ambitious climb up the corporate ladder. This is not to say that tendencies passed down from our ancestors do not influence our choices. The research suggests that they do. But our preferences for a physically attractive woman or a wealthy man might play a relatively small role in this process. In one study both men and women rated mutual love and affection the most important consideration when selecting a romantic partner (Ben Hamida et al., 1998). Moreover, researchers find gender differences in sexual behavior and mate preferences are significantly smaller in cultures that promote gender equality (Petersen & Hyde, 2010; Zentner & Mitura, 2012).

Common sense also tells us there are a number of exceptions to the rule. Many women no doubt prefer a man who is more sensitive than dominant. Many men prefer an older woman to a less mature partner. Evolutionary personality psychology also is limited to heterosexual mating choices. The prediction of partner choice based on parental investment says little or nothing about choices for lesbians and gays. The analysis also may not apply to women who are past their reproductive years and older men who are interested in an intimate relationship but not in raising a family.

Summary

1. Research suggests both genetics and the environment have an influence on the development of adult personalities. Psychologists use a variety of methods to determine the extent to which personality is inherited, most notably the twin-study method. However, questions surface when interpreting these studies, particularly with some of the underlying

assumptions of the methods. Nonetheless, the cumulative evidence argues strongly for a significant heritability component in adult personality.

2. Extraversion–introversion is probably the most widely researched aspect of Eysenck's personality theory. Evidence indicates that this personality variable has a large heritability component. Consistent with Eysenck's theory, researchers find extraverts seek out stimulating environments and perform better in these environments than introverts. Research also finds that extraverts are generally happier than introverts.

3. Evolutionary personality theory predicts that men and women look for different features when selecting romantic partners. Consistent with this view, research shows that men are more likely to consider physical attractiveness when selecting a dating partner or spouse. In addition, men are more likely to prefer a younger partner. Studies also indicate that women prefer a man who possesses the resources necessary for raising a family. Cross-cultural research suggests that these preferences may be universal

Key Term

twin-study method (p. 254)

Media Resources

Visit the book companion website at **www.cengagebrain.com** to find a glossary, flashcards, quizzing, and more.

CHAPTER 11

The Humanistic Approach

Theory, Application, and Assessment

I was once involved in a discussion about Jim Morrison, the leader of the 1960s rock group The Doors. For a few years Morrison was a rock legend who personified counterculture thinking. But he also abused his body with drugs and alcohol and died of an apparent heart attack at age 27. One man in this discussion blamed society for Morrison's self-destructive behavior and death. He argued that Morrison's alienation from his parents, harassment by police, and pressure from music industry executives pushed the singer to his tragic death. A woman in the group disagreed. She argued that no one forced Jim Morrison to take outrageous doses of dangerous drugs or to go on daily drinking binges. For that matter, no one kept him in the music business. If it was that much hassle, he could easily have gotten out.

Which of these views do you suppose is more "humanistic"? You may be surprised to find that the woman who blamed Morrison's problems on himself is probably more aligned with the view of humanistic psychology than the man who pointed to society and the hassles Morrison faced. This is not to say that humanistic psychologists are heartless or insensitive to the problems society tosses our way. But failure to take personal responsibility for how we react to those problems is completely foreign to the humanistic approach to personality and well-being.

This perspective is easier to understand if we look at the circumstances that gave birth to the humanistic view. By the middle of the 20th century, two major views of humanity had emerged from the discipline of psychology. One was the Freudian concept. According to this perspective, we are all victims of unconscious sexual and aggressive instincts that constantly influence our behavior. The other view came from the behaviorists (discussed in Chapter 13), who, in the extreme, view humans as little more than large, complex rats. Just as a rat is conditioned to respond to laboratory stimuli, humans are said to respond to stimuli in their living environments over which they have no control. We act the way we do because of the situation we are in or the situations we have been in before—not because of some personal choice or direction.

Many psychologists had difficulty accepting either of these descriptions of human nature. In particular, important aspects of human personality such as free will and human dignity were missing from the Freudians' and behaviorists' descriptions. In response to these concerns, a so-called third force was born. The humanistic approach (sometimes, perhaps incorrectly, referred to as *existential* or *phenomenological* psychology) paints a very different picture of our species.

A key distinction between the humanistic approach and other theories of personality is that people are assumed to be largely responsible for their actions. Although we sometimes respond automatically to events and may at times be motivated by unconscious impulses, most of the time we have the power to determine our own destiny and to decide our actions. We have free will. Jim Morrison may have found himself under tremendous pressure and difficulties, but how he responded to that situation was his own choice. Had Morrison seen a humanistic therapist, he probably would have been encouraged to accept this responsibility and make choices about his lifestyle consistent with his individuality and personal needs.

The third force in American psychology caught on rapidly with a large number of psychotherapists and personality theorists. The emphasis on individuality and personal expression in the 1960s (which gave rise to the counterculture movement personified by Jim Morrison) provided fertile soil for the growth of humanistic psychology. The election of prominent humanistic psychologist Abraham Maslow to president of the American Psychological Association in 1967 symbolized the acceptance of the humanistic approach as a legitimate alternative perspective.

Humanistic psychology never did overthrow psychoanalysis or behaviorism, but it did manage to make a niche for itself among the major approaches to understanding human personality. Although not as popular as it once was, there remains an active community of humanistic psychologists and a large number of psychotherapists who identify with this perspective.

The Roots of Humanistic Psychology

Although humanistic psychology evolved from many sources, its roots lie primarily in two areas: existential philosophy, which is decidedly European in flavor, and the work of some American psychologists, most notably Carl Rogers and Abraham Maslow.

Existential philosophy addresses many of the questions that later became cornerstones of the humanistic approach. Some of these include the meaning of our existence, the role of free will, and the uniqueness of each human being. Some psychologists align themselves so closely with existential philosophers that they have adopted the label *existential psychologists*. The list of prominent existential psychologists includes Ludwig Binswanger, Medard Boss, Viktor Frankl, R. D. Laing, and Rollo May. Existential psychotherapy frequently focuses on *existential anxiety*—the feelings of dread and panic that follow the realization that there is no meaning to one's life. Therapy often emphasizes the freedom to choose and develop a lifestyle that reduces feelings of emptiness, anxiety, and boredom.

At about the time existential philosophy was making its way into conversations among psychologists, two psychologists were writing about their personal transitions from traditional views of personality to a humanistic perspective. Carl Rogers found his early efforts as a psychotherapist were largely unsuccessful. He started to question his ability to understand his clients' problems or wondered whether he really could help people overcome their problems. "It began to occur to me," Rogers reflected many years later, "that unless I had a need to demonstrate my own cleverness ... I would do better to rely upon the client for direction" (1967, p. 359).

The turning point for Abraham Maslow came while watching a World War II parade. Although the parade was supposed to promote American patriotism and the war effort, it made Maslow aware of the scope of society's problems and just how little psychology had contributed to bettering the human condition. He became determined "to prove that human beings are capable of something grander than war and prejudice and hatred" (as cited in Hall, 1968, p. 55).

The new ideas promoted by Rogers and Maslow found a receptive audience among psychologists also bothered by the limitations and deficiencies they saw in the dominant approaches to personality at the time. Within a relatively short period, these ideas and contributions from many other psychologists developed into a comprehensive new approach for understanding personality. However, unlike psychoanalysis, there is no single authority we can point to as the definitive spokesperson for the humanistic perspective and no clearly agreed-upon definition of what constitutes a humanistic personality theory. Nonetheless, we can identify some elements that are central to the humanistic approach.

Key Elements of the Humanistic Approach

The problem of having no agreed-upon definition for humanistic psychology became obvious in the 1960s and early 1970s when it seemed nearly everyone identified himself or herself as "humanistic" in an effort to capitalize on the popularity of the approach at that time. As a result, humanistic psychology sometimes was associated with faddish therapies that promised to solve problems and provide the key to happiness for the price of a paperback book. Although no clear criteria exist for identifying which approaches to psychotherapy fall into the humanistic category, it is safe to say that the following four elements are central to the general viewpoint to which we apply the "humanistic" label: (1) an emphasis on personal responsibility, (2) an emphasis on the "here and now," (3) a focus on the experience of the individual, and (4) an emphasis on personal growth.

Personal Responsibility

Although we may try to deny it, we are ultimately responsible for what happens to us. This idea, borrowed from existential philosophers, is central to the humanistic approach to personality and is illustrated in the way we commonly use the phrase "I have to." We say, "I have to go to class," "I have to meet some friends," "I have to take care of my children," and so forth. But the truth is that we don't *have* to do any of these. Within limits, there is practically nothing we have to do. Rather, humanistic psychologists argue, virtually all our behaviors represent personal choices. People *choose* to remain in relationships; they do not have to. We choose to act passively; we could decide to act forcefully. We choose to go to work, call our friends, leave a party, or send a Christmas present. We do not have to do any of these things. The price we pay for making some of these choices can be steep, but they are choices nonetheless.

Unlike the Freudian or behavioral descriptions of people at the mercy of forces they cannot control, humanistic psychologists see people as active shapers of their own lives, with freedom to change limited only by physical constraints. Clients working with humanistic psychotherapists are often encouraged to accept that they have the power to do or to be whatever they desire. However, this power can be a two-edged sword. When speaking in the abstract, nearly everyone agrees that freedom of choice is a good thing.

But when applied at a personal level, accepting that our fate is in our own hands is often quite frightening. Taking responsibility means no more blaming others for your problems and no more feeling sorry for yourself. If things are going to change, it is up to you to do the changing.

The Here and Now

Think about the last time you walked to a class or some other appointment. Perhaps you spent the time thinking about what you did last weekend or ruminating over an embarrassing incident. Maybe you rehearsed something you wanted to say to someone or thought about how nice it would be just to get through this week. A humanistic psychologist might say that what you really did was to lose 10 minutes. You failed to experience fully the 10 minutes that life handed you. You could have enjoyed the fresh air, appreciated the blue sky, or learned something from observing or talking with other people.

According to the humanistic perspective, we can't become fully functioning individuals until we learn to live our lives as they happen. Some reflection on the past or future can be helpful, but most people spend far too much time thinking about events that have already happened or planning those that might. Time spent on these activities is time lost, for you can live life fully only if you live it in the here and now. Of course, potential distractions from living life to its fullest are everywhere. The writer Carl Sandburg once referred to television as "a thief of time." Were he alive today, one can only imagine what he might say about the countless hours lost to the many mindless diversions available through the Internet.

A popular poster reminds us, "Today Is the First Day of the Rest of Your Life." This phrase could well have been coined by a humanistic psychologist. The humanistic view maintains that we need not be victims of our past. Certainly our past experiences shape and influence who we are and how we behave. But these experiences should not dictate what we can become. People do not need to remain shy and unassertive just because they "have always been that way." You do not have to remain in an unhappy relationship simply because you don't know what else to do. Your past has guided you to where you are today, but it is not an anchor.

The Experience of the Individual

No one knows you better than yourself. This observation is a cornerstone of humanistic psychology. Humanistic psychologists argue that it's absurd for therapists to listen to clients, decide what the clients' problems are, and force clients' to accept the therapist's interpretation of what should be changed and how it should be changed. Instead, humanistic therapists seek to understand what their clients are experiencing and try to provide a therapeutic atmosphere that allows clients to help themselves.

People sometimes find this view of the therapist's role a bit puzzling. How would this approach help clients who don't know the cause of their problems? The answer is that, whereas some people may not understand the source of their difficulties at the moment, the therapist also has no access to this information. During the course of successful therapy, clients come to understand themselves and develop an appropriate strategy for resolving their problems. You may have had a similar experience when dealing with personal issues. Well-meaning friends may have provided plenty of advice, but it was only when you considered that advice and came to a decision on your own that you were able to resolve the problem.

Personal Growth

> "Whether one calls it a growth tendency, a drive toward self-actualization, or a forward-moving directional tendency, it is the mainspring of life."
>
> CARL ROGERS

Suppose tomorrow you inherited several million dollars, settled down with someone who will admire and love you always, and were promised a long and healthy life. Would you be happy? Most likely, your answer is "yes," or perhaps even, "Are you kidding?" No doubt having all these things is better than not having them. But a humanistic psychologist would probably predict that your happiness would be short-lived. That's because there is more to life than simply having all of our immediate needs met. Happiness also requires that that we grow in a positive direction. According to the humanistic psychology, we are all motivated to progress toward some ultimately satisfying state of being. Carl Rogers referred to this state as becoming a *fully functioning* individual. Abraham Maslow (1970) used the term *self-actualization*. A person becomes self-actualized when he or she becomes "more what one idiosyncratically is, to become everything that one is capable of becoming" (p. 46).

This growth process is assumed to be the natural manner of human development. That is, we progress toward this satisfying state unless life's difficulties prevent us from doing so. When obstacles block our personal growth, humanistic psychotherapy can be helpful. However, the therapist does not put clients back on track. Only the client can do that. Rather, the therapist creates a therapeutic atmosphere that allows clients to overcome their problems and continue growing. Rogers describes this ever-unfolding of one's self as a "process of becoming."

Carl Rogers

Humanistic psychology could ask for no better example of how to live life fully than the career of Carl Rogers. Rogers pioneered humanistic psychotherapy and was the first therapist to popularize a "person-centered" approach (Rogers, 1951). He also promoted encounter groups as a means of therapy (Rogers, 1970) and expanded his ideas about working with clients into a general theory of personality (Rogers, 1961). Late in his career, Rogers applied the humanistic approach to social issues such as education and world peace (Rogers, 1969, 1977, 1982). Throughout his career, Rogers espoused an optimistic view of humanity and a belief in each individual's potential for fulfillment and happiness.

The Fully Functioning Person

Like other humanistic theorists, Rogers maintained that each of us naturally strives to reach an optimal sense of satisfaction with our lives. He called people who reach this goal **fully functioning**. What is a fully functioning person

Carl R. Rogers

1902–1987

Roger Ressmeyer/Historical/Corbis

Like the inevitable unfolding of one's true self that he promoted, Carl Rogers' interest in science and his concern for people carried him from Midwest farm boy to leader of the humanistic movement in psychology. Carl was a shy but very intelligent boy growing up in Illinois. He had a particular fondness for science, and by the time he was 13 had developed a reputation as the local expert on biology and agriculture.

Ironically, the Rogers household was anything but warm and affectionate. Openly expressing emotions, later a key feature of Rogerian therapy, was not allowed. As a result, like two of his siblings, Carl developed an ulcer by age 15.

Rogers went to his mother and father's alma mater, the University of Wisconsin, in 1919 to study agriculture. He planned a career in farming but soon found agriculture unchallenging. He took a correspondence course in psychology one summer but found it boring. He finally settled on religious studies. In 1924, Carl moved with his new wife, Helen, to New York City to attend Union Theological Seminary as he prepared himself for a career as a minister.

But two developments in New York led to a change in plans. First, intensely studying theology caused Carl to question his religious beliefs. "It would be a horrible thing to have to profess to a set of beliefs in order to remain in one's profession," he observed. "I wanted to find a field in which I could be sure my freedom of thought would not be limited" (as cited in Kirschenbaum, 1979, pp. 51–52). A career in theology promised Rogers an opportunity to help people, but his faith continued to wane. The second development was a renewed introduction to psychology. While at the seminary, Rogers and several classmates took psychology courses across the street at Columbia University. These classmates included Theodore Newcomb and Ernest Hilgard, who

also went on to become important figures in psychology. Much to his parents' dismay, Rogers eventually left the church to pursue graduate study in psychology at Columbia.

After graduation, Rogers worked at a child guidance clinic in Rochester, New York. Later he joined the faculty at Ohio State University and the University of Chicago before returning to the University of Wisconsin in 1957. Throughout this time, Rogers battled with the established Freudian approach to psychotherapy and the dominant behavioral influence in academia. But in time he began to win many of these battles. When the American Psychological Association handed out its first annual award for distinguished scientific contribution in 1956, Carl Rogers was the recipient.

In 1963 Rogers moved to La Jolla, California, where he founded the Center for Studies of the Person. He devoted the last 15 years of his life to the issues of social conflict and world peace. Even in his 80s he led workshops and communication groups in such places as the Soviet Union and South Africa. Rogers continued to write extensively and to shape the discipline of psychology until his death in February 1987.

like? Rogers identified several characteristics. Fully functioning people are open to their experiences. Rather than falling into familiar patterns, they look to see what life will throw their way. Related to this, fully functioning people try to live each moment as it comes. The idea is to experience life, not just pass through.

Fully functioning people learn to trust their feelings. If something feels right, they'll probably do it. They aren't insensitive to the needs of others, but they aren't overly concerned with meeting the standards society sets for them. If a fully functioning woman wants to cut her hair or quit her job, she probably won't stop herself just because others might not approve. It's not that fully functioning people are rebellious. They may follow the traditional path of college, job, marriage, and family, but only if each of these choices is consistent with their own interests, values, and needs.

Fully functioning people aren't simply mellow folks who take everything in stride. On the contrary, they experience emotions—both positive and negative—more deeply and more intensely than most people. Fully functioning people accept and express their anger. To do otherwise would be to cut themselves off from their feelings. As a result of these intense emotions, fully functioning people have richer lives than most of us.

Anxiety and Defense

If we all have an innate desire to be fully functioning individuals, why is there so much unhappiness in the world? Why doesn't everyone get the maximum enjoyment out of life? Rogers was well aware that we often fall short of becoming happy, fully functioning adults. The world is full of disappointments and difficulties, all of which are potential sources of anxiety. Becoming a fully functioning person doesn't eliminate all our problems. But it does mean we acknowledge and deal with these problems directly rather than rely on psychological defenses to avoid them.

Rogers maintained that anxiety often is the result of coming into contact with information that is inconsistent with the way we think of ourselves. You may believe that you are a good tennis player, a kind person, a good student, or a pleasant conversationalist, but occasionally you receive information that contradicts this self-concept. For example, suppose you think of yourself as the kind of person everybody likes, but one day you overhear someone say what a jerk he thinks you are. How do you react? If you were fully functioning, you would accept the information. Here is someone who does not like you. You might acknowledge to yourself that, although you are a fine person, not everyone is going to find you pleasant and wonderful. Unfortunately, most of us are not capable of such a well-adjusted reaction. But for those of us who fall short of being a fully functioning person, hearing information that threatens our self-concept often leads to anxiety. And if the information is excessively threatening, the anxiety will be difficult to manage.

This is where Rogers' theory takes on a slight Freudian flavor. Rogers proposed that we initially process this threatening information at a level somewhere below consciousness, a process he called **subception**. When faced with particularly threatening information, we often rely on defenses to keep the information from entering consciousness. The most common defense is *distortion*. Returning to the example, you might convince yourself that the person who called you a jerk was in a bad mood or is just a rude person. In more extreme cases, you might resort to outright *denial*. No, you might convince yourself, he wasn't really talking about me but about someone else with a name that sounds like mine.

Rogers argued that using these defenses is not limited to situations in which we encounter unflattering assessments from other individuals. People who consider themselves socially undesirable also may turn to distortion and denial when they hear that someone is attracted to them. They might tell themselves the admirer is just being polite or perhaps is scheming to get something from them. Sometimes we defend ourselves from threatening observations we make about ourselves. Each of us on occasion acts in ways that fall short of our personal standards. Perhaps you have cheated a friend out of money, said some hurtful things to a loved one, or lied to take advantage of an acquaintance. Rather than acknowledge your shortcomings and try to learn from your mistakes, you may have distorted the situation ("She really shouldn't get that upset by what I said") or denied the facts ("I didn't know the money was his").

Distortion and denial often succeed in the short run by reducing anxiety. But this relief comes at a price. Each distortion takes us further and further away from experiencing life fully. In severe cases, people replace reality with fantasy. A man may think of himself as the world's most desirable bachelor when in fact there are no objective reasons to draw this conclusion. A student with poor grades might convince herself that she is a genius whose ideas are simply too sophisticated for her instructors to appreciate. However, at some point the gap between self-concept and reality may become so large that even our defenses are inadequate. In this case, people experience what Rogers called a state of disorganization. The protective barrier against threatening information collapses, and the result is extreme anxiety.

Conditions of Worth and Unconditional Positive Regard

Why is it so difficult to face facts and incorporate relevant information as we develop a sense of who we are? Rogers' answer is that most of us grow up in an atmosphere of **conditional positive regard**. As children, our parents and caregivers provide love and support. However, they rarely do this unconditionally. Rather, most parents communicate affection for their children as long as the children do what is expected of them. When parents disapprove of their children's behavior, they withhold their admiration and love. The children get the message they are loved, but only when they do what their parents want. The positive regard children need and want is conditional upon their behavior.

As a result of this conditioned esteem, children learn to accept only the parts of themselves their parents deem appropriate. They deny or distort their weaknesses and faults and as a result become less and less aware of who they really are. Unfortunately, this process continues when the child becomes an adult. Most of us have a tendency to incorporate into our self-concept only

Jerry Burger/Santa Clara University

Is the child a bad boy, or has he merely done a bad thing? Rogers argues that parents should provide children with unconditional positive regard. Although the boy may have done something the mother did not like, he is still loved and prized by her.

those aspects that are likely to win the approval of significant people in our lives. Instead of acknowledging and expressing characteristics that others might not approve of, we deny that we possess these characteristics. And as we lose touch with our real self, we become less and less fully functioning.

The antidote for this self-defeating sequence is **unconditional positive regard**. When we experience unconditional positive regard, we know we will be accepted and loved no matter what we say or do. Rogers advised parents to communicate to their children that although they don't approve of a specific behavior, they will always love and accept them. Under these conditions, children no longer feel a need to deny thoughts and feelings that might lead their parents to withdrawal affection. They are free to incorporate faults and weaknesses into their self-concepts and thereby able to more fully experience life.

Fortunately, parents are not the only source of unconditional positive regard, and growing up in a family without this acceptance does not condemn a person to a less-than-full life. Adult relationships with friends and romantic partners also can be based on unconditional positive regard.

Similarly, therapists can create an atmosphere of unconditional positive regard during psychotherapy. Rogers maintained that this type of accepting environment is a requirement for effective treatment. We'll examine more of Rogers' ideas about psychotherapy later in this chapter.

Abraham Maslow

"I'm someone who likes plowing new ground then walking away from it. I get bored. I like discovery, not proving."

ABRAHAM MASLOW

Abraham Maslow spent most of his career filling in the gaps he found in other approaches to personality. At a time when the field was largely concerned with psychological disorders, Maslow wondered what psychology could do for the happy, healthy side of personality. "Freud supplied to us the sick half of psychology," he wrote, "and we must now fill it out with the healthy half" (1968, p. 5). Maslow replaced Freud's pessimistic and dismal view of human nature with an optimistic and uplifting portrayal. In addition, although he acknowledged the existence of unconscious motives, Maslow focused his attention on the conscious aspects of personality.

Motivation and the Hierarchy of Needs

For a moment, contrast the concerns of the average middle-class American today with those of the typical blue-collar worker during the Great Depression of the 1930s. Today's financially secure professionals fret over their personal relationships and their standing in the social community. Many are concerned about making a contribution with their lives. Some find satisfaction working in community service projects and for charitable organizations. Others read novels, get involved with social causes, and take classes to develop their writing skills or appreciation for the arts. But things were very different when nearly a third of the workforce lost their jobs in the 1930s. Feeding oneself and one's family became the dominant concern of many Americans. A job, any job, was of primary importance. Spending time contemplating the direction of one's life and experimenting with various avenues to express one's potential were luxuries reserved for those who did not have to worry about day-to-day existence.

The contrasting experiences of today's middle-class citizens and those of Depression-era workers (and, sadly, the experiences of many impoverished people throughout the world today) illustrates a key aspect of Maslow's theory of personality. Maslow identified two types of motives. **Deficiency motives** result from a lack of some needed object. Basic needs such as hunger and thirst fall into this category. Once we obtain the needed object, deficiency motives are satisfied and for a period of time stop directing our behavior. In contrast, **growth needs** are not satisfied simply by finding the object of our need. Rather, growth needs are satisfied by expressing the motive. Growth needs include the unselfish giving of love to others and the development of one's unique potential. Satisfying a growth need may even lead to an increase in, rather than a satiation of, the need.

Maslow identified five basic categories of needs—both deficiency and growth—and arranged them in his well-known **hierarchy of needs**. As shown

Abraham H. Maslow

1908–1970

Bettmann/CORBIS

The evolution of Abraham Maslow's personal and professional life resembles in many ways the personal growth he described in his writings. Although generally regarded as a warm and gregarious adult, Maslow had a cold and lonely childhood. "I was the little Jewish boy in the non-Jewish neighborhood," he recalled. "I was isolated and unhappy. I grew up in libraries and among books, without friends" (cited in Hall, 1968, p. 37).

His professional career also started on a path far from his eventual position as one of the fathers of humanistic psychology. His parents, uneducated Russian immigrants, encouraged Maslow to go to law school. He went to City College of New York with a law career in mind, but he found the focus on law uninteresting and dropped out during the first year. Maslow later went to Cornell and then to the University of Wisconsin to study psychology. Ironically, what initially attracted him to psychology was behaviorism, particularly the works of John B. Watson. "I was so excited about Watson's program," he said. "I was confident that here was a real road to travel, solving one problem after another and changing the world" (cited in Hall, 1968, p. 37). Although his enthusiasm for behaviorism would eventually wane, Maslow's desire to solve the world's problems through psychology never diminished.

Maslow stayed at Wisconsin to finish his PhD in 1934. He remained a loyal behaviorist throughout this period, working closely with Harry Harlow in his animal lab. After graduation, Maslow went to Columbia University to work with the famous learning theorist E. L. Thorndike. But with the birth of his first daughter, Maslow went through a mystical experience similar to the peak experiences he later studied. Looking at his newborn child, Maslow realized that behaviorism was incapable of providing the understanding of human behavior he now needed. "I looked at this tiny, mysterious thing and felt so stupid," he said. "I was stunned by the mystery and by the sense of not really being in control.... Anyone who had a baby couldn't be a behaviorist" (cited in Hall, 1968, p. 56).

in Figure 11.1, he placed the five kinds of needs into a hierarchy of prominence. That is, some unsatisfied needs demand our attention more than others. Although there are exceptions, we typically attend to needs at the lower levels before focusing on higher level needs. If you are hungry, your attention will be focused on obtaining food. Until this need is met, you won't be very concerned about making new friends or developing a romantic relationship. Of course, once satisfied, the lower need may return, causing you to divert your attention again. But over the course of a lifetime, most of us generally progress up the hierarchy. Let's go through the hierarchy one step at a time.

After Columbia, Maslow taught at Brooklyn College for 14 years, where he came into contact with Karen Horney and Alfred Adler. Most important, he met Max Wertheimer, one of the founders of Gestalt psychology, and Ruth Benedict, a cultural anthropologist. It was his desire to better understand these two people, whom he called "the most remarkable human

FIGURE 11.1 Maslow's Hierarchy of Needs

beings," that led him to his exploration of self-actualized people (Maslow, 1970). Maslow moved to Brandeis University in 1951 and remained there until shortly before his death in 1970. He hoped to leave a new movement in psychology as his legacy. "I like to be the first runner in the relay race," he once said. "Then I like to pass on the baton to the next man" (cited in Hall, 1968, p. 56).

Physiological Needs

Physiological needs, including hunger, thirst, air, and sleep, are the most demanding in that they typically must be satisfied before we can move to higher level needs. In many places today—and throughout much of human history—many people's lives are focused on meeting these basic needs. Finding enough food and water for survival takes priority over concerns about gaining the respect of peers or developing potential as an artist.

Safety Needs

When physiological needs are met, we become increasingly motivated by our safety needs. These include the need for security, stability, protection, structure, order, and freedom from fear or chaos. These needs are likely to be prominent when the future is unpredictable or in locations where the political or social order is unstable. People motivated by safety needs may become obsessed about saving money for an uncertain future. They might settle for a job with a lot of security rather than pursue a better but riskier position. People stuck at the safety-need level in their personal development may tolerate an unhappy marriage if the arrangement provides stability and a sense of security.

Belongingness and Love Needs

For most middle-class American adults, the need for food and water and the need for security and stability are fairly well satisfied. Most of us have jobs, homes, and food on the table. But satisfaction of these lower level needs does not guarantee happiness. Soon the need for friendship and love is likely to make itself known. "Now the person will feel keenly, as never before, the absence of friends, or a sweetheart, or a wife, or children," Maslow wrote. "He will hunger for affectionate relations with people ... for a place in his group or family" (1970, p. 43). Although some adults remain slaves to their safety needs and devote most of their energy to their careers, most people eventually find work unsatisfying if it means sacrificing time spent with friends and loved ones.

Maslow identified two kinds of love. *D-love,* like hunger, is based on a deficiency. We need this love to satisfy the emptiness we experience without it. It is a selfish love, concerned with taking, not giving. But it is a necessary step in the development of the second type of love. *B-love* is a nonpossessive, unselfish love based on a growth need rather than a deficiency. B-love is not satisfied once a relationship is established. Rather, B-love is experienced and grows as a result of being in the relationship.

Esteem Needs

Although poets and songwriters might disagree, there is more to life than love. Satisfying our belongingness and love needs is likely to direct our attention to the esteem needs. Maslow divided esteem needs into two basic types: the need to perceive oneself as competent and achieving, and the need for admiration and respect. Satisfying one of these esteem needs often goes hand-in-hand with satisfying the other. It is difficult for others to admire you if you don't feel good about yourself. And knowing that you have earned the respect of people who are important to you most likely will contribute to your sense of personal esteem.

Need for Self-Actualization

Nearly every culture has a story about someone who, by virtue of a magic lamp or contact with a supernatural being, receives everything he or she wishes. But inevitably, the character discovers that acquiring wealth, love, and power is not enough to guarantee happiness. As Maslow explained, when all our lower level needs are satisfied, a new source of discontent often surfaces. We turn our attention inward and ask ourselves what we want out of life, where our lives are headed, and what we want to accomplish. The need for **self-actualization** is satisfied when we identify our true self and reach our full potential. "A musician must make music," Maslow wrote. "An artist must paint, a poet must write, if he is to be ultimately at peace with himself. What a man can be, he must be. He must be true to his own nature" (1970, p. 46).

Misconceptions About Maslow's Need Hierarchy

Maslow was quick to acknowledge that the five-level hierarchy is an oversimplification. Although the arrangement makes sense most of the time, there are some noteworthy exceptions. Some people have to satisfy their needs for self-esteem and respect before they can enter a romantic relationship. Some artists are so intent on expressing their creative desires that they forego basic needs and friendships. And we've all heard stories about martyrs who sacrifice life itself for an ideal.

People first encountering Maslow's need hierarchy sometimes assume that lower needs must be satisfied 100% before we turn to higher needs. But that was never Maslow's intent. He maintained that at any given moment our behavior is potentially influenced by needs from all five levels. Moreover, we rarely satisfy any of the five need levels for very long. Maslow estimated that for the average person in our culture, 85% of physiological needs, 70% of safety needs, 50% of belongingness and love needs, 40% of esteem needs, and 10% of self-actualization needs are satisfied.

Although Maslow described the need hierarchy as universal, he acknowledged that the means of satisfying a particular need varies across cultures. An individual can earn respect from others in our society by becoming a successful businessperson or a community leader. But in other societies this esteem is awarded for good hunting or farming skills. Nonetheless, Maslow maintained that the needs and their arrangement within the hierarchy are the same across cultures. Only the manner in which they are satisfied varies.

Another oversimplification of Maslow's theory is that any given behavior is motivated by a single need. Maslow maintained that most behavior is the result of multiple motivations. He used the example of sexual activity. It is easy to see that physiological needs are satisfied through sexual behavior. But that behavior can also be motivated by a desire to express affection, a need to feel masterful and competent, or a desire to act masculine or feminine. People engage in sexual activity to satisfy one or any combination of these needs.

The Study of Psychologically Healthy People

"Self-actualizing individuals have more free will than average people."
Abraham Maslow

As a rule, psychologists are focused on understanding and overcoming the psychological problems. But Maslow's research took him in the opposite direction. Instead of studying people who suffer from traumatic experiences or psychological disorders, Maslow turned his attention to psychologically healthy individuals. Knowing what self-actualized people are like, he reasoned, can provide lessons the rest of us can follow for fulfilling our true potential. So Maslow interviewed people he knew who appeared to have satisfied their need for self-actualization. But he also turned to records and documents to learn about historic figures who seemed to have lived a self-actualized life. That list included Thomas Jefferson, Albert Einstein, Eleanor Roosevelt, and Albert Schweitzer. By his own admission, Maslow's methods were far from scientifically rigorous. Rather than using statistical analyses, he relied on what he called "holistic analysis." He considered all of the information he collected about an individual and arrived at his own general impressions of that person. From these impressions, he created a list of characteristics common to psychologically healthy people.

Assessing Your Own Personality

Self-Actualization

Indicate the extent to which each of the following statements applies to you, using this 4-point scale: 1 = Disagree, 2 = Disagree somewhat, 3 = Agree somewhat, 4 = Agree.

_____ 1. I do not feel ashamed of any of my emotions.

_____ 2. I feel I must do what others expect of me.

_____ 3. I believe that people are essentially good and can be trusted.

_____ 4. I feel free to be angry at those I love.

_____ 5. It is always necessary that others approve of what I do.

_____ 6. I don't accept my own weaknesses.

_____ 7. I can like people without having to approve of them.

_____ 8. I fear failure.

_____ 9. I avoid attempts to analyze and simplify complex domains.

_____ 10. It is better to be yourself than to be popular.

_____ 11. I have no mission in life to which I feel especially dedicated.

_____ 12. I can express my feelings even when they may result in undesirable consequences.

_____ 13. I do not feel responsible to help anybody.

_____ 14. I am bothered by fears of being inadequate.

_____ 15. I am loved because I give love.

To calculate your score, first reverse the values for items 2, 5, 6, 8, 9, 11, 13, and 14 (1 = 4, 2 = 3, 3 = 2, 4 = 1). Then add the values for all 15 items. The higher the score, the more self-actualized you are said to be at this point in your life. You can compare your score with the norms for college students reported by the test developers:

	Standard	Mean Deviation
Men	45.02	4.95
Women	46.07	4.79

Scale: Index of Self-Actualization

Source: Personality & Social Psychology Bulletin by A. Jones and R. Crandall. Copyright 1986 by SAGE Publications Inc. Journals. Reproduced with permission of SAGE Publications Inc. Journals in the format Textbook via Copyright Clearance Center.

What are self-actualized people like? You may notice as we go through some of the list that these individuals sound a lot like the fully functioning people described by Rogers. To begin, self-actualized people tend to accept themselves for what they are. They admit to personal weaknesses, and they work to improve themselves where they can. But they don't spend a lot of time worrying about bad things they have done. They aren't perfect, but they respect and feel good about themselves for what they are.

Psychologically healthy people are also less restricted by cultural norms and customs than the average person. They express their thoughts and desires in a way that suits them, regardless of whether society approves. This freedom from social expectations is especially evident when it comes to self-expression. Self-actualized people often dress differently, live differently and spend their free time differently than the typical citizen. It's not that they are insensitive to or unaware of social rules and societal expectations. On the contrary, Maslow described them as very perceptive. They understand how they are "supposed" to act. They simply feel little need to structure their lives like everyone else's.

Maslow was surprised to find that every psychologically healthy person he studied was in some way quite creative. But not all expressed their creativity through traditional outlets like poetry and art. Rather, they often exhibited what he called *self-actualizing creativity*. This type of creativity shows up in the way people approach routine tasks. A self-actualized teacher develops innovative ways to communicate ideas to students. A self-actualized businessperson thinks of clever ways to improve sales. Maslow compared self-actualizing creativity with the spontaneous way a child interacts with the world. Just as a child uses fresh and naïve eyes to discover the little things that make the world an interesting place, self-actualizing people look at their world in an open-eyed way that helps them find new solutions to old problems.

People are often surprised to learn that self-actualized individuals have relatively few friends. However, the friendships they do have are deep and rewarding. Self-actualized people also have a "philosophical, unhostile" sense of humor. They poke fun at the human condition and at themselves but rarely target a particular person or group with their humor. These individuals also have a strong need for solitude, as we'll explore in the next chapter.

Perhaps the most intriguing characteristic Maslow discovered in psychologically healthy people is the tendency to have *peak experiences*. During a peak experience, time and place are transcended. Anxieties and fears disappear, replaced by a sense of unity with the universe and a momentary feeling of power and wonder. However, peak experiences are different for each person. Maslow likened them to "a visit to a personally defined Heaven." Above all else, they are growth experiences. Often problems that concerned people before a peak experience no longer seem as important afterward. Old fears are replaced with a sense of spontaneity and a greater appreciation of life.

However, Maslow soon discovered that psychologically healthy people are not the only ones who have these experiences, although self-actualized people do have more intense and more frequent peak experiences than the average person. Maslow also discovered that not all self-actualized people had peak experiences. This observation led him to talk about two kinds of psychologically healthy individuals, the "peakers" and the "nonpeakers." Nonpeaking self-actualizers are "the social world improvers, the politicians, the workers of society, the reformers, the crusaders." They have their feet planted firmly on the ground and have a clear direction in life. The peakers tend to be less conventional and more concerned with abstract notions. They "are more likely to write the poetry, the music, the philosophies, and the religions" (1970, p. 165).

The Psychology of Optimal Experience

What makes people happy? This question threads its way through much of the writings of the humanistic personality theorists. Of course, most of us point to family and friends as important sources of happiness. But what sorts of *activities* make you happy? That is, to increase our sense of well-being and happiness, how should we spend our time? Psychologist Mihaly Csikszentmihalyi (pronounced Chick-Sent-Me-High) has one suggestion. He maintains that opportunities for happiness lie all around us in many of the everyday, routine activities that fill our lives.

Optimal Experience

Can people structure the events in their daily lives in a way that promotes a sense of personal fulfillment and self-worth? One starting point for answering this question is simply to ask people to describe the activities that make them happy. That's what Csikszentmihalyi did. Try it yourself. Think of a time when you felt alive and totally engaged in an activity, when what you were doing was more than pleasurable, but truly enjoyable. When Csikszentmihalyi asked people to identify an experience that fits this description, he found a wide variety of answers (Csikszentmihalyi, 1990, 1999; Csikszentmihalyi & Csikszentmihalyi, 1988). Some people talked about mountain climbing, others about playing tennis, others about performing surgery. But when he asked people to *describe* the experience in their own words, he found they used surprisingly similar terms.

Csikszentmihalyi's participants talked about becoming so involved in what they were doing that nothing else seemed to matter. Whether it was climbing a mountain or performing surgery, the activity demanded all their attention. Although each step seemed to flow automatically to the next, the task was almost always challenging and demanded full concentration. Reaching their goal provided participants with a sense of mastery. But the real pleasure came from the process rather than the achievement.

Csikszentmihalyi refers to these kinds of moments as **optimal experience**. Because people typically describe a feeling of being caught up in a natural, almost effortless movement from one step to the next, psychologists sometimes refers to the experience as *flow*. Optimal experiences are intensely enjoyable, but they usually are not restful, relaxing moments. On the contrary, most often flow experiences are quite demanding (Abuhamdeh &

TABLE 11.1 Eight Components of Optimal Experience

1. *The Activity Is Challenging and Requires Skill.*
   The task is sufficiently challenging to demand full attention, but not so difficult that it denies a sense of accomplishment.

2. *One's Attention Is Completely Absorbed by the Activity.*
   People stop being aware of themselves as separate from their actions, which seem spontaneous and automatic.

3. *The Activity Has Clear Goals.*
   There is a direction, a logical point to work toward.

4. *There Is Clear Feedback.*
   We need to know if we have succeeded at reaching our goal, even if this is only self-confirmation.

5. *One Can Concentrate Only on the Task at Hand.*
   During flow, we pay no attention to the unpleasant parts of life.

6. *One Achieves a Sense of Personal Control.*
   People in flow enjoy the experience of exercising control over their environment.

7. *One Loses Self-Consciousness.*
   With attention focused on the activity and the goals, there is little opportunity to think about one's self.

8. *One Loses a Sense of Time.*
   Usually hours pass by in what seems like minutes, but the opposite can also occur.

Csikszentmihalyi, 2012; de Manzano, Theorell, Harmat, & Ullen, 2010). "The best moments usually occur when a person's body or mind is stretched to its limits in a voluntary effort to accomplish something difficult and worthwhile," Csikszentmihalyi explained. "Optimal experience is thus something that we make happen" (1990, p. 3).

Interestingly, the flow experience is described in fairly identical terms by people of all ages and in all cultures. After examining thousands of descriptions of people's most satisfying and enjoyable moments, Csikszentmihalyi (1990) identified eight characteristics of the flow experience. These are listed in Table 11.1. Not every flow experience contains each of these eight, but any flow experience you can think of probably includes many of these components.

Optimal Experience and Happiness in Everyday Activities

In a perfect world we all could enjoy life to its fullest by doing what we wanted when we wanted and filling our lives with one flow activity after another. But reality does not grant most of us such luxury. Most of us face a seemingly endless series of demands, with free time an increasingly rare commodity. This observation raises an important question: When are people more likely to experience flow—at work or during leisure hours? Most of us answer quickly that our leisure hours are far happier than time on the job. In fact, people often point to their long working hours as a cause of their unhappiness.

However, research suggests the opposite is the case. Certainly people often have flow-like experiences when engaging in recreational activities like playing a musical instrument or competing in sports (Stein, Kimiecik, Daniels, & Jackson, 1995). But flow experiences are far more likely to happen when people are at work than during off-hours (Csikszentmihalyi & LeFevre, 1989). A challenging job can create more opportunities for optimal experience than most of easygoing activities that typically fill our time away from work (Keller & Bless, 2008). Unfortunately, most of us buy into the conventional wisdom that says work is work and play is play. Consequently, we fail to recognize how often our jobs provide us with opportunities to experience a sense of mastery, accomplishment, and enrichment.

Fortunately, this is not true of all people. A woman I know, a writer, keeps her computer near her bed so that she can turn to her work even before her first cup of coffee in the morning. Friends say she often has to be pried away from her writing at night. She doesn't understand the fuss; she loves what she does for a living. Time spent writing is time spent learning and growing. Moviemaker Woody Allen is another example. Friends and colleagues are constantly amazed at the energy and attention he gives to his movies. "I love to work," he once said. "I'd work seven days a week. I don't care about hours. When we solve this problem, whether it's five o'clock or ten at night, we move on to something else. Hours or days mean nothing" (cited in Lax, 1991, p. 337). Woody Allen clearly experiences flow when he's working. That his movies also provide money and fame seems to a secondary concern.

Of course, not everyone can be a writer or a movie maker. What about the average person who puts in 40 hours a week at a less glamorous profession? Csikszentmihalyi argues that nearly any job can become a flow experience if we approach it the right way. Even mowing the lawn or making dinner can be a source of happiness if we look at these chores as challenges and take pride and satisfaction in a job well done. Rather than thinking of every job as something we have to do or something others expect us to do, we can approach daily tasks by searching for what we can get out of them.

This advice also applies to students (Schmidt, Shernoff, & Csikszentmihalyi, 2007). High school students are most content when they face academic assignments that are challenging but still within their power to accomplish (Moneta & Csikszentmihalyi, 1996). Researchers in one study identified students who were motivated to work hard because they found learning the material to be fascinating and satisfying (Wong & Csikszentmihalyi, 1991). Interestingly, these students' grades were not particularly high. But they did take more advanced courses than grade-driven students, probably because they wanted to learn more about the subjects they found most interesting. Intrinsically motivated undergraduates in another study were more likely to lose track of time and to report that study time passed quickly than students who were less interested in the learning experience (Conti, 2001).

In summary, Csikszentmihalyi's prescription for happiness contains many of the elements traditionally embraced by humanistic personality psychology.

Flow experiences require people to live in the present and to get the most out of their lives in the here and now. Achieving the goal is not the point. Rather, it is the struggle and experience along the way that provide the enjoyment. Moreover, happiness comes from taking control of your life rather than caving in to conventional standards or demands from others. In the flow state people are intensely in touch with themselves and their experiences. They feel a sense of mastery and an awareness of finding themselves. And like the peak experiences Maslow described, flow experiences are occasions for personal growth.

Application: Person-Centered Therapy and Job Satisfaction

Carl Rogers' developed many of his ideas about personality from his work with therapy clients. Among his most important contributions to the field was a new way to approach psychological counseling, an approach that places much of the responsibility for change in the hands of the client. Maslow's hierarchy of needs has influenced thinking and research in many areas outside of psychology. Among other applications, the need hierarchy has been used to address issues related to work environments and job satisfaction.

Person-Centered Therapy

"When I accept myself as I am, then I change."

CARL ROGERS

Carl Rogers' approach to counseling presents an interesting challenge for humanistic psychotherapists. According to Rogers, a therapist cannot possibly understand clients as well as clients understand themselves. He also maintained that clients, rather than the therapist, are responsible for changing themselves. So what is left for therapists to do with people who come to them for help?

Rogers' answer was that a therapist's job is not to change the client but to provide an atmosphere within which clients are able to help themselves. He called this approach *person-centered therapy*. Rogers believed each of us grows and develops in a positive, self-actualizing fashion unless our progress is in some way impeded. The therapist simply allows the client to get back on that positive growth track. After successful Rogerian therapy, clients should be more open to personal experience, more able to accept all aspects of themselves, and therefore less likely to use defenses when encountering information that threatens their self-concept. In short, they should be more fully functioning and happier people.

But how is this accomplished? Therapists must first create the proper relationship with their clients. The most important rule here is to be open and genuine. Therapists should be themselves rather than play the role of therapist they were taught in graduate school. This means being honest with clients, even if that includes being very frank (but not cruel) at times. Rogers believed clients can always tell when a therapist isn't being genuine with them, and the mistrust that comes from this perception can doom a therapeutic relationship.

The proper therapeutic relationship also requires unconditional positive regard from the therapist, something many clients have been denied elsewhere in their lives. Clients must feel free to express and accept all their thoughts and feelings during therapy without fear of rejection from the therapist. Unconditional positive regard does not mean therapists must approve of everything clients say and do. Indeed, in the safe atmosphere provided by the therapist, clients may disclose some disturbing information about themselves. But because therapists accept clients with positive regard despite these faults and weaknesses, clients learn to acknowledge—and eventually change—these aspects of themselves.

In addition to providing an accepting relationship, therapists can help clients understand their own thoughts and feelings through a process of reflection. Rather than interpret what clients really mean, as a Freudian therapist might, a Rogerian therapist helps clients listen to what they are saying. Part of this process is simply giving clients the opportunity to put their feelings into words. By translating vague feelings into precise words, clients come to understand their feelings. Clients listen to own their words and examine their thoughts, perhaps for the first time. One technique a therapist can use to further this process is to restate what the client says. Some people mistakenly think this means the therapist simply repeats the client's words verbatim. But as the following excerpt demonstrates, the goal is to help clients explore their thoughts and feelings by directing their attention to what they are saying. In this example, Rogers is working with a woman who is struggling with her sense of personal identity:

Client [C]: I suppose I want to know just what to do, but then maybe nobody could give me that.

Therapist [T]: You realize that you are probably looking for immediate answers that nobody could give you.

C: I just don't know. I don't know what I'm looking for. It's just that I wonder if I'm insane sometimes. I think I'm nuts.

T: It just gives you concern that you're as far from normal as you feel you are.

C: That's right. It's silly to tell me not to worry because I do worry. It's my life. ... Well, I don't know how I can change my concept of myself—because that's the way I feel.

T: You feel very different from others and you don't see how you can fix that.

C: I realize, of course, that it all began a long time ago—because everything begins somewhere. I wasn't just—somehow or other something failed somewhere along the line. And I guess we sort of have to get at it, a sort of reeducation. But I don't feel as though I can do it myself.

T: You realize that the roots must go a long way back, and that at some point you will have to start in reworking it, but you're not sure whether you can do it.

C: That's right. It's just the idea that I can see myself going through life this way, 50-, 60-, and 70-years-old—still thinking these horrible thoughts. And it just doesn't seem worthwhile—I mean, it's so ridiculous. While everybody else is going their way and living life, I'm sort of at the edge, and looking on. It just isn't right.

T: The future doesn't look very bright when you look at it that way.

C: No. I know I'm lacking in courage, that's the big thing I'm lacking. That must be it, 'cause other people aren't swayed so easily. ... It's a hard thing to explain these things. It's just as though—it's—true but I laugh at it in a way. ... It's a very confused feeling.

T: Logically, you realize that courage is one of your deficiencies, but inside yourself you find yourself laughing at that notion and feeling that it doesn't really have anything to do with you. Is that it?

C: That's right. I always sort of make myself different. That's it. (1947, pp. 138–140)

Therapists never tell clients what the client really means to say. Instead, therapists restate what they believe they are hearing. However, these restatements are only suggestions for the client to agree with or reject. If the process is effective, clients come to see themselves as others do and eventually accept or modify what they see. Clients may come to understand that they have been distorting or denying parts of their experiences. A man may realize he has been trying to live up to his father's impossibly high expectations, or a woman may come to understand she is afraid to commit herself to a serious relationship. In the freedom provided by the therapist's unconditional support, clients peel away their defenses, accept who they are, and begin to appreciate all of life's experiences.

Today a large number of psychotherapists identify their approach as humanistic (Cook, Biyanova, Elhai, Schnurr, & Coyne, 2010), and many others include aspects of person-centered therapy in their work (Cain & Seeman, 2002). One review of empirical studies found considerable evidence for the effectiveness of humanistic psychotherapy (Elliott, 2002). Not only do many clients benefit from the person-centered approach, but the effects of the treatment often can be seen many months after the therapy sessions end.

Job Satisfaction and the Hierarchy of Needs

Think for a moment of two or three careers you would like to have someday (maybe you already work at one of these). Ask yourself what it is about each of these jobs that makes it appealing. That is, what do you hope to gain from it that you can't get from just any job? Now, take the answers to this last question and apply them to Maslow's hierarchy of needs. Which of the five levels of needs will your chosen occupation satisfy? If a job pays a lot of money or promises job security, it probably will satisfy your safety needs. On the other hand, a job may appeal to you because it brings respect and admiration while allowing you to express yourself artistically. This latter example might go a long way toward satisfying your need for esteem or your need for self-actualization.

The point of this exercise is that your occupation can provide more than a paycheck. Besides sleeping, there is no single activity that will take up more of your adult life than your job. Maslow argued that to spend 40 hours a week at a job that pays well but that doesn't allow for personal growth is a tragic waste. "Finding one's lifework is a little like finding one's mate," he wrote. "If you are unhappy with your work, you have lost one of the most important means of self-fulfillment" (1971, p. 185). Maslow was critical of job counselors who direct young people into careers simply because the job pays well or fits the needs of the job market. A better approach matches a person's unique talents and potential to an occupation that allows the expression and development of that potential.

Maslow promoted what he called *Eupsychian management*—rearranging an organization to help employees satisfy higher level needs. Under this approach, employers can structure jobs so that workers take pride in their performance and thereby develop a sense of self-worth about what they do for a living. Employees might also be given opportunities to suggest creative solutions to problems. And employers can do what they can to foster a sense of belongingness and feelings of camaraderie among workers. In short, careers can provide an avenue for personal growth as well as a means for paying the bills.

It is difficult to gauge how much impact Maslow's ideas have had on businesses and organizations. No doubt many employers are concerned about their workers' sense of well-being and personal development. And it is probably the case that Maslow's notion of Eupsychian management has stimulated many discussions about how to improve worker satisfaction. But the widespread reshaping of the work environment Maslow envisioned has never come close to materializing (Payne, 2000).

Jerry Burger/Santa Clara University

Is the job a chore that must be endured 8 hours a day, or does this man get more out of work than just a paycheck? According to Maslow, occupations should provide opportunities for personal growth and the satisfaction of higher order needs. Besides money, a job can satisfy our needs for belongingness, self-esteem, and respect for others.

Assessment: The Q-Sort Technique

A persistent challenge for psychotherapists of all stripes is to demonstrate the effectiveness of their treatment. Carl Rogers was very aware of this challenge and strongly encouraged research on the effectiveness of person-centered psychotherapy. Too often therapy is declared a success simply because the therapist and client feel there has been improvement. However, without empirical evidence of therapeutic change, Rogers argued, psychologists are in danger of fooling themselves.

So how can a humanistic psychologist demonstrate that clients are more fully functioning or closer to self-actualization after a few months of therapy? One tool that has proven useful is a procedure called the **Q-Sort**. The basic procedure was developed several decades ago (Stephenson, 1953) and has been used to assess a wide variety of psychological concepts, including parent–child attachment (Tarabulsky et al., 2008), defense mechanisms (Davidson & MacGregor, 1996), temperament (Buckley, Klein, Durbin, Hayden, & Moerk, 2002), and strength of romantic relationships (Bengston & Grotevant, 1999). Rogers also saw that the procedure fit nicely with his approach to psychotherapy and quickly adopted it.

The California Q-Sort (Block, 2008) is a good example of a Q-Sort procedure used by many humanistic therapists. The materials for this test consist of a deck of 100 cards. A self-descriptive phrase is printed on each card, such as "is a talkative individual," "seeks reassurance from others," or "has high aspiration level for self."

If you were a client about to begin counseling with a Rogerian therapist, you might be instructed to read the cards and sort them into categories. On the first sort, you would be asked to place the cards into nine categories according to how much you believe the description on the card applies to you. The nine categories represent points on a normal distribution (Figure 11.2), with the categories on the extreme ends representing characteristics most descriptive of you (Category 9) and least descriptive of you (Category 1).

Let's suppose the description on the first card is "is a talkative individual." If this phrase describes you very well, you would place the card in Category 9 or 8. If this phrase describes you only slightly, you might place it in Category 6. If you think you are a very quiet person, you might put the card in Category 1 or 2. There is a limit to how many cards can be placed in each category, so indecisive test takers are forced to select cards that are *most* descriptive of them. In this manner, you would provide the therapist and yourself with a profile of your self-concept.

After recording which cards you placed into which categories, you would be asked to shuffle the deck and take the test again. However, this time you would distribute the cards according to your "ideal" self. Thus, if "is a talkative individual" does not describe you very well, but you want to become more talkative, you would move this card to a higher category than you used during the first sort. After you have laid out descriptions of your "real" and "ideal" selves, you and the therapist can compare the two profiles.

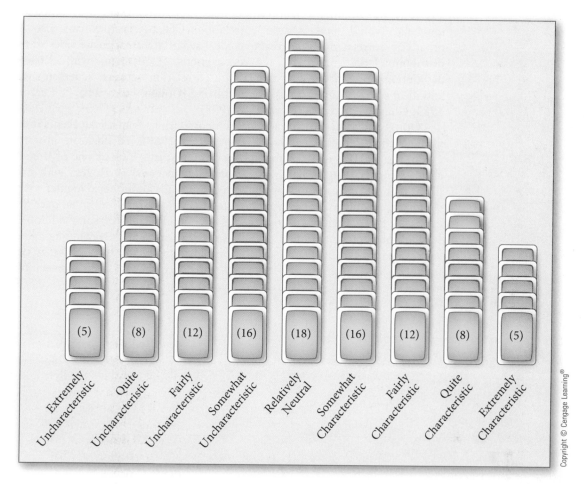

FIGURE 11.2 Distribution of Cards on Block's Q-Sort

The Q-Sort technique fits very nicely with Rogers' theory for several reasons. Consistent with Rogers' assumption that clients know themselves best, clients are allowed to describe themselves however they please. Of course, a therapist will not always agree with a client's placement of the cards. A client might describe herself as socially aware, polite, and sensitive to the needs of others when a perceptive therapist sees right away that her crude insensitivity may be part of her problem. The task for the therapist in this case is to help the client come to see herself in a more realistic light.

By assigning each card a number from 1 to 9 according to its category, we can compute a correlation coefficient (Chapter 2) between a client's real self and his or her ideal self. For a psychologically healthy person, the two should be very similar. If category values are identical for both profiles, a perfect 1.0 correlation would be obtained, although it is difficult to imagine people being just like their ideal selves in every way. The further the correlation is from 1.0, the less accepting people are of themselves and the less fully functioning. Clients whose real and ideal selves are completely unrelated would have a zero correlation. Clients' profiles can also be negatively correlated if their real and ideal selves are at opposite sides of the distribution on many of the descriptions. Consistent with Rogers' descriptions, researchers find that a high correlation between a person's real and ideal self is related to positive well-being (Gough, Fioravanti, & Lazzari, 1983; Gough, Lazzari, & Fioravanti, 1978).

Other studies find that real–ideal self correlations increase as clients move through client-centered psychotherapy (Butler, 1968). To illustrate how the Q-Sort can be used to track therapeutic progress, let's look at one of Rogers' clients (Rogers, 1961). This 40-year-old woman came to Rogers with problems that included an unhappy marriage and guilt about her daughter's psychological problems. The woman attended 40 therapy sessions over the course of 5 1/2 months and returned a few months later for some additional sessions. She completed the real and ideal self Q-Sorts at the beginning and at various stages during her treatment. She also completed the Q-Sort at two follow-up sessions, 7 and 12 months after her therapy. The correlations among the various Q-Sorts are presented in Figure 11.3.

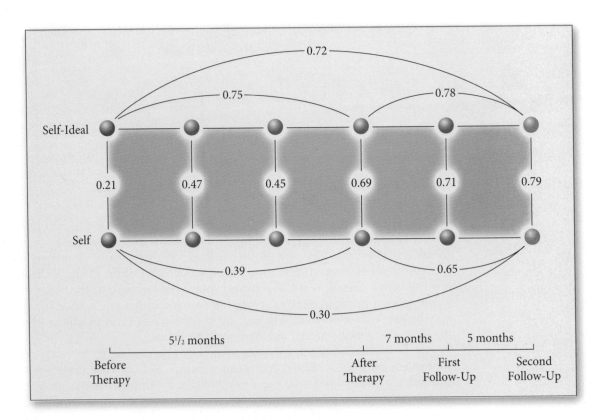

FIGURE 11.3 Changing Real and Ideal Self Q-Sorts for a 40-Year-Old Female Client

Source: From Rogers, C., *International Journal of Social Psychiatry*, June 1955; vol. 1: pp. 31–41, Copyright © 1955. Reprinted by Permission of SAGE.

Several important changes in the way the woman viewed her real self and her ideal self occurred during her treatment. The similarity between her real and ideal self increased significantly over the course of the therapy and continued to grow even after she discontinued the sessions. At the beginning of her treatment, her real and ideal self Q-Sorts were quite discrepant, correlating at only .21. In other words, when she first entered Carl Rogers' office, she did not see herself at all as the kind of person she wanted to be. However, as therapy progressed, the two descriptions became more and more alike. In particular, the client changed the way she viewed herself. We can tell this from the low correlation (.30) between the way she described herself at the beginning of the therapy and the way she described herself at the end. By exploring her feelings in these person-centered sessions, the client came to see herself in very different and presumably more accurate terms.

There also were some noticeable but less dramatic changes in the way the woman described her ideal self. She may have come to realize through therapy that the goals she set for herself were far too ideal. It is not uncommon for clients to enter therapy expecting near perfection of themselves and to consider themselves failures when they fall short of these impossible goals. It is clear from this example that Rogers' therapy was successful in bringing the client's real and ideal selves closer together. No doubt she was better able to experience life as a fully functioning person than she was before entering therapy.

Strengths and Criticisms of the Humanistic Approach

The humanistic movement hit psychology like a storm in the 1960s. Therapists from every perspective were converted to the person-centered approach, and humanistic-oriented encounter groups and workshops sprang up everywhere. Then, almost as quickly as it arrived, the third force movement seemed to fade in the late 1970s. Many converts became disenchanted, some humanistic-oriented programs in education and the workplace were declared failures, and the number of popular paperbacks capitalizing on the movement dwindled. But, also like a storm, the humanistic approach to personality has left reminders of its presence. Today a large number of practicing psychotherapists identify themselves as humanistic in their orientation, and many others have adopted various Rogerian techniques in their practice. Humanistic psychologists enjoy an active division in the American Psychological Association and publish their own journal. Although the movement never replaced the well-entrenched psychoanalytic or behavioral approaches, it remains an appealing alternative view of human nature for many people inside and outside of the discipline. This ebb and flow of popularity suggests that the humanistic approach, like other approaches to personality, has both strengths and points for criticism.

Strengths

Because personality theorists often dwell on psychological problems, the humanists' positive approach offers a welcome alternative. The writings of Rogers and Maslow remain popular with each new generation of students.

One enduring contribution of humanistic psychology is its emphasis on the healthy side of personality. Recently we have seen a huge interest in what has been called *positive psychology* (Lopez, 2009; Seligman, Steen, Park, & Peterson, 2005). That is, an increasing number of researchers are turning their attention to such topics as creativity, happiness, and sense of well-being.

Not surprisingly, humanistic psychology has had a huge impact on the way psychologists and counselors approach therapy. Many therapists identify themselves as "humanistic" (Cook et al., 2010). More important, several aspects of the humanistic approach to therapy have been adopted or modified in some form by a large number of therapists from other theoretical perspectives (Cain & Seeman, 2002). Many therapists embrace Rogers' suggestion to make their clients the center of therapy. In addition, many therapists include in their practices such Rogerian techniques as therapist empathy, positive regard for clients, giving clients responsibility for change, and self-disclosure by client and therapist. The humanistic approach also sparked the growth of encounter groups in the 1960s. Variations of encounter groups remain today in the form of group therapy and other self-improvement and personal-growth therapies.

Humanistic psychology's influence has not been limited to psychology and psychotherapy. Students in education, communication, and business are often introduced to Rogers' and Maslow's writings. Many employers and organizational psychologists are concerned about promoting job satisfaction by taking care of employees' higher needs. And many teachers and parents have adopted or modified some of Rogers' suggestions for education and child rearing. Because they focus on issues that many of us address in our lives—fulfilling personal potential, living in the here and now, finding happiness and meaning—books by Maslow, Rogers, and other humanistic psychologists can still be found in popular bookstores. One team of researchers went to the Internet to get an idea of humanistic psychology's popularity (Peterson & Park, 2010). A Google search for Maslow's hierarchy of needs produced more than 3,800,000 website hits. The researchers also located more than 766,000 images of the hierarchy of need pyramid, which is more than the number of Internet images for either *The Last Supper* or the *Mona Lisa*.

Criticisms

Like all influential personality theories, humanistic psychology has its critics. One area of controversy concerns humanistic psychology's reliance on the concept of free will to explain human behavior. Some psychologists argue that this reliance renders the humanistic approach unfit for scientific study. Science relies on the notion that events are determined by other events. Thus psychology relies on the assumption that behavior is determined and therefore predictable. However, if we accept the idea that behavior is sometimes caused by free will, which is not subject to these laws of determination, the assumption falls apart. Because we can explain any behavior as caused by "free will," no investigation will ever fail to support a free will interpretation. Free will by definition is not under the control of any observable or predictable force.

In response to this issue, humanistic psychologists and others have argued that, whereas we may not be able to predict any specific behavior with 100 percent certainty, we can identify patterns that allow us to predict the likelihood that a person will act a certain way in a certain situation. Some philosophers refer to this perspective as *statistical determinism.* That is, people may freely make choices about how they will behave, but those choices are still based on factors that scientists can often observe, measure and perhaps manipulate. We should also point out that critics of humanistic psychology's emphasis on free will typically do not argue that free will does not exist— only that it cannot be explored through scientific inquiry. Finally, Maslow responded to this concern by pointing out that there are more avenues for understanding human personality than the scientific method.

Another criticism of the humanistic approach is that many key concepts are poorly defined. What exactly is "self-actualization," "fully functioning," or "becoming"? How do we know if we're having a "peak experience" or just a particularly pleasant time? Maslow argued that we simply don't know enough about self-actualization and personal growth to provide clear definitions. But this defense is far from satisfying for most researchers. How can we investigate self-actualization if we can't decide who's got it and who hasn't? Because most psychologists are trained as researchers, the inability to pin down humanistic concepts causes many to challenge the usefulness of the approach.

Although many humanistic psychologists provide research findings to support their views, some psychologists have challenged these data as less than scientifically rigorous. Although Rogers is to be commended for his efforts to assess the effectiveness of person-centered therapy, he nonetheless often relied on his intuition when developing his ideas about personality. Similarly, Maslow selected people for his list of "self-actualized" individuals based on his own subjective impressions. Because of these weak data, much of what humanistic theorists say must be taken more as a matter of faith than as scientific fact. Most likely, psychologists and lay readers embrace the humanistic approach because it is consistent with their own observations and values, not because they are persuaded by the evidence.

Other psychologists point to the limited applicability of humanistic psychotherapy techniques. These critics argue that humanistic psychotherapy may be limited to a narrow band of problems. Creating the proper atmosphere for personal growth might have been useful for many of Rogers' clients, but that approach may be of little help to someone with an extreme psychological disorder. Similarly, reflecting on one's values and direction in life might prove beneficial for well-educated, middle-class clients. But these questions might be irrelevant to someone from a different background. Person-centered therapy may be useful for working through certain kinds of adjustment problems, but not for dealing with the myriad serious psychological disturbances that cause people to seek therapy.

Humanistic psychologists have also been criticized for making some overly naive assumptions about human nature. For example, most humanistic theorists assume that all people are basically good. Although this is more a theological than an empirical question, many people find the premise hard to accept. Another assumption many find difficult to swallow is that each of us has a desire to fulfill some hidden potential. Maslow's description of self-actualization implies that each individual is somehow destined to become, for example, a painter, a poet, or a carpenter. For Maslow the key is discovering which of these true selves lies bottled up inside waiting to be developed. But whether this bottled-up self really exists in all people is questionable. The predeterministic nature of this part of Maslow's theory also seems to contradict the general free will emphasis of the humanistic approach.

Summary

1. The humanistic approach to personality grew out of discontent with the psychoanalytic and behavioral descriptions of human nature prominent in the 1950s and 1960s. Humanistic psychology has its roots in European existential philosophy and the works of some American psychologists, most notably Carl Rogers and Abraham Maslow.

2. Although many approaches to psychotherapy have been described as humanistic, four criteria seem important for classifying a theory under this label. These criteria are an emphasis on personal responsibility, an emphasis on the here and now, focusing on the experience of the individual, and emphasizing personal growth.

3. Carl Rogers introduced the notion of a fully functioning person. According to his theory, we all progress toward a state of fulfillment and happiness unless derailed by life's obstacles. People who encounter evidence that contradicts their self-concept often rely on distortion and denial to avoid the anxiety this might create. People who grow up in families that give only conditional positive regard may come to deny certain aspects of themselves. Rogers advocated the use of unconditional positive regard by parents and therapists to overcome this denial.

4. Abraham Maslow introduced a hierarchy of human needs. According to this concept, people progress up the hierarchy as lower needs are satisfied. Maslow also examined psychologically healthy people. He found several characteristics typical of these self-actualized individuals, including the tendency by some to have frequent peak experiences.

5. One recent outgrowth of the humanistic approach to personality is presented by Mihaly Csikszentmihalyi. He finds people describe the happiest and most rewarding moments in their lives in terms of a "flow" experience. Csikszentmihalyi argues that turning one's life into a series of challenging and absorbing tasks, what he calls optimal experiences, is the key to happiness and personal fulfillment.

6. One of Rogers' contributions to psychology is the person-centered approach to psychotherapy. Rogers said the therapist's job is to create the proper atmosphere for clients' growth. This is accomplished by entering a genuine relationship with clients, providing unconditional positive

regard, and helping clients hear what they are saying. Maslow's hierarchy of needs concept has been applied to the problem of job satisfaction. He argued that one's career provides an opportunity for personal growth and that employers should arrange working situations to better meet employees' higher order needs.

7. Many person-centered therapists have adopted the Q-Sort assessment procedure. This procedure allows therapists and clients to see discrepancies between clients' images of themselves and the person they would like to be. Therapists can administer the Q-Sort at various points during treatment to measure therapy progress. Improvement is seen when clients close the gap between their real and ideal selves.

8. Among the strengths found in the humanistic approach to personality are the attention given to the positive side of personality and the influence this approach has had on psychotherapy and job satisfaction. Criticisms include the unscientific reliance on free will to explain behavior and the difficulty in dealing with many of the poorly defined constructs used by humanistic theorists. Some therapists have challenged the usefulness of person-centered therapy for many types of clients and psychological problems. The humanistic approach has also been criticized for making many naive assumptions about human nature.

Key Terms

conditional positive regard (p. 284)

deficiency motives (p. 286)

fully functioning person (p. 281)

growth needs (p. 286)

hierarchy of needs (p. 286)

optimal experience (p. 293)

Q-Sort (p. 300)

self-actualization (p. 289)

subception (p. 283)

unconditional positive regard (p. 285)

Media Resources

Visit the book companion website at **www.cengagebrain.com** to find a glossary, flashcards, quizzing, and more.

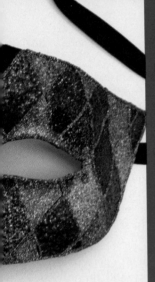

The Humanistic Approach

Relevant Research

Self-Disclosure

Loneliness

Self-Esteem

Solitude

Summary

The rapid growth of humanistic psychology a few decades ago was in part a reaction against the research-oriented approaches that had come to dominate psychology in American universities. Humanistic psychologists argued that people cannot be reduced to a set of numbers. Scores on a battery of personality tests don't capture a person's inner strength, feelings, and character. Most important, finding a person's place along a trait continuum erases that person's uniqueness and individuality. As the name implies, the third force in psychology was developed to attend to the "human" element lost in number-crunching approaches.

> "Facts are always friendly. Every bit of evidence one can acquire, in any area, leads one that much closer to what is true."
>
> CARL ROGERS

However, this strength also proves to be one of humanistic psychology's weaknesses. Critics sometimes refer to the approach as "soft" psychology. Flowery descriptions of a person's unique character are fine, but it's often difficult to translate these descriptions into testable hypotheses. Clinical observations and intuitive feelings may provide insights into personality and the therapy process, but they cannot replace reliable assessment procedures. This is not to say that humanistic psychologists don't conduct research. On the contrary, Carl Rogers continually evaluated the effectiveness of person-centered therapy, as do many other humanistic therapists (Cain & Seeman, 2002). But on the whole, advocates of the humanistic perspective have probably generated less empirical research than psychologists from the other approaches covered in this book.

Nonetheless, Rogers, Maslow, and other humanistic psychologists introduced a number of intriguing hypotheses and concepts that have led to extensive empirical work. Although the original investigations on some of these topics were conducted by humanistic psychologists, in most cases more extensive empirical research was done by investigators outside the humanistic circle. A good example of this is research on self-disclosure, the first topic we'll explore in this chapter. Rogers and other therapists argued that the act of revealing personal information has important psychological consequences. This notion stimulated decades of research, although most of this work has been conducted by psychologists who probably would shun the "humanistic" label. Nonetheless, the findings from this research have important implications for humanistic theory and therapy.

Similarly, research on the other three topics we'll examine in this chapter—loneliness, self-esteem, and solitude—was inspired in part by humanistic writers but largely conducted by more empirically oriented academic psychologists. Of course, there is some irony in this situation. The cold, empirical approach to understanding personality once rejected by many humanistic types has popularized many of the concepts central to the humanistic perspective.

Self-Disclosure

Imagine you are with someone you don't know very well but who seems to be a pleasant person. You both have time to kill, so you begin to talk. The conversation starts casually with a discussion about the classes you're taking. However, soon this person mentions some difficulties she's having with her parents. You find yourself talking about similar experiences you have had. Before the conversation is over, you learn quite a lot about this individual—problems with her family, with dating, with her self-confidence. You reveal that you, too, sometimes have difficulty with relationships. Perhaps you tell this person about an embarrassing dating situation you've been in. When the conversation ends, you feel good about her and maybe even about yourself.

Most of us have participated to some degree in similar conversations. If you think back to your own experience, you may recall that the conversation began with relatively impersonal topics and gradually worked toward more private information. Most likely, the conversation was anything but one-sided. You and this other person probably took turns sharing information about yourselves. And it's quite possible you left the conversation feeling good about your new acquaintance and perceiving that he or she also felt good about you. This may well have been the first step toward a long-lasting friendship. Moreover, the whole encounter may also have put you in a pleasant mood and kept you in good spirits for the rest of the day. Researchers find that these experiences are typical when two individuals share personal information.

People engage in **self-disclosure** when they reveal intimate information about themselves to another person. The discloser considers the information personal, and the choice of whom to disclose to is fairly selective. Many humanistic psychologists argue that self-disclosure is important for our personal growth and happiness. Rogers (1961) maintained that disclosing openly within a trusting relationship is a necessary step for understanding oneself.

However, humanistic theorists are quick to point out that the causal arrow between self-disclosure and well-being runs both ways (Jourard, 1971). People freely reveal information about themselves to others because they are psychologically healthy, and our psychological health increases because we disclose personal information to friends and loved ones. Of course, this is far from the way most people act. We often go to great lengths to keep others from finding out about bad habits or parts of our character they might not like. We're afraid of embarrassing ourselves or perhaps losing the respect of the people we love and admire. But Rogers argued that all this deception simply results in more to worry about and an ever-present fear that the real you might be revealed. More important, humanistic psychologists maintain that it is only through self-disclosure that we can truly come to know ourselves. Putting feelings into words allows us to understand those feelings in a way that simply thinking about emotions cannot. And if we are not aware of all aspects of ourselves, we cannot grow and become fully self-actualized.

Self-disclosure also plays a role in psychotherapy. Many humanistic psychologists argue that clients benefit most when they engage in an open exchange of thoughts and feelings with the therapist. When clients feel free to explore their true feelings, they move closer to understanding and becoming their true selves. Today, therapists from many approaches acknowledge the important role self-disclosure plays in the psychotherapeutic process (Farber, 2006).

Jerry Burger/Santa Clara University

Self-disclosure plays a key role in the development of personal relationships. However, researchers find that this is rarely one-sided. Instead, relationships develop as each person reveals intimate information about him- or herself at roughly the same level of intimacy.

But a therapeutic relationship is not one-sided. Rogers maintained that appropriate self-disclosure by the therapist is also beneficial. Disclosing therapists create an atmosphere of trust and elicit more disclosure from clients. However, research to date on the relationship between therapist disclosure and client progress is mixed (Henretty, 2010). Many psychologists are concerned about potential harm to the therapeutic process when therapists talk about themselves. Although many therapists reveal information about themselves on selected topics (Jeffrey & Austin, 2007), the appropriate level of self-disclosure for therapists remains a matter of debate (Barnett, 2011; Gibson, 2012; Zur, Williams, Lehavot, & Knapp, 2009).

Disclosure Reciprocity

If you are like me, you have had the unfortunate experience of being stuck on a plane or a bus sitting next to a stranger who wanted to tell you all about his or her life. During a recent plane trip, the woman next to me described her relationship with her husband, problems in raising her child, her opinions on drugs, sex education, and abortion—all without a single bit of encouragement or comparable disclosure from me.

What is notable about this "stranger on the bus" phenomenon is that it violates society's rules for the way social interaction is supposed to progress.

Like many social behaviors, the way we reveal information about ourselves is governed by a set of unstated but understood rules. Occasionally, parents teach us these rules directly ("Don't stare at people"), but more often we can't say how we learned what is expected and what is inappropriate when interacting with others. One of these social rules is known as **disclosure reciprocity**. According to this rule, people involved in a get-acquainted conversation reveal information about themselves at roughly the same level of intimacy: I reveal personal information to you as long as you continue to match that level of intimacy with personal information about yourself.

Investigators have demonstrated the rule of disclosure reciprocity in laboratory research (Davis, 1977; Taylor & Belgrave, 1986). Undergraduate students in one study were randomly paired with a member of the same gender whom they did not know (Davis, 1976). The students took turns getting to know one another by volunteering information about themselves. They were given a list of 72 discussion topics, previously ranked for level of intimacy, ranging from fairly trivial to extremely revealing. The winner of a coin toss began by talking for 1 minute on any one of the topics. The partner then talked for 1 minute on any one of the remaining topics. This procedure continued until both partners had spoken 12 times. As shown in Figure 12.1,

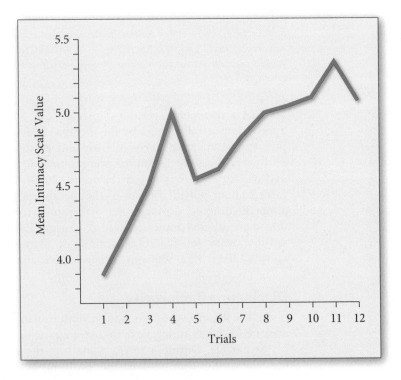

FIGURE 12.1 Progression of Intimacy During Dyad Conversation

Source: From "Self-disclosure in an acquaintance exercise: Responsibility for level of intimacy," by J. D. Davis, *Journal of Personality and Social Psychology*, 1976, 33, 787–792.

the students selected increasingly intimate topics as the interaction progressed. They typically began with something safe, perhaps discussing their favorite movies or foods. But they soon moved to more personal areas, such as problems with their parents or ways in which they felt personally inadequate. Moreover, participants tended to match their partners' intimacy levels. That is, if one person chose an intimate topic, the partner usually responded by selecting a similarly intimate topic. In other words, the students in this experiment followed the rule of disclosure reciprocity. Other studies show that children as young as 8 years of age seem to understand and follow the reciprocity rule (Cohn & Strassberg, 1983).

Why do we reciprocate disclosure intimacy? One reason is that self-disclosure leads to feelings of attraction and trust (Derlega, Winstead, & Greene, 2008). When people disclose information about themselves to us, we are attracted to them, and feelings of trust follow. We respond by disclosing personal information back, thus creating the reciprocity effect. Consistent with this explanation, studies find that we disclose to people we like and we like those who disclose to us (Collins & Miller, 1994). Because disclosure often leads to liking, people who understand the rule can use it to their advantage. For example, people who live in situations in which relationships come and go quickly, such as those who move frequently, tend to disclose a lot (Schug, Yuki, & Maddux, 2010). Presumably these individuals recognize that self-disclosure is a powerful tactic for making new friends. But disclosure alone does not lead to intimacy and liking. Relationships also require a responsive partner (Laurenceau, Feldman Barrett, & Pietromonaco, 1998; Reis & Patrick, 1996). When partners respond to personal disclosure with signs of caring and by revealing their own feelings, intimacy develops. Failure to respond appropriately likely ends the chance that the relationship will blossom.

Self-Disclosure Among Friends and Romantic Partners

If you apply the disclosure reciprocity rule to recent conversations you've had with friends, you may find that it doesn't always work. It's quite possible that one of you did most of the talking while the other one just listened. When a friend calls and says "I need to talk," we usually don't interrupt with personal examples of our own. Consistent with these observations, researchers find the reciprocity rule doesn't always apply to good friends. After a certain level of intimacy is reached in a relationship, we feel free to disclose to friends without requiring reciprocal disclosure (Altman & Taylor, 1973; Derlega, Wilson, & Chaikin, 1976). One researcher found the highest level of disclosure reciprocity among people who knew each other somewhat, but who were still in the process of developing their relationship (Won-Doornink, 1985). Apparently these individuals had made a commitment to learn more about each other, but they didn't know each other well enough to assume that the trust would be there without some sign of assurance.

However, these findings do not mean that strangers disclose more to each other than friends. On the contrary, friends are much more likely to talk about such intimate topics as their relationships, self-concepts, and sexual experiences (Bauminger, Finzi-Dottan, Chason, & Har-Even, 2008). In one demonstration of this difference, researchers recorded (with permission) the telephone conversations of female college students (Hornstein & Truesdell, 1988). The students talked about significantly more intimate information when they interacted with friends than when they spoke on the phone with someone they identified as only an acquaintance. Conversations among good friends also include many noticeable signs of intimacy that are lacking in conversations with strangers (Hornstein, 1985). These signs include the use of familiar terms, laughing at similar points, and understanding when to speak and when the conversation is coming to an end.

Willingness to self-disclose is also related to how easily one makes friends. One team of researchers asked incoming college freshmen how willing they were to reveal negative emotions like anxiety, fear, and sadness to others (Graham, Huang, Clark, & Helgeson, 2008). Students who were relatively willing to disclose their emotions developed more and more intimate social relationships during their first semester on campus than students who were reluctant to reveal personal information about themselves.

Studies with couples in long-term romantic relationships find similar patterns. The amount of self-disclosure in a marriage is a strong predictor of relationship satisfaction (Farber & Sohn, 2007; Harvey & Omarzu, 1997; Sprecher & Hendrick, 2004). The more couples talk to one another about what's personal and important to them, the better each of them feels about the marriage. Moreover, concealing personal information from a romantic partner is associated with less satisfaction and a reduced commitment to the relationship (Uysal, Lin, Knee, & Bush, 2012). Of course, it also may be that couples disclose *because* they feel good about each other. However, it is not the case that people who disclose a lot necessarily have more success at romance. Rather, researchers find that couples in good relationships have *selectively* chosen one another to disclose to rather than being high disclosers generally (Prager, 1986). And, as with good friends, married couples do not feel the need to reciprocate their partner's disclosure during every conversation (Morton, 1978).

Disclosing Men and Disclosing Women

Not long ago, my wife made an interesting observation about one of my male friends. "He interacts with people like a woman," she said. I immediately understood her point. My friend's voice is deep and masculine, and he doesn't use feminine hand gestures. But he often fills our conversations with fairly revealing information about his thoughts and feelings. This behavior would be appropriate, my wife continued, if my friend were a woman. But high levels of self-disclosure struck her as unusual for a man.

Consistent with my wife's observations, investigators find that women typically disclose more intimately and to more people than do men (Dindia & Allen, 1992). Moreover, this gender difference is expected by and perhaps reinforced by society. Participants in one study read about someone who was either highly disclosing or not very disclosing about personal problems (Derlega & Chaikin, 1976). Half the participants thought they were reading about a man, and half thought the person was a woman. The participants who thought they were reading about a female rated that person better adjusted when she was disclosing. However, when they thought the discloser was a male, revealing personal information was seen as a sign of poor psychological adjustment.

Other studies suggest at least a few exceptions to this rule. The freedom women feel to disclose may be limited by the nature of what they are talking about. Highly disclosing women in one study were liked more when they talked about their parents or about their sexual attitudes. However, women who disclosed about their personal aggressiveness were liked less (Kleinke & Kahn, 1980). Similarly, self-disclosing men are seen as well adjusted as long as they talk about masculine topics (Cunningham, Strassberg, & Haan, 1986). In other words, men and women are more likely to be accepted when they disclose within the appropriate societal roles for their gender. For men this usually means withholding information; for women it means being open and disclosing, but only on topics society deems appropriate. The result is an unfortunate limitation on personal expression.

Disclosing Traumatic Experiences

Students participating in a psychology experiment some years ago were asked to write anonymously about an upsetting or traumatic experience they once had, something they may have kept inside for years and told to no one (Pennebaker & Beall, 1986). One of the interesting findings from this and other studies like it is that nearly every participant is able to identify a secret trauma (Pennebaker, 1989, 2000). People write about personal failures and humiliations, illegal activities, drug and alcohol problems, and experiences with sexual abuse. They often express guilt over regrettable actions or great sadness about a personal loss. About a quarter of the participants cry. The students in this study wrote about themselves for 15 minutes each night for 4 consecutive November nights. Other students assigned to a control condition were instructed to spend this same amount of time writing about relatively trivial topics (for example, a description of their living room).

What impact did this writing exercise have on the students? Measures of blood pressure and self-reported mood indicated that writing about a traumatic experience led to more stress and a more negative mood immediately after the disclosure. However, the investigators contacted the students again in May, 6 months after they had written about their experiences. Students were asked about their health during the 6 months and about how many days they had been restricted because of an illness during this period. In addition, the number of visits each student had made to the campus health center was recorded.

Assessing Your Own Personality

Disclosure and Concealment

Indicate the extent to which you agree with each of the following statements. Use a 5-point scale to indicate your response, with 1 = Strongly disagree and 5 = Strongly agree.

_____   1. When I feel upset, I usually confide in my friends.

_____   2. I prefer not to talk about my problems.

_____   3. When something unpleasant happens to me, I often look for someone to talk to.

_____   4. I typically don't discuss things that upset me.

_____   5. When I feel depressed or sad, I tend to keep those feelings to myself.

_____   6. I try to find people to talk with about my problems.

_____   7. When I am in a bad mood, I talk about it with my friends.

_____   8. If I have a bad day, the last thing I want to do is talk about it.

_____   9. I rarely look for people to talk with when I am having a problem.

_____   10. When I'm distressed, I don't tell anyone.

_____   11. I usually seek out someone to talk to when I am in a bad mood.

_____   12. I am willing to tell others my distressing thoughts.

To score, reverse the answer values for items 2, 4, 5, 8, 9, and 10 (that is, 1 = 5, 2 = 4, etc.). Then add all 12 answer values together. High scores indicate a tendency to disclose distressing experiences to others, whereas low scores indicate a tendency to conceal information about distressing events. You can compare your score with norms from an undergraduate student sample (Kahn & Hessling, 2001). Men in this sample had a mean score of 36.33 (standard deviation = 8.98), and women had a mean score of 42.21 (standard deviation = 9.16).

Scale: The Distress Disclosure Index

Source: From "Measuring the tendency to conceal versus disclose psychological distress," by J. H. Kahn and R. M. Hessling, *Journal of Social and Clinical Psychology*, 2001, 20, 41–65. Copyright 2001 Guilford Publications, Inc. Reprinted by permission.

Some of the differences between the two groups are shown in Figure 12.2. Students in the trivial topic group showed a significant increase in the number of days they were restricted by illness and the number of visits they made to the health center. But this was not the case for the students who had written about their traumatic secrets. Similarly, only the disclosing students showed a decrease in the number of illnesses. In other words, although writing about

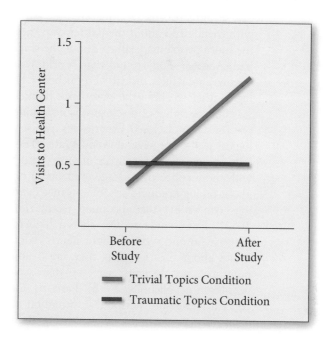

FIGURE 12.2 Mean Number of Visits to the Health Center as a Function of Experimental Condition

Source: From Pennebaker and Beall (1986).

their problems created some mild, short-term discomfort, it appears that the act of disclosing, even in the relatively mild form used in this study, improved the health of the already healthy college students.

The health benefits of disclosing traumatic experiences have been found in numerous subsequent investigations using this same basic procedure and with many different kinds of participants (Frattaroli, 2006; Frisina, Borod, & Lepore, 2004; Kelly & McKillop, 1996). Putting into words what has been kept under wraps for sometimes years consistently leads to improvements in physical health. Moreover, the benefits are found regardless of whether the disclosure is hand-written or typed or even if the information is disclosed orally (Frattaroli, 2006; Harrist, Carlozzi, McGovern, & Harrist, 2007). Participants also need not disclose about something as emotionally intense as a personal trauma. One team of investigators asked freshmen to write about the problems and emotions they encountered leaving home and adjusting to college (Pennebaker, Colder, & Sharp, 1990). Students who wrote about these thoughts and feelings for three consecutive nights made fewer visits to the health center over the next several months than those who wrote about trivial topics.

The connection between self-disclosure and health is also found in studies that look at how victims of specific traumas react to their experiences. One team of researchers contacted people who had lost a spouse either through an accidental death or because of suicide (Pennebaker & O'Heeron, 1984).

The investigators asked how often the participants had discussed the experience with friends and about the participants' health since the death. They found that the more people had talked about the tragedy, the fewer health problems they had. Another study found that World War II Holocaust survivors who spoke openly about their ordeal were in better health than those who were less willing to disclose about the experience (Finkelstein & Levy, 2006).

But the value of disclosure is not limited to physical health. Writing about previously undisclosed experiences also leads to better emotional and psychological well-being several months later (Frattaroli, 2006). Even putting our feelings about everyday sources of stress into words often makes it easier to cope with those concerns. College students in one study were less emotionally upset about taking graduate school entrance exams when they wrote about their feelings concerning the upcoming exam (Frattaroli, Thomas, & Lyubomirsky, 2011). These students also scored higher on the tests than a group of test-takers who had written about neutral topics. Freshmen in another study who wrote about the problems they faced adjusting to college had higher grade point averages their first semester than students who wrote about trivial topics (Cameron & Nicholls, 1998). Perhaps not surprisingly, people who typically conceal unpleasant personal information are more likely to experience depression and a lower sense of well-being than those who tend to be more open (Garrison & Kahn, 2010; Kahn & Garrison, 2009; Uysal, Lin & Knee, 2010).

But why does disclosure, even when written anonymously, result in better physical and psychological health? One reason is that actively inhibiting thoughts and feelings about unpleasant experiences requires a great deal of psychological and physiological work (Pennebaker, 1989). The impact of this stress is both immediate and long term. One investigation found an increase in immune system strength immediately after participants wrote about traumatic experiences (Petrie, Booth, & Pennebaker, 1998). Another study found participants slept better in the days following their disclosure (Mosher & Danoff-Burg, 2006). The cumulative effect of withholding secrets over time takes its toll in the form of increased illnesses and other stress-related problems.

Expressing thoughts and feelings also provides disclosers insight into their feelings that they might not have recognized otherwise, and this insight makes it easier to take steps to move beyond the experience (Kelly, Klusas, von Weiss, & Kenny, 2001; King, 2001; King & Miner, 2000; Langens & Schuler, 2007; Smyth, True, & Souto, 2001). As Rogers and other humanistic theorists argued, putting feelings into words allows us to "see" our emotions and thereby deal with them more effectively. Undergraduates in one study were asked to write about traumatic experiences during three 20-minute sessions (Hemenover, 2003). Three months later, these students scored higher on measures of mastery, personal growth, and self-acceptance than students who had written about trivial topics. In other words, the writing experience led to changes in the way participants thought about themselves. For this reason, the benefits of expressive writing may be limited to cultures that endorse the idea that personal insight can be gained by expressing emotions (Knowles, Wearing, & Campos, 2011).

Nonetheless, examples of beneficial self-disclosure can be found all around us. People often turn to friends, bartenders, and clergy members

Humanistic psychologists are concerned with loneliness for a number of reasons. Some people have argued that humanistic psychology's rise in popularity in the 1960s can be attributed to feelings of alienation and loneliness that had begun to creep into many American lives (Buhler & Allen, 1972). People faced with an increasingly dehumanized, mechanistic society welcomed the humanists' emphasis on the individual with his or her unique potential. Some psychologists believe feelings of loneliness reflect existential anxiety and a need to find meaning in one's life (Sadler & Johnson, 1980). And humanistic therapists often help clients develop meaningful encounters to overcome loneliness (Moustakas, 1968). Perhaps the most notable development in this area was the growth of encounter groups in the late 1960s and early 1970s. Within the safe confines of the group, humanistic therapists helped members discover the richness of intimate interpersonal encounters with others and thereby learn something about themselves (Rogers, 1970).

Defining and Measuring Loneliness

Loneliness is not the same as isolation. Some of the loneliest individuals are surrounded by people most of the day. Rather, *loneliness* concerns our perception of how much social interaction we have and the quality of that interaction. As one team of investigators explained, "Loneliness occurs when a person's network of social relationships is smaller or less satisfying *than the person desires*" (Peplau, Russell, & Heim, 1979, p. 55, italics added). You can have very little contact with people, but if you are satisfied with that contact, you won't feel lonely. On the other hand, you may have many friends, yet still feel a need for more or deeper friendships and thus become lonely.

Thinking of loneliness in terms of personal satisfaction with one's social relationships helps explain why some people who live in virtual isolation find the solitude enjoyable, whereas other individuals surrounded by people feel lonely. I commonly hear college students complain that, although they have a lot of acquaintances and people to hang around with, they don't have many real friends. For these students, the unmet need to interact with that special person in an intimate and honest way can create intense feelings of being alone.

Loneliness is often caused by the circumstances people find themselves in, such as moving to a new city or attending a new school. Moreover, the kinds of relationships we desire change as we pass through the life cycle (Green, Richardson, Lago, & Schatten-Jones, 2001; Pinquart & Sorensen, 2001). Young adults often require a larger number of friends to fend off loneliness, whereas older adults prefer fewer but closer friends. The causes and consequences of loneliness also vary as a function of culture (Anderson, 1999). The absence of an intimate friend or romantic partner often contributes to loneliness in Western societies. In fact, when people in individualistic cultures think of loneliness, they often imagine someone without a spouse or romantic partner. However, this source of loneliness is less common in Asian cultures, which emphasize instead associations with family members and the community (Rokach, 1998). On the other hand, because collectivist cultures emphasize one's place in a larger social network, feeling alone in these cultures is more likely to lower a person's sense of well-being (Goodwin, Cook, & Yung, 2001).

Although feelings of loneliness come and go as circumstances change, researchers also find loneliness can be thought of as a fairly stable personality trait. That is, although everyone feels lonely on occasion, some people are highly vulnerable to feelings of loneliness and seem to chronically suffer from not having enough close friends. Other people are relatively immune from these experiences. Several personality inventories have been developed to assess individual differences in our tendency to feel lonely (Cramer, Ofosu, & Barry, 2000; Rubenstein & Shaver, 1980; Russell, Peplau, & Cutrona, 1980; Schmidt & Sermat, 1983). Like other personality variables, our vulnerability to loneliness is relatively stable over time (Segrin, 1999; Weeks, Michela, Peplau, & Bragg, 1980).

Chronically Lonely People

Correlations between measures of loneliness and other personality variables paint a drab and sullen picture of chronically lonely people (Ernst & Cacioppo, 1999). High scores on loneliness scales are related to higher levels of social anxiety and self-consciousness and lower levels of self-esteem and assertiveness (Bruch, Kaflowitz, & Pearl, 1988; Jones, Freemon, & Goswick, 1981; Solano & Koester, 1989). Lonely people are more likely to be introverted, anxious, and sensitive to rejection (Russell et al., 1980) and more likely to suffer from depression (Vanhalst, Luyckx, Teppers, & Goossens, 2012; Wei, Russell, & Zakalik, 2005). High loneliness scores also are associated with pessimism and negative mood (Cacioppo et al., 2006).

Not surprisingly, lonely people have more than their share of social difficulties (Heinrich & Gullone, 2006). They have a hard time trusting other people (Rotenberg et al., 2010) and are often uncomfortable when others open up to them (Rotenberg, 1997). Lonely people spend less time with friends, date less frequently, attend fewer parties, and have fewer close friends than nonlonely people (Archibald, Bartholomew, & Marx, 1995). They have difficulty initiating social activity and participating in groups (Horowitz & de Sales French, 1979). Acquaintances of lonely people confirm the accuracy of these assessments. College students say their relationships with lonely people are noticeably less intimate than they are with nonlonely people (Williams & Solano, 1983).

In addition to the emotional and social toll that comes with feeling alone, a growing body of research indicates that loneliness also may be hazardous to your health (Cacioppo & Patrick, 2008; Cacioppo, Hawkley, Crawford et al., 2002; Cohen & Janicki-Deverts, 2009; Whisman, 2010). Compared to those who have few social contacts, people with a large and diverse social network have a decreased risk of cancer recurrence (Helgeson, Cohen, & Fritz, 1998), stroke (Rutledge et al., 2008), and heart disease (Kop et al., 2005). Not surprisingly, people with large social networks also live longer (Berkman, 1995). Healthy adults in one study were—with permission—deliberately exposed to a cold virus (Cohen, Doyle, Turner, Alper, & Skoner, 2003). Researchers found that the more social the participants, the less likely they were to come

TABLE 12.1 Pathways Between Loneliness and Health

Health Behaviors	Lonely people have poorer health habits
Stress Exposure	Lonely people experience more chronic stressors
Coping Styles	Lonely people use less effective coping strategies when dealing with stress
Stress Physiology	Lonely people experience unhealthy changes in physiology
Recuperation	Lonely people are less able to rely on natural restorative processes that improve health

Source: Adapted from Hawkley and Cacioppo (2007).

down with a cold. Lonely students in another study had a poorer antibody response to receiving a flu shot than did nonlonely students (Pressman, Cohen, Miller, Barkin, Rabin, & Treanor, 2005).

But why does loneliness affect health? As shown in Table 12.1, researchers have identified five possible pathways (Hawkley & Cacioppo, 2007). First, lonely people often have poorer health habits than nonlonely people. Most noteworthy, they tend to be less active physically (Hawkley, Thisted, & Cacioppo, 2009; Shankar, McMunn, Banks, & Steptoe, 2011). Whereas nonlonely people are out hiking, dancing, or golfing with friends, lonely people are staying home watching TV. This lack of activity combined with a poorer diet makes lonely people more prone to obesity than nonlonely individuals (Lauder, Mummery, Jones, & Caperchione, 2006). Lonely people also are more likely to smoke (Lauder et al., 2006). Second, lonely people are subject to more sources of stress than nonlonely individuals. People who suffer from chronic loneliness tend to experience stress in more areas of their lives (e.g., financial, social, employment) than nonlonely people (Hawkley, Burleson, Berntson, & Cacioppo, 2003). Third, lonely people do not cope with this stress as well as nonlonely people (Vanhalst et al., 2012). Seeking emotional support from friends when times are rough is an effective coping strategy. However, lonely individuals lack a network of friends they can turn to when feeling overwhelmed and helpless. Instead, they are more likely than most people to engage in less effective withdrawal strategies when experiencing stress (Cacioppo et al., 2000). Fourth, the excessive amount of stress experienced by lonely people leads to changes in physiological conditions that eventually affect their health. In particular, loneliness is associated with high blood pressure (Hawkley, Masi, Berry & Cacioppo, 2006). Fifth, loneliness interferes with some of the body's natural restorative processes. Most noteworthy, lonely people sleep less well than nonlonely people (Cacioppo, Hawkley, Berntson et al., 2002; Hawkley, Preacher, & Cacioppo, 2010). In short, a lifetime of chronic loneliness can grind away at a person's health.

The Causes of Loneliness

What is it about lonely people that continually frustrates their need for meaningful social contact? Researchers have identified two characteristics that seem to contribute to chronic loneliness—negative expectations and poorly developed social skills.

Lonely people often enter a social situation with the expectation that this encounter, like so many before, will not go well (Goswick & Jones, 1981; Hanley-Dunn, Maxwell, & Santos, 1985; Jones et al., 1981; Jones, Sansone, & Helm, 1983; Levin & Stokes, 1986). In one study, lonely and nonlonely college students were asked to participate in a series of group activities with three other students (Christensen & Kashy, 1998). The students discussed and solved problems together for 30 minutes. The participants were then separated and asked to rate the other members of the group in terms of their intelligence, friendliness, and so on. The participants also rated themselves on these dimensions and guessed what kind of ratings they would receive from the other group members. The researchers found that lonely participants evaluated themselves less favorably than they evaluated the other group members. Moreover, the lonely participants expected that the other three members of the group also would rate them poorly. However, they were wrong. Despite their low expectations for how the other students would see them, the lonely students were evaluated no differently from anyone else—with one exception. The lonely students were actually perceived as being friendlier than most of the people in the group. In short, the lonely students thought the others would not like them, yet as it turned out they were greatly mistaken.

These low expectations can be poisonous when trying to develop a friendship or romantic relationship. Lonely people doubt a new acquaintance will enjoy talking with them and suspect the person will find them boring or stupid by the end of the conversation. Consequently, lonely people often show little interest in getting to know other people and are quick to end the conversation and move on to something else. These negative expectations may also lead lonely people to interpret any small sign as rejection. Participants in one experiment spent 5 minutes talking with a stranger (Frankel & Prentice-Dunn, 1990). Later, participants saw a videotape of their partner's evaluation of them. The videotape contained positive and negative comments. As expected, the lonely people paid attention to and recalled the negative feedback better than the nonlonely participants. Because they believe their interactions have gone worse than they probably have, lonely people are unlikely to pursue a friendship with someone they've met or to seek out others to do things with.

Given this negative approach to social interactions, it is not surprising that lonely people have such a difficult time making friends. This research also helps explain why loneliness is a problem for many students on crowded college campuses. With so many potential friends around, there is little reason to seek out and nurture the friendship of someone who appears to be unfriendly.

Chronically lonely people also tend to have poorly developed social skills. Perhaps you are one of those lucky individuals for whom conversation comes easily. You enjoy meeting people, effortlessly finding out about them, and occasionally talking about yourself. If this is you, then you are probably puzzled by people who have difficulty interacting with others. Even for people who are not shy and who would like to meet new friends, engaging in more than a short and trivial conversation can be a chore. What these people may lack are basic social skills, the knowledge of how to carry on a conversation that both you and the other person find valuable and enjoyable.

Several studies implicate just such a lack of social skills as part of what keeps some people trapped in a cycle of loneliness (Segrin, 1999; Segrin & Flora, 2000; Vitkus & Horowitz, 1987). The best way to learn the art of conversation is to talk with others. Yet people without social skills may have such a difficult time developing relationships that they have little opportunity to develop these skills. They never learn how to initiate an interaction or how to keep the conversation lively, so their difficulty making friends continues.

Consider the interaction styles one team of researchers found when they examined conversations with lonely and nonlonely individuals (Jones, Hobbs, & Hockenbury, 1982). Lonely participants showed relatively little interest in their partners. They asked fewer questions, often failed to comment on what the other person said, and made fewer references to the partner. Instead, these lonely people were more likely to talk about themselves and introduce new topics unrelated to their partner's interests. Another study found lonely people were more likely to give advice to strangers and less likely to acknowledge what the other person said (Sloan & Solano, 1984). Little wonder, then, that we often fail to enjoy conversations with lonely people. It's not that lonely people are intentionally rude, but rather that they don't understand how their interaction style turns away potential friends.

Other researchers examine the way lonely and nonlonely people use self-disclosure. Studies find that lonely people generally reveal less about themselves than their partners (Berg & Peplau, 1982; Sloan & Solano, 1984). In one study lonely people selected relatively nonintimate topics to talk about in a get-acquainted conversation (Solano, Batten, & Parish, 1982). Not surprisingly, the lonely participants' partners reciprocated with nonintimate topics as well. Other studies find lonely people are often not aware of social rules about when and how much to disclose (Chelune, Sultan, & Williams, 1980; Solano & Koester, 1989; Wittenberg & Reis, 1986). They may disclose too much or fail to reveal enough about themselves when the other person expects it. Consequently, others may see them as either weird or aloof, and respond accordingly.

Fortunately, efforts to help people overcome their loneliness have been promising (Masi, Chen, Hawkley, & Cacioppo, 2011). Not surprisingly, many of these treatments are designed to improve social skills. Good social skills can lead to better interactions, which can lead to more socializing and better relationships. Therapists working with populations particularly vulnerable to loneliness, such as elderly individuals, often do what they can to create more opportunities for their clients to meet and interact with other people. Finally, some treatments help lonely people understand how they sometimes sabotage potential friendships with negative expectations and inaccurate interpretations of what others think of them.

Self-Esteem

If there is a single concept that threads its way through the writings of the humanistic psychologists, it may be how people feel about themselves. A central goal of Rogerian psychotherapy is to get clients to accept and appreciate themselves for who they are. Maslow wrote about the need for self-respect and the need to feel content about who we are and what we do with our lives. In short, humanistic personality theory is concerned with the individual's self-esteem.

Most researchers draw a distinction between self-esteem and self-concept. Your *self-concept* is the cumulation of what you see as your personal characteristics—that is, the kind of person you believe yourself to be. **Self-esteem** refers to your evaluation of your self-concept. In essence, do you like this person? Although we often speak of self-esteem in our everyday conversations, researchers face several challenges when trying to identify and measure this concept.

One problem is that the way we feel about ourselves can change from one situation to the next. Most people get a little down on themselves when they act in ways they know they shouldn't, and most of us can't help but think well of ourselves when someone heaps praise on us for a job well done (Heatherton & Polivy, 1991). However, these fluctuations in feelings should not be confused with self-esteem. Rather, psychologists often refer to these ups and downs as *feelings of self-worth* (Brown & Dutton, 1995). In contrast, self-esteem has to do with relatively stable self-evaluations. As with other personality variables, researchers find some people are prone to more positive self-evaluations than others. These individuals may have bad days and disappoint themselves on occasion, but in general they like themselves and feel good about who they are and what they do. Of course, we also can identify people who frequently experience negative self-evaluations. Although these low self-esteem people also have good days and feel good about much of what they do, compared to others they seem to lack a basic confidence in themselves or an appreciation for who they are.

Self-Esteem and Reaction to Failure

Evaluation is an unavoidable part of most of our lives. After only a few years of elementary school, most students become accustomed to having their schoolwork graded. Evaluation is commonplace in the business world, if not overtly in the form of an annual review, then implicitly in the size of one's raise. Any type of competition, from sports to chess to gardening, brings with it the possibility of both victory and defeat as we compare our abilities and accomplishments against those of others. All of this evaluation means that each of us has experienced our share of successes and failures.

However, not all people react the same to these evaluations. Several laboratory experiments have looked at how high and low self-esteem people respond when told they have done well or poorly on a test (Brockner, 1979; Brown & Dutton, 1995; Kernis, Brockner, & Frankel, 1989; Stake, Huff, & Zand, 1995; Tafarodi & Vu, 1997). Participants in these studies usually take a test supposedly measuring some intellectual aptitude or they work on a task calling for some specific ability. Researchers then give bogus feedback to participants, indicating they have done either very well or rather poorly. Although everyone responds well when told they have succeeded, how we respond to failure often depends on our level of self-esteem. When told they have done poorly, low self-esteem people typically don't try as hard on the next test. They perform more poorly and are more likely to give up early. In contrast, high self-esteem people work just as hard on the second test regardless of how they did on the initial test.

The importance of these findings for academic settings is obvious. Consider one study that examined college students' reactions to their grades on a midterm exam (Brockner, Derr, & Laing, 1987). The students took their first exam for the class 5 weeks into the term and received their grade 1 week later. The investigators found that high and low self-esteem students performed almost identically on the midterm test. The researchers then divided the students into those who had done well on the test (received an A or a B) and those who had not done as well (received a C or lower). As shown in Figure 12.3, like the laboratory participants who received false feedback, low self-esteem students who did well on the first test continued to perform well. However, low self-esteem students who had not done well on the first test performed significantly worse on the second exam.

Another study found that low self-esteem people do not have to actually experience failure to show these negative effects; rather, they only have to

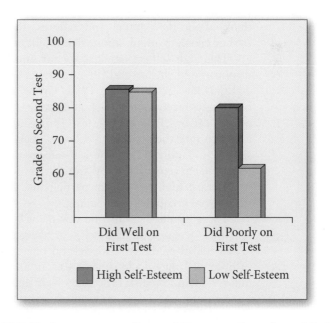

FIGURE 12.3 Performance on Second Test as a Function of Self-Esteem and Performance on First Test

Source: Adapted from Brockner et al. (1987).

imagine that they have failed (Campbell & Fairey, 1985). Participants in this investigation were asked to imagine they had done well or poorly on a 25-item anagram test. Low self-esteem people who imagined failing said they expected to do poorly on a subsequent test and indeed performed more poorly on the test than low self-esteem people who first imagined they had done well.

How can we explain these reactions? One possibility is that people are more likely to accept feedback consistent with their self-concept (Story, 1998; Wood, Heimpel, Manwell, & Whittington, 2009; Wood, Heimpel, Newby-Clark, & Ross, 2005). People with low self-esteem probably accept the fact that they fail more than most people. Consequently, it is easier for them to believe feedback confirming their negative self-image than information that violates their expectations. Another way to look at this is to say that the negative feedback reminds low self-esteem people about the low evaluations they have of themselves, which then triggers even more negative thoughts (Dutton & Brown, 1997; Tafarodi & Vu, 1997). This interpretation helps us understand why low self-esteem people perform more poorly on a task even when they have just imagined what it would be like to fail.

But we can also turn this question around. What is it about *high* self-esteem people that prevents them from becoming discouraged after failure? Why don't they give up when they fail a test or do poorly at work? The answer appears to be that high self-esteem people develop personal strategies for blunting the effects of negative feedback (van Dellen, Campbell, Hoyle, & Bradfield, 2011). Included in this arsenal is a tendency to respond to failure by focusing attention on their good qualities rather than on what they have done wrong. Whereas negative feedback causes people low in self-esteem to think about their faults and failures, this same feedback leads high self-esteem people to think about their abilities and achievements.

This high self-esteem strategy for blunting the effects of failure has been demonstrated in several investigations (Buckingham, Weber, & Sypher, 2012; Dodgson & Wood, 1998; Greve & Wentura, 2003). Participants in one study received feedback indicating they had performed either well or poorly on an achievement test (Brown & Smart, 1991). They were then asked to rate themselves on a list of social attributes (e.g., *sincere, kind*). As shown in Figure 12.4, low self-esteem participants reacted to their failure on the achievement test by rating themselves poorly on their social skills. In contrast, high self-esteem participants actually rated themselves *higher* on their social attributes after failing.

These results demonstrate one tactic high self-esteem people use to maintain their feelings of high self-worth even in the face of negative feedback. When told they did not do well on one task, they simply remind themselves of how well they do in other areas. In another study high self-esteem people quickly abandoned a task they were having trouble with when given an opportunity to work on something they could do well (Di Paula & Campbell, 2002). It's not that high self-esteem people think they're perfect; they just don't dwell on their failures (Li, Zeigler-Hill, Luo, Yang, & Zhang, 2012). If they mess up at work, they might remind themselves that they have

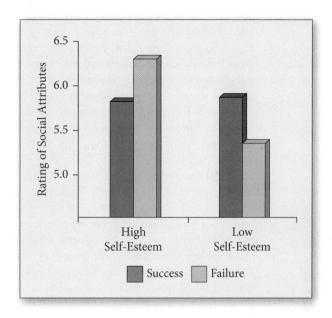

FIGURE 12.4 Ratings of Social Attributes Following Success and Failure
Source: Adapted from Brown and Smart (1991).

a lot of friends. If they lose badly at handball, they might recall how well they play chess. This strategy keeps high self-esteem people feeling good about themselves even when faced with life's inevitable downturns.

Contingencies of Self-Worth

To this point, we've concentrated on what researchers refer to as *global* self-esteem; that is, the overall evaluation we have about ourselves. But very few people feel entirely good or bad about themselves. Even the most content among us can point to deficiencies and weaknesses, areas where we feel less confident than others. Thus researchers sometimes find it useful to examine self-esteem within specific domains. For example, investigators might ask participants how they feel about themselves in terms of academic performance, personal ethics, or physical appearance. This strategy raises some interesting questions. Is global self-esteem simply the sum of how we feel about ourselves in these specific areas? Is high self-esteem restricted to those who feel good about themselves in most, if not all, major domains? Put another way, is it necessary to feel competent and virtuous in many different areas before we can feel good about who we are?

Fortunately, the answer to all of these questions is "No." Researchers find that global self-esteem seems to result from a two-step process (Crocker, Brook, Niiya, & Villacorta, 2006; Crocker & Park, 2003; Crocker & Wolfe, 2001). First, each of us identifies domains that we consider important to us; that is, areas we use to determine our self-worth. For one person these domains might be academic performance and acting in ethically sound ways. For someone else physical appearance and acceptance from family and friends might be most important. Researchers refer to these areas we use to evaluate ourselves as **contingencies of self-worth**. Second, we form evaluations of ourselves—that is, our global self-esteem—based on how we do in these selected areas. The woman who bases her self-esteem on academic performance will feel good about who she is as long as she performs well in class. The man whose contingencies of self-worth include his physical appearance will enjoy high self-esteem as long as he receives feedback that he is good-looking and desirable.

Looking at self-esteem in terms of contingencies of self-worth helps us understand why people with limitations and deficiencies can still feel good about who they are. You may be terrible at sports or math, but if you don't base your self-worth on how you perform in these areas, they probably will not affect your overall self-esteem. One team of researchers identified seven areas college students typically use as contingencies of self-worth (Crocker, Luhtanen, Cooper, & Bouvrette, 2003). As shown in Table 12.2, these contingencies range from some obvious areas (competence, appearance) to some you might not have considered (God's love).

Where do contingencies of self-worth come from? That is, why does one person base her self-esteem on competence, whereas another bases his self-esteem on God's love? For starters, people tend to select contingency areas in which they typically excel. Athletes often base their self-esteem on their ability to perform well in sports, whereas good students tend to rely on their grades. But this is only part of the story. We all know people who select contingencies of self-worth that are difficult to attain. Sometimes parents or peers influence these choices, such as a father who says he loves his little girl because of

TABLE 12.2 Contingencies of Self-Worth for College Students

Contingency	Description
Competencies	Abilities and performance in various areas, particularly academic performance for college students
Competition	Outperforming other people in various competitive situations
Approval from Generalized Others	Approval and acceptance from other people, based on what we believe they think of us
Family Support	Receiving approval and affection from the people closest to us, particularly from family members
Appearance	How physically attractive we believe others find us
God's Love	The belief that we are loved, valued, and unique in the eyes of God
Virtue	Adhering to personal ethical standards and judging ourselves as good and moral individuals

Source: Adapted from Crocker, Luhtanen et al. (2003).

how pretty she is and admires his son for his athletic skills. Culture also plays a role, placing different values on different personal attributes. For example, our society communicates in many ways that certain standards are more relevant for one gender than for the other (Fredrickson & Roberts, 1997; Strahan et al., 2008). Girls are often reminded by peers and media messages that their value depends on how they look. Boys are told that beating others in various competitions is a sign of their self-worth.

Using contingencies of self-worth to determine self-esteem has advantages and disadvantages. On the plus side, we don't have to be competent at everything—or even very many things—to feel good about who we are. The student who breezes through classes and the one who struggles can both have high self-esteem. Similarly, the star athlete and the ultimate physical klutz can both feel good about themselves. Returning to humanistic personality theory, it is ultimately up to us to choose which standards we use for this evaluation. On the down side, people sometimes select contingencies that are difficult to achieve. A young woman loved and admired by family and friends still might not feel good about herself if she feels academically inferior to some of her peers.

Thinking of self-esteem in terms of contingencies of worth also helps us understand why some people have relatively stable feelings of self-worth, whereas others fluctuate wildly between liking and not liking themselves. That's because some contingencies leave us at the mercy of other people and unmanageable forces. We can't always control whether we will be accepted by others, retain good looks, or succeed in competition. As a result, people who tie their self-esteem to uncontrollable forces may be more prone to bouts of anxiety and depression (Crocker & Park, 2004). Undergraduates who base their self-worth largely on academic performance often experience depression and a drop in self-esteem when they receive a low grade (Crocker, Karpinski, Quinn, & Chase, 2003; Park, Crocker & Kiefer, 2007) or a rejection letter from graduate school (Crocker, Sommers, & Luhtanen, 2002). In one study students who used academic performance as a contingency of self-worth experienced more stress—but did not obtain higher grades—than students who relied on other contingencies (Crocker & Luhtanen, 2003).

Making one's self-esteem contingent on physical appearance or the approval of others also can create an emotional roller coaster. A compliment or a pleasant conversation might lead to pride and self-liking, but a rude remark or a broken date can trigger self-doubt. People who make their self-esteem contingent on the state of their romantic relationships may be subject to strong emotional reactions when inevitable relationship issues surface (Knee, Canevello, Bush, & Cook, 2008). Similarly, individuals who base their self-esteem on the strength of their friendships are more prone to depression than those who don't embrace this contingency (Cambron, Acitelli, & Steinberg, 2010). Participants in one study who based their self-esteem on physical appearance felt alone and rejected when simply made aware of flaws in their appearance (Park, 2007). Another investigation found that college freshmen who based their self-worth on their appearance were more prone to drinking alcohol, presumably because their self-esteem was threatened in the kinds of situations (parties and social events, for example) in which drinking occurs (Luhtanen & Crocker, 2005).

In short, people who rely on uncontrollable self-esteem contingencies may be putting their emotional well-being on the line every day. On the other hand, people who base their self-esteem on contingencies largely under their control (such as virtue or God's love) are less prone to depression and anxiety than those who rely on more externally based contingencies (Sargent, Crocker, & Luhtanen, 2006).

Self-Esteem and Culture

People growing up in Western culture often assume that everyone wants to excel, to stand out from the crowd, to be recognized for personal accomplishments. Teachers and parents foster high self-esteem in children by identifying the child's unique strengths and helping the child develop and excel in these areas. Adolescents who say they are "no better than average" at anything might be readily labeled as poorly adjusted. Indeed, youth from disadvantaged backgrounds are encouraged to believe in themselves, to believe they can achieve whatever they set their minds to. In short, in most Western societies, the recipe for high self-esteem is feeling good about who you are and what you do to distinguish yourself.

However, some researchers have challenged the universality of these notions (Heine, 2001; Kitayama & Markus, 1994; Markus & Kitayama, 1991, 1994; Triandis, 1989, 2001). Recall from Chapter 1 that Western conceptions of the self are not shared by all cultures. People in collectivist cultures are more concerned with interdependence than with independence. Whereas individualistic countries like the United States emphasize the uniqueness of the individual, people in collectivist countries see themselves as part of a larger cultural unit.

One implication of these different views is that we may need to rethink the way we conceptualize self-esteem when working with people from different cultures. Self-esteem scales developed primarily for American research participants often ask test takers about feelings of competence and about how much they value their unique attributes. Such items make little sense to people who see their value in terms of belongingness and cooperation. Researchers sometimes illustrate the difference between an individualistic country like the United States and a collectivist country like Japan by pointing to a pair of expressions from these cultures. In the United States we sometimes say, "The squeaky wheel gets greased," meaning that one has to stand up and assert oneself to get ahead. In Japan one often hears, "The nail that stands up is the one that gets hammered," meaning that asserting one's individuality is unacceptable and is likely to result in negative consequences.

These different perspectives on the self also mean that people from the two types of cultures have different ideas about what leads to self-satisfaction and feeling good (Kang, Shaver, Sue, Min, & Jing, 2003; Tafarodi, Marshall, & Katsura, 2004). People in individualistic cultures typically feel good about themselves when they think about their unique value and personal accomplishments. In contrast, people from collectivist cultures derive self-satisfaction from their perceived relationships with others. People from collectivist cultures feel good when they obtain a sense of belonging within the culture, of occupying their appropriate place. Fitting in and doing one's duty are sources of pride in collectivist cultures. Personal achievements and independence are valued in individualistic cultures.

Consistent with these observations, research with American students finds a nearly universal tendency to see oneself in a better light than objective data might suggest. When American college students are asked to compare themselves to their peers on a variety of skills and aptitudes, they almost always report their superiority over those around them (Taylor, 1989). In this country, it seems, we are all better than average. However, when researchers present these same questions to students from collectivist cultures, they find relatively little evidence for such a bias (Heine & Hamamura, 2007). Typical citizens in a collectivist culture simply do not see themselves as any better than other members of society. In the United States these feelings of averageness might be taken as evidence of poor self-esteem. However, in other countries such a self-evaluation is considered quite healthy. In a collectivist culture, it is the person full of self-importance who is cause for concern, the nail that gets hammered down. Needless to say, this cultural difference can be a source of conflict for people who move from one culture to another. American baseball players, known for their elevated sense of self, often have a very difficult time playing for Japanese clubs, which emphasize the team above the individual (Whiting, 1989).

In an interesting demonstration of the relation between culture and self-esteem, one group of researchers compared average self-esteem scores for Asians as a function of their exposure to North American culture (Heine, Lehman, Markus, & Kitayama, 1999). Remember, the self-esteem scales were designed so that high scores reflect Western notions of individual accomplishment and pride in personal achievements. As shown in Figure 12.5, the participants' self-esteem scores changed with their amount of contact with individualistic cultures. Three generations after the participants' families had immigrated to Canada, the Asian Canadian self-esteem scores were no different from those of the European Canadians.

Culture also affects the standards people use to decide whether they are satisfied with their lives (Kuppens, Realo, & Diener, 2008; Oishi, Diener, Choi, Kim-Prieto, & Choi, 2007; Steger, Kawabata, Shimai, & Otake, 2008). Most Americans assume that happiness is the key to life satisfaction. That is, I will be satisfied with my life to the extent that I feel good about myself and experience positive emotions, such as happiness. Indeed, studies find this to be the case in individualistic cultures (Diener & Diener, 1995; Oishi & Diener, 2001; Suh, Diener, Oishi, & Triandis, 1998). However, this path to life satisfaction does not apply in collectivist cultures. Instead, how well people meet the culturally defined standard of proper behavior predicts life satisfaction in collectivist nations. Whereas feeling good is the key to a good life in individualistic cultures, fitting into the role prescribed by society is the key in collectivist cultures.

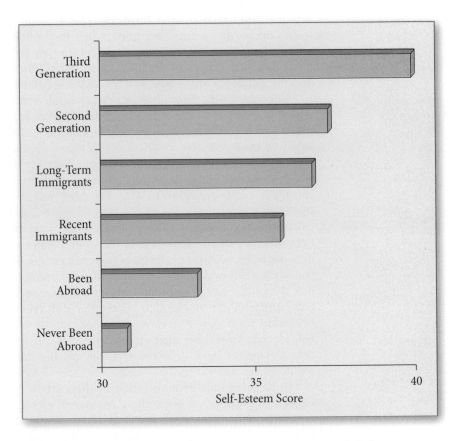

FIGURE 12.5 Average Self-Esteem Score of Asians and Asian Canadians as a Function of Exposure to Western Culture

Source: Adapted from "Is there a universal need for positive self-regard?" by S. J. Heine et al., *Psychological Review*, 1999, 106, 766–794. Copyright 1999 by the American Psychological Association. Adapted by permission of the American Psychological Association.

In short, the theory and research on self-esteem presented in this chapter is probably applicable only to people living in individualistic cultures. However, we should not take this to mean that people in collectivist cultures do not have self-esteem. Rather, we should recognize that concepts like the self and self-esteem have different meanings in different cultures. Personality researchers have come to appreciate these differences and are actively conducting research on these questions.

Solitude

In many ways Naomi is different from most people. Although she could easily join her coworkers in the company cafeteria, Naomi often chooses to have lunch alone. She'll eat a sandwich in the nearby park or sometimes spend her lunch hour taking a solitary walk around the neighborhood. When friends ask her to drop by on the weekend or to join them after work, she

> *"A desire for meaningful solitude is by no means neurotic; on the contrary, an incapacity for constructive solitude is itself a sign of neurosis."*
>
> KAREN HORNEY

frequently declines even when she has no other plans. Surprisingly, most people who know her describe Naomi as a warm and engaging person. And Naomi very much enjoys her friends and coworkers. Still, compared to most people, Naomi spends a significant amount of time by herself.

What might a personality psychologist say about Naomi? Research indicates that our interpersonal relationships are among our most important sources of happiness (Diener & Seligman, 2002; Myers, 1992). So why would someone frequently turn down opportunities to socialize? Several possible explanations can be found in earlier sections of this book. Perhaps Naomi is introverted (Chapter 10). She may not find the stimulation or rewards of social activity as attractive as more extraverted people do. On the other hand, Naomi might avoid people because she suffers from social anxiety (Chapter 8). Perhaps she is afraid that others will evaluate her negatively, so she reduces her anxiety by simply avoiding social interactions whenever possible. Then again, in some ways Naomi's behavior is similar to what Karen Horney called the neurotic style of "moving away from people" (Chapter 5). According to this analysis, Naomi may have adopted her avoidance style as a way to protect herself from anxiety when she was a child. Yet another possibility is that Naomi suffers from loneliness. As described earlier in this chapter, she may lack some basic social skills and spends time alone because she has difficulty interacting with people and developing relationships.

Although each of these explanations can account for a person's desire to spend time alone, there is at least one more interpretation, one that casts Naomi's quest for solitude in a different light. When Abraham Maslow studied psychologically healthy people, he found a curious similarity among members of this select group. Although these self-actualized people possessed characteristics that made them the warmest of friends, they also spent a surprisingly large amount of time by themselves. "For all my subjects it is true that they can be solitary without harm to themselves and without discomfort," Maslow (1970) observed. "Furthermore, it is true for almost all that they positively like solitude and privacy to a definitely greater degree than the average person" (p. 160).

Maslow's observations thus provide another explanation for Naomi's preference for solitude. It is possible that she is not introverted, socially anxious, or lonely. Perhaps Naomi's desire to spend time by herself is something positive. Her preference for solitude may be both a reflection of and a contributor to her personal growth and development. Maslow was quick to point out that psychologically healthy people also tend to express a great deal of interpersonal warmth and have especially close relationships with their dearest friends. People with a high desire for solitude are not necessarily trying to escape from relationships. Rather, some people who spend a great deal of time by themselves have come to recognize the benefits of solitude.

Time Alone

Although most of us live in social worlds, in truth we also spend a good deal of our day alone. To determine how often we spend time by ourselves, investigators sometimes use a procedure known as the *Experience Sampling*

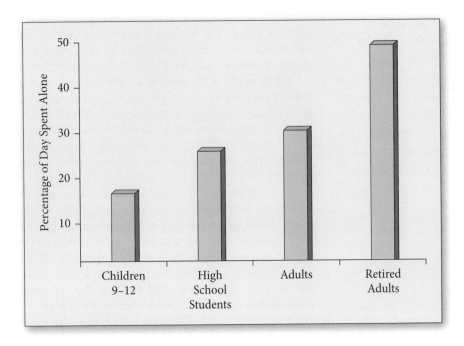

FIGURE 12.6 Percentage of Day Spent Alone as a Function of Age

Source: Adapted from Larson (1990).

Method (Larson & Csikszentmihalyi, 1980; Larson, Csikszentmihalyi, & Graef, 1982; Larson & Richards, 1991; Larson, Zuzanek, & Mannell, 1985). Participants in these studies carry pagers or handheld computers with them 24 hours a day for about a week. At random intervals throughout each day, the researchers signal participants that it is time to fill out a quick report on what they are doing and how they feel at that moment. The results of this research, shown in Figure 12.6, confirm that Americans spend a significant amount of their waking hours alone. Moreover, solitude becomes a more common experience as we age.

How do people react to time alone? As suggested by conventional wisdom, most of us find time by ourselves less pleasant than time spent with others (Larson, 1990). People typically complain of loneliness and boredom when they are by themselves. After spending a long period of time alone, most people eagerly seek out social interactions (O'Connor & Rosenblood, 1996). Emotional difficulties are often made worse when there is no one around. People prone to depression often experience negative emotion when alone. One study found that bulimics had a particularly negative reaction to solitude (Larson & Johnson, 1985). The researchers speculate that the loneliness and confusion experienced by bulimics when alone contributes to their eating disorder.

Clearly, time by oneself can be unpleasant and unsatisfying for many people. But consider the results of one national survey (Crossen, 1996). Only 6% of American adults in that survey said they wanted less time by themselves. In contrast, 31% wished they had more time alone in their lives. These numbers are consistent with observations of several researchers who argue that isolation from other people also has benefits (Buchholz & Helbraun, 1999; Burger, 1995; Larson, 1990; Long & Averill, 2003; Storr, 1988). To better understand the advantages of time alone, investigators sometimes divide solitude into three kinds of experiences (Burger, 1998). We can look at the effects of short periods of solitude during the day, usually measured in minutes. We also can study the effects of longer, planned time by oneself, typically measured in hours. Or we can examine the impact of extended periods of solitude, such as those measured in days. Each of these kinds of solitude has the potential to contribute to our well-being.

Even short periods of solitude spaced throughout the day can make a rough day go better. Sometimes we just need a break from constant social activity to organize our thoughts and psychologically prepare for future activities. Some writers have referred to this as a "self-restoration" process in which we reestablish a sense of who we are separate from the "social" self we present to others (Altman, 1975). Other psychologists describe these moments of solitude as a kind of emotional renewal. Adults and adolescents often say they feel more cheerful and more alert after spending short periods of time by themselves (Larson et al., 1982). Not surprisingly, a common complaint among people experiencing stress is that they have too little time to themselves (Webb, 1978).

But sometimes people need more than a few minutes alone. Occasionally, we need a more extended amount of time by ourselves to work through personal problems and make important decisions. Although consulting with others can be useful, many times people need extended time alone to think things through. Time for contemplation may be especially valuable for

Some people find time by themselves lonely and painful, but for others time alone is precious.

adolescents as they address personal questions about religion, values, personal identity, and life goals. To test this possibility, adolescents in one study were followed for one week through the Experience Sampling Procedure to determine how much time they spent by themselves (Larson, 1997). The investigator found that teenagers who spent a moderate amount of time by themselves, roughly between 25% and 45% of their nonclass hours, tended to be better adjusted and less depressed than either those who spent very little time in solitude or those who spent a great deal of their time alone. Teenagers who spent a moderate amount of time alone also had better grades than the other students. These findings also make it clear that although some time alone has positive benefits, more solitude is not necessarily better. Teenagers who spend an excessive amount of time away from others may fail to accrue some of the benefits that come from social contact.

For some, the benefits of solitude may be found in extended periods of isolation. Long periods of solitude—days or perhaps even weeks alone—can provide the opportunity to develop oneself spiritually, intellectually, and creatively. One psychologist found examples of several influential people whose contributions could be traced back to an extended period of isolation and introspection (Storr, 1988). The works of several famous writers, such as Beatrix Potter and Rudyard Kipling, were the result of inspiration that evolved during extended solitude. Similarly, many religious leaders, including Jesus and Buddha, are said to have come to their insights during extended periods alone (Storr, 1988). Even psychologists have been known to take advantage of extended solitude. You may recall from Chapter 5 that Carl Jung deliberately isolated himself for the better part of 7 years while he explored the contents of his own unconscious. Isolation from others can also be used during psychotherapy (Suedfeld, 1980, 1982). Volunteers who go through extended periods of social isolation and sensory restriction often describe the experience as pleasant and rewarding.

Individual Differences in Preference for Solitude

It seems clear that spending time alone can have both positive and negative consequences. Solitude can be boring and lonely, or it can bring insight and a sense of restoration. Whether people dislike or enjoy their time alone may be a function of their *preference for solitude*. As with other personality variables, researchers find people exhibit relatively stable patterns in the extent to which they seek out and enjoy time by themselves (Burger, 1995; Cramer & Lake, 1998; Haans, Kaiser, & de Kort, 2007; Larson & Lee, 1996; Pedersen, 1999). On one end of this individual difference dimension, we have people who avoid solitude whenever possible and who are eaten up by loneliness and sadness when forced to spend even a few hours by themselves. People on the other end of this dimension are more likely to resemble the self-actualized individuals Maslow described. They appreciate the benefits that come from solitude and probably arrange their days so they have at least a little time to themselves to collect their thoughts and reflect on matters that concern them.

In one demonstration of these individual differences, college students were asked to complete daily reports of their activities for 7 consecutive days

Assessing Your Own Personality

Preference for Solitude

For each of the following pairs of statements, select the one that best describes you. In some cases neither statement may describe you well or both may describe you somewhat. In those cases, please select the statement that best describes you or that describes you more often.

1. a. I enjoy being around people.
   b. I enjoy being by myself.

2. a. I try to structure my day so that I always have some time to myself.
   b. I try to structure my day so that I always am doing something with someone.

3. a. One feature I look for in a job is the opportunity to interact with interesting people.
   b. One feature I look for in a job is the opportunity to spend time by myself.

4. a. After spending a few hours surrounded by a lot of people, I usually find myself stimulated and energetic.
   b. After spending a few hours surrounded by a lot of people, I am usually eager to get away by myself.

5. a. Time spent alone is often productive for me.
   b. Time spent alone is often time wasted for me.

6. a. I often have a strong desire to get away by myself.
   b. I rarely have a strong desire to get away by myself.

7. a. I like to vacation in places where there are a lot of people around and a lot of activities going on.
   b. I like to vacation in places where there are few people around and a lot of serenity and quiet.

8. a. When I have to spend several hours alone, I find the time boring and unpleasant.
   b. When I have to spend several hours alone, I find the time productive and pleasant.

9. a. If I were to take a several-hour plane trip, I would like to sit next to someone who was pleasant to talk with.
   b. If I were to take a several-hour plane trip, I would like to spend the time quietly.

10. a. Time spent with other people is often boring and uninteresting.
    b. Time spent alone is often boring and uninteresting.

11. a. I have a strong need to be around other people.
    b. I do not have a strong need to be around other people.

(continues)

12. a. There are many times when I just have to get away and be by myself.
    b. There are rarely times when I just have to get away and be by myself.

To score, give yourself one point for each match: 1 – B, 2 – A, 3 – B, 4 – B, 5 – A, 6 – A, 7 – B, 8 – B, 9 – B, 10 – A, 11 – B, 12 – A. The higher your score, the more you prefer to experience solitude in a positive way. Here are some norms for undergraduate students:

	Mean	Standard Deviation
Women	4.52	2.61
Men	5.37	2.45
Total	4.87	2.57

Scale: The Preference for Solitude Scale
Source: Burger (1995)

(Burger, 1995). Students filled out a 24-hour report sheet indicating what they had done each hour of the day, whether they had been alone or with others, and whether they had found the experience enjoyable. The researcher also measured students' preference for solitude. After eliminating time spent in class, at work, and sleeping, students with a high and low preference for solitude were compared for how they spent their free time. As shown in Table 12.3, virtually all the students spent most of their free time with other people. In other words, it is not the case that people who enjoy solitude are hermits who avoid contact with others. However, the students with a high preference for solitude did manage to find more time for solitude in their days than the typical student. Moreover, whereas almost all the students said their time with others was pleasant, the students with a high preference for solitude were significantly more likely to report that their time alone was enjoyable.

In short, people with a high preference for solitude do not avoid social encounters and, in fact, enjoy their time with others quite a lot. Moreover,

TABLE 12.3 Free Time Spent by Students with High and Low Preference for Solitude

	Preference for Solitude	
	High	Low
Percentage of time spent alone	19.80	11.00
Percentage of time alone rated as pleasant	74.50	55.80
Percentage of time with others rated as pleasant	87.30	92.90

Source: From Burger (1995).

TABLE 12.4 Seven Positive Aspects of Solitude

Problem Solving	Opportunity to think about specific problems or decisions you are facing
Inner Peace	Feel calm and relaxed, away from the pressures of everyday life
Self-Discovery	Gain insight into your fundamental values and goals, come to realize your unique strengths and weaknesses
Creativity	Stimulates novel ideas or innovative ways of expressing yourself
Anonymity	Act in whatever ways you feel like at the moment, without concern for social niceties or what others might think
Intimacy	Although alone, you feel especially close to someone you care about
Spirituality	A sense of transcending everyday concerns, of being a part of something grander than yourself

Source: From Long et al. (2003).

people who enjoy time alone are not simply seeking an escape from social anxiety (Leary, Herbst, & McCrary, 2003). Rather, these individuals find something positive in being by themselves. What are these positive features of solitude? Undergraduate students in one study rated the importance of seven positive aspects of solitude they sometimes experience when by themselves (Long, Seburn, Averill, & More, 2003). As shown in Table 12.4, the list runs from solving problems to a spiritual experience. These findings are consistent with Maslow's observations of psychologically healthy people. Not only are a preference for solitude and well-being compatible, they may actually go hand in hand.

Summary

1. Although humanistic psychologists sometimes shun empirical studies, research on topics introduced or promoted by these psychologists has provided insight into some important aspects of humanistic personality theory.

2. Research on self-disclosure finds that people follow social rules concerning when and how to reveal information about themselves. Foremost among these is the rule of disclosure reciprocity. People in a get-acquainted situation tend to match the intimacy level of their conversation partner. However, friends who have already shared intimate information in a reciprocal manner need not always return to this pattern. Other studies find that men and women are restricted in what they disclose by what society deems appropriate. Holding traumatic secrets inside may take its toll on a person's health.

3. Loneliness is not the same as isolation. Researchers define loneliness as a discrepancy between the amount and quality of social contact we desire

and the amount and quality we receive. Although loneliness is influenced by social situations, people tend to suffer from loneliness at a fairly stable level. Research on chronically lonely people indicates they approach conversations with negative expectations and lack some basic social skills. Because of this tendency, they inadvertently stifle social interactions and discourage potential friends.

4. High and low self-esteem people react differently to failure. Low self-esteem people become discouraged and unmotivated when they receive negative feedback, whereas high self-esteem people employ tactics to blunt the effects of failure. Studies suggest that people base their self-esteem on how they perform in selected domains. Although people typically use areas in which they excel for their contingencies of self-worth, some individuals select contingencies that make it difficult for them to feel good about themselves. Research indicates that notions about the self and self-esteem taken from individualistic cultures may not apply to collectivist cultures.

5. Maslow observed that virtually all of his psychologically healthy people reported a high preference for solitude. Subsequent research finds that most people spend a large percentage of their time in solitude. Although some people typically find this time unpleasant, others seek out and enjoy their time alone. Researchers find that people differ in the extent to which they prefer solitude. People with a high preference for solitude enjoy their time alone but also enjoy time spent with others.

Key Terms

contingencies of self-worth (p. 330)

self-disclosure (p. 310)

self-esteem (p. 326)

Media Resources

Visit the book companion website at **www.cengagebrain.com** to find a glossary, flashcards, quizzing, and more.

CHAPTER 13

The Behavioral/ Social Learning Approach

Theory, Application, and Assessment

What do the following scenes have in common? A hospital patient suffering from depression makes her bed in the morning, dresses herself, and shows up to breakfast on time. A staff member hands the patient three tokens she can exchange for treats at the snack bar for completing these three acts. A middle-aged man attends a workshop to overcome a fear of snakes. He watches another middle-aged man, who shows no outward signs of fear, pick up a snake. A college student declines her friends' request to join them at a party. She knows people will be smoking there and is trying to break her habit.

In each of these scenes, someone is attempting to modify behavior by applying basic principles of learning. Psychologists have studied how people and animals learn for almost as long as there have been psychologists. The list of topics examined from the behaviorist's perspective includes attitude change, language acquisition, psychotherapy, student–teacher interactions, problem solving, gender roles, and job satisfaction. Naturally, such a far-reaching approach to the understanding of human behavior also provides a model for explaining why people engage in consistent behavior patterns—that is, a model for personality.

Behavioral accounts of personality have gone through a slow but steady transition over the years. Early behaviorists limited their descriptions to observable behaviors. Later, social learning theorists expanded the scope of their approach to include nonobservable concepts like thoughts, values, expectancies, and individual perceptions. Social learning psychologists also recognized that people can learn simply by watching someone else or even hearing about another person's behavior. More recently, many behavioral psychologists have moved toward invoking more cognitive explanations of behavior, so that today the line between behavioral and cognitive approaches to personality is sometimes blurred. It is not uncommon these days for counselors to refer to themselves as "cognitive-behavioral" therapists. Nonetheless, both traditional behaviorism—presented next—and the cognitive approaches to personality described in later chapters have a lot to tell us about the causes of personality and avenues for behavior change.

Behaviorism

In 1913 a young and brash psychologist named John B. Watson published an article titled "Psychology as the Behaviorist Views It." This article signaled the beginning of a new movement in psychology called *behaviorism*. By 1924, with the publication of his book *Behaviorism*, Watson had made significant progress in his effort to redefine the discipline. He argued that if psychology were to be a science, psychologists must stop examining mental states. Researchers who concerned themselves with consciousness, the mind, and thoughts were not engaging in legitimate scientific study. Only the observable was reasonable subject matter for a science. Because our subjective inner feelings cannot be observed or measured in an agreed-upon, accurate manner, they have no place in an objective science. The sooner psychology abandons these topics, Watson maintained, the sooner it can become a respectable member of the scientific community.

John B. Watson

1878–1958

Underwood & Underwood/Historical/Corbis

As a child growing up in Greenville, South Carolina, John Broadus Watson exhibited two characteristics that would later come to shape his career—he was a fighter, and he was a builder. He once wrote that his favorite activity in elementary school was fighting with classmates "until one or the other drew blood." But by age 12 he had also become something of a master carpenter. Later, during his first few years as a psychology professor, he built his own 10-room house virtually by himself.

Watson's lack of enthusiasm for contemporary standards also surfaced early. In grammar school, "I was lazy, somewhat insubordinate, and, so far as I know, I never made

above a passing grade." He also found that "little of my college life interested me. ... I was unsocial and had few close friends" (1936, p. 271). Watson bragged about being the only student to pass the Greek exam his senior year at Furman University. His secret was to cram the entire day before the test, powered only by a quart of Coca-Cola. "Today," he reported years later, "... I couldn't to save my life write the Greek alphabet or conjugate a verb" (1936, p. 272).

Watson began his doctoral work in philosophy at the University of Chicago (in part because Princeton required a reading knowledge of Greek). He soon switched to psychology, where, unlike his classmates, he preferred working with rats instead of humans. "Can't I find out by watching their behavior," he asked, "everything the other students are finding out?" (1936, p. 276).

Watson joined the faculty at Johns Hopkins University in 1908, where he began his quest to replace the psychology of the day with his new behavioral approach. His views received a surprisingly warm welcome from many scholars and academics, and in 1912 he was invited to give a series of public

lectures on his theory at Columbia University. He published an influential paper, "Psychology as the Behaviorist Views It," in 1913 and his first book in 1914. Soon behaviorism swept over the discipline. Watson was elected president of the American Psychological Association in 1915. Watson the fighter had taken on contemporary psychology and won, whereas Watson the builder had constructed an approach to understanding human behavior that would change the discipline for decades to come.

But his academic career was cut short in 1920. Watson suddenly divorced his wife of 17 years and married Rosalie Rayner, the research assistant with whom he had conducted the Little Albert experiments. The scandal that surrounded these actions forced Watson out of an intolerant Johns Hopkins and into the business world, where he eventually settled into a successful career in advertising. After writing a few popular articles and a book in 1925, Watson severed his ties with psychology while still in his late 40s. Several decades later, the foundation he built for the behavioral approach to personality still stands.

What, then, was the appropriate subject matter for psychology? Watson's answer was *overt* behavior—that which can be observed, predicted, and eventually controlled by scientists. We should appreciate just how much of psychology Watson was ready to jettison in his quest. Emotions, thoughts, expectancies, values, reasoning, insight, the unconscious, and the like were of interest to behaviorists only if they could be defined in terms of observable behaviors. Thus, according to Watson, thinking was simply a variant of verbal behavior, a "subvocal speech," as evidenced by the small vocal-cord movements he claimed accompanied it.

At about the same time, other researchers were beginning to study the basic processes of conditioning, or learning. Watson embraced these principles as the key to understanding human behavior. Like Watson, these researchers focused their efforts on predicting overt behaviors without introducing inner mental states to explain their findings. The famous Russian physiologist Ivan Pavlov demonstrated that animals could be made to respond to stimuli in their environment by pairing these stimuli with events that already elicited a response. This process soon became known as *classical conditioning*. At the same time, other psychologists were exploring what today is known as *operant conditioning*. For example, Edward Thorndike found that animals were less likely to repeat behaviors that met with negative consequences than were animals given no punishment.

This work convinced Watson that a few key conditioning principles would suffice to explain almost any human behavior. Personality, according to Watson, was "the end product of our habit systems." In other words, over the course of our lives we are conditioned to respond to certain stimuli in more or less predictable ways. You might have been conditioned by parents and teachers to respond to challenges with increased effort. Someone else might have learned to give up or try something new. Because each of us has a unique history of experiences that shaped our characteristic responses to stimuli, each adult has a slightly different personality.

Watson had tremendous faith in the power of conditioning. His most outrageous claim, which he admitted went "beyond my facts," was that given enough control over the environment, psychologists could mold a child into whatever kind of adult they wanted. "Give me a dozen healthy infants, well formed, and my own specified world to bring them up in," he wrote. "I'll guarantee to take any one at random and train him to become any type of specialist I might select—doctor, lawyer, artist, merchant—chief, and yes, even beggar-man and thief" (1924/1970, p. 104). This he promised regardless of the child's inherited abilities, intelligence, or ancestry. Although somewhat frightening in its implications for controlling human behavior, this type of thinking found a receptive audience among Americans who believed in the tradition of equal opportunity for all regardless of background or social class.

Watson's legacy was extended by the career of another influential psychologist, B. F. Skinner. Skinner, who identified his particular brand of behaviorism as *radical behaviorism*, took a small step away from the more extreme position Watson advocated. He did not deny the existence of thoughts and inner experiences. Rather, Skinner challenged the extent to which we are able to observe the inner causes of our own behavior. Suppose you are typically uncomfortable at social events. As you prepare for a party one evening, you begin to feel nervous. It's going to be a big party, and you don't think you will know very many people. At the last minute, your anxiety becomes intense and you decide to stay home. Why did you skip the party? Most people would answer that they avoided the party because they felt anxious. But Skinner (1974) argued that behavior does not change *because* you feel anxious. Rather, in this example, the decision to skip the party and the anxiety are both conditioned reactions to the situation.

B. F. Skinner

1904–1990

Bettmann/CORBIS

When Burrhus Frederick Skinner was born in Susquehanna, Pennsylvania, his father, a lawyer, announced the birth in the local paper: "The town has a new law firm: Wm. A. Skinner & Son." But all of the father's efforts to shape his son into the legal profession failed. After growing up in a "warm and stable" home, Skinner went to Hamilton College to study English. He planned a career as a professional writer, not a lawyer. This ambition was reinforced the summer before his senior year when an instructor introduced Skinner to the poet Robert Frost. Frost asked to see some of Skinner's work. Skinner sent three short stories, and several months later he received a letter from Frost encouraging him to continue writing.

Skinner devoted the 2 years after his graduation to writing, first at home and later in Greenwich Village in New York. At the end of this time he realized he had produced nothing and was not likely to become a great novelist. "I was to remain interested in human behavior, but the literary method had failed me," he wrote. "I would turn to the scientific. The relevant science appeared to be psychology, though I had only the vaguest idea of what that meant" (1967, p. 395).

So Skinner went to Harvard to study psychology. He immersed himself in his studies, rising at 6 o'clock each morning to hit the books. After teaching at the University of Minnesota and Indiana University, Skinner returned to Harvard in 1948, where he remained the rest of his career. Literature's loss was psychology's gain. A survey of psychology historians taken just about the time of his death ranked Skinner as the most influential of all contemporary psychologists (Korn, Davis, & Davis, 1991).

Although his work in psychology earned him numerous professional awards and recognitions, Skinner never relinquished his interest in literature. In the 1940s, he returned to fiction, writing a novel, *Walden Two*, about a utopian society based on the principles of

reinforcement he had found in his laboratory experiments. "It was pretty obviously a venture in self-therapy," Skinner wrote, sounding more psychoanalytic than behavioristic. "I was struggling to reconcile two aspects of my own behavior represented by [the characters] Burris and Frazier" (1967, p. 403). As this statement suggests, Skinner was not always as anti-Freudian as he is often described. Indeed, early in his career, he developed what he described as a projective test based on vague sounds emitted by a phonograph and once sought out an opportunity to go through psychoanalysis himself (Overskeid, 2007).

Nonetheless, Skinner remained an adamant believer in the power of the environment and eventually became an unwavering critic of those who introduce nonobservable concepts to explain human behavior. "I do not believe that my life shows a type of personality à la Freud, an archetypal pattern à la Jung, or a schedule of development à la Erikson," Skinner wrote nearly 8 decades after his birth. "There have been a few abiding themes, but they can be traced to environmental sources rather than to traits of character. They became part of my life as I lived it; they were not there at the beginning to determine its course" (1983, p. 401).

In other words, when we introduce an inner cause like anxiety to explain our actions, we may think we have identified the cause of the behavior, but we are mistaken. When you say you began eating because you were hungry, you have only put a label on your behavior. You have not explained why you are eating. Similarly, saying that people behave the way

> *"If I am right about human behavior, an individual is only the way in which a species and a culture produce more of a species and a culture."*
>
> B. F. Skinner

they do because they are friendly or aggressive or introverted does not explain where these behaviors come from. Although radically different in many ways, Skinner's view is much like Freud's in one respect. Both maintained that people simply do not know the reason for many of their behaviors, although we often think we do.

Naturally, Skinner's theory and some of the implications derived from it are highly controversial. Skinner described happiness as "a by-product of operant reinforcement." The things that bring happiness are the ones that reinforce us. In his most controversial work, *Beyond Freedom and Dignity* (1971), Skinner argued that it is time we moved beyond the illusion of personal freedom and the so-called dignity we award ourselves for our actions. We don't freely choose to do something as the result of inner moral decisions. We simply respond to environmental demands. We attribute dignity to people for admirable behavior, but because behavior is under the control of external contingencies, dignity is also an illusion. If you rush into a burning building to save people, it is not because you are heroic or foolish but because you have a history of reinforcements and contingencies in similar situations.

Basic Principles of Conditioning

Traditional behaviorists explain the causes of behavior in terms of learning experiences, or conditioning. They do not deny the influence of genetics but downplay its importance relative to the power of conditioning. According to behaviorists, if we are to understand the processes that shape our personalities as well as develop procedures for changing problem behaviors, we must examine basic conditioning principles. It is convenient to divide conditioning into two categories: classical (or Pavlovian) conditioning and operant (or instrumental) conditioning.

Classical Conditioning

Classical conditioning begins with an existing stimulus-response (S-R) association. For example, some people cringe (response) whenever they see a spider (stimulus). Although you may not be aware of them, your behavior repertoire contains a large number of S-R associations. You might feel faint when you see blood, want to eat whenever you smell chocolate, or become nervous when you find yourself more than a few feet off the ground.

In his classic demonstration of conditioning, Pavlov used the S-R association of food and salivation. He presented hungry dogs in his laboratory with meat powder (stimulus), to which they would always salivate (response). Because this S-R association existed without any conditioning from Pavlov, we call the meat powder the *unconditioned stimulus* (UCS) and the salivation the *unconditioned response* (UCR). Then Pavlov paired the old, unconditioned stimulus with a new, conditioned stimulus (CS). Whenever he presented the meat powder to the dogs, he also sounded a bell. After several trials of presenting the meat powder and the bell together, Pavlov simply sounded the bell without the powder. What happened? As nearly every psychology student knows, the dogs began to salivate at the sound of the bell, even though no meat powder had been presented. The salivation had become the *conditioned response* (CR), part of a new S-R association (bell tone-salivation) in the dogs' behavioral repertoire.

The classical conditioning procedure is diagramed in Figure 13.1. Once the new S-R association is established, it can be used to condition still another S-R association. If you were to pair a green light with Pavlov's bell tone, after a while the dogs would start to salivate when the green light came on. This process of building one conditioned S-R association on another is called *second-order conditioning*.

Because the stimuli you experience are often inadvertently paired with other aspects of your environment, you are probably not aware of the many S-R associations that influence your behavior. Research suggests that our preferences in food, clothing, and even friends can be determined through this process. A friend of mine guesses that he enjoys country and western music because his father used to play it on Saturday, his favorite day of the week. Anxious participants in one study sat in a waiting room with a stranger (Riordan & Tedeschi, 1983). Although the two did not interact, participants reported unpleasant impressions of this other person. The researchers reasoned that the incidental pairing of the anxiety with the stranger created a negative association with that person.

However, researchers have also uncovered several limitations of classical conditioning. For a new S-R association to persist, the unconditioned and conditioned stimuli must be paired occasionally or otherwise reinforced. When Pavlov presented his conditioned dogs with just the bell tone, the dogs salivated less and less until finally the dogs failed to salivate to the tone at all. This gradual disappearance of the conditioned S-R association is called *extinction*. Moreover, two events presented together will not always produce an association (Rescorla, 1988). Certain stimuli are easily associable, but it may be impossible to create some S-R bonds through classical conditioning.

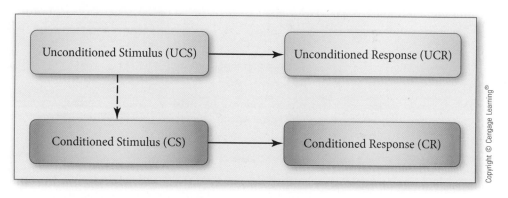

FIGURE 13.1 Classical Conditioning Diagram

Operant Conditioning

At about the time Pavlov was demonstrating classical conditioning in Russia; American psychologists were investigating another type of learning through association. Edward Thorndike put some stray cats into "puzzle boxes." To escape from the box and thereby obtain a piece of fish, hungry cats had to engage in a particular combination of actions. Before long, the cats learned what they had to do to receive their reward. These observations helped Thorndike (1911) formulate *the law of effect:* that behaviors are more likely to be repeated if they lead to satisfying consequences and less likely to be repeated if they lead to unsatisfying consequences. Thorndike's cats repeated the required behaviors because their actions led to the satisfying consequences of escape and food.

"Happiness is a ... by-product of operant reinforcement. The things which make us happy are the things which reinforce us."

B. F. SKINNER

At first glance Thorndike's observations hardly seem insightful. Do you know any parents who don't occasionally try rewards and punishments to mold their children's behavior? Teachers, judges, and employers also regularly rely on the connection between actions and consequences to shape behavior. But vague feelings that such a connection exists are not the same as understanding how this learning works or the most efficient and productive way to use it. Ask a group of parents the best way to deal with a problem child, and you will soon understand how little agreement there is among nonscientists on how to use rewards and punishments.

This poor understanding of basic learning principles is unfortunate, given the power of conditioning processes. It is especially tragic because several decades of research have provided psychologists with a relatively good understanding of how reinforcement and punishment shape and control behavior.

Much of what we know about the basic principles of conditioning was first demonstrated with laboratory animals. Here a researcher uses operant conditioning to teach a rat to press a bar. The rat receives positive reinforcement (a pellet of food) whenever it presses the bar.

Unlike classical conditioning, which begins with an existing S-R bond, operant conditioning begins with behaviors the organism (human or lower animal) emits spontaneously. We can observe these operant behaviors when a laboratory rat is placed in a new cage. The animal moves about, scratches, sniffs, and claws in a haphazard manner, for none of these responses have been reinforced or punished. However, if one of these behaviors is always followed by a pellet of food, its frequency will increase.

Operant conditioning concerns the effect certain kinds of consequences have on the frequency of behavior. A consequence that increases the frequency of a behavior that precedes it is called a *reinforcement,* one that decreases the behavior is called a *punishment.* Whether a consequence is reinforcing or punishing varies according to the person and the situation. If you are hungry, strawberry ice cream is probably a reinforcement. But if you don't like strawberry ice cream or if you are cold, the ice cream may serve as a punishment.

Psychologists have discovered two basic reinforcement strategies for increasing the frequency of a behavior (Table 13.1). With *positive reinforcement,* the behavior increases because it is followed by the presentation of a reward. Hungry rats that receive a pellet of food every time they press a bar will begin to press the bar frequently. Students who receive an A after dedicated studying for a test are likely to study hard for subsequent tests. We can also increase the frequency of a behavior by using *negative reinforcement,* the removal or lessening of an unpleasant stimulus when the behavior occurs. Rats that can turn off an electric shock by pulling a string will quickly learn to pull the string. People whose headaches go away when they take a few minutes to relax will soon learn to relax.

The other side of operant conditioning is the reduction of unwanted behaviors. As with the task of increasing desired behaviors, operant conditioning provides two methods for decreasing undesired behaviors. The most efficient method is to cease reinforcement and thereby allow the behavior to extinguish. Although this concept is simple enough, people often reinforce problem behaviors without realizing what they are doing. A teacher may react to a child who acts up in class by criticizing the child in front of the other students. The teacher may not realize that the attention the child gains from other students in the form of laughter and classroom status has turned the intended punishment into a reinforcement. An observant teacher might take disruptive children out into the hall for discipline, thereby removing the reinforcer.

TABLE 13.1 Operant Conditioning Procedures

Procedure	Purpose	Application
Positive reinforcement	Increase behavior	Give reward following behavior
Negative reinforcement	Increase behavior	Remove aversive stimulus following behavior
Extinction	Decrease behavior	Do not reward behavior
Punishment	Decrease behavior	Give aversive stimulus following behavior or take away positive stimulus

Alternatively, we can use *punishment* to eliminate unwanted behaviors. In theory, the frequency of a behavior is reduced when it is followed by an aversive stimulus, such as an electric shock, or the removal of a positive stimulus, such as taking away toys. The effects of punishment can be demonstrated in laboratory animals, and therapists have had some success applying this technique in special cases. But research shows the effectiveness of punishment is limited for several reasons.

First, punishment does not teach appropriate behaviors, it can only decrease the frequency of undesired ones. Rather than simply punish a child for hitting another student, it's better to help the child learn alternative ways to deal with frustrating situations. Second, to be effective, punishment must be delivered immediately and consistently. A parent needs to punish the problem behavior as soon as possible, not "when your father gets home." The punishment must also be fairly intense and should be administered after every instance of the undesired behavior. Parents who sometimes let their children use bad language but other times decide that to punish such talk will probably have little success in changing their children's vocabulary. Third, punishment can have negative side effects. Although parents or therapists intend to suppress a certain response, a child might associate other behaviors with the punishment. A child who is punished for hitting a toy against a window may stop playing with toys altogether. In addition, through classical conditioning, aversive feelings that accompany the punishment may be associated with the person doing the punishing. Children who are spanked by their parents may associate the parent with the pain of the spanking. Another side effect is that undesirable behaviors may be learned through modeling. Children who are spanked may learn that physical aggression is okay as long as you are bigger and stronger. Punishment can also create negative emotions, such as fear and anxiety, strong enough to interfere with learning appropriate responses. Taken together, these factors make punishment one of the least desirable choices for behavior therapists seeking to change problem behaviors. At most, punishment can temporarily suppress an undesirable response long enough for the therapist to begin reinforcing a desired behavior.

Shaping

Suppose you are hired to work with patients in a psychiatric hospital. Your job is to get reluctant patients more involved in some of the activities on the ward. You start with one patient who has never participated in any ward activities. Your goal is to get him into daily art therapy sessions, and positive reinforcement seems the right tool. Every time the patient joins one of the voluntary art sessions, you will reward him with coupons for free items in the hospital store. The patient skips art therapy the first day. So no reward. He skips art therapy the rest of the week. Still no reward. You wait 2 months, and still the patient has not attended one of the sessions. By now, one of the problems encountered when using operant conditioning is apparent to you: A behavior can be reinforced only after it is emitted.

Does this mean operant conditioning is useless in this situation? Fortunately, the answer is "No." A behavior therapist working with the reluctant patient might use a technique known as *shaping,* in which successive approximations of the desired behavior are reinforced. For example, you might reward the withdrawn patient for getting out of bed and sitting among the other patients. Once this behavior is established, you might reinforce him only when he is near or in the art therapy room. From here, rewards might be limited to time spent in the room during the sessions and later to time spent attending to and participating in the sessions. Shaping is particularly useful when teaching complex behaviors. Children will learn to enjoy reading if each step along the way is reinforced. If learning the alphabet, letter sounds, and short words is unpleasant, it will be difficult to get the child to move on to reading sentences and stories.

Generalization and Discrimination

Operant conditioning would be rather limited if every situation required that we learn a new response. Fortunately, because of **generalization,** this is not the case. Pigeons trained to peck at large red circles to receive food will also peck at small orange circles, although not as frequently. This process, called *stimulus generalization,* helps explain why personality characteristics generalize across situations. A child rewarded for acting politely around relatives will probably act politely around new acquaintances. The polite response has been generalized from the stimulus of the relative to the new stimulus, the stranger. When we observe polite behavior consistently across situations, we say this pattern is part of the child's personality.

As long as the generalized response is met with reinforcement, the behavior is likely to continue. But if the pigeon is not rewarded for pecking at orange circles, it will soon learn to **discriminate** between rewarded and nonrewarded stimuli and will peck only at the red ones. Similarly, the polite child may come in contact with adults who respond to friendly behavior with harshness. Soon the child will learn to discriminate between people who are friendly and people who aren't. The difference between a good and a great tennis player or between a second-string baseball player and a star may be the ability to make fine discriminations between those actions that lead to a reinforcement (a winning shot or a home run) and those that do not.

Social Learning Theory

It is difficult to overstate the impact traditional behaviorism had on psychology and subsequently on the field of personality. Watson and his followers provided a scientific, easily testable account of human behavior that complemented the growing empirical flavor of psychology in American universities. The basic principles of learning were so universal they could be tested on lower animals. The image many people have of the lab-coated psychologist, pencil in hand, watching rats running through mazes comes from this era. But somewhere in the 1950s or 1960s the enthusiasm for traditional behaviorism began to wane. Psychologists questioned the assertion that all human learning is the result of classical or operant conditioning. "The prospects for survival would be slim indeed if one could learn only from the consequences of trial and error," one psychologist wrote. "One does not teach children to swim, adolescents to drive automobiles, and novice medical students to perform surgery by having them discover the requisite behavior from the consequences of their successes and failures" (Bandura, 1986, p. 20). Psychologists also began to question whether behaviorism was too limited in the scope of its subject matter. Why couldn't "internal" events like thoughts and attitudes be conditioned the same way as overt behaviors? For example, paranoid individuals who believe evil agents are out to get them might have been reinforced in the past for these beliefs. Thus began the transition from traditional behaviorism to a number of approaches known collectively as *social learning theory.*

One of the concepts introduced by social learning theorists is the notion of *behavior-environment-behavior interactions* (Staats, 1996). That is, not only does the environment influence our behavior, but that behavior then determines the kind of environment we find ourselves in, which can then influence behavior, and so on. The way people treat you (environment) is partly the result of how you act (behavior). And, of course, how you act is partly a result of how people treat you. Other social learning theorists point out that people often provide their own reinforcers. It is rewarding to live up to your internal standards or to reach a personal goal even if no one else knows about it.

Social learning psychologists also helped to bridge traditional behaviorism and cognitive approaches to personality (Chapter 15) by incorporating into their theories a number of concepts once deemed unscientific by John B. Watson. Among the most influential of these social learning theorists is Julian Rotter (1954, 1982; Rotter, Chance, & Phares, 1972). Rotter argues that the causes of human behaviors are far more complex than those of lower animals. He introduced several "unobservable" concepts to account for human behavior and personality.

To get an idea of Rotter's approach, imagine someone has just insulted you at a party. How do you respond? You have several courses of action to choose from. You might attempt to top the remark with something clever and witty. You could calmly say the behavior was out of line and ask for an apology. You could get angry and hurl an equally rude insult at the offender, or you could simply leave the scene. The key to predicting your response lies in what Rotter refers to as the *behavior potential* for each option. The behavior potential is the likelihood that a given behavior will occur in a particular situation. Each possible response to the insult has a different behavior potential. If you decide to scream out your own insult, it means the behavior potential for that response was stronger than for any of the other possible responses. But what determines the strength of the behavior potential? According to Rotter, two variables need to be considered: expectancy and reinforcement value (Figure 13.2).

Before you decide to stay up all night studying for an exam, you probably ask yourself what the likelihood is that the all-nighter will help you do better on the test. Similarly, when debating whether to join a softball game, you try to figure out the probability that you will have a good time. Rotter referred to these estimations as *expectancies,* and whether you study all

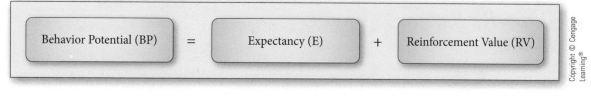

FIGURE 13.2 Rotter's Basic Formula for Predicting Behavior

night or play softball is determined by what you expect to happen. Of course, we base our expectancies largely on how things turned out other times we were in this situation. If you always do well after studying all night, you will develop an expectancy of receiving the reward again. If you never enjoy yourself playing softball, the expectancy of being rewarded for playing again is slim.

Of course, traditional behaviorists would make these same predictions. People are more likely to engage in a behavior when it has been reinforced. But Rotter and the behaviorists disagree on how to explain the behavior. Behaviorists say that an operant conditioning association or habit has been strengthened by the earlier experience. However, Rotter argues that the more often people are reinforced for a certain behavior (for example, studying all night and receiving an A), the stronger their expectancy that the behavior will be reinforced in the future. Of course, expectancies are not necessarily accurate. You might expect that studying for your Scholastic Assessment Test (SAT) will result in a higher score, even if in reality the studying has little effect. In this case, your expectancy will probably predict your behavior better than the actual contingencies.

But what about situations we encounter for the first time? In these situations we rely on *generalized expectancies*—beliefs we hold about how often our actions typically lead to reinforcements and punishments. According to Rotter (1966), each of us can be placed along a continuum called *locus of control*. At one end of this dimension we find individuals with an extreme *internal* orientation—those who believe that most of what happens to them is the result of their own actions or attributes. On the other end we find people who hold an extreme *external* orientation—those who maintain that much of what happens to them is the result of forces outside their control, such as chance or powerful others. As we will see in the next chapter, where we fall on this dimension has important implications in such areas as achievement and health.

The second component in Rotter's model is *reinforcement value*, the degree to which we prefer one reinforcer over another. Naturally, the reinforcement value we assign a certain outcome can vary from situation to situation. When we are lonely, social contact holds a higher reinforcement value than when we aren't. Yet each of us also has reinforcers we almost always value more than others. Some people consistently work hard, placing their job ahead of family and recreation. We might call these people obsessive or driven. But using Rotter's model, their personalities can be explained in terms of the consistently high value they put on achievement.

Julian B. Rotter

1916–2014

University of Connecticut

Julian Rotter first learned about psychology in the Avenue J Library in Brooklyn, where he spent a great deal of his grade school and high school years. One day, after exhausting most of the books in other sections of the library, he wandered over to the Philosophy and Psychology shelf. Among the first books he encountered were Alfred Adler's *Understanding Human Nature* and Sigmund Freud's

Psychopathology of Everyday Life. From that point on, he was hooked. But for a time his love of psychology took a backseat to the realities of the world. He decided to major in chemistry at Brooklyn College because "there was no profession of psychology that I knew of. And in 1933, in the depths of the Great Depression, one majored in a subject one could use to make a living" (1982, p. 343).

But circumstances soon intervened. One day during his junior year, Rotter discovered that Alfred Adler was teaching at the Long Island School of Medicine. Rotter began attending the lectures. Eventually, Adler invited Rotter to attend the monthly meetings of the Society of Individual Psychology held in Adler's home.

Unfortunately, Adler died the next year. Nonetheless, by then Rotter's enthusiasm for psychology dictated that he go to graduate

school. He chose the University of Iowa so that he could study with the famous Gestalt psychologist Kurt Lewin. He went to the University of Indiana for his PhD because it was one of the few schools at the time to offer a degree in clinical psychology. He wanted an academic position, but few were available when Rotter graduated in 1941. After working in a hospital for a year, Rotter served as a psychologist in the Army and later the Air Force during World War II.

Circumstances altered Rotter's career path again following the war. The need for clinical psychologists was suddenly high, but their numbers were few. Rotter took a position at Ohio State University, finally fulfilling his ambition to be a professional academic psychologist. He stayed there until 1963, when he moved to the University of Connecticut.

Social-Cognitive Theory

The evolution from traditional behavioral views of personality to more cognitive approaches is probably best illustrated by the work of Albert Bandura (1977a, 1986, 2001, 2006). Bandura rejects the behaviorist's depiction of human beings as passive recipients of whatever stimuli life throws their way. Certainly individuals respond to environmental events, and certainly they often learn characteristic behaviors as the result of rewards and punishments. But people possess other capacities that are distinctly human. By reducing the process through which people grow and change to the way a rat learns to press a bar, strict behaviorists overlook some of the most important causes of human behavior. Because these overlooked causes generally involve thinking and symbolic processing of information, Bandura refers to his approach as a *social-cognitive theory*.

Reciprocal Determinism

Bandura adds a new twist to the question of whether behavior is determined by internal or by external forces. He argues that there are both internal and external determinants of behavior, but behavior is not determined exclusively by either or by a simple combination. Bandura introduces instead the concept **reciprocal determinism.** That is, external determinants of behavior, such as rewards and punishments, and internal determinants, such as beliefs, thoughts, and expectations, are part of a system of interacting influences that affect not only behavior but the various parts of the system as well. Put more simply, each part of the system—behaviors, external factors, and internal factors—influences each of the other parts.

Some examples will help clarify the concept. Like Rotter, Bandura maintains that internal factors, such as our expectancies, affect our behavior. Suppose someone you don't like much asks you to play racquetball. You can just imagine what a dismal afternoon you would have with this person. Thus your internal expectation will probably cause you to reject the invitation. But what would happen if this person offered to buy you that new, expensive racket you've been eyeing if you play with him? Suddenly the external inducement is powerful enough to determine your behavior, and you say, "Let's play." Now imagine further that you have one of the most enjoyable sets of racquetball ever. You're evenly matched with this person, and he even cracks a few jokes to make the afternoon fun. You actually look forward to playing with him again. The behavior in this case has changed your expectations, which will affect future behavior and so on.

The reciprocal determinism process is diagrammed in Figure 13.3. You may notice that the arrows point in both directions, indicating that each of the three variables in the model is capable of influencing each of the other variables. This situation is very different from traditional behaviorism, which limits explanations of human behavior to a two-factor, one-way model in which external events cause behavior.

How can we predict which of the three parts in the reciprocal determinism model is going to influence which other part? That depends on the

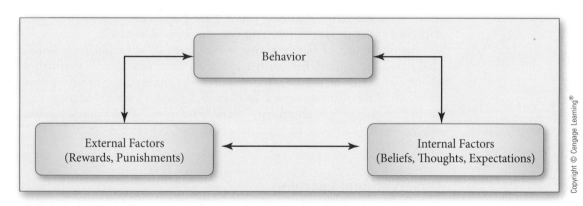

FIGURE 13.3 Bandura's Reciprocal Determinism Model

strength of each of the variables. At times, environmental forces are most powerful; at other times, internal forces dominate. The example used in Chapter 7 of both high and low self-esteem people fleeing a burning building illustrates how environmental factors can override internal individual factors on occasion. Though at times we mold our environment to meet our needs, at other times we are faced with environmental factors we cannot control. We often create our own opportunities and defeats, but they can also be created for us.

Imagination and Self-Regulation

Bandura identifies several features unique to humans that must be considered to understand personality. Unlike lower animals, people use symbols and forethought as guides for future action. Instead of working our way through rewards and punishments in a trial-and-error fashion every time we face a new problem, we imagine possible outcomes, calculate probabilities, set goals, and develop strategies. We do all of this in our mind without engaging in random actions and waiting to see which will be rewarded or punished. Of course, past experiences with reinforcements or punishments affect these judgments. But think about the way you prepare for a vacation. Most likely you think about several options of where and when to go, how to get there, who to go with, what to bring, what to do when you arrive, and so on. By imagining what a vacation will be like at various locations and with various people, you don't have to literally try out each option to see if the experience will be reinforcing or punishing.

Bandura also argues that most behavior is performed in the absence of external reinforcements and punishments. Our daily actions are largely controlled by what he calls **self-regulation**. Although we often strive to obtain external rewards, we also work toward self-imposed goals with internal rewards. Amateur runners push themselves in races, even though few expect to win. The reward comes from the feelings of accomplishment and self-worth they get from setting a personal record or perhaps for just finishing the race. Of course, self-regulation also includes self-punishment. When we fail to maintain personal standards, we often degrade and feel bad about ourselves. You may have chastised yourself for being rude to a stranger or not sticking to your diet, even when no one else seemed to notice.

Because much of our behavior is the result of self-regulation, Bandura challenges the radical behaviorist assertion that people will perform just about any action if the environmental contingencies are altered appropriately. "Anyone who attempted to change a pacifist into an aggressor or a devout religionist into an atheist," Bandura wrote, "would quickly come to appreciate the existence of personal sources of behavioral control" (1977a, pp. 128–129).

Observational Learning

Perhaps social-cognitive theory's most important contribution to the understanding of human behavior and personality is the concept of *vicarious* or

Albert Bandura

1925–

Linda A. Cicero/Stanford News Service

Albert Bandura was born in Mundare, a small farming community located among the wheat fields of Alberta, Canada. His parents had emigrated from Eastern Europe when they were teenagers. They had no formal schooling themselves, but communicated to their son the high value they placed on education.

Bandura attended the only school in the area, a combined elementary and high school with a total of about 20 students and two teachers. Summer jobs included filling in holes in the highways of the Yukon. He stayed in Canada for his undergraduate education, receiving a bachelor's degree from the University of British Columbia in 1949. He had intended to major in a biological science, but he became enamored with psychology after enrolling in an introductory course one term simply because the early-morning class fit his schedule.

Bandura chose the University of Iowa for graduate work, in part because of its strong tradition in learning theory. Among the Iowa faculty members who influenced Bandura was the learning theorist Kenneth Spence. The faculty at Iowa also emphasized the need for empirical research. This training left Bandura with the conviction that psychologists should "conceptualize clinical phenomena in ways that would make them amenable to experimental tests" (as cited in Evans, 1976, p. 243). He received his PhD in 1952.

After a year of clinical internship in Wichita, Bandura accepted a position at Stanford University in 1953 and has remained there ever since. While at Stanford, he has continued to build bridges between traditional learning theory and cognitive personality theories and between clinical psychology and empirically oriented approaches to understanding personality. Bandura has received numerous professional honors, including election to the presidency of the American Psychological Association in 1974.

observational learning. In addition to classical and operant conditioning, we can learn by observing or reading or just hearing about other people's actions. Many behaviors are too complex to be learned through the slow process of reinforcement and punishment. We don't teach pilots to fly by putting them in the cockpit and reinforcing correct behaviors and punishing incorrect ones. Bandura maintains that children would never learn to talk during their preschool years if they had to be reinforced for every correct utterance. Instead, the pilots and the toddlers watch others fly and talk, noting which behaviors work and which don't.

Bandura draws an important distinction between *learning* and *performance*. Behaviors learned through observation need not be performed. This idea again clashes with traditional behaviorists, who maintain that we cannot learn something until we have actually engaged in that behavior. But think for a moment of some of the behaviors you could perform if you wanted to, even though you never have. For example, although you have probably never picked up a pistol and shot another human being, you've observed this behavior in movies often enough for it to be part of your behavioral repertoire. You might even know to stand with your feet apart and to hold the weapon at eye level with both hands in front of you, just like the actors portraying police do. Fortunately, most of us will never perform this behavior, but it is one we have probably learned through observation.

Why do we perform some of the behaviors we learn through observation but not others? The answer lies in our expectations about the consequences. That is, do you believe the action will be rewarded or punished? In the case of shooting another person, most of us expect this behavior will be punished—if not in a legal sense, then through self-punishment in the form of guilt and lowered feelings of worth.

But if we have never performed the behavior, where do we get our expectations about consequences? Again, from observing others. Specifically, was your model for the behavior rewarded or punished? For example, a high school boy may watch an older friend ask someone for a date. He pays close attention to how the friend engages the potential date in conversation, what is said, and so on. If the friend's behavior is rewarded (a date is made), the boy may believe that he, too, will be rewarded if he acts just like his friend. Most likely, he'll soon get his courage up and ask out someone he's had his eye on for a while. And if the older friend is turned down? It's unlikely the boy will imitate the punished behavior. In both cases, the boy paid close enough attention to *learn* how his friend went about asking for a date. But whether he will *perform* the behavior depends on what he thinks will happen.

Bandura (1965) demonstrated this learning-performance distinction in a classic experiment with important social implications. Nursery school children watched a television program in which an adult model performed four novel aggressive acts on an adult-size plastic Bobo doll:

> First, the model laid the Bobo doll on its side, sat on it, and punched it in the nose while remarking, "Pow, right in the nose, boom, boom." The model then raised the doll and pommeled it on the head with a mallet. Each response was accompanied by the verbalization, "Sockeroo ... stay down." Following the mallet aggression, the model kicked the doll about the room, and these responses were interspersed with the comment, "Fly away." Finally, the model threw rubber balls at the Bobo doll, each strike punctuated with "Bang." (pp. 590–591)

The children saw one of three endings to the film. Some saw a second adult reward the aggressive model with soft drinks, candy, and lots of praise. Others saw the model spanked with a rolled-up magazine and warned not to act aggressively again. A third group was given no information about the consequences of the aggressive behavior. Next, each child was left alone for 10 minutes of free playing time. Among the many toys in the room were a Bobo doll and all the materials needed to perform the aggressive acts they had seen. An experimenter watched through a one-way window to see how many of the four acts of aggression the children would perform spontaneously. Each child was then offered fruit juice and small toys for each of the four aggressive acts he or she could perform for the experimenter. This last step was included to see if the children *could* perform the behavior—that is, had they learned the responses from watching the model?

The results are shown in Figure 13.4. Nearly all the children in all three groups could perform the behaviors when asked. However, whether they

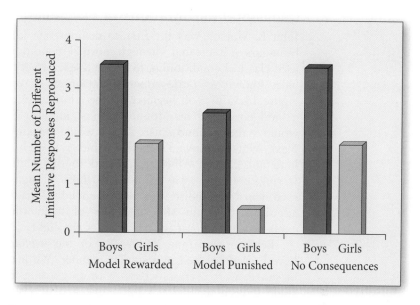

FIGURE 13.4 Mean Number of Aggressive Responses Performed

Source: From "Influence of models' reinforcement contingencies on the acquisition of imitative responses," by A. Bandura, *Journal of Personality and Social Psychology,* 1965, 1, 589–595.

chose to perform the behavior when left alone depended on the consequences they expected. Although all of the children had learned how to act aggressively, the ones who had seen the model rewarded were significantly more likely to perform the behaviors than those who had seen the model punished.

Application: Conditioning Principles and Self-Efficacy in Psychotherapy

One of the appeals of traditional behaviorism is its presentation of a simple, rational model of human nature. Looking at the world through a behaviorist's eyes, everything makes sense. Employees work hard when they are reinforced properly. Children stop fighting when aggressive behavior is punished and working together is reinforced. But what about some of the seemingly irrational behaviors we see in people suffering from psychological disorders? How can basic conditioning principles explain a fear of stairs or a belief that people are out to get you? As we will see next, not only can behaviorists account for these and other abnormal behaviors, but some of the therapeutic techniques designed to overcome these problems are based on basic conditioning principles. Concepts from social learning theory and social-cognitive theory also have been employed by psychotherapists. In particular, Bandura's notion of self-efficacy has been used to help people suffering from a wide variety of problems.

Behavioral Explanations of Psychological Disorders

John B. Watson was the first to demonstrate how seemingly "abnormal" behaviors are created through normal conditioning procedures. Watson used classical conditioning to create a fear of white rats in an 11-month-old baby known as Little Albert (Watson & Rayner, 1920). As shown in Figure 13.5, Watson began with the stimulus-response association between a loud noise and fear found in most infants. That is, whenever Watson would make the loud noise, Albert would cry and show other signs of fear. Next, Watson showed Albert a white rat, each time accompanied by the loud noise. Soon Albert responded to the white rat with fear responses (crying, crawling away) similar to those he had made to the loud noise, even when the noise was not sounded. Watson's point was that what appeared to be an abnormal fear of white rats in an infant could be explained by the past conditioning of the child.

Behaviorists argue that many of our seemingly irrational fears may have been developed in a similar manner. We may not recall when bridges or snakes were ever associated with an existing fear, but these associations could have taken place a long time ago or even without our awareness. However, there is a problem with this explanation. As Pavlov discovered, new associations formed through classical conditioning tend to extinguish once the pairing is removed. Why, then, do phobias not just become extinct on their own without psychological intervention? One answer is that operant conditioning may take over. Imagine a 3-year-old girl who falls off a tall slide. The pain and fear she experiences are paired with the slide, and those feelings re-emerge the next time she approaches the playground. Her anxiety increases as she gets closer and closer to the slide. Quite likely, she'll decide to turn away and try the slide some other time, thereby reducing the anxiety. What has happened in this situation is that the act of avoiding the slide has been reinforced through negative reinforcement. Running away was followed by a reduction in the aversive stimulus, the feelings of fear and anxiety. If this avoidance behavior is reinforced a few more

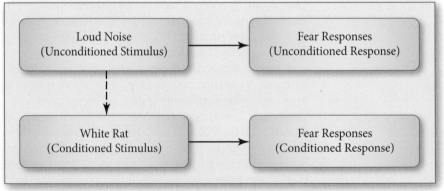

FIGURE 13.5 Diagram of Little Albert's Classical Conditioning

times, the girl could develop a strong fear of slides. The fear might then be generalized to a fear of all high places, and years later the woman may seek therapy for this debilitating phobia.

Psychologists also use conditioning principles to explain why some people develop fears after a traumatic experience whereas others do not (Mineka & Zinbarg, 2006). Sometimes previous learning can protect us from developing phobias. A boy who has had many pleasant experiences with dogs is not likely to develop a fear of the animal when one untrained dog snarls at and bites him. One study found children who had many uneventful trips to the dentist were less likely than new patients to develop a fear of dentists after one painful visit (Kent, 1997). On the other hand, a learning history with several small fearful experiences can make a person more vulnerable to developing a phobia when a very traumatic experience occurs (Mineka & Zinbarg, 2006). A girl who has been frightened several times by loud and splashing children at the local pool is especially vulnerable to developing a fear of water after a near-drowning experience.

Behaviorists explain other problem behaviors in terms of reinforcing the wrong behavior. A socially anxious girl may have found the only escape from the criticism and ridicule she received at home was to avoid family contact as much as possible (negative reinforcement), a behavior she then generalized to other people. A man suffering from paranoid delusions may believe he has thwarted a plan to kidnap him by staying in his house all day, thereby rewarding the behavior. Behavior theorists also point out that a lack of appropriate behaviors is often the result of too little reinforcement. For example, if the socially anxious woman's efforts to initiate conversations with others are never rewarded, she'll probably stop trying.

Conditioning Principles

If we accept that problem behavior is sometimes the result of unusual conditioning experiences, then it may be possible to treat the problem by using more appropriate conditioning. Several therapy procedures based on basic conditioning principles have been developed. These procedures differ from more traditional therapies in several respects. The treatment usually lasts for several weeks, as compared to perhaps years. The focus is on changing a few well-defined behaviors rather than changing the entire personality of the client. And therapists using these procedures are often unconcerned with discovering where the problem behavior originated. Their goal is simply to remove it or replace it with a more appropriate set of responses.

Classical Conditioning Applications

Pairing one stimulus with another is a powerful tool for creating new stimulus-response associations. Therapists often use classical conditioning to eliminate or replace stimulus-response associations that cause clients problems. Although these techniques traditionally use physical pairing of objects and reactions, psychologists also find that mental images can be classically conditioned (Dadds, Bovbjerg, Redd, & Cutmore, 1997). Thus, in the safety of a behavior therapist's office, clients can imagine themselves facing the situations they fear without actually visiting those places.

One treatment for phobias pairs images of the feared object with a relaxation response. Through *systematic desensitization* the old association between the feared stimulus and the fear response is replaced with a new association between the stimulus and relaxation. Clients and therapists begin the treatment by creating a list of imagined scenes ranging from mildly arousing to highly anxiety provoking. A man afraid of heights might begin his list with a scene of himself standing on a 2-foot-high footstool. The next scene might be walking up a flight of stairs, followed by a scene of him standing on an 8-foot ladder. Last on the hierarchy come the highly anxiety-provoking scenes, such as looking out from the top floor of a skyscraper or flying in a small airplane.

After clients complete relaxation training, they imagine the scenes while they practice relaxing. One step at a time, they slowly move through the list until they can imagine the scene without feeling anxious. In theory, the fear response is being replaced with a new, incompatible response—relaxation. If this therapy works, clients who used to be mildly anxious when thinking about standing on a 2-foot stool can imagine (and eventually perform) looking out over the city from the top of a tall building without experiencing fear.

Aversion therapy is another example of classical conditioning used to alter problem behaviors. Here therapists try to rid clients of undesirable behaviors by pairing aversive images with the behavior. For example, for a client trying to quit smoking, the image of a cigarette might be paired with images of becoming nauseated and vomiting.

Operant Conditioning Applications

Sometimes therapy can be as basic as reinforcing desired behaviors and punishing undesirable ones. However, this is more difficult than it may sound. Behavior therapists begin this type of treatment by identifying the target behavior and defining it in specific operational terms. For example, what would you reinforce or punish when a child's problem is "acting immature"? A behavior therapist would probably interview parents and teachers to determine which specific immature behaviors they wanted to reduce. Next, the therapist would want to determine a baseline of behavior frequency, because you cannot determine whether you are reducing the frequency of a behavior if you don't know how often it occurs before the treatment. Through observation or interviews, the therapist might find that a child throws an average of two and a half tantrums per week.

Once we know how often the behavior occurs under the current system of rewards and punishments, we change the contingencies. If it's a desired behavior, the environment is altered so the client is rewarded for it. If it's an undesired behavior, punishment is introduced or reinforcement is reduced. Ideally, appropriate responses are reinforced at the same time undesired behavior is extinguished or punished. In the case of the child throwing tantrums, parents might be told to stop rewarding the action with their attention and concern. In addition, punishments might be introduced, such as not allowing the child to watch television for 24 hours after a tantrum. At the same time, the child should be reinforced for handling frustrating situations in an appropriate way. The frequency of the target behavior should be monitored throughout the therapy. After a few weeks, the therapist can see whether the treatment is working or whether adjustments need to be made. If the child is down to one tantrum a week, the treatment will probably continue for a few more weeks until the tantrums disappear entirely. If they are still occurring two and a half times a week, a new therapy program may need to be developed.

Biofeedback is another type of operant conditioning used to treat psychological problems. Biofeedback requires special equipment that provides information about somatic processes. A woman suffering from anxiety might use a machine that tells her when she is tightening and relaxing certain facial and back muscles, a reaction she is otherwise not aware of. After several muscle relaxation sessions with the immediate feedback of the machine, she may learn to reduce tension on her own and thereby overcome her anxiety. In operant conditioning terms, the woman was reinforced for producing the response that lowered her muscle tension, as indicated by the machine. As with other reinforced behaviors, she soon learned to make the relaxation response.

One of the most common targets of biofeedback treatments is the tension headache. To reduce these headaches, psychologists use electromyography monitors to inform clients about muscle constriction that they otherwise might not be aware of. A review of studies using this procedure found it was highly effective in reducing the frequency, intensity, and duration of tension headaches (Nestoriuc, Rief, & Martin, 2008). Moreover, the procedure was relatively quick and efficient. Participants averaged fewer than 11 biofeedback sessions, and the improvements were seen in follow-up assessments 15 months later. Other bodily indicators that may be controlled through biofeedback include blood pressure, heart rate, and brain waves.

Self-Efficacy

Every year millions of Americans seek professional help to stop smoking or lose weight. Although many of these people go several weeks without cigarettes or succeed in dropping a few pounds, only a small percentage permanently end their habit or keep the lost pounds off. What is it about these few successful cases that separate them from the others? The answer may lie in what Bandura calls **self-efficacy**. People stop smoking and lose weight when they convince themselves they can do it. Many smokers complain that they have tried to quit many times but just can't. From a social-cognitive analysis, one reason these smokers are unable to kick their habit is precisely because they believe they cannot.

According to Bandura (1977b, 1997), people aren't likely to alter their behavior until they make a clear decision to expend the necessary effort. Bandura draws a distinction between outcome expectations and efficacy expectations. An *outcome expectation* is the extent to which people believe actions will lead to a certain outcome. An *efficacy expectation* is the extent to which people believe they can perform the actions that will bring about the particular outcome. Simply put, it is the difference between believing that something can happen and believing that you can make it happen. You may hold the outcome expectation that if you devote several hours to studying each night and abandon social life on weekends, you will get good grades this term. However, you may also hold the efficacy expectation that you are incapable of such devoted work and sacrifice.

Bandura argues that efficacy expectations are better predictors of behavior than outcome expectations. Students are unlikely to work hard for good grades if they don't think it possible. Therapy clients are unlikely to stop smoking, lose weight, or overcome a fear of flying if they don't believe they are capable of doing so.

Where do efficacy expectations come from, and how can therapists change these expectations in their clients? Bandura identifies four sources. The most important of these is *enactive mastery experiences*. These are successful attempts to achieve the outcome in the past. Sky divers suddenly struck with fear before a jump may tell themselves that they've done this many times before without incident and therefore can do it again. On the other hand, a history of failures can lead to low efficacy expectations. People with a fear of heights who have never been able to climb a ladder without coming back down in a fit of anxiety will probably conclude they can't perform this behavior.

Although not as powerful as actual performances, *vicarious experiences* also alter efficacy expectations. Seeing other people perform a behavior without adverse effects can lead us to believe that we can do it too. People who are afraid to speak in front of an audience may change their efficacy expectation from "I can't do that" to "maybe I can" after seeing other members of a public speaking class give their speeches without disastrous results. When you tell yourself something like "If she can do it, so can I," you are changing your efficacy expectation through vicarious experience.

A less effective way to alter efficacy expectations is through *verbal persuasion*. Telling someone who is reluctant to stand up to the boss "you can do it" might convince the person to assert his or her rights. However, this expectation will be easily crushed if the actual performance isn't met with the expected result.

Physiological and affective states can also be a source of efficacy expectations. A woman who has difficulty approaching men may find her heart beats rapidly and her palms perspire as she picks up the phone to call a man to ask for a date. If she interprets these physiological responses as signs of anxiety, she may decide she is too nervous to go through with it. However, if she notices how calm she is just before dialing, she may decide she is more courageous than she realized.

One key to successful treatment programs is changing a client's efficacy expectation through one or more of these means. In one study, therapists helped snake-phobic people overcome their fear of the reptiles by taking them through the process of touching and picking up snakes (enactive mastery experience) and/or watching someone else go through this procedure (vicarious experience). In nearly every case, whether the people believed they could approach and touch the snakes was the best predictor of whether they would actually do it (Bandura, Adams, & Beyer, 1977).

But if successful experiences are the most effective method for altering a client's efficacy expectations, this creates a bit of a problem. How can a therapist provide the client with a mastery experience of overcoming a fear of heights if the client is afraid to leave the first floor of a building? One answer is a procedure known as *guided mastery* (Bandura, 1997). Using this procedure, the therapist arranges the situation so that the client is almost guaranteed a successful experience. The treatment is broken down into small steps that can be accomplished with only a slight increase in the client's effort. A client with a fear of driving might begin by driving a short distance on a secluded street (Bandura, 1997). This step is followed with gradually longer drives on busier streets. With each successful experience, the client strengthens the belief that he or she is capable of driving an automobile. You may have noticed that this procedure sounds similar to systematic desensitization. Indeed, in many cases the distinction between the two therapy procedures may lie only in how they are interpreted. Behavior therapists explain successful systematic desensitization in terms of replacing old stimulus-response bonds with new ones. Social-cognitive therapists maintain that mastery experiences change efficacy expectations, leading to the change in behavior.

The other side of this process is that failure to instill a sense of efficacy in a client might very well doom therapeutic efforts. People battling alcohol and drug abuse typically do not succeed in treatment programs when they doubt their ability to overcome the problem (Ilgen, McKellar, & Tiet, 2005). Similarly, investigators find ex-smokers who are not confident they can stop smoking are the most likely to fall back into their habit, sometimes within a few weeks after quitting (Gwaltney, Shiffman, Balabanis, & Paty, 2005; Van Zundert, Ferguson, Shiffman, & Engels, 2010).

But the power of self-efficacy goes far beyond eliminating fears and bad habits. Self-efficacy beliefs have been found to play a role in overcoming a wide variety of psychological problems, including childhood depression (Bandura, Pastorelli, Babaranelli, & Caprara, 1999), post-traumatic stress disorder (Solomon, Weisenberg, Schwarzwald, & Mikulincer, 1988), test anxiety (Smith, 1989), phobias (Williams, 1995), and excessive bereavement (Bauer & Bonanno, 2001). Efficacy expectations also affect job performance (Stajkovic & Luthans, 1998), academic achievement (Richardson, Abraham, & Bond, 2012), exercise program persistence (McAuley et al., 2011), weight loss (Linde, Rothman, Baldwin, & Jeffery, 2006), and romantic relationships (Lent & Lopez, 2002). Heart attack patients who believe they can effectively participate in their rehabilitation have better cardiovascular health and lower mortality rates than those with low self-efficacy expectations about their health care (Burns & Evon, 2007; Sarkar, Ali, & Whooley, 2009). In short, believing that we are capable of making changes and moving forward is an important component for dealing with many of the challenges and problems life tosses our way.

Assessment: Behavior Observation Methods

Let's begin this section by thinking about one of your bad habits. Unless you are quite different from the rest of us, you probably chew your nails, eat junk food, lose your temper, use harsh language, smoke, talk too much, or engage in some other behavior you probably would like to change. Now imagine that you seek out a behavior therapist for help with this problem. The therapist asks you a simple question: How often do you perform the behavior? If you have been keeping track, you may be able to say exactly how many cigarettes you smoke per day or how often you chew your nails each week. But most likely your answer will be far from precise. Behavior therapists can't tell if a treatment program is effective unless they know how often the behavior occurs before treatment. Yet too often clients say they perform the unwanted behavior "every once in a while," "not too often," or "all the time."

Unlike those who practice other approaches to psychotherapy, behavior therapists typically do not spend much time trying to discover the initial cause of a client's problem. Instead, they focus on treating observable behaviors. Other therapists may see the behavior as a sign of some underlying conflict, but for behavior therapists, the behavior *is* the problem. Therefore, objective and reliable assessment of behavior is critical. Behavior therapists use assessment procedures for a variety of purposes. Obviously, they want to determine how often a problem behavior occurs. But they may also want to know about the events surrounding the behavior. Does the client smoke alone or with other people? Do the tantrums occur at a certain time of day or after a certain kind of experience, such as a scolding? These data can be very helpful in designing treatment programs.

So how do behavior therapists obtain accurate information about the frequency of target behaviors? When one team of researchers surveyed members of a behavior therapist organization, they found the therapists relied on a variety of procedures (Elliott, Miltenberger, Kaster-Bundgaard, & Lumley, 1996). Some of the most common methods of assessment mentioned by the therapists are shown in Table 13.2. Let's look at a few of these in depth.

TABLE 13.2 Behavior Therapists' Assessment

Method	Percentage of Cases Using
Interview with client	94.1
Direct observation	52.3
Client self-monitoring	44.1
Behavioral rating scales	43.7
Interview with client's significant others	42.0
Information from other professionals	38.0
Role playing	19.4

Source: Cognitive and behavioral practice by Elliot, A. J., Miltenberger, R. G., Kaster-Bundgaard, J. & Lumley, V. Copyright 1996 by *Elsevier Science & Technology Journals.* Reproduced with permission of Elsevier Science & Technology Journals in the format Textbook via Copyright Clearance Center.

Direct Observation

The most obvious way to find out how often a behavior occurs is to observe the person directly. Although a therapist usually can't watch a client all day long, it is often possible to observe a representative sample of the client's behavior. If you want to know how much time a girl spends interacting with children her own age, you can watch the child on the playground during several recesses. However, the therapist can't be everywhere. The therapist probably won't be around when a socially phobic person goes on a job interview or a married couple has an argument. In these cases, the psychologist might rely on *analogue behavioral observation* (Haynes, 2001). That is, the therapist creates a situation that resembles the real-world setting in which the problem behavior is likely to occur. For example, a therapist might stage a dance for clients suffering from acute shyness or ask a couple to enter into a discussion that recently sparked a disagreement. Occasionally behavior therapists ask clients to *role-play*. A therapist helping a man to be more assertive might ask the client to imagine that someone just cut in front of him in line. The client then acts out what he would do in that situation. In this case, the way the client acts in the role-playing exercise is probably similar to the way he acts when confronting real-life situations.

However, good behavioral assessment requires more than simply observing a person. The behaviors to be observed must first be defined as precisely as possible. This is fairly simple when talking about the number of cigarettes smoked, but what if the target behavior is "appropriate classroom responses"? In this case the therapist might define appropriate responses as those relevant to the topic being discussed or those in which the child waits for recognition before speaking. But even these definitions leave considerable room for observer interpretation. A good definition includes examples of behaviors to be counted and rules for dealing with borderline cases.

One way to improve the accuracy of behavior observation is to have two or more observers independently code the same behaviors. For example, two judges can watch the same child during the same set of recesses. If the two largely agree on how often they count the target behavior, we can be confident that the number is fairly accurate. However, if one coder sees few behaviors and a second coder sees many, we have no idea how often the target behavior actually occurs. One solution is to videotape the behavior so that many different judges can be used and disagreements can be resolved by replaying the tape. Behavior therapists must also be concerned about bias. Sometimes observers unintentionally see what they want or what they expect to see. To guard against this problem, therapists should define behaviors in a manner that minimizes subjective judgment. If possible, they can use observers who don't know what the therapist expects to find.

Self-Monitoring

Although direct observation provides a relatively accurate assessment of behavior frequency, it is often too costly and time consuming to be useful. An alternative is *self-monitoring*—clients observing themselves. However, simply asking clients how often they engage in a certain act may be of little

Marlene Somsak/University of Santa Clara

Psychologists working with children often use direct observation. This procedure allows them to assess how a child plays alone, how parents interact with their child, or how well a child interacts with other children. Many psychologists have also discovered the value of videotaping behavior samples for more extensive observation and coding later.

help. Clients frequently have a distorted idea about how often a behavior occurs. In addition, it is usually important to understand the circumstances surrounding the behavior. Are there places the client is particularly likely to smoke, such as with certain friends or at a party? Is the smoking associated with a certain time of day, a certain type of activity, or a certain mood?

Unfortunately, few clients can provide accurate information about these variables from memory. Therefore, therapists often ask clients to keep records of when and where they engage in certain behaviors. Clients are sometimes surprised by what they find. For example, people trying to watch their weight may discover that they eat more when they're alone, when watching television, or after they've had a drink. An interesting benefit of the self-monitoring method is that watching your own behavior can be therapeutic in itself. Clients forced to pay attention to their eating or smoking sometimes show improvement even before the treatment is started. Self-monitoring is also used to assess progress throughout the treatment period. Of course, one problem that sometimes surfaces when relying on self-monitoring is the client's honesty. Clients may not want to admit that they increased their smoking or lost their temper several times in one week. Therapists who suspect a problem may want to use other assessment methods, such as the one discussed next.

Observation by Others

Some clients are unwilling or simply unable to provide accurate information about themselves. For example, self-monitoring is probably inappropriate with children or those with severe psychological disorders. In these cases, it may be possible to rely on other people to make the observations. Parents and teachers can often record the frequency of a child's problem behaviors. A teacher might be asked to record each time she punishes a child for acting aggressively. Nurses and aides can record the occurrence of patients' behaviors. Although this process can introduce bias, it often provides the most accurate assessment of a client's behavior.

Many psychologists use these reports to complement data obtained through other methods. For example, children sometimes act differently in the presence of a therapist than they do at home. A client may be able to role-play the appropriate behaviors when confronting a make-believe manager but may become timid when facing the real boss at work. Getting family members involved in the process can have other advantages, such as making them aware of the client's problem and of how their reactions might affect his or her behavior.

Strengths and Criticisms of the Behavioral/Social Learning Approach

Behaviorism roared onto the psychology scene a century ago and put a grip on the discipline that didn't loosen for several decades. Although not as influential as it once was, behaviorism in various forms remains alive and well today. Explanations of behavior that evolved from behaviorism, such as social-cognitive theory, also remain popular. Obviously, the behavioral/social learning approach to personality could not have withstood this test of time without having some unique strengths. And of course, no theory as influential as this one can hope to escape criticism.

Strengths

One reason for the endurance of the behavioral/social learning approach is its solid foundation in empirical research. This contrasts with other approaches to personality, which are sometimes based on intuition or on data gathered from biased samples. Most of the theorists covered in this chapter relied on empirical data when developing and refining their theories. Critics often challenge the existence of Freud's Oedipus complex, but it would be difficult to deny the mountain of evidence demonstrating that behaviors sometimes change through operant and classical conditioning.

Another strength of the behavioral/social learning approach lies in the development of some useful therapeutic procedures. Studies find these procedures to be effective in treating a number of psychological problems, especially when combined with elements from cognitive therapies (Christensen, Atkins, Yi, Baucom, & George, 2006; Mitte, 2005; Shadish & Baldwin, 2005). Moreover, behavioral treatments are popular. One survey asked marriage and family therapists about their primary treatment approach when working with clients (Northey, 2002). By a large margin, "cognitive-behavioral" was the most commonly cited approach.

Treatments based on conditioning principles often have several advantages over other interventions. One advantage is the use of baseline data and objective criteria for determining success or failure. Other approaches often begin treatment without first determining the level of the problem; therapy is declared a success when the therapist or the client decides there has been some improvement. In addition, behavior therapy may be the most useful approach when working with certain populations, such as children or severely emotionally disturbed patients. These individuals might have a difficult time discussing abstract psychoanalytic concepts or dealing with some of the existential questions posed by humanistic therapists. Therapies based on conditioning principles also are relatively quick and easy to administer. Treatment often lasts a matter of weeks, compared with months or years with other approaches. The basic methods can be taught to parents, teachers, and hospital personnel, who can carry out the therapy without the therapist present. This means that more people can benefit from therapy procedures at a lower cost than is possible with most other types of psychotherapy.

The social learning theories and Bandura's social-cognitive theory added cognitive variables to the behavioral approach and thereby expanded the range of phenomena explained by this perspective. These theories have helped to fill in the gaps many psychologists see in traditional behaviorism. Social learning models of personality allow us to understand thoughts, expectancies, and values along with basic behavior conditioning principles within one theoretical framework. These models have also helped to bridge traditional behaviorism with cognitive approaches to personality.

Criticisms

A persistent criticism of the behavioral/social learning approach is that it is too narrow in its description of human personality. Although the approach touches on several crucial aspects of human experience such as thinking, emotion, and levels of consciousness, many psychologists feel that it does so in a limited way. Critics are particularly concerned with the Skinnerian brand of behaviorism, which rejects the usefulness of examining inner feelings and intuition. Others argue that the behavioral/social learning approach does not give inadequate attention to the role of heredity.

Another criticism, directed primarily at traditional behaviorism, is that human beings are more complex than the laboratory animals used in behavioral research. As Bandura and some of the social learning theorists recognize, people are capable of considering alternative courses of action, of weighing the probabilities and values of different reinforcers, of looking at long-term goals, and so forth. These critics do not deny that we often respond to stimuli in an automatic fashion or that some of our behaviors are conditioned. But they maintain that these are the least important and least interesting human behaviors. An example of the difficulty in generalizing from animal data to human behavior is seen in research on the effects of extrinsic reinforcers on intrinsically motivated behavior. Although this remains an area of controversy (Eisenberger & Cameron, 1996; Sansone & Harackiewicz, 1998), researchers often find that paying people to engage in a behavior they already enjoy results in a reduction in the frequency of the behavior. People seem to redefine the behavior as work instead of play ("I play the piano because I am paid") and therefore lose interest unless rewarded.

Despite the success of behavior therapists in dealing with many problem behaviors, some critics argue that these therapists sometimes distort the real therapy issues when they reduce everything to observable behaviors. For example, a man who complains that he has no meaning in his life might be asked to define this abstract issue in terms of measurable behaviors. A behavior therapist might count the number of times the man engages in pleasant activities and set up a treatment program that rewards him for going to parties, talking with friends, reading good books, and so on. These activities might make the man feel better. However, critics might argue that the therapy has not addressed the real problem but, instead, has temporarily diverted the client's attention from the concerns that caused him to seek out therapy.

Summary

1. Behaviorism was introduced a century ago by John B. Watson. In its most extreme form, behaviorism limits psychology to the study of observable behaviors. Classical conditioning and operant conditioning are used by behaviorists to explain the development and maintenance of behaviors. Personality is described as the end result of one's history of conditioning. B. F. Skinner later became the spokesperson for what he called radical behaviorism. He rejected the use of inner states, such as anxiety, as explanations of behavior in favor of observable external events.

2. Traditional behaviorism identifies two basic kinds of conditioning. Classical conditioning occurs when a new stimulus is paired with an existing stimulus-response bond. Operant conditioning results when a behavior is followed by either reinforcement or punishment.

3. Later social learning theorists expanded on the basic behaviorist position. Rotter argues that the probability of engaging in a behavior changes after rewards and punishments because our expectancies change. He uses these expectancies and the values given to particular reinforcers to predict which of many behavior options will be enacted.

4. Bandura proposes that internal states, the environment, and behavior all affect one another. He maintains that people often regulate their own behavior and that we engage in purposeful, future-oriented thinking. Bandura has added to classical and operant conditioning the notion that we learn through observing others, although whether we perform the behaviors we learn depends on our expectancies for rewards or punishments.

5. Therapists often apply basic conditioning principles when working with their clients. Some of these therapeutic procedures, such as systematic desensitization, are based on classical conditioning. Others are based on operant conditioning. Bandura has identified clients' self-efficacy beliefs as crucial for psychotherapy progress. Whether clients expect to succeed

is an important determinant of therapy success. These expectancies come from a variety of sources, including past performance accomplishments and vicarious learning.

6. Behavioral assessment includes a variety of techniques, including direct observation, self-monitoring, and observation by others. Each of these techniques can provide useful data for determining baseline frequencies, the conditions under which the target behavior occurs, and the success of the treatment procedure.

7. The behavioral/social learning approach has its strengths and its criticisms. Among the strengths are its empirical base and the useful therapeutic procedures it has generated. The criticisms include an inappropriate attention to important causes of behavior. People have also criticized the way behavior therapists interpret problems into observable behaviors.

Key Terms

classical conditioning (p. 348)

discriminate (p. 353)

generalization (p. 353)

observational learning (p. 359)

operant conditioning (p. 351)

reciprocal determinism (p. 357)

self-efficacy (p. 365)

self-regulation (p. 358)

Media Resources

Visit the book companion website at **www.cengagebrain.com** to find a glossary, flashcards, quizzing, and more.

CHAPTER 14

The Behavioral/ Social Learning Approach

Relevant Research

Behaviorists are sometimes portrayed as aloof, data-oriented scientists more concerned with how many times a rat presses a bar than with the people in their lives. Although it's true that these researchers often attend to minute experimental details and theoretical issues that seem overly esoteric to an outside observer, it is unfair to say they have lost sight of the human element or their goal of improving the human condition. Even B. F. Skinner, who conducted most of his research on rats, wrote extensively on how we can use the information coming out of animal laboratories to overcome many of the problems facing society today. This concern can be seen in each of the four research topics reviewed in this chapter. Each has something to say about pressing social problems or personal lifestyle issues.

First, society's expectations for men and women have undergone a great deal of reevaluation and change in the past few decades. In increasing numbers, women are abandoning traditional gender roles to take important positions in business and government. Some men are experimenting with nontraditional male roles, such as assuming child-rearing responsibilities. Understanding why we make some of the gender-related choices we do requires an examination of how operant conditioning and observational learning shape those choices. We'll look at these processes and individual differences in masculinity and femininity.

Second, in response to the ever-present issue of violence in our society, many psychologists have focused their attention on the impact aggressive models have on aggressive behavior. Bandura's observational learning model helps explain some of this process. We'll look at relevant research and the question of how mass media violence affects the behavior of those who consume it.

Third, applying animal research findings to human beings is a standard feature of the behavioral approach to personality. A particularly fruitful example of this application is the work on learned helplessness. From some surprising observations of dogs in a classical conditioning experiment, researchers have developed a theory with implications for depression and adjustment among the elderly.

Fourth, we'll look at one aspect of Rotter's social learning theory. Individual differences in locus of control have been the focus of an enormous amount of personality research. Some of these findings provide important information about how our expectancies are related to our well-being and our physical health.

Individual Differences in Gender-Role Behavior

I would like to describe two friends of mine. The first is a very caring and loving person. This friend never forgets my birthday, is sensitive to my needs and moods, and is the person I seek first when I need someone to talk to. This friend also confides in me and is not afraid to share intimate feelings. My other friend is on the way to becoming a leader in the business world. This friend knows how to be assertive when necessary, how to express opinions directly, and how to get others to do what is needed for the company.

Unlike the first person I described, this one sometimes has difficulty being intimate with others or sharing feelings. I've never seen this friend cry.

Unless you've already caught on to my point here, you probably imagined that the first person is a woman and the second is a man, even though I never identified the gender of either. If so, it doesn't mean you're gullible or sexist. Rather, it suggests you are aware of the gender-role stereotypes that affect the way men and women behave in this culture. Traditional stereotypes portray men as aggressive, independent, and unemotional, whereas women are depicted as passive, dependent, and affectionate. Much has been written recently about changes in these gender roles, with men being told it is all right to show emotion and women being encouraged to be assertive and businesslike. However, although some gender restrictions may have loosened in recent years, gender roles remain a part of our culture.

Why do women tend to behave in certain ways and men in others? Although biological differences between the sexes certainly play a role, behaviorists and social learning theorists point to a lifelong process of gender-role socialization. Children and adults acquire and maintain gender-appropriate behaviors largely through operant conditioning and observational learning. You can see the effects of operant conditioning whenever young children act in gender-inappropriate ways. Boys often tease one another for crying, playing with dolls, or showing an interest in cooking or sewing. Similarly, playmates make fun of girls when they act like tomboys. Boys are rewarded with camaraderie and parental nods for playing football and standing up to those

Most little girls occasionally play "dress up." Girls put on their mother's clothes, jewelry, and makeup after identifying that this is something females, but not males, do. We would not expect to find little boys imitating this behavior.

who try to push them around. Girls win approval for showing an interest in caring for babies and dressing up in pretty outfits.

You can appreciate the difficulty in changing these behavior patterns when you realize how early this operant conditioning starts. Even before the child can talk, parents speak to and play with their daughters differently than they do with their sons (Clearfield & Nelson, 2006). One team of researchers interviewed parents of sons and daughters within 24 hours after the birth of their first child (Rubin, Provenzano, & Luria, 1974). Parents rated daughters as softer, finer featured, smaller, and less attentive than sons. The daughters were also described as beautiful, pretty, and cute. In reality, the newborns did not differ in terms of weight, length, or measures of general health.

One team of investigators examined the choices parents made for boys and girls when the child was fewer than 25 months old (Pomerleau, Bolduc, Malcuit, & Cossette, 1990). Girls were more likely to receive dolls and toy furniture, whereas boys were more often given sports equipment, toy tools, and toy cars and trucks. Perhaps predictably, the girls were more likely to wear pink clothing, and the boys blue. In another study, researchers asked elementary school children prior to Christmas what they wanted and after Christmas asked what they had received (Etaugh & Liss, 1992). Most children asked for toys traditionally associated with their gender, and most of the time that's just what they got. However, a few children asked their parents for toys atypical for their gender. These boys and girls were much less likely to get what they wanted. In other words, many parents simply won't buy their daughter a football, no matter how much she wants one.

Messages about the different ways boys and girls are supposed to act are communicated to the child within the first few years of life. By the time children enter kindergarten, they are well aware of gender-role expectations (O'Brien et al., 2000; Vogel, Lake, Evans, & Karraker, 1991). Preschool boys and girls in one study were given a choice between traditional "boy" toys (tools) and "girl" toys (dishes) during a free-play period (Raag & Rackliff, 1998). Not only did most children select the toys traditionally associated with their gender, but most of the boys explained that their fathers would not approve of them playing with girls' toys. Preschoolers in another study were told that the other gender "really likes" a certain toy (Martin, Eisenbud, & Rose, 1995). After receiving this news, both boys and girls said they liked the toy less. In short, children are surrounded by adults and peers ready to reward gender-appropriate behaviors and punish inappropriate ones.

Gender-role behaviors are also acquired through observational learning. Children learn which behaviors are expected of males and which are expected of females by watching parents, neighbors, siblings, playmates, and television characters. When children are very young, parents are probably the most influential models, which may explain why people's gender-role behavior tends to resemble that of their mother or father (Jackson, Ialongo, & Stollak, 1986). Later, children are more likely to take their cues about appropriate and inappropriate behavior from their friends.

However, it is not the case that boys imitate only male models and girls only female models. Instead, the child must first notice that a certain behavior is performed more often by one gender than the other (Bandura & Bussey, 2004; Bussey & Bandura, 1999). Children may recognize that men, but rarely women, work on mechanical things. When an appliance needs fixing, father takes care of it. All the garage mechanics seem to be men, and if someone on television uses a screwdriver or a wrench, it is almost always a male. The children are likely to conclude that men are rewarded for mechanical behavior but women are not. Thus boys are likely to get involved with mechanical things, anticipating rewards, whereas girls seek out other activities. At this point, operant conditioning may also come into play, such as when a father rewards his son for showing an interest in cars and laughing when his daughter asks to help with an oil change.

Masculinity–Femininity

After a lifetime of socialization through operant conditioning and observational learning, we should not be surprised that most adult men and women act in gender-appropriate ways. But even casual observation of the people you meet in the next few hours will confirm that there are large individual differences in the extent to which people act in a masculine or feminine manner. Although men are generally more aggressive and independent than women, there are many exceptions. Similarly, finding women who do not fit the stereotypic affectionate, emotional, and sensitive pattern is not difficult.

As with other individual differences, personality psychologists are interested in identifying, measuring, and describing the way people typically act in terms of their gender-role behavior. Unfortunately, researchers do not always agree on what to call these traits. Originally, psychologists used the terms **masculinity** and **femininity**. People who act in ways that fit the traditional role expectations for men were classified as masculine, and those who acted like the traditional role expectations for women were feminine. Other psychologists argue that we should replace these terms with more specific and less emotionally loaded labels. In particular, many researchers prefer the terms *agency* and *communion* (Helgeson, 1994; Spence, 1993). Agency refers to independence, assertiveness, and control and is roughly similar to masculinity. Communion refers to attachment, cooperation, and interpersonal connection and is similar to femininity. Nonetheless, because many researchers continue to rely on the masculinity and femininity labels, we will also use these terms here.

Early scales developed to measure individual differences in gender-role behavior were based on two assumptions. First, masculinity and femininity were assumed to represent two extreme positions on a continuum. As shown in Figure 14.1, masculinity and femininity were considered opposites. The more a person was of one, the less he or she was of the other. Each of us can be placed on this continuum, with very masculine and very feminine people on the extremes and those who are both, but not much of either, toward the middle.

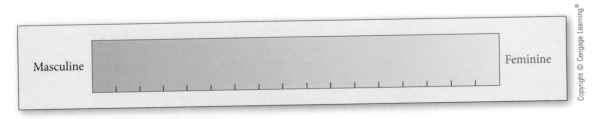

FIGURE 14.1 Traditional Masculinity–Femininity Model

The second assumption in this early research was that the more people's gender-role behavior matched the stereotype for their gender, the more psychologically healthy they were. Masculine men and feminine women were considered well adjusted. But a man who acted too much the way society said a woman was supposed to act or a woman who behaved too much like a stereotypic man was said to have adjustment problems. One of the original scales on the Minnesota Multiphasic Personality Inventory (MMPI) is the Mf (Masculinity–Femininity) Scale. Initially researchers maintained that scoring too far on the wrong side of this scale for one's gender was indicative of psychological disturbances.

Androgyny

Investigators eventually began to challenge the assumptions underlying this unidimensional masculinity–femininity model (Constantinople, 1973). In response, psychologists developed a new approach for measuring and identifying gender-role behaviors. The most influential of these new approaches is called the **androgyny** model (Bem, 1974, 1977). Coupled with society's rising concern for women's issues during these years, the androgyny model triggered an explosion in research on gender roles. The model begins by rejecting the notion that masculinity and femininity are opposites on a single continuum. Instead, masculinity and femininity are seen as independent traits. People can be high on both traits, on only one trait, or on neither. Further, because these traits are independent, knowing that someone is high or low in masculinity tells us nothing about how feminine that person is.

A great deal of research supports the notion that masculinity and femininity are best thought of as independent concepts. For example, researchers find that women tend to increase in both masculinity and femininity as they move through their middle adult years (Kasen, Chen, Sneed, Crawford, & Cohen, 2006; Strough, Leszczynski, Neely, Flinn, & Margrett, 2007). This pattern would not be possible if masculinity and femininity were opposite poles on a single dimension.

The androgyny model also challenges the assumption that a person's gender should match his or her gender type. Advocates of the model maintain that the most well-adjusted person is both masculine and feminine; that is, *androgynous*. According to this perspective, people who are only masculine or only feminine often find they lack the ability to engage in adaptive

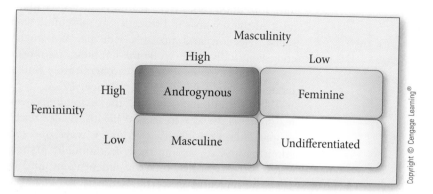

FIGURE 14.2 Androgyny Model

behavior. Masculine people do well as long as the situation calls for a masculine response, such as asserting one's rights or taking over the leadership of a group. But when masculine individuals are called on to act in a traditionally feminine manner, such as showing compassion or sensitivity, they falter. A well-adjusted person must have the flexibility to engage in masculine behaviors when the situation demands and in feminine behaviors when those are most appropriate.

Psychologists soon developed scales to measure the traits of masculinity and femininity separately (Bem, 1974; Lenney, 1991; Spence, Helmreich, & Stapp, 1974). By using the median score on each scale as a cutoff point, researchers can place people into one of four gender-type categories, as shown in Figure 14.2. Those who score high in both masculinity and femininity are classified as *androgynous*. People scoring high on one scale but not the other fall into either the *masculine* or *feminine* category. Those who score low on both scales are classified as *undifferentiated*.

Gender Type and Psychological Well-Being

The androgyny model was born out of a belief that possessing both masculine and feminine characteristics was important for psychological well-being. But how has that assumption held up under the scrutiny of research? In addition to the androgyny model, two other explanations for the relation between gender type and well-being have been proposed and tested.

The first explanation is the traditional *congruence model*. According to this account, masculine men and feminine women are the most well-adjusted. Although this approach reflects old-fashioned attitudes and may even border on sexism, a case can be made. Think about all the pressure society puts on men and women to act in gender-appropriate ways. What can we conclude about people who emerge from this socialization without developing the gender type dictated by society? Perhaps they are merely liberated from the restraints society attempts to place on them. But remember rewards and punishments for gender-appropriate behavior begin in childhood and continue into adulthood. Society is geared to give masculine men and feminine women most of the rewards in life, whereas masculine women and feminine men face social rejection and possibly ridicule. We might therefore expect gender-congruent individuals to be the happiest and most content. Although this reasoning makes some sense, researchers rarely find support for the congruence model (Taylor & Hall, 1982; Whitley, 1983).

The second explanation, the *masculinity model,* maintains that being masculine is the key to mental health. Before rejecting this view as masculine propaganda, consider that in many ways our society is still geared toward admiring and rewarding traits traditionally associated with men and masculinity. Stereotypically, men are independent, and women are dependent. Men are achieving and powerful; women are unassertive and conforming. Men are leaders, whereas women are followers. Given these descriptions, it makes sense that those who fit the masculine role might accomplish more and feel better about themselves than those who do not. Women do not have to abandon their femininity to get ahead in the traditionally male business world, but they may need some traditionally masculine attributes to be successful.

Several investigations find support for the masculinity model (Cheng, 1999; Marsh, Antill, & Cunningham, 1987; O'Heron & Orlofsky, 1990; Orlofsky & O'Heron, 1987; Roos & Cohen, 1987). Because masculine people are more likely to use direct, problem-focused strategies, they are better able to deal with stressors than those low in masculinity (Helgeson & Lepore, 1997). Masculine men in one study coped better with the loss of their spouse and the subsequent changes in their life than did other widowers (Bowers, 1999). Women who possess masculine traits are good at influencing others and getting what they want and are, therefore, less likely than most women to suffer from helplessness and depression (Sayers, Baucom, & Tierney, 1993). Support for the masculinity model is particularly strong when looking at the relationship between gender type and self-esteem (Whitley, 1983). People who possess traditionally masculine attributes (such as achieving, athletic, powerful) also feel good about themselves.

The third explanation is the *androgyny model.* According to this view, people whose behavioral repertoires lack either masculine or feminine behaviors are ill-prepared to respond to many situations they encounter. Without masculine characteristics such as decisiveness and assertiveness, both men and women are likely to falter in achievement situations. At the same time, people unable to express emotions have difficulty establishing good interpersonal relationships. Only androgynous people are capable of getting ahead on the job while relating well with friends and loved ones in their leisure time.

Several investigations find support for the androgyny model (Cheng, 2005; Lefkowitz & Zeldow, 2006; Shaw, 1982; Stake, 2000; Wolfram, Mohr, & Borchert, 2009). When taking care of a baby, feminine and androgynous—but not masculine—individuals show appropriate nurturing behavior. Feminine people are easily swayed by the opinions of others, whereas masculine and androgynous people better resist conformity pressures. Individuals who possess only masculine or feminine characteristics

Gender Roles and Toys

For generations, parents in Western cultures have encouraged traditional gender roles by giving their daughters dolls and tea sets and their sons footballs and toy trucks. Toy manufacturers have encouraged this pattern with commercials that typically portray girls playing with dolls and toy animals whereas boys are seen with construction sets and sports equipment (Kahlenberg & Hein, 2010). But a few recent developments suggest that some of this adherence to gender-specific toys may be breaking down.

In 2012, the Lego toy company announced a line of products called Lego Friends aimed specifically at girls age 5 and up (Wieners, 2011). The building block sets include female figures and come in colors like lavender and azure that are designed to be more appealing to girls. Prior to these new products, the market for Legos had been almost exclusively made up of boys. Later that same year, the Mattel toy company introduced a

Barbie construction set—The Mega Bloks Barbie Build 'n Style line (Clifford, 2012). The sets include small Barbie figures and allow girls to build structures like a mansion and an ice cream cart. All advertising and promotion of the products has been aimed specifically at girls. Initial reactions to the new products have been encouraging. Some retailers estimate that construction sets designed for girls now make up about 20 percent of the construction toy market (Clifford, 2012).

Predictably, this development has not escaped controversy. Although most people applaud the notion of loosening traditional rules concerning gender-appropriate toys, some see elements of sexism in the girls' construction toys. They point out that the Lego sets include a beauty parlor and a fashion studio, and that the luxury mansions that Barbie builds are pink—features that would never be found in toys designed for boys. Nonetheless, many parents are eager to see their daughters playing

with construction toys, even if those toys are largely pastels.

Changes in the way toys are marketed to boys and girls has the potential to have more of an impact than just giving children play time options. There is some evidence that playing with puzzles, blocks, and other types of building toys helps young children develop spatial skills (Levine, Ratliff, Huttenlocher, & Cannon, 2012). And children with good spatial skills are more likely to study and eventually move into careers in the so-called STEM fields—science, technology, engineering, and math. These are all fields in which women are significantly under-represented. It would be a gross overstatement to suggest that simply changing the way toys are manufactured and promoted will someday result in equal gender representation in STEM occupations. Nonetheless, it is not difficult to imagine the five year old girl building objects with her Legos as a future architect or engineer.

often do poorly when faced with stressful situations where taking action and seeking comfort from others is beneficial.

However, overall support for the androgyny model is mixed. Whereas many studies show the superior adaptability of androgynous individuals, others do not (Taylor & Hall, 1982; Woodhill & Samuels, 2004). Although androgynous people may be well-prepared to deal with many situations, this does not always translate into a sense of well-being or high self-esteem.

So what are we to conclude? First, very little research supports the congruence model. Second, some of the inconsistent findings may reflect the way masculinity and femininity are measured. For example, the most widely used measure in this research, the Bem Sex Role Inventory, asks people the extent to which 20 masculine and 20 feminine terms describe them. Unfortunately, the masculine terms in the scale tend to be more desirable than the feminine terms (Pedhazur & Tetenbaum, 1979). It makes sense that people who describe themselves with the more flattering and positive masculine terms (for example, self-reliant, ambitious) have higher self-esteem than those who describe themselves with some of the less-desirable feminine terms (for example, gullible, shy). Third, it seems quite possible that some aspects of a healthy personality, such as dealing with stress and personal achievement, are related to masculinity, whereas other aspects, such as developing good interpersonal relationships, are not (Marsh & Byrne, 1991). Individual differences in gender-role behavior are clearly tied to well-being in some way. However, just how these two are related remains the fuel for continued research.

Gender Type and Interpersonal Relationships

Who would you turn to if you needed to talk to someone about a personal problem—a masculine, feminine, androgynous, or undifferentiated person? Who would you prefer for a friend? For a romantic partner? Advertisements and TV shows often portray masculine men and feminine women as the most desirable partners for romantic encounters. And Americans spend a considerable amount of money on makeup, body-building equipment, and the like to make themselves appear more feminine or masculine. But is this the road to a perfect relationship? Some research suggests it may not be.

A simple way to examine how people react to different gender types is to ask participants about hypothetical character sketches of masculine, feminine, androgynous, and undifferentiated individuals. In general, researchers using this procedure find the androgynous character is liked more than the other three (Brooks-Gunn & Fisch, 1980; Gilbert, Deutsch, & Strahan, 1978; Jackson, 1983; Korabik, 1982; Kulick & Harackiewicz, 1979; Slavkin & Stright, 2000). Undergraduates in one study said the androgynous person was more popular, more interesting, better adjusted, more competent, more intelligent, and more successful than people described in masculine, feminine, or undifferentiated terms (Major, Carnevale, & Deaux, 1981). And when researchers asked college students to estimate the desirability of hypothetical romantic partners, both men and women showed a preference for the androgynous person (Green & Kenrick, 1994).

But do these impressions of hypothetical people translate into actual behaviors? To answer this question, one team of researchers created four types of male–female pairs: a masculine man and a feminine woman, an androgynous woman and a masculine man, a feminine woman and an androgynous man, and two androgynous people (Ickes & Barnes, 1978). The couples, who did not know each other before the study, were left alone in a room for 5 minutes. The participants were free to carry on a conversation or simply sit quietly and wait. Their behavior was recorded with a hidden video camera for later evaluation. Participants also were asked to rate afterward how much they had enjoyed the interaction. As shown in Figure 14.3, members of the masculine man–feminine woman dyads enjoyed their interactions the least. Analyses of the videotapes revealed that these couples talked to each other less, looked at each other less, used fewer expressive gestures, and smiled and laughed less than people in the other combinations.

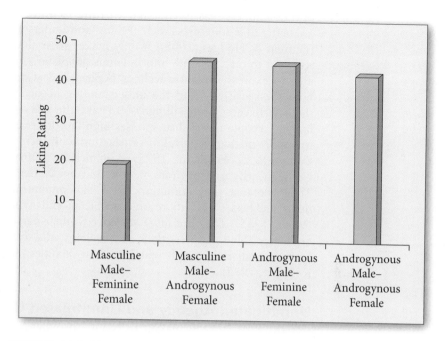

FIGURE 14.3 Mean Liking Rating Between Couples During 5-Minute Interaction

Source: From "Boys and girls together—and alienated: On enacting stereotyped sex roles in mixed-sex dyads," by W. Ickes and R. D. Barnes, *Journal of Personality and Social Psychology,* 1978, 36, 669–683.

These results argue against the masculine man–feminine woman combination as the ideal couple. When we examine the different ways masculine and feminine people approach an interpersonal encounter, some of the reasons for this finding become clear. The masculine style emphasizes control, self-monitoring, and self-restraint, whereas femininity is associated with interpersonal warmth and actively expressing one's feelings. Little wonder, then, that this combination didn't work out well in this or other experiments (Ickes, 1993; Ickes, Schermer, & Steeno, 1979; Lamke & Bell, 1982).

But what about long-term relationships? After the initial awkwardness, it's possible a masculine man and a feminine woman will get along well once they get to know one another. However, this notion is also not supported by the evidence. Researchers find the highest level of relationship satisfaction in people married to someone with feminine characteristics (Antill, 1983). That is, people with either a feminine or an androgynous spouse tend to be satisfied with their relationship. Marrying a partner who lacks feminine characteristics (i.e., a masculine or undifferentiated partner) may lead to an unhappy marriage. This same pattern has been found in cohabiting heterosexuals, gay couples, and lesbian couples (Kurdek & Schmitt, 1986).

What is it that makes feminine and androgynous people preferable partners? Research suggests at least three reasons. First, look at the characteristics that make up the feminine trait. People scoring high on this scale are affectionate, compassionate, and sensitive to others' needs. Feminine people are better able to express their feelings and understand the feelings of others (Laurent & Hodges, 2009). It only makes sense that we turn to them when we want to talk. Second, androgynous people are more aware of and better able to express romantic feelings (Coleman & Ganong, 1985). They have both the sensitivity and the understanding needed for intimacy as well as the assertiveness and willingness to take the risks required to make things happen. People married to spouses high in both expressiveness and sensitivity report the highest level of satisfaction with their relationships (Bradbury, Campbell, & Fincham, 1995; Zammichieli, Gilroy, & Sherman, 1988). Consequently, androgynous people may make the best romantic partners. Third, because they communicate well, feminine and androgynous individuals are better able to resolve problems and avoid unnecessary disputes (Voelz, 1985). They are more sensitive to their partners' feelings and needs, are better able to express their own feelings, and are thus more likely to live harmoniously than people who lack these qualities (Aube, Norcliffe, Craig, & Koestner, 1995).

Unmitigated Agency and Unmitigated Communion

Clearly, there are advantages to being either masculine or feminine. People with masculine attributes can be effective when they need to be decisive and independent. Feminine individuals clearly have an advantage when interacting with others in a nurturing and loving way. But what if we take either of these characteristics to an extreme? Imagine a woman who is not simply sensitive to others' problems but subjugates her own needs to the needs of the people around her. Is it possible to be so focused on taking care of other people that you fail to take care of yourself? On the other hand, what might we say about a man who is insensitive to the needs of others and who always opts to go his own way? Is this approach always in the man's best interests? These questions lead some researchers to draw a distinction between *communion* and *unmitigated communion* and between *agency* and *unmitigated agency* (Helgeson, 1994).

Communion—interacting with others in a compassionate and caring manner—is a positive attribute. But people high in unmitigated communion are so concerned with taking care of others that they tend to sacrifice their own needs and interests. A woman high in unmitigated communion may put her own educational and career ambitions aside to concentrate on the needs of her spouse, children, and friends. Unmitigated communion typically includes low masculinity. Thus, unmitigated communion is also associated with difficulty asserting oneself, a fear of expressing feelings that might lead to conflict, and a vulnerability to being exploited by others.

Failure to take care of one's own needs can exact a heavy toll. People high in unmitigated communion tend to score low on measures of well-being and self-esteem (Aube, 2008; Fritz & Helgeson, 1998; Helgeson & Fritz, 1999; Saragovi, Koestner, Di Dio, & Aube, 1997). These individuals tend to view their personal value in terms of what others think of them (Fritz & Helgeson, 1998). Thus, as discussed in Chapter 12, their sense of self-worth is fragile and highly vulnerable to events outside their control. Not surprisingly, researchers find unmitigated communion is related to high scores on measures of depression (Helgeson & Fritz, 1999). One investigator collected measures of unmitigated communion from a group of men and women when they were 31 years old (Aube, 2008). The participants were contacted again at age 41 and assessed for their level of depression. For both men and women, high scores on unmitigated communion predicted higher levels of depression 10 years later. Because women are more likely than men to suffer from unmitigated communion, these findings suggest one reason for the higher rates of depression found in women.

The problems associated with unmitigated communion are especially evident when facing health issues (Helgeson & Fritz, 2000). People high in

Assessing Your Own Personality

Unmitigated Communion

Indicate the extent to which you agree or disagree with each statement using the following scale: 1 = Strongly disagree, 2 = Slightly disagree, 3 = Neither agree nor disagree, 4 = Slightly agree, 5 = Strongly agree.

————— 1. I always place the needs of others above my own.

————— 2. I never find myself getting overly involved in others' problems.

————— 3. For me to be happy, I need others to be happy.

————— 4. I worry about how other people get along without me when I am not there.

————— 5. I have great difficulty getting to sleep at night when other people are upset.

————— 6. It is impossible for me to satisfy my own needs when they interfere with the needs of others.

————— 7. I can't say no when someone asks me for help.

————— 8. Even when exhausted, I will always help other people.

————— 9. I often worry about others' problems.

To determine your score, reverse the answer value for item # 2 (i.e., for this item only, 1 = 5, 2 = 4, 3 = 3, 4 = 2, 5 = 1). Then add all nine answer values together. The test creators found mean scores of 29.97 (sd = 6.14) for undergraduate women and 28.55 (sd = 5.53) for undergraduate men. The higher your score, the more you tend to subjugate your own needs to the needs of other people.

Scale: Unmitigated Communion

Source: Copyright © 1998 by the American Psychological Association. Reproduced with permission. Fritz, H. L., & Helgeson, V. S. (1998). Distinctions of unmitigated communion from communion: Self-neglect and overinvolvement with others. *Journal of Personality and Social Psychology,* 75, 121–140. doi: 10.1037/0022-3514.75.1.12. No further reproduction or distribution is permitted without written permission from the American Psychological Association.

unmitigated communion may neglect their own needs at a time when self-attention is called for. Resting, eating well, attending rehabilitation sessions, and other steps necessary to improve their health may take a back seat to taking care of the family. In one study, unmitigated communion was associated with poor psychological and physical health among women diagnosed with breast cancer (Helgeson, 2003). In another investigation, women high in unmitigated communion who were diagnosed with rheumatoid arthritis became more psychologically distressed than other patients as the disease progressed (Danoff-Burg, Revenson, Trudeau, & Paget, 2004). One team of researchers looked at how teenagers responded to being diagnosed with diabetes, a disease that requires a good deal of personal monitoring and treatment (Helgeson, Escobar, Siminerio, & Becker, 2007). High levels of unmitigated communion predicted more depression and higher anxiety among these adolescents one year after the diagnosis. In short, being compassionate and nurturing is a good thing, but on occasion people need to devote some of that nurturing to themselves.

Like communion, agency can also be a positive attribute that can become a liability when taken too far. People high in unmitigated agency often act narcissistically, focusing on themselves to the exclusion of others (Ghaed & Gallo, 2006; Helgeson, 1994). As a result, their interactions with other people are often strained if not unpleasant (Helgeson & Fritz, 1999). This interpersonal style obviously creates problems for the people who have to interact with individuals high in unmitigated agency. But, because they turn potential friends away, people high in unmitigated agency may also find themselves in trouble when they encounter a situation in which they need to rely on other people.

Imagine what happens when this kind of person encounters serious health issues. In addition to helping with practical needs, other people can provide important emotional support and encouragement. Yet, people high in unmitigated agency are reluctant to seek or receive help from others (Helgeson & Lepore, 2004). As a result, individuals high in unmitigated agency who become ill do not do as well on physical or psychological measures as those low in this trait (Helgeson & Lepore, 1997, 2004; Helgeson & Palladino, 2012; Hoyt & Stanton, 2011).

Observational Learning of Aggression

On May 25, 2009, a 17-year-old set off a bomb outside a Manhattan Starbucks. When arrested weeks later, the boy confessed to plans for a series of similar attacks. He explained he was just imitating Brad Pitt's character in his favorite movie, *Fight Club*. The incident was just one in a long string of violent crimes linked to violence in a motion picture. The list goes back many years, and many of the examples on that list have ended in tragedy. In December 1997 a 14-year-old boy entered his Kentucky high school carrying five guns. The boy opened fire on classmates who had gathered for a prayer meeting, and three students were killed. Later the boy said he was acting out a scene from the movie *The Basketball Diaries*. In July 1991 the motion picture *Boyz 'n the Hood* opened around the country. Although calm was the norm at most of the theaters, some became the setting for real-life violence, including several shootings. Thirty-five people were reported wounded or injured the first night the movie was shown. A man in Chicago was killed. In May 1981 John Hinckley tried to assassinate President Ronald Reagan. Investigators soon discovered that Hinckley had viewed the motion picture *Taxi Driver* several times before the shooting. The film portrays a man who falls in love with a young prostitute, played by Jodie Foster, and who later attempts to shoot a presidential candidate. The subsequent investigation uncovered that Hinckley also had a strong attraction to Jodie Foster.

These incidents are painful examples of one of the most widely researched aspects of Bandura's social-cognitive theory, the relationship between modeled aggression and performed aggression. Studies not only demonstrate how people often learn behaviors through observing models, but the findings also raise some important questions about the portrayal of violence in the mass media.

Bandura's Four-Step Model

As you will see, decades of research demonstrate that people exposed to aggressive models sometimes imitate the aggressive behavior. Before reviewing some of that research, an observation is in order. Anyone who watches television or goes to an occasional movie (which is just about all of us) undoubtedly has seen quite a few murders, beatings, shootings, and the like. Yet rarely do we step away from our TV set or leave the theater in search of victims. Obviously, simple exposure to an aggressive model is not enough to turn us into violent people. Why, then, do individuals sometimes imitate aggression when most of the time they do not?

Bandura's (1973, 1986) answer to this question is that observational learning and performance consist of four interrelated processes. People must go through each of four steps before exposure to aggression leads them to act aggressively. They must *attend* to the aggressive action, *remember* the information, *enact* what they have seen, and *expect* that rewards will be forthcoming. Fortunately, most of the time circumstances prevent people from moving through the entire process. Unfortunately, sometimes they do. Let's look at each of the four steps in the process more closely.

For observational learning to take place, people must first *attend* to the significant features of the model's behavior. We can sit in front of violent TV programs all day long, but the aggressive models will have little or no impact unless we pay attention to them. Children who watch a lot of television have probably seen so many TV characters punched in the face or shot that only the most graphic and spectacular action grabs their attention. Children in one study imitated aggressive models only when the acts were carried out quite vigorously (Parton & Geshuri, 1971). Less intense action apparently failed to hold their attention. A viewer's mental state can also make him or her more attentive to the aggression. Children in one study were more likely to pay attention to an aggressive model when they were frustrated

(Parker & Rogers, 1981). This finding ties back to the connection between frustration and aggression described in Chapter 6.

But attending to an aggressive act is only the first step in the observational learning process. People must also *remember* information about the model's behavior. You are unlikely to recall any specific aggressive act you saw on television a few weeks ago unless that act was quite gripping. And if you can't recall what the model did, you are not likely to imitate the model. Unfortunately, although most aggressive acts we witness soon fade from our memories, not all do. Practice and mental rehearsal can keep the action fresh in our minds. Children who play with toy guns and plastic combat equipment may embed the actions of their aggressive heroes permanently into their memories.

The importance of this recall was demonstrated in a study with first- and second-grade children (Slife & Rychlak, 1982). The researchers asked the children how much they liked each of the aggressive acts they saw on a videotape. They also determined which toys used by the aggressive model each child liked. Then, as in Bandura's classic study, the children were watched for 5 minutes while they played in a room containing all the equipment necessary to imitate the aggressive acts they had just seen. As shown in Figure 14.4, the children were most likely to imitate the aggression when it was an act they liked and when it was performed with a toy they liked. The researchers argue that these are the acts the children remember. This interpretation helps to explain why the boys in the study

Research indicates that children learn aggression by imitating aggressive models. Rehearsing aggression, as when children play with toy guns, is one step in this process.

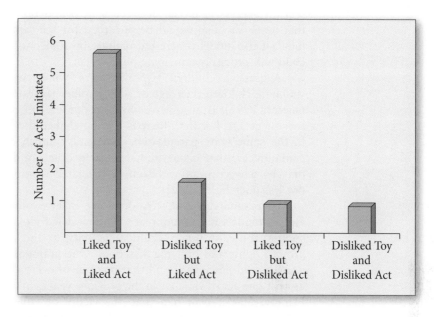

FIGURE 14.4 Mean Number of Aggressive Acts Imitated

Source: From "Role of affective assessment in modeling aggressive behavior," by B. D. Slife and J. F. Rychlak, *Journal of Personality and Social Psychology,* 1982, 43, 861–868.

were more aggressive than the girls: They liked and recalled the aggressive behavior more.

The third step in the observational learning process is that people must *enact* what they have seen. Remember that Bandura draws a distinction between learning and performance. One reason we don't carry out every aggressive act we recall is that we may lack the ability to do so. Few of us can imitate the behavior of a martial arts champion, even after watching a dozen movies. But even if we knew what to do, we would still need an opportunity to carry out the violent act. I may remember from repeated exposure in movies how to hold and fire a gun. But because I don't have access to a gun and because I hope I am never in a situation where a gun would be useful, shooting someone with a handgun is one learned behavior I will probably never enact.

The final step in the process requires individuals to *expect* that the aggressive act will lead to rewards and not to punishment. One study of elementary school children found that aggressive boys were particularly attracted to what they saw as the positive consequences of aggression, such as controlling other children (Boldizar, Perry, & Perry, 1989). These same boys were not very concerned about potentially negative consequences, such as causing suffering or being rejected by their classmates.

Where do aggressive children develop these expectancies? As described in the previous chapter, we not only learn what to do from models, we also learn what is likely to happen to us as a result of imitating them. If a child sees an aggressive model declared a hero and praised, the child may expect that he or she also would be rewarded for the same behavior. On the other hand, if the model is arrested or hurt by someone even more aggressive, the child will probably anticipate punishment.

Aggressive children typically learn what consequences to expect by watching children their age or slightly older (Huesmann, 1988; Huesmann & Guerra, 1997). If an older child who pushes and punches gets his choice of toys or gets to bat first, there is a good chance the behavior will be imitated. In the same way, parents who physically punish children for fighting may communicate that bigger and stronger people can do what they want, which may be why corporal punishment is related to more aggression in children, not less (Gershoff, 2002).

Unfortunately, many children live in environments where exposure to violent models is commonplace. The modeled violence comes in the form of spouse abuse at home, criminal activity in the neighborhood, and play-ground fights and bullying at school. One national survey of American children and adolescents found that one out of every three youth had witnessed at least one act of violence in the previous year (Finkelhor, Ormrod, Turner, & Hamby, 2005). Half had been the victim of violence themselves, and only 29% had been shielded from any form of violence. Researchers find that the more children are exposed to this type of violence, the more likely it is that they will turn to violence themselves (Wilson, Smith Stover, & Berkowitz, 2009). Over time, the children come to see violence as normal; that is, as a common and appropriate way to get what they want (Orue et al., 2011).

Finally, people are more likely to imitate aggressive behavior that is por-trayed as justified (Paik & Comstock, 1994). Children are more likely to imitate a superhero who smacks around a bad guy for the good of society than a supervillain who acts violently only for his own good. Children see that the villain is punished, but they also see the good guy's aggressive behavior rewarded. Unfortunately, in most cases people believe *their* side in a conflict is the correct and just one. Therefore, like the superhero, people may come to think of aggression as an appropriate way to solve their pro-blems (Smith & Donnerstein, 1998). One study found that the more adoles-cents generally believed that violence was sometimes justified, the more likely they were to become physically aggressive themselves over the next six months (Calvete, 2008).

Mass Media Aggression and Aggressive Behavior

If you watch even a small amount of television, you are surely aware that the average American receives a heavy dose of modeled aggression almost daily. For several decades, psychologists and other professionals have been con-cerned about how this constant exposure to stabbings, shootings, beatings, and so on affects viewers, especially children. Although today the action may consist of a space monster being killed by a superhero's laser beam instead of a bank robber felled by a bullet from a sheriff's gun, one estimate claimed the average American child will view about 8,000 murders and more than

100,000 other acts of violence on television before leaving elementary school (Smith & Donnerstein, 1998). And the situation isn't getting any better. Studies find there is more violence on prime-time television today than ever before (Bauder, 2005).

As the examples at the beginning of this section suggest, there are some very convincing instances of people witnessing and then imitating media violence. However, we can't determine conclusively from these examples that viewing the aggressive act actually caused the person to behave violently. It is possible that John Hinckley would have committed some other violent act if he hadn't watched *Taxi Driver*. After all, millions of people saw the movie without reacting aggressively. Although most of us find it difficult not to see a link between viewing aggression and performing aggression in these examples, these incidents supply only weak evidence for this connection.

Fortunately, we don't have to rely on this circumstantial evidence. Researchers have generated a wealth of experimental data concerning the impact of viewing aggression on performing aggression. The vast majority of these studies find the causal link irrefutable: Viewing aggression increases the likelihood of acting aggressively, especially over a short time span (Anderson & Bushman, 2002b; Bushman & Huesmann, 2001; Friedrich-Cofer & Huston, 1986; Geen, 1998; Paik & Comstock, 1994; Smith & Donnerstein, 1998; Wood, Wong, & Chachere, 1991). Most of the data come from controlled laboratory experiments. Typically, participants watch a segment from either a violent or an arousing but nonviolent program or movie. Then they are given the opportunity to act aggressively against another individual, often by administering electric shocks or loud noise they believe will hurt the other person. In almost all cases, participants who watch the violence act more aggressively than those who see the nonviolent clip.

Although impressive, this research also contains some limitations. The effects typically are short-lived, and the opportunity to hurt another person provided by the experimenter is unique. Therefore, it is reasonable to wonder how much these studies tell us about the impact of aggressive movies and television shows in real-life situations.

In response to this question, several investigators have conducted long-term field studies to gauge the impact of exposure to violence and aggressive behavior outside the laboratory (Eron, 1987; Gentile, Coyne, & Walsh, 2011; McCarthy, Langner, Gersten, Eisenberg, & Orzeck, 1975; Singer & Singer, 1981). In each case the researchers use the amount and kind of television children watched at one point in their lives to predict how aggressive the children will be at a later date. Like the laboratory studies, these investigations find significant evidence indicating that watching a lot of aggressive television leads to more aggression in children and adults.

One team of researchers began their investigation by determining how much television a group of 8-year-old children watched (Eron, 1987; Huesmann, Eron, Dubow, & Seebauer, 1987; Lefkowitz, Eron, Walder, & Huesmann, 1977). They then waited 22 years before measuring aggressive behavior in these same individuals at age 30. The researchers found a significant relationship between the amount of television the participants watched

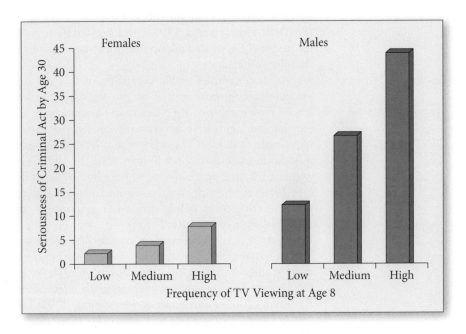

FIGURE 14.5 Seriousness of Criminal Act at Age 30 as a Function of Frequency of TV Viewing at Age 8

Source: From Eron (1987).

as children and the likelihood that they would have been convicted for criminal behavior by age 30. As shown in Figure 14.5, the seriousness of the criminal act was directly related to the amount of television watched. The more TV the 8-year-old had watched, the more serious the adult crime.

Another investigation measured the amount of television boys and girls watched at age 14 and incidences of aggression over the next 8 years (Johnson, Cohen, Smailes, Kasen, & Brook, 2002). As shown in Figure 14.6, the percentages of men and women who engaged in some act of aggression (assault, physical fights resulting in injury, robbery, crime committed with a weapon) increased dramatically with an increase in television viewing.

One potential difficulty in interpreting this research concerns the possibility that the children watched television *because* they were aggressive, not the other way around. Not surprisingly, research shows that aggressive people prefer aggressive television programs (Bushman, 1995). However, when researchers control for the child's initial aggressiveness level, the findings still suggest that watching television causes the later aggressive behavior. Moreover, when researchers account for other possible influences on aggressive behavior, such as neighborhood violence, childhood neglect, and family income, they still find the association between television viewing and aggression (Johnson et al., 2002).

In short, frequent exposure to aggressive models on television appears to increase aggressive behavior over the short run and many years later. Some of this relationship can be explained through Bandura's observational learning

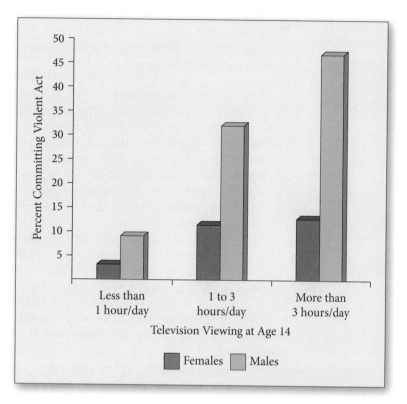

FIGURE 14.6 Violence as a Function of Television Viewing

Source: Adapted from Johnson et al. (2002).

model. However, a close examination of the model suggests imitation may be only part of the picture. In many studies the aggressive acts displayed by participants are different from the acts modeled in the films the participants are shown (Geen & Thomas, 1986). That is, exposure to an aggressive motion picture increases aggressive acts, but not necessarily the acts shown in the movie. Why might this be so? As we will see in Chapter 16, some concepts borrowed from the cognitive approach to personality help us complete the picture. Essentially, researchers find that exposure to violence makes access to violent thoughts and emotions more accessible. The research also is a good example of how psychologists often blend aspects of the behavioral approach with features from the cognitive approach to obtain a better understanding of complex phenomena.

Violent Video Games

Over the past three decades, the video game business has grown from a few quarter-eating machines in restaurants and arcades to a multibillion dollar industry. Along the way, the nature of many of these games also changed: they became violent. In some cases, very violent. Players of violent video games are rewarded for killing police, prostitutes, and innocent bystanders. Weapons include cars, guns, flame-throwers, and chain saws. In some games, the player takes on the role of a criminal on a violent crime spree.

Given what we know about the effects of violent movies and television, many psychologists and other professionals are concerned about the impact of all this exposure to simulated violence in video games. A couple of video games' features are especially worrisome. First, players do not merely watch the action. They pay close attention and actively engage in practicing violent acts. Second, virtually all violent video games are designed to reward violence. The more thugs, monsters, evil-doers, and police you kill, the higher your score. Thus, some of the necessary elements for imitating aggression identified by Bandura—attending to the behavior, enhanced recall through rehearsal, seeing the behavior rewarded—are built into most violent video games.

Numerous studies on the effects of violent video games have now been conducted. Although there remain some unanswered questions (Ferguson, 2013), for the most part the findings consistently point to the same conclusion—playing violent video games increases the likelihood that the player will act aggressively (Anderson, 2004; Anderson et al., 2010; Anderson & Bushman, 2001). As with research on the effects of media violence, we can look at the short-term and the long-term effects of violent video games.

Participants who play violent video games are more aggressive immediately afterward than participants who play nonviolent video games (Anderson & Dill, 2000; Bartholow, Bushman, & Sestir, 2006; Engelhardt, Bartholow, & Saults, 2011; Fischer, Kastenmuller, & Greitemeyer, 2010). Undergraduate men and women in one study played a car-driving video game (Carnagey & Anderson, 2005). In one condition players were rewarded for killing pedestrians and opponents. In a second condition players lost points when they hit other cars or pedestrians. In a third condition all pedestrians were removed from the screen and players earned points simply by passing checkpoints. A little later, participants were given an opportunity to hurt someone who had insulted them by administering what they thought were blasts of loud noise to their insulter. As shown in Figure 14.7, participants who had been rewarded for video game violence gave louder and longer blasts of noise than participants who either had been punished for violence or who played the nonviolent game. Other studies find that playing violent video games increases feelings of hostility (Saleem, Anderson, & Gentile, 2012) and causes players to think of their video victims as less than human (Greitemeyer & McLatchie, 2011).

This increased aggressiveness from playing violent video games typically lasts for several minutes after people stop playing (Barlett, Branch, Rodeheffer, & Harris, 2009). But researchers have found effects even 24 hours after the game was turned off (Bushman & Gibson, 2011). Investigators also find that the more realistic the violence in the game, the stronger the effect (Barlett & Rodeheffer, 2009). And, consistent with Bandura's theory, the fact that players are actively engaged in the simulated violence may

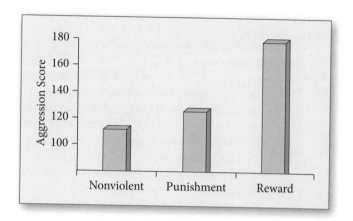

FIGURE 14.7 Aggression as a Function of Video Game Violence
Source: Adapted from Carnagey and Anderson (2005).

make the impact of the violence more powerful. This last observation explains why participants who play violent video games act more aggressively than participants who simply watch someone else play (Polman, de Castro, & van Aken, 2008).

Psychologists have also looked at the long-term effects of playing violent video games. One study found that adolescents who play a lot of violent video games are more likely to argue with teachers and get into physical fights (Gentile, Lynch, Linder, & Walsh, 2004). A study with juvenile delinquents found that playing violent video games was associated with more severe delinquent behavior and higher levels of violence (DeLisi, Vaughn, Gentile, Anderson, & Shook, 2013). Similarly, college students who frequently play these games were more likely to have engaged in violent acts (destroying property, hitting, threatening to hurt someone) during the past year than students who rarely play such games (Anderson & Dill, 2000). One team of researchers measured how often young adolescents (average age 13 years) played violent video games and how often they engaged in violent behavior 30 months later (Moller & Krahe, 2009). The investigators found a significant increase in violence (hitting, threatening to hit, pulling hair) among those who had played a lot of violent video games. The take-away message from all of this research is that, like exposure to other types of mass media violence, playing violent video games appears to contribute to subsequent aggressive behavior.

Learned Helplessness

Consider the following three cases. A woman is fired from her job because her employer believes the position is too demanding for her abilities. After a few frustrating weeks of job-hunting, she decides to just stay home. She stops going out with friends and shuts down other parts of her life she once enjoyed—dancing, movies, jogging. She becomes more and more depressed, develops lower and lower self-esteem, and has little faith in her ability to get another job. An elderly man is moved to a senior residential community and is told the staff will take care of all the chores he used to do. He no longer has to cook for himself or clean his room or even do the shopping. Shortly after the move, he becomes less active. He is less talkative and less cheerful. His health begins to fail. A fourth-grade boy does poorly on a math test. He becomes frustrated and distressed on his next few math assignments and eventually refuses to even try. He begins to struggle in other subjects and soon loses interest in school altogether.

What these three hypothetical people have in common is that they are all examples of what researchers refer to as **learned helplessness**. Psychology's interest in learned helplessness began with the curious behavior of some dogs in a classical conditioning study but soon evolved into a widely applied phenomenon.

Learning to Be Helpless

Like so many of the topics to come out of the behaviorist tradition, research on learned helplessness began with studies on laboratory animals. In the original learned helplessness experiments, harnessed dogs were subjected to a series of electric shocks from which they could not escape (Overmier & Seligman, 1967; Seligman & Maier, 1967). After several trials of inescapable electric shock, the animals were placed in an avoidance learning situation. Whenever a signal sounded, the dogs could avoid electric shocks by jumping over a small partition to the other side of a shuttle-box (Figure 14.8). Naturally, dogs that had not gone through the earlier shock experience scurried about frantically when the electric shock came on and quickly learned to leap over the barrier to safety whenever they heard the signal. But the researchers were completely surprised by the response of the dogs that

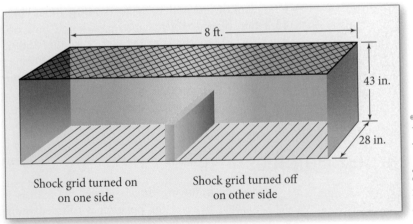

FIGURE 14.8 Shuttle-Box for Learned Helplessness Experiments

had first gone through the inescapable shock experience. These dogs also ran around for a few seconds after the shock came on, but then the dogs stopped moving. "To our surprise, it lay down and quietly whined," a researcher explained. "After one minute of this we turned the shock off; the dog had failed to cross the barrier and had not escaped from the shock" (Seligman, 1975, p. 22).

What had happened to these dogs? According to the researchers, the animals had learned that they were helpless. During the inescapable shock trials, the dogs tried various moves to avoid the shock and found that none were rewarded. The animals eventually learned there was nothing they could do to turn off the shock, and they became resigned to their helplessness. Of course, this reaction was no surprise. It's probably the most reasonable response to inescapable shock. The problem became apparent when the dogs experienced shock in the shuttle-box situation—shock from which they *could* escape. In behavioral terms, the dogs inappropriately generalized what they had learned in the first situation to the second situation. Although the dogs could easily have escaped the shock in the shuttle-box, they responded with the helplessness they had learned earlier. In fact, before the animals could learn the simple response, researchers had to physically move the dogs to the other side of the shuttle-box to show them the shock was escapable.

Learned Helplessness in Humans

Soon after the first demonstrations of learned helplessness in animals, psychologists wondered if learned helplessness could also be found in people. Ethically, we can't put human volunteers in a harness and subject them to inescapable shock. But with a few modifications in the basic procedure, researchers figured out a way to test whether humans were also susceptible to this effect (Hiroto, 1974; Hiroto & Seligman, 1975). Instead of inescapable shock, irritating (but not painful) loud noise was used. Participants were told they could turn off the noise by solving a problem (e.g., pressing some buttons in the correct sequence). Some participants quickly worked through dozens of these problems, turning off each noise blast by figuring out the answer. However, other participants were given problems for which there were no solutions. Like the dogs in the earlier studies, these people soon learned there was no way to escape the aversive stimulus.

Would these people generalize their feelings of helplessness to other situations? Participants were taken out of the noise situation and given a different kind of problem to work on. Participants who had found the earlier problems solvable had little difficulty with the new problems. In fact, they did no worse than a comparison group of participants who received no noise. However, participants who had felt helpless to turn off the noise performed significantly worse on the second set of problems. Like the dogs in the shuttle-box, they appeared to have inappropriately generalized their perception of helplessness in one situation to a new, controllable situation.

Numerous replications of this experiment confirm that humans are as susceptible as laboratory animals to learned helplessness (Overmier, 2002;

Marlene Somsak/University of Santa Clara

Residents of old-age homes often have many of their daily tasks, such as cooking and cleaning, taken care of by the staff. However, a learned helplessness analysis suggests that this reduction in control may lead to problems with adjustment and health for the elderly.

Peterson, Maier, & Seligman, 1993). People learn they are helpless in the initial uncontrollable setting and can't break out of that association in subsequent situations. Sometimes people learn to be helpless by simply observing other people who are helpless (Brown & Inouye, 1978; DeVellis, DeVellis, & McCauley, 1978). Imagine your reaction when you see several people with ability similar to yours trying yet failing to pass an important test. You might conclude that you also can't pass the test, even though you have yet to try ("There's no use in trying; nobody ever passes"). These feelings of helplessness might then be generalized to a new situation, and you could suffer from learned helplessness without ever experiencing failure yourself.

Some Applications of Learned Helplessness

Since it was first demonstrated in humans, learned helplessness has been studied in numerous investigations and used to explain a wide variety of human problems. We'll look at two of those problems here—well-being among older individuals and psychological disorders.

Learned Helplessness in the Elderly

We commonly assume in Western society that elderly people deserve to rest after a lifetime of hard work. Retirement is structured to relieve older individuals of their daily concerns and responsibilities. Retirement communities are often designed to take care of the cooking and cleaning and structuring of daily activities. But is this approach really in the best interests of the retired person? If we apply a learned helplessness analysis to the situation, we see that these living situations may be taking away the older persons' control over their daily experiences. For formerly active people used to exercising a great deal of control, living under such conditions may be similar to the experience of research participants presented with uncontrollable noise. And, like the research participants, the elderly may generalize this perception of uncontrollability to other areas of their lives. In short, the lack of motivation and activity seen in many retired individuals may be a form of highly generalized learned helplessness.

One team of investigators tested this possibility in a classic study that involved residents on two floors of a retirement residence (Langer & Rodin, 1976). With the administrators' cooperation, they altered the usual treatment given to one of these groups. The researchers increased the amount of responsibility and control typically exercised by these residents in several ways. Administrators gave a presentation urging the residents to take control of their lives. Here is an excerpt from that talk:

> You have the responsibility of caring for yourselves, of deciding whether or not you want to make this a home you can be proud of and happy in. You should be deciding how you want your rooms to be arranged—whether you want the staff to help you rearrange the furniture. You should be deciding how you want to spend your time, for example, whether you want to be visiting friends or whether you want to be watching television, listening to the radio, writing, reading, or planning social events. In other words, it's your life and you can make of it whatever you want. (Langer & Rodin, 1976, p. 194)

In addition, participants were offered a small plant as a gift. The residents decided whether they wanted a plant and which plant they wanted, and were told they were responsible for taking care of it. Residents on the other floor served as the comparison group. They listened to a talk about allowing the staff to take care of things for them. They were given a plant (chosen by the staff) and were told the staff would take care of the plant for them.

The differences between the two floors were soon evident. Within a few weeks, the residents in the responsibility-induced condition reported feeling happier. Staff members noted they were visiting more and sitting around less. Nurses, who did not know a study was going on, reported 93% of the residents showed improved adjustment. Only 21% of the residents in the comparison group showed improvement. But the effects of the treatment did not stop there.

The researchers returned to the home 18 months later to find that many of the differences in happiness and activity level remained (Rodin & Langer, 1977). Most dramatically, only 15% of the responsibility-induced residents had died during the 18-month period, compared to 30% of the comparison group.

Several subsequent investigations have discovered similar advantages when elderly people retain a sense of control over their lives (Chipperfield & Perry, 2006; Schulz & Heckhausen, 1999; Wrosch, Schulz, & Heckhausen, 2002). One team of researchers looked at mortality rates from all causes over a 5-year period for 20,323 middle-aged and older adults living in Norfolk, England (Surtees, Wainwright, Luben, Khaw, & Day, 2006). Citizens who had indicated on earlier psychological tests that they felt a sense of mastery over their lives were significantly more likely to survive than those who expressed a general sense of helplessness. These findings do not mean we should abandon those who genuinely need assistance, but sometimes letting people take care of themselves is in everyone's best interest.

Learned Helplessness and Psychological Disorders

Soon after the demonstrations of learned helplessness in humans, psychologists noticed some striking parallels between research participants and people suffering from depression (Seligman, 1976). Clinical psychologists have long observed that depressed patients often act as if they are helpless to control what happens to them (Beck, 1972). Severely depressed people sometimes lack the motivation even to get out of bed in the morning. Little interests them, and they often believe that nothing they do will turn out well. Like the dogs that lie whimpering in the shuttle-box, they seem to have given up on their ability to do anything about their problems.

These observations led psychologists to suggest that depression sometimes develops in a manner similar to the way research participants acquire learned helplessness (Seligman, 1975). That is, people perceive a lack of control over one important part of their lives and inappropriately generalize that perception to other situations. A college student might have difficulty in a particular class. No matter how hard she tries, she can't improve her test scores. At first she studies harder and gets advice from other students, but it doesn't seem to help. If it's important to her to do well in school, she may continue her efforts to change her grade. However, at some point she may decide that no matter what she does, she can't avoid the bad grade that is bound to come at the end of the term. In other words, she has learned she is helpless in this class. As a result, she may become mildly depressed.

Unless other information is forthcoming to counteract these feelings, this student may soon conclude there is no sense trying in other classes or in other parts of her life, such as sports, friendships or keeping up her appearance. She may decide she lacks control over most of life's outcomes and may eventually lose the motivation to try. In learned helplessness terms, she has inappropriately generalized her feelings of helplessness in one situation she can't control to others that she might be able to control.

Consistent with this interpretation of depression, people who find they cannot control relatively simple laboratory tasks, such as escaping the irritating noise, show significant increases in depressed feelings (Bodner & Mikulincer, 1998; Burger & Arkin, 1980). Other support for a learned helplessness–depression connection comes from research with animals. Investigators find changes in neurotransmitters and receptors in animals exposed to inescapable shock similar to what we see in the neurotransmitters and receptors of depressed individuals (Aznar et al., 2010; Dwivedi, Mondal, Payappagoudar, & Rizavi, 2005; Hammack, Cooper, & Lezak, 2012; Joca, Zanelati, & Guimaraes, 2006; Maier & Watkins, 2005). In particular, the neurotransmitter *serotonin* appears to play a role in the development of both learned helplessness and depression.

In short, data from many different sources suggest exposure to uncontrollable events can be a cause of depression. But one difference between laboratory-induced learned helplessness and genuine depression needs to be addressed. Learned helplessness in laboratory animals is short, typically lasting no more than a few days in rats and dogs (Maier, 2001). But clinical depression often lasts considerably longer, in some cases for years. One explanation for this discrepancy is that there are many different causes of depression, only one of which is learned helplessness. Another possibility is that, in a sense, people suffering from depression continually relive the initial helplessness induction. Depressed patients typically ruminate about the causes of their depression (Nolen-Hoeksema, 2000). By frequently thinking about the circumstances leading up to their depression, people may re-experience the helplessness-inducing events. Recall that even imagining oneself in an uncontrollable situation sometimes is sufficient to generate learned helplessness. Occasional reminders about the initial helplessness event can also reactivate depression. Consistent with this observation, when rats in one study were exposed periodically to the location in which their initial learned helplessness experience had occurred, researchers found no decline in learned helplessness over time (Maier, 2001).

In sum, learned helplessness has become an important model for understanding some kinds of depression. Experiences with uncontrollable aversive events may become the first step into a downward spiral of helplessness. Fortunately, research also suggests a treatment. People who experience success at controlling outcomes soon overcome feelings of helplessness (Klein & Seligman, 1976). Thus, all the failing student may need is a good grade in another class to appreciate that she still has the ability to succeed in school, make friends, and generally control her life. Moreover, as you'll discover in Chapter 16, whether people fall into learned helplessness may depend on how they explain their lack of control.

Locus of Control

If you're in good health, is it because you take care of yourself or because you're lucky? Are lonely people without friends because they don't try to meet other people or because they don't have many opportunities? When you win in a sporting contest, is it because you did your best or because of some lucky breaks? These are the kinds of questions researchers ask when they investigate individual differences in **locus of control.**

Research on locus of control developed out of Julian Rotter's concept of *generalized expectancies* described in Chapter 13. In a new situation, we have no information to draw upon when generating an expectation of what might happen. In these cases, Rotter argued, we rely on general beliefs about our ability to influence events. If you answered that good health comes from taking care of yourself, that loneliness is caused by not trying, and that winning a sporting contest is the result of effort, you probably maintain an *internal* locus of control orientation. Your generalized expectancy is that people can affect what happens to them and that good and bad experiences are generally of our own making. However, if you feel that health is a matter of luck, that people are lonely because of the circumstances they find themselves in, and that winning

●●● Assessing Your Own Personality

Locus of Control

Indicate the extent to which each of the following statements applies to you. Use the following scale: 1 = Disagree strongly, 2 = Disagree, 3 = Disagree slightly, 4 = Neither agree nor disagree, 5 = Agree slightly, 6 = Agree, 7 = Agree strongly.

_____   1. When I get what I want, it's usually because I worked hard for it.

_____   2. When I make plans, I am almost certain to make them work.

_____   3. I prefer games involving some luck over games requiring pure skill.

_____   4. I can learn almost anything if I set my mind to it.

_____   5. My major accomplishments are entirely due to my hard work and ability.

_____   6. I usually don't set goals because I have a hard time following through on them.

_____   7. Competition discourages excellence.

_____   8. Often people get ahead just by being lucky.

_____   9. On any sort of exam or competition I like to know how well I do relative to everyone else.

_____   10. It's pointless to keep working on something that's too difficult for me.

To determine your score, reverse the point values for items 3, 6, 7, 8, and 10 (1 = 7; 2 = 6; 3 = 5; 5 = 3; 6 = 2; 7 = 1). Then add the point values for each of the 10 items together. A recent sample of college students found a mean of 51.8 for males and 52.2 for females, with a standard deviation of about 6 for each. The higher your score, the more you tend to believe that you are generally responsible for what happens to you in personal achievement situations.

Scale: Personal Efficacy Scale

Source: Copyright 1998 by the American Psychological Association. Reproduced with permission. Paulhus, Delroy (1983) Sphere-specific measures of perceived control. *Journal of Personality and Social Psychology.* 44, 1253–1265. doi 10.1037/0022- 3514.44.6.1253. No further reproduction or distribution is permitted without written permission from the American Psychological Association.

means you got some lucky breaks, you probably fall on the *external* end of the locus of control dimension. More than most people, you believe that what happens to you and others is outside of your control. Because locus of control represents a generalized set of beliefs, it can potentially play a role in many areas of your life. In this chapter, we'll look at two of these areas—your psychological well-being and your physical health.

Locus of Control and Well-Being

Who is happier—internals who believe they can control most things or externals who recognize the limits that outside forces place on them? Which person is more productive, better liked, and better adjusted? A case can be made for either position. On one hand, we could argue that internals probably work harder and thus achieve more because they feel they control outcomes. Externals, who give up in the face of setbacks and who quickly conclude there is nothing they can do to correct a problem, are unlikely to get far in a world filled with obstacles and challenges. On the other hand, just because people believe they are in control does not mean they actually exercise control. Internal people may invest their efforts inefficiently chasing rainbows or making plans at odds with reality. Perhaps externals understand their limits and work to achieve only what is reasonably attainable.

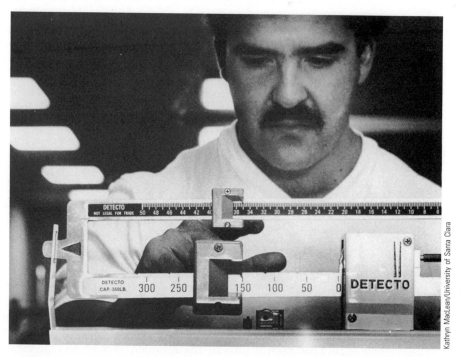

Kathryn MacLean/University of Santa Clara

Of the millions who try to lose weight each year, only a small number of people succeed in taking it off and keeping it off. One variable that may affect a diet's success or failure is the extent to which the dieter believes he or she is capable of losing the weight.

Of course, happiness is determined by many factors, and we can point to happy and unhappy people at any point on the locus of control spectrum. Nonetheless, researchers find that, with a few exceptions, internals tend to be happier than externals (DeNeve & Cooper, 1998; Ng, Sorensen, & Eby, 2006). To better understand why this might be the case, let's look at the connection between locus of control and three common markers of psychological well-being: psychological disorders, achievement, and psychotherapy results.

Psychological Disorders

People suffering from psychological disorders tend to be more external than internal (Cheng, Cheung, Chio, & Chun, 2013; Lefcourt, 1982). Researchers are particularly interested in the relationship between locus of control and depression. One review found an average correlation of .31 between locus of control scores and measures of depression, with external scores associated with higher levels of depression (Benassi, Sweeney, & Dufour, 1988).

The reasons for this connection between locus of control and depression tie back to the research on learned helplessness. It may be that externals often find themselves in situations similar to that of research participants who cannot control important outcomes. Consider a study in which recently diagnosed cancer patients were tested for level of depression (Marks, Richardson, Graham, & Levine, 1986). For external patients, the more severe the diagnosis, the more depressed they became. However, the severity of the disease had no impact on the depression experienced by internal patients. These patients believed they could still control the course of the disease, and this belief shielded them from giving up and becoming depressed about their situation. A similar pattern was found in a study with individuals suffering from Parkinson's Disease (Zampieri & de Souza, 2011).

A dramatic example of how locus of control is related to depression was demonstrated in a study of suicidal patients (Melges & Weisz, 1971). Patients who had recently attempted suicide were asked to relive the events that took place immediately before the attempt. Patients were left alone with a tape recorder and asked to describe in the present tense what had happened to them during this time. Analysis of the recordings revealed that patients described themselves in more external terms as they became more suicidal. Other studies find that suicide attempters often experience an increase in events outside their personal control just prior to the attempt (Slater & Depue, 1981) and that external adolescents and college students report more suicidal thoughts than internals (Burger, 1984; Evans, Owens, & Marsh, 2005).

Although research has established a link between locus of control and depression, we need to add a few notes of caution when interpreting the findings. First, the vast majority of people scoring on the external end of locus of control scales are happy and well-adjusted. Second, because the relationship is correlational, it is difficult to make strong statements about external locus of control causing the disorder. It may be that externals are susceptible to depression, but it is also possible that depressed people become more external. Third, the strength of the relationship between locus of control and depression may vary from culture to culture. One team of reviewers found the tendency for externals to experience more depression than internals is weaker in collectivist cultures in which personal demonstrations of masterful accomplishments are less likely to be valued (Cheng et al., 2013).

Achievement

One indicator of well-being in Western society is how much we achieve in school and in our careers. Although high achievers are by no means shielded from psychological problems, we often point to a deteriorating job performance as a reason for concern. Similarly, improved performance in school or work is often seen as evidence that a therapy client is getting better. When researchers use locus of control scores to predict achievement, they consistently find that internal students receive higher grades and better teacher evaluations than externals (Cappella & Weinstein, 2001; Findley & Cooper, 1983; Kalechstein & Nowicki, 1997; Richardson, Abraham & Bond, 2012). This finding is true of elementary, high school, and college students, but the relationship is especially strong among adolescents.

Why do internals do better in school? One reason is that they see themselves as being responsible for their achievements. Internal students believe studying for tests pays off, whereas externals are less likely to feel that their efforts affect their grades. Internals and externals also respond differently to feedback (Martinez, 1994). Internal students are likely to attribute high test scores to their abilities or to studying hard, whereas externals who do well might say they were lucky or that the test was easy. Internals also are better at adjusting their expectancies following feedback, which means they have a better idea of how to prepare for the next exam. Externals are more likely to make excuses following a poor performance (Basgall & Snyder, 1988). An external student who decides the teacher is an unfair grader probably will not prepare much for the next test. Because they believe academic success is up to them, internal students also pay attention to information that will help them reach their goals. One investigator found internal undergraduates were more likely than externals to know test dates, grading policies, and other relevant information that would help them do well in their classes (Dollinger, 2000). Internal students also are more ambitious than external students. Because they see outcomes as under their control, they are more likely to work to reach their goals. Internal college students are more likely than externals to complete their degrees in a timely fashion (Hall, Smith, & Chia, 2008). They also are more likely to apply to graduate school (Nordstrom & Segrist, 2009).

Higher achievement by internals is not limited to the classroom. Studies in career settings also find higher levels of performance for internal workers than for externals (Judge & Bono, 2001; Ng et al., 2006; Wang, Bowling, & Eschleman, 2010). People who believe that making a sale, inspiring employees, or completing a job on time is largely up to them are more likely to reach those goals than workers who fail to see their role in achieving work objectives (Judge, Erez, & Bono, 1998). Not surprisingly, researchers find internals score higher than externals on measures of job satisfaction (Judge & Bono, 2001, Ng et al., 2006). Externals also are less likely to miss work, complain about work-related stress or experience burnout (Wang et al., 2010).

Although ideas about achievement vary across cultures, the relationship between perceived control and achievement appears to be widespread. One team of investigators examined locus of control and job satisfaction among managers in large corporations in 24 countries (Spector et al., 2001). Across different cultures, managers who experienced a great deal of control over their work environment reported consistently higher levels of satisfaction with their jobs than managers who felt they had little control.

Psychotherapy

As a general rule, clients tend to become more internal as they pass through successful psychotherapy (Strickland, 1978). Consider the case of Israeli soldiers suffering from post-traumatic stress disorder following their experiences with intense combat (Solomon, Mikulincer, & Avitzur, 1988). These men suffered from a variety of symptoms often found after a profoundly stressful experience. When tested shortly after combat, the soldiers scored fairly external on locus of control measures. However, as they recovered from their trauma over the next 3 years, they became increasingly internal. As the soldiers came to appreciate the control they could exercise over many parts of their lives, they took an important step toward recovery.

Does this mean that therapists should focus on giving clients more control over therapy? Not necessarily. Although internals respond well when given control over their treatment, externals sometimes do better when treatment remains in the therapist's hands (Schwartz & Higgins, 1979). One team of investigators looked at depression levels in patients with rheumatoid arthritis (Reich & Zautra, 1997). The external patients became less depressed when their spouses provided them with a lot of support and assistance. However, internal patients showed an increase in depression when their spouse gave this same amount of assistance. The researchers speculate that the spouse's care was seen as helpful by the externals but as an indication of dependence by the internals.

Locus of Control and Health

One of the most frustrating problems health care professionals face is lack of patient cooperation. Many patients discontinue their therapy programs or simply stop taking their medicines. But this is not true of everyone. Some patients do an excellent job of watching their diets, taking medication, attending therapy, and keeping appointments. Observations like these lead some psychologists to suggest that locus of control might have an impact on our health (Strickland, 1989; Wallston, 2005). Those who believe their health is largely in their own hands will do what they can to get better. Those who attribute poor health to bad genes or fate may see little reason to make the effort.

Researchers generally find that internals are in better health than externals. One study followed 5,114 middle-aged men and women for an eight and half year period (Sturmer & Hasselbach, 2006). Locus of control scores taken at the beginning of the study were strong predictors of which participants would suffer from heart attacks and cancer by the end of the study. Internals were significantly less likely to experience these health problems than externals.

Another investigation measured locus of control in 10 year olds (Gale, Batty, & Deary, 2008). When the researchers contacted these individuals again 20 years later, they found the participants identified as internals two decades earlier were in significantly better health than those identified as externals.

Psychologists explain these effects in terms of the way internals and externals approach their physical health. People who take an external orientation toward their health believe there is little they can do to improve their physical condition or avoid disease. Whether they become ill is out of their control, and when they become ill they depend on health professionals to make them well again. On the other hand, people with an internal locus of control believe they have a significant role in maintaining good health. Because they see a relationship between what they do and how they feel, internals are more likely than externals to eat well and participate in health-maintaining exercise programs, such as aerobics or jogging.

Consistent with these descriptions, several studies find that internals practice better health habits and are generally healthier than externals (Johansson et al., 2001; Klonowicz, 2001; Ng et al., 2006; O'Hea, Grothe, Bodenlos, Boudreaux, White, & Brantley, 2005; Perrig-Chiello, Perrig, & Staehelin, 1999; Simoni & Ng, 2002). One investigation found college students who held an external locus of control toward their health were more likely to smoke, drink alcohol, skip breakfast, eat fatty foods, and consume less fruit and fiber than internals (Steptoe & Wardle, 2001). Internals also have more confidence in their ability to control stressful situations and, therefore, are less likely to suffer the health-harming consequences of stress (Weinstein & Quigley, 2006). A study of business executives in high-stress positions found that internals were less likely to become ill than externals (Kobasa, 1979).

Internals also are more likely than externals to seek out information about health problems (Grotz, Hapke, Lampert, & Baumeister, 2011). However, as with psychotherapy success, a match between locus of control and the health message may be the most effective approach. One study looked at the effectiveness of campaigns encouraging middle-aged women to obtain a mammogram (Williams-Piehota, Schneider, Pizarro, Mowad, & Salovey, 2004). Half the women received a brochure and a phone call that were targeted to internals. The brochure was titled "The Best Thing *You* Can Do for Your Health," and contained messages like, "You hold the key to your health." The other half received messages targeted to externals. The brochure was titled, "The Best Thing Medical Science Has to Offer for Your Health," with messages like, "Health care providers hold the key to your health." As shown in Figure 14.9, internal women were more likely to get a mammogram within the next 6 months when they received the internally worded messages. In contrast, external women were more likely to get a mammogram when receiving the externally oriented message.

Although researchers often find a connection between locus of control and health, this is not always the case. Some investigations fail to find health differences between internals and externals or find only weak effects (Bettencourt, Talley, Molix, Schlegel, & Westgate, 2008; Norman &

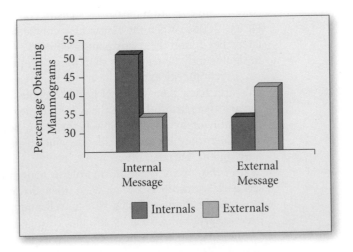

FIGURE 14.9 Percentage of Women Obtaining Mammograms

Source: Adapted from Williams-Piehota et al. (2004).

Bennett, 1996). Why might this be so? To answer this question, we need to return to Rotter's theory. Recall that Rotter said behavior was a function of both expectancy and reinforcement value. That is, I might expect that studying for a test will result in a good grade. However, if I don't value that grade, I am still unlikely to make the effort.

Psychologists make similar predictions when they apply Rotter's model to health behaviors (Wallston, 1992; Wallston & Smith, 1994). That is, believing that your actions can affect your health is not enough. You also need to place great value on good health. Of course, everyone wants good health. But if you think about some of the people you know, you probably can identify those who place health at the top of their concerns and those who don't. According to the theory, people who place a high value on their health *and* who believe there is something they can do to control their health are the ones who watch what they eat, exercise, and get regular checkups. You might believe that daily exercise leaves you feeling fit and full of energy. But if you don't particularly value these effects (especially if you value less-exhausting activities more), it's unlikely you'll enroll in a fitness program.

Several investigations find evidence for this reasoning (Norman & Bennett, 1996; Wallston & Smith, 1994). Internal participants in one study who placed a high value on health were found to eat more fruits and vegetables and fewer fatty foods and snacks than either external participants or internals who did not value physical health (Bennett, Moore, Smith, Murphy, & Smith, 1994). Similar results have been found in studies looking at breast self-examination (Lau, Hartman, & Ware, 1986) and efforts to stop smoking (Kaplan & Cowles, 1978). In short, health professionals face two tasks when trying to get patients to take better care of themselves. Patients must place their health high on their list of things they value, and they must believe that they can influence the extent to which they are healthy.

Summary

1. From the day we are born, most of us face tremendous socialization pressures to take on the gender roles deemed appropriate by society. Through a combination of operant conditioning and observational learning, boys tend to act like other boys, and girls like other girls. Research on individual differences in gender-role behavior was originally stifled by a model that viewed masculinity and femininity as polar opposites. The androgyny model sees these as two independent traits and argues that the most well-adjusted people are those who are androgynous—that is, high in both masculinity and femininity.

2. Researchers agree that exposure to aggressive models increases a person's likelihood of acting aggressively. Bandura's four-step model helps explain why people sometimes imitate aggressive acts they see and sometimes do not. Before people imitate aggression, they must attend to the act, recall it, have the opportunity to engage in the behavior, and believe the aggression will lead to rewards. Research from laboratory and long-term field studies indicates that exposure to mass media violence increases aggressive behavior.

3. Like much behavioral research, work on learned helplessness began with experiments on laboratory animals. Researchers observed that dogs that learned they were helpless to escape shock in one situation inappropriately generalized this perception of helplessness to a new situation. Subsequent research found that humans are also susceptible to this effect. Research suggests elderly people may adjust better to retirement communities when they are allowed to retain some control over their situation. Depression may develop when people perceive a lack of control over an important event and inappropriately generalize that perception to other aspects of their lives.

4. The most widely researched aspect of Rotter's social learning theory is the notion of individual differences in generalized expectancies, or locus of control. At one end of this dimension we find internals, who generally believe they control what happens to them. On the other end are externals, who generally hold that what happens to them is under the control of outside forces. Internals generally do better than externals on measures of well-being and health.

Key Terms

androgyny (p. 380)

learned helplessness (p. 398)

locus of control (p. 403)

masculinity–femininity (p. 379)

Media Resources

Visit the book companion website at **www.cengagebrain.com** to find a glossary, flashcards, quizzing, and more.

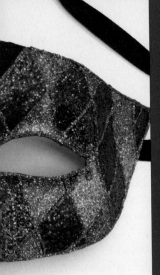

CHAPTER 15

The Cognitive Approach

Theory, Application, and Assessment

I went to a social gathering with a friend of mine recently. We talked with old friends, met some new people, and mingled, sampling conversations, music, food, and drink. As is our custom, we immediately shared our perceptions after leaving the party. "Did you notice how casually some people were dressed?" my friend asked. Actually, I hadn't. I asked him what he thought of a man we had both met. "Wasn't he the most arrogant person?" I asked. My friend hadn't seen anything to indicate so. As we continued to exchange impressions, I began to wonder if my friend had been at the same party interacting with the same people I had. I couldn't believe he hadn't noticed how weird the music was or realized how ill at ease the hostess seemed. My friend didn't understand how I had failed to recognize the architecture of the house or even the furniture I sat on. "I guess we learned one lesson," I said. "Never go to a party at their house again." My friend stared at me in disbelief. "Are you kidding?" he said. "I had a great time!"

How can two people participate in the same situation yet leave with very different impressions of what happened? The answer from the cognitive approach to personality is that my friend and I have very different ways of processing information. Whereas I was attending to and processing information about the weirdness of the music and the arrogance of the guests, my friend entered the party prepared to notice clothing styles and furniture. Because we attended to different features of the party, we had very different perceptions of it and very different experiences. These different perceptions no doubt affected how we acted that night and how we will respond to future invitations.

The cognitive approach explains differences in personality as differences in the way people process information. Because I have developed relatively stable ways of processing information in social settings, I probably respond to parties and other social gatherings in a similar way most of the time. Other people respond differently than I do because they consistently perceive something different from what I perceive.

Cognitive models of personality have become popular in recent years, but they are not entirely new. An early predecessor can be found in Kurt Lewin's (1938) field theory of behavior. Lewin described the mental representations we form of the important elements in our lives and how we organize those cognitive elements within our "life space." A more recent and, for the purposes of this book, more important cognitive personality theory was developed by George Kelly. Since the publication of his book *The Psychology of Personal Constructs* in 1955, Kelly's work has evolved into a rich source of ideas for personality researchers and psychotherapists (Fransella, 2003, 2005). It is interesting that Kelly did not think of himself as a cognitive psychologist. "I have been so puzzled over the early labeling of [my] theory as cognitive," he wrote, "that several years ago I set out to write another short book to make it clear that I wanted no part of cognitive theory" (1969, p. 216). Despite his protests, Kelly's writings have become the starting point for many of the approaches to personality we now identify as "cognitive."

Personal Construct Theory

George Kelly's approach to personality begins with a unique conception of humankind. He called it a *man-the-scientist* perspective. Like scientists, people constantly generate and test hypotheses about their world. Just as scientists try to predict and control the things they study, we all want to predict and control as many events in our lives as possible. Not knowing why things happen or how the people around us might act can be unsettling. So to satisfy our need for predictability, we engage in a process Kelly compared to template matching. That is, our ideas about the world are similar to transparent templates. We place these templates over the events we encounter. If they match, we retain the templates. If not, we modify them for a better prediction next time. For example, based on past observations, you may have generated a few hypotheses about one of your instructors. One hypothesis is that this man is stuffy and arrogant. Whenever you see this instructor, you collect more information and compare the new data with your hypothesis. If it is verified (the instructor acts the way stuffy people act), you continue using it. If not (outside of the classroom he is warm and charming), you discard the hypothesis and replace it with a new one. The process resembles the one used by scientists who retain and reject hypotheses based on empirical findings.

Kelly called the cognitive structures we use to interpret and predict events **personal constructs**. No two people use identical personal constructs, and no two people organize their constructs in an identical manner. What do these constructs look like? Kelly described them as bipolar. That is, we classify relevant objects in an either/or fashion within our constructs. When I meet someone for the first time, I might apply the personal constructs *friendly–unfriendly, tall–short, intelligent–unintelligent,* and *masculine–feminine* in constructing an image of this person. I might decide that this person is friendly, tall, intelligent, and feminine. But the bipolar nature of personal constructs does not mean that we see the world as black and white with no shades of gray. After applying our first construct, we often use other bipolar constructs to determine the extent of the blackness or whiteness. For example, after determining that this new acquaintance is intelligent, I might then apply an *academically intelligent–commonsense intelligent* construct to get an even clearer picture of what this person is like.

How can personal constructs be used to explain personality? Kelly maintained that differences in personality result largely from differences in the way people "construe the world." If you and I interact with Jacob, I might use *friendly–unfriendly, fun–boring,* and *outgoing–shy* constructs in forming my impression. But you might interpret Jacob in terms of *refined–gross, sensitive–insensitive,* and *intelligent–unintelligent* constructs. After we both talk to Jacob for a while, I might act as if I'm interacting with a friendly, fun, and outgoing person. You might respond to Jacob as if dealing with a gross, insensitive, and unintelligent person. We're both in the same situation, but because we interpret that situation very differently, we respond in very different ways. In addition, because I tend to use these same constructs when meeting other individuals, I probably have a characteristic way I interact with

George Kelly

1905–1967

National Library of Medicine

George Alexander Kelly was born in a farming community near Wichita, Kansas, in 1905. He attended Friends University in Wichita for 3 years before graduating from Park College in Missouri in 1926. He was an active member of the intercollegiate debate team during these years and developed a keen ability to challenge arguments and conventional positions. Although these skills would eventually become an asset, they may have kept him away from

the field of psychology for many years. Kelly described his first psychology course as boring and unconvincing. The instructor spent considerable time discussing learning theories, but Kelly was unimpressed. "The most I could make of it was that the S was what you had to have in order to account for the R, and the R was put there so the S would have something to account for," he wrote. "I never did find out what that arrow stood for" (1969, pp. 46–47). He was also skeptical when he first read Freud. "I don't remember which one of Freud's books I was trying to read," he recalled, "but I do remember the mounting feeling of incredulity that anyone could write such nonsense, much less publish it" (p. 47).

After graduating with a degree in physics and mathematics, Kelly went to the University of Kansas to study educational sociology. After a series of odd jobs, including teaching speech and working as an aeronautical engineer, he went to

the University of Edinburgh to study education in 1929. While there, he developed a growing interest in psychology and received his PhD in psychology from the University of Iowa a few years later.

Kelly spent the next 10 years at Fort Hays Kansas State College. During this time he set up a network of clinics to provide psychological services to the poor and destitute Dust Bowl victims of the 1930s. "I listened to people in trouble," he wrote, "and tried to help them figure out what they could do about it" (p. 50). He soon came to see that what these people needed most was an explanation for what had happened to them and an ability to predict what would happen to them in the future. Personal construct theory evolved from this insight. After serving in the navy in World War II, Kelly spent a year at the University of Maryland and then 20 years at Ohio State University. He moved to Brandeis University in 1965 and died soon after.

people that is different from yours. In other words, the relatively stable patterns in our behavior are the result of the relatively stable way we construe the world.

Personal Construct Systems

To get a rough idea of your own personal constructs, ask yourself what you tend to notice about people when you first meet them. The first few thoughts that come to mind are probably some of the constructs you typically use to make sense of other people and their behavior. It is also possible that two people use the same constructs but construe the world differently. That is, I might think someone intelligent, and you might see the same person as unintelligent. Further, two people's constructs might be similar on one pole but not the other. I might use an *outgoing–reserved* construct, whereas you use an *outgoing–melancholy* construct. If that were the case, what I see as reserved behavior you might see as sadness.

One reason you and I act differently from each other is that we use different constructs. Another reason is that we organize our constructs differently. After I determine that a new acquaintance appears friendly, I might want to know if the person is outgoing or quiet. We could diagram the relation between my constructs this way:

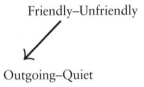

Note that within this construct system, I could not see an unfriendly person as either outgoing or quiet, just unfriendly. On the other hand, you might use the same constructs but organize them this way:

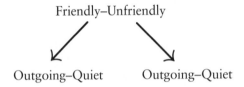

In this case, whether you judge someone as friendly or unfriendly, you can still judge that person as either outgoing or quiet. Of course, it is also possible to organize these same two constructs this way:

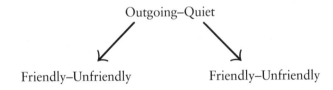

In this case, after deciding someone is a quiet person, you might want to know if she is a quiet–friendly person or a quiet–unfriendly one. In short, not only do we use a limitless number of constructs to make sense of our world, but the ways we organize and use these constructs also are practically endless.

Inadequate Personal Constructs

Like many personality theorists, Kelly was a practicing psychotherapist who applied his ideas about personality to treating psychological problems. However, unlike many theorists, Kelly rejected the notion that psychological disorders are caused by past traumatic experiences. Rather, he argued, people suffer from psychological problems because of defects in their construct systems. Past experiences with an unloving parent or a tragic incident may explain *why* people construe the world as they do, but they are not the *cause* of the person's problems.

Kelly placed anxiety at the heart of most psychological problems. We become anxious when our personal constructs fail to make sense of the events in our lives. We have all had this experience on occasion. An upcoming interview will cause more anxiety if you have no idea who you will meet or what kind of questions you will be asked. Similarly, when you can't understand why certain people treat you the way they do or you don't know how to behave in certain situations, you probably feel confused, disoriented, and anxious. Relationship problems are particularly unsettling when you don't know why things are going poorly and have no idea how to put the relationship back on track.

The problem is that construct systems are never perfect. For a variety of reasons, our constructs occasionally fail us. Most of the time, we simply generate a new construct to replace the inadequate one. If you anticipate that a conversation with Anna is going to be boring but then find it interesting, you will probably alter your expectations for future encounters with Anna. But failure to consider this new information lessens your ability to predict what will happen the next time you interact with Anna. You may have experienced this frustration when you said to someone, "I just don't understand you anymore."

Cognitive Personality Variables

In the early days of behaviorism (Chapter 13), psychologists sometimes used a "black box" metaphor to describe the relationship between stimuli and responses. In this model, features in the environment (e.g., a loud noise) cause behaviors (e.g., running away). But what happens inside the organism between the stimulus and response is unknown and unknowable, that is, the black box. In contrast, the elements between stimulus and response are extremely important to cognitive personality psychologists. In recent years, these psychologists have introduced a large number of cognitive variables to account for individual differences (Mischel & Shoda, 1995, 2008; Shoda, Tiernan, & Mischel, 2002). Some of these cognitive variables, sometimes called *cognitive-affective units,* are shown in Table 15.1.

TABLE 15.1 Cognitive-Affective Units

Encodings	Categories (constructs) for encoding information about one's self, other people, events, and situations
Expectations and Beliefs	Expectations for what will happen in certain situations, for outcomes for certain behaviors, and for one's personal efficacy
Affects	Feelings, emotions, and emotional responses
Goals and Values	Individual goals and values, and life projects
Competencies and Self-Regulatory Plans	Perceived abilities, plans, and strategies for changing and maintaining one's behavior and internal states

Source: From A Cognitive-Affective System Theory of Personality: Reconceptualizing Situations, Disposition, Dynamics, and Invariance in Personality Structure, by W. Mischel and Y. Shoda, *Psychological Review*, 1995, 102, 246–148. Copyright © 1995 American Psychological Association.

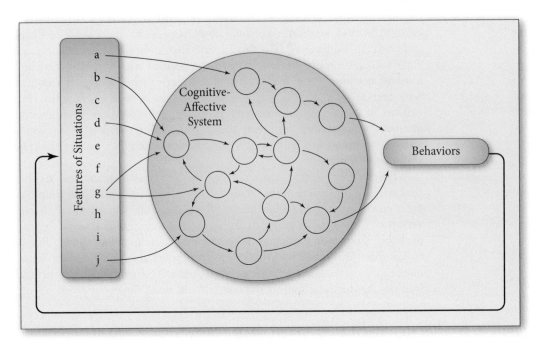

FIGURE 15.1 Cognitive Model of Personality

Source: From A Cognitive-Affective System Theory of Personality: Reconceptualizing Situations, Disposition, Dynamics, and Invariance in Personality Structure, by W. Mischel and Y. Shoda, *Psychological Review*, 1995, 102, 246148. Copyright 1995 American Psychological Association.

Cognitive variables are part of a complex system that links the situations we encounter with our behavior. An oversimplified illustration of this process is shown in Figure 15.1. How we react to features in the environment, and even whether we notice these features, depends on our cognitive structures. Once perceived, various mental representations, such as expectations, values and goals, interact with one another to determine how we respond to the situation. Notice also that, as in some of the social learning models, our behavior can then affect the situation.

How do we explain individual differences within this cognitive framework? The answer is that each of us possesses a different set of mental representations. In addition, how easily we access certain kinds of information stored in memory varies from individual to individual. As a result, two people often react to the same situation differently. What one person hears as a clever retort someone else might take as an insult. A Christmas tree will remind one person of religious values, another of family and seasonal joy, and a third of sad memories from childhood.

Cognitive Representations of the Self

Of all the cognitive structures studied by researchers, the most important for understanding personality are the mental representations that are unique to you. Beginning at a very early age, each of us develops a cognitive representation of ourselves. Psychologists sometimes refer to this representation as our self-concept. As with other personality constructs, researchers find that our self-concepts are relatively stable over time (Markus & Kunda, 1986). Moreover, research indicates that cognitive representations of the self play a central role in the way we process information and thus in how we interact with the world around us.

Self-Schemas

Surveys tell us that most Americans believe exercise is good for their physical and mental health. The majority of adults periodically take up jogging, swimming, aerobic dancing, or some other type of exercise program. However, a large number of people rarely, if ever, exercise. And about half of those who begin an exercise program quit within the first year. Why do some people succeed in making exercise a part of their lives, whereas others fail? One explanation has to do with whether the would-be exerciser incorporates exercise into his or her self-schema.

Self-schemas are cognitive representations of ourselves that we use to organize and process self-relevant information (Markus, 1977, 1983). Your self-schema consists of the behaviors and attributes that are most important to you. Because each part of your life is not equally important, not everything you do becomes part of your self-schema. If both you and I occasionally play softball and write poetry, we can't assume that these two activities play an equally important role in our self-schemas. Softball might be an important part of how I think of myself, but not poetry, whereas the opposite might be the case for you.

If you could see your self-schema, what would it look like? An example is shown in Figure 15.2. Basic information about you makes up the core of your self-schema. This includes your name, information about your physical appearance, and information about your relationships with significant people, such as with a spouse or parents. Although different for each of us, these basic elements are found in nearly everyone's self-schema. More interesting to personality psychologists are the unique features within your self-schema (Markus & Sentis, 1982; Markus & Smith, 1981). Returning to the exercise question, some people include *athlete* or *physically fit* in their self-schemas. Another way of saying this is that these individuals consider their athletic activities a part of who they are. Researchers find that people who incorporate these identities into their self-schemas are more likely to stick with regular exercise programs than those who do not (Kendzierski, 1988, 1990). When exercising becomes a part of who you are, you are much less likely to give it up when the weather turns bad or you experience a few aches and pains.

Trait concepts, such as independence or friendliness, can also be part of your self-schema. That is, you might think of yourself as a friendly person. If that is the case, you frequently evaluate your behavior by asking yourself, "Was that a friendly thing to do?" However, it might never occur to me to evaluate my actions in terms of friendliness. In this example, friendliness is a feature of your self-schema, but not mine. Because the elements that constitute

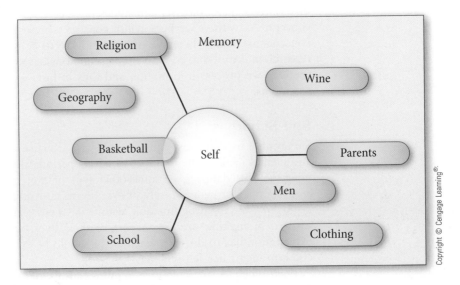

FIGURE 15.2 Example of a Self-Schema Diagram

self-schemas vary from person to person, we process information about ourselves differently. And because of these individual differences in self-schemas, we behave differently. In one study, elementary school children with *prosocial* as a part of their self-schemas were more likely to give valuable tokens to others than children who did not include *prosocial* as part of their self-concepts (Froming, Nasby, & McManus, 1998). In another investigation, men and women whose self-schemas included *sexuality* reported higher levels of sexual desire and stronger romantic attachments than those whose self-schemas did not include *sexuality* (Andersen, Cyranowski, & Espindle, 1999; Cyranowski & Andersen, 2000). One team of researchers found that Latino Americans were more likely than White Americans to include *simpatico* (an interpersonal style emphasizing hospitality and graciousness) in their self-schemas (Holloway, Waldrip, & Ickes, 2009). Participants with *simpatico* as part of their self-schema were found to interact with others in a warmer, more engaged style.

But how do psychologists determine what a person's self-schema looks like? Although examining something as abstract as self-schemas presents a challenge, cognitive personality researchers have developed some creative procedures to test their hypotheses. Essentially, these psychologists look at how people perceive and use information presented to them. For example, answer the following question yes or no: Are you a competitive person? When faced with this question on a personality inventory, some people answer immediately and decisively, whereas others have to pause to think about what it means to be competitive and whether they possess those qualities. In taking the various personality tests in this book, you probably found some items were easy to answer and some for which you simply couldn't make up your mind. According to a self-schema analysis, the items that were easy to answer are those for which you have a well-defined schema. People who say yes immediately when asked if they are competitive have a strong *competitive* schema that is part of their self-schema. The schema enables them to understand the question, retrieve relevant information and respond immediately. People without a strong *competitive* schema are unable to process the information as quickly.

Much of the early research on self-schemas was based on this reasoning. Participants in one study were classified as possessing either a strong *independence* schema or a strong *dependence* schema or as aschematic (Markus, 1977). Later these participants were presented with a series of adjectives on a computer screen. Their task was to press either a ME or a NOT ME button to indicate whether the adjective described them. Fifteen of the adjectives were related to independence (e.g., *individualistic, outspoken*) and 15 to dependence (e.g., *conforming, submissive*). As Figure 15.3 shows, people with strong *independence* schemas pressed the ME button quickly on the independence-related adjectives but took longer to respond on the

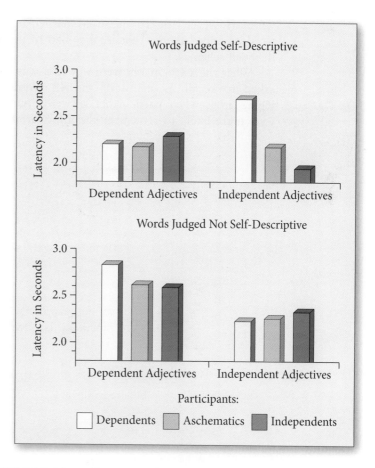

FIGURE 15.3 Mean Response Latencies for Adjectives

Source: From "Self-schemata and processing information about the self," by H. Markus, *Journal of Personality and Social Psychology*, 1977, 35, 63–78. Reprinted by permission of the American Psychological Association.

dependence-related adjectives. Participants with strong *dependence* schemas responded in the opposite pattern. Aschematics showed no difference in making these judgments for any of the words. Researchers find similar results when they divide participants along other personality dimensions (Shah & Higgins, 2001).

In addition to allowing for rapid processing of schema-relevant information, self-schemas provide a framework for organizing and storing this information. Consequently, we would expect people to retrieve information from memory more readily when they have a strong schema for a topic than when the information is stored in a less organized manner. To test this hypothesis, researchers presented college students with a series of 40 questions on a computer screen (Rogers, Kuiper, & Kirker, 1977). Participants answered each question by pressing a YES or a NO button as quickly as possible. Thirty of the questions were written so that people could answer easily without using their self-schemas to process the information. For these questions, participants simply answered whether a word was printed in big letters, whether it rhymed with another word, or whether it meant the same thing as another word. However, for 10 questions participants had to decide whether the word described them. That is, they had to process the information through their self-schemas.

What the participants were not told was that afterward they would be asked to recall as many of the 40 words as possible. As shown in Figure 15.4, when participants answered questions about themselves, they were more likely to remember the information than when the question was

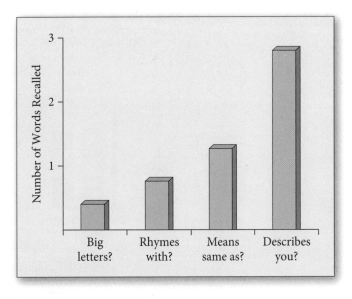

FIGURE 15.4 Mean Number of Words Recalled as a Function of Cue Question

Source: From Rogers, et al. (1977). Self-reference and the encoding of personal information. *Journal of Personality and Social Psychology, 35,* 677–688. Reprinted by permission of the American Psychological Association.

processed in other ways. The researchers point to this finding as evidence for a self-schema. When asked whether a word describes them, participants processed the question through their self-schemas. Because information in our self-schemas is easy to access, the self-referent words were easier to remember than those not processed through self-schemas. But might this finding be explained in other ways? Could it be that the self-referent question was simply harder than the other questions, thus causing participants to think about it more? Apparently not. When people are asked if a word describes a celebrity—a question that also requires some thinking—they don't recall the words as well as when they are asked about themselves (Lord, 1980).

This *self-reference effect* has been found in a large number of investigations using a wide variety of memory material (Klein, 2012; Symons & Johnson, 1997). It also seems to be the case that we often relate new information we encounter to something about ourselves. For example, when a friend tells you she went to Paris, you might think of your own visit to Paris. Moreover, information processed in this self-related manner should be more readily accessible in memory than information we are unable to relate to ourselves. To test this possibility, one team of researchers asked undergraduates to list friends' birthdays they could recall (Kesebir & Oishi, 2010). Consistent with other research on self-schemas, the students were significantly more likely to remember a friend's birthday when that birthday was close to their own. That is, if you and your friend both have birthdays in November, you are more likely to recall that friend's birthday than if your friend had been born in April.

Possible Selves

Suppose two college students, Denise and Carlos, receive an identical poor grade in a course on deductive logic and argumentation. Neither of them is pleased with the grade, but Denise quickly dismisses it as a bad semester, whereas Carlos frets about the grade for weeks. Denise turns her attention to the next term, but Carlos looks over his final exam several times and thinks about taking another course in this area. Although many explanations can be suggested to account for the two students' different reactions, a key piece of information may be that Carlos is thinking about going to law school and becoming a trial attorney someday, but Denise is not. A negative evaluation of his deductive logic and argumentation skills means something quite different to Carlos than it does to Denise.

Our behavior is directed not only by cognitive representations of the way we think of ourselves at the moment, but also by representations of what we might become. You might think about a future self with a lot of friends, with a medical degree, or with a physically fit body. Psychologists refer to these images as our possible selves (Markus & Nurius, 1986; Ruvolo & Markus, 1992; Vignoles, Manzi, Regalia, Jemmolo, & Scabini, 2008). **Possible selves** are cognitive representations of the kind of person we might become someday. These include roles and occupations we aspire to, such as police officer or community leader, as well as the roles we fear we might fall into, such as alcoholic or divorced parent. Possible selves also include the attributes we think we might possess in the future, such as being a warm and loving person, an overworked and underappreciated employee, or a contributor to society. In a sense, possible selves represent our dreams and aspirations as well as our fears and anxieties. Like other personality constructs, possible selves are fairly stable over time (Frazier, Hooker, Johnson, & Kaus, 2000; Morfei, Hooker, Fiese, & Cordeiro, 2001).

Possible selves serve two important functions (Markus & Nurius, 1986). First, they provide incentives for future behavior. When making decisions, we ask ourselves whether a choice will take us closer to or further away from one of our future selves. A woman might enter an MBA program because this decision moves her closer to becoming her *powerful business executive* possible self. A man might stop seeing old friends if he thinks the association could lead him to the *criminal* self he fears he might become.

The second function of possible selves is to help us interpret the meaning of our behavior and the events in our lives. A man with a *professional baseball pitcher* possible self will attach a very different meaning to an arm injury than someone who does not think of himself this way. A woman with a possible self of *cancer patient* will react differently to small changes in her health than someone without this cognitive representation. In other words, we pay more attention to and have a stronger emotional reaction to events that are relevant to our possible selves.

Because possible selves guide many of our choices and reactions, they can be useful in predicting future behavior. Researchers have used measures of possible selves to look at such varied behaviors as binge drinking (Quinlan, Jaccard, & Blanton, 2006), academic performance (Oyserman et al., 2006; Oyserman, Johnson, & James, 2011), weight loss (Granberg, 2006), and adherence to an exercise program (Ouellette, Hessling, Gibbons, Reis-Bergan, & Gerrard, 2005). Other research has tied possible selves to problem behaviors. One team of investigators examined possible selves in juvenile delinquents (Oyserman & Markus, 1990; Oyserman & Saltz, 1993). Significantly, more than one-third of the juvenile delinquents had developed a *criminal* possible self. In addition, very few of these adolescents possessed possible selves for more conventional goals, such as having a job. Because possible selves are indicative of our goals, fears, and aspirations, we should not be surprised if many of these youthful offenders were to become adult criminals.

Researchers also find gender differences in the possible selves of young men and young women. In particular, female high school and college students are less likely than males to see themselves in traditionally masculine roles in the future. University women are less likely than men to have a possible self that includes a career in a math, science or business (Lips, 2004). Male students are less likely than women to see themselves in careers related to arts, culture, and communication. However, research also points to solutions for these gender discrepancies. High school girls who have female friends interested in science and who receive encouragement from their peers are more likely to develop a *scientist* possible self (Buday, Stake, & Peterson, 2012; Stake & Nickens, 2005). Same-gender role models also help. High school girls who see women scientists and business leaders are more likely to incorporate these occupations into their possible selves. People are more optimistic about reaching their hoped-for occupation when they know someone already in that position (Robinson, Davis, & Meara, 2003).

Self Discrepancies

While reading the previous section, you may have been struck by the similarities between possible selves and Carl Rogers' description of the *real-self* and *ideal-self* (Chapter 11). Rogers described the difficulties people face when the person they believe themselves to be is very different from the person they would like to be. Cognitive personality psychologists have also explored the relation between different self-concepts. One approach, called *self-discrepancy theory*, proposes three different cognitive representations of the self (Higgins, 1987, 1989). First, each of us possesses an *actual self*. The actual self contains all the information you have about the kind of person you are (or believe you are), similar to the notion of self-concept used by other personality psychologists. Second, you also possess an *ideal self*, which is your mental image of the kind of person you would like to be. The ideal self includes your dreams and aspirations and the goals you have set for yourself in life. Third, there is the *ought self*. This is the self you believe you should be, the kind of person who fulfills all the duties and obligations various sources (parents, religion) have defined for you. Your ought self might be a devoted parent, a patriotic citizen, or someone who gets involved in community activities.

According to the theory, we often compare the way we act (our actual self) with the way we want to be (ideal self) or the way we should be (ought self). Not surprisingly, we often fall short in these comparisons. Discrepancies between our actual self and ideal self result in disappointment, dejection, and sometimes sadness. This is the reaction of a would-be honors student who becomes lax in his or her study habits and receives low grades. On the other hand, discrepancies between the actual self and the ought self lead to agitation, anxiety, and guilt. These are the emotions we might expect when we act selfishly or take advantage of someone, in contrast with the generous and kind person we think we ought to be. As with other cognitive processes, this comparison is said to take place outside of conscious awareness. Thus you can experience sadness or guilt without being aware of why you feel that way.

Researchers find support for many of the predictions generated from self-discrepancy theory. In particular, individuals made aware of a gap between their actual and ideal self often experience sadness, whereas those with discrepant actual and ought selves suffer from anxiety (Cornette, Strauman, Abramson, & Busch, 2009; Hardin & Lakin, 2009; Petrocelli & Smith, 2005; Phillips & Silva, 2005; Renaud & McConnell, 2007). Researchers also find that, like other personality variables, measures of an adult's ideal-self and ought-self are fairly consistent over time (Strauman, 1996). Although little is known about how self-discrepancies affect emotions in other cultures, one study found Japanese undergraduates had larger discrepancies between their actual and ideal selves than did Canadian students (Heine & Lehman,

1999). Interestingly, this increase in self-criticism by the Japanese students did not translate into higher levels of depression.

Application: Cognitive (Behavior) Psychotherapy

"The best scientist is one who approaches his subject [as] intimately as a clinician ... and the best clinician is one who invites his client to join him in a controlled investigation of life."

GEORGE KELLY

The increased attention given to cognitive structures by personality researchers in recent years has been paralleled by the growing popularity of cognitive approaches to psychotherapy. As described in Chapter 13, today many therapists combine cognitive approaches to therapy with procedures from traditional behavioral therapies. But whether they call themselves cognitive therapists or cognitive-behavior therapists, each identifies inappropriate thoughts as a cause of mood disorders and self-defeating behavior. People become anxious and depressed because they harbor anxiety-provoking and depressing thoughts. Consequently, the goal of most cognitive therapies is to help clients recognize inappropriate thoughts and replace them with more appropriate ones. A cognitive therapist's role usually falls somewhere between that of the intrusive Freudian therapist and the Rogerian therapist who relies on the client for clinical progress. Although clients must come to see how their cognitions affect their emotions and behaviors, the therapist plays an active role in the process.

In addition to addressing current issues, cognitive psychologists often teach clients how to deal with future and recurring problems (Meichenbaum & Deffenbacher, 1988). One cause of recurring problems is *self-defeating thinking* (Meichenbaum & Cameron, 1983). A man who suffers from shyness probably approaches a party telling himself something like this: "I don't know why I'm going to this dumb party. No one ever wants to talk with me. And when they do, I usually sound awkward and stupid." This man has set himself up to fail. At the first awkward moment, he will conclude that things are going as poorly as anticipated. All the nervousness and embarrassment he dreaded are likely to follow.

What can be done for this man? A cognitive therapist might try to replace these self-defeating thoughts with more appropriate, positive ones. This is not to say the man should expect that everything will always go well. Rather, he should be prepared for some disappointments and failures and learn to interpret these in appropriate ways. Some psychologists compare this process to inoculation. Like a medical vaccine that prevents a patient from becoming ill, the treatment is designed to keep negative thoughts from creating undue psychological distress.

Like any approach to treatment, cognitive psychotherapy does not work for everyone and may be limited to psychological problems that are based in irrational and self-defeating thinking. Nonetheless, the success many therapists have had with this approach has been encouraging (Butler, Chapman, Forman, & Beck, 2006; Gaudiano, 2005). Cognitive-behavioral therapies have been found to be especially effective for treating emotional disorders like depression and anxiety (Aderka, Nickerson, Boe, & Hofmann, 2012; Hollon, Stewart, & Strunk, 2006; Stewart & Chambless, 2009; Vittengl, Clark, Dunn, & Jarrett, 2007). Not only do these treatments relieve the symptoms of emotional disorders, but people who have gone through cognitive-behavioral therapies are less likely to experience a relapse in the future. Presumably these individuals have learned how to identify unhealthy thoughts and how to replace them with positive ones.

Rational Emotive (Behavior) Therapy

One of the earliest advocates of cognitive therapy was Albert Ellis, who developed **rational emotive therapy** (Ellis & Joffe Ellis, 2011). Consistent with the tendency to blend cognitive and behavioral treatments, toward the end of his career, Ellis referred to his approach as *rational emotive behavior therapy*. According to Ellis, people become depressed, anxious, upset, and the like because of faulty reasoning and a reliance on irrational beliefs. Ellis described this as an A-B-C process. For example, suppose your boyfriend/girlfriend calls tonight and tells you the relationship is over. This is the A, which Ellis calls the *Activating experience*. However, when clients seek out psychotherapy, they usually identify the reason as the C, the *emotional Consequence*. In this case, you are probably depressed, guilty, or angry. Of course, an emotional reaction to breaking up is entirely appropriate. But if your reaction is severe and starts interfering with your ability to go to work or attend classes, you might benefit from some cognitive counseling.

And if you were to seek that counseling from someone like Ellis, you would be asked how you could logically go from A (the experience) to C (the emotion). Why should a personal setback or loss cause such strong negative emotions? The answer is that you must be using a middle step in this sequence, B—the *irrational Belief*. The only way you could logically conclude from breaking up with your partner that you should be severely depressed is that you are also saying to yourself something like "It is necessary for me to be loved and approved by virtually every person in my life," or "I can never be happy without this person." Of course, when isolated like this, the belief is obviously irrational. But these irrational beliefs are so entrenched in our thoughts that it often takes professional help to see the flaws in our thinking.

Ellis maintained that each of us harbors and relies on a large number of these irrational beliefs. Imagine that you fail an important class (A). If you then fall back on the irrational belief "I need to do well at everything to be considered worthwhile" (B), you'll lead yourself to the conclusion that this is a catastrophe and become excessively anxious (C). A rational emotive therapist would point out that, whereas failing is certainly an unfortunate event—and something you'd prefer didn't happen—it does not warrant extreme anxiety. Expecting everything to work out well all the time will only lead to disappointment and frustration. Some of the more commonly used irrational beliefs are listed in Table 15.2. Ellis (1987) maintained that some of these beliefs are blatantly irrational and therefore easily identified and corrected during therapy. However, other beliefs are more subtle or trickier and thus are more resistant to change.

The goal of rational emotive therapy is twofold. First, clients must see how they rely on irrational beliefs and thereby identify the fault in their reasoning. Second, the therapist works with the client to replace irrational beliefs with rational ones. For example, instead of deciding that your romantic

TABLE 15.2 Some Common Irrational Beliefs

Obvious Irrational Beliefs

Because I strongly desire to perform important tasks competently and successfully, I absolutely must perform them well at all times.

Because I strongly desire to be approved by people I find significant, I absolutely must always have their approval.

Because I strongly desire people to treat me considerately and fairly, they absolutely must at all times and under all conditions do so.

Because I strongly desire to have a safe, comfortable, and satisfying life, the conditions under which I live absolutely must at all times be easy, convenient, and gratifying.

Subtle and Tricky Irrational Beliefs

Because I strongly desire to perform important tasks competently and successfully, and because I want to succeed at them only some of the time, I absolutely must perform these tasks well.

Because I strongly desire to be approved by people I find significant, and because I only want a little approval from them, I absolutely must have it.

Because I strongly desire people to treat me considerately and fairly, and because I am almost always considerate and fair to others, they absolutely must treat me well.

Because I strongly desire to have a safe, comfortable, and satisfying life, and because I am a nice person who tries to help others lead this kind of life, the conditions under which I live absolutely must be easy, convenient, and gratifying.

Source: From "The impossibility of achieving consistently good mental health," by A. Ellis, *American Psychologist*, 1987, 42, 364–375. Reprinted by permission of the American Psychological Association.

breakup is a reason to be depressed, you might tell yourself that, although you enjoy a stable romantic relationship and wish this one could have continued, you know that not all relationships work out. You also know that this doesn't mean no one else can love you or that you are never going to have a good relationship again. Thus, whereas the A statement is the same—"I broke up with my partner"—the B statement is different. Because the situation is identified as unpleasant but not catastrophic, there is no need to become overly depressed, the old C.

In the following sample, taken from one of Ellis' therapy sessions with a young woman (Ellis, 1971), you can see how a rational emotive therapist tries to change faulty thoughts:

Client[C]: Well, this is all a part of something that's bothered me for a long time. I'm always afraid of making a mistake.

Ellis[E]: Why? What's the horror?

C: I don't know.

E: You're saying that you're a bitch, you're a louse when you make a mistake.

C: But this is the way I've always been. Every time I make a mistake, I die a thousand deaths over it.

E: You blame yourself. But why? What's the horror? Is it going to make you better next time? Is it going to make you make fewer mistakes?

C: No.

E: Then why blame yourself? Why are you a louse for making a mistake? Who said so?

C: I guess it's one of those feelings I have.

E: One of those beliefs. The belief is: "I am a louse!" And then you get the feeling: "Oh, how awful! How shameful!" But the feeling follows the belief. And again, you're saying, "I should be different; I shouldn't make mistakes!" instead of, "Oh, look: I made a mistake. It's undesirable to make mistakes. Now, how am I going to stop making one next time?"...

C: It might all go back to, as you said, the need for approval. If I don't make mistakes, then people will look up to me. If I do it all perfectly—

E: Yes, that's part of it. That is the erroneous belief: that if you never make mistakes everybody will love you and that it is necessary that they do.... But is it true? Suppose you never did make mistakes—would people love you? They'd sometimes hate your guts, wouldn't they?

Rational emotive therapists challenge clients to identify their irrational beliefs and see how these beliefs lead them to their faulty conclusions. Of course, this is not easy. Most of us can readily identify what's wrong with our friends' thinking, but it's quite another matter when we're the ones with an emotional problem. Nonetheless, the success of rational emotive therapy with a large number of clients has contributed to the increased popularity of cognitive approaches to psychotherapy in recent years (Dryden, David, & Ellis, 2010).

Assessment: The Repertory Grid Technique

George Kelly made personal constructs the key concept in his theory of personality as well as the focus of his approach to psychotherapy. But this emphasis created a bit of a problem. Specifically, how does one go about measuring a person's personal constructs? Of course, a therapist might obtain some idea of a client's construct system during the course of therapy sessions. But Kelly and his colleagues needed a more efficient way to examine construct systems that could then be communicated fairly easily to the client. Kelly's answer was the *Repertory Grid Technique.* Kelly and his followers developed several variations of this technique (Caputi, Viney, Walker, & Crittenden, 2012; Fransella, Bell, & Bannister, 2003), but the essential procedure consists of two steps (Bell, 1990). First, the test taker creates a list of *elements.* The items on this list can be anything the person encounters in life, but most often the list consists of specific people the test taker knows. Second, the test taker's personal constructs are elicited by comparing and contrasting various elements on the list.

The most common version of the grid technique is the *Role Construct Repertory Test,* or more commonly, the Rep Test. A shortened version of the basic Rep Test procedure is presented on pages 433–434. Therapists begin by asking clients to provide a list of 24 people from various personal experiences—for example, a teacher they liked, the most interesting person they know, and so on. The therapist then presents clients with three of the names from this list and asks, "In what important way are two of these people alike but different from the third?" A client might say that two of them are *warm* people and that the third person is *cold*. In Kelly's terms, this client has used a *warm–cold* construct to categorize the three people. The process is repeated with three different names from the list. Perhaps this time the client will divide the people along an *outgoing–shy* or a *generous–miserly* construct. Kelly suggested that about 20 trials, or "sorts," provide the therapist with a useful sample of the client's principal constructs.

In one variation of the Rep Test, the therapist takes away one of the three names and replaces it with a new one. This procedure can be useful in identifying clients' difficulties in applying new constructs to new situations. To examine self-concepts, therapists sometimes present the client's name along with two names from the list. Again, clients are asked how two of the three are alike and one is different. Many therapists take the list of constructs generated from the client's initial Rep Test and ask the client to evaluate each person on the list according to the construct. This step creates a grid similar to the one shown in Table 15.3 and allows the therapist and client to look for patterns across a broad set of information.

The Repertory Grid Technique has been widely used by therapists and clinical psychologists to obtain a visual map of how clients and those suffering from various psychological disorders construe the world (Feixas, Erazo-Caicedo, Harter, & Bach, 2008; Winter, 2003). But the grid technique has also been used by researchers when studying such diverse topics as communication within a large organization (Coopman, 1997), teaching effectiveness (Chitsabesan, Corbett, Walker, Spencer, & Barton, 2006), profiles of specific criminal types (Horley, 1996), and career counseling (Savickas, 1997). Since its inception, thousands of studies using variations of the Repertory Grid Technique have been published (Neimeyer, 2001; Saul et al., 2012).

Like other assessment procedures, the grid technique also has its limitations. One concern is that, unlike other personality measures, the Repertory Grid Technique does not generate a simple test score (Horley, 1996).

TABLE 15.3 Sample Grid

	Mom	Dad	Sister	Brother	Boss	Neighbor	Friend	Coworker	
Pleasant	P	U	U	U	U	U	P	U	Unpleasant
Trustworthy	U	U	U	U	U	U	?	U	Untrustworthy
Competitive	N	N	C	C	?	N	C	C	Not Competitive
Warm	W	C	C	C	C	C	?	C	Cold
Intelligent	N	I	I	I	I	?	N	I	Not Intelligent
Fun	D	D	D	D	D	D	F	D	Dull

Although various number-generating systems have been developed, the procedure still allows for a large degree of interpretation on the part of the therapist. Another limitation concerns the many assumptions underlying the test. One assumption when using the Rep Test is that the constructs clients provide are not limited to the people on the list but also would apply to new people in new situations. It is also assumed that the constructs elicited during the test have some degree of permanence. That is, we assume clients are not using these constructs for the first time in the testing session and never again. A related assumption is that the people on the list are representative of the kind of people clients are likely to deal with in their daily lives. Constructs used only for unique people that clients rarely encounter are of little use in understanding how clients deal with the majority of people with whom they interact.

 Assessing Your Own Personality

Personal Constructs

To begin, write down the names of the following 12 people. Although a person may fit more than one category, you need to compile a list of 12 different people. If there is no one who fits a category, name someone who is similar to the category description. For example, if you do not have a brother, select someone who is like a brother to you.

_____ 1. A teacher you liked

_____ 2. A teacher you disliked

_____ 3. Your wife (husband) or boyfriend (girlfriend)

_____ 4. An employer, supervisor, or officer you found hard to get along with

_____ 5. An employer, supervisor, or officer you liked

_____ 6. Your mother

_____ 7. Your father

_____ 8. Brother nearest your age

_____ 9. Sister nearest your age

_____ 10. A person with whom you have worked who was easy to get along with

_____ 11. A person with whom you have worked who was hard to understand

_____ 12. A neighbor with whom you get along well

Next, take three of these people at a time, as indicated by the numbers in the following list. Then describe in what important way two of them are alike but different from the third. Put a word or phrase describing the two

(continues)

alike people in the *Construct* list and a description of the remaining person in the *Contrast* list.

Names	Construct	Contrast
3, 6, 7	_____	_____
1, 4, 10	_____	_____
4, 7, 8	_____	_____
1, 6, 9	_____	_____
4, 5, 8	_____	_____
2, 11, 12	_____	_____
8, 9, 10	_____	_____
2, 3, 5	_____	_____
5, 7, 11	_____	_____
1, 10, 12	_____	_____

This is an abbreviated version of Kelly's Rep Test (the Minimum Context Form). The test provides a quick idea of the constructs you use to organize information about the people you know and meet. You may want to compare your responses with those of other test takers. No doubt you will find a few overlapping constructs, but also many you hadn't thought of. Of course, these differences in personal constructs represent differences in personality that should translate into individual differences in your behavior.

Scale: The Role Construct Repertory (Rep) Test

Source: From *A Theory of Personality: The Psychology of Personal Constructs* by George A. Kelly. Copyright © 1955, 1963 by George A. Kelly, renewed 1983, 1991 by Gladys Kelly. Used by permission of W.W. Norton & Company, Inc.

But Kelly maintained that the most precarious assumption about the procedure is that people are able to describe the constructs they use. Although clients may supply words that come close to what they mean, they might not accurately capture what the client means. Kelly did not assume that words necessarily exist for describing all constructs. In fact, he described "preverbal" constructs, those developed before we learn to speak. And even when clients do use appropriate words, therapists may interpret those words differently. For example, a client's definition of aggressive may be quite different from a therapist's. In this case the therapist may still end up with a false impression of how the client views the world.

Strengths and Criticisms of the Cognitive Approach

Strengths

One strength of the cognitive approach to personality is that many of the ideas evolved out of and were developed through empirical research findings.

Most of the cognitive structures used to account for individual differences have been subjected to extensive investigation in controlled laboratory experiments. In many cases personality psychologists have borrowed ideas and research procedures from social and cognitive psychologists investigating similar phenomena. Moreover, cognitive models of personality have been modified as investigators learn more about cognitive structures and processes through their ongoing research.

Another strength of the cognitive approach is that it fits well with the current mood, or Zeitgeist, of psychology. The number of journal articles and doctoral dissertations examining cognitive concepts has risen dramatically over the past few decades. Researchers in other areas of psychology, such as developmental and social psychologists, are conducting research that often complements and extends what is known from the cognitive personality perspective.

Related to the preceding point, cognitive approaches to psychotherapy have become particularly popular in recent years. Even therapists who identify with other approaches to personality sometimes incorporate aspects of cognitive therapy in their practice. A survey of practitioners in the Association for the Advancement of Behavior Therapy, a group originally composed of behavior therapists, found that 67% described their therapy orientation as "cognitive behavioral" (Elliott et al., 1996). Nearly half said they occasionally use rational emotive therapy with their clients.

Criticisms

A frequent criticism of the cognitive approach is that the concepts are sometimes too abstract for empirical research. What exactly is a "personal construct" or a "possible self"? How do we know if a schema is being used? How many schemas are there, and how are they related? More important, how can we study their influence on behavior if we can't agree on clear operational definitions? Some of the answers may come with more research, but the nature of cognitions probably renders them more nebulous than many constructs used by personality theorists.

A related question is whether we need to introduce these concepts to account for individual differences in behavior. For example, strict behaviorists might argue that they can explain the same phenomena with fewer constructs. Introducing schemas or possible selves may be unnecessary and perhaps even an obstacle to understanding personality. Applying the law of parsimony, it is incumbent upon cognitive theorists to demonstrate how their approach can explain personality better than other, less complicated approaches.

Another source of concern about the cognitive approach to personality is that there is no single model to organize and guide theory and research. Basic questions about how various cognitive structures relate to one another and to other aspects of information processing, such as memory, remain unanswered. A related problem concerns the relationship between the various cognitive structures different theorists have introduced. Is a personal construct different from a schema? A comprehensive model would help researchers understand precisely what these terms mean and how they are related.

Summary

1. The cognitive approach to personality describes consistent behavior patterns in terms of the way people process information. George Kelly was an early pioneer in this approach with his personal construct theory. Kelly maintained that we are motivated to make sense out of our world. He compared people to scientists, always striving for better predictions about what will happen to them. Kelly described the cognitive structures we use in this regard as personal constructs. He maintained that psychological problems stem from anxiety, which results from a person's inability to predict events.

2. Psychologists have described a number of cognitive structures to help explain individual differences and intrapersonal processes. Perhaps the most important cognitive structures for personality psychologists are the cognitive representations we have for our selves. Much research in this area is concerned with self-schemas. Studies demonstrate that we perceive information more readily and recall it better when it is relevant to our self-schemas. Researchers also find that cognitive representations of future selves guide our behavior, but that discrepancies between different self-concepts can result in negative emotions.

3. Cognitive approaches to psychotherapy have become increasingly popular in the last few decades. These therapies focus on changing the clients' thoughts. Albert Ellis, an early advocate of this approach, argued that people have emotional problems when they use irrational beliefs. Rational emotive therapy helps clients see how they use these beliefs and how to replace them with more rational ones.

4. Kelly introduced the Repertory Grid Technique to measure individual differences in personal constructs. In one example, test takers typically develop a list of people in their lives and then divide these people into various categories. This procedure helps therapists see the constructs clients use to make sense of the world. Kelly acknowledged several assumptions behind this approach, including that people can adequately communicate the constructs they use.

5. Among the strengths of the cognitive approach is its strong empirical background. The cognitive approach also fits nicely with the current trend in psychology toward cognitive explanations of behavior. Some critics of the cognitive approach have complained that many of the concepts used by cognitive theorists are too abstract. Others have questioned whether it is always necessary to introduce cognitions to explain behavior. The cognitive approach also suffers from the lack of a general model to organize all of the work that falls under this approach.

Key Terms

personal constructs (p. 414)

possible selves (p. 423)

rational emotive therapy (p. 427)

self-schemas (p. 419)

Media Resources

Visit the book companion website at **www.cengagebrain.com** to find a glossary, flashcards, quizzing, and more.

The Cognitive Approach

Relevant Research

If you think back to the first chapter, you may recall the story about the blind men trying to describe an elephant. The point was that obtaining a complete understanding of human personality requires that we examine personality from several different perspectives. Although each perspective offers useful information, each also provides only a limited view of this complex topic. That lesson is clearly illustrated in this chapter. Each program of research examines from a cognitive perspective a topic covered elsewhere in the book. It's not that the research covered earlier is wrong or needs updating. Rather, the point is that we need to examine important topics from more than one perspective if we want to obtain a complete picture. We'll begin with aggression, a topic we've looked at in depth from a psychoanalytic and behavioral/social learning perspective. Next, we'll return to the topic of gender. In addition to the many gender differences we've touched on throughout the book, researchers find that men and women also differ in the way they remember information. Finally, we'll examine cognitive explanations for depression, another topic that has surfaced often in this book. Investigators find that the way we process information plays a crucial role in this psychological disorder.

Cognitions and Aggression

Imagine you are strolling alone through a park. Two teenage boys walking about 30 feet behind you suddenly quicken their pace and draw closer. What is your reaction? Perhaps the boys are in a hurry to get somewhere. Perhaps they are simply more energetic and walk faster than you do. Maybe they are interested in catching up to you to ask for the time or directions. Or maybe they want to harm you. This situation, like many we encounter, contains a fair degree of ambiguity, and people react to it differently.

How you respond in this scenario depends on how you interpret the information available to you. Whether you see the circumstances as threatening, annoying, or benign will cause you to run away, prepare to fight, or move out of the way. This example illustrates a key concept that cognitive researchers rely on when trying to predict aggressive behavior. It's not enough to know that a person is high in aggressiveness, has just witnessed someone model aggression, or has a history of being rewarded for violence. Although all of these variables play a role, a full understanding of aggressive behavior requires that we also examine the cognitions that come into play when people encounter a potentially threatening or dangerous situation (Anderson & Huesmann, 2003; Crick & Dodge, 1996; Fontaine & Dodge, 2006; Wilkowski & Robinson, 2010).

General Aggression Model

Whether a potentially violent encounter passes uneventfully or leads to aggression depends on a large number of factors. To explain this complex process, one team of psychologists combined research findings from a number of areas to create a *General Aggression Model* (Anderson & Bushman, 2002a). Although the model relies heavily on cognitive variables, you will notice that it also includes many of the factors related to aggression discussed in earlier chapters.

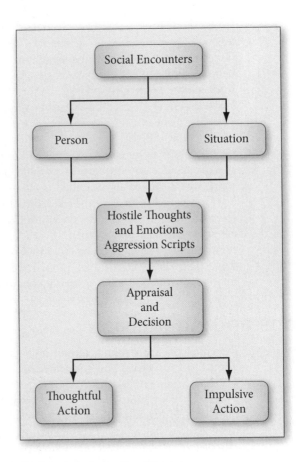

FIGURE 16.1 General Aggression Model

Source: Adapted from Anderson and Bushman (2002a).

As shown in Figure 16.1, the model begins with a social encounter that has the potential for triggering aggression. This encounter might be an insult, a threat, a shove, or any action that could be interpreted along these lines. How we respond to the event depends first on the kind of person we are and the kind of situation we are in. Because of differences in traits, attitudes, past experiences, genetic predispositions, and so on, some people are more prone to aggression than others. Moreover, some situations lend themselves to violence more than others. Aggression is more likely when the situation includes provocation, frustration, or encouragement to act violently.

However, according to the model, these personal and situational factors are relevant only to the extent that they activate aggression-relation thoughts and emotions. That is, to some degree, each of us has within our memories some hostile thoughts and feelings. For most of us most of the time, these thoughts remain outside our awareness and therefore have little or no impact on how we act. But certain experiences can tap into these cognitions. When aggressive thoughts enter our awareness and remain easily accessible, acts of violence become a real possibility.

What activates these potentially dangerous thoughts and emotions? Just about any aspect of the situation that we associate with violence can do the job. Visual images like weapons, fists, and blood certainly can tap into hostile thoughts. But these cognitions also can be activated by any sound, smell, or sight that we happen to associate with aggression. There also are times when hostile thoughts and feelings are more accessible than usual. People recently exposed to violent images, such as scenes from violent movies or violent video games, have highly accessible hostile cognitions (Anderson & Huesmann, 2003; Carlson, Marcus-Newhall, & Miller, 1990; Gentile, Coyne, & Walsh, 2011; Todorov & Bargh, 2002). Even exposure to songs with violent lyrics has been found to increase aggressive thoughts and feelings (Anderson, Carnagey, & Eubanks, 2003; Fischer & Greitemeyer, 2006).

It is also the case that some people are more prone to seeing hostile associations with events than are others. For a highly aggressive person, even a mild insult can generate violent thoughts and anger. Cognitive psychologists would say that these individuals have a well-developed and easily accessible network of hostile cognitions. Researchers find that people who watch a lot of violent movies and television programs are able to bring these aggression-related thoughts into awareness more easily than individuals who have not been exposed to a lot of violent media images (Krahe et al., 2011). In a sense, aggressive people move through their worlds ready to think aggressively about whatever they might encounter.

But how do these hostile thoughts lead to aggressive acts? Among the hostile cognitions potentially activated in this process are aggressive behavior *scripts*. Like scripts for plays or movies, these behavior scripts represent ways to act that we have learned and sometimes practiced. Although there are many possible sources, we often learn aggressive scripts by watching aggressive models. Even though you may never have punched someone in the face, you have seen the behavior modeled often enough in various media outlets that you probably could act out this script if you needed to.

Aggressive scripts that have been practiced are even more likely to be acted out. People practice their aggressive scripts when they physically rehearse the behavior, such as during karate drills or target practice. But people also practice aggressive scripts simply by imagining themselves acting violently or by reliving in their minds a violent sequence they may have experienced or seen. The more accessible the behavior script, the more likely the person will act aggressively. However, psychologists are quick to point out that a great deal of aggression takes place in a more-or-less automatic or impulsive manner (Berkowitz, 2012; Fontaine & Dodge, 2006). Sometimes when someone steps on our toes or bumps us from behind we respond almost immediately. In these instances, highly accessible aggressive scripts can be particularly dangerous.

Cognitive scripts also are more likely to lead to aggression when people ruminate about the events that led to their aggressive thoughts (Wilkowski & Robinson, 2010). If cooler heads prevail and tensions are allowed to pass quickly without incident, violence usually can be avoided. Unfortunately, violence-prone people often are slow to forgive and forget. Because these individuals continue to revisit the provoking incident in their minds, they remain angry and their hostile thoughts and aggressive scripts remain highly accessible (Bushman, Bonacci, Pedersen, Vasquez, & Miller, 2005; Gerin, Davidson, Christenfeld, Goyal, & Schwartz, 2006). As a result, the likelihood of acting on some of these aggressive impulses remains high.

The General Aggression Model helps us understand why certain conditions and experiences make us more prone to acting violently. In essence, some experiences make it easier for people to activate aggressive thoughts. For example, an angry person is more likely to interpret information in an aggressive manner than someone who is not experiencing anger (Baumann & DeSteno, 2010). Alcohol, which is often involved in violence, and even images associated with alcohol also have been found to increase aggressive cognitions (Subra, Muller, Begue, Bushman, & Delmas, 2010). Similarly, frustrated people are likely to have highly accessible hostile thoughts.

Finally, aggressive cognitions not only trigger aggressive behavior scripts, but also affect the way we interpret situations. Returning to the example of the teenage boys in the park, if hostile thoughts and emotions were easily accessible for you (perhaps you just came from a violent movie), you might very well have interpreted the situation as a threat. But if you were in a pleasant mood and had not recently activated thoughts related to violence, the idea that these boys wanted to hurt you might never have entered your mind.

Reactive Aggression in Boys

Few people will be surprised to learn that adolescent and preadolescent boys are much more likely to engage in physical acts of aggression than girls (Card, Stucky, Sawalani, & Little, 2008). Although aggression at any age is a concern for parents, educators, and psychologists, some researchers are particularly interested in boys who exhibit *reactive aggression*. As the name suggests, this research focuses on the angry and aggressive way some boys respond to even mild frustrations or provocations. These are the boys who react to a little teasing by threatening to beat up the teaser and who are likely to turn an accidental bump in the hallway into a fist fight.

To better understand these reactions, some psychologists examine the way these boys interpret the events that preceded their physical aggression (Hubbard, McAuliffe, Morrow, & Romano, 2010). One team of researchers presented a series of hypothetical situations to boys with a history of reactive aggression (Crick & Dodge, 1996). For example, in one scenario another student breaks the boy's radio while the boy is out of the room. For each situation, the boys were asked why the other student did what he did and whether the act was intentional. As shown in Figure 16.2, the boys with a history of reactive aggression were more likely to see the act as intentional and hostile than were nonaggressive boys. Another way to say this is that the aggressive boys had chronically accessible hostile thoughts that led them to interpret harmless acts as threatening. Not surprisingly, researchers find that these types of interpretations often lead to aggression (Dodge, 2006; Dodge et al., 2003; Reijntjes et al., 2011).

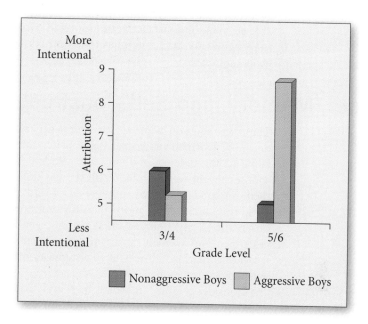

FIGURE 16.2 Mean Attribution Score

Source: Adapted from Crick and Dodge (1996).

If easily accessible hostile thoughts play a large role in some children's aggressive behavior, then targeting those thoughts might be a successful strategy for reducing the level of violence in these children. Several intervention programs have been developed to reduce reactive aggression, and many of these prevention programs include efforts to change the child's aggression-related cognitions (Barlett & Anderson, 2011; Metropolitan Area Child Study Research Group, 2007).

One of these prevention programs was conducted in a number of schools in North Carolina, Tennessee, Pennsylvania, and Washington (Conduct Problems Prevention Research Group, 2011). Researchers find that physically aggressive boys and girls often exhibit disruptive behavior early in life, which allows investigators to identify children at risk of becoming aggressive later in life. At-risk Kindergarten students in this study were randomly assigned to either the Fast Track intervention program or to a control condition. The intervention started in the first grade with home visits and "enrichment" programs that included, among other aspects, social skill training, academic tutoring, and lessons on developing friendships. The interventions continued until the students were in the tenth grade. Initial reports indicate that the program is a success. Students in the Fast Track condition were significantly less likely to commit antisocial acts like assault and theft than children in the control condition (Dodge, Godwin, & Conduct Problems Prevention Research Group, 2013). In particular, the reduction in antisocial behavior was associated with changes in the student's thoughts. The students in the Fast Track program were less likely than the control condition students to attribute a classmate's actions to something provocative. These students also were better able to think of constructive solutions to social problems and were better able to recognize the bad outcomes that were likely to follow if they became physically aggressive.

Gender, Memory, and Self-Construal

The next time you want to stir things up at a dull social gathering, raise this question: Do men or women have better memories? Inevitably, I find people come to the defense of their own gender. Men complain about times their spouses forgot to pay bills or fill the gas tank, and women point out the way their husbands overlook anniversaries and the names of in-laws. Although these responses reflect more than an ounce of stereotype, they also highlight observations psychologists make about gender and memory. Research suggests men and women do not differ in their general ability to memorize and recall information. However, investigators often find differences in *what* men and women remember.

Consider a study in which men and women were asked to recall several different kinds of information (Seidlitz & Diener, 1998). Participants first were given 3 minutes to list as many positive and negative events as they could recall from the previous 3 years of their lives. Later the participants were asked to recall, among other things, emotional events from the previous year and from a randomly selected 1-hour interval from the previous week. Participants were also given a limited amount of time to recall events from American history.

Who had the better recall? As shown in Figure 16.3, the answer depends on what kind of information the participants were asked to remember. The women recalled significantly more personal events than the men. This was true for both negative events and positive events. On the other hand, men did better recalling the impersonal information about American history. In short, women were better able to remember happy occasions with friends and times they embarrassed themselves, whereas men recalled better the facts they had learned in school or read about.

Psychologists explain these differences in memory by pointing to the way people process self-relevant information. Specifically, investigators identify two differences in the way men and women organize information in memory. First, the genders differ in the extent to which self-relevant information is associated with emotions. Second, men and women differ in the extent to which information about themselves is connected with information about personal relationships.

Emotional Memories

From an early age, females learn to pay attention to their emotions and the emotions of others. Consequently, women are more likely than men to encode information about themselves in terms of emotions (Bloise & Johnson, 2007; Feldman Barrett, Lane, Sechrest, & Schwartz, 2000; Kuebli,

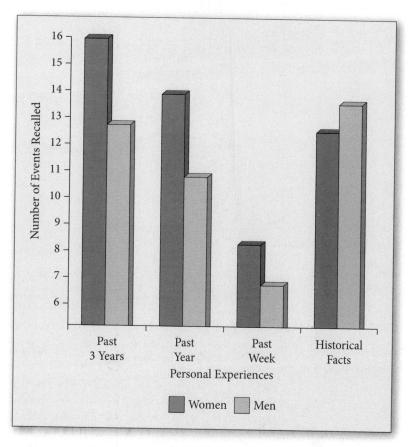

FIGURE 16.3 Number of Events Recalled

Source: Adapted from "Sex differences in the recall of affective experience," by L. Seidlitz and E. Diener, *Journal of Personality and Social Psychology*, 1998, 74, 262–271. Copyright © 1998 by the American Psychological Association. Adapted with permission of the author.

Butler, & Fivush, 1995). And if women organize their memories around emotions, we should not be surprised to find that they are better able to recall both positive and negative emotional experiences (Fujita, Diener, & Sandvik, 1991). Memories for both happy and sad experiences are more accessible for women. Moreover, the cognitive link between one emotional memory and another is stronger for women than for men. As a result, recalling one sad experience is likely to trigger another sad memory for women, but this is less likely to be the case for men.

These gender differences were demonstrated in a study in which adult men and women were asked to recall childhood experiences (Davis, 1999). Participants were cued with a series of emotional words and phrases, such as "feeling rejected" or "getting something you really wanted." As shown in Figure 16.4, women recalled more emotional memories from childhood than did men. Moreover, this was true for each emotion examined, whether positive or

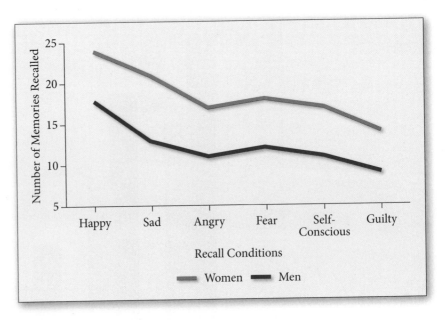

FIGURE 16.4 Recall of Emotional Childhood Memories

Source: Adapted from "Gender differences in autobiographical memory of childhood emotional experience," by P. J. Davis, *Journal of Personality and Social Psychology*, 1999, 76, 498–510. Copyright © 1999 by the American Psychological Association. Adapted with permission of the American Psychological Association.

negative. When the investigator compared similar recall in male and female students in grades 3, 5, 8, and 11, she found a similar pattern. That is, regardless of age, females are better able to recall emotional memories than males. Interestingly, the researcher found no gender differences when men and women were asked to recall nonemotional memories.

This tendency for women to recall more emotional memories could help explain why women suffer from depression more often than men (Nolen-Hoeksema, 2001). Not only do women remember sad experiences more often, but recalling one unhappy incident is also likely to activate memories about other sad events.

Memories About Relationships

Another line of research looks at the extent to which men and women consider relationships when they organize self-relevant information. Drawing from the work on individualist and collectivist cultures (Chapter 1), some psychologists argue that the way men and women are raised in our society causes them to form different cognitive representations of themselves (Cross, Hardin, & Gercek-Swing, 2011; Cross & Madson, 1997). Men are said to develop *independent self-construals*. That is, men's self-concepts are relatively unrelated to the cognitive representations they have for other people. On the other hand, women in our society tend to develop *interdependent self-construals*. Their self-concepts are highly related to the cognitive representations they have of others and their relationships with those people.

In particular, women's self-concepts are tied to those with whom women feel close and personal relations (Gabriel & Gardner, 1999).

Put another way, relationships with friends and loved ones are an important part of how women think of themselves. It's not just that they enjoy their relationships more than men, but rather that women are more likely to define themselves in terms of the relationships they share with others. Returning to the memory data, perhaps one reason women recall certain kinds of experiences more readily than men is that these events may have involved other people. Because of their interdependent self-construal, information involving relationships is more accessible for women than for men.

Assessing Your Own Personality

Self-Construal

Indicate the extent to which you agree with the following statements. Use a 7-point scale to indicate your response, with 1 = Strongly disagree and 7 = Strongly agree.

_____ 1. My close relationships are an important reflection of who I am.

_____ 2. When I feel very close to someone, it often feels to me like that person is an important part of who I am.

_____ 3. I usually feel a strong sense of pride when someone close to me has an important accomplishment.

_____ 4. I think one of the most important parts of who I am can be captured by looking at my close friends and understanding who they are.

_____ 5. When I think of myself, I often think of my close friends or family also.

_____ 6. If a person hurts someone close to me, I feel personally hurt as well.

_____ 7. In general, my close relationships are an important part of my self-image.

_____ 8. Overall, my close relationships have very little to do with how I feel about myself.

_____ 9. My close relationships are unimportant to my sense of what kind of person I am.

_____ 10. My sense of pride comes from knowing who I have as close friends.

_____ 11. When I establish a close friendship with someone, I usually develop a strong sense of identification with that person.

(continues)

To obtain your score, reverse the answer values for items 8 and 9 (that is, $1 = 7$, $2 = 6$, etc.). Then add all 11 answer values. High scores indicate a tendency to think of oneself in terms of your relationships with close others. That is, those scoring high on the scale have self-concepts closely tied to the cognitive representations they have of the people they feel emotionally closest to (Cross, Morris, & Gore, 2002). You can compare your score with those obtained from a sample of American undergraduates (Cross, Bacon, & Morris, 2000):

	Men	Women	Total
Mean	52.89	55.11	54.10
Standard Deviation	8.07	10.03	9.29

Scale: The Relational-Interdependent Self-Construal Scale

Source: Copyright © 1998 by the American Psychological Association. Reproduced with permission. Cross, S. E., Bacon, P. L., & Morris, M. L. (2000). The relational interdependent self-construal and relationships. *Journal of Personality and Social Psychology, 78*, 791–808. doi: 10.1037/0022-3514.78.4.791. No further reproduction or distribution is permitted without written permission from the American Psychological Association.

Consistent with this analysis, several studies find women are more likely than men to define themselves in terms of their relationships (Foels & Tomcho, 2009; Guimond, Chatard, Martinot, Crisp, & Redersdorff, 2006). Participants in one investigation were asked simply to list as many statements as they could in response to the question "Who am I?" (Mackie, 1983). Compared to male participants, the women in the study included more statements about their roles as parents and family members. Similar findings were uncovered when elementary and high school students were asked to "tell us about yourself" (McGuire & McGuire, 1982). Another group of researchers gave participants a camera and asked to take (or have someone else take) 12 photographs that "describe who you are as you see yourself" (Clancy & Dollinger, 1993). In other words, the photographs provided a rough indication of the cognitive representations the men and women held of themselves. As shown in Figure 16.5, the women's photographs were more likely to include other people. When the women portrayed the way they thought of themselves, they chose to include pictures with good friends and loved ones. In contrast, the men more often portrayed their self-concept with images of themselves alone.

Other research finds gender differences in the way men and women perceive and recall information about significant people in their lives. Participants in one study were asked if certain words described them, their best friend, a group they belong to, or the president of the United States (Josephs, Markus, & Tafarodi, 1992). As described in the previous chapter, researchers assume information processed through a strong schema will be more accessible than information processed through weaker schemas. When participants were later asked to recall as many of the words as possible, the women remembered words processed through their *best friend* and *group* schemas

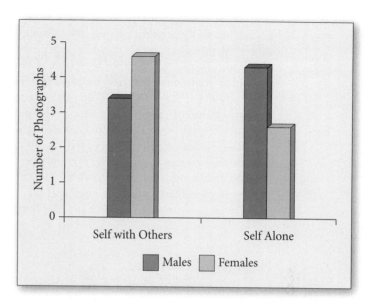

FIGURE 16.5 Number of Photographs Used to Portray Self

Source: Adapted from "Photographic depictions of the self: Gender and age differences in social connectedness," by S. M. Clancy and S. J. Dollinger, *Sex Roles,* 1993, 29, 477–495. Copyright © 1993 by Plenum Publishing Corporation. Reprinted by permission of Springer.

better than the men. Married couples in another study were asked to talk about their first date together, their last vacation together, and a recent argument between the two of them (Ross & Holmberg, 1992). The stories told by the wives were more vivid and contained more details than those described by the husbands. In sum, evidence from many sources makes a strong case that men and women differ in the way they store and recall information about relationships and thus about themselves.

Cognitions and Depression

For a moment, try to think of a time when you felt a little depressed. One of the first things you may notice is that this is relatively easy if you already feel a little down today and relatively difficult if you feel pretty good. Depressed people not only remember sad experiences more easily but may also have difficulty keeping themselves from generating one depressing thought after another. Sad people easily recall times when they felt lonely and unloved. They tend to dwell on their problems and worry about all the things that might go wrong. They recall embarrassing mishaps, things they wish they had never said, and experiences they wish they could erase. Even when good things happen, depressed people look for the gray cloud to go with the silver lining. Just got accepted into a good school? Think of all that pressure and what happens if you fail. Been invited to a party? What if you don't know anyone or you embarrass yourself there? In short, when you're depressed, your mind fills with depressing thoughts.

These observations make it clear that depressing thoughts are tied to depressing feelings. Although negative thoughts are often considered a symptom of depression, the cognitive perspective argues that these thoughts can also *cause* people to become depressed (Clark, Beck, & Alford, 1999). Psychologists sometimes describe the thoughts of depressed people as a *depressive cognitive triad* (Beck, 1972). That is, depressed people typically have negative thoughts about themselves, are pessimistic about the future, and tend to interpret ongoing experiences in a negative manner.

Many psychologists look for clues about the causes and treatment of depression by examining the way people perceive, organize, and recall emotionally laden information (Rusting, 1998). Among other questions, these investigators want to know if some people are prone to depression because of the way they process information. We'll look at two concepts investigators use in this research—negative schemas and negative cognitive style.

Negative Schemas

Each day we encounter some good events, a few bad events, and an occasional incident with ambiguous emotional meaning. Which ones will you think about today and which will you ignore? From a cognitive perspective, the happiest people are those who pay attention to the positive information, dismiss the negative information, and interpret the ambiguous information as positively as possible. In fact, most of us have an unrealistically positive outlook on life (Taylor, 1989). We believe we are better than most at almost everything we do, certain that good things will happen to us, and convinced unfortunate events happen to other people. Because most of us look at life through rose-colored glasses, we remain content and in good psychological health (Alloy & Abramson, 1988).

Unfortunately, many people look at life through glasses that are tinted blue. Psychologists from a cognitive perspective say that depressed people process information through an active negative schema (Dozois & Beck, 2008; Hertel & Brozovich, 2010). A **negative schema,** sometimes referred to as a *depressive schema,* is a cognitive structure containing memories about and associations with depressing events and thoughts. People processing information through this schema attend to negative information, ignore positive information, and interpret ambiguous information in a depressing way. They also recall depressing memories easily and often associate current sad experiences with sad incidents from their past. In short, depressed people are set to process information in a way that keeps negative thoughts prominent and positive thoughts away. Little wonder, then, that these people remain depressed.

Researchers have developed a number of procedures to study negative schemas. Along with clinical observations about how depressed people think and act, these experiments provide an impressive body of evidence pointing to the role cognitive structures play in the development and maintenance of depression. Much of the evidence for negative schemas comes from studies employing the self-schema research techniques described in the previous chapter. Researchers sometimes ask depressed and nondepressed individuals to answer questions about a series of words. In one study, depressed patients

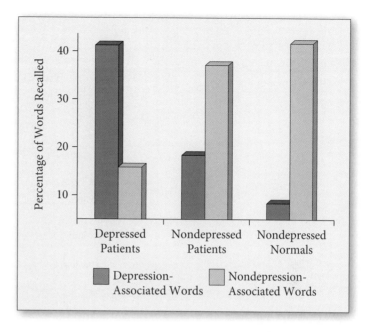

FIGURE 16.6 Proportion of Self-Descriptive Words Recalled with Self-Referent Processing

Source: From "Schematic processing and self-reference in clinical depression," by P. A. Derry and N. A. Kuiper, *Journal of Abnormal Psychology,* 1981, 90, 286–297.

responded to a list of adjectives by pressing a YES or a NO button to indicate whether the word described them (Derry & Kuiper, 1981). Half the words were related to depression (e.g., *bleak, dismal, helpless*), and half were not. The researchers then surprised the participants by giving them 3 minutes to recall as many of the words as they could.

The results of the study are shown in Figure 16.6. As predicted, depressed patients remembered the depression-associated words better, whereas two groups of nondepressed participants recalled the other words better. This finding has been replicated with clinically depressed patients (Lim & Kim, 2005) and mildly depressed college students (Moilanen, 1993). Depressed people recall words like *dismal* and *helpless* better because they process these words through a negative schema. They are more likely to attend to the depression-related words, associate them with aspects of themselves, and readily recall them later on.

If depressed people process information through a negative schema, we would also expect them to recall sad memories more readily than people who are not depressed. If I ask you to quickly think of something that happened to you in high school, most likely you will think of a pleasant time. You might recall a star performance in a play or perhaps just the fun you had hanging out with friends. But if you are a little depressed today, you might instead recall a test you failed or a time you were rejected by friends. This is because people processing information through a negative schema have greater access

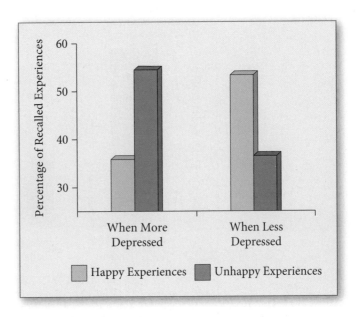

FIGURE 16.7 Percentages of Happy and Unhappy Experiences Recalled

Source: From "Diurnal variation in clinical depression and accessibility of memories of positive and negative experiences," by D. M. Clark and J. D. Teasdale, *Journal of Abnormal Psychology,* 1982, 91, 87–95. Reprinted by permission of the American Psychological Association.

to the depressing memories stored there. When you are depressed, it should not take long to recall times when you were sad, lonely, or embarrassed because using a negative schema makes these memories readily accessible.

This easy access to sad memories was demonstrated in an experiment with depressed clients (Clark & Teasdale, 1982). Clients were given a series of words (such as *train, ice*) and asked to recall a real-life experience each word brought to mind. For example, a client might describe a train ride to visit her favorite aunt or a time she missed a train. Clients were tested twice, once when they were feeling particularly depressed and once when they were less depressed. As shown in Figure 16.7, most of the memories recalled during the depressed period were unhappy ones. However, when clients were less depressed, they recalled happier experiences. Presumably the negative schemas were activated more when the clients' depression levels were higher. A similar pattern is found when depressed people are asked to think about the future. Depressed individuals in one study could more easily come up with reasons something bad is likely to happen to them someday than could nondepressed participants (Vaughn & Weary, 2002).

Because depressed people filter information through a negative schema, they also tend to interpret ambiguous information in the most negative light possible. When depressed people consider their performances, they tend to dwell on what they did wrong and fail to give themselves enough credit for what they did right (Crowson & Cromwell, 1995; Moretti et al., 1996). Participants in one study were given the choice of looking at either the favorable or unfavorable scores from a battery of tests they had taken (Giesler, Josephs, &

Swann, 1996). Eighty-two percent of the depressed participants chose the unfavorable feedback, significantly more than the nondepressed participants. Thus, if an instructor tells a depressed student he did well on five essay answers but was a little weak on one, the student will most likely focus his or her attention on the one weak answer and conclude that the performance was poor.

Not surprisingly, negative schemas go hand-in-hand with other depression symptoms, such as sad mood and decreased activity (Dozois & Beck, 2008; Dozois et al., 2009). Cognitive theorists see the causal arrow between negative cognitions and these other symptoms running both ways. That is, depressing thoughts can cause depression, and depression can lead to an increase in depressing thoughts. However, studies suggest that although negative thoughts decline as people recover from an episode of depression, the underlying cognitive network often remains in place (Dozois, 2007; Dozois & Dobson, 2001; Ingram & Ritter, 2000; Seeds & Dozois, 2010). If a strong negative schema stays intact, the individual may be vulnerable to future bouts of depression (Havermans, Nicolson, & deVries, 2007; Lewinsohn, Joiner, & Rohde, 2001). In fact, people with strong negative schemas may face a daily battle to fend off depression. Formerly depressed patients in one study showed an increase in negative thoughts simply after listening to a sad piece of music (Gemar, Segal, Sagrati, & Kennedy, 2001).

Negative Cognitive Style

In Chapter 14 we looked at research on learned helplessness. As you recall, psychologists initially demonstrated this effect in dogs that failed to escape from electric shocks after first experiencing inescapable shocks. The dogs learned they were helpless in one situation and inappropriately generalized that perception to the new situation. Not long after the demonstrations with animals, researchers found that people also sometimes generalize helpless feelings to controllable situations. Similarities between learned helplessness participants and depressed patients led some psychologists to propose learned helplessness as a model for understanding depression.

However, investigators soon found the simple model used to explain animal behavior was insufficient for understanding learned helplessness in people. Human research participants reacted to some uncontrollable situations with helplessness, but not others. Feelings of helplessness generalized to some tasks, but not every task. People exposed to inescapable noise sometimes became less motivated, but occasionally motivation increased (Costello, 1978; Depue & Monroe, 1978; Roth, 1980).

The limitations of the original model led some investigators to argue that negative life experiences alone are not sufficient to produce depression. Rather, how we *interpret* these events is the key (Abramson, Seligman, & Teasdale, 1978; Miller & Norman, 1979). If you attribute the loss of a job to a general lack of skills and aptitude that will keep you from getting a good job anywhere else, you may be headed for depression. However, if you fail an algebra class and conclude it's because this particular instructor used a strange and unfair grading system, it is unlikely you'll generalize feelings of helplessness to other math classes or other subjects.

Psychologists soon observed individual differences in the way people explain the events they encounter. In particular, researchers identified what they called a **negative cognitive style** (Alloy, Abramson, Keyser, Gerstein, & Sylvia, 2008). Individuals who possess a negative cognitive style tend to attribute their problems to stable (enduring) and global (widespread) causes. They also tend to anticipate the most dreadful consequences possible and often believe problems they encounter are the result of or reflect their own personal shortcomings. Investigators have developed procedures to measure the extent to which people rely on this type of thinking (Alloy et al., 2000; Beevers, Strong, Meyer, Pilkonis, & Miller, 2007; Peterson et al., 1982; Peterson & Villanova, 1988; Rodriguez-Naranjo & Cano, 2010). Like other personality variables, negative cognitive style tends to be fairly stable over time (Burns & Seligman, 1989; Hankin, 2008).

Not surprisingly, researchers find that negative cognitive style is related to depression (Goldberg, Gerstein, Wenze, Beck & Welker, 2008; Haeffel et al., 2003; Hankin, Fraley, & Abela, 2005; Lau & Eley, 2008; Otto et al., 2007; Riso et al., 2003). People who interpret negative events as the result of personal shortcomings that are enduring and widespread are vulnerable to depression when one of life's unfortunate experiences inevitably comes their way. One pair of investigators looked at the psychological effects of physical and emotional abuse in a group of battered women (Palker-Corell & Marcus, 2004). The researchers contacted the women within 2 weeks after their arrival at a battered women's shelter. They found the women with a negative cognitive style suffered from depression and other symptoms of trauma more often than the women who did not rely on this style of thinking. Another study looked at emotional reactions following a strong earthquake (Greening, Stoppelbein, & Docter, 2002). Participants with a negative cognitive style were more likely to be depressed after the earthquake than those without this cognitive style.

Investigators also use negative cognitive style to predict who might be vulnerable to future episodes of depression (Evans, Heron, Lewis, Araya, & Wolke, 2005; Fresco, Alloy, & Reilly-Harrington, 2006; Kleiman & Riskind, 2012; Robinson & Alloy, 2003). One team of researchers measured negative cognitive style in incoming college freshmen (Alloy, Abramson, Whitehouse, Hogan, Panzarella, & Rose, 2006). They divided the students into those who had previously suffered from an episode of depression and those who had not. The researchers contacted the students again every 6 weeks for the next 2 1/2 years. As shown in Figure 16.8, the students who were identified as high risk for depression based on their negative cognitive style were much more likely to experience at least one episode of major depression during this time than the other students. This was not only the case for those who had bouts of depression prior to college, but also for those who had never before suffered from depression. In fact, the high-risk students in the latter group were six times more likely to experience depression than their low-risk classmates.

Other researchers have used negative cognitive style to predict how adolescents react when encountering the stressors we often associate with the teenage years (Auerbach & Ho, 2012; Carter & Garber, 2011; Lee, Hankin,

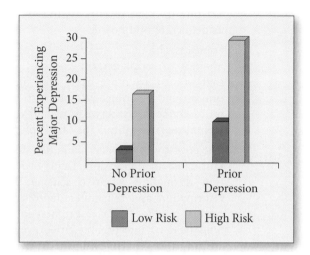

FIGURE 16.8 Students Experiencing Depression

Source: Alloy et al. (2006).

& Mermelstein, 2010). Many young people experience high levels of stress from academic pressure, relationships with peers, and conflicts with parents. However, those who typically rely on a negative cognitive style to explain these difficulties are significantly more likely to respond to these troubling times by becoming depressed.

We should also note that the link between cognitive style and depression may be affected by culture. Recall from earlier chapters that people in collectivist cultures tend to emphasize their role in the community, whereas people in individualistic cultures focus on their individual aspirations and accomplishments. One team of researchers found that college students in China (a collectivist culture) had a more pessimistic cognitive style than American students (Lee & Seligman, 1997). Consistent with their individualistic emphasis, the Americans were more likely to attribute successes to their own efforts and failures to other people or unfortunate circumstances. However, investigators comparing American and Chinese students also find that the kinds of explanations that predict depression in the United States also predict depression in China (Abela et al., 2011; Anderson, 1999). Thus, although the way people in two cultures typically explain events may be different, the cognitive style that leads to depression is the same.

Summary

1. Psychologists have looked at the role hostile cognitions play in aggressive behavior. They find that aggressive responses are more likely when a situation activates hostile thoughts and emotions. Hostile cognitions include aggressive behavior scripts. When hostile cognitions are highly accessible, the likelihood of acting aggressively increases. Boys with a history of

reacting to minor events aggressively tend to interpret unintentional acts as deliberate and hostile.

2. Some psychologists have looked at differences in men's and women's abilities to recall certain kinds of information. These researchers find that women are more likely than men to organize self-relevant information around emotions. Women also have been found to have strong cognitive connections between mental representations of themselves and the mental representations they have of close friends and loved ones.

3. The cognitive approach maintains that depressing thoughts are an important cause of depression. Depressed people are said to process information through a negative schema. Depressed people recall depressing information and remember depressing events more readily than nondepressed people. Other researchers look at negative cognitive style. People who tend to interpret negative events in terms of enduring and widespread causes are more prone to depression than those who do not rely on this cognitive style.

Key Terms

negative schema (p. 448)   negative cognitive style (p. 452)

Media Resources

Visit the book companion website at **www.cengagebrain.com** to find a glossary, flashcards, quizzing, and more.

Appendix

Your Personality

If you have completed each of the personality inventories that appear throughout this book, you have probably learned quite a bit about yourself. By comparing your scores with the norms for other people who have taken the same tests, you can see some of the ways your personality is different from or similar to the personalities of the people around you. In total, you have had the opportunity to collect data from 13 personality measures, which yield 17 test scores (not to mention descriptive information about your personal constructs in Chapter 15). No doubt this information proved useful as you read about the personality variables and related research. But you can also use these test scores to obtain a broad picture of your personality. If you have not already done so, enter your scores for each of the personality inventories below.

	Your Score	Mean	Standard Deviation
Identity versus Identity Diffusion Scale (Chapter 5)	_____	56.79	7.84
Coping Flexibility Scale (Chapter 6)			
Evaluation Coping	_____	10.10	3.12
Adaptive Coping	_____	7.29	3.20
Big Five Factor Markers for Conscientiousness (Chapter 7)	_____	123.11	23.99
Impression Management Scale (Chapter 7)	_____	4.9 (f)	3.2
		4.3 (m)	3.1
Achievement Goal Questionnaire (Chapter 8)			
Master-Approach	_____	5.52	1.18
Master-Avoidance	_____	3.89	1.53

(Continued)

	Your Score	Mean	Standard Deviation
Performance-Approach	_____	4.82	1.68
Performance-Avoidance	_____	4.49	1.67
Shyness Scale (Chapter 8)	_____	14.4 (f)	5.9
		14.8 (m)	5.6
Emotional Expressivity Scale (Chapter 8)	_____	66.60 (f)	12.71
		61.15 (m)	12.69
Index of Self-Actualization (Chapter 11)	_____	46.07 (f)	4.79
		45.02 (m)	4.95
Distress Disclosure Index (Chapter 12)	_____	42.21 (f)	9.16
		36.33 (m)	8.98
Preference for Solitude Scale (Chapter 12)	_____	4.52 (f)	2.61
		5.37 (m)	2.45
Unmitigated Communion Scale (Chapter 14)	_____	29.97 (f)	6.14
		28.55 (m)	5.53
Personal Efficacy Scale (Chapter 14)	_____	52.2 (f)	
		51.8 (m)	
Relational-Interdependent Self-Construal Scale (Chapter 16)	_____	55.11 (f)	10.03
		52.89 (m)	8.07

How to Interpret Your Scores

A score by itself is pretty meaningless. You also need to know the scores other people like you receive when they take the same test. In particular, you need two numbers—the mean and the standard deviation. The *mean* is the arithmetic average of all the scores from the norm sample. By comparing your score with the mean, you can see whether you scored higher or lower than the average test-taker. The *standard deviation* is the average amount scores differ from the mean. If the standard deviation is small, we know that most test takers' scores fall within a small range of possible scores. If the standard deviation is large, it means test takers' scores are more spread out. As a rule, about two-thirds of all people who take the inventory will receive a score that is within one standard deviation of the mean. Thus, if the mean for the norm sample is 20 and the standard deviation is 5, two out of every three people who take the test will probably receive a score between 15 and 25. About one-sixth of all test-takers will receive a score more than one standard deviation above the mean, and about one-sixth will receive a score more than one standard deviation below the mean. In many ways, these scores toward the ends of the distribution are the most interesting. These are the personality characteristics that differentiate us from the typical person. When I describe someone's personality, it's these distinctive characteristics that I am most likely to mention.

Caution: Don't Overinterpret

Scores from personality tests can be interesting, but, like all data, they need to be interpreted. There are many reasons why a test score may not accurately reflect your personality. It also is the case that a single test score is best interpreted within the context of other information about your personality. If a score on a personality inventory is consistent with your own observations, with objective evidence, and with feedback you have received from other people, then it most likely is a valid indicator of your personality. However, if the test score contradicts these other sources of information, it is probably best to take it with a grain of salt.

Another reason for caution is that labels like "high" and "low" can sometimes be misleading. What we mean by these terms is that the test taker received a score that is higher or lower than the average person who has taken the test. People who consider themselves to be shy are sometimes surprised to find that their score on the Shyness Scale or other social anxiety measures is near the mean or maybe even below the mean for the scale. But an average score on the scale does not mean the person is not shy or does not on occasion experience social anxiety. Rather, it suggests that a lot of people experience shyness and perhaps that this test taker is not as shy as many others who have taken the test.

Getting the Big Picture

Knowing how you score on a reliable and valid personality scale can be useful. But getting an idea about the kind of person you are requires considerably more information. Your personality is made up of many characteristics that come together to make you a unique individual. Thus, although you may be a conscientious person, this one characteristic alone does not define you. Similarly, if I want to predict how a person acts in certain areas of his or her life, I can do a much better job when I have scores from several relevant measures rather than relying on a single score.

You probably noticed that some research topics tended to surface repeatedly in the book. For example, personality researchers find that health is related to

Type A and hostility, negative affect, optimism and pessimism, loneliness, unmitigated communion, and locus of control, among other characteristics. Similarly, there are at least three areas of your life that research suggests are related to scores on more than one of the personality inventories listed earlier. These three areas are psychological well-being, social relationships, and achievement.

Psychological Well-Being

Many of the personality variables covered in this book are in some way related to psychological well-being. In some cases, the connection is a broad one; that is, scores on relevant personality tests predict general levels of personal satisfaction and happiness. Other personality variables have been linked to more specific aspects of well-being, such as depression or anxiety. Personality scores related to psychological well-being include the *Identity versus Identity Diffusion Scale*, the *Coping Flexibility Scale*, the *Shyness Scale*, the *Emotional Expressivity Scale*, the *Index of Self-Actualization*, the *Distress Disclosure Scale*, the *Unmitigated Communion Scale*, and the *Personal Efficacy Scale*.

Social Relationships

In many ways, our ability to establish and maintain good social relationships is affected by the kind of person we are. Our personalities also play a role in the kinds of relationships we establish, the amount of social interaction we engage in, and how much we enjoy interacting with other people. Some of the personality inventories researchers use to predict these social behaviors include the *Shyness Scale*, the *Emotional Expressivity Scale*, the *Preference for Solitude Scale*, and the *Relational-Interdependent Self-Construal Scale*.

Achievement

Achievement in academic and career settings is another topic that shows up repeatedly in personality theory and research. Although how we define and evaluate achievement varies as a function of culture and gender, achieving goals is an important part of most people's lives and is often an indicator of general well-being. Researchers have identified several personality traits that predict how people approach achievement situations, how they respond to challenges and setbacks, and how much they accomplish in achievement settings. Some of the personality tests used in this research include the *Big Five Factor Markers for Conscientiousness*, the *Achievement Goal Questionnaire*, and the *Personal Efficacy Scale*.

Glossary

absorption The ability to become highly involved in sensory and imaginative experiences.

achievement goals Targets people aspire to in achievement situations.

affect intensity The strength or degree to which people typically experience their emotions.

androgyny A personality trait consisting of masculine as well as feminine characteristics.

avoidance strategies Coping strategies designed to distract us from thinking about the source of anxiety.

behavioral approach system A hypothetical biological system that is focused on seeking out and achieving pleasurable goals.

behavioral inhibition system A hypothetical biological system that is focused on avoiding dangerous and unpleasant experiences.

Big Five The five basic dimensions of personality found in many factor analytic studies.

case study method An in-depth examination of one person or one group.

catharsis A release of tension or anxiety.

cerebral asymmetry Higher levels of brain activity in one cerebral hemisphere than the other.

classical conditioning Learning resulting from pairing a conditioned stimulus with a new, unconditioned stimulus.

collective unconscious The part of the unconscious mind containing thoughts, images, and psychic characteristics common to all members of a culture.

collectivist culture Culture that emphasizes the importance of belonging to a larger group, such as a family, tribe, or nation.

conditional/unconditional positive regard Acceptance and respect for people either only when they act as we desire (conditional) or regardless of their behavior (unconditional).

conscious In Freud's topographic model, the part of personality that contains the thoughts we are currently aware of.

contingencies of self-worth The domains of self-concept an individual uses to evaluate his or her self.

coping strategies Conscious efforts to reduce anxiety in the face of a perceived threat.

correlation coefficient A statistic that indicates the strength and direction of a relationship between two variables.

defense mechanisms Devices the ego uses to keep threatening material out of awareness and thereby reduce or avoid anxiety.

deficiency motive A need that is reduced when the object of the need is attained.

dependent variable The experimental variable measured by the experimenter and used to compare groups.

discrimination A learned tendency to respond only to stimuli that result in reinforcement and not to similar, but unrewarded, stimuli.

dispositional optimism The extent to which a person typically adopts an optimistic or pessimistic approach to dealing with life's challenges.

ego In Freud's structural model, the part of personality that considers external reality while mediating between the demands of the id and the superego.

emotional affectivity The extent to which people typically experience positive and negative emotions.

emotional expressiveness The extent to which people outwardly express their emotions.

emotion-focused strategies Coping strategies designed to reduce emotional distress.

evaluation apprehension A strong concern about receiving negative evaluations from others.

factor analysis A statistical procedure used to determine the number of dimensions in a data set.

free association A procedure used in psychoanalysis in which patients say whatever comes into their mind.

Freudian slip A seemingly innocent misstatement that reveals unconscious associations.

fully functioning person A psychologically healthy individual who is able to enjoy life as completely as possible.

generalization The tendency to respond to stimuli similar to the one used in the initial conditioning.

growth need A need that leads to personal growth and that persists after the need object is attained.

hierarchy of needs In Maslow's theory, the order in which human needs demand attention.

hypothesis A formal prediction about the relationship between two or more variables that is logically derived from a theory.

id In Freud's structural model, the part of personality concerned with immediate gratification of needs.

independent variable The experimental variable used to divide participants into groups.

individualistic culture Culture that places great emphasis on individual needs and accomplishments.

inhibited/uninhibited children Inhibited children show strong anxiety about novel and unfamiliar situations; uninhibited children show very little of this anxiety.

learned helplessness The cognitive, motivational, and emotional deficits that follow a perceived lack of control over important aversive events.

locus of control A personality trait that divides people along a continuum according to the extent to which they believe what happens to them and others is controllable.

manipulated independent variable An independent variable for which participants have been randomly assigned to an experimental group.

masculinity-femininity A personality trait indicating the extent to which a person possesses sex-typed characteristics, with masculine characteristics at one end of the trait continuum and feminine characteristics at the other end.

need for Achievement The motive to engage in and succeed at entrepreneurial achievement behavior.

negative cognitive style A style of processing information in which people attribute their problems to stable and global causes, anticipate dreadful consequences, and believe the problems reflect their own personal shortcomings.

negative schema A cognitive structure that allows people to readily make negative associations.

neodissociation theory Hilgard's theory, which maintains that consciousness is divided into aware and unaware parts during hypnosis.

nonmanipulated independent variable An independent variable for which condition assignment is determined by a characteristic of the participant.

observational learning Learning that results from watching or hearing about a person modeling the behavior.

operant conditioning Learning resulting from the response an organism receives following a behavior.

optimal experience A state of happiness and satisfaction characterized by absorption in a challenging and personally rewarding task.

personal constructs In Kelly's theory, the bipolar cognitive structures through which people process information.

personal narratives Assessment procedure that asks individuals to provide autobiographical descriptions of important events in their lives.

personality Consistent behavior patterns and intrapersonal processes originating within the individual.

person-by-situation approach An approach to understanding behavior that maintains behavior is a function of the person as well as the situation.

possible selves Cognitive representations of the kind of people we think we might become some day.

preconscious In Freud's topographic model, the part of personality that contains thoughts that can be brought into awareness with little difficulty.

problem-focused strategies Coping strategies directed at taking care of the problem causing the anxiety.

projective tests Tests designed to assess unconscious material by asking test takers to respond to ambiguous stimuli.

psychoanalysis The system of psychotherapy developed by Freud that focuses on uncovering the unconscious material responsible for a patient's disorder.

psychosexual stages of development The innate sequence of development made up of stages characterized by primary erogenous zones and sexual desires.

Q-Sort An assessment procedure in which test takers distribute personal descriptions along a continuum.

rational emotive therapy A psychotherapy procedure introduced by Ellis that examines the irrational reasoning causing emotional problems.

reciprocal determinism The notion that external determinants of behavior, internal determinants of behavior, and behavior all influence one another.

reliability The extent to which a test measures consistently.

self-actualization A state of personal growth in which people fulfill their true potential.

self-disclosure The act of revealing intimate information about oneself to another person.

self-efficacy A person's expectancy that he or she can successfully perform a given behavior.

self-esteem Evaluation of one's self-concept, usually measured in terms of a relatively stable and global assessment of how a person feels about him- or herself.

self-regulation The ability to develop and apply rewards and punishments for internal standards of behavior.

self-schema A schema consisting of aspects of a person's life most important to him or her.

social anxiety A trait dimension indicating the extent to which people experience anxiety during social encounters or when anticipating social encounters.

social desirability The extent to which test takers tend to respond to items in a manner that presents them in a positive light.

statistical significance The likelihood that a research finding represents a genuine effect rather than a chance fluctuation of measurement.

striving for superiority The primary motivational force in Adler's theory, which is the person's effort to overcome feelings of inferiority.

structural model Freud's model of personality that divides personality into the id, the ego, and the superego.

subception The perception of information at a less-than-conscious level.

superego In Freud's structural model, the part of personality that represents society's values.

temperaments General behavioral predispositions present in infancy and assumed to be inherited.

theory A general statement about the relationship between constructs or events.

topographic model Freud's original model of personality structure, in which personality is divided into three different levels of awareness.

trait A dimension of personality used to categorize people according to the degree to which they manifest a particular characteristic.

twin-study method A procedure for examining the role of genetics on personality in which pairs of monozygotic and dizygotic twins are compared.

unconscious In Freud's topographic model, the part of personality that contains material that cannot easily be brought into awareness.

validity The extent to which a test measures what it is designed to measure.

References

AARP. (2010). *Loneliness among older adults: A national survey of adults 45+*. Washington, DC: Author.

Abela, J. R. Z., Stolow, D., Mineka, S., Yao, S., Zhu, X. Z., & Hankin, B. L. (2011). Cognitive vulnerability to depressive symptoms in adolescents in urban and rural Hunan, China: A multiwave longitudinal study. *Journal of Abnormal Psychology, 120*, 765–778.

Abramson, L. Y., Seligman, M. E. P., & Teasdale, J. D. (1978). *Learned helplessness in humans: Critique and reformulation. Journal of Abnormal Psychology, 87*, 49–74.

Abuhamdeh, S., & Csikszentmihalyi, M. (2012). The importance of challenge for the enjoyment of intrinsically motivated, goal-directed activities. *Personality and Social Psychology Bulletin, 38*, 317–330.

Accortt, E. E., & Allen, J. J. B. (2006). Frontal EEG asymmetry and premenstrual dysphoric symptomatology. *Journal of Abnormal Psychology, 115*, 179–184.

Aderka, I. M., Nickerson, A., Boe, H. J., & Hofmann, S. G. (2012). Sudden gains during psychological treatments of anxiety and depression: A meta-analysis. *Journal of Consulting and Clinical Psychology, 80*, 93–101.

Ainsworth, M. D. S. (1989). Attachments beyond infancy. *American Psychologist, 44*, 709–716.

Ainsworth, M. D. S., Blehar, M. C., Waters, E., & Wall, S. (1978). *Patterns of attachment*. Hillsdale, NJ: Erlbaum.

Aldwin, C. M., & Revenson, T. A. (1987). Does coping help? A reexamination of the relation between coping and mental health. *Journal of Personality and Social Psychology, 53*, 337–348.

Alloy, L. B., & Abramson, L. Y. (1988). Depressive realism: Four theoretical perspectives. In L. B. Alloy (Ed.), *Cognitive processes in depression* (pp. 223–265). New York: Guilford.

Alloy, L. B., Abramson, L. Y., Hogan, M. E., Whitehouse, W. G., Rose, D. T., Robinson, M. S. et al. (2000). The Temple-Wisconsin cognitive vulnerability to depression project: Lifetime history of Axis I psychopathology in individuals at high and low cognitive risk for depression. *Journal of Abnormal Psychology, 109*, 403–418.

Alloy, L. B., Abramson, L. Y., Keyser, J., Gerstein, R. K., & Sylvia, L. G. (2008). Negative cognitive style. In K. S. Dobson & D. J. A. Dozois (Eds.), *Risk factors in depression* (pp. 237–262). San Diego, CA: Academic Press.

Alloy, L. B., Abramson, L. Y., Whitehouse, W. G., Hogan, M. E., Panzarella, C., & Rose, D. T. (2006). Prospective incidence of first onsets and recurrences of depression in individuals at high and low cognitive risk for depression. *Journal of Abnormal Psychology, 115*, 145–156.

Allport, G. W. (1961). *Pattern and growth in personality*. New York: Holt, Rinehart & Winston.

Allport, G. W. (1965). *Letters from Jenny*. New York: Harcourt, Brace & World.

Allport, G. W. (1967). Gordon W. Allport. In E. G. Boring & G. Lindzey (Eds.), *A history of psychology in autobiography* (Vol. 5, pp. 3–25). New York: Appleton-Century-Crofts.

Allport, G. W. (1968). *The person in psychology: Selected essays*. Boston: Beacon.

Almagor, M., Tellegen, A., & Waller, N. G. (1995). The Big Seven model: A cross-cultural replication and further exploration of the basic dimensions of natural language trait descriptors. *Journal of Personality and Social Psychology, 69*, 300–307.

Altman, I. (1975). *The environment and social behavior*. Monterey, CA: Brooks/Cole.

Altman, I., & Taylor, D. A. (1973). *Social penetration: The development of interpersonal relationships*. New York: Holt, Rinehart & Winston.

American Psychological Association (APA). (1997). Gold medal award for life achievement in psychological science: Raymond, 1997 Raymond B. Cattell. *American Psychologist, 52*, 797–799.

Amir, N., Beard, C., & Bower, E. (2005). Interpretation bias and social anxiety. *Cognitive Therapy and Research, 29*, 433–443.

Amirkhan, J. H., Risinger, R. T., & Swickert, R. J. (1995). Extraversion: A "hidden" personality factor in coping? *Journal of Personality, 63,* 189–212.

Andersen, B. L., Cyranowski, J. M., & Espindle, D. (1999). Men's sexual self-schema. *Journal of Personality and Social Psychology, 76,* 645–661.

Anderson, C. A. (1999). Attributional style, depression, and loneliness: A cross-cultural comparison of American and Chinese students. *Personality and Social Psychology Bulletin, 15,* 482–499.

Anderson, C. A. (2004). An update on the effects of playing violent video games. *Journal of Adolescence, 27,* 113–122.

Anderson, C. A., & Anderson, K. B. (1998). Temperature and aggression: Paradox, controversy, and a (fairly) clear picture. In R. Geen & E. Donnerstein (Eds.), *Human aggression: Theories, research, and implications for public policy* (pp. 247–298). New York: Academic Press.

Anderson, C. A., & Bushman, B. J. (2001). Effects of violent video games on aggressive behavior, aggressive cognition, aggressive affect, physiological arousal, and prosocial behavior: A meta-analytic review of the scientific literature. *Psychological Science, 12,* 353–359.

Anderson, C. A., & Bushman, B. J. (2002a). Human aggression. *Annual Review of Psychology, 53,* 27–51.

Anderson, C. A., & Bushman, B. J. (2002b). The effects of media violence on society. *Science, 295,* 2377–2378.

Anderson, C. A., Carnagey, N. L., & Eubanks, J. (2003). Exposure to violent media: The effects of songs with violent lyrics on aggressive thoughts and feelings. *Journal of Personality and Social Psychology, 84,* 960–971.

Anderson, C. A., & Dill, K. E. (2000). Video games and aggressive thoughts, feelings, and behavior in the laboratory and in life. *Journal of Personality and Social Psychology, 78,* 772–790.

Anderson, C. A., & Harvey, R. J. (1988). Discriminating between

problems in living: An examination of measures of depression, loneliness, shyness, and social anxiety. *Journal of Social and Clinical Psychology, 6,* 482–491.

Anderson, C. A., & Huesmann, L. R. (2003). Human aggression: A social-cognitive view. In M. A. Hogg & J. Cooper (Eds.), *Handbook of social psychology* (pp. 296–323). London: Sage.

Anderson, C. A., Shibuya, A., Ihori, N., Swing, E. L., Bushman, B. J., Sakamoto, A. et al. (2010). Violent video game effects on aggression, empathy, and prosocial behavior in Eastern and Western countries: A meta-analytic review. *Psychological Bulletin, 136,* 151–173.

Ansbacher, H. L., & Ansbacher, R. R. (Eds.). (1956). *The individual psychology of Alfred Adler.* New York: Basic Books.

Antill, J. K. (1983). Sex role complementarity versus similarity in married couples. *Journal of Personality and Social Psychology, 45,* 145–155.

Anusic, I., Lucas, R. E., & Donnellan, M. B. (2012). Cross-sectional age differences in personality: Evidence from nationally representative samples from Switzerland and the United States. *Journal of Research in Personality, 46,* 116–120.

Archer, J. (1996). Sex differences in social behavior: Are the social role and evolutionary explanations compatible? *American Psychologist, 51,* 909–917.

Archibald, F. S., Bartholomew, K., & Marx, R. (1995). Loneliness in early adolescence: A test of the cognitive discrepancy model of loneliness. *Personality and Social Psychology Bulletin, 21,* 296–301.

Arkin, A. M., Antrobus, J. S., & Ellman, S. J. (1978). *The mind in sleep: Psychology and psychophysiology.* Hillsdale, NJ: Erlbaum.

Arkin, R. M., & Grove, T. (1990). Shyness, sociability and patterns of everyday affiliation. *Journal of Social and Personal Relationships, 7,* 273–281.

Aron, A., Aron, E. N., & Allen, J. (1998). Motivations for unreciprocated love. *Personality and Social Psychology Bulletin, 24,* 787–796.

Arthur, W., & Graziano, W. G. (1996). The five-factor model, conscientiousness, and driving accident involvement. *Journal of Personality, 64,* 593–618.

Asendorpf, J. B., & Wilpers, S. (1998). Personality effects on social relationships. *Journal of Personality and Social Psychology, 74,* 1531–1544.

Aserinsky, E., & Kleitman, N. (1953). Regularly occurring periods of eye motility and concomitant phenomena during sleep. *Science, 118,* 273–274.

Ashton, M. C., & Lee, K. (2007). Empirical, theoretical, and practical advantages of the HEXACO model of personality structure. *Personality and Social Psychology Review, 11,* 150–166.

Ashton, M. C., Lee, K., Goldberg, L. R., & de Vries, R. E. (2009). Higher order factors of personality: Do they exist? *Personality and Social Psychology Review, 13,* 79–91.

Aspinwall, L. G., & Brunhart, S. M. (1996). Distinguishing optimism from denial: Optimistic beliefs predict attention to health threats. *Personality and Social Psychology Bulletin, 22,* 993–1003.

Aspinwall, L. G., & Taylor, S. E. (1992). Modeling cognitive adaptation: A longitudinal investigation of the impact of individual differences and coping on college adjustment and performance. *Journal of Personality and Social Psychology, 63,* 989–1003.

Aube, J. (2008). Balancing concern for other with concern for self: Links between unmitigated communion, communion, and psychological well-being. *Journal of Personality, 76,* 101–133.

Aube, J., Norcliffe, H., Craig, J., & Koestner, R. (1995). Gender characteristics and adjustment-related outcomes: Questioning the masculinity model. *Personality and Social Psychology Bulletin, 21,* 284–295.

Auerbach, R. P., & Ho, M.-H. R. (2012). A cognitive-interpersonal model of adolescent depression: The impact of family conflict and depressogenic cognitive styples. *Journal of Clinical Child & Adolescent Psychology, 41,* 792–802.

Austenfeld, J. L., & Stanton, A. L. (2004). Coping through emotional approach: A new look at emotion, coping, and health-related outcomes. *Journal of Personality, 72,* 1335–1363.

Aznar, S., Klein, A. B., Santini, M. A., Knudsen, G. M., Henn, F., Gass, P., & Vollmayr, B. (2010). Aging and depression vulnerability interaction results in decreased serotonin innervation associated with reduced BDNF levels in hippocampus of rats bred for learned helplessness. *Synapse, 64,* 561–565.

Bagby, R. M., Rogers, R., Nicholson, R. A., Buis, T., Seeman, M. V., & Rector, N. A. (1997). Effectiveness of the MMPI-2 validity indicators in the detection of defensive responding in clinical and nonclinical samples. *Psychological Assessment, 9,* 406–413.

Baker, E. L., & Nash, M. R. (2008). Psychoanalytic approaches to clinical hypnosis. In M. R. Nash & A. J. Barnier (Eds.), *The Oxford handbook of hypnosis: Theory, research and practice* (pp. 439–456). New York: Oxford University Press.

Baker, L. A., & Daniels, D. (1990). Nonshared environmental influences and personality differences in adult twins. *Journal of Personality and Social Psychology, 58,* 103–110.

Baker, L., & McNulty, J. K. (2010). Shyness and marriage: Does shyness shape even established relationships? *Personality and Social Psychology Bulletin, 36,* 665–676.

Baker, S. R. (2007). Dispositional optimism and health status, symptoms and behaviours: Assessing idiothetic relationships using a prospective daily diary approach. *Psychology and Health, 22,* 431–455.

Bandura, A. (1965). Influences of models' reinforcement contingencies on the acquisition of imitative responses. *Journal of Personality and Social Psychology, 1,* 589–595.

Bandura, A. (1973). *Aggression: A social learning analysis.* Englewood Cliffs, NJ: Prentice Hall.

Bandura, A. (1977a). Self-efficacy: Toward a unifying theory of behavioral change. *Psychological Review, 84,* 191–215.

Bandura, A. (1977b). *Social learning theory.* Englewood Cliffs, NJ: Prentice Hall.

Bandura, A. (1986). *Social foundations of thought and action: A social cognitive theory.* Englewood Cliffs, NJ: Prentice Hall.

Bandura, A. (1997). *Self-efficacy: The exercise of control.* New York: Freeman.

Bandura, A. (2001). Social cognitive theory: An agentic perspective. *Annual Review of Psychology, 52,* 1–26.

Bandura, A. (2006). Toward a psychology of human agency. *Perspectives on Psychological Science, 1,* 164–180.

Bandura, A., Adams, N. E., & Beyer, J. (1977). Cognitive processes mediating behavioral change. *Journal of Personality and Social Psychology, 35,* 125–139.

Bandura, A., & Bussey, K. (2004). On broadening the cognitive, motivational, and sociostructural scope of theorizing about gender development and functioning: Comment on Martin, Ruble, and Szkrybalo (2002). *Psychological Bulletin, 130,* 691–701.

Bandura, A., Pastorelli, C., Barbaranelli, C., & Caprara, G. V. (1999). Self-efficacy pathways to childhood depression. *Journal of Personality and Social Psychology, 76,* 258–269.

Barber, T. S., & Calverley, D. S. (1964). Toward a theory of hypnotic behavior: Effects on suggestibility of defining the situation as hypnosis and defining responses to suggestion as easy. *Journal of Abnormal and Social Psychology, 68,* 585–592.

Barber, T. X. (1969). *Hypnosis: A scientific approach.* New York: Van Nostrand Reinhold.

Barber, T. X. (1999). A comprehensive three-dimensional theory of hypnosis. In I. Kirsch, A. Capafons, E. Cardena-Buelna, & S. Amigo (Eds.), *Clinical hypnosis and self-regulation: Cognitive-behavioral perspectives* (pp. 21–48). Washington, DC: American Psychological Association.

Bardos, A. N., & Powell, S. (2001). Human figure drawings and the Draw-A-Person: Screening procedures for emotional disturbances. In W. I. Dorfman & M. Hersen (Eds.), *Understanding psychological assessment* (pp. 275–294). New York: Plenum.

Bar-Haim, Y., Fox, N. A., Benson, B., Guyer, A. E., Williams, A., Nelson, E. E. et al. (2009). Neural correlates of reward processing in adolescents with a history of inhibited temperament. *Psychological Science, 20,* 1009–1018.

Barlett, C. P., & Anderson, C. A. (2011). Reappraising the situation and its impact on aggressive behavior. *Personality and Social Psychology Bulletin, 37,* 1564–1573.

Barlett, C., Branch, O., Rodeheffer, C., & Harris, R. (2009). How long do the short-term violent video game effects last? *Aggressive Behavior, 35,* 225–236.

Barlett, C. P., & Rodeheffer, C. (2009). Effects of realism on extended violent and nonviolent video game play on aggressive thoughts, feelings, and physiological arousal. *Aggressive Behavior, 35,* 213–224.

Barlow, D. H. (1988). *Anxiety and its disorders.* New York: Guilford.

Barnett, J. E. (2011). Psychotherapist self-disclosure: Ethical and clinical considerations. *Psychotherapy, 48,* 315–321.

Baron, R. A. (1978a). Aggression-inhibiting influence of sexual behavior. *Journal of Personality* and Social Psychology, 36, 189–197.

Baron, R. A. (1978b). The influence of hostile and nonhostile humor upon physical aggression. *Personality and Social Psychology Bulletin, 4,* 77–80.

Barrett, P., & Eysenck, S. B. G. (1984). The assessment of personality factors across 25 countries. *Personality and Individual Differences, 5,* 615–632.

Barrick, M. R., & Mount, M. K. (1991). The Big Five personality dimensions and job performance: A meta-analysis. *Personnel Psychology, 44,* 1–26.

Barrick, M. R., Mount, M. K., & Judge, T. A. (2001). Personality and performance at the beginning of the new millennium: What do we know and where to we go next? *International Journal of Selection and Assessment, 91,* 9–30.

Barrick, M. R., Mount, M. K., & Strauss, J. P. (1993). Conscientiousness and performance of sales representatives: Test of the mediating effects of goal setting. *Journal of Applied Psychology, 78,* 715–722.

Barrick, M. R., Mount, M. K., & Strauss, J. P. (1994). Antecedents of involuntary turnover due to a reduction in force. *Personnel Psychology, 47,* 515–535.

Barron, K. E., & Harackiewicz, J. M. (2001). Achievement goals and optimal motivation: Testing multiple goal models. *Journal of Personality and Social Psychology, 80,* 706–722.

Bartholomew, K. (1990). Avoidance of intimacy: An attachment perspective. *Journal of Social and Personal Relationships, 7,* 147–178.

Bartholomew, K., & Horowitz, L. M. (1991). Attachment styles among young adults: A test of a four-category model. *Journal of Personality and Social Psychology, 61,* 226–244.

Bartholomew, K., & Shaver, P. R. (1998). Methods of assessing adult attachment. In J. A. Simpson & W. S. Rholes (Eds.), *Attachment theory and close relationships* (pp. 25–45). New York: Guilford.

Bartholow, B. D., Bushman, B. J., & Sestir, M. A. (2006). Chronic violent video game exposure and desensitization to violence: Behavioral and event-related brain potential data. *Journal of Experimental Social Psychology, 42,* 532–539.

Basgall, J. A., & Snyder, C. R. (1988). Excuses in waiting: External locus of control and reactions to success-failure feedback. *Journal of Personality and Social Psychology, 54,* 656–662.

Bates, J. E., Wachs, T. D., & Emde, R. N. (1994). Toward practical uses for biological concepts of temperament. In J. E. Bates & T. D. Wachs (Eds.), *Temperament: Individual differences at the interface of biology and behavior* (pp. 275–306). Washington, DC: American Psychological Association.

Bauder, D. (2005, November 29). Violence surging on networks. *San Jose Mercury News*, p. 2E.

Bauer, J. J., & Bonanno, G. A. (2001). I can, I do, I am: The narrative differentiation of self-efficacy and other self-evaluations while adapting to bereavement. *Journal of Research in Personality, 35,* 424–448.

Baumann, J., & DeSterno, D. (2010). Emotion guided threat detection: Expecting guns where there are none. *Journal of Personality and Social Psychology, 99,* 595–610.

Baumeister, R. F. (1991). On the stability of variability: Retest reliability of metatraits. *Personality and Social Psychology Bulletin, 17,* 633–639.

Baumeister, R. F., & Leary, M. R. (1995). The need to belong: Desire for interpersonal attachments as a fundamental human motivation. *Psychological Bulletin, 117,* 497–529.

Baumeister, R. F., & Tice, D. M. (1988). Metatraits. *Journal of Personality, 56,* 571–598.

Baumeister, R. F., & Tice, D. M. (1990). Anxiety and social exclusion. *Journal of Social and Clinical Psychology, 9,* 165–195.

Bauminger, N., Finzi-Dottan, R., Chason, S., & Har-Even, D. (2008). Intimacy in adolescent friendship: The roles of attachment, coherence, and self-disclosure. *Journal of Social and Personal Relationships, 25,* 409–428.

Bechtle, R. (1984). The religion of the unconscious. In C. G. Jung & J. Heaney (Eds.), *Psyche and spirit* (pp. 138–163). New York: Paulist.

Beck, A. T. (1972). *Depression: Causes and treatments.* Philadelphia: University of Pennsylvania Press.

Beck, A. T., & Bhar, S. S. (2009). Effectiveness of long-term psychodynamic psychotherapy: A meta-analysis': Comment. *Journal of the American Medical Association, 301,* 931.

Beevers, C. G., Strong, D. R., Meyer, B., Pilkonis, P. A., & Miller, I. W. (2007). Efficiently assessing negative cognition in depression: An item response theory analysis of the Dysfunctional Attitude Scale. *Psychological Assessment, 19,* 199–209.

Bell, R. C. (1990). Analytic issues in the use of Repertory Grid Technique. In G. J. Neimeyer & R. A. Neimeyer (Eds.), *Advances in personal construct psychology* (Vol. 1, pp. 25–48). Greenwich, CT: JAI Press.

Bem, D. J., & Allen, A. (1974). On predicting some of the people some of the time: The search for cross-situational consistencies in behavior. *Psychological Review, 81,* 506–520.

Bem, S. L. (1974). The measurement of psychological androgyny. *Journal of Consulting and Clinical Psychology, 42,* 155–162.

Bem, S. L. (1977). On the utility of alternative procedures for assessing psychological androgyny. *Journal of Consulting and Clinical Psychology, 45,* 196–205.

Benassi, V. A., Sweeney, P. D., & Dufour, C. L. (1988). Is there a relationship between locus of control orientation and depression? *Journal of Abnormal Psychology, 97,* 357–367.

Benet-Martinez, V., & Oishi, S. (2008). Personality and culture. In O. P. John, R. W. Robins, & L. A. Pervin (Eds.), *Handbook of personality* (3rd ed., pp. 542–567). New York: Guilford.

Benet-Martinez, V., & Waller, N. G. (1997). Further evidence for the cross-cultural generality of the Big Seven factor model: Indigenous and imported Spanish personality constructs. *Journal of Personality, 65,* 567–598.

Bengston, P. L., & Grotevant, H. D. (1999). The individuality and connectedness Q-Sort: A measure for assessing individuality and connectedness in dyadic relationships. *Personal Relationships, 6,* 213–225.

Benham, G., Woody, E. Z., Wilson, K. S., & Nash, M. R. (2006). Expect the unexpected: Ability, attitude, and responsiveness to hypnosis. *Journal of Personality and Social Psychology, 91,* 342–350.

Ben Hamida, S., Mineka, S., & Bailey, J. M. (1998). Sex differences in perceived controllability of mate value: An evolutionary perspective. *Journal of Personality and Social Psychology, 75,* 953–966.

Benish, S. G., Quintana, S., & Wampold, B. E. (2011). Culturally adapted psychotherapy and the legitimacy of myth: A direct-comparison meta-analysis. *Journal of Counseling Psychology, 58,* 279–289.

Bennett, P., Moore, L., Smith, A., Murphy, S., & Smith, C. (1994). Health locus of control and value for health as predictors of dietary behaviour. *Psychology and Health, 10,* 41–54.

Berg, J. H., & Peplau, L. A. (1982). Loneliness: The relationship of self-disclosure and androgyny. *Personality and Social Psychology Bulletin, 8,* 624–630.

Berkman, L. F. (1995). The role of social relations in health promotion. *Psychosomatic Medicine, 57,* 245–254.

Berkowitz, L. (1970). Aggressive humor as a stimulus to aggressive responses. *Journal of Personality and Social Psychology, 16,* 710–717.

Berkowitz, L. (1989). The frustration-aggression hypothesis: An examination and reformulation. *Psychological Bulletin, 106,* 59–73.

Berkowitz, L. (1994). Is something missing? Some observations prompted by the cognitive-neoassociationist view of anger and emotional aggression. In L. R. Huesmann (Ed.), *Aggressive behavior: Current perspectives* (pp. 35–57). New York: Plenum.

Berkowitz, L. (1998). Affective aggression: The role of stress, pain, and negative affect. In R. G. Geen & E. Donnerstein (Eds.), *Human aggression: Theories, research, and implications for social policy* (pp. 49–72). San Diego: Academic Press.

Berkowitz, L. (2012). A different view of anger: The cognitive-neoassociation conception of the relation of anger to aggression. *Aggressive Behavior, 38,* 322–333.

Berman, M. E., McCloskey, M. S., Fanning, J. R., Schumacher, J. A., & Coccaro, E. F. (2009). Serotonin augmentation reduces response to attack in aggressive individuals. *Psychological Science, 20,* 714–720.

Berman, M. I., & Frazier, P. A. (2005). Relationship power and betrayal experience as predictors of reactions to infidelity. *Personality and Social Psychology Bulletin, 31,* 1617–1627.

Berry, D. S., & Hansen, J. S. (1996). Positive affect, negative affect, and social interaction. *Journal of Personality and Social Psychology, 71,* 796–809.

Berry, D. S., & Willingham, J. K. (1997). Affective traits, responses to conflict, and satisfaction in romantic relationships. *Journal of Research in Personality, 31,* 564–576.

Berry, D. S., Willingham, J. K., & Thayer, C. A. (2000). Affect and personality as predictors of conflict and closeness in young adults' friendships. *Journal of Research in Personality, 34,* 84–107.

Bettencourt, B. A., Talley, A. E., Benjamin, A. J., & Valentine, J. (2006). Personality and aggressive behavior under provoking and neutral conditions: A meta-analytic review. *Psychological Bulletin, 132,* 751–777.

Bettencourt, B. A., Talley, A. E., Molix, L., Schlegel, R., & Westgate, S. J. (2008). Rural and urban breast cancer patients: Health locus of control and psychological adjustment. *Psycho-Oncology, 17,* 932–939.

Bezdjian, S., Baker, L. A., & Tuvblad, C. (2011). Genetic and environmental influences on impulsivity: A meta-analysis of twin, family and adoption studies. *Clinical Psychology Review, 31,* 1209–1223.

Bianchi, E. C. (1988). Jungian psychology and religious experience. In R. L. Moore (Ed.), *Carl Jung and Christian spirituality* (pp. 16–37). New York: Paulist.

Biederman, J., Hirshfeld-Becker, D. R., Rosenbaum, J. F., Herot, C., Friedman, D., Snidman, N. et al. (2001). Further evidence of association between behavioral inhibition and social anxiety in children. *American Journal of Psychiatry, 158,* 1673–1679.

Blankenship, V., Vega, C. M., Ramos, E., Romero, K., Warren, K., Keenan, K. et al. (2006). Using the multifaceted Rasch model to improve the TAT/PSE measure of need for Achievement. *Journal of Personality Assessment, 86,* 100–114.

Bleidorn, W., Kandler, C., Riemann, R., Angleitner, A., & Spinath, F. M. (2009). Patterns and sources of adult personality development: Growth curve analysis of the NEO PI-R Scales in a longitudinal twin study. *Journal of Personality and Social Psychology, 97,* 142–155.

Block, J. (2008). *The Q-Sort in character appraisal.* Washington, DC: American Psychological Association.

Block, J. H., Gjerde, P. F., & Block, J. H. (1991). Personality antecedents of depressive tendencies in 18-year-olds: A prospective study.

Journal of Personality and Social Psychology, 60, 726–738.

Bloise, S. M., & Johnson, M. K. (2007). Memory for emotional and neutral information: Gender and individual differences in emotional sensitivity. *Memory, 15,* 192–204.

Bodner, E., & Mikulincer, M. (1998). Learned helplessness and the occurrence of depressive-like and paranoid-like responses: The role of attentional focus. *Journal of Personality and Social Psychology, 74,* 1010–1023.

Boldizar, J. P., Perry, D. G., & Perry, L. C. (1989). Outcome values and aggression. *Child Development, 60,* 571–579.

Bond, M. (1992). An empirical study of defensive style: The Defense Style Questionnaire. In G. Vaillant (Ed.), *Ego mechanisms of defense: A guide for clinicians and researchers* (pp. 127–158). Washington, DC: American Psychiatric Press.

Bonanno, G. A., Papa, A., Lalande, K., Westphal, M., & Coifman, K. (2004). The importance of being flexible: The ability to both enhance and suppress emotional expression predicts long-term adjustment. *Psychological Science, 15,* 482–487.

Bonanno, G. A., Pat-Horenczyk, R., & Noll, J. (2011). Coping flexibility and trauma: The Perceived Ability to Cope with Trauma (PACT) Scale. *Psychological Trauma: Theory, Research, Practice, and Policy, 3,* 117–129.

Booth-Kewley, S., & Vickers, R. R. (1994). Associations between major domains of personality and health behavior. *Journal of Personality, 62,* 281–298.

Borkenau, P., Riemann, R., Angleitner, A., & Spinath, F. M. (2001). Genetic and environmental influences on observed personality: Evidence from the German observational study of adult twins. *Journal of Personality and Social Psychology, 80,* 655–668.

Bowers, S. P. (1999). Gender role identity and the caregiving experience of widowed men. *Sex Roles, 41,* 645–655.

Bowlby, J. (1969). *Attachment and loss: Attachment* (Vol. 1). New York: Basic Books.

Bowlby, J. (1973). *Attachment and loss: Separation: Anger and anxiety* (Vol. 2). New York: Basic Books.

Bowlby, J. (1980). *Attachment and loss: Loss, sadness, and depression* (Vol. 3). New York: Basic Books.

Bradbury, T. N., Campbell, S. M., & Fincham, F. D. (1995). Longitudinal and behavioral analysis of masculinity and femininity in marriage. *Journal of Personality and Social Psychology, 68,* 328–341.

Braffman, W., & Kirsch, I. (1999). Imaginative suggestibility and hypnotizability: An empirical analysis. *Journal of Personality and Social Psychology, 77,* 578–587.

Brebner, J., & Cooper, C. (1978). Stimulus-or response-induced excitation: A comparison of behavior in introverts and extraverts. *Journal of Research in Personality, 12,* 306–311.

Brennan, K. A., Clark, C. L., & Shaver, P. R. (1998). Self-report measurement of adult attachment. In J. A. Simpson & W. S. Rholes (Eds.), *Attachment theory and close relationships* (pp. 46–76). New York: Guilford.

Brennan, K. A., & Shaver, P. R. (1993). Attachment styles and parental divorce. *Journal of Divorce and Remarriage, 21,* 161–175.

Brennan, K. A., & Shaver, P. R. (1995). Dimensions of adult attachment, affect regulation, and romantic relationship functioning. *Personality and Social Psychology Bulletin, 21,* 267–283.

Bresin, K., & Gordon, K. H. (2013). Aggression as affect regulation: Extending catharsis theory to evaluate aggression and experiential anger in the laboratory and daily life. *Journal of Social and Clinical Psychology, 32,* 400–423.

Brissette, I., & Cohen, S. (2002). The contribution of individual differences in hostility to the associations between daily interpersonal conflict, affect, and sleep. *Personality*

and *Social Psychology Bulletin, 28,* 1265–1274.

Brissette, I., Scheier, M. F., & Carver, C. S. (2002). The role of optimism in social network development, coping, and psychological adjustment during a life transition. *Journal of Personality and Social Psychology, 82,* 102–111.

Britt, T. W. (1993). Metatraits: Evidence relevant to the validity of the construct and its implications. *Journal of Personality and Social Psychology, 65,* 544–562.

Britt, T. W., & Shepperd, J. A. (1999). Trait relevance and trait assessment. *Personality and Social Psychology Review, 3,* 108–122.

Brockner, J. (1979). The effects of self-esteem, success-failure, and self-consciousness on task performance. *Journal of Personality and Social Psychology, 37,* 1732–1741.

Brockner, J., Derr, W. R., & Laing, W. N. (1987). Self-esteem and reactions to negative feedback: Toward greater generalizability. *Journal of Research in Personality, 21,* 318–333.

Brody, J. E. (2000, April 25). Memories of things that never were. *New York Times,* p. D8.

Brody, L. R., Rozek, M. K., & Muten, E. O. (1985). Age, sex, and individual differences in children's defensive styles. *Journal of Clinical Child Psychology, 14,* 132–138.

Brooks-Gunn, J., & Fisch, M. (1980). Psychological androgyny and college students' judgments of mental health. *Sex Roles, 6,* 575–580.

Brown, J., & Inouye, D. K. (1978). Learned helplessness through modeling: The role of perceived similarity in competence. *Journal of Personality and Social Psychology, 36,* 900–908.

Brown, J. D., & Dutton, K. A. (1995). The thrill of victory, the complexity of defeat: Self-esteem and people's emotional reactions to success and failure. *Journal of Personality and Social Psychology, 68,* 712–722.

Brown, J. D., & Marshall, M. A. (2001). Great expectations: Optimism and pessimism in achievement settings. In E. C. Chang (Ed.), *Optimism and pessimism: Implications for theory, research, and practice* (pp. 239–255). Washington, DC: American Psychological Association.

Brown, J. D., & Smart, S. A. (1991). The self and social conduct: Linking self-representations to prosocial behavior. *Journal of Personality and Social Psychology, 60*, 368–375.

Brown, R. J., & Donderi, D. C. (1986). Dream content and self-reported well-being among recurrent dreamers, past-recurrent dreamers, and nonrecurrent dreamers. *Journal of Personality and Social Psychology, 50*, 612–623.

Bruch, M. A., Hamer, R. J., & Heimberg, R. G. (1995). Shyness and public self-consciousness: Additive or interactive relation with social interaction? *Journal of Personality, 63*, 47–63.

Bruch, M. A., Kaflowitz, N. G., & Pearl, L. (1988). Mediated and nonmediated relationships of personality components to loneliness. *Journal of Social and Clinical Psychology, 6*, 346–355.

Brunstein, J. C., & Maier, G. W. (2005). Implicit and self-attributed motives to achieve: Two separate but interacting needs. *Journal of Personality and Social Psychology, 89*, 205–222.

Brunstein, J. C., & Schmitt, C. H. (2004). Assessing individual differences in achievement motivation with the Implicit Association Test. *Journal of Research in Personality, 38*, 536–555.

Buchholz, E. S., & Helbraun, E. (1999). A psychobiological developmental model for an "alonetime" need in infancy. *Bulletin of the Menninger Clinic, 63*, 143–158.

Buckingham, J. T., Weber, A. M., & Sypher, A. K. (2012). Self-esteem and self-perpetuating effects of threat on contingencies of self-worth. *Self and Identity, 11*, 360–385.

Buckley, M. E., Klein, D. N., Durbin, C. E., Hayden, E. P., & Moerk, K. C. (2002). Development and validation of a Q-Sort procedure to assess temperament and behavior in preschool-age children. *Journal of Clinical Child and Adolescent Psychology, 31*, 525–539.

Buday, S. K., Stake, J. E., & Peterson, Z. D. (2012). Gender and choice of a science career: The impact of social support and possible selves. *Sex Roles, 66*, 197–209.

Buhler, C., & Allen, M. (1972). *Introduction to humanistic psychology.* Monterey, CA: Brooks/ Cole.

Bulkeley, K. (1997). *An introduction to the psychology of dreaming.* Westport, CT: Praeger.

Bullock, W. A., & Gilliland, K. (1993). Eysenck's arousal theory of introversion-extraversion: A converging measures investigation. *Journal of Personality and Social Psychology, 64*, 113–123.

Bunde, J., & Suls, J. (2006). A quantitative analysis of the relationship between the Cook-Medley Hostility Scale and traditional coronary artery disease risk factors. *Health Psychology, 25*, 493–500.

Burger, J. M. (1984). Desire for control, locus of control, and proneness to depression. *Journal of Personality, 52*, 71–89.

Burger, J. M. (1995). Individual differences in preference for solitude. *Journal of Research in Personality, 29*, 85–108.

Burger, J. M. (1998). Solitude. In H. S. Friedman (Ed.), *The encyclopedia of mental health* (pp. 563–569). San Diego, CA: Academic Press.

Burger, J. M., & Arkin, R. M. (1980). Prediction, control and learned helplessness. *Journal of Personality and Social Psychology, 38*, 482–491.

Burger, J. M., & Cosby, M. (1999). Do women prefer dominant men? The case of the missing control condition. *Journal of Research in Personality, 33*, 358–368.

Burgess, A. (2007). On the contribution of neurophysiology to hypnosis research: Current state and future directions. In G. A. Jamieson (Ed.), *Hypnosis and conscious states: The cognitive neuroscience perspective* (pp. 195–219). New York: Oxford University Press.

Burns, J. W., & Evon, D. (2007). Common and specific process factors in cardiac rehabilitation: Independent and interactive effects of the working alliance and self-efficacy. *Health Psychology, 26*, 684–692.

Burns, M. O., & Seligman, M. E. P. (1989). Explanatory style across the life span: Evidence for stability over 52 years. *Journal of Personality and Social Psychology, 56*, 471–477.

Bushman, B. J. (1995). Moderating role of trait aggressiveness in the effects of violent media on aggression. *Journal of Personality and Social Psychology, 69*, 950–960.

Bushman, B. J. (2002). Does venting anger feed or extinguish the flame? Catharsis, rumination, distraction, anger, and aggressive responding. *Personality and Social Psychology Bulletin, 28*, 724–731.

Bushman, B. J., Baumeister, R. F., & Phillips, C. M. (2001). Do people aggress to improve their mood? Catharsis beliefs, affect regulation opportunity, and aggressive responding. *Journal of Personality and Social Psychology, 81*, 17–32.

Bushman, B. J., Baumeister, R. F., & Stack, A. D. (1999). Catharsis, aggression, and persuasive influence: Self-fulfilling or self-defeating prophecies? *Journal of Personality and Social Psychology, 76*, 367–376.

Bushman, B. J., Bonacci, A. M., Pedersen, W. C., Vasquez, E. A., & Miller, N. (2005). Chewing on it can chew you up: Effects of rumination on triggered displaced aggression. *Journal of Personality and Social Psychology, 88*, 969–983.

Bushman, B. J., & Gibson, B. (2011). Violent video games cause an increase in aggression long after the game has been turned off. *Social Psychological and Personality Science, 2*, 29–32.

Bushman, B. J., & Huesmann, L. R. (2001). Effects of televised violence on aggression. In D. G. Singer &

J. L. Singer (Eds.), *Handbook of children and the media* (pp. 223–254). Thousand Oaks, CA: Sage.

Bushman, B. J., & Whitaker, J. L. (2010). Like a magnet: Catharsis beliefs attract angry people to violent video games. *Psychological Science, 21,* 790–792.

Buss, A. H. (1980). *Self-consciousness and social anxiety.* San Francisco: W. H. Freeman.

Buss, A. H., & Plomin, R. (1984). *Temperament: Early developing personality traits.* Hillsdale, NJ: Erlbaum.

Buss, A. H., & Plomin, R. (1986). The EAS approach to temperament. In R. Plomin & J. Dunn (Eds.), *The study of temperament: Changes, continuities and challenges* (pp. 67–79). Hillsdale, NJ: Erlbaum.

Buss, D. M. (1988). The evolution of human intrasexual competition: Tactics of mate attraction. *Journal of Personality and Social Psychology, 54,* 616–628.

Buss, D. M. (1989). Sex differences in human mate preferences: Evolutionary hypotheses tested in 37 cultures. *Behavioral and Brain Sciences, 12,* 1–49.

Buss, D. M. (1990). The evolution of anxiety and social exclusion. *Journal of Social and Clinical Psychology, 9,* 196–201.

Buss, D. M. (1991). Evolutionary personality psychology. *Annual Review of Psychology, 42,* 459–491.

Buss, D. M. (2008). Human nature and individual differences: Evolution of human personality. In O. P. John, R. W. Robins, & L. A. Pervin (Eds.), *Handbook of personality* (3rd ed., pp. 29–60). New York: Guilford.

Buss, D. M. (2009). The great struggles of life: Darwin and the emergence of evolutionary psychology. *American Psychologist, 64,* 140–148.

Buss, D. M., & Barnes, M. (1986). Preferences in human mate selection. *Journal of Personality and Social Psychology, 50,* 559–570.

Buss, D. M., & Shackelford, T. K. (1997). From vigilance to violence: Mate retention tactics in married couples. *Journal of Personality and Social Psychology, 72,* 346–361.

Bussey, K., & Bandura, A. (1999). Social cognitive theory of gender development and differentiation. *Psychological Review, 106,* 676–713.

Butcher, J. N. (Eds.). (2006). *MMPI-2: A practitioner's guide.* Washington, DC: American Psychological Association.

Butler, A. C., Chapman, J. E., Forman, E. M., & Beck, A. T. (2006). The empirical status of cognitive-behavioral therapy: A review of meta-analyses. *Clinical Psychology Review, 26,* 17–31.

Butler, J. M. (1968). Self-ideal congruence in psychotherapy. *Psychotherapy: Theory, Research and Practice, 5,* 13–17.

Byrne, D. (1964). Repression sensitization as a dimension of personality. In B. A. Maher (Ed.), *Progress in experimental personality research* (Vol. 1, pp. 169–220). New York: Academic Press.

Cacioppo, J. T., Ernest, J. M., Burleson, M. H., McClintock, M. K., Malarkey, W. B., Hawkley, L. C. et al. (2000). Lonely traits and concomitant physiological processes: The Macarthur Social Neuroscience Studies. *International Journal of Psychophysiology, 35,* 143–154.

Cacioppo, J. T., Hawkley, L. C., Berntson, G. G., Ernst, J. M., Gibbs, A. C., Stickgold, R. et al. (2002). Do lonely days invade the night? Potential social modulation of sleep efficiency. *Psychological Science, 13,* 384–387.

Cacioppo, J. T., Hawkley, L. C., Crawford, E., Ernst, J. M., Burleson, M. H., Kowalewski, R. B. et al. (2002). Loneliness and health: Potential mechanisms. *Psychosomatic Medicine, 64,* 407–417.

Cacioppo, J. T., Hawkley, L. C., Ernst, J. M., Burleson, M., Berntson, G. G., & Nouriani, B. (2006). Loneliness within a nomological net: An evolutionary perspective. *Journal of Research in Personality, 40,* 1054–1085.

Cacioppo, J. T., & Patrick, B. (2008). *Loneliness: Human nature and the need for social connection.* New York: Norton.

Cain, D. J., & Seeman, J. (2002). *Humanistic psychotherapies: Handbook of research and practice.* Washington, DC: American Psychological Association.

Cairns, R. B. (1986). An evolutionary and developmental perspective on aggressive patterns. In C. Zahn-Waxler, E. M. Cummings, & R. Iannotti (Eds.), *Altruism and aggression: Biological and social origins* (pp. 58–87). Cambridge: Cambridge University Press.

Caldwell, D. F., & Burger, J. M. (1998). Personality characteristics of job applicants and success in screening interviews. *Personnel Psychology, 51,* 119–136.

Calvete, E. (2008). Justification of violence and grandiosity schemas as predictors of antisocial behavior in adolescents. *Journal of Abnormal Child Psychology, 36,* 1083–1095.

Camara, W. J., Nathan, J. S., & Puente, A. E. (2000). Psychological test usage: Implications in professional psychology. *Professional Psychology: Research and Practice, 31,* 141–154.

Cambron, M. J., Acitelli, L. K., & Steinberg, L. (2010). When friends make you blue: The role of friendship contingent self-esteem in predicting self-esteem and depressive symptoms. *Personality and Social Psychology Bulletin, 36,* 384–397.

Cameron, L. D., & Nicholls, G. (1998). Expression of stressful experiences through writing: Effects of a self-regulation manipulation for pessimists and optimists. *Health Psychology, 17,* 84–92.

Campbell, J. B. (1983). Differential relationships of extraversion, impulsivity, and sociability to study habits. *Journal of Research in Personality, 17,* 308–314.

Campbell, J. B., & Hawley, C. W. (1982). Study habits and eysenck's theory of extraversion-introversion. *Journal of Research in Personality, 16,* 139–146.

Campbell, J. D., & Fairey, P. J. (1985). Effects of self-esteem, hypothetical explanations, and verbalization of expectancies on future performance. *Journal of Personality and Social Psychology, 48,* 1097–1111.

Campbell, L., Simpson, J. A., Boldry, J., & Kashy, D. A. (2005). Perceptions of conflict and support in romantic relationships: The role of attachment anxiety. *Journal of Personality and Social Psychology, 88,* 510–531.

Campos, J. J., Barrett, K. C., Lamb, M. E., Goldsmith, H. H., & Stenberg, C. (1983). Socioemotional development. In M. M. Haith & J. J. Campos (Eds.), *Handbook of child psychology: Infancy and psychobiology* (Vol. 2, pp. 783–915). New York: Wiley.

Canli, T. (2004). Functional brain mapping of extraversion and neuroticism: Learning from individual differences in emotion processing. *Journal of Personality, 72,* 1105–1132.

Canli, T. (2006). Genomic imaging of extraversion. In T. Canli (Ed.), *Biology of personality and individual differences* (pp. 93–115). New York: Guilford.

Canli, T. (2008). Toward a "molecular psychology" of personality. In O. P. John, R. W. Robins, & L. A. Pervin (Eds.), *Handbook of personality* (3rd ed., pp. 311–327). New York: Guilford.

Cappella, E., & Weinstein, R. S. (2001). Turning around reading achievement: Predictors of high school students' academic resilience. *Journal of Educational Psychology, 93,* 758–771.

Caputi, P., Viney, L. L., Walker, B. M., & Crittenden, N. (2012). *Personal construct methodology.* Hoboken, NJ: Wiley & Sons.

Card, N. A., Stucky, B. D., Sawalani, G. M., & Little, T. D. (2008). Direct and indirect aggression during childhood and adolescence: A meta-analytic review of gender differences, intercorrelations, and relations to maladjustment. *Child Development, 79,* 1185–1229.

Carlson, M., Marcus-Newhall, A., & Miller, N. (1990). Effects of situational aggression cues: A quantitative review. *Journal of Personality and Social Psychology, 58,* 622–633.

Carnagey, N. L., & Anderson, C. A. (2005). The effects of reward and punishment in violent video games on aggressive affect, cognition, and behavior. *Psychological Science, 16,* 882–889.

Carnelley, K. B., Pietromonaco, P. R., & Jaffe, K. (1994). Depression, working models of others, and relationship functioning. *Journal of Personality and Social Psychology, 66,* 127–140.

Carter, J. M., & Garber, J. (2011). Predictors of the first onset of a major depressive episode and changes in depressive symptoms across adolescence: Stress and negative cognitions. *Journal of Abnormal Psychology, 120,* 779–796.

Carvajal, S. C., Clair, S. D., Nash, S. G., & Evans, R. I. (1998). Relating optimism, hope, and self-esteem to social influences in deterring substance use in adolescents. *Journal of Social and Clinical Psychology, 17,* 443–465.

Carver, C. S. (1997). Adult attachment and personality: Converging evidence and a new measure. *Personality and Social Psychology Bulletin, 23,* 865–883.

Carver, C. S., Lehman, J. M., & Antoni, M. H. (2003). Dispositional pessimism predicts illness-related disruption of social and recreational activities among breast cancer patients. *Journal of Personality and Social Psychology, 84,* 813–821.

Carver, C. S., Pozo, C., Harris, S. D., Noriega, V., Scheier, M. F., Robinson, D. S. et al. (1993). How coping mediates the effect of optimism on distress: A study of women with early stage breast cancer. *Journal of Personality and Social Psychology, 65,* 375–390.

Carver, C. S., Scheier, M. F., & Segerstrom, S. C. (2010). Optimism. *Clinical Psychology Review, 30,* 879–889.

Carver, C. S., Smith, R. G., Antoni, M. H., Petronis, V. M., Weiss, S., & Derhagopian, R. P. (2005). Optimistic personality and psychological well-being during treatment predict psychosocial well-being among long-term survivors of breast cancer. *Health Psychology, 24,* 508–516.

Caspi, A. (1998). Personality development across the life course. In N. Eisenberg (Ed.), *Handbook of child psychology: Social, emotional and personality development* (5th ed., Vol. 3, pp. 311–388). New York: Wiley.

Caspi, A. (2000). The child is father of the man: Personality continuities from childhood to adulthood. *Journal of Personality and Social Psychology, 78,* 158–172.

Caspi, A., Harrington, H., Milne, B., Amell, J. W., Theodore, R. F., & Moffitt, T. E. (2003). Children's behavioral styles at age 3 are linked to their adult personality traits at age 26. *Journal of Personality, 71,* 495–513.

Catalano, R., Dooley, D., Novaco, R. W., Wilson, G., & Hough, R. (1993). Using ECA survey data to examine the effect of job layoffs on violent behavior. *Hospital and Community Psychiatry, 44,* 874–879.

Catalino, L. I., Furr, R. M., & Bellis, F. A. (2012). A multilevel analysis of the self-presentation theory of social anxiety: Contextualized, dispositional, and interactive perspectives. *Journal of Research in Personality, 46,* 361–373.

Cattell, H. E. P. (2004). The Sixteen Personality Factor (16PF) Questionnaire. In M. J. Hilsenroth & M. Hersen (Eds.), *Comprehensive handbook of psychological assessment* (Vol. 2, pp. 39–49). New York: Wiley.

Cattell, H. E. P., & Mead, A. D. (2008). The Sixteen Personality Factor Questionnaire (16PF). In G. J. Boyle, G. Matthews, & D. H. Saklofske (Eds.), *The Sage handbook of personality theory and assessment* (Vol. 2, pp. 135–159). Thousand Oaks, CA: Sage.

Cattell, R. B. (1974). Raymond B. Cattell. In G. Lindzey (Ed.), *A history of psychology in autobiography* (Vol. 6, pp. 61–100). Englewood Cliffs, NJ: Prentice Hall.

Cepeda-Benito, A., & Short, P. (1998). Self-concealment, avoidance of psychological services, and perceived likelihood of seeking professional help. *Journal of Counseling Psychology, 45*, 58–64.

Chang, E. C. (1996). Cultural differences in optimism, pessimism and coping: Predictors of subsequent adjustment in Asian American and Caucasian American college students. *Journal of Counseling Psychology, 43*, 113–123.

Chang, E. C. (1998). Dispositional optimism and primary and secondary appraisal of a stressor: Controlling for confounding influences and relations to coping and psychological and physical adjustment. *Journal of Personality and Social Psychology, 74*, 1109–1120.

Chang, E. C. (2001). Cultural influences on optimism and pessimism: Differences in Western and Eastern construals of the self. In E. C. Chang (Ed.), *Optimism and pessimism: Implications for theory, research, and practice* (pp. 257–280). Washington, DC: American Psychological Association.

Charles, S. T., Reynolds, C. A., & Gatz, M. (2001). Age-related differences and change in positive and negative affect over 23 years. *Journal of Personality and Social Psychology, 80*, 136–151.

Cheek, J. M., & Buss, A. H. (1981). Shyness and sociability. *Journal of Personality and Social Psychology, 41*, 330–339.

Chelune, G. J., Sultan, F. E., & Williams, C. L. (1980). Loneliness, self-disclosure, and interpersonal effectiveness. *Journal of Counseling Psychology, 27*, 462–468.

Chen, X., Chen, H., Li, D., & Wang, L. (2009). Early childhood behavioral inhibition and social and school adjustment in Chinese children: A 5-year longitudinal study. *Child Development, 80*, 1692–1704.

Cheng, C. (1999). Gender-role differences in susceptibility to the influence of support availability and depression. *Journal of Personality, 67*, 439–467.

Cheng, C. (2001). Assessing coping flexibility in real-life and laboratory settings: A multi-method approach. *Journal of Personality and Social Psychology, 80*, 814–833.

Cheng, C. (2005). Processes underlying gender-role flexibility: Do androgynous individuals know more or know how to cope? *Journal of Personality, 73*, 645–673.

Cheng, C. (2009). Dialectical thinking and coping flexibility: A multi-method approach. *Journal of Personality, 77*, 471–493.

Cheng, C., & Cheung, M. W. L. (2005). Cognitive processes underlying coping flexibility: Differentiation and integration. *Journal of Personality, 73*, 859–886.

Cheng, C., Cheung, S., Chio, J. H., & Chan, M. P. (2013). Cultural meaning of perceived control: A meta-analysis of locus of control and psychological symptoms across 18 cultural regions. *Psychological Bulletin, 139*, 152–188.

Chess, S., & Thomas, A. (1986). *Temperament in clinical practice*. New York: Guilford.

Chess, S., & Thomas, A. (1991). Temperament and the concept of goodness of fit. In J. Strelau & A. Angleitner (Eds.), *Explorations in temperament* (pp. 15–28). London: Plenum.

Chess, S., & Thomas, A. (1996). *Temperament: Theory and practice*. New York: Brunner/Mazel.

Cheung, F. M., van de Vijver, F. J. R., & Leong, F. T. L. (2011). Toward a new approach to the study of personality and culture. *American Psychologist, 66*, 593–603.

Chipperfield, J. G., & Perry, R. P. (2006). Primary- and secondary-control strategies in later life: Predicting hospital outcomes in men and women. *Health Psychology, 25*, 226–236.

Chitsabesan, P., Corbett, S., Walker, L., Spencer, J., & Barton, J. R. (2006). Describing clinical teachers' characteristics and behaviours using critical incidents and repertory grids. *Medical Education, 40*, 645–653.

Choca, J. P. (2013). *The Rorschach Inkblot Test*. Washington, DC: American Psychological Association.

Christensen, A., Atkins, D. C., Yi, J., Baucom, D. H., & George, W. H. (2009). Couple and individual adjustment for 2 years following a randomized clinical trial comparing traditional versus integrative behavioral couple therapy. *Journal of Clinical and Consulting Psychology, 74*, 1180–1191.

Christensen, P. N., & Kashy, D. A. (1998). Perceptions of and by lonely people in initial social interaction. *Personality and Social Psychology Bulletin, 24*, 322–329.

Chronis-Tuscano, A., Degnan, K. A., Pine, D. S., Perez-Edgar, K., Henderson, H. A., Diaz, Y. et al. (2009). Stable early maternal report of behavioral inhibition predicts lifetime social anxiety disorder in adolescence. *Journal of the American Academy of Child & Adolescent Psychiatry, 48*, 928–935.

Churchill, S. L. (2003). Goodness-of-fit in early childhood settings. *Early Childhood Education Journal, 31*, 113–118.

Clancy, S. M., & Dollinger, S. J. (1993). Photographic depictions of the self: Gender and age differences in social connectedness. *Sex Roles, 29*, 477–495.

Clark, D. A., Beck, A. T., & Alford, B. A. (1999). *Scientific foundations of cognitive theory and therapy for depression*. New York: Wiley.

Clark, D. M., & Teasdale, J. D. (1982). Diurnal variations in clinical depression and accessibility of memories of positive and negative experiences. *Journal of Abnormal Psychology, 91*, 87–95.

Clark, L. A. (2005). Temperament as a unifying basis for personality and psychopathology. *Journal of Abnormal Psychology, 114*, 505–521.

Clark, L. A., & Watson, D. (1988). Mood and the mundane: Relations between daily life events and self-reported mood. *Journal of Personality and Social Psychology, 54*, 296–308.

Clauss, J. A., & Blackford, J. U. (2012). Behavioral inhibition and risk for developing social anxiety disorder: A meta-analytic study. *Journal of the American Academy of Child & Adolescent Psychiatry, 51*, 1066–1075.

Clearfield, M. W., & Nelson, N. M. (2006). Sex differences in mothers' speech and play behavior with 6-9- and 14-month infants. *Sex Roles, 54*, 127–137.

Clifford, S. (2012, December 4). More dads buy the toys, so Barbie, and stories, get makeovers. *New York Times*, pp. A1, A4.

Coe, W. C. (1989). Posthypnotic amnesia: Theory and research. In N. P. Spanos & J. F. Chaves (Eds.), *Hypnosis: The cognitive-behavioral perspective* (pp. 110–148). Buffalo, NY: Prometheus.

Coe, W. C., & Sarbin, T. R. (1991). Role theory: Hypnosis from a dramaturgical and narrational perspective. In S. J. Lynn & J. W. Rhue (Eds.), *Theories of hypnosis: Current models and perspective* (pp. 303–323). New York: Guilford.

Cohen, D. B. (1979). *Sleep and dreaming: Origins, nature and function*. New York: Pergamon.

Cohen, S., Doyle, W. J., Skoner, D. P., Fireman, P., Gwaltney, J. M., Jr., & Newsom, J. T. (1995). State and trait affect as predictors of objective and subjective symptoms of respiratory viral infections. *Journal of Personality and Social Psychology, 68*, 159–169.

Cohen, S., Doyle, W., Turner, R., Alper, C. M., & Skoner, D. P. (2003). Sociability and susceptibility to the common cold. *Psychological Science, 14*, 389–395.

Cohen, S., & Janicki-Deverts, D. (2009). Can we improve our physical health by altering our social networks? *Perspectives on Psychological Science, 4*, 375–378.

Cohen, S., & Pressman, S. D. (2006). Positive affect and health. *Current Directions in Psychological Science, 15*, 122–125.

Cohen, S., & Wills, T. A. (1985). Stress, social support, and the buffering hypothesis. *Psychological Bulletin, 98*, 310–357.

Cohn, N. B., & Strassberg, D. S. (1983). Self-disclosure reciprocity among preadolescents. *Personality and Social Psychology Bulletin, 9*, 97–102.

Coleman, M., & Ganong, L. H. (1985). Love and sex-role stereotypes: Do "macho" men and "feminine" women make better lovers? *Journal of Personality and Social Psychology, 49*, 170–176.

Collins, N. L., Cooper, M. L., Albino, A., & Allard, L. (2002). Psychosocial vulnerability from adolescence to adulthood: A prospective study of attachment style differences in relationship functioning and partner choice. *Journal of Personality, 70*, 965–1008.

Collins, N. L., & Feeney, B. C. (2000). A safe haven: An attachment theory perspective on support seeking and caregiving in intimate relationships. *Journal of Personality and Social Psychology, 78*, 1053–1073.

Collins, N. L., Ford, M. B., Guichard, A. C., & Allard, L. M. (2006). Working models of attachment and attribution process in intimate relationships. *Personality and Social Psychology Bulletin, 32*, 201–219.

Collins, N. L., & Miller, L. C. (1994). Self-disclosure and liking: A meta-analytic review. *Psychological Bulletin, 116*, 457–475.

Collins, N. L., & Read, S. J. (1990). Adult attachment, working models, and relationship quality in dating couples. *Journal of Personality and Social Psychology, 58*, 644–663.

Compas, B. E., Worsham, N. L., Ey, S., & Howell, D. C. (1996). When Mom or Dad has cancer: II. Coping, cognitive appraisals, and psychological distress in children of cancer patients. *Health Psychology, 15*, 167–175.

Condren, M., & Greenglass, E. R. (2011). Optimism, emotional support, and depression among first-year university students. In G. M. Reevy & E. Prydenberg (Eds.), *Personality, Stress, and Coping: Implications for Education* (pp. 133–151). Charlotte, NC: Information Age Publishing.

Conduct Problems Prevention Research Group. (2011). The effects of the Fast Track prevention intervention on the development of conduct disorder across childhood. *Child Development, 82*, 331–245.

Conley, J. J. (1984). Longitudinal consistency of adult personality: Self-reported psychological characteristics across 45 years. *Journal of Personality and Social Psychology, 47*, 1325–1333.

Conley, J. J. (1985). Longitudinal stability of personality traits: A multitrait-multimethod-multioccasion analysis. *Journal of Personality and Social Psychology, 49*, 1266–1282.

Constantinople, A. (1973). Masculinity-femininity: An exception to a famous dictum. *Psychological Bulletin, 80*, 389–407.

Conti, D. (2005, February 1). Convicted murderer will get new trial. *Pittsburgh Tribune Review*.

Conti, R. (2001). Time flies: Investigating the connection between intrinsic motivation and the experience of time. *Journal of Personality, 69*, 1–26.

Conway, F., Magai, C., Springer, C., & Jones, S. C. (2008). Optimism and pessimism as predictors of physical and psychological health among grandmothers raising their grandchildren. *Journal of Research in Personality, 42*, 1352–1357.

Conway, M. A., & Holmes, A. (2004). Psychosocial stages and the accessibility of autobiographical memories across the life cycle. *Journal of Personality, 72*, 461–480.

Cook, J. M., Biyanova, T., Elhai, J., Schnurr, P. P., & Coyne, J. C. (2010). What do psychotherapists really do in practice? An Internet study of over 2,000 practitioners.

Psychotherapy Theory, Research, Practice, Training, 47, 260–267.

Cooper, H. M., & Good, T. E. (1983). *Pygmalion grows up: Studies in the expectation communication process.* New York: Longman.

Cooper, M. L., Wood, P. K., Orcutt, H. K., & Albino, A. (2003). Personality and the predisposition to engage in risky or problem behaviors during adolescence. *Journal of Personality and Social Psychology, 84*, 390–410.

Cooper, T., Detre, T., & Weiss, S. M. (1981). Coronary-prone behavior and coronary heart disease: A critical review. *Circulation, 63*, 1199–1215.

Coopman, S. J. (1997). Personal constructs and communication in interpersonal and organizational contexts. In G. J. Neimeyer & R. A. Neimeyer (Eds.), *Advances in personal construct psychology* (Vol. 4, pp. 101–147). Greenwich, CT: JAI Press.

Coplan, R. J., Barber, A. M., & Lagace-Seguin, D. G. (1999). The role of child temperament as a predictor of early literacy and numeracy skills in preschoolers. *Early Childhood Research Quarterly, 14*, 537–553.

Coplan, R. J., Bowker, A., & Cooper, S. M. (2003). Parenting daily hassles, child temperament, and social adjustment in preschool. *Early Childhood Research Quarterly, 18*, 376–395.

Cordova, J. V., Gee, C. B., & Warren, L. Z. (2005). Emotional skillfulness in marriage: Intimacy as a mediator of the relationship between emotional skillfulness and marital satisfaction. *Journal of Social and Clinical Psychology, 24*, 218–235.

Cornell, D. G. (1997). Post hoc explanation is not prediction. *American Psychologist, 52*, 1380.

Cornette, M. M., Strauman, T. J., Abramson, L. Y., & Busch, A. M. (2009). Self-discrepancy and suicidal ideation. *Cognition and Emotion, 23*, 504–527.

Costa, P. T., & McCrae, R. R. (1992). *Professional manual for the NEO PI-R.* Odessa, FL: Psychological Assessment Resources.

Costa, P. T., & McCrae, R. R. (2006). Age changes in personality and their origins: Comment on Roberts, Walton, and Viechtbauer (2006). *Psychological Bulletin, 132*, 28–30.

Costa, P. T., Terracciano, A., & McCrae, R. R. (2001). Gender differences in personality traits across cultures: Robust and surprising findings. *Journal of Personality and Social Psychology, 81*, 322–331.

Costello, C. G. (1978). A critical review of seligman's laboratory experiments on learned helplessness and depression in humans. *Journal of Abnormal Psychology, 87*, 21–31.

Cowen, E. I., Wyman, P. A., & Work, W. C. (1992). The relationship between retrospective reports of early child temperament and adjustment at ages 10–12. *Journal of Abnormal Child Psychology, 20*, 39–50.

Cox-Fuenzalida, L., Angie, A., Holloway, S., & Sohl, L. (2006). Extraversion and task performance: A fresh look through the workload history lens. *Journal of Research in Personality, 40*, 432–439.

Cox-Fuenzalida, L., Gilliland, K., & Swickert, R. J. (2001). Congruency of the relationship between extraversion and the brainstem auditory evoked response based on the EPI versus the EPQ. *Journal of Research in Personality, 35*, 117–126.

Crabbe, J. C. (2002). Genetic contributions to addiction. *Annual Review of Psychology, 53*, 435–462.

Craik, K. H. (1986). Personality research methods: An historical perspective. *Journal of Personality, 54*, 18–51.

Cramer, K. M., & Lake, R. P. (1998). The Preference for Solitude Scale: Psychometric properties and factor structure. *Personality and Individual Differences, 24*, 193–199.

Cramer, K. M., Ofosu, H. B., & Barry, J. E. (2000). An abbreviated form of the social and emotional loneliness scale for adults (SELSA). *Personality and Individual Differences, 28*, 1125–1131.

Cramer, P. (1991). *The development of defense mechanisms: Theory, research, and assessment.* New York: Springer-Verlag.

Cramer, P. (1997). Evidence for change in children's use of defense mechanisms. *Journal of Personality, 65*, 233–247.

Cramer, P. (1998). Threat to gender representation: Identity and identification. *Journal of Personality, 66*, 335–357.

Cramer, P. (1999). Personality, personality disorders, and defense mechanisms. *Journal of Personality, 67*, 535–554.

Cramer, P. (2000). Defense mechanisms in psychology today: Further processes for adaptation. *American Psychologist, 55*, 637–646.

Cramer, P. (2002). Defense mechanisms, behavior, and affect in young adulthood. *Journal of Personality, 70*, 103–126.

Cramer, P. (2006). *Protecting the self: Defense mechanisms in action.* New York: Guilford.

Cramer, P. (2007). Longitudinal study of defense mechanisms: Late childhood to late adolescence. *Journal of Personality, 75*, 1–23.

Cramer, P. (2012). Psychological maturity and change in adult defense mechanisms. *Journal of Research in Personality, 46*, 306–316.

Cramer, P., Blatt, S. J., & Ford, R. Q. (1988). Defense mechanisms in the anaclitic and introjective personality configuration. *Journal of Consulting and Clinical Psychology, 56*, 610–616.

Cramer, P., & Block, J. (1998). Preschool antecedents of defense mechanism use in young adults: A longitudinal study. *Journal of Personality and Social Psychology, 74*, 159–169.

Cramer, P., & Brilliant, M. A. (2001). Defense use and defense understanding in children. *Journal of Personality, 69*, 297–322.

Cramer, R. E., Manning-Ryan, B., Johnson, L. M., & Barbo, E. (2000). Sex differences in subjective distress to violations of trust: Extending an evolutionary perspective. *Basic and Applied Social Psychology, 22,* 101–109.

Crane, F. G., & Crane, E. C. (2007). Dispositional optimism and entrepreneurial success. *Psychologist-Manager Journal, 10,* 13–25.

Crick, F., & Mitchison, G. (1983). The function of dream sleep. *Nature, 304,* 111–114.

Crick, N. R., & Dodge, K. A. (1996). Social information-processing mechanisms in reactive and proactive aggression. *Child Development, 67,* 993–1002.

Crocker, J., Brook, A. T., Niiya, Y., & Villacorta, M. (2006). The pursuit of self-esteem: Contingencies of self-wroth and self-regulation. *Journal of Personality, 74,* 1749–1177.

Crocker, J., Karpinski, A., Quinn, D. M., & Chase, S. K. (2003). When grades determine self-worth: Consequences of contingent self-worth for male and female engineering and psychology majors. *Journal of Personality and Social Psychology, 85,* 507–516.

Crocker, J., & Luhtanen, R. K. (2003). Level of self-esteem and contingencies of self-worth: Unique effects on academic, social, and financial problems in college students. *Personality and Social Psychology Bulletin, 29,* 701–712.

Crocker, J., Luhtanen, R. K., Cooper, M. L., & Bouvrette, A. (2003). Contingencies of self-worth in college students: Theory and measurement. *Journal of Personality and Social Psychology, 85,* 894–908.

Crocker, J., & Park, L. E. (2003). Seeking self-esteem: Construction, maintenance, and protection of self-worth. In M. R. Leary & J. P. Tangney (Eds.), *Handbook of self and identity* (pp. 291–313). New York: Guilford.

Crocker, J., & Park, L. E. (2004). The costly pursuit of self-esteem. *Psychological Bulletin, 130,* 392–414.

Crocker, J., Sommers, S. R., & Luhtanen, R. K. (2002). Hopes dashed and dreams fulfilled: Contingencies

of self-worth and graduate school admissions. *Personality and Social Psychology Bulletin, 28,* 1275–1286.

Crocker, J., & Wolfe, C. T. (2001). Contingencies of self-worth. *Psychological Review, 108,* 593–623.

Cross, S. E., Bacon, P. L., & Morris, M. L. (2000). The relational-interdependent self-construal and relationships. *Journal of Personality and Social Psychology, 78,* 791–808.

Cross, S. E., Hardin, E. E., & Gercek-Swing, B. (2011). The what, how, why, and where of self-construal. *Personality and Social Psychology Review, 15,* 142–179.

Cross, S. E., & Madson, L. (1997). Models of the self: Self-construals and gender. *Psychological Bulletin, 122,* 5–37.

Cross, S. E., Morris, M. L., & Gore, J. S. (2002). Thinking about oneself and others: The relational-interdependent self-construal and social cognition. *Journal of Personality and Social Psychology, 82,* 399–418.

Crossen, C. (1996, March 8). Solitude is a casualty of the war with time. *Wall Street Journal,* p. R4.

Crost, N. W., Pauls, C. A., & Wacker, J. (2008). Defensiveness and anxiety predict frontal EEG asymmetry only in specific situational contexts. *Biological Psychology, 78,* 43–52.

Crowson, J. J., & Cromwell, R. L. (1995). Depressed and normal individuals differ both in selection and in perceived tonal quality of positive-negative messages. *Journal of Abnormal Psychology, 104,* 305–311.

Csikszentmihalyi, M. (1990). *Flow: The psychology of optimal experience.* New York: Harper & Row.

Csikszentmihalyi, M. (1999). If we are so rich, why aren't we happy? *American Psychologist, 54,* 821–827.

Csikszentmihalyi, M., & Csikszentmihalyi, I. S. (1988). *Optimal experience: Psychological studies of flow in consciousness.* New York: Cambridge.

Csikszentmihalyi, M., & LeFevre, J. (1989). Optimal experience in work and leisure. *Journal of Personality and Social Psychology, 56,* 815–822.

Cunningham, J. A., Strassberg, D. S., & Haan, B. (1986). Effects of intimacy and sex-role congruency of self-disclosure. *Journal of Social and Clinical Psychology, 4,* 393–401.

Cunningham, M. R. (1988). Does happiness mean friendliness? Induced mood and heterosexual self-disclosure. *Personality and Social Psychology Bulletin, 14,* 283–297.

Curran, J. P., Wallander, J. L., & Fischetti, M. (1980). The importance of behavioral and cognitive factors in heterosexual-social anxiety. *Journal of Personality, 48,* 285–292.

Cury, F., Elliot, A. J., Da Fonseca, D., & Moller, A. C. (2006). The social-cognitive model of achievement motivation and the 2 x 2 achievement goal framework. *Journal of Personality and Social Psychology, 90,* 666–679.

Cutrona, C. E. (1982). Transition to college: Loneliness and the process of social adjustment. In L. A. Peplau & D. Perlman (Eds.), *Loneliness* (pp. 291–309). New York: Wiley.

Cyranowski, J. M., & Andersen, B. L. (2000). Evidence of self-schematic cognitive processing of women with differing sexual self-views. *Journal of Social and Clinical Psychology, 19,* 519–543.

Dadds, M. R., Bovbjerg, D. H., Redd, W. H., & Cutmore, T. R. H. (1997). Imagery in human classical conditioning. *Psychological Bulletin, 122,* 89–103.

Danoff-Burg, S., Revenson, T. A., Trudeau, K. J., & Paget, S. A. (2004). Unmitigated communion, social constraints, and psychological distress among women with rheumatoid arthritis. *Journal of Personality, 72,* 29–46.

Darnon, C., Dompnier, B., Delmas, F., Pulfrey, C., & Butera, F. (2009). Achievement goal promotion at university: Social desirability and social utility of mastery and performance goals. *Journal of Personality and Social Psychology, 96,* 119–134.

Darnon, C., Harackiewicz, J. M., Butera, F., Mugny, G., & Quiamzade, A. (2007). Performance-approach and performance-avoidance goals: When uncertainty makes a difference. *Personality and Social Psychology Bulletin, 33,* 813–827.

Davidson, K., & MacGregor, M. W. (1996). Reliability of an idiographic Q-Sort measure of defense mechanisms. *Journal of Personality Assessment, 66,* 624–639.

Davidson, K., & MacGregor, M. W. (1998). A critical appraisal of self-report defense mechanism measures. *Journal of Personality, 66,* 965–992.

Davidson, K., MacGregor, M. W., Johnson, E. A., Woody, E. Z., & Chaplin, W. F. (2004). The relation between defense use and adaptive behavior. *Journal of Research in Personality, 38,* 105–129.

Davidson, K. W., Gidron, Y., Mostofsky, E., & Trudeau, K. J. (2007). Hospitalization cost offset of a hostility intervention for coronary heart disease patients. *Journal of Consulting and Clinical Psychology, 75,* 657–662.

Davidson, R. J. (1991). Biological approaches to the study of personality. In V. J. Derlega, B. A. Winstead, & W. H. Jones (Eds.), *Personality: Contemporary theory and research* (pp. 87–112). Chicago: Nelson-Hall.

Davidson, R. J., Ekman, P., Saron, C. D., Senulis, J. A., & Friesen, W. V. (1990). Approach-withdrawal and cerebral asymmetry: Emotional expression and brain physiology I. *Journal of Personality and Social Psychology, 58,* 330–341.

Davidson, R. J., & Fox, N. A. (1982). Asymmetrical brain activity discriminates between positive versus negative affective stimuli in human infants. *Science, 218,* 1235–1237.

Davidson, R. J., & Fox, N. A. (1989). Frontal brain asymmetry predicts infants' response to maternal separation. *Journal of Abnormal Psychology, 98,* 127–131.

Davidson, R. J., & Tomarken, A. J. (1989). Laterality and emotion: An electrophysiological approach. In F. Boller & J. Grafman (Eds.), *Handbook of neuropsychology* (Vol. 3, pp. 419–441). New York: Elsevier Science.

Davila, J., Burge, D., & Hammen, C. (1997). Why does attachment style change? *Journal of Personality and Social Psychology, 73,* 826–838.

Davila, J., Karney, B. R., & Bradbury, T. N. (1999). Attachment change processes in the early years of marriage. *Journal of Personality and Social Psychology, 76,* 783–802.

Davis, J. D. (1976). Self-disclosure in an acquaintance exercise: Responsibility for level of intimacy. *Journal of Personality and Social Psychology, 33,* 787–792.

Davis, J. D. (1977). Effects of communication about interpersonal process on the evolution of self-disclosure in dyads. *Journal of Personality and Social Psychology, 35,* 31–137.

Davis, P. J. (1999). Gender differences in autobiographical memory for childhood emotional experiences. *Journal of Personality and Social Psychology, 76,* 498–510.

Dawes, R. M. (1994). *House of cards: Psychology and psychotherapy built on myth.* New York: Free Press.

Deffenbacher, J., Huff, M., Lynch, R., Oetting, E., & Salvatore, N. (2000). Characteristics and treatments of high-anger drivers. *Journal of Counseling Psychology, 47,* 5–17.

DeLisi, M., Vaughn, M. G., Gentile, D. A., Anderson, C. A., & Shook, J. J. (2013). Violent video games, delinquency, and youth violence: New evidence. *Youth Violence and Juvenile Justice, 11,* 132–142.

de Manzano, O., Theorell, T., Harmat, L., & Ullen, F. (2010). The psychophysiology of flow during piano playing. *Emotion, 10,* 301–311.

Dembroski, T. M., & Costa, P. T. (1987). Coronary prone behavior: Components of the Type A pattern and hostility. *Journal of Personality, 55,* 211–235.

DeNeve, K. M. (1999). Happy as an extraverted clam? The role of personality for subjective well-being. *Current Directions in Psychological Science, 8,* 141–144.

DeNeve, K. M., & Cooper, H. (1998). The happy personality: A meta-analysis of 137 personality traits and subjective well-being. *Psychological Bulletin, 124,* 197–229.

Denson, T. F., Aviles, F. E., Pollock, V. E., Earleywine, M., Vasquez, E. A., & Miller, N. (2008). The effects of alcohol and the salience of aggressive cues on triggered displaced aggression. *Aggressive Behavior, 34,* 25–33.

Denson, T. F., Pedersen, W. C., & Miller, N. (2006). The displaced aggression questionnaire. *Journal of Personality and Social Psychology, 90,* 1032–1051.

DePaulo, B. M., Dull, W. R., Greenberg, J. M., & Swaim, G. W. (1989). Are shy people reluctant to ask for help? *Journal of Personality and Social Psychology, 56,* 834–844.

DePaulo, B. M., Epstein, J. A., & LeMay, C. S. (1990). Responses of the socially anxious to the prospect of interpersonal evaluation. *Journal of Personality, 58,* 623–640.

DePaulo, B. M., Kenny, D. A., Hoover, C. W., Webb, W., & Oliver, P. V. (1987). Accuracy of person perception: Do people know what kinds of impressions they convey? *Journal of Personality and Social Psychology, 52,* 303–315.

Depue, R. A., & Monroe, S. M. (1978). Learned helplessness in the perspective of the depressive disorders: Conceptual and definitional issues. *Journal of Abnormal Psychology, 87,* 3–20.

De Raad, B., Barelds, D. P. H., Levert, E., Ostendorf, F., Mlacic, B., Di Blas, L. et al. (2010). Only three factors of personality description are fully replicable across languages: A comparison of 14 trait taxonomies. *Journal of Personality and Social Psychology, 98,* 160–173.

de Rivera, J. (1997). The construction of false memory syndrome: The experience of retractors. *Psychological Inquiry, 8,* 271–292.

Derlega, V. J., & Chaikin, A. L. (1976). Norms affecting self-disclosure in men and women. *Journal of Consulting and Clinical Psychology, 44,* 376–380.

Derlega, V. J., Wilson, M., & Chaikin, A. L. (1976). Friendship and disclosure reciprocity. *Journal of Personality and Social Psychology, 34,* 578–582.

Derlega, V. J., Winstead, B. A., & Greene, K. (2008). Self-disclosure and starting a close relationship. In S. Sprecher, A. Wenzel, & J. Harvey (Eds.), *Handbook of relationship initiation* (pp. 153–174). New York: Psychology Press.

Derry, P. A., & Kuiper, N. A. (1981). Schematic processing and self-reference in clinical depression. *Journal of Abnormal Psychology, 90,* 286–297.

De Schipper, J. C., Tavecchio, L. W. C., Van IJzendoorn, M. H., & Van Zeijl, J. (2004). Goodness-of-fit in center day care: Relations of temperament, stability, and quality of care with the child's adjustment. *Early Childhood Research Quarterly, 19,* 257–272.

DeSteno, D., Bartlett, M. Y., Braverman, J., & Salovey, P. (2002). Sex differences in jealousy: Evolutionary mechanism or artifact of measurement? *Journal of Personality and Social Psychology, 83,* 1103–1116.

DeVellis, R. F., DeVellis, B. M., & McCauley, C. (1978). Vicarious acquisition of learned helplessness. *Journal of Personality and Social Psychology, 36,* 894–899.

DeWall, C. N., Lambert, N. M., Slotter, E. B., Pond, R. S., Deckman, T., Finkel, E. J. et al. (2011). So far away from one's partner, yet so close to romantic alternatives: Avoidant attachment, interest in alternatives, and infidelity. *Journal of Personality and Social Psychology, 101,* 1302–1316.

Diehl, M., Elnick, A. B., Bourbeau, L. S., & Labouvie-Vief, G. (1998). Adult attachment styles: Their relations to family context and personality. *Journal of Personality and Social Psychology, 74,* 1656–1669.

Diener, E. (1984). Subjective well-being. *Psychological Bulletin, 95,* 542–575.

Diener, E., & Diener, M. (1995). Cross-cultural correlates of life satisfaction and self-esteem. *Journal of Personality and Social Psychology, 68,* 653–663.

Diener, E., & Emmons, R. A. (1984). The independence of positive and negative affect. *Journal of Personality and Social Psychology, 47,* 1105–1117.

Diener, E., & Seligman, M. E. P. (2002). Very happy people. *Psychological Science, 13,* 81–84.

Digman, J. M. (1990). Personality structure: Emergence of the five-factor model. *Annual Review of Psychology, 41,* 417–440.

Digman, J. M., & Inouye, J. (1986). Further specification of the five robust factors of personality. *Journal of Personality and Social Psychology, 50,* 116–123.

DiLalla, D. L., Carey, G., Gottesman, I. I., & Bouchard, T. J. (1996). Heritability of MMPI personality indicators of psychopathology in twins reared apart. *Journal of Abnormal Psychology, 105,* 491–499.

Dindia, K., & Allen, M. (1992). Sex differences in self-disclosure: A meta-analysis. *Psychological Bulletin, 112,* 106–124.

Di Paula, A., & Campbell, J. D. (2002). Self-esteem and persistence in the face of failure. *Journal of Personality and Social Psychology, 83,* 711–724.

Dobbs, S., Furnham, A., & McClelland, A. (2011). The effect of background music and noise on the cognitive test performance of introverts and extraverts. *Applied Cognitive Psychology, 25,* 307–313.

Dodge, K. A. (2006). Translational science in action: Hostile attributional style and the development of aggressive behavior problems. *Development and Psychopathology, 18,* 791–814.

Dodge, K. A., Godwin, J., & Conduct Problems Prevention Research Group. (2013). Social-information-processing patterns mediate the impact of preventive intervention on adolescent antisocial behavior. *Psychological Science.*

Dodge, K. A., Lansford, J. E., Burks, V. S., Pettit, G. S., Price, J. M., Fontaine, R. et al. (2003). Peer rejection and social information-processing factors in the development of aggressive behavior problems in children. *Child Development, 74,* 374–393.

Dodgson, P. G., & Wood, J. V. (1998). Self-esteem and the cognitive accessibility of strengths and weaknesses after failure. *Journal of Personality and Social Psychology, 75,* 178–197.

Dollard, J., Doob, L., Miller, N. E., Mowrer, O. H., & Sears, R. R. (1939). *Frustration and aggression.* New Haven, CT: Yale University Press.

Dollinger, S. J. (2000). Locus of control and incidental learning: An application to college student success. *College Student Journal, 34,* 537–540.

Domhoff, G. W. (1996). *Finding meaning in dreams: A quantitative approach.* New York: Plenum.

Domhoff, G. W. (1999). New directions in the study of dream content using the Hall and Van de Castle coding system. *Dreaming, 9,* 115–137.

Domhoff, G. W. (2001). A new neuro-cognitive theory of dreams. *Dreaming, 11,* 13–33.

Domhoff, G. W. (2004). Why did empirical dream researchers reject Freud? A critique of historical claims by Mark Solms. *Dreaming, 14,* 3–17.

Dompnier, B., Darnon, C., & Butera, F. (2009). Faking the desire to learn: A clarification of the link between mastery goals and academic achievement. *Psychological Science, 20,* 939–943.

Donnellan, M. B., Conger, R. D., & Bryant, C. M. (2004). The big five and enduring marriages. *Journal of*

Research in Personality, 38, 481–504.

Donnelly, D. A., & Murray, E. J. (1991). Cognitive and emotional changes in written essays and therapy interviews. *Journal of Social and Clinical Psychology, 10,* 334–350.

Doob, L. W., & Sears, R. R. (1939). Factors determining substitute behavior and the overt expression of aggression. *Journal of Abnormal and Social Psychology, 34,* 293–313.

Doucet, C., & Stelmack, R. M. (2000). An event-related potential analysis of extraversion and individual differences in cognitive processing speed and response execution. *Journal of Personality and Social Psychology, 78,* 956–964.

Douthat, R. (2013, May 19). All the lonely people. *New York Times,* p. SR11.

Dozios, D. J. A. (2007). Stability of negative self-structures: A longitudinal comparison of depressed, remitted, and nonpsychiatric controls. *Journal of Clinical Psychology, 63,* 319–338.

Dozois, D. J. A., & Beck, A. T. (2008). Cognitive schemas, beliefs, and assumptions. In K. S. Dobson & D. J. A. Dozois (Eds.), *Risk factors in depression* (pp. 121–143). San Diego: Academic Press.

Dozois, D. J. A., Bieling, P. J., Patelis-Siotis, I., Hoar, L., Chudzik, S., McCabe, K., & Westra, H. A. (2009). Changes in self-schema structure in cognitive therapy for major depressive disorder: A randomized clinical trial. *Journal of Consulting and Clinical Psychology, 77,* 1078–1088.

Dozois, D. J. A., & Dobson, K. S. (2001). A longitudinal investigation of information processing and cognitive organization in clinical depression: Stability of schematic interconnectedness. *Journal of Consulting and Clinical Psychology, 69,* 914–925.

Draguns, J. G. (2008). What have we learned about the interplay of culture with counseling and psychotherapy? In U. P. Gielen, J.

Draguns, & J. M. Fish (Eds.), *Principles of multicultural counseling and therapy* (pp. 393–417). New York: Routledge/ Taylor & Francis.

Dryden, W., David, D., & Ellis, A. (2010). Rational emotive behavior therapy. In K. S. Dobson (Ed.), *Handbook of cognitive-behavioral therapies* (3rd ed., pp. 226–276). New York: Guilford.

Duke, T., & Davidson, J. (2002). Ordinary and recurrent dream recall of active, past and nonrecurrent dreamers during and after academic stress. *Dreaming, 12,* 185–197.

Dunbar, E. (2006, April 1). *Bizarre death four years after trial leads to tossed conviction. Associated Press State and Local Wire.* Retrieved November 27, 2006, from http://www.lexis-nexis.com

Dunkel, C. S., & Sefcek, J. A. (2009). Eriksonian lifespan theory and life history theory: An integration using the example of identity formation. *Review of General Psychology, 13,* 13–23.

Durante, K. M., Li, N. P., & Haselton, M. G. (2008). Changes in women's choice of dress across the ovulatory cycle: Naturalistic and laboratory task-based evidence. *Personality and Social Psychology Bulletin, 34,* 1451–1460.

Dutton, K. A., & Brown, J. D. (1997). Global self-esteem and specific self-views as determinants of people's reactions to success and failure. *Journal of Personality and Social Psychology, 73,* 139–148.

Dwivedi, Y., Mondal, A. C., Payappagoudar, G. V., & Rizavi, S. (2005). Differential regulation of serotonin (5HT)-sub(2A) receptor mRNA and protein levels after single and repeated stress in rat brain: Role in learned helplessness behavior. *Neuropharmacology, 48,* 204–214.

Dyson, M. W., Olino, T. M., Durbin, C. E., Goldsmith, H. H., & Klein, D. N. (2012). The structure of temperament in preschoolers: A two-stage factor analytic approach. *Emotion, 12,* 44–57.

Eagly, A. H. (1997). Sex differences in social behavior: Comparing social role theory and evolutionary psychology. *American Psychologist, 52,* 1380–1382.

Eastwick, P. W., & Finkel, E. J. (2008). Sex differences in mate preferences revisted: Do people know what they initially desire in a romantic partner? *Journal of Personality and Social Psychology, 94,* 245–264.

Eccles, J. (1985). Sex differences in achievement patterns. In T. B. Sonderegger (Ed.), *Nebraska symposium on motivation* (Vol. 32, pp. 97–132). Lincoln: University of Nebraska Press.

Eccles, J. (2005). Subjective task value and the Eccles et al. model of achievement-related choices. In A. J. Elliott & C. W. Dweck (Eds.), *Handbook of competence and motivation* (pp. 105–121). New York: Guilford Press.

Eisen, M. R. (2010). Psychoanalytic and psychodynamic models of hypnoanalysis. In S. J. Lynn, J. W. Rhue, & I. Kirsch (Eds.), *Handbook of clinical hypnosis* (2nd ed., pp. 121–149). Washington, DC: American Psychological Association.

Eisenberger, R., & Cameron, J. (1996). Detrimental effects of reward: Reality or myth? *American Psychologist, 51,* 1153–1166.

Elliot, A. J., & McGregor, H. A. (2001). A 2 x 2 achievement goal framework. *Journal of Personality and Social Psychology, 80,* 501–519.

Elliot, A. J., Shell, M. M., Bouas, H. K., & Maier, M. A. (2005). Achievement goals, performance contingencies, and performance attainment: An experimental test. *Journal of Educational Psychology, 97,* 630–640.

Elliott, A. J., Miltenberger, R. G., Kaster-Bundgaard, J., & Lumley, V. (1996). A national survey of assessment and therapy techniques used by behavior therapists. *Cognitive and Behavioral Practice, 3,* 107–125.

Elliott, R. (2002). The effectiveness of humanistic therapies: A meta-analysis. In D. J. Cain & J. Seeman (Eds.), *Humanistic* psychotherapies: Handbook of research and practice (pp. 57–81). Washington, DC: American Psychological Association.

Ellis, A., & Joffe Ellis, D. (2011). Rational emotive behavior therapy. Washington, DC: American Psychological Association.

Ellis, A. E. (1971). Growth through reason: Verbatim cases in rational-emotive therapy. North Hollywood, CA: Wilshire.

Ellis, A. E. (1987). The impossibility of achieving consistently good mental health. American Psychologist, 42, 364–375.

Else-Quest, N. M., Hyde, J. S., Goldsmith, H. H., & Van Hulle, C. A. (2006). Gender differences in temperament: A meta-analysis. Psychological Bulletin, 132, 33–72.

Emmons, R. A., & Diener, E. (1986). Influence of impulsivity and sociability on subjective well-being. Journal of Personality and Social Psychology, 50, 1211–1215.

Endler, N. S., & Hunt, J. M. (1966). Sources of behavioral variance as measured by the S-R inventory of anxiousness. Psychological Bulletin, 65, 336–346.

Endler, N. S., & Hunt, J. M. (1968). S-R inventories of hostility and comparisons of the proportions of variance from persons, responses, and situations for hostility and anxiousness. Journal of Personality and Social Psychology, 9, 309–315.

Engelhardt, C. R., Bartholow, B. D., & Saults, J. S. (2011). Violent and nonviolent video games differentially affect physical aggression for individuals high vs. low in dispositional anger. Aggressive Behavior, 37, 539–546.

Epstein, S. (1979). The stability of behavior: I. On predicting most of the people much of the time. Journal of Personality and Social Psychology, 37, 1097–1126.

Epstein, S. (1980). The stability of behavior: II. Implications for psychological research. American Psychologist, 35, 790–806.

Epstein, S. (1983). Aggregation and beyond: Some basic issues on the

prediction of behavior. Journal of Personality, 51, 360–392.

Erikson, E. H. (1950/1963). Childhood and society (2nd ed.). New York: Norton.

Erikson, E. H. (1968). Identity: Youth and crisis. New York: Norton.

Erikson, E. H. (1975). Life history and the historical moment. New York: Norton.

Ersner-Hershfield, H., Mikels, J. A., Sullivan, S. J., & Carstensen, L. L. (2008). Poignancy: Mixed emotional experience in the face of meaningful endings. Journal of Personality and Social Psychology, 94, 158–167.

Ernst, J. M., & Cacioppo, J. T. (1999). Lonely hearts: Psychological perspectives on loneliness. Applied Preventive Psychology, 8, 1–22.

Eron, L. D. (1987). The development of aggressive behavior from the perspective of a developing behaviorism. American Psychologist, 42, 435–442.

Etaugh, C., & Liss, M. B. (1992). Home, school, and playroom: Training grounds for adult gender roles. Sex Roles, 26, 129–147.

Evans, D. E., & Rothbart, M. K. (2007). Developing a model for adult temperament. Journal of Research in Personality, 41, 868–888.

Evans, D. M., Gillespie, N. A., & Marting, N. G. (2002). Biometrical genetics. Biological Psychology, 61, 33–51.

Evans, J., Heron, J., Lewis, G., Araya, R., & Wolke, D. (2005). Negative self-schemas and the onset of depression in women: Longitudinal study. British Journal of Psychiatry, 186, 302–307.

Evans, K. K., & Singer, J. A. (1995). Studying intimacy through dream narratives: The relationship of dreams to self-report and projective measures of personality. Imagination, Cognition and Personality, 14, 211–226.

Evans, R. I. (1976). The making of psychology. New York: Knopf.

Evans, W. P., Owens, P., & Marsh, S. C. (2005). Environmental factors, locus of control, and adolescent

suicide risk. Child & Adolescent Social Work Journal, 22, 301–319.

Eysenck, H. J. (1967). The biological basis of personality. Springfield, IL: Charles C. Thomas.

Eysenck, H. J. (1982). Development of a theory. In C. D. Spielberger (Ed.), Personality, genetics and behavior: Selected papers (pp. 1–38). New York: Praeger.

Eysenck, H. J. (1990). Biological dimensions of personality. In L. Pervin (Ed.), Handbook of personality theory and research (pp. 244–276). New York: Guilford.

Eysenck, H. J., & Eysenck, S. B. G. (1968). Manual for the Eysenck Personality Inventory. San Diego, CA: Educational and Industrial Testing Service.

Eysenck, S. B. G., & Long, F. Y. (1986). A cross-cultural comparison of personality in adults and children: Singapore and England. Journal of Personality and Social Psychology, 50, 124–130.

Fancher, R. E. (2000). Snapshots of Freud in America, 1899-1999. American Psychologist, 55, 1025–1028.

Farabee, D. J., Holcom, M. L., Ramsey, S. L., & Cole, S. G. (1993). Social anxiety and speaker gaze in a persuasive atmosphere. Journal of Research in Personality, 27, 365–376.

Farber, B. A. (2006). Self-disclosure in psychotherapy. New York: Guilford.

Farber, B. A., & Sohn, A. E. (2007). Patterns of self-disclosure in psychotherapy and marriage. Psychotherapy: Theory, Research, Practice, Training, 44, 226–231.

Farley, F. (2000). Hans J. Eysenck (1916-1997). American Psychologist, 55, 674–675.

Fassler, O., Lynn, S. J., & Knox, J. (2008). Is hypnotic suggestibility a stable trait? Consciousness and Cognition, 17, 240–253.

Feeney, B. C., & Collins, N. L. (2001). Predictors of caregiving in adult intimate relationships: An attachment theoretical perspective. Journal of Personality and Social Psychology, 80, 972–994.

Feeney, B. C., & Kirkpatrick, L. A. (1996). Effects of adult attachment and presence of romantic partners on physiological responses to stress. *Journal of Personality and Social Psychology, 70*, 255–270.

Feeney, J. A., & Noller, P. (1990). Attachment style as a predictor of adult romantic relationships. *Journal of Personality and Social Psychology, 58*, 281–291.

Feeney, J. A., Noller, P., & Patty, J. (1993). Adolescents' interactions with the opposite sex: Influence of attachment style and gender. *Journal of Adolescence, 16*, 169–186.

Feingold, A. (1990). Gender differences in effects of physical attractiveness on romantic attraction: A comparison across five research paradigms. *Journal of Personality and Social Psychology, 59*, 981–993.

Feingold, A. (1992). Gender differences in mate selection preferences: A test of the parental investment model. *Psychological Bulletin, 112*, 125–139.

Feist, G. J. (1998). A meta-analysis of personality in scientific and artistic creativity. *Personality and Social Psychology Review, 2*, 290–309.

Feixas, G., Erazo-Caicedo, M. I., Harter, S. L., & Bach, L. (2008). Construction of self and others in unipolar depressive disorders: A study using repertory grid technique. *Cognitive Therapy and Research, 32*, 386–400.

Feldman Barrett, L., Lane, R. D., Sechrest, L., & Schwartz, G. E. (2000). Sex differences in emotional awareness. *Personality and Social Psychology Bulletin, 26*, 1027–1035.

Fenichel, O. (1945). *The psychoanalytic theory of neurosis.* New York: Norton.

Ferguson, C. J. (2010). A meta-analysis of normal and disordered personality across the life span. *Journal of Personality and Social Psychology, 98*, 659–667.

Ferguson, C. J. (2013). Violent video games and the *Supreme Court:* Lessons for the scientific community in the wake of *Brown v. Entertainment Merchants*

Association. *American Psychologist, 68*, 57–74.

Fernandez, E. (2010). Toward an integrative psychotherapy for maladaptive anger. In M. Potegal, G. Stemmler, & C. Spielberger (Eds.), *International handbook of anger: Constituent and concomitant biological, psychological, and social processes* (pp. 499–513). New York: Springer.

Fernandez, K. C., Levinson, C. A., & Rodebaugh, T. L. (2012). Profiling: Predicting social anxiety from Facebook profiles. *Social Psychological and Personality Science, 3*, 706–713.

Finch, J. F., Baranik, L. E., Liu, Y., & West, S. G. (2012). Physical health, positive and negative affect, and personality: A longitudinal analysis. *Journal of Research in Personality, 46*, 537–545.

Findley, M. J., & Cooper, H. M. (1983). Locus of control and academic achievement: A literature review. *Journal of Personality and Social Psychology, 44*, 419–427.

Finkel, D., & McGue, M. (1997). Sex differences and nonadditivity in heritability of the multidimensional personality questionnaire scales. *Journal of Personality and Social Psychology, 72*, 929–938.

Finkelhor, D., Ormrod, R., Turner, H., & Hamby, S. L. (2005). The victimization of children and youth: A comprehensive, national survey. *Child Maltreatment, 10*, 5–25.

Finkelstein, L. E., & Levy, B. R. (2006). Disclosure of Holocaust experiences: Reasons, attributions and health implications. *Journal of Social and Clinical Psychology, 25*, 117–140.

Fischer, P., Kastenmuller, A., & Greitemeyer, T. (2010). Media violence and the self: The impact of personalized gaming characters in aggressive video games on aggressive behavior. *Journal of Experimental Social Psychology, 46*, 192–195.

Fischer, P., & Greitemeyer, T. (2006). Music and aggression: The impact of sexual-aggressive song lyrics on aggression-related thoughts,

emotions, and behavior toward the same and the opposite sex. *Personality and Social Psychology Bulletin, 32*, 1165–1176.

Fischer, R., & Chalmers, A. (2008). Is optimism universal? A meta-analytical investigation of optimism across 22 nations. *Personality and Individual Differences, 45*, 378–382.

Fisher, M. (1995, December 6). *Freudian slip. San Jose Mercury News*, p. 25A.

Fiske, D. W. (1949). Consistency of the factorial structures of personality ratings from different sources. *Journal of Abnormal and Social Psychology, 44*, 329–344.

Fletcher, G. J. O., Tither, J. M., O'Loughlin, C., Friesen, M., & Overall, N. (2004). Warm and homely or cold and beautiful? Sex differences in trading off traits in mate selection. *Personality and Social Psychology Bulletin, 30*, 659–672.

Floderus-Myrhed, B., Pedersen, N., & Rasmuson, I. (1980). Assessment of heritability for personality, based on a short-form of the Eysenck Personality Inventory: A study of 12,898 twin pairs. *Behavior Genetics, 10*, 153–162.

Foel, R., & Tomcho, T. J. (2009). Gender differences in interdependent self-construals: It's not the type of group, it's the way you see it. *Self and Identity, 8*, 396–417.

Fok, C. C. T., Allen, J., Henry, D. Mohattt, G. V., & People Awakening Team (2012). Multicultural Mastery Scale for Youth: Multidimensional assessment of culturally mediated coping strategies. *Psychological Assessment, 24*, 313–327.

Folkman, S., & Lazarus, R. S. (1980). An analysis of coping in a middle-aged community sample. *Journal of Health and Social Behavior, 21*, 219–239.

Fontaine, R. G., & Dodge, K. A. (2006). Real-time decision making and aggressive behavior in youth: A heuristic model of response evaluation and decision (RED). *Aggressive Behavior, 32*, 604–624.

Foulkes, D., & Cavallero, C. (1993). *Dreaming as cognition.* New York: Harvester Wheatsheaf.

Fox, N. A., & Davidson, R. J. (1986). Taste-elicited changes in facial signs of emotion and the asymmetry of brain electrical activity in human newborns. *Neuropsychologia, 24,* 417–422.

Fox, N. A., & Davidson, R. J. (1987). Electroencephalogram asymmetry in response to the approach of a stranger and maternal separation of 10-month-old infants. *Developmental Psychology, 23,* 233–240.

Fox, N. A., & Davidson, R. J. (1988). Patterns of electrical activity during facial signs of emotion in 10-month-old infants. *Developmental Psychology, 24,* 230–236.

Fox, N. A., Henderson, H. A., Rubin, K. H., Calkins, S. D., & Schmidt, L. A. (2001). Continuity and discontinuity of behavioral inhibition and exuberance: Psychophysiological and behavioral influences across the first four years of life. *Child Development, 72,* 1–21.

Fraley, R. C., Roisman, G. I., Booth-LaForce, C., Owen, M. T., & Holland, A. S. (2013). Interpersonal and genetic origins of adult attachment styles: A longitudinal study from infancy to early adulthood. *Journal of Personality and Social Psychology, 104,* 817–838.

Fraley, R. C., & Shaver, P. R. (1998). Airport separation: A naturalistic study of adult attachment dynamics in separating couples. *Journal of Personality and Social Psychology, 75,* 1198–1212.

Fraley, R. C., Vicary, A. M., Brumbaugh, C. C., & Roisman, G. I. (2011). Patterns of stability in adult attachment: An empirical test of two models of continuity and change. *Journal of Personality and Social Psychology, 101,* 974–992.

Frankel, A., & Prentice-Dunn, S. (1990). Loneliness and the processing of self-relevant information. *Journal of Social and Clinical Psychology, 9,* 303–315.

Fransella, F. (2003). *International handbook of personal construct psychology.* London: Wiley.

Fransella, F. (2005). *The essential practitioner's handbook of personal construct psychology.* London: Wiley.

Fransella, F., Bell, R., & Bannister, D. (2003). *A manual for repertory grid technique* (2nd ed.). London: Wiley.

Frattaroli, J. (2006). Experimental disclosure and its moderators: A meta-analysis. *Psychological Bulletin, 132,* 823–865.

Frattaroli, J., Thomas, M., & Lyubomirsky, S. (2011). Opening up in the classroom: Effects of expressive writing on graduate school entrance exam performance. *Emotion, 11,* 691–696.

Frazier, L. D., Hooker, K., Johnson, P. M., & Kaus, C. R. (2000). Continuity and change in possible selves in later life: A 5-year longitudinal study. *Basic and Applied Social Psychology, 22,* 237–243.

Fredrickson, B. L., & Roberts, T. A. (1997). Objectification theory: Toward understanding women's lived experience and mental health risks. *Psychology of Women Quarterly, 21,* 173–206.

Frensch, K. M., Pratt, M. W., & Norris, J. E. (2007). Foundations of generativity: Personal and family correlates of emerging adults' generative life-story themes. *Journal of Research in Personality, 41,* 45–62.

Fresco, D. M., Alloy, L. B., & Reilly-Harrington, N. (2006). Association of attributional style for negative and positive events and the occurrence of life events with depression and anxiety. *Journal of Social and Clinical Psychology, 25,* 1140–1159.

Freud, A. (1965). *Normality and pathology in childhood.* New York: International Universities Press.

Freud, S. (1886–1936/1964). *The complete psychological works of Sigmund Freud* (Vols. 1–24). London: Hogarth.

Friedman, H. S., & Miller-Herringer, T. (1991). Nonverbal display of emotion in public and private: Self-monitoring, personality, and expressive cues. *Journal of Personality and Social Psychology, 61,* 766–775.

Friedman, H. S., Prince, L. M., Riggio, R. E., & DiMatteo, M. R. (1980). Understanding and assessing nonverbal expressiveness: The Affective Communication Test. *Journal of Personality and Social Psychology, 39,* 333–351.

Friedman, L. C., Nelson, D. V., Baer, P. E., Lane, M., Smith, F. E., & Dworkin, R. J. (1992). The relationship of dispositional optimism, daily life stress, and domestic environment to coping methods used by cancer patients. *Journal of Behavioral Medicine, 15,* 127–141.

Friedman, M., & Rosenman, R. (1974). *Type A behavior and your heart.* New York: Knopf.

Friedrich-Cofer, L., & Huston, A. C. (1986). Television violence and aggression: The debate continues. *Psychological Bulletin, 100,* 364–371.

Frisell, T., Pawitan, Y., Langstrom, N., & Lichtenstein, P. (2012). Heritability, assortative mating and gender differences in violent crime: Results from a total population sample using twin, adoption, and sibling models. *Behavior Genetics, 42,* 3–18.

Frisina, P. G., Borod, J. C., & Lepore, S. J. (2004). A meta-analysis of the effects of written emotional disclosure on the health outcomes in clinical populations. *Journal of Nervous and Mental Disease, 192,* 629–634.

Fritz, H. L., & Helgeson, V. S. (1998). Distinctions of unmitigated communion from communion: Self-neglect and overinvolvement with others. *Journal of Personality and Social Psychology, 75,* 121–140.

Froming, W. J., Nasby, W., & McManus, J. (1998). Pro-social self-schemas, self-awareness, and children's prosocial behavior. *Journal of Personality and Social Psychology, 75,* 766–777.

Fromm, E. (1950). *Psychoanalysis and religion.* New Haven, CT: Yale University Press.

Fromm, E. (1966). *You shall be as gods.* Greenwich, CT: Fawcett.

Fromm, E., & Nash, M. R. (1997). *Psychoanalysis and hypnosis.* Madison, CT: International Universities Press.

Fujita, F., Diener, E., & Sandvik, E. (1991). Gender differences in negative affect and well-being: The case for emotional intensity. *Journal of Personality and Social Psychology, 61,* 427–434.

Fulmer, C. A., Gelfand, M. J., Kruglanski, A. W., Kim-Prieto, C., Diener, E., Pierro, A. et al. (2010). On "feeling right" in cultural contexts: How person-culture match affects self-esteem and subjective well-being. *Psychological Science, 21,* 1563–1569.

Funder, D. C. (2009). Persons, behaviors and situations: An agenda for personality psychology in the postwar era. *Journal of Research in Personality, 43,* 120–126.

Funder, D. C., & Ozer, D. J. (1983). Behavior as a function of the situation. *Journal of Personality and Social Psychology, 44,* 107–112.

Gabbard, G. O., Gunderson, J. G., & Fonagy, P. (2002). The place of psychoanalytic treatments within psychiatry. *Archives of General Psychiatry, 59,* 505–510.

Gabriel, S., & Gardner, W. L. (1999). Are there "his" and "her" types of interdependence? The implications of gender differences in collective versus relational interdependence for affect, behavior, and cognition. *Journal of Personality and Social Psychology, 77,* 642–655.

Gacono, C. B., & Evans, F. B. (Eds.). (2008). *The handbook of forensic Rorschach assessment.* New York: Routledge.

Gaeddert, W. P. (1985). Sex and sex role effects on achievement strivings: Dimensions of similarity and difference. *Journal of Personality, 53,* 286–305.

Galatzer-Levy, I. R., Burton, C. L., & Bonanno, G. A. (2012). Coping flexibility, potentially traumatic life events, and resilience: A prospective study of college student adjustment. *Journal of Social and Clinical Psychology, 31,* 542–567.

Gale, C. R., Batty, G. D., & Deary, I. J. (2008). Locus of control at age 10 years and health outcomes and behaviors at age 30 years: The 1970 British Cohort Study. *Psychosomatic Medicine, 70,* 397–403.

Gangestad, S. W., & Thornhill, R. (1997). Human sexual selection and developmental stability. In J. A. Simpson & D. T. Kenrick (Eds.), *Evolutionary social psychology* (pp. 169–195). Mahwah, NJ: Erlbaum.

Ganiban, J. M., Saudino, K. J., Ulbricht, J., Neiderhiser, J. M., & Reiss, D. (2008). Stability and change in temperament during adolescence. *Journal of Personality and Social Psychology, 95,* 222–236.

Garb, H. N., Wood, J. M., Lilienfeld, S. O., & Nezworski, M. T. (2005). Roots of the Rorschach controversy. *Clinical Psychology Review, 25,* 97–118.

Garcia, S., Stinson, L., Ickes, W., Bissonnette, V., & Briggs, S. R. (1991). Shyness and physical attractiveness in mixed-sex dyads. *Journal of Personality and Social Psychology, 61,* 35–49.

Garrison, A. M., & Kahn, J. H. (2010). Intraindividual relations between the intensity and disclosure of daily emotional events: The moderating role of depressive symptoms. *Journal of Counseling Psychology, 57,* 187–197.

Garrison, A. M., Kahn, J. H., Sauer, E. M., & Florczak, M. A. (2012). Disentangling the effects of depression symptoms and adult attachment on emotional disclosure. *Journal of Counseling Psychology, 59,* 230–239.

Gastorf, J. W. (1980). Time urgency of the type A behavior pattern. *Journal of Consulting and Clinical Psychology, 48,* 299.

Gaudiano, B. A. (2005). Cognitive behavior therapies for psychotic disorders: Current empirical status and future directions. *Clinical Psychology: Science and Practice, 12,* 33–50.

Geary, D. C. (2000). Evolution and proximate expression of human paternal investment. *Psychological Bulletin, 126,* 55–77.

Geen, R. G. (1983). The psychophysiology of extraversion-introversion. In J. T. Cacioppo & R. E. Petty (Eds.), *Social psychophysiology: A sourcebook* (pp. 391–416). New York: Guilford.

Geen, R. G. (1984). Preferred stimulation levels in introverts and extraverts: Effects on arousal and performance. *Journal of Personality and Social Psychology, 46,* 1303–1312.

Geen, R. G. (1998). Aggression and antisocial behavior. In D. T. Gilbert, S. T. Fiske, & G. Lindzey (Eds.), *The handbook of social psychology* (4th ed., Vol. 2, pp. 317–356). Boston: McGraw-Hill.

Geen, R. G., & Quanty, M. B. (1977). The catharsis of aggression: An evaluation of a hypothesis. In L. Berkowitz (Ed.), *Advances in experimental social psychology* (Vol. 10, pp. 1–37). New York: Academic Press.

Geen, R. G., Stonner, D., & Shope, G. L. (1975). The facilitation of aggression by aggression: Evidence against the catharsis hypothesis. *Journal of Personality and Social Psychology, 31,* 721–726.

Geen, R. G., & Thomas, S. L. (1986). The immediate effects of media violence on behavior. *Journal of Social Issues, 42,* 7–27.

Geers, A. L., Wellman, J. A., & Lassiter, G. D. (2009). Dispositional optimism and engagement: The moderating influence of goal prioritization. *Journal of Personality and Social Psychology, 96,* 913–932.

Geers, A. L., Wellman, J. A., Seligman, L. D., Wuyek, L. A., & Neff, L. A. (2010). Dispositional optimism, goals, and engagement in health treatment programs. *Journal of Behavioral Medicine, 33,* 123–134.

Gemar, M. C., Segal, Z. V., Sagrati, S., & Kennedy, S. J. (2001). Mood-induced changes on the implicit association test in recovered depressed patients. *Journal of*

Abnormal Psychology, 110, 282–289.

Gentile, D. A., Coyne, S., & Walsh, D. A. (2011). Media violence, physical aggression, and relational aggression in school age children: A short-term longitudinal study. *Aggressive Behavior, 37,* 193–206.

Gentile, D. A., Lynch, P. J., Linder, J. R., & Walsh, D. A. (2004). The effects of violent video game habits on adolescent hostility, aggressive behaviors, and school performance. *Journal of Adolescence, 27,* 5–22.

Geraerts, E., Lindsay, D. S., Merckelbach, H., Jelicic, M., Raymaekers, L., Arnold, M. M. et al. (2009). Cognitive mechanisms underlying recovered memory experiences of childhood sexual abuse. *Psychological Science, 20,* 92–98.

Gerin, W. D., Davidson, K. W., Christenfeld, N. J. S., Goyal, T., & Schwartz, J. E. (2006). The role of angry rumination and distraction in blood pressure recovery from emotional arousal. *Psychosomatic Medicine, 68,* 64–72.

Gershoff, E. T. (2002). Corporal punishment by parents and associated child behaviors and experiences: A meta-analytic and theoretical review. *Psychological Bulletin, 128,* 539–579.

Gersten, M. (1989). Behavioral inhibition in the classroom. In J. S. Reznick (Ed.), *Perspectives on behavioral inhibition* (pp. 71–91). Chicago: University of Chicago Press.

Gest, S. D. (1997). Behavioral inhibition: Stability and associations with adaptation from childhood to early adulthood. *Journal of Personality and Social Psychology, 72,* 467–475.

Geuens, M., & De Pelsmacker, P. (1999). Affect intensity revisited: Individual differences and the communication effects of emotional stimuli. *Psychology and Marketing, 16,* 195–209.

Ghaed, S. G., & Gallo, L. C. (2006). Distinctions among agency, communion, and unmitigated agency and communion according to the interpersonal circumplex, Five-Factor Model, and social-emotional correlates. *Journal of Personality Assessment, 86,* 77–88.

Gibbons, F. X., Blanton, H., Gerrard, M., Buunk, B., & Eggleston, T. (2000). Does social comparison make a difference? Optimism as a moderator of the relation between comparison level and academic performance. *Personality and Social Psychology Bulletin, 26,* 637–648.

Gibson, H. B. (1981). *Hans Eysenck: The man and his work.* London: Peter Owen.

Gibson, M. F. (2012). Opening up: Therapist self-disclosure in theory, research, and practice. *Clinical Social Work Journal, 40,* 287–296.

Gidron, Y., Davidson, K., & Bata, I. (1999). The short-term effects of a hostility-reduction intervention on male coronary heart disease patients. *Health Psychology, 18,* 416–420.

Giesler, R. B., Josephs, R. A., & Swann, W. B. (1996). Self-verification in clinical depression: The desire for negative evaluation. *Journal of Abnormal Psychology, 105,* 358–368.

Gilbert, L., Deutsch, C. L., & Strahan, R. F. (1978). Feminine and masculine dimensions of the typical, desirable and ideal woman and man. *Sex Roles, 4,* 767–778.

Gillespie, N. A., Zhu, G., Evans, D. M., Medland, S. E., Wright, M. J., & Marti, N. G. (2008). A genome-wide scan for Eysenckian personality dimensions in adolescent twin sibships: Psychoticism, extraversion, neuroticism and lie. *Journal of Personality, 76,* 1415–1445.

Giltay, E. J., Geleijnse, K. M., Zitman, F. G., Buijsse, B., & Kromhout, D. (2007). Lifestyle and dietary correlates of dispositional optimism in men: The Zutphen Elderly Study. *Journal of Psychosomatic Medicine, 63,* 483–490.

Glasberg, R., & Aboud, F. (1982). Keeping one's distance from sadness: Children's self-reports of emotional experience. *Developmental Psychology, 18,* 287–293.

Glass, C. R., & Shea, C. A. (1986). Cognitive therapy for shyness and social anxiety. In W. H. Jones, J. M. Cheek, & S. R. Briggs (Eds.), *Shyness: Perspectives on research and treatment* (pp. 315–327). New York: Plenum.

Glass, D. C. (1977). *Behavior patterns, stress, and coronary disease.* Hillsdale, NJ: Erlbaum.

Glass, K., Flory, K., Hanking, B. L., Kloos, B., & Turecki, G. (2009). Are coping strategies, social support, and hope associated with psychological distress among Hurricane Katrina survivors? *Journal of Social and Clinical Psychology, 28,* 779–795.

Glisky, M. L., Tataryn, D. J., Tobias, B. A., Kihlstrom, J. F., & McConkey, K. M. (1991). Absorption, openness to experience, and hypnotizability. *Journal of Personality and Social Psychology, 60,* 263–272.

Goetz, J. L., Keltner, D., & Simon-Thomas, E. (2010). Compassion: An evolutionary analysis and empirical review. *Psychological Bulletin, 136,* 351–374.

Gohm, C. L., & Clore, G. L. (2000). Individual differences in emotional experience: Mapping available scales to processes. *Personality and Social Psychology Bulletin, 26,* 679–697.

Gohm, C. L., & Clore, G. L. (2002). Four latent traits of emotional experience and their involvement in well-being, coping, and attributional style. *Cognition and Emotion, 16,* 495–518.

Gol, A. R., & Cook, S. W. (2004). Exploring the underlying dimensions of coping: A concept mapping approach. *Journal of Social and Clinical Psychology, 23,* 155–171.

Goldberg, J. F., Gerstein, R. K., Wenze, S. J., Beck, A. T., & Welker, T. A. (2008). Dysfunctional attitudes and cognitive schemas in bipolar manic and unipolar depressed outpatients: Implications for cognitively based psychotherapeutics. *Journal of Nervous and Mental Disease, 196,* 207–210.

Goldberg, L. R. (1992). The development of markers for the Big-Five factor structure. *Psychological Assessment, 4*, 26–42.

Goldberg, L. R. (1993). The structure of phenotypic personality traits. *American Psychologist, 48*, 26–34.

Goldberg, L. R. (2001). Analyses of Digman's child-personality data: Derivation of Big-Five factor scores from each of six samples. *Journal of Personality, 69*, 709–743.

Goode, E. (1999, April 23). Homosexuality-gene study released: Research fails to support report of chromosomal link. *San Jose Mercury News*, p. 8A.

Goodwin, R., Cook, O., & Yung, Y. (2001). Loneliness and life satisfaction among three cultural groups. *Personal Relationships, 8*, 225–230.

Gorassini, D. R., Sowerby, D., Creighton, A., & Fry, G. (1991). Hypnotic susceptibility enhancement through brief cognitive skill training. *Journal of Personality and Social Psychology, 61*, 289–297.

Gorassini, D. R., & Spanos, N. P. (1986). A social-cognitive skills approach to the successful modification of hypnotic susceptibility. *Journal of Personality and Social Psychology, 50*, 1004–1012.

Goswick, R. A., & Jones, W. H. (1981). Loneliness, self-concept, and adjustment. *Journal of Psychology, 88*, 258–261.

Gotay, C. C. (1981). Cooperation and competition as a function of type A behavior. *Personality and Social Psychology Bulletin, 7*, 386–392.

Gough, H. G., Fioravanti, M., & Lazzari, R. (1983). Some implications of self versus ideal-self congruence on the Revised Adjective Check List. *Journal of Personality and Social Psychology, 44*, 1214–1220.

Gough, H. G., Lazzari, R., & Fioravanti, M. (1978). Self versus ideal self: A comparison of five adjective check list indices. *Journal of Consulting and Clinical Psychology, 46*, 1085–1091.

Graham, S. M., Huang, J. Y., Clark, M. S., & Helgeson, V. S. (2008). The positives of negative emotions: Willingness to express negative emotions promotes relationships. *Personality and Social Psychology Bulletin, 34*, 394–406.

Granberg, E. (2006). "Is that all there is?" Possible selves, self-change, and weight loss. *Social Psychology Quarterly, 69*, 109–126.

Gray, J. A. (1982). *The neuropsychology of anxiety: An inquiry of the septo-hippocampal system.* Oxford, England: Oxford University Press.

Gray, J. A. (1987). Perspectives on anxiety and impulsivity: A commentary. *Journal of Research in Personality, 21*, 493–509.

Gray, J. A., & McNaughton, N. (2000). *The neuropsychology of anxiety.* Oxford, England: Oxford University Press.

Graziano, W. G., & Habashi, M. M. (2010). Motivational processes underlying both prejudice and helping. *Personality and Social Psychology Review, 14*, 313–331.

Graziano, W. G., Jensen-Campbell, L. A., Steele, R. G., & Hair, E. C. (1998). Unknown words in self-reported personality: Lethargic and provincial in Texas. *Personality and Social Psychology Bulletin, 24*, 893–905.

Graziano, W. G., Jensen-Campbell, L. A., & Sullivan-Logan, G. M. (1998). Temperament, activity, and expectations for later personality development. *Journal of Personality and Social Psychology, 74*, 1266–1277.

Graziano, W. G., Jensen-Campbell, L. A., Todd, M., & Finch, J. F. (1997). Interpersonal attraction from an evolutionary psychology perspective: Women's reactions to dominant and prosocial men. In J. A. Simpson & D. T. Kenrick (Eds.), *Evolutionary social psychology* (pp. 141–167). Mahwah, NJ: Erlbaum.

Green, B. L., & Kenrick, D. T. (1994). The attractiveness of gender-typed traits at different relationship levels: Androgynous characteristics may be desirable after all. *Personality and Social Psychology Bulletin, 20*, 244–253.

Green, J. P. (2004). The five factor model of personality and hypnotizability: Little variance in common. *Contemporary Hypnosis, 21*, 161–168.

Green, J. P., Page, R. A., Handley, G. W., & Rasekhy, R. (2005). The "hidden observer" and ideomotor responding: A real-simulator comparison. *Contemporary Hypnosis, 22*, 123–137.

Green, L. R., Richardson, D. S., Lago, T., & Schatten-Jones, E. C. (2001). Network correlates of social and emotional loneliness in young and older adults. *Personality and Social Psychology Bulletin, 27*, 281–288.

Greenberg, M. A., Wortman, C. B., & Stone, A. A. (1996). Emotional expression and physical health: Revising traumatic memories or fostering self-regulation? *Journal of Personality and Social Psychology, 71*, 588–602.

Greenberg, R., Pillard, R., & Pearlman, C. (1978). The effect of dream (stage REM) deprivation on adaptation to stress. In S. Fisher & R. P. Greenberg (Eds.), *The scientific evaluation of Freud's theories and therapy* (pp. 40–48). New York: Basic Books.

Greening, L., Stoppelbein, L., & Docter, R. (2002). The mediating effects of attributional style and event-specific attributions on postdisaster adjustment. *Cognitive Therapy and Research, 26*, 261–274.

Greitemeyer, T., & McLatchie, N. (2011). Denying humanness to others: A newly discovered mechanism by which violent video games increase aggressive behavior. *Psychological Science, 22*, 659–665.

Greve, W., & Wentura, D. (2003). Immunizing the self: Self-concept stabilization through reality-adaptive self-definitions. *Personality and Social Psychology Bulletin, 29*, 39–50.

Gronnerod, C. (2004). Rorschach assessment of changes following psychotherapy: A meta-analytic review. *Journal of Personality Assessment, 83*, 256–276.

Gross, J. J., & John, O. P. (1998). Mapping the domain of expressivity: Multimethod evidence for a hierarchical model. *Journal of Personality and Social Psychology, 74,* 170–191.

Grotz, M., Hapke, U., Lampert, T., & Baumeister, H. (2011). Health locus of control and health behavior: Results from a nationally representative survey. *Psychology, Health & Medicine, 16,* 129–140.

Grove, J. R., Hanrahan, S. J., & McInman, A. (1991). Success/ failure bias in attributions across involvement categories in sport. *Personality and Social Psychology Bulletin, 17,* 93–97.

Gruzelier, J. H. (2006). Frontal functions, connectivity and neural efficiency underpinning hypnosis and hypnotic susceptibility. *Contemporary Hypnosis, 23,* 15–23.

Guerra, N. G., Huesmann, L. R., Tolan, P. H., Van Acker, R., & Eron, L. D. (1995). Stressful events and individual beliefs as correlates of economic disadvantage and aggression among urban children. *Journal of Consulting and Clinical Psychology, 63,* 518–528.

Guimond, S., Chatard, A., Martinot, D., Crisp, R. J., & Redersdorff, S. (2006). Social comparison, self-stereotyping, and gender differences in self-construal. *Journal of Personality and Social Psychology, 90,* 221–242.

Gunthert, K. C., Cohen, L. H., & Armeli, S. (1999). The role of neuroticism in daily stress and coping. *Journal of Personality and Social Psychology, 77,* 1087–1100.

Gur, R. C., & Reivich, M. (1980). Cognitive task effects on hemispheric blood flow in humans: Evidence for individual differences in hemispheric activation. *Brain and Language, 9,* 78–92.

Guyll, M., & Contrada, R. J. (1998). Trait hostility and ambulatory cardiovascular activity: Responses to social interaction. *Health Psychology, 17,* 30–39.

Gwaltney, C. J., Shiffman, S., Balabanis, M. H., & Paty, J. A. (2005). Dynamic self-efficacy and outcome expectancies: Prediction of smoking lapse and relapse. *Journal of Abnormal Psychology, 114,* 661–675.

Haans, A., Kaiser, F. G., & de Kort, Y. A. W. (2007). Privacy needs in office environments: Development of two behavior-based scales. *European Psychologist, 12,* 93–102.

Haeffel, G. J., Abramson, L. Y., Voelz, Z. R., Metalsky, G. I., Halberstadt, L., Dykman, B. M. et al. (2003). Cognitive vulnerability to depression and lifetime history of Axis I psychopathology: A comparison of negative cognitive styles (CSQ) and dysfunctional attitudes (DAS). *Journal of Cognitive Psychotherapy, 17,* 3–22.

Haemmerlie, F. M., & Montgomery, R. L. (1986). Self-perception theory and the treatment of shyness. In W. H. Jones, J. M. Cheek, & S. R. Briggs (Eds.), *Shyness: Perspectives on research and treatment* (pp. 329–342). New York: Plenum.

Hall, C., Smith, K., & Chia, R. (2008). Cognitive and personality factors in relation to timely completion of a college degree. *College Student Journal, 42,* 1087–1098.

Hall, C. S. (1953). A cognitive theory of dream symbols. *Journal of General Psychology, 48,* 169–186.

Hall, C. S. (1984). "A ubiquitous sex difference in dreams" revisited. *Journal of Personality and Social Psychology, 46,* 1109–1117.

Hall, C. S., & Domhoff, B. (1963). A ubiquitous sex difference in dreams. *Journal of Abnormal and Social Psychology, 66,* 278–280.

Hall, M. H. (1968, August). A conversation with the president of the American Psychological Association: The psychology of universality. *Psychology Today,* 35–37, 54–57.

Hammack, S. E., Cooper, M. A., & Lezak, K. R. (2012). Overlapping neurobiology of learned helplessness and conditioned defeat: Implications for PTSD and mood disorders. *Neuropharmacology, 62,* 565–575.

Handler, L. (1996). The clinical use of drawings: Draw-a-person, house-tree-person, and kinetic family drawings. In C. S. Newmark (Ed.), *Major psychological assessment instruments* (2nd ed., pp. 206–293). Needham Heights, MA: Allyn & Bacon.

Hankin, B. L. (2008). Stability of cognitive vulnerabilities to depression: A short-term prospective multiwave study. *Journal of Abnormal Psychology, 117,* 324–233.

Hankin, B. L., Fraley, R. C., & Abela, J. R. Z. (2005). Daily depression and cognitions about stress: Evidence for a traitlike depressogenic cognitive style and the prediction of depressive symptoms in a prospective daily diary study. *Journal of Personality and Social Psychology, 88,* 673–685.

Hanley-Dunn, P., Maxwell, S. E., & Santos, J. F. (1985). Interpretation of interpersonal interaction: The influence of loneliness. *Personality and Social Psychology Bulletin, 11,* 445–456.

Harackiewicz, J. M., Barron, K. E., Pintrich, P. R., Elliot, A. J., & Thrash, T. M. (2002). Revision of achievement goal theory: Necessary and illuminating. *Journal of Educational Psychology, 94,* 638–645.

Hardin, E. E., & Lakin, J. L. (2009). The integrated self-discrepancy index: A reliable and valid measure of self-discrepancies. *Journal of Personality Assessment, 91,* 245–253.

Harmon-Jones, E., & Allen, J. J. B. (1997). Behavioral activation sensitivity and resting frontal EEG asymmetry: Covariation of putative indicators related to risk for mood disorders. *Journal of Abnormal Psychology, 106,* 159–163.

Harmon-Jones, E., Lueck, L., Fearn, M., & Harmon-Jones, C. (2006). The effect of personal relevance and approach-related action expectation on relative left frontal cortical activity. *Psychological Science, 17,* 434–440.

Harmon-Jones, E., & Sigelman, J. (2001). State anger and prefrontal brain activity: Evidence that insult-related relative left-prefrontal activation is associated with experienced anger and aggression. *Journal of Personality and Social Psychology, 80,* 797–803.

Harris, C. R. (2003). A review of sex differences in sexual jealousy, including self-report data, psycho-physiological responses, interpersonal violence, and morbid jealousy. *Personality and Social Psychology Review, 7,* 102–128.

Harris, M. B. (1974). Mediators between frustration and aggression in a field experiment. *Journal of Experimental Social Psychology, 10,* 561–571.

Harrison, A. A., & Saeed, L. (1977). Let's make a deal: An analysis of revelations and stipulations in lonely hearts advertisements. *Journal of Personality and Social Psychology, 35,* 257–264.

Harrist, S., Carlozzi, B. L., McGovern, A. R., & Harrist, A. W. (2007). Benefits of expressive writing and expressive talking about life goals. *Journal of Research in Personality, 41,* 923–930.

Hartshorne, H., & May, M. A. (1928). *Studies in the nature of character: Studies in deceit.* New York: Macmillan.

Harvey, J. H., & Omarzu, J. (1997). Minding the close relationship. *Personality and Social Psychology Review, 1,* 224–240.

Havermans, R., Nicolson, N. A., & deVries, M. W. (2007). Daily hassles, uplifts, and time use in individuals with bipolar disorder in remission. *Journal of Nervous and Mental Disease, 195,* 745–751.

Hawkley, L. C., Burleson, M. H., Berntson, G. G., & Cacioppo, J. T. (2003). Loneliness in everyday life: Cardiovascular activity, psychosocial context, and health behaviors. *Journal of Personality and Social Psychology, 85,* 105–120.

Hawkley, L. C., & Cacioppo, J. T. (2007). Aging and loneliness: Downhill quickly? *Current Directions in Psychological Science, 16,* 187–191.

Hawkley, L. C., Masi, C. M., Berry, J. D., & Cacioppo, J. T. (2006). Loneliness is a unique predictor of age-related differences in systolic blood pressure. *Psychology and Aging, 21,* 152–164.

Hawkley, L. C., Preacher, K. J., & Cacioppo, J. T. (2010). Loneliness impairs daytime functioning but not sleep duration. *Health Psychology, 29,* 124–129.

Hawkley, L. C., Thisted, R. A., & Cacioppo, J. T. (2009). Loneliness predicts reduced physical activity: Cross-sectional & longitudinal analyses. *Health Psychology, 28,* 354–363.

Haynes, S. N. (2001). Introduction to the special section on clinical applications of analogue behavioral observation. *Psychological Assessment, 13,* 3–4.

Hazan, C., & Shaver, P. (1987). Romantic love conceptualized as an attachment process. *Journal of Personality and Social Psychology, 52,* 511–524.

Headey, B., & Wearing, A. (1989). Personality, life events, and subjective well-being: Toward a dynamic equilibrium model. *Journal of Personality and Social Psychology, 57,* 731–739.

Heath, A. C., Neale, M. C., Kessler, R. C., Eaves, L. J., & Kendler, K. S. (1992). Evidence for genetic influences on personality from self-reports and informant ratings. *Journal of Personality and Social Psychology, 63,* 85–96.

Heatherton, T. F., & Polivy, J. (1991). Development and validation of a scale for measuring state self-esteem. *Journal of Personality and Social Psychology, 60,* 895–910.

Heery, E. A., & Kring, A. M. (2007). Interpersonal consequences of social anxiety. *Journal of Abnormal Psychology, 116,* 125–134.

Heine, S. J. (2001). Self as cultural product: An examination of East Asian and North American selves. *Journal of Personality, 69,* 881–906.

Heine, S. J., & Hamamura, T. (2007). In search of East Asian self-enhancement. *Personality and Social Psychology Review, 11,* 4–27.

Heine, S. J., & Lehman, D. R. (1995). Cultural variation in unrealistic optimism: Does the West feel more invulnerable than the East? *Journal of Personality and Social Psychology, 68,* 595–607.

Heine, S. J., & Lehman, D. R. (1999). Culture, self-discrepancies, and self-satisfaction. *Personality and Social Psychology Bulletin, 25,* 915–925.

Heine, S. J., Lehman, D. R., Markus, H. R., & Kitayama, S. (1999). Is there a universal need for positive self-regard? *Psychological Review, 106,* 766–794.

Heinrich, L. M., & Gullone, E. (2006). The clinical significance of loneliness: A literature review. *Clinical Psychology Review, 26,* 695–718.

Heinrichs, N., Rapee, R. M., Alden, L. A., Bogels, S., Hofmann, S. G., Oh, K. J. et al. (2005). Cultural differences in perceived social norms and social anxiety. *Behaviour Research and Therapy, 44,* 1187–1197.

Helfinstein, S. M., Fox, N. A., & Pine, D. S. (2012). Approach-withdrawal and the role of the striatum in the temperament of behavioral inhibition. *Developmental Psychology, 48,* 815–826.

Helgeson, V. S. (1994). Relation of agency and communion to well-being: Evidence and potential explanations. *Psychological Bulletin, 116,* 412–428.

Helgeson, V. S. (2003). Unmitigated communion and adjustment to breast cancer: Associations and explanations. *Journal of Applied Social Psychology, 33,* 1643–1661.

Helgeson, V. S., Cohen, S., & Fritz, H. L. (1998). Social ties and cancer. In J. C. Holland & W. Breitbart (Eds.), *Psycho-oncology* (pp. 99–109). New York: Oxford University Press.

Helgeson, V. S., Escobar, O., Siminerio, L., & Becker, D. (2007). Unmitigated communion and health among adolescents with and without diabetes: The mediating role of eating disturbances. *Personality and Social Psychology Bulletin, 33,* 519–536.

Helgeson, V. S., & Fritz, H. L. (1999). Unmitigated agency and unmitigated communion: Distinctions from agency and communion.

Journal of Research in Personality, 33, 131–158.

Helgeson, V. S., & Fritz, H. L. (2000). The implications of unmitigated agency and unmitigated communion for domains of problem behavior. *Journal of Personality, 68,* 1031–1057.

Helgeson, V. S., & Lepore, S. J. (1997). Men's adjustment to prostate cancer: The role of agency and unmitigated agency. *Sex Roles, 37,* 251–267.

Helgeson, V. S., & Lepore, S. J. (2004). Quality of life following prostate cancer: The role of agency and unmitigated agency. *Journal of Applied Social Psychology, 34,* 2559–2585.

Helgeson, V. S., & Palladino, D. K. (2012). Agentic and communal traits and health: Adolescents with and without diabetes. *Personality and Social Psychology Bulletin, 38,* 415–428.

Helmes, E., & Reddon, J. R. (1993). A perspective on developments in assessing psychopathology: A critical review of the MMPI and MMPI-2. *Psychological Bulletin, 113,* 453–471.

Hemenover, S. H. (2003). The good, the bad, and the healthy: Impacts of emotional disclosure of trauma on resilient self-concept and psychological distress. *Personality and Social Psychology Bulletin, 29,* 1236–1244.

Henretty, J. R. (2010). The role of therapist self-disclosure in psychotherapy: A qualitative review. *Clinical Psychology Review, 30,* 63–77.

Henriques, J. B., & Davidson, R. J. (1990). Regional brain electrical asymmetries discriminate between previously depressed and healthy control subjects. *Journal of Abnormal Psychology, 99,* 22–31.

Herrnstein, R. J., & Murray, C. (1994). *The bell curve: Intelligence and class structure in American life.* New York: Free Press.

Hertel, P. T., & Brozovich, F. (2010). Cognitive habits and memory distortions in anxiety and depression. *Current Directions in Psychological Science, 19,* 155–160.

Higgins, E. T. (1987). Self-discrepancy: A theory relating self and affect. *Psychological Review, 94,* 319–340.

Higgins, E. T. (1989). Self-discrepancy theory: What patterns of self-beliefs cause people to suffer? In L. Berkowitz (Ed.), *Advances in experimental social psychology* (Vol. 22, pp. 93–136). San Diego: Academic Press.

Hilgard, E. R. (1973). A neodissociation interpretation of pain reduction in hypnosis. *Psychological Review, 80,* 396–411.

Hilgard, E. R. (1977). *Divided consciousness: Multiple controls in human thought and action.* New York: Wiley.

Hilgard, E. R. (1992). Dissociation and theories of hypnosis. In E. Fromm & M. R. Nash (Eds.), *Contemporary hypnosis research* (pp. 69–101). New York: Guilford.

Hilgard, E. R. (1994). Neodissociation theory. In S. J. Lynn & J. W. Rhue (Eds.), *Dissociation: Clinical, theoretical and research perspectives* (pp. 32–51). New York: Guilford.

Hill, C. E. (1996). *Working with dreams in psychotherapy.* New York: Guilford.

Hill, G. J. (1989). An unwillingness to act: Behavioral appropriateness, situational constraint, and self-efficacy in shyness. *Journal of Personality, 57,* 871–890.

Hill, P. L., Turiano, N. A., Hurd, M. D., Mroczek, D. K., & Roberts, B. W. (2011). Conscientiousness and longevity: An examination of possible mediators. *Health Psychology, 30,* 536–541.

Hill, S. E., Rodeheffer, C. D., Griskevicius, V., Durante, K., & White, A. E. (2012). Boosting beauty in an economic decline: Mating, spending, and the lipstick effect. *Journal of Personality and Social Psychology, 103,* 275–291.

Hiroto, D. S. (1974). Locus of control and learned helplessness. *Journal of Experimental Psychology, 102,* 187–193.

Hiroto, D. S., & Seligman, M. E. P. (1975). Generality of learned helplessness in man. *Journal of*

Personality and Social Psychology, 31, 311–327.

Hodson, G., Rush, J., & MacInnis, C. C. (2010). A joke is just a joke (except when it isn't): Cavalier humor beliefs facilitate the expression of group dominance motives. *Journal of Personality and Social Psychology, 99,* 660–682.

Hoffman, L. W. (1985). The changing genetics/socialization balance. *Journal of Social Issues, 41,* 127–148.

Hoffman, L. W. (1991). The influence of the family environment on personality: Accounting for sibling differences. *Psychological Bulletin, 110,* 187–203.

Hogan, R. (1991). Personality and personality measurement. In M. D. Dunnette & L. M. Hough (Eds.), *Handbook of industrial and organizational psychology* (2nd ed., Vol. 2, pp. 873–919). Palo Alto, CA: Consulting Psychologists Press.

Hojnoski, R. L., Morrison, R., Brown, M., & Matthews, W. J. (2009). Projective test use among school psychologists. *Journal of Psychoeducational Assessment, 24,* 145–159.

Hollon, S. D., Stewart, M. O., & Strunk, D. (2006). Enduring effects for cognitive behavior therapy in the treatment of depression and anxiety. *Annual Review of Psychology, 57,* 285–315.

Holloway, R. A., Waldrip, A. M., & Ickes, W. (2009). Evidence that a simpatico self-schema accounts for differences in the self-concepts and social behavior of Latinos versus Whites (and Blacks). *Journal of Personality and Social Psychology, 96,* 1012–1028.

Hoobler, J. M., & Brass, D. J. (2006). Abusive supervision and family undermining as displaced aggression. *Journal of Applied Psychology, 91,* 1125–1133.

Hooker, K., Monahan, D., Shifren, K., & Hutchinson, C. (1992). Mental and physical health of spouse caregivers: The role of personality. *Psychology and Aging, 7,* 367–375.

Hopkins, J. R. (1995). Erik Homburger Erikson (1902-1994). *American Psychologist, 50*, 796–797.

Horley, J. (1996). Content stability in the repertory grid: An examination using a forensic sample. *International Journal of Offender Therapy and Comparative Criminology, 40*, 26–31.

Horn, J. (2001). Raymond Bernard Cattell (1905-1998). *American Psychologist, 56*, 71–72.

Horney, K. (1945/1966). *Our inner conflicts: A constructive theory of neurosis.* New York: Norton.

Horney, K. (1967). *Feminine psychology.* New York: Norton.

Hornstein, G. A. (1985). Intimacy in conversational style as a function of the degree of closeness between members of a dyad. *Journal of Personality and Social Psychology, 49*, 671–681.

Hornstein, G. A., & Truesdell, S. E. (1988). Development of intimate conversation in close relationships. *Journal of Social and Clinical Psychology, 7*, 49–64.

Horowitz, L. M., & de Sales French, R. (1979). Interpersonal problems of people who describe themselves as lonely. *Journal of Consulting and Clinical Psychology, 47*, 762–764.

Houts, R. M., Caspi, A., Pianta, R. C., Arseneault, L., & Moffitt, T. E. (2010). The challenging pupil in the classroom: The effect of the child on the teacher. *Psychological Science, 21*, 1802–1810.

Howard, M. L., & Coe, W. C. (1980). The effects of context and subjects' perceived control in breaching posthypnotic amnesia. *Journal of Personality, 48*, 342–359.

Howren, M. B., & Suls, J. (2011). The symptom perception hypothesis revisited: Depression and anxiety play different roles in concurrent and retrospective physical symptom reporting. *Journal of Personality and Social Psychology, 100*, 182–195.

Hoyt, M. A., & Stanton, A. L. (2011). Unmitigated agency, social support, and psychological adjustment in men with cancer. *Journal of Personality, 79*, 259–276.

Hoyt, M. F., & Singer, J. L. (1978). Psychological effects of REM ("dream") deprivation upon waking mentation. In A. M. Arkin, J. S. Antrobus, & S. J. Ellman (Eds.), *The mind in sleep: Psychology and psychophysiology* (pp. 487–510). Hillsdale, NJ: Erlbaum.

Hubbard, J. A., McAuliffe, M. D., Morrow, M. T., & Romano, L. J. (2010). Reactive and proactive aggression in childhood and adolescence: Precursors, outcomes, processes, experiences, and measurement. *Journal of Personality, 78*, 95–118.

Huesmann, L. R. (1988). An information-processing model for the development of aggression. *Aggressive Behavior, 14*, 13–24.

Huesmann, L. R., Eron, L. D., Dubow, E. F., & Seebauer, E. (1987). Television viewing habits in childhood and adult aggression. *Child Development, 58*, 357–367.

Huesmann, L. R., Eron, L. D., & Yarmel, P. W. (1987). Intellectual functioning and aggression. *Journal of Personality and Social Psychology, 52*, 232–240.

Huesmann, L. R., & Guerra, N. G. (1997). Children's normative beliefs about aggression and aggressive behavior. *Journal of Personality and Social Psychology, 72*, 408–419.

Hunsley, J., & Bailey, J. M. (1999). The clinical utility of the Rorschach: Unfulfilled promises and an uncertain future. *Psychological Assessment, 11*, 266–277.

Hurtz, G. M., & Donovan, J. J. (2000). Personality and job performance: The Big Five revisited. *Journal of Applied Psychology, 85*, 869–879.

Hyde, J. S., & Kling, K. C. (2001). Women, motivation and achievement. *Psychology of Women Quarterly, 25*, 364–378.

Ickes, W. (1993). Traditional gender roles: Do they make, and then break, our relationships? *Journal of Social Issues, 49*, 71–85.

Ickes, W., & Barnes, R. D. (1978). Boys and girls together and alienated: On enacting stereotyped sex roles in mixed-sex dyads. *Journal of*

Personality and Social Psychology, 36, 669–683.

Ickes, W., Robertson, E., Tooke, W., & Teng, G. (1986). Naturalistic social cognition: Methodology, assessment, and validation. *Journal of Personality and Social Psychology, 51*, 66–82.

Ickes, W., Schermer, B., & Steeno, J. (1979). Sex and sex-role influence in same-sex dyads. *Social Psychology Quarterly, 42*, 373–385.

Ihilevich, D., & Gleser, G. C. (1993). *Defense mechanisms: Their classification, correlates, and measurement with the Defense Mechanism Inventory.* Odessa, FL: Psychological Assessment Resources.

Ilgen, M., McKellar, J., & Tiet, Q. (2005). Abstinence self-efficacy and abstinence 1 year after substance use disorder treatment. *Journal of Consulting and Clinical Psychology, 73*, 1175–1180.

Ingram, R. E., & Ritter, J. (2000). Vulnerability to depression: Cognitive reactivity and parental bonding in high-risk individuals. *Journal of Abnormal Psychology, 109*, 588–596.

Jackson, B., Kubzansky, L. D., Cohen, S., Jacobs, D. R., & Wright, R. J. (2007). Does harboring hostility hurt? Associations between hostility and pulmonary function in the Coronary Artery Risk Development in (young) Adults (CARDIA) study. *Health Psychology, 26*, 333–340.

Jackson, C. J. (2009). Jackson-5 scales of revised Reinforcement Sensitivity Theory (r-RST) and their application to dysfunctional real world outcomes. *Journal of Research in Personality, 43*, 556–569.

Jackson, L. A. (1983). The perception of androgyny and physical attractiveness: Two is better than one. *Personality and Social Psychology Bulletin, 9*, 405–413.

Jackson, L. A., Ialongo, N., & Stollak, G. E. (1986). Parental correlates of gender role: The relations between parents' masculinity, femininity, and child-rearing behaviors and their children's gender roles.

Journal of Social and Clinical Psychology, 4, 204–224.

Jahoda, M. (1977). *Freud and the dilemmas of psychology.* New York: Basic Books.

Jang, K. L., Livesley, W. J., & Vernon, P. A. (1996). Heritability of the Big Five personality dimensions and their facets: A twin study. *Journal of Personality, 64,* 577–591.

Jang, K. L., McCrae, R. R., Angleitner, A., Riemann, R., & Livesley, W. J. (1998). Heritability of facet-level traits in a cross-cultural twin sample: Support for a hierarchical model of personality. *Journal of Personality and Social Psychology, 74,* 1556–1565.

Janoff-Bulman, R. (1992). *Shattered assumptions: Towards a new psychology of trauma.* New York: Free Press.

Jefferson, T., Herbst, J. H., & McCrae, R. R. (1998). Associations between birth order and personality traits: Evidence from self-reports and observer ratings. *Journal of Research in Personality, 32,* 498–509.

Jeffrey, A., & Austin, T. (2007). Perspectives and practices of clinician self-disclosure to clients: A pilot comparison study of two disciplines. *American Journal of Family Therapy, 35,* 95–108.

Jenkins, C. D. (1971). Psychologic and social precursors of coronary disease. *New England Journal of Medicine, 284,* 244–255, 307–317.

Jenkins, C. D. (1976). Recent evidence supporting psychologic and social risk factors for coronary disease. *New England Journal of Medicine, 294,* 987–994, 1033–1038.

Jenkins, C. D., Zyzanski, S. J., & Rosenman, R. H. (1976). Risk of new myocardial infarction in middle-age men with manifest coronary heart disease. *Circulation, 53,* 342–347.

Jenkins, S. R. (1987). Need for achievement and women's careers over 14 years: Evidence for occupational structure effects. *Journal of Personality and Social Psychology, 53,* 922–932.

Jensen, A. R. (1969). How much can we boost IQ and scholastic achievement? *Harvard Educational Review, 39,* 1–123.

Jensen-Campbell, L. A., & Graziano, W. G. (2001). Agreeableness as a moderator of interpersonal conflict. *Journal of Personality, 69,* 323–362.

Jensen-Campbell, L. A., Graziano, W. G., & West, S. G. (1995). Dominance, prosocial orientation, and female preferences: Do nice guys really finish last? *Journal of Personality and Social Psychology, 68,* 427–440.

Joca, S. R. L., Zanelati, T., & Guimaraes, F. S. (2006). Post-stress facilitation of serotonergic, but not noradrenergic, neurotransmission in the dorsal hippocampus prevents learned helplessness development in rats. *Brain Research, 1087,* 67–74.

Johansson, B., Grant, J. D., Plomin, R., Pedersen, N. L., Ahern, F., Berg, S. et al. (2001). Health locus of control in late life: A study of genetic and environmental influences in twins aged 80 years and older. *Health Psychology, 20,* 33–40.

John, O. P., Nauman, L. P., & Soto, C. J. (2008). Paradigm shift to the integrative Big Five trait taxonomy: History, measurement, and conceptual issues. In O. P. John, R. W. Robins, & L. A. Pervin (Eds.), *Handbook of personality* (3rd ed., pp. 114–158). New York: Guilford.

Johnson, J. G., Cohen, P., Smailes, E. M., Kasen, S., & Brook, J. S. (2002). Television viewing and aggressive behavior during adolescence and adulthood. *Science, 295,* 2468–2471.

Johnson, W., Turkheimer, E., Gottesman, I. I., & Bouchard, T. J. (2009). Beyond heritability: Twin studies in behavioral research. *Current Directions in Psychological Science, 18,* 217– 220.

Jones, A., & Crandall, R. (1986). Validation of a short index of self-actualization. *Personality and*

Social Psychology Bulletin, 12, 63–73.

Jones, E. (1953–1957). *The life and work of Sigmund Freud* (Vols. 1–3). New York: Basic Books.

Jones, R. E., Leen-Felder, E. W., Olatunji, B. O., Reardon, L. E., & Hawks, E. (2009). Psychometric properties of the affect intensity and reactivity measure adapted for youth (AIR-Y). *Psychological Assessment, 21,* 162–175.

Jones, W. H., Freemon, J. E., & Goswick, R. A. (1981). The persistence of loneliness: Self and other determinants. *Journal of Personality, 49,* 27–48.

Jones, W. H., Hobbs, S. A., & Hockenbury, D. (1982). Loneliness and social skill deficits. *Journal of Personality and Social Psychology, 42,* 682–689.

Jones, W. H., Sansone, C., & Helm, B. (1983). Loneliness and interpersonal judgments. *Personality and Social Psychology Bulletin, 9,* 437–441.

Jorgensen, R. S., Johnson, B. T., Kolodziej, M. E., & Schreer, G. E. (1996). Elevated blood pressure and personality: A meta-analytic review. *Psychological Bulletin, 120,* 293–320.

Josephs, R. A., Markus, H. R., & Tafarodi, R. W. (1992). Gender and self-esteem. *Journal of Personality and Social Psychology, 63,* 391–402.

Jourard, S. M. (1971). *The transparent self* (2nd ed.). New York: Van Nostrand.

Judge, T. A., & Bono, J. E. (2001). Relationship of core self-evaluations traits—self-esteem, generalized self-efficacy, locus of control, and emotional stability—with job satisfaction and job performance: A meta-analysis. *Journal of Applied Psychology, 86,* 80–92.

Judge, T. A., Erez, A., & Bono, J. E. (1998). The power of being positive: The relationship between positive self-concept and job performance. *Human Performance, 11,* 167–187.

Judge, T. A., Higgins, C. A., Thoresen, C. J., & Barrick, M. R. (1999). The

Big Five personality traits, general mental ability, and career success across the life span. *Personnel Psychology, 52,* 621–652.

Jung, C. G. (1902–1961). *The collected works of Carl Jung* (Vols. 1–17). Princeton, NJ: Princeton University Press.

Jung, C. G. (1961). *Memories, dreams, reflections.* New York: Pantheon.

Jung, C. G. (1964). Approaching the unconscious. In C. G. Jung (Ed.), *Man and his symbols* (pp. 3–94). New York: Dell.

Kagan, J. (1989). Temperamental contributions to social behavior. *American Psychologist, 44,* 668–674.

Kagan, J. (2003). Biology, context, and developmental inquiry. *Annual Review of Psychology, 54,* 1–23.

Kagan, J., & Moss, H. A. (1962). *Birth to maturity.* New York: Wiley.

Kagan, J., & Snidman, N. (1991a). Infant predictors of inhibited and uninhibited profiles. *Psychological Science, 2,* 40–44.

Kagan, J., & Snidman, N. (1991b). Temperamental factors in human development. *American Psychologist, 46,* 856–862.

Kagan, J., & Snidman, N. (2004). *The long shadow of temperament.* Cambridge, MA: Harvard University Press.

Kahn, J. H., & Garrison, A. M. (2009). Emotional self-disclosure and emotional avoidance: Relations with symptoms of depression and anxiety. *Journal of Counseling Psychology, 56,* 573–584.

Kahn, J. H., & Hessling, R. M. (2001). Measuring the tendency to conceal versus disclose psychological distress. *Journal of Social and Clinical Psychology, 20,* 41–65.

Kahlenberg, S. G., & Hein, M. M. (2010). Progression on Nickelodeon? Gender-role stereotypes in toy commercials. *Sex Roles, 62,* 830–847.

Kalechstein, A. D., & Nowicki, S. (1997). A meta-analytic examination of the relationship between control expectancies and academic achievement: An 11-yr. follow-up to Findley and Cooper. *Genetic,*

Social and General Psychology Monographs, 123, 27–56.

Kallio, S., & Revonsuo, A. (2003). Hypnotic phenomena and altered states of consciousness: A multilevel framework of description and explanation. *Contemporary Hypnosis, 20,* 111–164.

Kallio, S., & Revonsuo, A. (2005). Altering the state of the altered state debate: Reply to commentaries. *Contemporary Hypnosis, 20,* 46–55.

Kamen-Siegel, L., Rodin, J., Seligman, M. E. P., & Dwyer, J. (1991). Explanatory style and cell-mediated immunity in elderly men and women. *Health Psychology, 10,* 229–235.

Kandler, C., Bleidorn, W., Riemann, R., Angleitner, A., & Spinath, F. M. (2011). The genetic links between the Big Five personality traits and general interest domains. *Personality and Social Psychology Bulletin, 37,* 1633–1643.

Kandler, C., Bleidorn, W., Riemann, R., Spinath, F. M., Thiel, W., & Angleitner, A. (2010). Sources of cumulative continuity in personality: A longitudinal multiple-rater twin study. *Journal of Personality and Social Psychology, 98,* 995–1008.

Kandler, C., Riemann, R., & Algleitner, A. (2013). Patterns and sources of continuity and change of energetic and temporal aspects of temperament in adulthood: A longitudinal twin study of self- and peer reports. *Developmental Psychology, 49,* 1739–1753.

Kandler, C., Riemann, R., Spinath, F. M., & Angleitner, A. (2010). Sources of variance in personality facets: A multiple-rater twin study of self-peer, peer-peer, and self-self (dis)agreement. *Journal of Personality, 78,* 1565–1594.

Kang, S.-M., Shaver, P. R., Sue, S., Min, K.-H., & Jing, H. (2003). Culture-specific patterns in the prediction of life satisfaction: Roles of emotion, relationship quality, and self-esteem. *Personality and Social Psychology Bulletin, 29,* 1596–1608.

Kaplan, A., & Maehr, M. L. (2007). The contributions and prospects of goal orientation theory. *Educational Psychology Review, 19,* 141–184.

Kaplan, G. D., & Cowles, A. (1978). Health locus of control and health value in the prediction of smoking cessation. *Health Education Monographs, 6,* 129–137.

Kappe, R., & van der Flier, H. (2010). Using multiple and specific criteria to assess the predictive validity of the Big Five personality factors on academic performance. *Journal of Research in Personality, 44,* 142–145.

Kasen, S., Chen, H., Sneed, J., Crawford, T., & Cohen, P. (2006). Social role and birth cohort influences on gender-linked personality traits in women: A 20-year longitudinal analysis. *Journal of Personality and Social Psychology, 91,* 944–958.

Kashdan, T. B., & Roberts, J. E. (2006). Affective outcomes in superficial and intimate interactions: Roles of social anxiety and curiosity. *Journal of Research in Personality, 40,* 140–167.

Kato, T. (2012). Development of the Coping Flexibility Scale: Evidence for the coping flexibility hypothesis. *Journal of Counseling Psychology, 59,* 262–273.

Katz, I. M., & Campbell, J. D. (1994). Ambivalence over emotional expression and well-being: Nomothetic and idiographic tests of the stress-buffering hypothesis. *Journal of Personality and Social Psychology, 67,* 513–524.

Kawachi, I., Sparrow, D., Spiro, A., Vokonas, P., & Weiss, S. T. (1996). A prospective study of anger and coronary heart disease: The Normative Aging Study. *Circulation, 94,* 2090–2095.

Keelan, J. P. R., Dion, K. L., & Dion, K. K. (1994). Attachment style and heterosexual relationships among young adults: A short-term panel study. *Journal of Social and Personal Relationships, 11,* 201–214.

Keller, J., & Bless, H. (2008). Flow and regulatory compatibility: An experimental approach to the flow model of intrinsic motivation. *Personality and Social Psychology Bulletin, 34,* 196–209.

Kelley, J. M., & Malouf, R. A. (2013). Blind dates and mate preferences: An analysis of newspaper match-making columns. *Evolutionary Psychology, 11,* 1–8.

Kelley, N. J., Hortensius, R., & Harmon-Jones, E. (2013). When anger leads to rumination: Induction of relative right frontal cortical activity with transcranial direct current stimulation increases anger-related rumination. *Psychological Science, 24,* 475–481.

Kelly, A. E. (1998). Clients' secret keeping in outpatient therapy. *Journal of Counseling Psychology, 45,* 50–57.

Kelly, A. E., & Archer, J. A. (1995). Self-concealment and attitudes toward counseling in university students. *Journal of Counseling Psychology, 42,* 40–46.

Kelly, A. E., Klusas, J. A., von Weiss, R. T., & Kenny, C. (2001). What is it about revealing secrets that is beneficial? *Personality and Social Psychology Bulletin, 27,* 651–665.

Kelly, A. E., & McKillop, K. J. (1996). Consequences of revealing personal secrets. *Psychological Bulletin, 120,* 450–465.

Kelly, G. A. (1955). *The psychology of personal constructs.* New York: Norton.

Kelly, G. A. (1969). *Clinical psychology and personality: The selected papers of George Kelly.* New York: Wiley.

Kendzierski, D. (1988). Self-schemata and exercise. *Basic and Applied Social Psychology, 9,* 45–61.

Kendzierski, D. (1990). Exercise self-schemata: Cognitive and behavioral correlates. *Health Psychology, 9,* 69–82.

Kenrick, D. T., Keefe, R. C., Gabrielidis, C., & Cornelius, J. S. (1996). Adolescents' age preferences for dating partners: Support for an evolutionary model of life-history strategies. *Child Development, 67,* 1499–1511.

Kent, G. (1997). Dental phobias. In G. C. Davey (Ed.), *Phobias: A*

handbook of theory, research and treatment (pp. 107–127). Chichester, England: Wiley.

Keogh, B. K. (1986). Temperament and schooling: Meaning of "Goodness of Fit"? In J. V. Lerner & R. M. Lerner (Eds.), *Temperament and social interaction during infancy and childhood* (pp. 89–108). San Francisco: Jossey-Bass.

Keogh, B. K. (1989). Applying temperament research to schools. In G. A. Kohnstamm, J. E. Bates, & M. K. Rothbart (Eds.), *Temperament in childhood* (pp. 437–450). New York: Wiley.

Keogh, B. K. (2003). *Temperament in the classroom: Understanding individual differences.* Baltimore, MD: Paul H. Brookes.

Kernis, M. H., Brockner, J., & Frankel, B. S. (1989). Self-esteem and reactions to failure: The mediating role of overgeneralization. *Journal of Personality and Social Psychology, 57,* 707–714.

Kesebir, S., & Oishi, S. (2010). A spontaneous self-reference effect in memory: Why some birthdays are harder to remember than others. *Psychological Science, 21,* 1525–1531.

Kihlstrom, J. F. (1985). Hypnosis. *Annual Review of Psychology, 36,* 385–418.

Kihlstrom, J. F. (1998). Dissociations and dissociation theory in hypnosis: Comment on Kirsch and Lynn (1998). *Psychological Bulletin, 123,* 186–191.

Kihlstrom, J. F. (2005). Is hypnosis an altered state of consciousness or what? *Contemporary Hypnosis, 22,* 34–38.

King, L. A. (1998). Ambivalence over emotional expression and reading emotions in situations and faces. *Journal of Personality and Social Psychology, 74,* 753–762.

King, L. A. (2001). The health benefits of writing about life goals. *Personality and Social Psychology Bulletin, 27,* 798–807.

King, L. A., & Emmons, R. A. (1990). Conflict over emotional expression: Psychological and physical correlates. *Journal of Personality*

and Social Psychology, 58, 864–877.

King, L. A., & Miner, K. N. (2000). Writing about the perceived benefits of traumatic events: Implications for physical health. *Personality and Social Psychology Bulletin, 26,* 220–230.

Kirkpatrick, L. A., & Davis, K. E. (1994). Attachment style, gender, and relationship stability: A longitudinal analysis. *Journal of Personality and Social Psychology, 66,* 502–512.

Kirsch, I. (1996). Hypnotic enhancement of cognitive-behavioral weight loss treatments—another meta-reanalysis. *Journal of Consulting and Clinical Psychology, 64,* 517–519.

Kirsch, I. (2000). The response set theory of hypnosis. *American Journal of Clinical Hypnosis, 42,* 274–292.

Kirsch, I. (2005). Empirical resolutions of the altered state debate. *Contemporary Hypnosis, 22,* 18–23.

Kirsch, I., & Council, J. R. (1992). Situational and personality correlates of hypnotic responsiveness. In E. Fromm & M. R. Nash (Eds.), *Contemporary hypnosis research* (pp. 267–291). New York: Guilford.

Kirsch, I., & Lynn, J. L. (1998). Dissociation theories of hypnosis. *Psychological Bulletin, 123,* 100–115.

Kirsch, I., & Lynn, S. J. (1995). The altered state of hypnosis: Changes in the theoretical landscape. *American Psychologist, 50,* 846–858.

Kirschenbaum, H. (1979). *On becoming Carl Rogers.* New York: Delacorte.

Kitayama, S., & Markus, H. R. (Eds.). (1994). *Emotion and culture: Empirical studies of mutual influence.* Washington, DC: American Psychological Association.

Kivimaki, M., Vahtera, J., Elovainio, M., Helenius, H., Singh-Manoux, A., & Pentti, J. (2005). Optimism and pessimism as predictors of change in health after death or onset of severe illness in family. *Health Psychology, 24,* 413–421.

Kleiman, E. M., & Riskind, J. H. (2012). Cognitive vulnerability to comorbidity: Looming cognitive style and depressive cognitive style as synergistic predictors of anxiety and depression symptoms. *Journal of Behavior Therapy and Experimental Psychiatry, 43,* 1109–1114.

Klein, D. C., & Seligman, M. E. P. (1976). Reversal of performance deficits and perceptual deficits in learned helplessness and depression. *Journal of Abnormal Psychology, 85,* 11–26.

Klein, S. B. (2012). Self, memory, and the self-reference effect: An examination of conceptual and methodological issues. *Personality and Social Psychology Review, 16,* 283–300.

Kleinke, C. L., & Kahn, M. L. (1980). Perceptions of self-disclosers: Effects of sex and physical attractiveness. *Journal of Personality, 48,* 190–205.

Klinesmith, J., Kasser, T., & McAndrew, F. T. (2006). Guns, testosterone, and aggression: An experimental test of a mediational hypothesis. *Psychological Science, 17,* 568–572.

Klinger, B. I. (1970). Effect of peer model responsiveness and length of induction procedure on hypnotic responsiveness. *Journal of Abnormal Psychology, 75,* 15–18.

Klohnen, E. C., & Bera, S. (1998). Behavioral and experiential patterns of avoidantly and securely attached women across adulthood: A 31-year longitudinal perspective. *Journal of Personality and Social Psychology, 74,* 211–223.

Klonowicz, T. (2001). Discontented people: Reactivity and locus of control as determinants of subjective well-being. *European Journal of Personality, 15,* 29–47.

Klump, K. L., Suisman, J. L., Burt, S. A., McGue, M., & Iacono, W. G. (2009). Genetic and environmental influences on disordered eating: An adoption study. *Journal of Abnormal Psychology, 118,* 797–805.

Knee, C. R., Canevello, A., Bush, A. L., & Cook, A. (2008). Relationship-contingent self-esteem and the ups and downs of romantic relationships. *Journal of Personality and Social Psychology, 95,* 608–627.

Knowles, E. D., Wearing, J. R., & Campos, B. (2011). Culture and the health benefits of expressive writing. *Social Psychological and Personality Science, 2,* 408–415.

Knowles, E. S., & Nathan, K. T. (1997). Acquiescent responding in self-reports: Cognitive style or social concern? *Journal of Research in Personality, 31,* 293–301.

Kobasa, S. C. (1979). Stressful life events, personality, and health: An inquiry into hardiness. *Journal of Personality and Social Psychology, 37,* 1–11.

Konecni, V. J., & Doob, A. N. (1972). Catharsis through displacement of aggression. *Journal of Personality and Social Psychology, 23,* 379–387.

Kop, W. J., Berman, D. S., Gransar, H., Wong, N. D., Miranda-Peats, R., White, M. D. et al. (2005). Social network and coronary artery calcification in asymptomatic individuals. *Psychosomatic Medicine, 67,* 343–352.

Koppitz, E. M. (1968). *Psychological evaluation of children's human figure drawings.* New York: Grune & Stratton.

Korabik, K. (1982). Sex-role orientation and impressions: A comparison of differing genders and sex roles. *Personality and Social Psychology Bulletin, 8,* 25–30.

Koriat, A., Melkman, R., Averill, J. R., & Lazarus, R. S. (1972). The self-control of emotional reactions to a stressful film. *Journal of Personality, 40,* 601–619.

Korn, J. H., Davis, R., & Davis, S. F. (1991). Historians' and chairpersons' judgments of eminence among psychologists. *American Psychologist, 46,* 789–792.

Kotov, R., Gamez, W., Schmidt, F., & Watson, D. (2010). Linking "big" personality traits to anxiety, depressive, and substance use disorders: A meta-analysis. *Psychological Bulletin, 136,* 768–821.

Krahe, B., Moller, I., Huesmann, L. R., Kirwil, L., Felber, J., & Berger, A. (2011). Desensitization to media violence: Links with habitual media violence exposure, aggressive cognitions, and aggressive behavior. *Journal of Personality and Social Psychology, 100,* 630–646.

Krantz, D. S., & McCeney, M. K. (2002). Effects of psychological and social factors on organic disease: A critical assessment of research on coronary heart disease. *Annual Review of Psychology, 53,* 341–369.

Kring, A. M., & Gordon, A. H. (1998). Sex differences in emotion: Expression, experience, and physiology. *Journal of Personality and Social Psychology, 74,* 686–703.

Kring, A. M., Smith, D. A., & Neale, J. M. (1994). Individual differences in dispositional expressiveness: Development and validation of the Emotional Expressivity Scale. *Journal of Personality and Social Psychology, 66,* 934–949.

Krokoff, L. J. (1990). Job distress is no laughing matter in marriage, or is it? *Journal of Social and Personal Relationships, 8,* 5–25.

Krueger, R. F., & Johnson, W. (2008). Behavioral genetics and personality: A new look at the integration of nature and nurture. In L. A. Pervin, O. P. John, & R. W. Robins (Eds.), *Handbook of personality: Theory and research* (3rd ed., pp. 287–310). New York: Guilford.

Krueger, R. F., South, S., Johnson, W., & Iacono, W. (2008). The heritability of personality is not always 50%: Gene-environment interactions and correlations between personality and parenting. *Journal of Personality, 76,* 1485–1521.

Kuebli, J., Butler, S., & Fivush, R. (1995). Mother-child talk about past emotions: Relations of maternal language and child gender over time. *Cognition and Emotion, 9,* 265–283.

Kuhlman, T. L. (1985). A study of salience and motivational theories of humor. *Journal of Personality and Social Psychology, 49,* 281–286.

Kuiper, N. A., & Martin, R. A. (1998). Laughter and stress in daily life: Relation to positive and negative affect. *Motivation and Emotion, 22*, 133–143.

Kuiper, N. A., McKenzie, S. D., & Belanger, K. A. (1995). Cognitive appraisal and individual differences in sense of humor: Motivational and affective implications. *Personality and Individual Differences, 19*, 359–372.

Kulick, J. A., & Harackiewicz, J. (1979). Opposite-sex interpersonal attraction as a function of the sex roles of the perceiver and the perceived. *Sex Roles, 5*, 443–452.

Kuppens, P., Realo, A., & Diener, E. (2008). The role of positive and negative emotions in life satisfaction judgment across nations. *Journal of Personality and Social Psychology, 95*, 66–75.

Kurdek, L. A., & Schmitt, J. P. (1986). Interaction of sex role self-concept with relationship quality and relationship beliefs in married, heterosexual cohabiting, gay and lesbian couples. *Journal of Personality and Social Psychology, 51*, 365–370.

Kwon, P. (2000). Hope and dysphoria: The moderating role of defense mechanisms. *Journal of Personality, 68*, 199–223.

LaFraniere, S. (2009, June 13). An all-nighter? For this test, some Chinese cram all year. *New York Times*, p. A4.

LaGasse, L., Gruber, C., & Lipsitt, L. P. (1989). The infantile expression of activity in relation to later assessments. In J. S. Reznick (Ed.), *Perspectives on behavioral inhibition* (pp. 159–176). Chicago: University of Chicago Press.

Lahey, B. B. (2009). Public health significance of neuroticism. *American Psychologist, 64*, 241–256.

Lamers, S. M. A., Westerhof, G. J., Kovacs, V., & Bohlmeijer, E. T. (2012). Differential relationships in the association of the Big Five personality traits with positive mental health and psychopathology. *Journal of Research in Personality, 46*, 517–524.

Lamke, L. K., & Bell, N. J. (1982). Sex-role orientation and relationship development in same-sex dyads. *Journal of Research in Personality, 16*, 343–354.

Landau, S. F. (1988). Violent crime and its relation to subjective social stress indicators: The case of Israel. *Aggressive Behavior, 14*, 337–362.

Landau, S. F., & Raveh, A. (1987). Stress factors, social support, and violence in Israeli society: A quantitative analysis. *Aggressive Behavior, 13*, 67–85.

Landy, F. J., Shankster, L. J., & Kohler, S. S. (1994). Personnel selection and placement. *Annual Review of Psychology, 45*, 261–296.

Langens, T. A., & Schuler, J. (2007). Effects of written emotional expression: The role of positive expectancies. *Health Psychology, 26*, 174–182.

Langer, E. J., & Rodin, J. (1976). The effects of choice and enhanced personal responsibility for the aged: A field experiment in an institutional setting. *Journal of Personality and Social Psychology, 34*, 191–198.

Lankton, S. R., & Matthews, W. J. (2010). An Ericksonian model of clinical hypnosis. In S. J. Lynn, J. W. Rhue, & I. Kirsch (Eds.), *Handbook of clinical hypnosis* (2nd ed., pp. 209–237). Washington, DC: American Psychological Association.

Larsen, J. T., & McGraw, A. P. (2011). Further evidence for mixed emotions. *Journal of Personality and Social Psychology, 100*, 1095–1110.

Larsen, R. J. (1987). The stability of mood variability: A spectral analytic approach to daily mood assessments. *Journal of Personality and Social Psychology, 52*, 1195–1204.

Larsen, R. J., Billings, D. W., & Cutler, S. E. (1996). Individual differences in informational style: Associations with dispositional affect intensity. *Journal of Personality, 64*, 185–207.

Larsen, R. J., & Diener, E. (1987). Affect intensity as an individual difference characteristic: A review. *Journal of Research in Personality, 21*, 1–39.

Larsen, R. J., Diener, E., & Cropanzano, R. S. (1987). Cognitive operations associated with individual differences in affect intensity. *Journal of Personality and Social Psychology, 53*, 767–774.

Larsen, R. J., Diener, E., & Emmons, R. A. (1985). An evaluation of subjective well-being measures. *Social Indicators Research, 17*, 1–17.

Larsen, R. J., Diener, E., & Emmons, R. A. (1986). Affect intensity and reactions to daily life events. *Journal of Personality and Social Psychology, 51*, 803–814.

Larsen, R. J., & Kasimatis, M. (1990). Individual differences in entrainment of mood to the weekly calendar. *Journal of Personality and Social Psychology, 58*, 164–171.

Larsen, R. J., & Ketelaar, T. (1989). Extraversion, neuroticism and susceptibility to positive and negative mood induction procedures. *Personality and Individual Differences, 10*, 1221–1228.

Larson, R. W. (1990). The solitary side of life: An examination of the time people spend alone from childhood to old age. *Developmental Review, 10*, 155–183.

Larson, R. W. (1997). The emergence of solitude as a constructive domain of experience in early adolescence. *Child Development, 68*, 80–93.

Larson, R. W., & Csikszentmihalyi, M. (1980). The significance of solitude in adolescents' development. *Journal of Current Adolescent Medicine, 2*, 33–40.

Larson, R. W., Csikszentmihalyi, M., & Graef, R. (1982). Time alone in daily experience: Loneliness or renewal? In L. A. Peplau & D. Perlman (Eds.), *Loneliness: A sourcebook of current theory, research and therapy* (pp. 40–53). New York: Wiley.

Larson, R. W., & Johnson, C. (1985). Bulimia: Disturbed patterns of solitude. *Addictive Behaviors, 10*, 281–290.

Larson, R. W., & Lee, M. (1996). The capacity to be alone as a stress buffer. *Journal of Social Psychology, 136,* 5–16.

Larson, R. W., & Richards, M. H. (1991). Daily companionship in late childhood and early adolescence: Changing developmental contexts. *Child Development, 62,* 284–300.

Larson, R. W., Zuzanek, J., & Mannell, R. (1985). Being alone versus being with people: Disengagement in the daily experience of older adults. *Journal of Gerontology, 40,* 375–381.

Lau, J. Y. F., & Eley, T. C. (2008). Attributional style as a risk marker of genetic effects for adolescent depressive symptoms. *Journal of Abnormal Psychology, 117,* 849–859.

Lau, R. R., Hartman, K. A., & Ware, J. E. (1986). Health as value: Methodological and theoretical considerations. *Health Psychology, 5,* 25–43.

Lauder, W., Mummery, K., Jones, M., & Caperchione, C. (2006). A comparison of health behaviours in lonely and non-lonely populations. *Psychology, Health, & Medicine, 11,* 233–245.

Laurence, J.-R., Beaulieu-Prevost, D., & du Chene, T. (2008). Measuring and understanding individual differences in hypnotizability. In M. R. Nash & A. J. Barnier (Eds.), *The oxford handbook of hypnosis: Theory, research and practice* (pp. 225–253). New York: Oxford University Press.

Laurenceau, J.-P., Feldman Barrett, L., & Pietromonaco, P. R. (1998). Intimacy as an interpersonal process: The importance of self-disclosure, partner disclosure, and perceived partner responsiveness in interpersonal exchanges. *Journal of Personality and Social Psychology, 74,* 1238–1251.

Laurent, S. M., & Hodges, S. D. (2009). Gender roles and empathic accuracy: The role of communion in reading minds. *Sex Roles, 60,* 387–398.

Lavee, Y., & Ben-Ari, A. (2004). Emotional expressiveness and neuroticism: Do they predict marital quality? *Journal of Family Psychology, 18,* 620–627.

Lax, E. (1991). *Woody Allen: A biography.* New York: Knopf.

Lazarus, R. (1968). Emotions and adaptation. In W. J. Arnold (Ed.), *Nebraska symposium on motivation* (pp. 175–266). Lincoln: University of Nebraska Press.

Lazarus, R. S. (1974). Cognitive and coping processes in emotion. In B. Weiner (Ed.), *Cognitive views of human motivation* (pp. 21–32). New York: Academic Press.

Lazarus, R. S. (2006). Emotions and interpersonal relationships: Toward a person-centered conceptualization of emotions and coping. *Journal of Personality, 74,* 9–46.

Leak, G. K. (1974). Effects of hostility arousal and aggressive humor on catharsis and humor preference. *Journal of Personality and Social Psychology, 30,* 736–740.

Leary, M. R. (1983a). Social anxiousness: The construct and its measurement. *Journal of Personality Assessment, 47,* 66–75.

Leary, M. R. (1983b). *Understanding social anxiety: Social, personality, and clinical perspectives.* Beverly Hills, CA: Sage.

Leary, M. R. (1986). The impact of interactional impediments on social anxiety and self-presentation. *Journal of Experimental Social Psychology, 22,* 122–135.

Leary, M. R., & Atherton, S. C. (1986). Self-efficacy, social anxiety, and inhibition in interpersonal encounters. *Journal of Social and Clinical Psychology, 4,* 256–267.

Leary, M. R., Herbst, K. C., & McCrary, F. (2003). Finding pleasure in solitary activities: Desire for aloneness or disinterest in social contact? *Personality and Individual Differences, 35,* 59–68.

Leary, M. R., Knight, P. D., & Johnson, K. A. (1987). Social anxiety and dyadic conversation: A verbal response analysis. *Journal of Social and Clinical Psychology, 5,* 34–50.

Leary, M. R., & Kowalski, R. M. (1995). *Social anxiety.* New York: Guilford.

Leary, M. R., & Meadows, S. (1991). Predictors, elicitors, and concomitants of social blushing. *Journal of Personality and Social Psychology, 60,* 254–262.

Ledley, D. R., & Heimberg, R. G. (2006). Cognitive vulnerability to social anxiety. *Journal of social and Clinical Psychology, 25,* 755–778.

Lee, A., Hankin, B. L., & Mermelstein, R. J. (2010). Perceived social competence, negative social interactions, and negative cognitive style predict depressive symptoms during adolescence. *Journal of Clinical Child & Adolescent Psychology, 39,* 603–615.

Lee, Y.-T., & Seligman, M. E. P. (1997). Are Americans more optimistic than the Chinese? *Personality and Social Psychology Bulletin, 23,* 32–40.

Leedham, B., Meyerowitz, B. E., Muirhead, J., & Frist, W. H. (1995). Positive expectations predict health after heart transplant. *Health Psychology, 14,* 74–79.

Lefcourt, H. M. (1982). *Locus of control: Current trends in theory and research* (2nd ed.). Hillsdale, NJ: Erlbaum.

Lefcourt, H. M., Davidson, K., Prkachin, K. M., & Mills, D. E. (1997). Humor as a stress moderator in the prediction of blood pressure obtained during five stressful tasks. *Journal of Research in Personality, 31,* 523–542.

Lefkowitz, E. S., & Zeldow, P. B. (2006). Masculinity and femininity predict optimal mental health: A belated test of the androgyny hypothesis. *Journal of Personality Assessment, 87,* 95–101.

Lefkowitz, M. M., Eron, L. D., Walder, L. O., & Huesmann, L. R. (1977). *Growing up to be violent: A longitudinal study of the development of aggression.* New York: Pergamon.

Leichsenring, F. (2007). Psychodynamic psychotherapy: A systematic review of techniques, indications and empirical evidence. *Psychology and Psychotherapy: Theory, Research and Practice, 80,* 217–228.

Leichsenring, F., & Rabung, S. (2008). Effectiveness of long-term psychodynamic psychotherapy: A meta-analysis. *Journal of the American Medical Association, 300,* 1551–1565.

Lenney, E. (1991). Sex roles: The measurement of masculinity, femininity, and androgyny. In J. P. Robinson, P. R. Shaver, & L. S. Wrightsman (Eds.), *Measures of personality and social psychological attitudes* (pp. 573–660). San Diego, CA: Academic Press.

Lent, R. W., & Lopez, F. G. (2002). Cognitive ties that bind: A tripartite view of efficacy beliefs in growth-promoting relationships. *Journal of Social and Clinical Psychology, 21,* 256–286.

Leon, G. R., Gillum, B., Gillum, R., & Gouze, M. (1979). Personality stability and change over a 30-year period—middle age to old age. *Journal of Consulting and Clinical Psychology, 47,* 517–524.

Lerner, P., & Lerner, H. (1990). Rorschach measures of psychoanalytic theories of defense. In J. N. Butcher & C. D. Spielberger (Eds.), *Advances in personality assessment* (Vol. 8, pp. 121–160). Hillsdale, NJ: Erlbaum.

Leue, A., & Beauducel, A. (2011). The PANAS structure revisited: On the validity of a bifactor model in community and forensic samples. *Psychological Assessment, 23,* 215–225.

Levin, I., & Stokes, J. P. (1986). An examination of the relation of individual difference variables to loneliness. *Journal of Personality, 54,* 717–733.

Levine, S. C., Ratliff, K. R., Huttenlocher, J., & Cannon, J. (2012). Early puzzle play: A predictor of preschoolers' spatial transformation skill. *Developmental Psychology, 48,* 530–542.

Levy, K. N., Blatt, S. J., & Shaver, P. R. (1998). Attachment styles and parental representations. *Journal of Personality and Social Psychology, 74,* 407–419.

Levy, K. N., & Kelly, K. M. (2010). Sex differences in jealousy: A contribution from attachment theory. *Psychological Science, 21,* 168–173.

Lewin, K. (1938). *The conceptual representation and measurement of psychological forces.* Durham, NC: Duke University Press.

Lewinsohn, P. M., Joiner, T. E., & Rohde, P. (2001). Evaluation of cognitive diathesis-stress models in predicting major depressive disorder in adolescents. *Journal of Abnormal Psychology, 110,* 203–215.

Li, H., Zeigler-Hill, V., Luo, J., Yang, J., & Zhang, Q. (2012). Self-esteem modulates attentional responses to rejection: Evidence from event-related brain potentials. *Journal of Research in Personality, 46,* 459–464.

Lim, S.-L., & Kim, J.-H. (2005). Cognitive processing of emotional information in depression, panic, and somatoform disorder. *Journal of Abnormal Psychology, 114,* 50–61.

Linde, J. A., Rothman, A. J., Baldwin, A. S., & Jeffery, R. W. (2006). The impact of self-efficacy on behavior change and weight change among overweight participants in a weight loss trial. *Health Psychology, 25,* 282–291.

Lindsay, J. L., & Anderson, C. A. (2000). From antecedent conditions to violent actions: A general affective aggression model. *Personality and Social Psychology Bulletin, 26,* 533–547.

Lips, H. M. (2004). The gender gap in possible selves: Divergence of academic self-views among high school and university students. *Sex Roles, 50,* 357–371.

Littig, L. W., & Yeracaris, C. A. (1965). Achievement motivation and intergenerational occupational mobility. *Journal of Personality and Social Psychology, 1,* 386–389.

Loehlin, J. C. (1992). *Genes and the environment in personality development.* Newbury Park, CA: Sage.

Loehlin, J. C. (2012). How general across inventories is a general factor of personality? *Journal of Research in Personality, 46,* 258–263.

Loehlin, J. C., McCrae, R. R., & Costa, P. T. (1998). Heritabilities of common and measure-specific components of the Big Five personality factors. *Journal of Research in Personality, 32,* 431–453.

Loehlin, J. C., Willerman, L., & Horn, J. M. (1982). Personality resemblances between unwed mothers and their adopted-away offspring. *Journal of Personality and Social Psychology, 42,* 1089–1099.

Loehlin, J. C., Willerman, L., & Horn, J. M. (1987). Personality resemblance in adoptive families: A 10-year follow-up. *Journal of Personality and Social Psychology, 53,* 961–969.

Long, B. C., & Sangster, J. I. (1993). Dispositional optimism/pessimism and coping strategies: Predictors of psychosocial adjustment of rheumatoid and osteoarthritis patients. *Journal of Applied Social Psychology, 23,* 1069–1091.

Long, C. R., & Averill, J. R. (2003). Solitude: An exploration of benefits of being alone. *Journal for the Theory of Social Behaviour, 33,* 21–44.

Long, C. R., Seburn, M., Averill, J. R., & More, T. A. (2003). Solitude experiences: Varieties, settings, and individual differences. *Personality and Social Psychology Bulletin, 29,* 578–583.

Lopez, S. J. (Ed.). (2009). *The encyclopedia of positive psychology.* New York: Wiley-Blackwell.

Lord, C. G. (1980). Schemas and images as memory aids: Two modes of processing social information. *Journal of Personality and Social Psychology, 38,* 257–269.

Lucas, R. E., & Baird, B. M. (2004). Extraversion and emotional reactivity. *Journal of Personality and Social Psychology, 86,* 473–485.

Lucas, R. E., & Diener, E. (2001). Understanding extraverts' enjoyment of social situations: The importance of pleasantness. *Journal of Personality and Social Psychology, 81,* 343–356.

Lucas, R. E., Diener, E., Grob, A., Suh, E. M., & Shao, L. (2000). Cross-cultural evidence for the fundamental features of extraversion. *Journal of Personality and Social Psychology, 79*, 452–468.

Lucas, R. E., Le, K., & Dyrenforth, P. S. (2008). Explaining the extraversion/positive affect relation: Sociability cannot account for extraverts' greater happiness. *Journal of Personality, 76*, 385–414.

Luhtanen, R. K., & Crocker, J. (2005). Alcohol use in college students: Effects of level of self-esteem, narcissism, and contingencies of self-worth. *Psychology of Addictive Behaviors, 19*, 99–103.

Lyness, S. A. (1993). Predictors of differences between type A and B individuals in heart rate and blood pressure reactivity. *Psychological Bulletin, 114*, 266–295.

Lynn, R., & Martin, T. (1995). National differences for thirty-seven nations in extraversion, neuroticism, psychoticism and economic, demographic and other correlates. *Personality and Individual Differences, 19*, 403–406.

Lynn, S. J., Fassler, O., & Knox, J. (2005). Hypnosis and the altered state debate: Something more or nothing more? *Contemporary Hypnosis, 22*, 39–45.

Lynn, S. J., Kirsch, I., Knox, J., Fassler, O., & Lilienfeld, S. O. (2007). Hypnosis and neuroscience: Implications for the altered state debate. In G. A. Jamieson (Ed.), *Hypnosis and conscious states: The cognitive neuroscience perspective* (pp. 145–165). New York: Oxford University Press.

Lynn, S. J., & Sherman, S. J. (2000). The clinical importance of sociocognitive models of hypnosis: Response set theory and Milton Erickson's strategic interventions. *American Journal of Clinical Hypnosis, 42*, 294–315.

Lynn, S. J., Weekes, J. R., Neufeld, V., Zivney, O., Brentar, J., & Weiss, F. (1991). Interpersonal climate and hypnotizability level: Effects on hypnotic performance, rapport, and archaic involvement. *Journal*

of *Personality and Social Psychology, 60*, 739–743.

Lytton, H. (1977). Do parents create, or respond to, differences in twins? *Developmental Psychology, 13*, 456–459.

MacDonald, D. A. (2000). Spirituality: Description, measurement, and relation to the five factor model of personality. *Journal of Personality, 68*, 153–197.

Mackie, M. (1983). The domestication of self: Gender comparisons of self-imagery and self-esteem. *Social Psychology Quarterly, 46*, 343–350.

Mackinnon, S. P., Nosko, P., Pratt, M. W., & Norris, J. E. (2011). Intimacy in young adults' narratives of romance and friendship predicts Eriksonian generativity: A mixed method analysis. *Journal of Personality, 79*, 587–617.

Maddux, J. E., Norton, L. W., & Leary, M. R. (1988). Cognitive components of social anxiety: An investigation of the integration of self-presentation theory and self-efficacy theory. *Journal of social and Clinical Psychology, 6*, 180–190.

Magnus, K., Diener, E., Fujita, F., & Pavot, W. (1993). Extraversion and neuroticism as predictors of objective life events: A longitudinal analysis. *Journal of Personality and Social Psychology, 65*, 1046–1053.

Mahalik, J. R., Cournoyer, R. J., DeFranc, W., Cherry, M., & Napolitano, J. M. (1998). Men's gender role conflict and use of psychological defenses. *Journal of Counseling Psychology, 45*, 247–255.

Mahoney, M. J., & Arnkoff, D. B. (1979). Self-management. In O. F. Pomerleau & J. P. Brady (Eds.), *Behavioral medicine: Theory and practice* (pp. 75–96). Baltimore: Williams & Wilkins.

Maier, S. F. (2001). Exposure to the stressor environment prevents the temporal dissipation of behavioral depression/learned helplessness. *Biological Psychiatry, 49*, 763–773.

Maier, S. F., & Watkins, L. R. (2005). Stressor controllability and learned helplessness: The roles of dorsal raphe nucleus, serotonin, and corticotropin-releasing factor. *Neuroscience & Biobehavioral Reviews, 29*, 829–841.

Major, B., Carnevale, P. J. D., & Deaux, K. (1981). A different perspective on androgyny: Evaluations of masculine and feminine personality characteristics. *Journal of Personality and Social Psychology, 41*, 988–1001.

Mallon, S. D., Kingsley, D., Affleck, G., & Tennen, H. (1998). Methodological trends in *Journal of Personality*: 1970-1995. *Journal of Personality, 66*, 671–685.

Malouff, J. M., Thorsteinsson, E. B., Schutte, N. S., Bhullar, N., & Rooke, S. E. (2010). The Five-Factor Model of personality and relationship satisfaction of intimate partners: A meta-analysis. *Journal of Research in Personality, 44*, 124–127.

Mansfield, E. D., & McAdams, D. P. (1996). Generativity and themes of agency and communion in adult autobiography. *Personality and Social Psychology Bulletin, 22*, 721–731.

Many Americans fed up with diet advice. (2001, January 2). *New York Times*, p. F10.

Marcus-Newhall, A., Pedersen, W. C., Carlson, M., & Miller, N. (2000). Displaced aggression is alive and well: A meta-analytic review. *Journal of Personality and Social Psychology, 78*, 670–689.

Markey, P. M., Markey, C. N., Tinsley, B. J., & Ericksen, A. J. (2002). A preliminary validation of preadolescents' self-reports using the Five-Factor Model of personality. *Journal of Research in Personality, 36*, 173–181.

Marks, G., Richardson, J. L., Graham, J. W., & Levine, A. (1986). Role of health locus of control beliefs and expectations of treatment efficacy in adjustment to cancer. *Journal of Personality and Social Psychology, 51*, 443–450.

Markus, H. (1977). Self-schemata and processing information

about the self. *Journal of Personality and Social Psychology, 35,* 63–78.

Markus, H. (1983). Self-knowledge: An expanded view. *Journal of Personality, 51,* 543–565.

Markus, H. R., & Kitayama, S. (1991). Culture and the self: Implications for cognition, emotion, and motivation. *Psychological Review, 98,* 224–253.

Markus, H. R., & Kitayama, S. (1994). A collective fear of the collective: Implications for selves and theories of selves. *Personality and Social Psychology Bulletin, 20,* 568–579.

Markus, H. R., & Kitayama, S. (2010). Cultures and selves: A cycle of mutual constitution. *Perspectives on Psychological Science, 5,* 420–430.

Markus, H. R., & Kunda, Z. (1986). Stability and malleability of the self-concept. *Journal of Personality and Social Psychology, 51,* 858–866.

Markus, H. R., & Nurius, P. (1986). Possible selves. *American Psychologist, 41,* 954–969.

Markus, H. R., & Sentis, K. (1982). The self and social information processing. In J. Suls (Ed.), *Psychological perspectives on the self* (Vol. 1, pp. 41–70). Hillsdale, NJ: Erlbaum.

Markus, H. R., & Smith, J. (1981). The influence of self-schemata on the perception of others. In N. Cantor & J. F. Kihlstrom (Eds.), *Personality, cognition, and social interaction* (pp. 233–262). Hillsdale, NJ: Erlbaum.

Marsh, H. W., Antill, J. K., & Cunningham, J. D. (1987). Masculinity, femininity, and androgyny: Relations to self-esteem and social desirability. *Journal of Personality, 55,* 661–683.

Marsh, H. W., & Byrne, B. M. (1991). Differentiated additive androgyny model: Relations between masculinity, femininity, and multiple dimensions of self-concept. *Journal of Personality and Social Psychology, 61,* 811–828.

Marshall, G. N., Wortman, C. B., Vickers, R. R., Kusulas, J. W., & Hervig, L. K. (1994). The Five-Factor Model of personality as a framework for personality-health research. *Journal of Personality and Social Psychology, 67,* 278–286.

Martin, C. L., Eisenbud, L., & Rose, H. (1995). Children's gender-based reasoning about toys. *Child Development, 66,* 1453–1471.

Martin, R., & Watson, D. (1997). Style of anger expression and its relation to daily experience. *Personality and Social Psychology Bulletin, 23,* 285–294.

Martinez, J. C. (1994). Perceived control and feedback in judgment and memory. *Journal of Research in Personality, 28,* 374–381.

Masi, C. M., Chen, H.-Y., Hawkley, L. C., & Cacioppo, J. T. (2011). A meta-analysis of interventions to reduce loneliness. *Personality and Social Psychology Review, 15,* 219–266.

Maslow, A. H. (1968). *Toward a psychology of being* (2nd ed.). New York: Van Nostrand.

Maslow, A. H. (1970). *Motivation and personality* (2nd ed.). New York: Harper & Row.

Maslow, A. H. (1971). *The farther reaches of human nature.* New York: Viking.

Massachusetts: Court upholds ex-priest's conviction. (2010, January 16). *New York Times.* Retrieved from http:www.nytimes.com/2010/01/16/us/16brfs-COURTU-PHOLDS_BRF.html/

Mather, M., Cacioppo, J. T., & Kanwisher, N. (2013). How fMRI can inform cognitive theories. *Perspectives on Psychological Science, 8,* 108–113.

Mathersul, D., Williams, L. M., Hopkinson, P. J., & Kemp, A. H. (2008). Investigating models of affect: Relationships among EEG alpha asymmetry, depression, and anxiety. *Emotion, 8,* 560–572.

Matthews, K. A., & Haynes, S. G. (1986). Type A behavior pattern and coronary risk: Update and critical evaluation. *American Journal of Epidemiology, 123,* 923–960.

Matto, H. C. (2002). Investigating the validity of the Draw-A-Person: Screening procedure for emotional disturbance: A measurement validation study with high-risk youth. *Personality Assessment, 14,* 221–225.

Mayer, J. D. (2005). A tale of two visions. Can a new view of personality help integrate psychology? *American Psychologist, 60,* 294–307.

Mayer, J. D., & Gaschke, Y. N. (1988). The experience and meta-experience of mood. *Journal of Personality and Social Psychology, 55,* 102–111.

McAdams, D. P. (1993). *Stories we live by: Personal myths and the making of the self.* New York: Morrow.

McAdams, D. P. (2004). Generativity and the narrative ecology of family life. In M. W. Pratt & B. H. Fiese (Eds.), *Family stories and the life course: Across time and generations.* Mahwah, NJ: Erlbaum.

McAdams, D. P. (2008). Personal narratives and the life story. In O. P. John, R. W. Robins, & L. A. Pervin (Eds.), *Handbook of personality* (3rd ed., pp. 242–262). New York: Guilford.

McAdams, D. P., Bauer, J. J., Sakaeda, A. R., Anyidoho, N. A., Machado, M. A., Magrino-Failla, K. et al. (2006). Continuity and change in the life story: A longitudinal study of autobiographical memories in emerging adulthood. *Journal of Personality, 74,* 1371–1400.

McAdams, D. P., Diamond, A., de St. Aubin, E., & Mansfield, E. (1997). Stories of commitment: The psychosocial construction of generative lives. *Journal of Personality and Social Psychology, 72,* 678–694.

McAdams, D. P., Hart, H. M., & Maruna, S. (1998). The anatomy of generativity. In D. P. McAdams & E. de St. Aubin (Eds.), *Generativity and adult development: How and why we care for the next generation* (pp. 7–43). Washington, DC: American Psychological Association.

McAdams, D. P., & McLean, K. C. (2013). Narrative identity. *Current Directions in Psychological Science, 22,* 233–238.

McAdams, D. P., & Pals, J. L. (2006). A new big five. Fundamental principles for an integrative science of personality. *American Psychologist, 61*, 204–217.

McAdams, D. P., Reynolds, J., Lewis, M., Patten, A. H., & Bowman, P. J. (2001). When bad things turn good and good things turn bad: Sequences of redemption and contamination in life narrative and their relation to psychosocial adaptation in midlife adults and in students. *Personality and Social Psychology Bulletin, 27*, 474–485.

McAuley, E., Mailey, E. L., Mullen, S. P., Szabo, A. N., Wojcicki, T. R., White, S. M. et al. (2011). Growth trajectories of exercise self-efficacy in older adults: Influence of measures and initial status. *Health Psychology, 30*, 75–83.

McCarthy, E. D., Langner, T. S., Gersten, J. C., Eisenberg, J. G., & Orzeck, L. (1975). Violence and behavior disorders. *Journal of Communication, 25*, 71–85.

McCauley, C., Woods, K., Coolidge, C., & Kulick, W. (1983). More aggressive cartoons are funnier. *Journal of Personality and Social Psychology, 44*, 817–823.

McClelland, D. C. (1961). *The achieving society*. Princeton, NJ: Van Nostrand.

McClelland, D. C. (1980). Motive dispositions: The merits of operant and respondent measures. In L. Wheeler (Ed.), *Review of personality and social psychology* (Vol. 1, pp. 10–41). Beverly Hills, CA: Sage.

McClelland, D. C. (1985). How motives, skill, and values determine what people do. *American Psychologist, 40*, 812–825.

McClelland, D. C., Atkinson, J. W., Clark, R. A., & Lowell, E. L. (1953). *The achievement motive*. New York: Appleton-Century-Crofts.

McClelland, D. C., & Boyatzis, R. E. (1982). Leadership motive pattern and long-term success in management. *Journal of Applied Psychology, 67*, 737–743.

McClelland, D. C., & Pilon, D. A. (1983). Sources of adult motives in patterns of parent behavior in early childhood. *Journal of Personality and Social Psychology, 44*, 564–574.

McClure, E. B. (2000). A meta-analytic review of sex differences in facial expression processing and their development in infants, children, and adolescents. *Psychological Bulletin, 126*, 424–453.

McCrae, R. R. (2001). 5 years of progress: A reply to *Block*. *Journal of Research in Personality, 35*, 108–113.

McCrae, R. R., & Costa, P. T. (1986). Personality, coping, and coping effectiveness in an adult sample. *Journal of Personality, 54*, 385–405.

McCrae, R. R., & Costa, P. T. (1995). Positive and negative valence within the Five-Factor Model. *Journal of Research in Personality, 29*, 443–460.

McCrae, R. R., & Costa, P. T. (1997). Personality trait structure as a human universal. *American Psychologist, 52*, 509–516.

McCrae, R. R., & Costa, P. T. (2008). The five-factor theory of personality. In O. P. John, R. W. Robins, & L. A. Pervin (Eds.), *Handbook of personality* (3rd ed., pp. 159–181). New York: Guilford.

McCrae, R. R., Costa, P. T., Martin, T. A., Oryol, V. E., Rukavishnikov, A. A., Senin, I. G. et al. (2004). Consensual validation of personality traits across cultures. *Journal of Research in Personality, 38*, 179–201.

McCrae, R. R., Jang, K. L., Livesley, W. J., Riemann, R., & Angleitner, A. (2001). Sources of structure: Genetic, environmental and artifactual influences on the covariation of personality traits. *Journal of Personality, 69*, 511–535.

McCrae, R. R., Scally, M., Terraccianno, A., Abecasis, G. R., & Costa, P. T. (2010). An alternative to the search for single polymorphisms: Toward molecular personality scales for the Five-Factor Model. *Journal of Personality and Social Psychology, 99*, 1014–1024.

McCrae, R. R., & Terracciano, A. (2005). Personality profiles of cultures: Aggregate personality traits. *Journal of Personality and Social Psychology, 89*, 407–425.

McCrae, R. R., Terracciano, A., & Personality Profiles of Cultures Project. (2005). Universal features of personality traits from observer's perspective: Data from 50 cultures. *Journal of Personality and Social Psychology, 88*, 547–561.

McDonald, M. (2012, June 7). Putting Chinese students to the test. *New York Times*. Retrieved from http://rendezvous.blogs.nytimes.com/2012/06/07/putting-chinese-students-to-the-test/

McGhee, P. E. (1979). *Humor: Its origin and development*. San Francisco: W. H. Freeman.

McGrath, M. J., & Cohen, D. B. (1978). REM sleep facilitation of adaptive waking behavior: A review of the literature. *Psychological Bulletin, 85*, 24–57.

McGrath, R. E., Mitchell, M., Kim, B. H., & Hough, L. (2010). Evidence for response bias as a source of error variance in applied assessment. *Psychological Bulletin, 136*, 450–470.

McGue, M., & Christensen, K. (1997). Genetic and environmental contributions to depression symptomatology: Evidence from Danish twins 75 years of age and older. *Journal of Abnormal Psychology, 106*, 439–448.

McGuire, M. T., & Troisi, A. (1990). Anger: An evolutionary view. In R. Plutchik & H. Kellerman (Eds.), *Emotion: Theory, research, and experience* (Vol. 5, pp. 43–57). San Diego, CA: Academic Press.

McGuire, P. A. (1999, March). Therapists see new sense in use of humor. *APA Monitor*, pp. 1, 10.

McGuire, W. J., & McGuire, C. V. (1982). Significant others in self-space: Sex differences and developmental trends in the social self. In J. Suls (Ed.), *Psychological perspectives on the self* (Vol. 1, pp. 71–96). Hillsdale, NJ: Erlbaum.

McKay, D. (2011). Methods and mechanisms in the efficacy of psychodynamic psychotherapy. *American Psychologist, 66,* 147–148.

McNally, R. J., & Geraerts, E. (2009). A new solution to the recovered memory debate. *Perspectives on Psychological Science, 4,* 126–134.

McPherson, M., Smith-Lovin, L., & Brashears, M. E. (2006). Social isolation in America: Changes in core discussion networks over two decades. *American Sociological Review, 71,* 353–375.

Measelle, J. R., John, O. P., Ablow, J. C., Cowan, P. A., & Cowan, P. (2005). Can children provide coherent, stable, and valid self-reports on the Big Five dimensions? A longitudinal study from ages 5 to 7. *Journal of Personality and Social Psychology, 89,* 90–106.

Mednick, M., & Thomas, V. (2008). Women and achievement. In F. L. Denmark & M. A. Paludi (Eds.), *Psychology of women: A handbook of issues and theories* (2nd ed., pp. 625–651). Westport, CT: Praeger.

Meece, J. L., Anderman, E. M., & Anderman, L. H. (2006). Classroom goal structure, student motivation, and academic achievement. *Annual Review of Psychology, 57,* 487–503.

Meeker, W. B., & Barber, T. X. (1971). Toward an explanation of stage hypnosis. *Journal of Abnormal Psychology, 77,* 61–70.

Meichenbaum, D. H. (1985). *Stress inoculation training.* New York: Pergamon.

Meichenbaum, D. H., & Cameron, R. (1983). Stress inoculation training: Toward a general paradigm for training coping skills. In D. Meichenbaum & M. E. Jaemko (Eds.), *Stress reduction and prevention* (pp. 115–157). New York: Plenum.

Meichenbaum, D. H., & Deffenbacher, J. L. (1988). Stress inoculation training. *Counseling Psychologist, 16,* 69–90.

Meissner, W. W. (1984). *Psychoanalysis and religious experience.* New Haven, CT: Yale University Press.

Meleshko, K. G. A., & Alden, L. E. (1993). Anxiety and self-disclosure: Toward a motivational model. *Journal of Personality and Social Psychology, 64,* 1000–1009.

Melges, F. T., & Weisz, A. E. (1971). The personal future and suicidal ideation. *Journal of Nervous and Mental Disease, 153,* 244–250.

Mellman, T. A., David, D., Bustamante, V., Torres, J., & Fins, A. (2001). Dreams in the acute aftermath of trauma and their relationship to PTSD. *Journal of Traumatic Stress, 14,* 241–247.

Mershon, B., & Gorsuch, R. L. (1988). Number of factors in the personality sphere: Does increase in factors increase predictability of real-life criteria? *Journal of Personality and Social Psychology, 55,* 675–680.

Merz, E. L., & Roesch, S. C. (2011). Modeling trait and state variation using multilevel factor analysis with PANAS daily diary data. *Journal of Research in Personality, 45,* 2–9.

Metropolitan Area Child Study Research Group. (2007). Changing the way children "think" about aggression: Social-cognitive effects of a preventive intervention. *Journal of Consulting and Clinical Psychology, 75,* 160–167.

Meyer, G. J., & Shack, J. R. (1989). The structural convergence of mood and personality: Evidence for old and new directions. *Journal of Personality and Social Psychology, 57,* 691–706.

Michalski, R. L., & Shackelford, T. K. (2002). An attempted replication of the relationships between birth order and personality. *Journal of Research in Personality, 36,* 182–188.

Mickelson, K. D., Kessler, R. C., & Shaver, P. R. (1997). Adult attachment in a nationally representative sample. *Journal of Personality and Social Psychology, 73,* 1092–1106.

Mihura, J. L., Meyer, G. J., Dumitrascu, N., & Bombel, G. (2013). The validity of individual Rorschach variables: Systematic reviews and meta-analyses of the comprehensive system. *Psychological Bulletin, 139,* 548–605.

Miles, D. R., & Carey, G. (1997). Genetic and environmental architecture of human aggression. *Journal of Personality and Social Psychology, 72,* 207–217.

Miller, I. W., & Norman, W. H. (1979). Learned helplessness in humans: A review and attribution theory model. *Psychological Bulletin, 86,* 93–118.

Miller, M. G., & Ostlund, N. M. (2006). The effect of a parenting prime on sex differences in mate selection criteria. *Personality and Social Psychology Bulletin, 32,* 1459–1468.

Miller, N., Pedersen, W. C., Earleywine, M., & Pollock, V. E. (2003). A theoretical model of triggered displaced aggression. *Personality and Social Psychology Review, 7,* 75–97.

Miller, N. E. (1941). The frustration-aggression hypothesis. *Psychological Review, 48,* 337–346.

Milling, L. S., Reardon, J. M., & Carosella, G. M. (2006). Mediation and moderation of psychological pain treatments: Response expectancies and hypnotic suggestibility. *Journal of Consulting and Clinical Psychology, 74,* 253–262.

Mineka, S., & Zinbarg, R. (2006). A contemporary learning theory perspective on the etiology of anxiety disorders. *American Psychologist, 61,* 10–26.

Mischel, W. (1968). *Personality and assessment.* New York: Wiley.

Mischel, W. (1973). Toward a cognitive social learning reconceptualization of personality. *Psychological Review, 80,* 252–283.

Mischel, W. (1990). Personality dispositions revisited and revised: A view after three decades. In L. A. Pervin (Ed.), *Handbook of personality: Theory and research* (pp. 111–134). New York: Guilford.

Mischel, W. (2009). From personality and assessment (1968) to personality science 2009. *Journal of Research in Personality, 43,* 282–290.

Mischel, W., & Shoda, Y. (1995). A cognitive-affective system theory of personality: Reconceptualizing situations, dispositions, dynamics, and invariance in personality structure. *Psychological Review, 102*, 246–268.

Mischel, W., & Shoda, Y. (2008). Toward a unified theory of personality: Integrating dispositions and processing dynamics within the cognitive-affective processing system. In O. P. John, R. W. Robins, & L. A. Pervin (Eds.), *Handbook of personality: Theory and research* (3rd ed., pp. 208–241). New York: Guilford.

Mitchell, R. E., Cronkite, R. C., & Moos, R. H. (1983). Stress, coping, and depression among married couples. *Journal of Abnormal Psychology, 92*, 433–448.

Mitte, K. (2005). Meta-analysis of cognitive-behavioral treatments for generalized anxiety disorder: A comparison with pharmacotherapy. *Psychological Bulletin, 131*, 785–795.

Moehler, E., Kagan, J., Brunner, R., Wiebel, A., Kaufmann, C., & Resch, F. (2006). Association of behavioral inhibition with hair pigmentation in a European sample. *Biological Psychology, 72*, 344–346.

Moehler, E., Kagan, J., Oelkers-Ax, R., Brunner, R., Poustka, L., Haffner, J. et al. (2008). Infant predictors of behavioral inhibition. *British Journal of Developmental Psychology, 26*, 145–150.

Moffitt, T. E., Caspi, A., Milne, B. J., Melchior, M., Goldberg, D., & Poulton, R. (2007). Generalized anxiety disorder and depression: Childhood risk factors in a birth cohort followed to age 32. *Psychological Medicine, 37*, 441–452.

Moilanen, D. L. (1993). Depressive information processing among nonclinic, nonreferred college students. *Journal of Counseling Psychology, 40*, 340–347.

Moller, I., & Krahe, B. (2009). Exposure to violent video games and aggression in German adolescents: A longitudinal analysis. *Aggressive Behavior, 35*, 75–89.

Moneta, G. B., & Csikszentmihalyi, M. (1996). The effect of perceived challenges and skills on the quality of subjective experience. *Journal of Personality, 64*, 275–310.

Moretti, M. M., Segal, Z. V., McCann, C. D., Shaw, B. F., Miller, D. T., & Vella, D. (1996). Self-referent versus other-referent information processing in dysphoric, clinically depressed, and remitted depressed subjects. *Personality and Social Psychology Bulletin, 22*, 68–80.

Morfei, M. Z., Hooker, K., Fiese, B. H., & Cordeiro, A. M. (2001). Continuity and change in parenting possible selves: A longitudinal follow-up. *Basic and Applied Social Psychology, 23*, 217–223.

Morton, T. L. (1978). Intimacy and reciprocity of exchange: A comparison of spouses and strangers. *Journal of Personality and Social Psychology, 36*, 72–81.

Mosher, C. E., & Danoff-Burg, S. (2006). Health effects of expressive letter writing. *Journal of Social and Clinical Psychology, 25*, 1122–1139.

Mount, M. K., Barrick, M. R., & Strauss, J. P. (1994). Validity of observer ratings of the Big Five personality factors. *Journal of Applied Psychology, 79*, 272–280.

Moustakas, C. E. (1968). *Individuality and encounter.* Cambridge, MA: Doyle.

Mullineaux, P. Y., Deater-Deckard, K., Petrill, S. A., Thompson, L. A., & DeThrone, L. S. (2009). Temperament in middle childhood: A behavioral genetic analysis of fathers' and mothers' reports. *Journal of Research in Personality, 43*, 737–746.

Mund, M., & Mitte, K. (2012). The costs of repression: A meta-analysis of the relation between repressive coping and somatic diseases. *Health Psychology, 31*, 640–649.

Mundorf, N., Bhatia, A., Zillmann, D., Lester, P., & Robertson, S. (1988). Gender differences in humor appreciation. *Humor, 1*, 231–243.

Murayama, K., & Elliot, A. J. (2009). The joint influence of personal achievement goals and classroom goal structures on achievement-related outcomes. *Journal of Educational Psychology, 101*, 432–447.

Murray, E. J., Lamnin, A. D., & Carver, C. S. (1989). Emotional expression in written essays and psychotherapy. *Journal of Social and Clinical Psychology, 8*, 414–429.

Murray, H. A. (1938). *Explorations in personality: A clinical and experimental study of fifty men of college age.* New York: Oxford University Press.

Murray, H. A. (1967). Henry A. Murray. In E. G. Boring & G. Lindzey (Eds.), *A history of psychology in autobiography* (Vol. 5, pp. 285–310). New York: Appleton-Century-Crofts.

Murray, J. A., & Terry, D. J. (1999). Parental reactions to infant death: The effects of resources and coping strategies. *Journal of Social and Clinical Psychology, 18*, 341–369.

Myers, D. G. (1992). *The pursuit of happiness: Who is happy—and why.* New York: Morrow.

Nadon, R., Hoyt, I. P., Register, P. A., & Kihlstrom, J. F. (1991). Absorption and hypnotizability: Context effects reexamined. *Journal of Personality and Social Psychology, 60*, 144–153.

Naik, G. (2011, December 2). Scientists' elusive goal: Reproducing study results. *Wall Street Journal*, pp. A1, A16.

Nasby, W., & Read, N. W. (1997). The life voyage of a solo circumnavigator: Integrating theoretical and methodological perspectives. *Journal of Personality, 65*, 785–1068.

Nash, M. (1987). What, if anything, is regressed about hypnotic age regression? A review of the empirical literature. *Psychological Bulletin, 102*, 42–52.

Neimeyer, R. A. (2001). Repertory grid technique. In W. E. Craighead & C. B. Nemeroff (Eds.), *The Corsini encyclopedia of psychology and behavioral science* (3rd ed., Vol. 4, pp. 1394–1395). New York: Wiley.

Neisser, U., Boodoo, G., Bourchard, T. J., Boykin, A. W., Brody, N., Ceci, S. J. et al. (1996). Intelligence:

Knowns and unknowns. *American Psychologist, 51,* 77–101.

Nelson, B. D., Sarapas, C., Robison-Andrew, E. J., Altman, S. E., Campbell, M. L., & Shankman, S. A. (2012). Frontal brain asymmetry in depression with comorbid anxiety: A neuropsychological investigation. *Journal of Abnormal Psychology, 121,* 579–591.

Nelson, N. W., Sweet, J. J., & Demakis, G. J. (2006). Meta-analysis of the MMPI-2 Fake Bad Scale: Utility in forensic practice. *Clinical Neuropsychologist, 20,* 39–58.

Nes, L. S., & Segerstrom, S. C. (2006). Dispositional optimism and coping: A meta-analytic review. *Personality and Social Psychology Review, 10,* 235–251.

Nestoriuc, Y., Rief, W., & Martin, A. (2008). Meta-analysis of biofeedback for tension-type headache: Efficacy, specificity, and treatment moderators. *Journal of Clinical and Consulting Psychology, 76,* 379–396.

Nevid, J. S., & Spencer, S. A. (1978). Multivariate and normative data pertaining to the RAS with the college population. *Behavior Therapy, 9,* 675.

Nevo, O., & Nevo, B. (1983). What do you do when asked to answer humorously? *Journal of Personality and Social Psychology, 44,* 188–194.

Newman, M. L., Holden, G. W., & Delville, Y. (2011). Coping with the stress of being bullied: Consequences of coping strategies among college students. *Social Psychological and Personality Science, 2,* 205–211.

Ng, T. W. H., Sorensen, K. L., & Eby, L. T. (2006). Locus of control at work: A meta-analysis. *Journal of Organizational Behavior, 27,* 1057–1087.

Niaura, R., Todaro, J. F., Stroud, L., Spiro, A., Ward, K. D., & Weiss, S. (2002). Hostility, the metabolic syndrome, and incident of coronary heart disease. *Health Psychology, 21,* 588–593.

Nicholson, I. A. M. (1997). To "Correlate Psychology and Social Ethics": Gordon Allport and the first course in American personality psychology. *Journal of Personality, 65,* 733–742.

Nicholson, R. A., Mouton, G. J., Bagby, R. M., Buis, T., Peterson, S. A., & Buigas, R. A. (1997). Utility of MMPI-2 indicators of response distortion: Receiver operating characteristic analysis. *Psychological Assessment, 9,* 471–479.

Nikles, C. D., Brecht, D. L., Klinger, E., & Bursell, A. L. (1998). The effects of current-concern-and nonconcern-related waking suggestions on nocturnal dream content. *Journal of Personality and Social Psychology, 75,* 242–255.

Niles, S. (1998). Achievement goals and means: A cultural comparison. *Journal of Cross-Cultural Psychology, 29,* 656–667.

Nisbett, R. E. (2007, December 9). All brains are the same color. *New York Times.*

Nisbett, R. E. (2009). *Intelligence and how to get it: Why schools and culture count.* New York: Norton.

Nisbett, R. E., Aronson, J., Blair, C., Dickens, W., Flynn, J., Halpern, D. F. et al. (2012). Intelligence: New findings and theoretical developments. *American Psychologist, 67,* 130–159.

Noguchi, K., Gohm, C. L., & Dalsky, J. (2006). Cognitive tendencies of focusing on positive and negative information. *Journal of Research in Personality, 40,* 891–910.

Nolen-Hoeksema, S. (2000). The role of rumination in depressive disorders and mixed anxiety/depressive symptoms. *Journal of Abnormal Psychology, 109,* 504–511.

Nolen-Hoeksema, S. (2001). Gender differences in depression. *Current Directions in Psychological Science, 10,* 173–176.

Noll, R. (1997). *The Aryan Christ: The secret life of Carl Jung.* New York: Random House.

Noller, P. (1984). *Nonverbal communication and marital interaction.* Oxford: Pergamon.

Nordstrom, C. R., & Segrist, D. J. (2009). Predicting the likelihood of going to graduate school: The importance of locus of control. *College Student Journal, 43,* 200–206.

Norman, P., & Bennett, P. (1996). Health locus of control. In M. Conner & P. Norman (Eds.), *Predicting health behaviour: Research and practice within social cognition models* (pp. 62–94). Buckingham, England: Open University Press.

Northey, W. F. (2002). Characteristics and clinical practices of marriage and family therapists: A national survey. *Journal of Marital and Family Therapy, 28,* 487–494.

Nusslock, R., Harmon-Jones, E., Alloy, L. B., Urosevic, S., Goldstein, K., & Abramson, L. Y. (2012). Elevated left mid-frontal cortical activity prospectively predicts conversion to bipolar I disorder. *Journal of Abnormal Psychology, 121,* 592–601.

Nusslock, R., Shackman, A. J., Harmon-Jones, E., Alloy, L. B., Coan, J. A., & Abramson, L. Y. (2011). Cognitive vulnerability and frontal brain asymmetry: Common predictors of first prospective depressive episode. *Journal of Abnormal Psychology, 121,* 497–503.

Oakley, D. A. (2008). Hypnosis, trance and suggestion: Evidence from neuroimaging. In M. R. Nash & A. J. Barnier (Eds.), *The oxford handbook of hypnosis: Theory, research and practice* (pp. 365–392). New York: Oxford University Press.

O'Brien, M., Peyton, V., Mistry, R., Hruda, L., Jacobs, A., Caldera, Y. et al. (2000). Gender-role cognition in three-year-old boys and girls. *Sex Roles, 42,* 1007–1025.

Ochse, R., & Plug, C. (1986). Cross-cultural investigation of the validity of Erikson's theory of personality development. *Journal of Personality and Social Psychology, 50,* 1240–1252.

O'Connor, S. C., & Rosenblood, L. K. (1996). Affiliation motivation in everyday experience: A theoretical comparison. *Journal of Personality and Social Psychology, 70,* 513–522.

O'Hea, E. L., Grothe, K. B., Bodenlos, J. S., Boudreaux, E. D., White, M. A., & Brantley, P. J. (2005). Predicting medical regimen adherence: The interactions of health locus of control beliefs. *Journal of Health Psychology, 10*, 705–717.

O'Heron, C. A., & Orlofsky, J. L. (1990). Stereotypic and nonstereotypic sex role trait and behavior orientations, gender identity, and psychological adjustment. *Journal of Personality and Social Psychology, 58*, 134–143.

Oishi, S., & Diener, E. (2001). Goals, culture, and subjective well-being. *Personality and Social Psychology Bulletin, 27*, 1674–1682.

Oishi, S., Diener, E., Choi, D.-W., Kim-Prieto, C., & Choi, I. (2007). The dynamics of daily events and well-being across cultures: When less is more. *Journal of Personality and Social Psychology, 93*, 685–698.

Okazaki, S. (1997). Sources of ethnic differences between Asian American and White American college students on measures of depression and social anxiety. *Journal of Abnormal Psychology, 106*, 52–60.

Orgler, H. (1963). *Alfred Adler: The man and his work*. New York: Liveright.

Orlofsky, J. L., & O'Heron, C. A. (1987). Stereotypic and nonstereotypic sex role trait and behavior orientations: Implications for personal adjustment. *Journal of Personality and Social Psychology, 52*, 1034–1042.

Orue, I., Bushman, B. J., Calvete, E., Thomaes, S., de Castro, B. O., & Hutteman, R. (2011). Monkey see, monkey do, monkey hurt: Longitudinal effects of exposure to violence on children's aggressive behavior. *Social Psychological and Personality Science, 2*, 432–437.

Otto, M. W., Teachman, B. A., Cohen, L. S., Soares, C. N., Vitonis, A. F., & Harlow, B. L. (2007). Dysfunctional attitudes and episodes of major depression: Predictive validity and temporal stability in never-depressed, depressed, and recovered women. *Journal of Abnormal Psychology, 116*, 475–483.

Ouellette, J. A., Hessling, R., Gibbons, F. X., Reis-Bergan, M., & Gerrard, M. (2005). Using images to increase exercise behavior: Prototypes versus possible selves. *Personality and Social Psychology Bulletin, 31*, 610–620.

Ovcharchyn, C. A., Johnson, H. H., & Petzel, T. P. (1981). Type A behavior, academic aspirations, and academic success. *Journal of Personality, 49*, 248–256.

Overmier, J. B. (2002). On learned helplessness. *Integrative Physiological & Behavioral Science, 37*, 4–8.

Overmier, J. B., & Seligman, M. E. P. (1967). Effects of inescapable shock upon subsequent escape and avoidance learning. *Journal of Comparative and Physiological Psychology, 63*, 28–33.

Overskeid, G. (2007). Looking for Skinner and finding Freud. *American Psychologist, 62*, 590–595.

Oyserman, D., Bybee, D., & Terry, K. (2006). Possible selves and academic outcomes: How and when possible selves impel action. *Journal of Personality and Social Psychology, 91*, 188–204.

Oyserman, D., Johnson, E., & James, L. (2011). Seeing the destination but not the path: Effects of socioeconomic disadvantage on school-focused possible self content and linked behavioral strategies. *Self and Identity, 10*, 474–492.

Oyserman, D., & Markus, H. R. (1990). Possible selves and delinquency. *Journal of Personality and Social Psychology, 59*, 112–125.

Oyserman, D., & Saltz, E. (1993). Competence, delinquency, and attempts to attain possible selves. *Journal of Personality and Social Psychology, 65*, 360–374.

Paik, H., & Comstock, G. (1994). The effects of television violence on antisocial behavior: A meta-analysis. *Communication Research, 21*, 516–546.

Palker-Corell, A., & Marcus, D. K. (2004). Partner abuse, learned helplessness, and trauma symptoms. *Journal of Social and Clinical Psychology, 23*, 445–462.

Papsdorf, M., & Alden, L. (1998). Mediators of social rejection in social anxiety: Similarity, self-disclosure, and overt signs of anxiety. *Journal of Research in Personality, 32*, 351–369.

Park, C. L., & Adler, N. E. (2003). Coping style as a predictor of health and well-being across the first year of medical school. *Health Psychology, 22*, 627–631.

Park, L. E. (2007). Appearance-based rejection sensitivity: Implications for mental and physical health, affect, and motivation. *Personality and Social Psychology Bulletin, 33*, 490–504.

Park, L. E., Crocker, J., & Kiefer, A. K. (2007). Contingencies of self-worth, academic failure, and goal pursuit. *Personality and Social Psychology Bulletin, 33*, 1503–1517.

Parker, D. R., & Rogers, R. W. (1981). Observation and performance of aggression: Effects of multiple models and frustration. *Personality and Social Psychology Bulletin, 7*, 302–308.

Parker, K. C. H., Hanson, R. K., & Hunsley, J. (1988). MMPI, Rorschach, and WAIS: A meta-analytic comparison of reliability, stability, and validity. *Psychological Bulletin, 103*, 367–373.

Parker, W. D. (1998). Birth order effects in the academically talented. *Gifted Child Quarterly, 42*, 29–38.

Parton, D. A., & Geshuri, Y. (1971). Learning of aggression as a function of presence of a human model, response intensity, and target of the response. *Journal of Experimental Child Psychology, 20*, 304–318.

Pasupathi, M., McLean, K. C., & Weeks, T. (2009). To tell or not to tell: Disclosure and the narrative self. *Journal of Personality, 77*, 89–123.

Patterson, D. R., & Jensen, M. P. (2003). Hypnosis and clinical pain. *Psychological Bulletin, 129*, 495–521.

Paulhus, D. (1983). Sphere-specific measures of perceived control.

Journal of Personality and Social Psychology, 44, 1253–1265.

Paulhus, D. L. (1984). Two-component models of socially desirable responding. *Journal of Personality and Social Psychology, 46,* 598–609.

Paulhus, D. L. (1991). Measurement and control of response bias. In J. P. Robinson, P. S. Shaver, & L. S. Wrightsman (Eds.), *Measures of personality and social psychological attitudes* (Vol. 1, pp. 17–59). San Diego, CA: Academic Press.

Paulhus, D. L., Duncan, J. H., & Yik, M. S. M. (2002). Patterns of shyness in East-Asian and European-heritage students. *Journal of Research in Personality, 36,* 442–462.

Paulhus, D. L., & Martin, C. L. (1987). The structure of personality capabilities. *Journal of Personality and Social Psychology, 52,* 354–365.

Paulhus, D. L., & Morgan, K. L. (1997). Perception of intelligence in leaderless groups: The dynamic effects of shyness and acquaintance. *Journal of Personality and Social Psychology, 72,* 581–591.

Paunonen, S. V. (1998). Hierarchical organization of personality and prediction of behavior. *Journal of Personality and Social Psychology, 74,* 538–556.

Paunonen, S. V., & Ashton, M. C. (2001). Big Five factors and facets and the prediction of behavior. *Journal of Personality and Social Psychology, 81,* 524–539.

Paunonen, S. V., & Jackson, D. N. (2000). What is beyond the Big Five? Plenty! *Journal of Personality, 68,* 821–835.

Paunonen, S. V., & LeBel, E. P. (2012). Socially desirable responding and its elusive effects on the validity of personality assessments. *Journal of Personality and Social Psychology, 103,* 158–175.

Payne, R. L. (2000). Eupsychian management at the millennium. *Journal of Managerial Psychology, 15,* 219–226.

Payne, S. C., Youngcourt, S. S., & Beaubein, J. M. (2007). A meta-analytic examination of the goal

orientation nomological net. *Journal of Applied Psychology, 92,* 128–150.

Pedersen, D. M. (1999). Model for types of privacy by privacy functions. *Journal of Environmental Psychology, 19,* 397–405.

Pedersen, J. L., & Hyde, J. S. (2010). A meta-analytic review of research on gender differences in sexuality, 1993-2007. *Psychological Bulletin, 136,* 21–38.

Pedersen, N. L., Plomin, R., McClearn, G. E., & Friberg, L. (1988). Neuroticism, extraversion, and related traits in adult twins reared apart and reared together. *Journal of Personality and Social Psychology, 55,* 950–957.

Pedersen, P. B. (2008). Ethics, competence, and professional issues in cross-cultural counseling. In P. B. Pedersen, J. G. Draguns, W. J. Lonner, & J. E. Trimble (Eds.), *Counseling across cultures* (6th ed., pp. 5–20). Thousand Oaks, CA: Sage.

Pedersen, W. C., Bushman, B. J., Vasquez, E. A., & Miller, N. (2008). Kicking the (barking) dog effect: The moderating role of target attributes on triggered displaced aggression. *Personality and Social Psychology Bulletin, 34,* 1382–1395.

Pedhazur, E. J., & Tetenbaum, T. J. (1979). Bem Sex Role Inventory: A theoretical and methodological critique. *Journal of Personality and Social Psychology, 37,* 996–1016.

Pennebaker, J. W. (1989). Confession, inhibition, and disease. In L. Berkowitz (Ed.), *Advances in experimental social psychology* (Vol. 22, pp. 211–244). New York: Academic Press.

Pennebaker, J. W. (2000). The effects of traumatic disclosure on physical and mental health: The values of writing and talking about upsetting events. In J. M. Violanti, D. Paton, & C. Dunning (Eds.), *Posttraumatic stress intervention: Challenges, issues, and perspectives* (pp. 97–114). Springfield, IL: Charles C. Thomas.

Pennebaker, J. W., & Beall, S. K. (1986). Confronting a traumatic event:

Toward an understanding of inhibition and disease. *Journal of Abnormal Psychology, 95,* 274–281.

Pennebaker, J. W., Colder, M., & Sharp, L. K. (1990). Accelerating the coping process. *Journal of Personality and Social Psychology, 58,* 528–537.

Pennebaker, J. W., & O'Heeron, R. C. (1984). Confiding in others and illness rates among spouses of suicide and accidental-death victims. *Journal of Abnormal Psychology, 93,* 473–476.

Peplau, L. A., Russell, D., & Heim, M. (1979). The experience of loneliness. In I. Frieze, D. Bar-Tel, & J. Carroll (Eds.), *New approaches to social problems* (pp. 53–78). San Francisco: Jossey-Bass.

Perez-Edgar, K., Bar-Haim, V., McDermott, J. M., Chronis-Tuscano, A., Pine, D. S., & Fox, N. A. (2010). Attention biases to threat and behavioral inhibition in early childhood shape adolescent social withdrawal. *Emotion, 10,* 349–357.

Perez-Edgar, K., Roberson-Nay, R., Hardin, M. G., Poeth, K., Guyer, A. E., Nelson, E. E. et al. (2007). Attention alters neural responses to evocative faces in behaviorally inhibited adolescents. *NeuroImage, 35,* 1538–1546.

Perrig-Chiello, P., Perrig, W. G., & Staehelin, H. B. (1999). Health control beliefs in old age: Relationship with subjective and objective health, and health behaviour. *Psychology, Health and Medicine, 4,* 83–94.

Perry, R. P., Stupnisky, R. H., Hall, N. C., Chipperfield, J. G., & Weiner, B. (2010). Bad starts and better finishes: Attributional retraining and initial performance in competitive achievement settings. *Journal of Social and Clinical Psychology, 29,* 668–700.

Petersen, J. L., & Hyde, J. S. (2010). A meta-analytic review of research on gender differences in sexuality, 1993-2007. *Psychological Bulletin, 136,* 21–38.

Peterson, C., & Bossio, L. M. (2001). Optimism and physical well-being.

In E. C. Chang (Ed.), *Optimism and pessimism: Implications for theory, research, and practice* (pp. 127–145). Washington, DC: American Psychological Association.

Peterson, C., Maier, S. F., & Seligman, M. E. P. (1993). *Learned helplessness: A theory for the age of personal control.* New York: Oxford University Press.

Peterson, C., & Park, N. (2010). What happened to self-actualization? Commentary on Kenrick et al. (2010). *Perspectives on Psychological Science, 5,* 320–322.

Peterson, C., Seligman, M. E. P., & Vaillant, G. E. (1988). Pessimistic explanatory style is a risk factor for physical illness: A thirty-five-year longitudinal study. *Journal of Personality and Social Psychology, 55,* 23–27.

Peterson, C., Seligman, M. E. P., Yurko, K. H., Martin, L. R., & Friedman, H. S. (1998). Catastrophizing and untimely death. *Psychological Science, 9,* 127–130.

Peterson, C., Semmel, A., von Baeyer, C., Abramson, L. Y., Metalsky, G. I., & Seligman, M. E. P. (1982). The Attributional Style Questionnaire. *Cognitive Therapy and Research, 6,* 287–300.

Peterson, C., & Villanova, P. (1988). An expanded Attributional Style Questionnaire. *Journal of Abnormal Psychology, 97,* 87–89.

Petrie, K. J., Booth, R. J., & Pennebaker, J. W. (1998). The immunological effects of thought suppression. *Journal of Personality and Social Psychology, 75,* 1264–1272.

Petrocelli, J. V., & Smith, E. R. (2005). Who I am, who we are, and why: Links between emotions and causal attributions for self-and group discrepancies. *Personality and Social Psychology Bulletin, 31,* 1628–1642.

Phillips, A. G., & Silva, P. J. (2005). Self-awareness and the emotional consequences of self-discrepancies. *Personality and Social Psychology Bulletin, 31,* 703–713.

Phillips, S. D., & Bruch, M. A. (1988). Shyness and dysfunction in career

development. *Journal of Counseling Psychology, 35,* 159–165.

Piccione, C., Hilgard, E. R., & Zimbardo, P. G. (1989). On the degree of stability of measured hypnotizability over a 25-year period. *Journal of Personality and Social Psychology, 56,* 289–295.

Piedmont, R. L. (1999). Does spirituality represent the sixth factor of personality? Spiritual transcendence and the Five-Factor Model. *Journal of Personality, 67,* 985–1013.

Piedmont, R. L., McCrae, R. R., Riemann, R., & Angleitner, A. (2000). On the invalidity of validity scales: Evidence from self-reports and observer ratings in volunteer samples. *Journal of Personality and Social Psychology, 78,* 582–593.

Pilkonis, P. A. (1977a). Shyness, public and private, and its relationship to other measures of social behavior. *Journal of Personality, 45,* 585–595.

Pilkonis, P. A. (1977b). The behavioral consequences of shyness. *Journal of Personality, 45,* 596–611.

Pinquart, M., & Sorensen, S. (2001). Influences on loneliness in older adults: A meta-analysis. *Basic and Applied Social Psychology, 23,* 245–266.

Piotrowski, C., & Keller, J. W. (1989). Psychological testing in outpatient mental health facilities: A national study. *Professional Psychology: Research and Practice, 20,* 423–425.

Piotrowski, C., & Zalewski, C. (1993). Training in psychodiagnostic testing in APA-approved PsyD and PhD clinical psychology programs. *Journal of Personality Assessment, 61,* 394–405.

Pistole, M. C. (1989). Attachment in adult romantic relationships: Style of conflict resolution and relationship satisfaction. *Journal of Social and Personal Relationships, 6,* 505–510.

Pizzagalli, D. A., Sherwood, R. J., Henriques, J. B., & Davidson, R. J. (2005). Frontal brain asymmetry and reward responsiveness. *Psychological Science, 16,* 805–813.

Plomin, R., & Caspi, A. (1999). Behavioral genetics and personality. In L. A. Pervin & O. P. John (Eds.), *Handbook of personality: Theory and research* (2nd ed., pp. 251–276). New York: Guilford.

Plomin, R., Corley, R., Caspi, A., Fulker, D. W., & DeFries, J. (1998). Adoption results for self-reported personality: Evidence for nonadditive genetic effects? *Journal of Personality and Social Psychology, 75,* 211–218.

Plomin, R., & DeFries, J. C. (1998, May). Genetics of cognitive abilities and disabilities. *Scientific American,* 62–69.

Pollet, T. V., Dijkstra, P., Barelds, D. P. H., & Buunk, A. P. (2010). Birth order and the dominance aspect of extraversion: Are firstborns more extraverted, in the sense of being dominant, than laterborns? *Journal of Research in Personality, 44,* 742–745.

Polman, H., de Castro, B. O., & van Aken, M. A. G. (2008). Experimental study of the differential effects of playing versus watching violent video games on children's aggressive behavior. *Aggressive Behavior, 34,* 256–264.

Pomerleau, A., Bolduc, D., Malcuit, G., & Cossette, L. (1990). Pink or blue: Environmental gender stereotypes in the first two years of life. *Sex Roles, 22,* 359–367.

Pontari, B. A. (2009). Appearing socially competent: The effects of a friend's presence on the socially anxious. *Personality and Social Psychology Bulletin, 35,* 283–294.

Pontari, B. A., & Glenn, E. J. (2012). Engaging in less protective self-presentation: The effects of a friend's presence on the socially anxious. *Basic and Applied Social Psychology, 34,* 516–526.

Poortvliet, P. M., & Darnon, C. (2010). Toward a more social understanding of achievement goals: The interpersonal effects of mastery and performance goals. *Current Directions in Psychological Science, 19,* 324–328.

Porcerelli, J. H., Cogan, R., Kamoo, R., & Miller, K. (2010). Convergent validity of the Defense Mechanisms Manual and the Defensive Functioning Scale. *Journal of Personality Assessment, 92*, 432–438.

Poropat, A. E. (2009). A meta-analysis of the Five-Factor Model of personality and academic performance. *Psychological Bulletin, 135*, 322–338.

Powch, I. G., & Houston, B. K. (1996). Hostility, anger-in, and cardiovascular reactivity in White women. *Health Psychology, 15*, 200–208.

Powers, S. I., Pietromonaco, P. R., Gunlicks, M., & Sayer, A. (2006). Dating couples' attachment styles and patterns of cortisol reactivity and recovery in response to a relationship conflict. *Journal of Personality and Social Psychology, 90*, 613–628.

Pozo, C., Carver, C. S., Wellens, A. R., & Scheier, M. F. (1991). Social anxiety and social perception: Construing others' reactions to the self. *Personality and Social Psychology Bulletin, 17*, 355–362.

Prager, K. J. (1986). Intimacy status: Its relationship to locus of control, self-disclosure, and anxiety in adults. *Personality and Social Psychology Bulletin, 12*, 91–109.

Pratt, M. W., Norris, J. E., Hebblethwaite, S., & Arnold, M. L. (2008). Intergenerational transmission of values: Family generativity and adolescents' narratives of parent and grandparent value teaching. *Journal of Personality, 76*, 171–198.

Pressman, S. D., Cohen, S., Miller, G. E., Barkin, A., Rabin, B. S., & Treanor, J. J. (2005). Loneliness, social network size, and immune response to influenza vaccination in college freshmen. *Health Psychology, 24*, 297–306.

Ptacek, J. T., Pierce, G. R., & Thompson, E. L. (2006). Finding evidence of dispositional coping. *Journal of Research in Personality, 40*, 1137–1151.

Ptacek, J. T., Smith, R. E., & Dodge, K. L. (1994). Gender differences in coping with stress: When stressor and appraisals do not differ. *Personality and Social Psychology Bulletin, 20*, 421–430.

Puca, R. M., & Schmalt, H.-D. (2001). The influence of the achievement motive on spontaneous thoughts in pre-and postdecisional action phases. *Personality and Social Psychology Bulletin, 27*, 302–308.

Quinlan, S. L., Jaccard, J., & Blanton, H. (2006). A decision theoretic and prototype conceptualization of possible selves: Implications for the prediction of risk behavior. *Journal of Personality, 74*, 599–630.

Raag, T., & Rackliff, C. L. (1998). Preschoolers' awareness of social expectations of gender: Relationships to toy choices. *Sex Roles, 38*, 685–700.

Raikkonen, K., & Matthews, K. A. (2008). Do dispositional pessimism and optimism predict ambulatory blood pressure during schooldays and nights in adolescents? *Journal of Personality, 76*, 605–629.

Raikkonen, K., Matthews, K. A., Flory, J. D., & Owens, J. F. (1999). Effects of hostility on ambulatory blood pressure and mood during daily living in healthy adults. *Health Psychology, 18*, 44–53.

Rammstedt, B., & Kemper, C. J. (2011). Measurement equivalence of the Big Five: Shedding further light on the potential causes of the educational bias. *Journal of Research in Personality, 45*, 121–125.

Rasmussen, H. N., Scheier, M. F., & Greenhouse, J. B. (2009). Optimism and physical health: A meta-analytic review. *Annals of Behavioral Medicine, 37*, 239–256.

Rasmussen, H. N., Wrosch, C., Scheier, M. F., & Carver, C. S. (2006). Self-regulation processes and health: The importance of optimism and goal adjustment. *Journal of Personality, 74*, 1721–1747.

Rathus, S. A. (1973). A 30-item schedule for assessing assertive behavior. *Behavior Therapy, 4*, 398–406.

Rawsthorne, L. J., & Elliot, A. J. (1999). Achievement goals and intrinsic motivation: A meta-analytic review. *Personality and Social Psychology Review, 3*, 326–344.

Raz, A., Kirsch, I., Pollard, J., & Nitkin-Kaner, Y. (2006). Suggestion reduces the Stroop effect. *Psychological Science, 17*, 91–95.

Regalado, A. (2006, June 16). Scientist's study of brain genes sparks a backlash. *Wall Street Journal*, pp. A1, A12.

Reich, J. W., & Zautra, A. J. (1997). Locus of control influences diathesis-stress effects in rheumatoid arthritis patients. *Journal of Research in Personality, 31*, 423–438.

Reijntjes, A., Kamphuis, J. H., Thomaes, S., Bushman, B. J., & Telch, M. J. (2012). Too calloused to care: An experimental examination of factors influencing youths' displaced aggression against their peers. *Journal of General Psychology: General, 142*, 28–33.

Reijntjes, A., Thomaes, S., Kamphuis, J. H., Bushman, B. J., de Castro, B. O., & Telch, M. J. (2011). Explaining the paradoxical rejection-aggression link: The mediating effects of hostile intent attributions, anger, and decreases in state self-esteem on peer rejection-induced aggression in youth. *Personality and Social Psychology Bulletin, 37*, 955–963.

Reilly, R. R., & Chao, G. T. (1982). Validity and fairness of some alternative employee selection procedures. *Personnel Psychology, 35*, 1–62.

Reis, H. T., & Patrick, B. C. (1996). Attachment and intimacy: Component processes. In E. T. Higgins & A. W. Kruglanski (Eds.), *Social psychology: Handbook of basic principles* (pp. 523–563). New York: Guilford.

Reise, S. P., & Waller, N. G. (1993). Traitedness and the assessment of response pattern scalability. *Journal of Personality and Social Psychology, 65*, 143–151.

Renaud, J. M., & McConnell, A. R. (2007). Wanting to be better but thinking you can't: Implicit theories of personality moderate the impact of self-discrepancies on self-esteem. *Self and Identity, 6*, 41–50.

Rescorla, R. A. (1988). Pavlovian conditioning: It's not what you think it is. *American Psychologist, 43*, 160.

Revelle, W., & Oehlberg, K. (2008). Integrating experimental and observational personality research the contributions of Hans Eysenck. *Journal of Personality, 76,* 1387–1414.

Reznick, J. S., Kagan, J., Snidman, N., Gersten, M., Baak, K., & Rosenberg, A. (1986). Inhibited and uninhibited children: A follow-up study. *Child Development, 57,* 660–680.

Rhee, S. H., & Waldman, I. D. (2002). Genetic and environmental influences on antisocial behavior: A meta-analysis of twin and adoption studies. *Psychological Bulletin, 128,* 490–529.

Rhodewalt, F., & Comer, R. (1982). Coronary-prone behavior and reactance: The attractiveness of an eliminated choice. *Personality and Social Psychology Bulletin, 8,* 158.

Rhodewalt, F., & Davison, J. (1983). Reactance and the coronary-prone behavior pattern: The role of self-attribution in responses to reduced behavioral freedom. *Journal of Personality and Social Psychology, 44,* 220–228.

Rholes, W. S., Simpson, J. A., Campbell, L., & Grich, J. (2001). Adult attachment and transition to parenthood. *Journal of Personality and Social Psychology, 81,* 421–435.

Riemann, R., Angleitner, A., & Strelau, J. (1997). Genetic and environmental influences on personality: A study of twins reared together using the self-and peer-report NEO-FFI scales. *Journal of Personality, 65,* 449–475.

Richards, J. C., Hof, A., & Alvarenga, M. (2000). Serum lipids and their relationships with hostility and angry affect and behaviors in men. *Health Psychology, 19,* 393–398.

Richardson, M., Abraham, C., & Bond, R. (2012). Psychological correlates of university students' academic performance: A systematic review and meta-analysis. *Psychological Bulletin, 138,* 353–387.

Rimer, S. (2008, September 22). College panel calls for less focus on SATs. *New York Times,* p. A14.

Rimm-Kaufman, S. E., & Kagan, J. (2005). Infant predictors of kindergarten behavior: The contribution of inhibited and uninhibited temperament types. *Behavioral Disorders, 30,* 331–347.

Riordan, C. A., & Tedeschi, J. T. (1983). Attraction in aversive environments: Some evidence for classical conditioning and negative reinforcement. *Journal of Personality and Social Psychology, 44,* 683–692.

Riso, L. P., du Toit, P. L., Blandino, J. A., Penna, S., Dacey, S., Duin, J. S. et al. (2003). Cognitive aspects of chronic depression. *Journal of Abnormal Psychology, 112,* 72–80.

Ritts, V., & Patterson, M. L. (1996). Effects of social anxiety and action identification on impressions and thoughts in interaction. *Journal of Social and Clinical Psychology, 15,* 191–205.

Robbins, P. R., Tanck, R. H., & Houshi, F. (1985). Anxiety and dream symbolism. *Journal of Personality, 53,* 17–22.

Roberts, B., & Hogan, R. (2001). *Personality psychology in the workplace.* Washington, DC: American Psychological Association.

Roberts, B. W., Kuncel, N. R., Shiner, R., Caspi, A., & Goldberg, L. R. (2007). The power of personality: The comparative validity of personality traits, socioeconomic status, and cognitive ability for predicting important life outcomes. *Perspectives on Psychological Science, 2,* 313–345.

Roberts, B. W., & Mroczek, D. (2008). Personality trait change in adulthood. *Current Directions in Psychological Science, 17,* 31–35.

Roberts, B. W., Walton, K. E., & Viechtbauer, W. (2006). Patterns of mean-level change in personality traits across the life course: A meta-analysis of longitudinal studies. *Psychological Bulletin, 132,* 1–25.

Robins, R. W., Caspi, A., & Moffitt, T. E. (2002). It's not just who you're with, it's who you are: Personality and relationship experiences across multiple relationships. *Journal of Personality, 70,* 925–964.

Robinson, B. S., Davis, K. L., & Meara, N. M. (2003). Motivational attributes of occupational possible selves for low-income rural women. *Journal of Counseling Psychology, 50,* 156–164.

Robinson, M. S., & Alloy, L. B. (2003). Negative cognitive styles and stress-reactive rumination interact to predict depression: A prospective study. *Cognitive Therapy and Research, 27,* 275–292.

Robles, T. F., Brooks, K. P., & Pressman, S. D. (2009). Trait positive affect buffers the effects of acute stress on skin barrier recovery. *Health Psychology, 28,* 373–378.

Roche, S. M., & McConkey, K. M. (1990). Absorption: Nature, assessment, and correlates. *Journal of Personality and Social Psychology, 59,* 91–101.

Rodgers, J. L., Cleveland, H. H., van den Oord, E., & Rowe, D. C. (2000). Resolving the debate over birth order, family size, and intelligence. *American Psychologist, 55,* 599–612.

Rodin, J., & Langer, E. J. (1977). Long-term effects of a control-relevant intervention with the institutionalized aged. *Journal of Personality and Social Psychology, 35,* 897–902.

Rodriguez-Naranjo, C., & Cano, A. (2010). Development and validation of an Attributional Style Questionnaire for adolescents. *Psychological Assessment, 22,* 837–851.

Roepke, S., & Renneberg, B. (2009). "Effectiveness of long-term psychodynamic psychotherapy: A meta-analysis": Comment. *Journal of the American Medical Association, 301,* 931–932.

Rogers, C. R. (1947). The case of Mary Jane Tildon. In W. U. Snyder (Ed.), *Casebook of nondirective counseling* (pp. 128–203). Cambridge, MA: Houghton Mifflin.

Rogers, C. R. (1951). *Client-centered therapy: Its current practice, implications, and theory.* Boston: Houghton Mifflin.

Rogers, C. R. (1954). The case of Mrs. Oak: A research analysis. In C. R. Rogers & R. F. Dymond (Eds.), *Psychotherapy and personality change* (pp. 259–348). Chicago: University of Chicago Press.

Rogers, C. R. (1961). *On becoming a person: A therapist's view of psychotherapy.* Boston: Houghton Mifflin.

Rogers, C. R. (1967). Carl R. Rogers. In E. G. Boring & G. Lindzey (Eds.), *A history of psychology in autobiography* (Vol. 5, pp. 341–384). New York: Appleton-Century-Crofts.

Rogers, C. R. (1969). *Freedom to learn: A view of what education might become.* Columbus, OH: Merrill.

Rogers, C. R. (1970). *Carl Rogers on encounter groups.* New York: Harper & Row.

Rogers, C. R. (1977). *Carl Rogers on personal power.* New York: Delacorte.

Rogers, C. R. (1982, August). Nuclear war: A personal response. *APA Monitor,* pp. 6–7.

Rogers, M. E., Hansen, N. B., Levy, B. R., Tate, D. C., & Sikkema, K. J. (2005). Optimism and coping with loss in bereaved HIV-infected men and women. *Journal of Social and Clinical Psychology, 24,* 341–360.

Rogers, T. B., Kuiper, N. A., & Kirker, W. S. (1977). Self-reference and the encoding of personal information. *Journal of Personality and Social Psychology, 35,* 677–688.

Rokach, A. (1998). The relation of cultural background to the causes of loneliness. *Journal of Social and Clinical Psychology, 17,* 75–88.

Roney, C. J. R., & O'Connor, M. C. (2008). The interplay between achievement goals and specific target goals in determining performance. *Journal of Research in Personality, 42,* 482–489.

Roos, P. E., & Cohen, L. H. (1987). Sex roles and social support as moderators of life stress adjustment. *Journal of Personality and Social Psychology, 52,* 576–585.

Rose, R. J., Koskenvuo, M., Kaprio, J., Sarna, S., & Langinvainio, H. (1988). Shared genes, shared experiences, and similarity of personality: Data from 14,288 adult Finnish co-twins. *Journal of Personality and Social Psychology, 54,* 161–171.

Rosenberg, A., & Kagan, J. (1989). Physical and physiological correlates of behavioral inhibition. *Developmental Psychobiology, 22,* 753–770.

Rosenman, R. H., Brand, R. J., Jenkins, D., Friedman, M., Straus, R., & Wurm, M. (1975). Coronary heart disease in the Western Collaborative Group Study: Final follow-up experience of 8 1/2 years. *Journal of the American Medical Association, 233,* 872–877.

Rosenthal, E. (2012, June 3). Let's (not) get physical. *New York Times,* pp. SR1, SR8.

Rosenthal, R. (1979). The "file drawer problem" and tolerance for null results. *Psychological Bulletin, 86,* 638–641.

Rosenthal, R. (1990). How are we doing in soft psychology? *American Psychologist, 45,* 775–777.

Ross, M., & Holmberg, D. (1992). Are wives' memories for events in relationships more vivid than their husbands' memories? *Journal of Social and Personal Relationships, 9,* 585–604.

Rosse, J. G., Stecher, M. D., Miller, J. L., & Levin, R. A. (1998). The impact of response distortion on preemployment personality testing and hiring decisions. *Journal of Applied Psychology, 83,* 634–644.

Rotenberg, K. J. (1997). Loneliness and the perception of the exchange of disclosures. *Journal of Social and Clinical Psychology, 16,* 259–276.

Rotenberg, K. J., Addis, N., Betts, L. R., Corrigan, A., Fox, C., Hobson, Z. et al. (2011). The relation between trust beliefs and loneliness during early childhood, middle childhood, and adulthood. *Personality and Social Psychology Bulletin, 36,* 1086–1100.

Roth, S. (1980). A revised model of learned helplessness in humans. *Journal of Personality, 48,* 103–133.

Rothbart, M. K. (2007). Temperament, development, and personality. *Current Directions in Psychological Science, 16,* 207–212.

Rothbart, M. K., & Ahadi, S. A. (1994). Temperament and the development of personality. *Journal of Abnormal Psychology, 103,* 55–66.

Rotter, J. B. (1954). *Social learning and clinical psychology.* Englewood Cliffs, NJ: Prentice-Hall.

Rotter, J. B. (1966). Generalized expectancies for internal versus external control of reinforcement. *Psychological Monographs, 80*(1).

Rotter, J. B. (1982). *The development and applications of social learning theory: Selected papers.* New York: Praeger.

Rotter, J. B., Chance, J. E., & Phares, E. J. (Eds.). (1972). *Applications of a social learning theory of personality.* New York: Holt, Rinehart & Winston.

Rowe, D. C. (1987). Resolving the person-situation debate: Invitation to an interdisciplinary dialogue. *American Psychologist, 42,* 218–227.

Rubenstein, C. M., & Shaver, P. (1980). Loneliness in two northern cities. In J. Hartog, J. R. Andy, & Y. A. Cohen (Eds.), *The anatomy of loneliness* (pp. 319–337). New York: International Universities Press.

Rubin, J. A., Provenzano, F. J., & Luria, Z. (1974). The eye of the beholder: Parents' views of sex of newborns. *American Journal of Orthopsychiatry, 44,* 512–519.

Rubins, J. L. (1978). *Karen Horney: Gentle rebel of psychoanalysis.* New York: Dial.

Rubinstein, G., & Strul, S. (2007). The Five Factor Model (FFM) among four groups of male and female professionals. *Journal of Research in Personality, 41,* 931–937.

Rudasill, K. M., & Konold, T. R. (2008). Contribution of children's temperament to teacher's judgments of social competence from kindergarten through second grade. *Early Education and Development, 19,* 643–666.

Rudasill, K. M., & Rimm-Kaufman, S. E. (2009). Teacher-child relationship quality: The roles of child temperament and teacher-child interactions. *Early Childhood Research Quarterly, 24*, 107–120.

Rudasill, K. M., Rimm-Kaufman, S. E., Justice, L. M., & Pence, K. (2006). Temperament and language skills as predictors of teacher-child relationship quality in preschool. *Early Education and Development, 17*, 271–291.

Russell, D., Peplau, L. A., & Cutrona, C. E. (1980). The revised UCLA Loneliness Scale: Concurrent and discriminant validity. *Journal of Personality and Social Psychology, 39*, 472–480.

Russell, J. A., & Carroll, J. M. (1999). On the bipolarity of positive and negative affect. *Psychological Bulletin, 125*, 3–30.

Rusting, C. L. (1998). Personality, mood, and cognitive processing of emotional information: Three conceptual frameworks. *Psychological Bulletin, 124*, 165–196.

Rusting, C. L. (1999). Interactive effects of personality and mood on emotion-congruent memory and judgment. *Journal of Personality and Social Psychology, 77*, 1073–1086.

Rusting, C. L., & Larsen, R. J. (1998). Personality and cognitive processing of affective information. *Personality and Social Psychology Bulletin, 24*, 200–213.

Rutledge, T., Linke, S. E., Olson, M. B., Francis, J., Johnson, B. D., Bittner, V. et al. (2008). Social networks and incident stroke among women with suspected myocardial ischemia. *Psychosomatic Medicine, 70*, 282–287.

Ruvolo, A. P., & Markus, H. R. (1992). Possible selves and performance: The power of self-relevant imagery. *Social Cognition, 10*, 95–124.

Sackett, P. R., Kuncel, N. R., Arneson, J. J., Cooper, S. R., & Waters, S. D. (2009). Does socioeconomic status explain the relationship between admissions tests and post-secondary academic performance? *Psychological Bulletin, 135*, 1–22.

Sadalla, E. K., Kenrick, D. T., & Vershure, B. (1987). Dominance and heterosexual attraction. *Journal of Personality and Social Psychology, 52*, 730–738.

Sadler, P., & Woody, E. (2010). Dissociation in hypnosis: Theoretical frameworks and psychotherapeutic implications. In S. J. Lynn, J. W. Rhue, & I. Kirsch (Eds.), *Handbook of clinical hypnosis* (2nd ed., pp. 151–178). Washington, DC: American Psychological Association.

Sadler, W. A., & Johnson, T. B. (1980). From loneliness to anomie. In J. Hartog, J. R. Audy, & Y. A. Cohen (Eds.), *The anatomy of loneliness* (pp. 34–64). New York: International Universities Press.

Saleem, M., Anderson, C. A., & Gentile, D. A. (2012). Effects of prosocial, neutral, and violent video games on college students' affect. *Aggressive Behavior, 38*, 263–271.

Salgado, J. F. (1997). The five factor model of personality and job performance in the European community. *Journal of Applied Psychology, 82*, 30–43.

Salili, F. (1994). Age, sex, and cultural differences in the meaning and dimensions of achievement. *Personality and Social Psychology Bulletin, 20*, 635–648.

Sandstrom, M. J., & Cramer, P. (2003). Girls' use of defense mechanisms following peer rejection. *Journal of Personality, 71*, 603–627.

Sanford, S., & Eder, D. (1984). Adolescent humor during peer interaction. *Social Psychology Quarterly, 47*, 235–243.

Sansone, C., & Harackiewicz, J. M. (1998). "Reality" is complicated. *American Psychologist, 53*, 673–674.

Saragovi, C., Koestner, R., Di Dio, L., & Aube, J. (1997). Agency, communion, and well-being: Extending Helgeson's (1994) model. *Journal of Personality and Social Psychology, 73*, 593–609.

Sarbin, T. R., & Coe, W. C. (1972). *Hypnosis: A social psychological analysis of influence communication*. New York: Holt, Rinehart & Winston.

Sarbin, T. R., & Coe, W. C. (1979). Hypnosis and psychopathology: Replacing old myths with fresh metaphors. *Journal of Abnormal Psychology, 88*, 506–526.

Sargent, R. T., Crocker, J., & Luhtanen, R. K. (2006). Contingencies of self-worth and depressive symptoms in college students. *Journal of Social and Clinical Psychology, 25*, 628–646.

Sarkar, U., Ali, S., & Whooley, M. A. (2009). Self-efficacy as a marker of cardiac function and predictor of heart failure hospitalization and mortality in patients with stable coronary heart disease: Findings from the Heart and Soul study. *Health Psychology, 28*, 166–173.

Saucier, G., & Goldberg, L. R. (1998). What is beyond the Big Five? *Journal of Personality, 66*, 495–524.

Saul, L. A., Lopez-Gonzales, M. A., Moreno-Pulido, A., Corbella, S., Compan, V., & Feixas, G. (2012). Bibliometric review of the reperatory grid technique: 1998-2007. *Journal of Constructivist Psychology, 25*, 112–131.

Saulny, S. (2009, November 18). Claims of child abuse remembered divide town and lead to charges against 6. *New York Times*. Retrieved from http://www.nytimes.com/2009/11/18/us/18family.html

Savickas, M. L. (1997). Constructivist career counseling: Models and methods. In G. J. Neimeyer & R. A. Neimeyer (Eds.), *Advances in personal construct psychology* (Vol. 4, pp. 149–182). Greenwich, CT: JAI Press.

Sayers, S. L., Baucom, D. H., & Tierney, A. M. (1993). Sex roles, interpersonal control, and depression: Who can get their way? *Journal of Research in Personality, 27*, 377–395.

Scarr, S., & Carter-Saltzman, L. (1979). Twin method: Defense of a critical assumption. *Behavior Genetics, 9*, 527–542.

Scarr, S., Webber, P. L., Weinberg, R. A., & Wittig, M. A. (1981).

Personality resemblances among adolescents and their parents in biologically related and adoptive families. *Journal of Personality and Social Psychology, 40,* 885–898.

Scarr-Salapatek, S. (1971). Race, social class, and IQ. *Science, 174,* 1286–1295.

Scheier, M. F., & Carver, C. S. (1985). Optimism, coping, and health: Assessment and implications of generalized outcome expectancies. *Health Psychology, 4,* 219–247.

Scheier, M. F., Carver, C. S., & Bridges, M. W. (2001). Optimism, pessimism, and psychological well-being. In E. C. Chang (Ed.), *Optimism and pessimism: Implications for theory, research, and practice* (pp. 189–216). Washington, DC: American Psychological Association.

Scheier, M. F., Matthews, K. A., Owens, J. F., Magovern, G. J., Lefebvre, R. C., Abbott, R. A. et al. (1989). Dispositional optimism and recovery from coronary artery bypass surgery: The beneficial effects on physical and psychological well-being. *Journal of Personality and Social Psychology, 57,* 1024–1040.

Schimmack, U., & Diener, E. (1997). Affect intensity: Separating intensity and frequency in repeatedly measured affect. *Journal of Personality and Social Psychology, 73,* 1313–1329.

Schlenker, B. R., & Leary, M. R. (1982). Social anxiety and self-presentation: A conceptualization and model. *Psychological Bulletin, 92,* 641–669.

Schmalt, H.-D. (1999). Assessing the achievement motive using the grid technique. *Journal of Research in Personality, 33,* 109–130.

Schmidt, J. A., Shernoff, D. J., & Csikszentmihalyi, M. (2007). Individual and situational factors related to the experience of flow in adolescence: A multilevel approach. In A. D. Ong & M. H. M. van Dulmen (Eds.), *Oxford handbook of methods in positive psychology* (pp. 542–558). New York: Oxford University Press.

Schmidt, N., Gooding, R. Z., Noe, R. A., & Kirsch, M. (1984). Meta-analyses of validity studies published between 1964 and 1982 and the investigation of study characteristics. *Personnel Psychology, 37,* 407–422.

Schmidt, N., & Sermat, V. (1983). Measuring loneliness in different relationships. *Journal of Personality and Social Psychology, 44,* 1038–1047.

Schmukle, S. C., Egloff, B., & Burns, L. R. (2002). The relationship between positive and negative affect in the Positive and Negative Affect Schedule. *Journal of Research in Personality, 36,* 463–475.

Schollgen, I., Huxhold, O., Schuz, B., & Tesch-Romer, C. (2011). Resources for health: Differential effects of optimistic self-beliefs and social support according to socioeconomic status. *Health Psychology, 30,* 326–335.

Schug, J., Yuki, M., & Maddux, W. (2010). Relational mobility explains between- and within-culture differences in self-disclosure to close friends. *Psychological Science, 21,* 1471–1478.

Schulz, R., & Heckhausen, J. (1999). Aging, culture and control: Setting a new research agenda. *Journal of Gerontology: Psychological Sciences, 54B,* 139–145.

Schuyler, B. A., & Coe, W. C. (1981). A physiological investigation of volitional and nonvolitional experience during posthypnotic amnesia. *Journal of Personality and Social Psychology, 40,* 1160–1169.

Schwartz, C. E., Snidman, N., & Kagan, J. (1996). Early childhood temperament as a determinant of externalizing behavior in adolescence. *Development and Psychopathology, 8,* 527–537.

Schwartz, C. E., Snidman, N., & Kagan, J. (1999). Adolescent social anxiety as an outcome of inhibited temperament in childhood. *Journal of the American Academy of Child and Adolescent Psychiatry, 38,* 1008–1015.

Schwartz, C. E., Wright, C. I., Shin, L. M., Kagan, J., & Rauch, S. L. (2003). Inhibited and uninhibited infants "grown up": Adult amygdalar response to novelty. *Science, 300,* 1952–1953.

Schwartz, R. D., & Higgins, R. L. (1979). Differential outcome from automated assertion training as a function of locus of control. *Journal of Consulting and Clinical Psychology, 47,* 686–694.

Sears, R. R. (1941). Non-aggressive reactions to frustration. *Psychological Review, 48,* 343–346.

Seeds, P. M., & Dozois, D. J. A. (2010). Prospective evaluation of a cognitive vulnerability-stress model for depression: The interaction of schema self-structures and negative life events. *Journal of Clinical Psychology, 66,* 1307–1323.

Segal, D. L., Coolidge, F. L., & Mizuno, H. (2007). Defense mechanism differences between younger and older adults: A cross-sectional investigation. *Aging & Mental Health, 11,* 415–422.

Segal, D. L., & Murray, E. J. (1993). Emotional processing in cognitive therapy and vocal expression of feeling. *Journal of Social and Clinical Psychology, 13,* 189–206.

Segerstrom, S. C. (2007). Optimism and resources: Effects on each other and on health over 10 years. *Journal of Research in Personality, 41,* 772–786.

Segerstrom, S. C., & Sephton, S. E. (2010). Optimistic expectancies and cell-mediated immunity: The role of positive affect. *Psychological Science, 21,* 448–455.

Segrin, C. (1999). Social skills, stressful life events, and the development of psychosocial problems. *Journal of Social and Clinical Psychology, 18,* 14–34.

Segrin, C., & Flora, J. (2000). Poor social skills are a vulnerability factor in the development of psychosocial problems. *Human Communication Research, 26,* 489–514.

Segura, S. L., & Gonzalez-Roma, V. (2003). How do respondents construe ambiguous response formats of affect items? *Journal of Personality and Social Psychology, 85,* 956–968.

Seidlitz, L., & Diener, E. (1998). Sex differences in the recall of affective experiences. *Journal of Personality and Social Psychology, 74,* 262–271.

Selfhout, M., Burk, W., Branje, S., Denissen, J., van Aken, M., & Meeus, W. (2010). Emerging late adolescent friendship networks and Big Five personality traits: A social network approach. *Journal of Personality, 78,* 509–538.

Seligman, M. E. P. (1975). *Helplessness: On depression, development and death.* San Francisco: W. H. Freeman.

Seligman, M. E. P. (1976). *Learned helplessness and depression in animals and men.* Morristown, NJ: General Learning Press.

Seligman, M. E. P., & Maier, S. F. (1967). Failure to escape traumatic shock. *Journal of Experimental Psychology, 74,* 1–9.

Seligman, M. E. P., & Schulman, P. (1986). Explanatory style as a predictor of productivity and quitting among life insurance sales agents. *Journal of Personality and Social Psychology, 50,* 832–838.

Seligman, M. E. P., Steen, T. A., Park, N., & Peterson, C. (2005). Positive psychology progress: Empirical validation of interventions. *American Psychologist, 60,* 410–421.

Senko, C., & Harackiewicz, J. M. (2005). Achievement goals, task performance, and interest: Why perceived goal difficulty matters. *Personality and Social Psychology Bulletin, 31,* 1739–1753.

Shadish, W. R., & Baldwin, S. A. (2005). Effects of behavioral marital therapy: A meta-analysis of randomized controlled trials. *Journal of Consulting and Clinical Psychology, 73,* 6–18.

Shah, J., & Higgins, E. T. (2001). Regulatory concerns and appraisal efficiency: The general impact of promotion and prevention. *Journal of Personality and Social Psychology, 80,* 693–705.

Shankar, A., McMunn, A., Banks, J., & Steptoe, A. (2011). Loneliness, social isolation, and behavioral and biological health indicators in older adults. *Health Psychology, 30,* 377–385.

Shaw, J. S. (1982). Psychological androgyny and stressful life events. *Journal of Personality and Social Psychology, 43,* 145–153.

Shechter, O. G., Durik, A. M., Miyamoto, Y., & Harackiewicz, J. M. (2011). The role of utility value in achievement behavior: The importance of culture. *Personality and Social Psychology Bulletin, 37,* 303–317.

Shedler, J. (2010). The efficacy of psychodynamic psychotherapy. *American Psychologist, 65,* 98–109.

Shedler, J., Mayman, M., & Manis, M. (1993). The illusion of mental health. *American Psychologist, 48,* 1117–1131.

Sheldon, K. M. (1994). Emotionality differences between artists and scientists. *Journal of Research in Personality, 28,* 481–491.

Sheldon, W. H. (1942). *The varieties of temperament: A psychology of constitutional differences.* New York: Harper & Row.

Shepperd, J. A., & Arkin, R. M. (1990). Shyness and self-presentation. In W. R. Crozier (Ed.), *Shyness and embarrassment: Perspectives from social psychology* (pp. 286–314). Cambridge: Cambridge University Press.

Shepperd, J. A., Maroto, J. J., & Pbert, L. A. (1996). Dispositional optimism as a predictor of health changes among cardiac patients. *Journal of Research in Personality, 30,* 517–534.

Shimizu, M., Seery, M. D., Weisbuch, M., & Lupien, S. P. (2011). Trait social anxiety and physiological activation: Cardiovascular threat during social interaction. *Personality and Social Psychology Bulletin, 37,* 94–106.

Shiner, R. L. (1998). How shall we speak of children's personalities in middle childhood? A preliminary taxonomy. *Psychological Bulletin, 124,* 308–332.

Shoda, Y., Tiernan, S. L., & Mischel, W. (2002). Personality as a dynamical system: Emergence of stability and distinctiveness from intra-and interpersonal interactions. *Personality and Social Psychology Review, 6,* 316–325.

Shulevitz, J. (2013, May 27). The lethality of loneliness. *The New Republic,* pp. 22–29.

Shurcliff, A. (1968). Judged humor, arousal, and the relief theory. *Journal of Personality and Social Psychology, 4,* 360–363.

Siegel, B. (2007, June 12). Stressful times for Chinese students. *Time.*

Siegler, I. C. (1994). Hostility and risk: Demographic and lifestyle variables. In A. W. Siegman & T. W. Smith (Eds.), *Anger, hostility, and the heart* (pp. 199–214). Hillsdale, NJ: Erlbaum.

Siegman, A. W. (1994). From type A to hostility to anger: Reflections on the history of coronary-prone behavior. In A. W. Siegman & T. W. Smith (Eds.), *Anger, hostility, and the heart* (pp. 1–21). Hillsdale, NJ: Erlbaum.

Siem, F. M. (1998). Metatraits and self-schemata: Same or different? *Journal of Personality, 66,* 783–803.

Simms, L. J. (2007). The Big Seven Model of personality and its relevance to personality pathology. *Journal of Personality, 75,* 65–94.

Simoni, J. M., & Ng, M. T. (2002). Abuse, health locus of control, and perceived health among HIV-positive women. *Health Psychology, 21,* 89–93.

Simpson, J. A. (1990). Influence of attachment styles on romantic relationships. *Journal of Personality and Social Psychology, 59,* 971–980.

Simpson, J. A., Collins, A., Tran, S., & Haydon, K. C. (2007). Attachment and the experience and expression of emotion in romantic relationships: A developmental perspective. *Journal of Personality and Social Psychology, 92,* 355–367.

Simpson, J. A., Ickes, W., & Grich, J. (1999). When accuracy hurts: Reactions of anxious-ambivalent dating partners to a relationship threatening situation. *Journal of Personality and Social Psychology, 76,* 754–769.

Simpson, J. A., Rholes, W. S., & Nelligan, J. S. (1992). Support seeking and support giving within couples in an anxiety-provoking situation: The role of attachment styles. *Journal of Personality and Social Psychology, 62*, 434–446.

Simpson, J. A., Rholes, W. S., Orina, M. M., & Grich, J. (2002). Working models of attachment, support giving, and support seeking in a stressful situation. *Personality and Social Psychology Bulletin, 28*, 598–608.

Simpson, T. L., & Arroyo, J. A. (1998). Coping patterns associated with alcohol-related negative consequences among college women. *Journal of Social and Clinical Psychology, 17*, 150–166.

Simsek, O. F., Koydemir, S., & Schutz, A. (2012). A multigroup multitrait-multimethod study in two countries supports the validity of a two-factor higher order model of personality. *Journal of Research in Personality, 46*, 442–449.

Singer, J. A. (2004). Narrative identity and meaning making across the adult lifespan: An introduction. *Journal of Personality, 72*, 437–459.

Singer, J. L., & Singer, D. G. (1981). *Television, imagination, and aggression: A study of preschoolers.* Hillside, NJ: Erlbaum.

Sipley, C. G., Fischer, R., & Lui, J. H. (2005). Reliability and validity of the Revised Experiences in Close Relationships (ECR-R) self-report measure of adult romantic attachment. *Personality and Social Psychology Bulletin, 31*, 1524–1536.

Skinner, B. F. (1967). B. F. Skinner. In E. G. Boring & G. Lindzey (Eds.), *A history of psychology in autobiography* (Vol. 5, pp. 387–413). New York: Appleton-Century-Crofts.

Skinner, B. F. (1971). *Beyond freedom and dignity.* New York: Bantam.

Skinner, B. F. (1974). *About behaviorism.* New York: Vintage Books.

Skinner, B. F. (1983). *A matter of consequences.* New York: Knopf.

Skinner, E. A., Edge, K., Altman, J., & Sherwood, H. (2003). Searching for the structure of coping: A review and critique of category systems for classifying ways of coping. *Psychological Bulletin, 129*, 216–269.

Slater, J., & Depue, R. A. (1981). The contribution of environmental events and social support to serious suicide attempts in primary depressive disorder. *Journal of Abnormal Psychology, 90*, 275–285.

Slavkin, M., & Stright, A. D. (2000). Gender role differences in college students from one-and two-parent families. *Sex Roles, 42*, 23–37.

Slife, B., & Rychlak, J. F. (1982). Role of affective assessment in modeling aggressive behavior. *Journal of Personality and Social Psychology, 43*, 861–868.

Sloan, W. W., & Solano, C. H. (1984). The conversational styles of lonely males with strangers and roommates. *Personality and Social Psychology Bulletin, 10*, 293–301.

Sloman, L. (2008). A new comprehensive evolutionary model of depression and anxiety. *Journal of Affective Disorders, 106*, 219–228.

Slotter, E. B., & Finkel, E. J. (2009). The strange case of sustained dedication to an unfulfilling relationship: Predicting commitment and breakup from attachment anxiety and need fulfillment within relationships. *Personality and Social Psychology Bulletin, 35*, 85–100.

Slutske, W. S., Moffitt, T. E., Poulton, R., & Caspi, A. (2012). Undercontrolled temperament at age 3 predicts disordered gambling at age 32: A longitudinal study of a complete birth cohort. *Psychological Science, 23*, 510–516.

Smillie, L. D. (2013). Extraversion and reward processing. *Current Directions in Psychological Science, 22*, 167–172.

Smillie, L. D., Cooper, A. J., Wilt, J., & Revelle, W. (2012). Do extraverts get more bang for the buck? Refining the affective-reactivity hypothesis of extraversion. *Journal of Personality and Social Psychology, 103*, 306–326.

Smillie, L. D., Pickering, A. D., & Jackson, C. J. (2006). The new reinforcement sensitivity theory: Implications for personality measurement. *Personality and Social Psychology Review, 10*, 320–335.

Smith, C. A., Wallston, K. A., & Dwyer, K. A. (1995). On babies and bath water: Disease impact and negative affectivity in the self-reports of persons with rheumatoid arthritis. *Health Psychology, 14*, 64–73.

Smith, C. E., Fernengel, K., Holcroft, C., Gerald, K., & Marien, M. (1994). Meta-analysis of the associations between social support and health outcomes. *Annals of Behavioral Medicine, 16*, 352–362.

Smith, R. E. (1989). Effects of coping skills training on generalized self-efficacy and locus of control. *Journal of Personality and Social Psychology, 56*, 228–233.

Smith, S. L., & Donnerstein, E. (1998). Harmful effects of exposure to media violence: Learning of aggression, emotional desensitization, and fear. In R. G. Geen & E. Donnerstein (Eds.), *Human aggression: Theories, research, and implications for social policy* (pp. 167–202). San Diego: Academic Press.

Smith, T. W. (2006). Personality as risk and resilience in physical health. *Current Directions in Psychological Science, 15*, 227–231.

Smith, T. W., Glazer, K., Ruiz, J. M., & Gallo, L. C. (2004). Hostility, anger, aggressiveness, and coronary heart disease: An interpersonal perspective on personality, emotion, and health. *Journal of Personality, 72*, 1217–1270.

Smyth, J., True, N., & Souto, J. (2001). Effects of writing about traumatic experiences: The necessity for narrative structuring. *Journal of Social and Clinical Psychology, 20*, 161–172.

Snyder, C. R. (1988). From defenses to self-protection: An evolutionary perspective. *Journal of Social and Clinical Psychology, 6*, 155–158.

Solano, C. H., Batten, P. G., & Parish, E. A. (1982). Loneliness and patterns of self-disclosure. *Journal of Personality and Social Psychology, 43*, 524–531.

Solano, C. H., & Koester, N. H. (1989). Loneliness and communication problems: Subjective anxiety or objective skills? *Personality and Social Psychology Bulletin, 15,* 126–133.

Solberg Nes, L., Evans, D. R., & Segerstrom, S. C. (2009). Optimism and college retention: Mediation by motivation, performance and adjustment. *Journal of Applied Social Psychology, 39,* 1887–1912.

Soldz, S., & Vaillant, G. E. (1999). The Big Five personality traits and the life course: A 45-year longitudinal study. *Journal of Research in Personality, 33,* 208–232.

Solomon, Z., Mikulincer, M., & Avitzur, E. (1988). Coping, locus of control, social support, and combat-related posttraumatic stress disorder: A prospective study. *Journal of Personality and Social Psychology, 55,* 279–285.

Solomon, Z., Weisenberg, M., Schwarzwald, J., & Mikulincer, M. (1988). Combat stress reaction and posttraumatic stress disorder as determinants of perceived self-efficacy in battle. *Journal of Social and Clinical Psychology, 6,* 356–370.

Soto, C. J., John, O. P., Gosling, S. D., & Potter, J. (2011). Age differences in personality traits from 10 to 65: Big Five domains and facets in a large cross-sectional sample. *Journal of Personality and Social Psychology, 100,* 330–348.

Spangler, W. D., & House, R. J. (1991). Presidential effectiveness and the leadership motive profile. *Journal of Personality and Social Psychology, 60,* 439–455.

Spanos, N. P., & Hewitt, E. C. (1980). The hidden observer in hypnotic analgesia: Discovery or experimental creation? *Journal of Personality and Social Psychology, 39,* 1201–1214.

Spanos, N. P., & Katsanis, J. (1989). Effects of instructional set on attributions of nonvolition during hypnotic and nonhypnotic analgesia. *Journal of Personality and Social Psychology, 56,* 182–188.

Spanos, N. P., Liddy, S. J., Baxter, C. E., & Burgess, C. A. (1994). Long-term and short-term stability of behavioral and subjective indexes of hypnotizability. *Journal of Research in Personality, 28,* 301–313.

Spanos, N. P., Radtke, H. L., & Dubreuil, D. L. (1982). Episodic and semantic memory in posthypnotic amnesia: A reevaluation. *Journal of Personality and Social Psychology, 43,* 565–573.

Specht, J., Egloff, B., & Schmukle, S. C. (2011). Stability and change of personality across the life course: The impact of age and major life events on mean-level and rankorder stability of the Big Five. *Journal of Personality and Social Psychology, 101,* 862–882.

Spector, P. E., Cooper, C. L., Sanchez, J. L., O'Driscoll, M., Sparks, K., Bernin, P. et al. (2001). Do national levels of individualism and internal locus of control relate to well-being: An ecological level international study. *Journal of Organizational Behavior, 22,* 815–832.

Spence, J. T. (1993). Gender-related traits and gender ideology: Evidence for a multifactorial theory. *Journal of Personality and Social Psychology, 64,* 624–635.

Spence, J. T., & Helmreich, R. L. (1983). Achievement-related motives and behaviors. In J. T. Spence (Ed.), *Achievement and achievement motives: Psychological and sociological approaches* (pp. 7–74). San Francisco: W. H. Freeman.

Spence, J. T., Helmreich, R. L., & Stapp, J. (1974). The Personal Attributes Questionnaire: A measure of sex-role stereotypes and masculinity-femininity. *JSAS Catalog of Selected Documents in Psychology, 4,* 127 (Ms. No. 617).

Spiegel, D. (2005). Multileveling the playing field: Altering our state of consciousness to understand hypnosis. *Contemporary Hypnosis, 22,* 31–33.

Spielmann, S. S., Maxwell, J. A., MacDonald, G., & Baratta, P. L. (2013). Don't get your hopes up: Avoidantly attached individuals perceive lower social reward when there is potential for intimacy. *Personality and Social Psychology Bulletin, 39,* 219–236.

Sprecher, S., & Hendrick, S. S. (2004). Self-disclosure in intimate relationships: Associations with individual and relationship characteristics over time. *Journal of Social and Clinical Psychology, 23,* 857–877.

Sprecher, S., Sullivan, Q., & Hatfield, E. (1994). Mate selection preferences: Gender differences examined in a national sample. *Journal of Personality and Social Psychology, 66,* 1074–1080.

Srivastava, S., Angelo, K. M., & Vallereux, S. R. (2009). Extraversion and positive affect: A day reconstruction study of person-environment transactions. *Journal of Research in Personality, 42,* 1613–1618.

Staats, A. W. (1996). *Behaviorism and personality: Psychological behaviorism.* New York: Springer.

Stajkovic, A. D., & Luthans, F. (1998). Self-efficacy and work-related performance: A meta-analysis. *Psychological Bulletin, 124,* 240–261.

Stake, J. E. (2000). When situations call for instrumentality and expressiveness: Resource appraisal, coping strategy choice, and adjustment. *Sex Roles, 42,* 865–885.

Stake, J. E., Huff, L., & Zand, D. (1995). Trait self-esteem, positive and negative events, and event-specific shifts in self-evaluation and affect. *Journal of Research in Personality, 29,* 223–241.

Stake, J. E., & Nickens, S. D. (2005). Adolescent girls' and boys' science peer relationships and perceptions of the possible self as scientist. *Sex Roles, 52,* 1–11.

Stanton, A. L., Kirk, S. B., Cameron, C. L., & Danoff-Burg, S. (2000). Coping through emotional approach: Scale construction and validation. *Journal of Personality and Social Psychology, 78,* 1150–1169.

Steel, P., & Ones, D. S. (2002). Personality and happiness: A national-level analysis. *Journal of Personality and Social Psychology, 83,* 767–781.

Steger, M. F., Kawabata, Y., Shimai, S., & Otake, K. (2008). The meaningful life in Japan and the United States: Levels and correlates of meaning in life. *Journal of Research in Personality, 42,* 660–678.

Stein, G. L., Kimiecik, J. C., Daniels, J., & Jackson, S. A. (1995). Psychological antecedents of flow in recreational sports. *Personality and Social Psychology Bulletin, 21,* 125–135.

Stelmack, R. M. (1990). Biological bases of extraversion: Psychophysiological evidence. *Journal of Personality, 58,* 293–311.

Stelmack, R. M., & Pivik, R. T. (1996). Extraversion and the effects of exercise on spinal motoneuronal excitability. *Personality and Individual Differences, 21,* 69–76.

Stephenson, W. (1953). *The study of behavior: Q-technique and its methodology.* Chicago: University of Chicago Press.

Steptoe, A., Dockray, S., & Wardle, J. (2009). Positive affect and psychobiological processes relevant to health. *Journal of Personality, 77,* 1746–1775.

Steptoe, A., & Wardle, J. (2001). Locus of control and health behaviour revisited: A multivariate analysis of young adults from 18 countries. *British Journal of Psychology, 92,* 659–672.

Sternberg, R. J., Grigorenko, E. L., & Kidd, K. K. (2005). Intelligence, race, and genetics. *American Psychologist, 60,* 46–59.

Stewart, A. J. (1982). *Motivation and society.* San Francisco: Jossey-Bass.

Stewart, J. L., Bismark, A. W., Towers, D. N., Coan, J. A., & Allen, J. J. B. (2010). Resting frontal EEG asymmetry as an endophenotype for depression risk: Sex-specific patterns of frontal brain asymmetry. *Journal of Abnormal Psychology, 119,* 502–512.

Stewart, R. E., & Chambless, D. L. (2009). Cognitive-behavioral therapy for adult anxiety disorders in clinical practice: A meta-analysis of effectiveness studies. *Journal of Consulting and Clinical Psychology, 77,* 595–606.

Stoolmiller, M. (1999). Implications of the restricted range of family environments for estimates of heritability and nonshared environment in behavior-genetic adoption studies. *Psychological Bulletin, 125,* 392–409.

Storr, A. (1988). *Solitude: A return to the self.* New York: Free Press.

Story, A. L. (1998). Self-esteem and memory for favorable and unfavorable personality feedback. *Personality and Social Psychology Bulletin, 24,* 51–64.

Strahan, E. J., Lafrance, A., Wilson, A. E., Ethier, N., Spencer, S. J., & Zanna, M. (2008). Victoria's dirty secret: How sociocultural norms influence adolescent girls and women. *Personality and Social Psychology Bulletin, 34,* 288–301.

Strauman, T. J. (1996). Stability within the self: A longitudinal study of the structural implications of self-discrepancy theory. *Journal of Personality and Social Psychology, 71,* 1142–1153.

Strentz, T., & Auerbach, S. M. (1988). Adjustment to the stress of simulated captivity: Effects of emotion-focused versus problem-focused preparation on hostages differing in locus of control. *Journal of Personality and Social Psychology, 55,* 652–660.

Strickland, B. R. (1978). Internal-external expectancies and health-related behaviors. *Journal of Consulting and Clinical Psychology, 46,* 1192–1211.

Strickland, B. R. (1989). Internal-external control expectancies: From contingency to creativity. *American Psychologist, 44,* 1–12.

Stright, A. D., Gallagher, K. C., & Kelley, K. (2008). Infant temperament moderates relations between maternal parenting in early childhood and children's adjustment in first grade. *Child Development, 79,* 186–200.

Strough, J., Leszczynski, J. P., Neely, T. L., Flinn, J. A., & Margrett, J. (2007). From adolescence to later adulthood: Femininity,

masculinity, and androgyny in six age groups. *Sex Roles, 57,* 385–396.

Strube, M. J. (1982). Time urgency and Type A behavior: A methodological note. *Personality and Social Psychology Bulletin, 8,* 563–565.

Strube, M. J., Berry, J. M., & Moergen, S. (1985). Relinquishment of control and the Type A behavior pattern: The role of performance evaluation. *Journal of Personality and Social Psychology, 49,* 831–842.

Sturmer, T., & Hasselbach, P. (2006). Personality, lifestyle, and risk of cardiovascular disease and cancer: Follow-up of population based cohort. *British Medical Journal, 332,* 1359.

Subra, B., Muller, D., Begue, L., Bushman, B. J., & Delmas, F. (2010). Automatic effects of alcohol and aggressive cues on aggressive thoughts and behaviors. *Personality and Social Psychology Bulletin, 36,* 1052–1057.

Suedfeld, P. (1980). *Restricted environmental stimulation: Research and clinical applications.* New York: Wiley.

Suedfeld, P. (1982). Aloneness as a healing experience. In L. A. Peplau & D. Perlman (Eds.), *Loneliness: A sourcebook of current theory, research and therapy* (pp. 54–67). New York: Wiley.

Suh, E., Diener, E., Oishi, S., & Triandis, H. C. (1998). The shifting basis of life satisfaction judgments across cultures: Emotions versus norms. *Journal of Personality and Social Psychology, 74,* 482–493.

Suinn, R. M. (2001). The terrible twos—anger and anxiety: Hazardous to your health. *American Psychologist, 56,* 27–36.

Suls, J., & Fletcher, B. (1985). The relative efficacy of avoidant and nonavoidant coping strategies: A meta-analysis. *Health Psychology, 4,* 249–288.

Sundie, J. M., Kenrick, D. T., Griskevicius, V., Tybur, J. M., Vohs, K. D., & Beal, D. J. (2011). Peacocks, Porsches, and Thorstein Veblen:

Conspicuous consumption as a sexual signaling system. *Journal of Personality and Social Psychology, 100*, 664–680.

Surtees, P. G., Wainwright, N. W. J., Luben, R., Khaw, K.-T., & Day, N. E. (2006). Mastery, sense of coherence, and mortality: Evidence of independent associations from the EPIC-Norfolk prospective cohort study. *Health Psychology, 25*, 102–110.

Suvak, M. K., Vogt, D. S., Savarese, V. W., King, L. A., & King, D. W. (2002). Relationship of war-zone coping strategies to long-term general life adjustment among Vietnam veterans: Combat exposure as a moderator variable. *Personality and social Psychology Bulletin, 28*, 974–985.

Swann, W. B., & Seyle, C. (2005). Personality psychology's comeback and its emerging symbiosis with social psychology. *Personality and Social Psychology Bulletin, 31*, 155–165.

Swickert, R. J., & Gilliland, K. (1998). Relationship between the brainstem auditory evoked response and extraversion, impulsivity, and sociability. *Journal of Research in Personality, 32*, 314–330.

Symons, C. S., & Johnson, B. T. (1997). The self-reference effect in memory: A meta-analysis. *Psychological Bulletin, 121*, 371–394.

Tafarodi, R. W., Marshall, T. C., & Katsura, H. (2004). Standing out in Canada and Japan. *Journal of Personality, 72*, 785–814.

Tafarodi, R. W., & Vu, C. (1997). Two-dimensional self-esteem and reactions to success and failure. *Personality and Social Psychology Bulletin, 23*, 626–635.

Tamir, M. (2009). Differential preferences for happiness: Extraversion and trait-consistent emotion regulation. *Journal of Personality, 77*, 447–470.

Tamres, L. K., Janicki, D., & Helgeson, V. S. (2002). Sex differences in coping behavior: A meta-analytic review and an examination of relative coping. *Personality*

and *Social Psychology Review, 6*, 2–30.

Tarabulsky, G. M., Provost, M. A., Larose, S., Moss, E., Lemelin, J.-P., Moran, G. et al. (2008). Similarities and differences in mothers' and observers' ratings of infant security on the attachment Q-Sort. *Infant Behavior & Development, 31*, 10–22.

Taubes, G. (1998, May–June). Telling time by the second hand. *Technology Review, 101*, 76.

Taylor, D. A., & Belgrave, F. Z. (1986). The effects of perceived intimacy and valence on self-disclosure reciprocity. *Personality and Social Psychology Bulletin, 12*, 247–255.

Taylor, M. C., & Hall, J. A. (1982). Psychological androgyny: Theories, methods and conclusions. *Psychological Bulletin, 92*, 347–366.

Taylor, S. E. (1989). *Positive illusions: Creative self-deception and the healthy mind*. New York: Basic Books.

Tellegen, A., & Atkinson, G. (1974). Openness to absorbing and self-altering experiences ("absorption"), a trait related to hypnotic susceptibility. *Journal of Abnormal Psychology, 83*, 268–277.

Terracciano, A., Costa, P. T., & McCrae, R. R. (2006). Personality plasticity after age 30. *Personality and Social Psychology Bulletin, 32*, 999–1009.

Terracciano, A., McCrae, R. R., & Costa, P. T. (2010). Intra-individual change in personality stability and age. *Journal of Research in Personality, 44*, 31–37.

Terracciano, A., McCrae, R. R., Hagemann, D., & Costa, P. T. (2003). Individual difference variables, affective differentiation, and the structure of affect. *Journal of Personality, 71*, 669–703.

Terry, D. J., & Hynes, G. J. (1998). Adjustment to a low-control situation: Reexamining the role of coping responses. *Journal of Personality and Social Psychology, 74*, 1078–1092.

Tett, R. P., Jackson, D. N., & Rothstein, M. (1991). Personality measures as predictors of job performance: A meta-analytic review. *Personnel Psychology, 44*, 703–739.

Thibodeau, R., Jorgensen, R. S., & Kim, S. (2006). Depression, anxiety, and resting frontal EEG asymmetry: A meta-analytic review. *Journal of Abnormal Psychology, 115*, 715–729.

Thoma, N. C., & Cecero, J. J. (2009). Is integrative use of techniques in psychotherapy the exception or the rule? Results of a national survey of doctoral-level practitioners. *Psychotherapy Theory, Research, Practice, Training, 46*, 405–417.

Thomas, A., & Chess, S. (1977). *Temperament and development*. New York: Brunner/Mazel.

Thompson, R. J., Dizen, M., & Berenbaum, H. (2009). The unique relations between emotional awareness and facets of affective instability. *Journal of Research in Personality, 43*, 875–879.

Thorndike, E. L. (1911). *Animal intelligence: Experimental studies*. New York: Macmillan.

Thrash, T. M., & Elliot, A. J. (2002). Implicit and self-attributed achievement motives: Concordance and predictive validity. *Journal of Personality, 70*, 729–755.

Thrash, T. M., Elliot, A. J., & Schultheiss, O. C. (2007). Methodological and dispositional predictors of congruence between implicit and explicit need for achievement. *Personality and Social Psychology Bulletin, 33*, 961–974.

Tidwell, M.-C. O., Reis, H. T., & Shaver, P. R. (1996). Attachment, attractiveness, and social interaction: A diary study. *Journal of Personality and Social Psychology, 71*, 729–745.

Timmers, M., Fischer, A. H., & Manstead, A. S. R. (1998). Gender differences in motives for regulating emotions. *Personality and Social Psychology Bulletin, 24*, 974–985.

Todorov, A., & Bargh, J. A. (2002). Automatic sources of aggression.

Aggression and Violent Behavior, 7, 53–68.

Torges, C. M., Stewart, A. J., & Duncan, L. E. (2009). Appreciating life's complexities: Assessing narrative ego integrity in late midlife. *Journal of Research in Personality, 43*, 66–74.

Tracy, J. L., Robins, R. W., & Sherman, J. W. (2009). The practice of psychological science: Searching for Cronbach's two streams in social-personality psychology. *Journal of Personality and Social Psychology, 96*, 1206–1225.

Triandis, H. C. (1989). The self and social behavior in differing cultural contexts. *Psychological Review, 96*, 506–520.

Triandis, H. C. (2001). Individualism-collectivism and personality. *Journal of Personality, 69*, 907–924.

Tripathi, R., & Cervone, D. (2008). Cultural variations in achievement motivation despite equivalent motivational strength: Motivational concerns among Indian and American corporate professionals. *Journal of Research in Personality, 42*, 456–464.

Trivers, R. L. (1972). Parental investment and sexual selection. In B. Campbell (Ed.), *Sexual selection and the descent of man: 1871-1971* (pp. 136–179). Chicago: Aldine.

Tucker, J. S., & Anders, S. L. (1999). Attachment style, interpersonal perception accuracy, and relationship satisfaction in dating couples. *Personality and Social Psychology Bulletin, 15*, 403–412.

Tuerlinckx, F., De Boeck, P., & Lens, W. (2002). Measuring needs with the Thematic Apperception Test: A psychometric study. *Journal of Personality and Social Psychology, 82*, 448–461.

Twenge, J. M. (2000). The age of anxiety? Birth cohort change in anxiety and neuroticism, 1952-1993. *Journal of Personality and Social Psychology, 79*, 1007–1021.

Uchino, B. N., Cacioppo, J. T., & Kiecolt-Glaser, J. K. (1996). The relationship between social support and physiological processes: A review with emphasis on

underlying mechanisms and implications for health. *Psychological Bulletin, 119*, 488–531.

Ungerer, J. A., Waters, B., & Barnett, B. (1997). Defense style and adjustment in interpersonal relationships. *Journal of Research in Personality, 31*, 375–384.

Urbina, S. P., & Grey, A. (1975). Cultural and sex differences in the sex distribution of dream characters. *Journal of Cross-Cultural Psychology, 6*, 358–364.

Uysal, A., Lin, H. L., & Knee, C. R. (2010). The role of need satisfaction in self-concealment and well-being. *Personality and Social Psychology Bulletin, 36*, 187–199.

Uysal, A., Lin, H. L., Knee, C. R., & Bush, A. L. (2012). The association between self-concealment from one's partner and relationship well-being. *Personality and Social Psychology Bulletin, 38*, 39–51.

Vaidya, J. G., Gray, E. K., Haig, J., & Watson, D. (2002). On the temporal stability of personality: Evidence for differential stability and the role of life experiences. *Journal of Personality and Social Psychology, 83*, 1469–1484.

Vaillant, G. E. (1977). *Adaptation to life.* Boston: Little, Brown.

Vaillant, G. E. (1992). *Ego mechanisms of defense: A guide for clinicians and researchers.* Washington, DC: American Psychiatric Press.

Valentiner, D. P., Foa, E. B., Riggs, D. S., & Gershuny, B. S. (1996). Coping strategies and posttraumatic stress disorder in female victims of sexual and nonsexual assault. *Journal of Abnormal Psychology, 105*, 455–458.

Valli, K., Revonsuo, A., Palkas, O., & Punamaki, R.-L. (2006). The effect of trauma on dream content—a field study of Palestinian children. *Dreaming, 16*, 63–87.

van Dellen, M. R., Campbell, W. K., Hoyle, R. H., & Bradfield, E. K. (2011). Compensating, resisting, and breaking: A meta-analytic examination of reactions to self-esteem threat. *Personality and Social Psychology Review, 15*, 51–74.

van der Linden, D., Scholte, R. H. J., Cillessen, A. H. N., te Nijenhuis, J., & Segers, E. (2010). Classroom ratings of likeability and popularity are related to the Big Five and the general factor of personality. *Journal of Research in Personality, 44*, 669–672.

Vanhalst, J., Luyckx, K., Teppers, E., & Goossens, L. (2012). Disentangling the longitudinal relation between loneliness and depressive symptoms: Prospective effects and the intervening role of coping. *Journal of Social and Clinical Psychology, 31*, 810–834.

van Ijendoorn, M. H., Vereijken, C. M. J. L., Bakermans-Kranenburg, M. J., & Riksen-Walraven, J. M. (2004). Assessing attachment security with the attachment Q-Sort: Meta-analytic evidence for the validity of the observer AQS. *Child Development, 75*, 1188–1213.

Van Yperen, N. W. (2006). A novel approach to assessing achievement goals in the context of the 2 X 2 framework: Identifying distinct profiles and individuals with different dominant achievement goals. *Personality and Social Psychology Bulletin, 32*, 1432–1445.

Van Zalk, N., Van Zalk, M., Kerr, M., & Stattin, H. (2011). Social anxiety as a basis for friendship selection and socialization in adolescents' social networks. *Journal of Personality, 79*, 499–526.

Van Zundert, R. M. P., Ferguson, S. G., Shiffman, S., & Engels, R. C. M. E. (2010). Dynamic effects of self-efficacy on smoking lapses and relapse among adolescents. *Health Psychology, 29*, 246–254.

Vasquez, E. A. (2009). Cognitive load, trigger salience, and the facilitation of triggered displaced aggression. *European Journal of Social Psychology, 39*, 684–693.

Vasquez, E. A., Denson, T. F., Pedersen, W. C., Stenstrom, D. M., & Miller, N. (2005). The moderating effect of trigger intensity on triggered displaced aggression. *Journal of Experimental Social Psychology, 41*, 61–67.

Vasquez, E. A., Osman, S., & Wood, J. L. (2012). Rumination and the displacement of aggression in United Kingdom gang-affiliated youth. *Aggressive Behavior, 38,* 89–97.

Vasquez, E. A., Pedersen, W. C., Bushman, B. J., Kelley, N. J., Demeestere, P., & Miller, N. (2013). Lashing out after stewing over public insults: The effects of public provocation, provocation intensity, and rumination on triggered displaced aggression. *Aggressive Behavior, 39,* 13–29.

Vaughn, L. A., & Weary, G. (2002). Roles of the availability of explanations, feelings of ease, and dysphoria in judgments about the future. *Journal of Social and Clinical Psychology, 21,* 686–704.

Veroff, J., Depner, C., Kulka, R., & Douvan, E. (1980). Comparison of American motives: 1957 versus 1976. *Journal of Personality and Social Psychology, 39,* 1249–1262.

Verona, E., & Sullivan, E. A. (2008). Emotional catharsis and aggression revisited: Heart rate reduction following aggressive responding. *Emotion, 8,* 331–340.

Viglione, D. J. (1999). A review of recent research addressing the utility of the Rorschach. *Psychological Assessment, 11,* 251–265.

Viglione, D. J., & Hilsenroth, M. J. (2001). The Rorschach: Facts, fictions, and future. *Psychological Assessment, 13,* 452–471.

Vignoles, V. L., Manzi, C., Regalia, C., Jemmolo, S., & Scabini, E. (2008). Identity motives underlying desired and feared possible future selves. *Journal of Personality, 76,* 1165–1200.

Vitaliano, P. P., DeWolfe, D. J., Maiuro, R. D., Russo, J., & Katon, W. (1990). Appraised changeability of a stressor as a modifier of the relationship between coping and depression: A test of the hypothesis of fit. *Journal of Personality and Social Psychology, 59,* 582–592.

Vitkus, J., & Horowitz, L. M. (1987). Poor social performance of lonely people: Lacking a skill or adopting a role? *Journal of Personality and Social Psychology, 52,* 1266–1273.

Vittengl, J. R., Clark, L. A., Dunn, T. W., & Jarrett, R. B. (2007). Reducing relapse and recurrence in unipolar depression: A comparative meta-analysis of cognitive-behavioral therapy's effects. *Journal of Consulting and Clinical Psychology, 75,* 475–488.

Vo, K., & Ostrov, B. F. (2006, February 19). Women seek reliable health advice in vain: Studies keep contradicting the conventional wisdom. *San Jose Mercury News,* pp. 1A, 15A.

Voelz, C. J. (1985). Effects of gender role disparity on couples' decision-making processes. *Journal of Personality and Social Psychology, 49,* 1532–1540.

Vogel, D. A., Lake, M. A., Evans, S., & Karraker, K. H. (1991). Children's and adults' sex-stereotyped perceptions of infants. *Sex Roles, 24,* 605–616.

Vogel, G. W. (1975). Review of REM sleep deprivation. *Archives of General Psychiatry, 32,* 749–761.

Wacker, J., Chavanon, M., Leue, A., & Stemmler, G. (2008). Is running away right? The behavioral activation-behavioral inhibition model of anterior asymmetry. *Emotion, 8,* 232–249.

Wagstaff, G. F., David, D., Kirsch, I., & Lynn, S. J. (2010). The cognitive-behavioral model of hypnotherapy. In S. J. Lynn, J. W. Rhue, & I. Kirsch (Eds.), *Handbook of clinical hypnosis* (2nd ed., pp. 179–208). Washington, DC: American Psychological Association.

Walker, M. P., & van der Helm, E. (2009). Overnight therapy? The role of sleep in emotional brain processing. *Psychological Bulletin, 135,* 731–748.

Wallston, K. A. (1992). Hocus-pocus, the focus isn't strictly on locus: Rotter's social learning theory modified for health. *Cognitive Therapy and Research, 16,* 183–199.

Wallston, K. A. (Ed.). (2005). Research with the Multidimensional Health Locus of Control (MHLC) Scales [Special issue]. *Journal of Health Psychology, 10*(5), 619–621.

Wallston, K. A., & Smith, M. S. (1994). Issues of control and health: The action is in the interaction. In G. N. Penney, P. Bennett, & M. Herbert (Eds.), *Health psychology: A lifespan perspective* (pp. 153–168). London, England: Harwood.

Wang, Q., Bowling, N. A., & Eschleman, K. J. (2010). A meta-analytic examination of work and general locus of control. *Journal of Applied Psychology, 95,* 761–768.

Ward, C. H., & Eisler, R. M. (1987). Type A behavior, achievement striving, and a dysfunctional self-evaluation system. *Journal of Personality and Social Psychology, 53,* 318–326.

Watkins, C. E., Campbell, V. L., Nieberding, R., & Hallmark, R. (1995). Contemporary practice of psychological assessment by clinical psychologists. *Professional Psychology: Research and Practice, 26,* 54–60.

Watson, D. (1988). Intraindividual and interindividual analyses of positive and negative affect: Their relation to health complaints, perceived stress, and daily activities. *Journal of Personality and Social Psychology, 54,* 1020–1030.

Watson, D., & Clark, L. A. (1991). Self-versus peer-ratings of specific emotional traits: Evidence of convergent and discriminant validity. *Journal of Personality and Social Psychology, 60,* 927–940.

Watson, D., Clark, L. A., McIntyre, C. W., & Hamaker, S. (1992). Affect, personality, and social activity. *Journal of Personality and Social Psychology, 63,* 1011–1025.

Watson, D., Clark, L. A., & Tellegen, A. (1988). Development and validation of brief measures of positive and negative affect: The PANAS Scales. *Journal of Personality and Social Psychology, 54,* 1063–1070.

Watson, D., Hubbard, B., & Wiese, D. (2000). Self-other agreement in personality and affectivity: The role of acquaintanceship, trait visibility, and assumed similarity. *Journal of Personality and Social Psychology, 78,* 546–558.

Watson, D., & Naragon, K. (2009). Positive affectivity: The disposition to experience positive emotional states. In S. J. Lopez & C. R. Snyder (Eds.), *Oxford handbook of positive psychology* (2nd ed., pp. 207–215). New York: Oxford University Press.

Watson, D., & Tellegen, A. (1985). Toward a consensual structure of mood. *Psychological Bulletin, 98,* 219–235.

Watson, J. B. (1924/1970). *Behaviorism.* New York: Norton.

Watson, J. B. (1936). John Broadus Watson. In C. Murchison (Ed.), *A history of psychology in autobiography* (Vol. 3, pp. 271–281). Worcester, MA: Clark University Press.

Watson, J. B., & Rayner, R. (1920). Conditioned emotional reactions. *Journal of Experimental Psychology, 3,* 1–14.

Webb, S. D. (1978). Privacy and psychosomatic stress: An empirical analysis. *Social Behavior and Personality, 6,* 227–234.

Weeks, D. G., Michela, J. L., Peplau, L. A., & Bragg, M. E. (1980). Relation between loneliness and depression: A structural equation analysis. *Journal of Personality and Social Psychology, 39,* 1238–1244.

Weeks, J. W., Jakatdar, T. A., & Heimberg, R. G. (2010). Comparing and contrasting fears of positive and negative evaluation as facets of social anxiety. *Journal of Social and Clinical Psychology, 29,* 68–94.

Wegner, D. M., Wenzlaff, R. M., & Kozak, M. (2004). Dream rebound: The return of suppressed thoughts in dreams. *Psychological Science, 15,* 232–236.

Wei, M., Russell, D. W., & Zakalik, R. A. (2005). Adult attachment, social self-efficacy, self-disclosure, loneliness, and subsequent depression for freshman college students: A longitudinal study. *Journal of Counseling Psychology, 52,* 602–614.

Weiner, B. (1985). An attributional theory of achievement motivation and emotion. *Psychological Bulletin, 92,* 548–573.

Weiner, B. (1990). Attribution in personality psychology. In L. A. Pervin (Ed.), *Handbook of personality: Theory and research* (pp. 465–485). New York: Guilford.

Weiner, B. (2006). *Social motivation, justice, and the moral emotions: An attributional approach.* Mahwah, NJ: Erlbaum.

Weiner, I. B. (1995). Methodological considerations in Rorschach research. *Psychological Assessment, 7,* 330–337.

Weiner, I. B. (1996). Some observations on the validity of the Rorschach inkblot method. *Psychological Assessment, 8,* 206–213.

Weiner, I. B. (2001). Advancing the science of psychological assessment: The Rorschach inkblot method as exemplar. *Psychological Assessment, 13,* 423–432.

Weinstein, N., Hodgins, H. S., & Ostvik-White, E. (2011). Humor as aggression: Effects of motivation on hostility expressed in humor appreciation. *Journal of Personality and Social Psychology, 100,* 1043–1055.

Weinstein, S. E., & Quigley, K. S. (2006). Locus of control predicts appraisals and cardiovascular reactivity to a novel active coping task. *Journal of Personality, 74,* 911–931.

Wenzel, A., & Emerson, T. (2009). Mate selection in socially anxious and nonanxious individuals. *Journal of Social and Clinical Psychology, 28,* 341–363.

Westen, D. (1998). The scientific legacy of Sigmund Freud: Toward a psychodynamically informed psychological science. *Psychological Bulletin, 124,* 333–371.

Wheeler, R. E., Davidson, R. J., & Tomarken, A. J. (1993). Frontal brain asymmetry and emotional reactivity: A biological substrate of affective style. *Psychophysiology, 30,* 82–89.

Whisman, M. A. (2010). Loneliness and the metabolic syndrome in a population-based sample of middle-aged and older adults. *Health Psychology, 29,* 550–554.

Whiting, R. (1989). *You gotta have Wa.* New York: Vintage.

Whitley, B. E. (1983). Sex-role orientation and self-esteem: A critical meta-analytic review. *Journal of Personality and Social Psychology, 44,* 765–778.

Whyte, L. L. (1978). *The unconscious before Freud.* New York: St. Martin's.

Wichman, A. L., Rodgers, J. L., & MacCallum, R. C. (2006). A multilevel approach to the relationship between birth order and intelligence. *Personality and Social Psychology Bulletin, 32,* 117–127.

Wicker, F. W., Barron, W. L., & Willis, A. C. (1980). Disparagement humor: Dispositions and resolutions. *Journal of Personality and Social Psychology, 39,* 701–709.

Widiger, T. A., & Costa, P. T. (2013). *Personality disorders and the Five-Factor Model of personality* (3rd ed.). Washington, DC: American Psychological Association.

Wieners, B. (2011, December 14). Lego is for girls. *Bloomberg Business Week.* Retrieved from http://www.businessweek.com/printer/articles/21120-lego-is-for-girls

Wilkowski, B. M., & Robinson, M. D. (2010). The anatomy of anger: An integrative cognitive model of trait anger and reactive aggression. *Journal of Personality, 78,* 9–38.

Williams, J. E. (2010). Anger/hostility and cardiovascular disease. In M. Potegal, G. Stemmler, & C. Spielberger (Eds.), *International handbook of anger: Constituent and concomitant biological, psychological, and social processes* (pp. 435–447). New York: Springer.

Williams, J. E., Nieto, F. J., Sanford, C. P., Couper, D. J., & Tyroler, A. (2002). The association between trait anger and incident stroke risk: The Atherosclerosis Risk in Communities (ARIC) Study. *Stroke, 33,* 13–20.

Williams, J. E., Nieto, F. J., Sanford, C. P., & Tyroler, H. A. (2001). Effects of an angry temperament on coronary heart disease risk: The

Atherosclerosis Risk in Communities Study. *American Journal of Epidemiology, 154,* 230–235.

Williams, J. E., Paton, C. C., Seigler, C., Eigenbrodt, M. L., Nieto, F. J., & Tyroler, H. A. (2000). Anger proneness predicts coronary heart disease risk: Prospective analysis from the Atherosclerosis Risk in Communities (ARIC) Study. *Circulation, 101,* 2034–2039.

Williams, J. G., & Solano, C. H. (1983). The social reality of feeling lonely: Friendship and reciprocation. *Personality and Social Psychology Bulletin, 9,* 237–242.

Williams, P. G., Colder, C. R., Lane, J. D., McCaskill, C. C., Feinglos, M. N., & Surwit, R. S. (2002). Examination of the neuroticism-symptom reporting relationship in individuals with Type 2 diabetes. *Personality and Social Psychology Bulletin, 28,* 1015–1025.

Williams, S. L. (1995). Self-efficacy and anxiety and phobic disorders. In J. E. Maddux (Ed.), *Self-efficacy, adaptation, and adjustment: Theory, research, and application* (pp. 69–108). New York: Plenum.

Williams-Piehota, P., Schneider, T. R., Pizarro, J., Mowad, L., & Salovey, P. (2004). Matching health messages to health locus of control beliefs for promoting mammography utilization. *Psychology and Health, 19,* 407–423.

Wilner, M. A. (2013, March 1). Getting in without the SAT. *New York Times.* Retrieved from http://thechoice.blogs.nytimes.com/2013/03/01/getting-in-without-the-sat/

Wilson, H. W., Smith Stover, C., & Berkowitz, S. J. (2009). The relationship between childhood violence exposure and juvenile antisocial behavior: A meta-analytic review. *Journal of Child Psychology and Psychiatry, 50,* 769–779.

Windle, M., & Windle, R. C. (1996). Coping strategies, drinking motives, and stressful life events among middle adolescents: Associations with emotional and behavioral problems and with academic functioning. *Journal of*

Abnormal Psychology, 105, 551–560.

Winter, D. A. (2003). Repertory grid technique as a psychotherapy research measure. *Psychotherapy Research, 13,* 25–42.

Winter, D. G. (2010). Why achievement motivation predicts success in business but failure in politics: The importance of personal control. *Journal of Personality, 78,* 1637–1668.

Wittenberg, M. T., & Reis, H. T. (1986). Loneliness, social skills, and social perception. *Personality and Social Psychology Bulletin, 12,* 121–130.

Woike, B. A. (2008). A functional framework for the influence of implicit and explicit motives on autobiographical memory. *Personality and Social Psychology Review, 12,* 99–117.

Wolfe, R. N., & Kasmer, J. A. (1988). Type versus trait: Extraversion, impulsivity, sociability, and preferences for cooperative and competitive activities. *Journal of Personality and Social Psychology, 54,* 864–871.

Wolfram, H.-J., Mohr, G., & Borchert, J. (2009). Gender role self-concept, gender-role conflict, and well-being in male primary school teachers. *Sex Roles, 60,* 114–127.

Won-Doornink, M. J. (1985). Self-disclosure and reciprocity in conversation: A cross-national study. *Social Psychology Quarterly, 48,* 97–107.

Wong, E. (2012, July 1). Test that can determine the course of life in China gets a closer examination. *New York Times.* Retrieved from www.nytimes.com/2012/07/01/world/asia/burden-of-chinas-college-entrance-test/

Wong, M. M., & Csikszentmihalyi, M. (1991). Motivation and academic achievement: The effects of personality traits and the quality of experience. *Journal of Personality, 59,* 539–574.

Wood, J. M., Garb, H. N., Lilienfeld, S. O., & Nezworski, M. T. (2002). Clinical assessment. *Annual Review of Psychology, 53,* 519–543.

Wood, J. M., Lilienfeld, S. O., Nezworski, M. T., Garb, H. N., Allen, K. H., & Wildermuth, J. L. (2010). Validity of Rorschach inkblot scores for discriminating psychopaths from nonpsychopaths in forensic populations: A meta-analysis. *Psychological Assessment, 22,* 336–349.

Wood, J. M., Nezworski, M. T., & Stejskal, W. J. (1996). Thinking critically about the comprehensive system for the Rorschach: A reply to Exner. *Psychological Science, 7,* 14–17.

Wood, J. M., Nezworski, M. T., & Stejskal, W. J. (1997). The reliability of the comprehensive system for the Rorschach: A comment on Meyer (1997). *Psychological Assessment, 9,* 490–494.

Wood, J. V., Heimpel, S. A., Manwell, L. A., & Whittington, E. J. (2009). This mood is familiar and I don't deserve to feel better anyway: Mechanisms underlying self-esteem differences in motivation to repair sad moods. *Journal of Personality and Social Psychology, 96,* 363–380.

Wood, J. V., Heimpel, S. A., Newby-Clark, I. R., & Ross, M. (2005). Snatching defeat from the jaws of victory: Self-esteem differences in the experience and anticipation of success. *Journal of Personality and Social Psychology, 89,* 764–780.

Wood, W., & Eagly, A. H. (2002). A cross-cultural analysis of the behavior of women and men: Implications for the origins of sex differences. *Psychological Bulletin, 128,* 699–727.

Wood, W., Wong, F. Y., & Chachere, J. G. (1991). Effects of media violence on viewers' aggression in unconstrained social interaction. *Psychological Bulletin, 109,* 371–383.

Woodhill, B. M., & Samuels, C. A. (2004). Desirable and undesirable androgyny: A prescription for the twenty-first century. *Journal of Gender Studies, 13,* 15–28.

Woodward, S. A., McManis, M. H., Kagan, J., Deldin, P., Snidman, N., Lewis, M. et al. (2001). Infant temperament and the brainstem auditory evoked response in later childhood. *Developmental Psychology, 37,* 533–538.

Wrosch, C., & Miller, G. E. (2009). Depressive symptoms can be useful: Self-regulatory and emotional benefits of dysphoric mood in adolescence. *Journal of Personality and Social Psychology, 96,* 1181–1190.

Wrosch, C., Schulz, R., & Heckhausen, J. (2002). Health stresses and depressive symptomatology in the elderly: The importance of health engagement control strategies. *Health Psychology, 21,* 340–348.

Wu, K. D., & Clark, L. A. (2003). Relations between personality traits and self-reports of daily behavior. *Journal of Research in Personality, 37,* 231–256.

Yarnold, P. R., Mueser, K. T., & Grimm, L. G. (1985). Interpersonal dominance of Type As in group discussions. *Journal of Abnormal Psychology, 94,* 233–236.

You, J., Fung, H. H. L., & Isaacowitz, D. M. (2009). Age differences in dispositional optimism: A cross-cultural study. *European Journal of Ageing, 6,* 247–252.

Zadra, A., Desjardins, S., & Marcotte, E. (2006). Evolutionary function of dreams: A test of the threat simulation theory in recurrent dreams. *Consciousness and Cognition, 15,* 450–463.

Zadra, A. L., O'Brien, S. A., & Donderi, D. C. (1998). Dream content, dream recurrence and well-being: A replication with a younger sample. *Imagination, Cognition and Personality, 17,* 293–311.

Zajonc, R. B. (2001). The family dynamics of intellectual development. *American Psychologist, 56,* 490–496.

Zajonc, R. B., & Sulloway, F. J. (2007). The confluence model: Birth order as a within-family or between-family dynamic? *Personality and Social Psychology Bulletin, 33,* 1187–1194.

Zammichieli, M. E., Gilroy, F. D., & Sherman, M. F. (1988). Relations between sex-role orientation and marital satisfaction. *Personality and Social Psychology Bulletin, 14,* 747–754.

Zampieri, M., & de Souza, E. A. P. (2011). Locus of control, depression, and quality of life in Parkinson's disease. *Journal of Health Psychology, 16,* 980–987.

Zayas, V., Mischel, W., Shoda, Y., & Aber, L. (2011). Roots of adult attachment: Maternal caregiving at 18 months predicts adult peer and partner attachment. *Social Psychological and Personality Science, 2,* 289–297.

Zeidner, M. (2007). Anxiety and coping with community disasters: The Israeli experience. *Journal of Research in Personality, 41,* 213–220.

Zeidner, M., & Hammer, A. L. (1992). Coping with missile attack: Resources, strategies, and outcomes. *Journal of Personality, 60,* 709–746.

Zeigler-Hill, V., Chadha, S., & Osterman, L. (2008). Psychological defense and self-esteem instability: Is defense style associated with unstable self-esteem? *Journal of Research in Personality, 42,* 348–364.

Zelenski, J. M., Santoro, M. S., & Whelan, D. C. (2012). Would introverts be better off if they acted more like extraverts? Exploring emotional and cognitive consequences of counterdispositional behavior. *Emotion, 12,* 290–303.

Zentner, M., & Mitura, K. (2012). Stepping out of the caveman's shadow: Nations' gender gap predicts degree of sex differentiation in mate preferences. *Psychological Science, 23,* 1176–1185.

Zernike, K. (2000, August 25). Academic race gap grows again. *San Jose Mercury News,* p. 21A.

Zezima, K., & Carey, B. (2009, September 11). Ex-priest challenges abuse conviction on repressed memories. *New York Times,* p. A13.

Zillmann, D. (1979). *Hostility and aggression.* Hillsdale, NJ: Erlbaum.

Zimbardo, P. G. (1986). The Stanford shyness project. In W. H. Jones, J. M. Cheek, & S. R. Briggs (Eds.), *Shyness: Perspectives on research and treatment* (pp. 17–25). New York: Plenum.

Zuckerman, M., & Gagne, M. (2003). The COPE revised: Proposing a 5-factor model of coping strategies. *Journal of Research in Personality, 37,* 169–204.

Zur, O., Williams, M. H., Lehavot, K., & Knapp, S. (2009). Psychotherapist self-disclosure and transparency in the Internet age. *Professional Psychology: Research and Practice, 40,* 22–30.

Name Index

Subject Index